*Major Problems
in the Gilded Age
and the Progressive Era*

MAJOR PROBLEMS IN AMERICAN HISTORY SERIES

GENERAL EDITOR

THOMAS G. PATERSON

Major Problems in the Gilded Age and the Progressive Era

DOCUMENTS AND ESSAYS

EDITED BY
LEON FINK
UNIVERSITY OF NORTH CAROLINA, CHAPEL HILL

D. C. HEATH AND COMPANY
Lexington, Massachusetts   Toronto

Address editorial correspondence to:

D. C. Heath
125 Spring Street
Lexington, MA 02173

Copyright © 1993 by D. C. Heath and Company.

Published simultaneously in Canada.

Printed in the United States of America.

International Standard Book Number: 0-669-21680-1

Library of Congress Catalog Number: 92-70798

10   9   8   7   6   5   4   3   2   1

TO ANNA AND SIMON—
for helping to preserve a sense of humor
in my historical process

Preface

"The Republic thunders past with the rush of the express," exclaimed steel-company executive Andrew Carnegie in 1885. This volume invites readers to board the mighty train that was the United States around the turn of the last century, and to experience its thunderous ride. The Gilded Age and the Progressive Era, spanning approximately 1877 to 1920, form the gateway to the modern America that we have inherited.

The term "the Gilded Age" originated in the 1873 novel of the same name by Mark Twain and Charles Dudley Warner. Satirizing the "all-pervading speculativeness" and "shameful corruption" rampant during the presidency of Ulysses S. Grant, Twain and Warner set the tone for much future commentary on late-nineteenth-century public affairs. "The Gilded Age," in short, identified a period of rapid economic advance simultaneously associated with shady practices in business and politics. The term "the Progressive Era," on the other hand, initially summoned up more positive associations. A label that urban, middle-class reformers applied to themselves (in preference to *liberal, populist,* or *socialist*) in the first decade of the twentieth century, *progressive*, at least in the view of its defenders, evoked a beneficent and rational reckoning with the excesses of the Gilded Age.

For years, the scholarly debates surrounding both periods tended to revolve around these initial judgments, essentially trying to separate the "good guys" from the "bad guys." Were the Gilded Age industrialists "robber barons" or "captains of industry," scholars pondered—and they vigorously debated and defended their conclusions. Were American workers supporters or, rather, critics of capitalism? Were the populists spouting mere demagoguery, or did they offer a legitimate radical alternative? Was urban government a partial success or an utter failure? Were the progressives enlightened reformers or instead bigoted agents of social condescension? While still digesting some of these earlier historiographic controversies, recent treatments of the Gilded Age and the Progressive Era tend to adopt a more thematic, and unifying, analytical framework. It is with such newer perspectives in mind that this volume attempts to define the major problems of the age.

Dominated by the new wealth and technology associated with the consolidation of the Industrial Revolution, this period is marked both by stupendous innovation and by stupefying conflicts on almost every front. The transformation of landscape and cityscape was no more dramatic than was the metamorphosis of personal values, political ideas, and group identities. In one sense, the nation's very material progress carried it to the threshold of world superpower. But what did power mean at home and abroad? Who benefited from economic development, and at what cost? Who led the country into a new age, and against which competing or alternative visions of social purpose and national well-being?

Proceeding in roughly chronological fashion, our journey emphasizes themes that continue to resonate even today. We begin with a panorama of sweeping material change, a prospect of abundance and opportunity on the one hand and of poverty and growing inequality on the other. Moving from the workshops and factories of sprawling northern cities to the farms and reservations of the once-wild West to the post-plantation South, bubbling with great expectations, the first five chapters illuminate the social challenges posed in very different settings by explosive economic development. The next six chapters focus on the political and cultural ramifications of development: the struggle for public power as reflected in Gilded Age partisan rivalry; the farmers' revolt; the movements for women's rights and for temperance; African-American strategies in the face of segregation and political exclusion; the voluntary and coerced Americanization of immigrants; and the multifaceted burst of social reform and state regulation known as progressivism. One area of progressive concern, the effort to manage environmental resources, receives special attention. Following these chapters spotlighting the "public" sphere, the next two chapters examine twentieth-century innovations in private conduct and popular taste: first, with reference to questions of sexuality and gender roles; and second, in relation to the growing commercialization of leisure time. The last two chapters, the final leg of our journey, explore America's new social order on a world stage: first, in the ideology and debate over expansionism and imperialism; and finally, in the full-scale national mobilization for the First World War.

In applying these overarching themes, I have tried to overcome the fragmentation of perspective and of subfield that too often bedevils the historical discipline. The rich scholarship in women's history over the past two decades, in particular, allows this volume to venture further than previous collections in integrating a discussion of gender differences into the treatment of political and social issues.

Following the general format of the Major Problems in American History series, each chapter brings together historically significant, readable documents and essays accenting the provocative encounter of the past with the present. In each chapter a brief introduction sets the historical scene and defines the central issues. Headnotes to the documents and essays place the issues in historical and interpretive perspective. Each chapter closes with an invitation to further reading. Although the choice of topics inevitably reflects my own sense of the critical questions and turning points of the period, the array and the arrangement of the selections are open-ended enough to encourage readers to debate the issues and to formulate their own understanding of the nation's "major problems" during these years.

In preparing this volume, I have had significant help along the way. For their thematic and bibliographic suggestions, I would like particularly to thank William Barney, Henry Binford, Eileen Boris, Peter Coclanis, Sarah Deutsch, John Kasson, James Leloudis, Susan Levine, Roger Lotchin,

David Moltke-Hansen, Malcolm Rohrbough, and Jeffrey Stewart. I am also indebted to the thoughtful advice of the various reviewers consulted by D. C. Heath: Betty Brandon, University of South Alabama; Priscilla J. Brewer, University of South Florida; John D. Buenker, University of Wisconsin, Parkside; Mark T. Carleton, Louisiana State University; Francis J. Couvares, Amherst College; Jack D. Elenbaas, California State University, Fullerton; Lewis L. Gould, University of Texas, Austin; H. Roger Grant, University of Akron; Martin R. Haas, Adelphi University; D. Alan Harris, Old Dominion University; Gerald W. McFarland, University of Massachusetts, Amherst; Samuel T. McSeveney, Vanderbilt University; Donald W. Rogers, University of Hartford; Jack Tager, University of Massachusetts, Amherst; and Mark Wyman, Illinois State University. These colleagues undertook their task with an impressive sense of responsibility. In addition, I have profited greatly from the suggestions of series editor Thomas G. Paterson and the D. C. Heath staff, especially managing editor Sylvia Mallory, history editor James Miller, permissions editor Margaret Roll, and production editor Bryan Woodhouse. Finally, I extend special gratitude to my research assistant Georg Leidenberger for his thoughtful and painstaking contributions in the editorial process.

L.F.

Contents

C H A P T E R 3
"Civilizing" the Wild West
Page 70

C H A P T E R 4
New South Image Versus New South Reality
Page 103

CHAPTER 5
City and Suburb: New Vistas, New Walls
Page 137

CHAPTER 6
Power in the Gilded Age: Political Parties and Social Movements
Page 175

C H A P T E R 14
The Language of Empire
Page 487

C H A P T E R 15
America and the Great War
Page 526

*Major Problems
in the Gilded Age
and the Progressive Era*

C H A P T E R

1

The Price of Progress: Capitalism and Its Discontents

❧

Late-nineteenth-century American capitalism was more than a means for the production and distribution of goods and services. It was also a system of meanings, imparting purpose and justification to the manifold physical and social disruptions wrought by economic development in a comparatively free, or unregulated, marketplace. In place of the economic independence and rough equality widespread among farmers and artisans in the early republic, industrialization—the application of machine processes, fueled by outside power sources, to production—promoted new virtues even as it threatened older ones. Industrialists and their apostles defended capitalism's new order on grounds of natural law, scientific progress, and the expansion of individual economic opportunity. Critics argued that the instruments of technological progress, left in the hands of a relative few, were being used to stifle rather than to liberate the potential of a democratic citizenry.

❧ D O C U M E N T S

Contemporaries sharply disagreed about the gain versus the pain of an industrial, corporate capitalist social order, as the opening passages of the first two selections suggest. In the first document, steel baron Andrew Carnegie marvels at the astounding success of American civilization. Carnegie stresses free labor, public education, and the advantages of British racial stock as key sources of America's Great Leap Forward. What most strikes Henry George, on the other hand, is that "the 'tramp' comes with the locomotive." The second selection is excerpted from his introduction to *Progress and Poverty,* one of the nineteenth century's most influential works of social and economic criticism. In this passage, George, a labor reformer whose distinctive nostrum is the "single tax" on unimproved land, promises to get to the root of capitalism's paradox.

The remaining documents present similarly vivid contrasts. In the third document, iron manufacturer Abram S. Hewitt salutes the beauty of the Brooklyn Bridge, the magnificent product of a successful marriage between science and industry, whereas in the fourth selection, Chicago anarchist Gerhard Lizius finds an alternate use for the wonders of technology and human engineering. A selection by the Reverend Alexander Lewis from the vast outpouring of self-help literature, together with an excerpt from Baptist businessman Russell H. Conwell's famous lecture "Acres of Diamonds," suggests a broad popular and even religious sanction for the ethics of the marketplace. But the closing document, Mark Twain's acerbic satire ("Poor Little Stephen Girard") on the success ideology popularized by the preachings of Lewis and Conwell and in the stories of Horatio Alger, reveals not only contemporary ambivalence but open conflict about the nation's proper goals and values.

Andrew Carnegie on the Triumph of America, 1885

The old nations of the earth creep on at a snail's pace; the Republic thunders past with the rush of the express. The United States, the growth of a single century, has already reached the foremost rank among nations, and is destined soon to out-distance all others in the race. In population, in wealth, in annual savings, and in public credit; in freedom from debt, in agriculture, and in manufactures, America already leads the civilized world. . . .

Into the distant future of this giant nation we need not seek to peer; but if we cast a glance forward, as we have done backward, for only fifty years, and assume that in that short interval no serious change will occur, the astounding fact startles us that in 1935, fifty years from now, when many in manhood will still be living, one hundred and eighty millions of English-speaking republicans will exist under one flag and possess more than two hundred and fifty thousand millions of dollars, or fifty thousand millions sterling of national wealth. Eighty years ago the whole of America and Europe did not contain so many people; and, if Europe and America continue their normal growth, it will be little more than another eighty years ere the mighty Republic may boast as many loyal citizens as all the rulers of Europe combined, for before the year 1980 Europe and America will each have a population of about six hundred millions.

The causes which have led to the rapid growth and aggrandizement of this latest addition to the family of nations constitute one of the most interesting problems in the social history of mankind. What has brought about such stupendous results—so unparalleled a development of a nation within so brief a period! The most important factors in this problem are three: the ethnic character of the people, the topographical and climatic conditions under which they developed, and the influence of political institutions founded upon the equality of the citizen.

Certain writers in the past have maintained that the ethnic type of a people has less influence upon its growth as a nation than the conditions of life under which it is developing. The modern ethnologist knows better. We have only to imagine what America would be to-day if she had fallen, in the beginning, into the hands of any other people than the colonizing British, to see how vitally important is this question of race. America was indeed fortunate in the seed planted upon her soil. With the exception of a few Dutch and French it was wholly British; and . . . the American of to-day remains true to this noble strain and is four-fifths British. The special aptitude of this race for colonization, its vigor and enterprise, and its capacity for governing, although brilliantly manifested in all parts of the world, have never been shown to such advantage as in America. Freed here from the pressure of feudal institutions no longer fitted to their present development, and freed also from the dominion of the upper classes, which have kept the people at home from effective management of affairs and sacrificed the nation's interest for their own, as is the nature of classes, these masses of the lower ranks of Britons, called upon to found a new state, have proved themselves possessors of a positive genius for political administration.

The second, and perhaps equally important factor in the problem of the rapid advancement of this branch of the British race, is the superiority of the conditions under which it has developed. The home which has fallen to its lot, a domain more magnificent than has cradled any other race in the history of the world, presents no obstructions to unity—to the thorough amalgamation of its dwellers, North, South, East, and West, into one homogeneous mass— for the conformation of the American continent differs in important respects from that of every other great division of the globe. In Europe the Alps occupy a central position, forming on each side watersheds of rivers which flow into opposite seas. In Asia the Himalaya, the Hindu Kush, and the Altai Mountains divide the continent, rolling from their sides many great rivers which pour their floods into widely separated oceans. But in North America the mountains rise up on each coast, and from them the land slopes gradually into great central plains, forming an immense basin where the rivers flow together in one valley, offering to commerce many thousand miles of navigable streams. The map thus proclaims the unity of North America, for in this great central basin, three million square miles in extent, free from impassable rivers or mountain barriers great enough to hinder free intercourse, political integration is a necessity and consolidation a certainty. . . .

The unity of the American people is further powerfully promoted by the foundation upon which the political structure rests, the equality of the citizen. There is not one shred of privilege to be met with anywhere in all the laws. One man's right is every man's right. The flag is the guarantor and symbol of equality. The people are not emasculated by being made to feel that their own country decrees their inferiority, and holds them unworthy of privileges accorded to others. No ranks, no titles, no hereditary dignities, and therefore no classes. Suffrage is universal, and votes are of equal weight. Representatives are paid, and political life and usefulness thereby thrown open to all. Thus there is brought about a community of interests and aims which a Briton, accustomed to monarchical and aristocratic institutions, dividing the people into classes with separate interests, aims, thoughts, and feelings, can only with difficulty understand.

The free common school system of the land is probably, after all, the greatest single power in the unifying process which is producing the new American race. Through the crucible of a good common English education, furnished free by the State, pass the various racial elements—children of Irishmen, Germans, Italians, Spaniards, and Swedes, side by side with the native American, all to be fused into one, in language, in thought, in feeling, and in patriotism. The Irish boy loses his brogue, and the German child learns English. The sympathies suited to the feudal systems of Europe, which they inherit from their fathers, pass off as dross, leaving behind the pure gold of the only noble political creed: "All men are created free and equal." Taught now to live and work for the common weal, and not for the maintenance of a royal family or an overbearing aristocracy, not for the continuance of a social system which ranks them beneath an arrogant class of drones, children of Russian and German serfs, of Irish evicted tenants, Scotch crofters, and other victims of feudal tyranny, are transmuted into republican Americans, and are made one in love for a country which provides equal rights and privileges for all her children. There is no class so intensely patriotic, so wildly devoted to the Republic as the naturalized citizen and his child, for little does the native-born citizen know of the value of rights which have never been denied. Only the man born abroad, like myself, under institutions which insult him at his birth, can know the full meaning of Republicanism. . . .

It is these causes which render possible the growth of a great homogeneous nation, alike in race, language, literature, interest, patriotism—an empire of such overwhelming power and proportions as to require neither army nor navy to ensure its safety, and a people so educated and advanced as to value the victories of peace.

The student of American affairs to-day sees no influences at work save those which make for closer and closer union. The Republic has solved the problem of governing large areas by adopting the federal, or home-rule system, and has proved to the world that the freest self-government of the parts produces the strongest government of the whole.

Henry George and the Paradox of Capitalist Growth, 1879

The present century has been marked by a prodigious increase in wealth-producing power. The utilization of steam and electricity, the introduction of improved processes and labor-saving machinery, the greater subdivision and grander scale of production, the wonderful facilitation of exchanges, have multiplied enormously the effectiveness of labor.

At the beginning of this marvelous era it was natural to expect, and it was expected, that labor-saving inventions would lighten the toil and improve the condition of the laborer; that the enormous increase in the power of producing wealth would make real poverty a thing of the past. Could a man of the last century—a Franklin or a Priestley—have seen, in a vision of the future, the steamship taking the place of the sailing vessel, the railroad train of the wagon, the reaping machine of the scythe, the threshing machine of the flail; could he have heard the throb of the engines that in obedience to human will, and for the satisfaction of human desire, exert a power greater than that of all the men and all the beasts of burden of the earth combined; could he have seen the forest tree transformed into finished lumber—into doors, sashes, blinds, boxes or barrels, with hardly the touch of a human hand; the great workshops where boots and shoes are turned out by the case with less labor than the old-fashioned cobbler could have put on a sole; the factories where, under the eye of a girl, cotton becomes cloth faster than hundreds of stalwart weavers could have turned it out with their handlooms; could he have seen steam hammers shaping mammoth shafts and mighty anchors, and delicate machinery making tiny watches; the diamond drill cutting through the heart of the rocks, and coal oil sparing the whale; could he have realized the enormous saving of labor resulting from improved facilities of exchange and communication—sheep killed in Australia eaten fresh in England, and the order given by the London banker in the afternoon executed in San Francisco in the morning of the same day; could he have conceived of the hundred thousand improvements which these only suggest, what would he have inferred as to the social condition of mankind? . . .

. . . Out of these bounteous material conditions he would have seen arising, as necessary sequences, moral conditions realizing the golden age of which mankind has always dreamed. Youth no longer stunted and starved; age no longer harried by avarice; the child at play with the tiger; the man with the muck-rake drinking in the glory of the stars. Foul things fled, fierce things tame; discord turned to harmony! For how could there be greed where all had enough? How could the vice, the crime, the ignorance, the brutality, that spring from poverty and the fear of poverty, exist where poverty had vanished? Who should crouch where all were freemen; who oppress where all were peers? . . .

Now, however, we are coming into collision with facts which there can be no mistaking. From all parts of the civilized world come complaints of industrial depression; of labor condemned to involuntary idleness; of capital massed and wasting; of pecuniary distress among business men; of want and suffering and anxiety among the working classes. All the dull, deadening pain, all the keen, maddening anguish, that to great masses of men are involved in the words "hard times," afflict the world to-day. This state of things, common to communities differing so widely in situation, in political institutions, in fiscal and financial systems, in density of population and in social organization, can hardly be accounted for by local causes. . . .

That there is a common cause, and that it is either what we call material progress or something closely connected with material progress, becomes more than an inference when it is noted that the phenomena we class together and speak of as industrial depression are but intensifications of phenomena which always accompany material progress, and which show themselves more clearly and strongly as material progress goes on. . . .

Just as . . . a community realizes the conditions which all civilized communities are striving for, and advances in the scale of material progress—just as closer settlement and a more intimate connection with the rest of the world, and greater utilization of labor-saving machinery, make possible greater economies in production and exchange, and wealth in consequence increases, not merely in the aggregate, but in proportion to population—so does poverty take a darker aspect. Some get an infinitely better and easier living, but others find it hard to get a living at all. The "tramp" comes with the locomotive, and almshouses and prisons are as surely the marks of "material progress" as are costly dwellings, rich warehouses, and magnificent churches. Upon streets lighted with gas and patrolled by uniformed policemen, beggars wait for the passer-by, and in the shadow of college, and library, and museum, are gathering the more hideous Huns and fiercer Vandals of whom Macaulay prophesied.

This fact—the great fact that poverty and all its concomitants show themselves in communities just as they develop into the conditions toward which material progress tends—proves that the social difficulties existing wherever a certain stage of progress has been reached, do not arise from local circumstances, but are, in some way or another, engendered by progress itself.

And, unpleasant as it may be to admit it, it is at last becoming evident that the enormous increase in productive power which has marked the present century and is still going on with accelerating ratio, has no tendency to extirpate poverty or to lighten the burdens of those compelled to toil. It simply widens the gulf between Dives and Lazarus, and makes the struggle for existence more intense. The march of invention has clothed mankind with powers of which a century ago the boldest imagination could not have dreamed. But in factories where labor-saving machinery has reached its most wonderful development, little children are at work; wherever the new forces are anything like fully utilized, large classes are maintained by charity or live on the verge of recourse to it; amid the greatest accumulations of wealth, men die of starvation, and puny infants suckle dry breasts; while everywhere the greed of gain, the worship of wealth, shows the force of the fear of want. The promised land flies before us like the mirage. The fruits of the tree of knowledge turn as we grasp them to apples of Sodom that crumble at the touch.

It is true that wealth has been greatly increased, and that the average of comfort, leisure, and refinement has been raised; but these gains are not general. In them the lowest class do not share. I do not mean that the condition of the lowest class has nowhere nor in anything been improved; but that there is nowhere any improvement which can be credited to increase productive power. I mean that the tendency of what we call material progress is in nowise to improve the condition of the lowest class in the essentials of healthy, happy human life. Nay, more, that it is still further to depress the condition of the lowest class. The new forces, elevating in their nature though they be, do not act upon the social fabric from underneath, as was for a long time hoped and believed, but strike it at a point intermediate between top and bottom. It is as though an immense wedge were being forced, not underneath society, but through society. Those who are above the point of separation are elevated, but those who are below are crushed down. . . .

This association of poverty with progress is the great enigma of our times. It is the central fact from which spring industrial, social, and political difficulties that perplex the world, and with which statesmanship and philanthropy and education grapple in vain. From it come the clouds that overhang the future of the most progressive and self-reliant nations. It is the riddle which the Sphinx of Fate puts to our civilization, and which not to answer is to be destroyed. So long as all the increased wealth which modern progress brings goes but to build up great fortunes, to increase luxury and make sharper the contrast between the House of Have and the House of Want, progress is not real and cannot be permanent. The reaction must come. The tower leans from its foundations, and every new story but hastens the final catastrophe. To educate men who must be condemned to poverty, is but to make them restive; to base on a state of most glaring social inequality political institutions under which men are theoretically equal, is to stand a pyramid on its apex. . . .

Abram S. Hewitt on the Wonders of the Brooklyn Bridge, 1883

Could there be a more astounding exhibition of the power of man to change the face of nature than the panoramic view which presents itself to the spectator standing upon the crowning arch of the bridge whose completion we are here today to celebrate in the honored presence of the President of the United States, with their fifty millions; of the governor of the state of New York, with its five millions; and of the mayors of the two cities, aggregating over two million of inhabitants? In the place of stillness and solitude, the footsteps of these millions of human beings; instead of the smooth waters "unvexed by any keel," highways of commerce ablaze with the flags of all the nations; and where once was the green monotony of forested hills, the piled and towering splendors of a vast metropolis, the countless homes of industry, the echoing marts of trade, the gorgeous palaces of luxury, the silent and steadfast spires of worship! . . .

"What hath God wrought!" were the words of wonder, which ushered into being the magnetic telegraph, the greatest marvel of the many marvelous inventions of the present century. It was the natural impulse of the pious maiden who chose this first message of reverence and awe to look to the Divine Power as the author of a new gospel. For it was the invisible, and not the visible, agency which addressed itself to her perceptions. Neither the bare poles nor the slender wire, nor the magnetic battery, could suggest an adequate explanation of the extinction of time and space which was manifest to her senses, and she could only say, "What hath God wrought!"

But when we turn from the unsightly telegraph to the graceful structure at whose portal we stand, and when the airy outline of its curves of beauty, pendant between massive towers suggestive of art alone, is contrasted with the over-reaching vault of heaven above and the ever-moving flood of waters beneath, the work of omnipotent power, we are irresistibly moved to exclaim, What hath man wrought!

Man hath indeed wrought far more than strikes the eye in this daring undertaking, by the general judgment of engineers, without a rival among the wonders of human skill. It is not the work of any one man or of any one age. It is the result of the study, of the experience, and of the knowledge of many men in many ages. It is not merely a creation; it is a growth. It stands before us today as the sum and epitome of human knowledge; as the very heir of the ages; as the latest glory of centuries of patient observation, profound study and accumulated skill, gained, step by step, in the never-ending struggle of man to subdue the forces of nature to his control and use.

In no previous period of the world's history could this bridge have been built. Within the last hundred years the greater part of the knowledge necessary for its erection has been gained. Chemistry was not born until 1776, the year when political economy was ushered into the world by Adam Smith, and the Declaration of Independence was proclaimed by the Continental Congress, to be maintained at the point of the sword by George Washington. In the same year Watt produced his successful steam engine, and a century has not elapsed since the first specimen of his skill was erected on this continent. The law of gravitation was indeed known a hundred years ago, but the intricate laws of force, which now control the domain of industry, had not been developed by the study of physical science, and their practical applications have only been effectually accomplished within our own day, and indeed, some of the most important of them during the building of the bridge. For use in the caissons, the perfecting of the electric light came too late, though happily in season for the illumination of the finished work.

This construction has not only employed every abstract conclusion and formula of mathematics, whether derived from the study of the earth or the heavens, but the whole structure may be said to rest upon a mathematical foundation. The great discoveries of chemistry, showing the composition of water, the nature of gases, the properties of metals; the laws and processes of physics, from the strains and pressures of mighty masses, to the delicate vibrations of molecules, are all recorded here. Every department of human industry is represented, from the quarrying and the cutting of the stones, the mining and smelting of the ores, the conversion of iron into steel by the pneumatic process, to the final shaping of the masses of metal into useful forms, and its reduction into wire, so as to develop in the highest degree, the tensile strength which fits it for the work of suspension. Every tool which the ingenuity of man has invented, has somewhere, in some special detail, contributed its share in the accomplishment of the final result.

> Ah! what a wondrous thing it is
> To note how many wheels of toil
> One word, one thought can set in motion.

But without the most recent discoveries of science, which have enabled steel to be substituted for iron—applications made since the original plans of the bridge were devised—we should have had a structure fit, indeed, for use, but of such moderate capacity that we could not have justified the claim which we are now able to make, that the cities of New York and Brooklyn have constructed, and today rejoice in the possession of, the crowning glory of an age memorable for great industrial achievements. . . .

An Anarchist Celebrates the Potential of Dynamite, 1885

Dynamite! of all the good stuff, this is the stuff. Stuff several pounds of this sublime stuff into an inch pipe, gas or water pipe, plug up both ends, insert a cap with fuse attached, place this in the immediate neighborhood of a lot of rich loafers, who live by the sweat of other people's brows, and light the fuse. A most cheerful and gratifying result will follow. In giving dynamite to the downtrodden millions of the globe, science has done its best work. The dear stuff can be carried around in the pocket without danger, while it is a formidable weapon against any force of militia, police or detectives that may want to stifle the cry for justice that goes forth from the plundered slaves. It is something not very ornamental, but exceedingly useful. It can be used against persons and things; it is better to use it against the former than against bricks and masonry. It is a genuine boon for the disinherited, while it brings terror and fear to the robbers. It brings terror only to the guilty, and consequently the Senator who introduced a bill in congress to stop its manufacture and use, must be guilty of something. He fears the wrath of an outraged people that has been duped and swindled by him and his like. The same must be the case with the "servant" of the people who introduced a like measure in the senate of the Indiana Legislature. All the good this will do. Like everything else, the more you prohibit it, the more will it be done. Dynamite is like Banquo's ghost, it keeps on fooling around somewhere or other in spite of his satanic majesty. A pound of this good stuff bears a bushel of ballots all hollow, and don't you forget it. Our law makers might as well try to sit down on the crater of a volcano or a bayonet as to endeavor to stop the manufacture and use of dynamite. It takes more justice and right than is contained in laws to quiet the spirit of unrest. If workingmen would be truly free, they must learn to know why they are slaves. They must rise above petty prejudice and learn to think. From thought to action is not far, and when the worker has seen the chains, he need but look a little closer to find near at hand the sledge with which to shatter every link. The sledge is dynamite. . . .

An Ode to Upward Mobility, 1902

There is always a way to rise, my boy,
Always a way to advance;
Yet the road that leads to Mount Success
Does not pass by the way of Chance,
But goes through the stations of Work and
      Strive,
through the valley of Persevere;
And the man that succeeds while others fail,
Must be willing to pay most dear.

For there's always a way to fall my boy,
Always a way to slide,
And the men you find at the foot of the hill

All sought for an easy ride.
So on and up, though the road be rough,
And the storms come thick and fast;
There is room at the top for the man who tries,
And victory comes at last.

Russell H. Conwell Sanctifies Wealth, 1915

Now then, I say again that the opportunity to get rich, to attain unto great wealth, is here in Philadelphia now, within the reach of almost every man and woman who hears me speak tonight, and I mean just what I say. I have not come to this platform even under these circumstances to recite something to you. I have come to tell you what in God's sight I believe to be the truth, and if the years of life have been of any value to me in the attainment of common sense, I know I am right; that the men and women sitting here, who found it difficult perhaps to buy a ticket to this lecture or gathering to-night, have within their reach "acres of diamonds," opportunities to get largely wealthy. There never was a place on earth more adapted than the city of Philadelphia to-day, and never in the history of the world did a poor man without capital have such an opportunity to get rich quickly and honestly as he has now in our city. I say it is the truth, and I want you to accept it as such; for if you think I have come to simply recite something, then I would better not be here. I have no time to waste in any such talk, but to say the things I believe, and unless some of you get richer for what I am saying to-night my time is wasted.

I say that you ought to get rich, and it is your duty to get rich. How many of my pious brethren say to me, "Do you, a Christian minister, spend your time going up and down the country advising young people to get rich, to get money?" "Yes, of course I do." They say, "Isn't that awful! Why don't you preach the gospel instead of preaching about man's making money?" "Because to make money honestly is to preach the gospel." That is the reason. The men who get rich may be the most honest men you find in the community.

"Oh," but says some young man here to-night, "I have been told all my life that if a person has money he is very dishonest and dishonorable and mean and contemptible." My friend, that is the reason why you have none, because you have that idea of people. The foundation of your faith is altogether false. Let me say here clearly, and say it briefly, though subject to discussion which I have not time for here, ninety-eight out of one hundred of the rich men of America are honest. That is why they are rich. That is why they are trusted with money. That is why they carry on great enterprises and find plenty of people to work with them. It is because they are honest men.

Says another young man, "I hear sometimes of men that get millions of dollars dishonestly." Yes, of course you do, and so do I. But they are so rare a thing in fact that the newspapers talk about them all the time as a matter of news until you get the idea that all the other rich men got rich dishonestly.

My friend, you take and drive me—if you furnish the auto—out into the suburbs of Philadelphia, and introduce me to the people who own their homes around this great city, those beautiful homes with gardens and flowers, those magnificent homes so lovely in their art, and I will introduce you to the very best people in character as well as in enterprise in our city, and you know I will. A man is not really a true man until he owns his own home, and they that own their homes are made more honorable and honest and pure, and true and economical and careful, by owning the home.

For a man to have money, even in large sums, is not an inconsistent thing. We preach against covetousness, and you know we do, in the pulpit, and oftentimes preach against it so long and use the terms about "filthy lucre" so extremely that Christians get the idea that when we stand in the pulpit we believe it is wicked for any man to have money—until the collection-basket goes around, and then we almost swear at the people because they don't give more money. Oh, the inconsistency of such doctrines as that!

Money is power, and you ought to be reasonably ambitious to have it. You ought because you can do more good with it than you could without it. Money printed your Bible, money builds your churches, money sends your missionaries, and money pays your preachers, and you would not have many of them, either, if you did not pay them. I am always willing that my church should raise my salary, because the church that pays the largest salary always raises it the easiest. You never knew an exception to it in your life. The man who gets the largest salary can do the most good with the power that is furnished to him. Of course he can if his spirit be right to use it for what it is given to him.

I say, then, you ought to have money. If you can honestly attain unto riches in Philadelphia, it is your Christian and godly duty to do so. It is an awful mistake of these pious people to think you must be awfully poor in order to be pious.

Some men say, "Don't you sympathize with the poor people?" Of course I do, or else I would not have been lecturing these years. I won't give in but what I sympathize with the poor, but the number of poor who are to be sympathized with is very small. To sympathize with a man whom God has punished for his sins, thus to help him when God would still continue a just punishment, is to do wrong, no doubt about it, and we do that more than we help those who are deserving. While we should sympathize with God's poor—that is, those who cannot help themselves—let us remember there is not a poor person in the United States who was not made poor by his own shortcomings, or by the shortcomings of some one else. It is all wrong to be poor anyhow. Let us give in to that argument and pass that to one side.

A gentleman gets up back there, and says, "Don't you think there are some things in this world that are better than money?" Of course I do, but I am talking about money now. Of course there are some things higher than money. Oh yes, I know by the grave that has left me standing alone that there are some things in this world that are higher and sweeter and purer than money. Well do I know there are some things higher and grander than gold. Love is the grandest thing on God's earth, but fortunate the lover who has plenty of money. Money is power, money is force, money will do good as well as harm. In the hands of good men and women it could accomplish, and it has accomplished, good.

Mark Twain on the Great American Myth, 1879

Poor Little Stephen Girard

The man lived in Philadelphia who, when young and poor, entered a bank, and says he: "Please, sir, don't you want a boy?" And the stately personage said: "No, little boy, I don't want a little boy." The little boy, whose heart was too full for utterance, chewing a piece of licorice stick he had bought with a cent stolen from his good and pious aunt, with sobs plainly audible, and with great globules of water rolling down his cheeks, glided silently down the marble steps of the bank. Bending his noble form, the bank man dodged behind a door, for he thought the little boy was going to shy a stone at him. But the little boy picked up something, and stuck it in his poor but ragged jacket. "Come here, little boy," and the little boy did come here; and the bank man said: "Lo, what pickest thou up?" And he answered and replied: "A pin." And the bank man said: "Little boy, are you good?" and he said he was. And the bank man said: "How do you vote?—excuse me, do you go to Sunday school?" and he said he did. Then the bank man took down a pen made of pure gold, and flowing with pure ink, and he wrote on a piece of paper, "St. Peter;" and he asked the little boy what it stood for, and he said "Salt Peter," Then the bankman said it meant "Saint Peter." The little boy said; "Oh!"

Then the bank man took the little boy to his bosom, and the little boy said, "Oh!" again, for he squeezed him. Then the bank man took the little boy into partnership, and gave him half the profits and all the capital, and he married the bank man's daughter, and now all he has is all his, and all his own too.

My uncle told me this story, and I spent six weeks in picking up pins in front of a bank. I expected the bank man would call me in and say: "Little boy, are you good?" and I was going to say "Yes"; and when he asked me what "St. John" stood for, I was going to say "Salt John." But the bank man wasn't anxious to have a partner, and I guess the daughter was a son, for one day says he to me: "Little boy, what's that you're picking up?" Says I, awful meekly, "Pins." Says he: "Let's see 'em." And he took 'em, and I took off my cap, all ready to go in the bank, and become a partner, and marry his daughter. But I didn't get an invitation. He said: "Those pins belong to the bank, and if I catch you hanging around here any more I'll set the dog on you!" Then I left, and the mean old fellow kept the pins. Such is life as I find it.

☙ *E S S A Y S*

In generally more moderate tones than those of their Gilded Age counterparts, historians continue to debate the pros and cons of America's industrial revolution. In the first selection, H. Wayne Morgan of the University of Oklahoma offers a relatively benign view of late-nineteenth-century America, correcting the image, popularized by Mark Twain, of the Gilded Age as a predatory Great Barbecue. But in the second essay, which focuses on the literary self-representation of the period, Alan Trachtenberg, professor of American studies at Yale University, stresses the darkness of the clouds that bore American capitalism's silver linings.

Building a Mighty Nation

H. WAYNE MORGAN

The picture is compelling; one sees it half in mirth and half in a muffled pity. There is Colonel Beriah Sellers, surrounded by doting or incredulous towns-folk, plotting with a magisterial wave of a well-tailored arm the future of an inland empire. Its seat will be at this unlikely spot, to be named after a great historical event or man. A gilt cane marks out in the muddy ruts the streets and avenues of riches and success. Here, he says grandly in the overblown rhetoric the age loves so well, will converge the river traffic, despite the absence of rivers soon to be remedied by a huge canal grant from an all-wise national government. Here will be the railroad, despite the hopeless terrain. Here will sit the city, ablaze with color and aglow with the lights of wealth and power, rising from these unlikely dunes and hills. And from here the glory of America will radiate outward toward lesser peoples who may yet come to partake of this bounty at a reasonable price.

The picture is familiar. It is the Gilded Age, or at least it is the stereotype of the bloated dreams, foolish optimism, seedy rhetoric of the generation which followed the Civil War, and no man caught that side of it as well as Mark Twain, who named it. No human vanity, no pomposity, no trace of the overblown or flatulent escaped his pen. In drawing Colonel Sellers and his compatriots, Twain delineated a view of the whole generation, throwing it into a relief that is compelling almost a century later.

Though this view of the age may be partly discounted because it is fiction, there is too often the sterner stuff of facts to corroborate it. The generation that emerged from the Civil War embarked upon a seemingly endless development of America's natural resources, commercial riches, and opportunities for equality in most spheres of life, to stage what Vernon Parrington called "the Great Barbecue." The feast of material plenty was set at the national table for everyone, who purchased this bonanza only at the price of bad taste, corruption in politics and economics, and dangerous refusals to face the harder and deeper facts of life. Yet whether these facts be true or false, the age presents a compelling charm in many of its aspects. It was a time of peace, of relative prosperity, of growth and change which seemed the more important and exciting because they occurred in a vacuum of international affairs when the United States could afford the luxury of self-interest. Moreover, the age believed in itself, something its successors cannot always claim. Optimism, a belief in progress, however foolish it may sometimes have become, was the keynote of the time.

H. Wayne Morgan. *The Gilded Age,* (Syracuse University Press, 1963), pp. 1–2. By permission of the publisher.

A famous jurist once said that the Constitution is what the judges say it is. By the same token, history is often what the historians say it is, and the Gilded Age has fared poorly in that light. Only in very recent years has it begun to emerge in detailed studies which reveal it in true relation to its own time and its successors. For three generations of viewers and students, the era has been either a result of one thing, the Civil War, or a prelude to something better and different in the twentieth century. It seems lifeless in historical print. It is something standing between the huge mountain range of the Civil War and the lesser plateaus of Populism and the Progressive movement. It is popular to call it a watershed, and historical watersheds seem to have no life of their own. Few students have seriously attempted to view it in proper perspective, as it was to itself, and for the things that it produced in itself.

The stereotype picture of the Gilded Age, presented in almost all secondary studies, is the result of the work of relatively few scholars. Chief among these is one of America's most celebrated critics and scholars, Vernon Lewis Parrington, whose *The Beginnings of Critical Realism in America* sets a tone which few subsequent students have materially altered. Though primarily literary criticism and cultural history, Parrington's widely read study profoundly influenced historians and scholars interested in American culture. To Parrington, a man of acute social consciousness, reared in the traditions of Progressive America, the Gilded Age seemed an appalling low in national morals and manners. It was to him frankly and crassly materialistic, a spectacular national feast labeled "the Great Barbecue." It surrendered the country's affairs into the hands of a few men of business who looted, overbuilt, and ultimately almost ruined the economy and political and social system: "With no social conscience, no concern for civilization, no heed for the future of democracy it talked so much about, the Gilded Age threw itself into the business of money-getting."

From Parrington's view, the era's chief fault was the transfer of power from the people to the economic masters. With this, the Jacksonian agrarian frontier of freedom and mobility disappeared, and in its stead came the monolithic and oppressive grandeur of an industrial system producing many goods, but devouring labor and wasting materials while building fortunes and power for the wrong men. America was on the road to economic plenty and social goodness in the Gilded Age, but not until some distant future date would they become real. In the meantime, the generation of the Gilded Age was an interregnum of waste, corruption, and inefficiency.

The evil of corrupt politics and lopsided economics was compounded by a nadir of taste. "It was in the seventies that good taste reached its lowest ebb," Parrington wrote, without explaining either his own view of good taste, or what the seventies thought of taste, good or bad. With his blanket condemnations, qualified now and then by a reserved, hopeful prognostication for the future, Parrington set the tone for dealing with the Gilded Age. His thesis, covered in the bright gloss of a happy style, lent itself to quotation for two generations of college students and serious scholars who also liked to smash idols. The glamor of much of his theory and the wide-spread appeal of his thinking lie largely in the ease with which they are repeated, as a generation of uncritical historians should know. Parrington saw the age from a special viewpoint; in many ways he was the last great agrarian critic among American scholars, and inevitably he did not take kindly to a generation or a morality that overthrew his ideal.

Of the other major figures who dealt with the period, Charles A. Beard is easily the most important. Perhaps because he was a trained historian presumably with a broader view and deeper knowledge, or perhaps because his purposes were different, Beard produced a critical and biased yet more substantial and even commentary on the era. Though he too viewed history within a famous framework, "the economic interpretation," Beard had the common sense, at least in the 1930's, not to become totally imprisoned in his theories at the expense of the facts of history.

Like Parrington, Beard deplored the waste of resources and the gravitation of power into the hands of the economically minded few. But he also saw that the period was far more complex than Parrington sketched it. He saw that the urban middle class, growing wealthy from the Civil War and the industrial and transportation system it produced, ruled society; but he also saw that this class was greatly expanded in a bloodless revolution. The new culture it produced was "without form and void" save for the older parts of the East. Money ruled, "the cash nexus pure and simple," but the wealth was more widely spread and far more easily obtained than in the prewar era. The age was ruled by "the onrushing plutocracy"; yet that plutocracy was not fixed or hereditary, and the nation avoided revolution because of its innate conservatism and flexible social structure. "Among American working classes, all save the most wretched had aspirations; there was a baton in every tool kit."

His criticism no less strong than that of others, Beard also saw much that other students missed, much that redeemed the age and helped its children forgive its sudden and massive interest in boundless wealth and power. Not all men were blind to the era's faults; there were reformers and reform movements in most spheres of life, and political criticism was especially harsh. After all, it was the age of E. L. Godkin, Thomas Nast, and free-wheeling editorializing on a scale later generations might not accept. Beginnings are not always what men desire, but they are beginnings nonetheless. The Gilded Age witnessed pioneer efforts in education, when a few of the "Robber Barons" endowed institutions of higher learning; when most major eastern cities established art galleries; when states began to expand their educational systems and social services, forming molds which the twentieth century would expand. How curious and how often overlooked is the fact of great scientific and philosophical development in the period; it was the age of Charles S. Peirce, William James, and the Social Darwinists.

Doubtless because of its materialism, the energy it showed among its people, and its fascinating studies in power, the Gilded Age has lent itself to deterministic analysis. No recent student approached the era with more bias than did Matthew Josephson, three of whose works have remained standard interpretations of the period for a generation. Frankly Marxist in his approach, Josephson saw the period in terms of economic, political, and social exploitation of the many by the few, for whom he coined the telling phrase "Robber Barons." He dealt with the period in terms of stark power, showing vividly how within his interpretive framework the late nineteenth century was a breeding ground for tyranny and corruption in every sphere of American life. His black-white interpretation of the period, chosen largely because of the ease of its generalizations, has influenced many, but on the whole it has presented no total view of the period or its actors.

Few if any students of the period have chosen to see it as it saw itself. Any historical problem or person should be approached in two stages: first, the student must decide how it appeared at the time of the event; second, using analysis and hindsight, he must determine its relevance and importance in the mainstream of its time and circumstance. This test has been applied without consistency to the Gilded Age. Because of its activity and transitional nature it does not lend itself to accurate, easy generalizations.

The nation's pent-up forces and emotions, focused by the tragic but compelling events of the early 1860's, burst forth with peace in the Gilded Age to seek wealth, power, and general material advancement. Of the great institutions that touched daily life, politics was doubtless the most real and most immediate to Americans of the Gilded Age. This may well have been the last generation of Americans who freely indulged a national taste for personal participation in the rough and tumble sport of American politics. Free from formal polls, advertising techniques, and what a later generation calls "the Madison Avenue approach," our grandparents and great-grandparents participated freely and often with vehemence in the picnics, rallies, parades, stump speaking, and public dealings that marked the progress of elections, whether state or national. Politics was not only more strongly emphasized by, but more important to the men of this period. If, as most historians have judged, the parties of the era avoided the issues of the day and were in fact as much alike as peas in a pod, how explain this great public interest in such long-dead issues as the tariff, currency reform, and internal improvements? One answer must surely be that the parties were not alike to the people of the time, and that the issues were fully as diversified, clear, and different as those of a later generation.

It is true that much of these political fireworks and most of these issues seem distant and even unreal today, but that does not invalidate their earlier appeal. Some of these issues—the currency and the tariff, for instance—survive in modified form to arouse interest among politicians and constituents alike.

The importance of politics to Americans of that period showed the vitality of the democratic spirit. Public interest in government was very much alive, working within a viable tradition of changing party politics. No one can blink away the massive corruption in many areas of politics in the period, especially in city and state government; but these festering sores, many of which were healed during the Gilded Age, should not blind students to the real accomplishments in politics. The closeness of all the national elections of the period illustrates the degree and kind of labor necessary for any party's victory and the extent to which it could marshal support among constituents. The Gilded Age and its interest in government and politics, whatever its faults in both spheres, must not be forgotten when the accounts are cast up for an analysis of democratic rule in the American party system.

Few generations produced a more striking set of party leaders, contrary to the views of many scholars who portray it as an age of drab issues and dull men. The Republicans, long dominant on the national scene, could count on a host of glamorous if not always wise or successful military heroes to fill its rosters. The defected South after 1876 could return its men in grey to public office with equal fanfare, if often with worse results. Few are the generations that can match for political effectiveness and appeal such figures as Grant, James G. Blaine, "Lord Roscoe" Conkling and his New York cohorts, or the Boys in Blue. There were also the less colorful but perhaps more effective men like Hayes, Arthur, McKinley, and a powerful senatorial group. Nor were the reformers silent. Thomas Nast, Horace Greeley, E. L. Godkin, Henry and Brooks Adams, Peter Cooper, and others raised the standard of reform in many fields. Public and private probity and integrity were never eclipsed, no matter to what depths certain departments of government fell under some men. Newspaper reporting and editorializing were merciless. It was also a time of free-wheeling third party movements in both politics and labor—the Greenbackers, Socialists, Anarchists, Prohibitionists, and even a few early Communists kept the pot of political change simmering, if not at times boiling.

Contrary to accepted textbook clichés, the Republican party was a vital organization, composed of more than retired colonels and grafting politicians. Fighting for its life and for the consolidation of the great gains made under Lincoln, it dominated the White House during most of this era. It controlled most of the northern and western states by adopting and enacting the greatest program of nationalism and government spending since Federalism. Far from fearing strong central government, the Republicans of this era wrote into law most of Hamilton's theories, arguing that whatever their faults, their merits were greater when viewed in the context of the whole nation's welfare. This centralization, repugnant to many unsuspecting latter-day Republicans, accounted for the party's success and also for much of lasting good within the country's economic and social structure. Its cost, as is the case with any program, is another matter, largely of alternatives available at the time. Perhaps it is not too much to say that the country as a whole benefited more quickly under this Republican theory than it would have under a Democratic administration committed largely to states' rights and the trappings of prewar theory.

And what of the society of the time, its culture, taste, manners, and morals? Was it, as most students would believe, made up of the gauche mob now risen to affluence and to new middle-class status on the war's wealth and the postwar period's endless opportunities? How familiar is the standard historical picture of the age: the tasteless reading matter, the lack of interest in the arts and music, the garish architecture rearing up on avenues of small country hamlets as well as proud cities, and the aping of English and French manners and style. Where, critics then and later asked, was the native American architecture, art, music, manners? It was an age of extremes—of low wages and huge dividends, of garish display and of poverty, of opulent richness in one row of houses and of degrading poverty a block away. Socially the gulf between the haves and the have-nots was greater than our generation would recognize. Who can forget the huge balls and parties thrown by the gentry, and who can visit Newport, Saratoga Springs, or Greenbriar without staring in awe at the "cottages" and hostelries built to house the idle rich?

But is this the whole story, this stereotype dealing in extremes? The answer, . . . is not quite so clearly cut and dried. It seems a human failing to expect the worst of mankind. Students of the Gilded Age have fastened upon popular culture as proof of the period's tastelessness, ignoring or forgetting the rich vitality which the arts and culture displayed in many fields. The Chautauqua, for instance, was not the thing of chaff and wind depicted by many, and like the lyceum before the Civil War, served a real educational purpose. That it sought basically to perpetuate the manners and morals of the age hardly condemns it, for all such institutions do likewise. That it dealt largely with accepted themes should not blind us also to the new ideas and attitudes it brought to countless towns, large and small alike, enlivening with a combination of entertainment and culture the isolated and dull existence of a predominantly rural nation.

It is easy also to forget the amount of good or at least respectable literature both written and read, the flourishing and often culturally important magazines and newspapers, and the popular interest in both applied and theoretical science. This generation supported more intellectual organs of print than a far richer twentieth century does. The arts were by no means stagnant. The theater, music, the opera all drew large and appreciative audiences, presented tasteful and great works, and reflected new developments as well as their counterparts did elsewhere in the world. Surely there was bad taste, especially among the crassest *nouveaux riches*. But there was also a solid stratum of good taste, intellectual ferment, and artistic endeavor to redeem at least some of the more public and therefore better remembered faults and lapses.

It is easy also to forget the writers and artists, the thinkers and scientists of the period, who seem somehow unreal or small in stature compared to successors. Literature was not limited to women's fiction, Horatio Alger, or the cruder humor of Mark Twain. There was William Dean Howells, the nascent school of realism centering on Hamlin Garland, Edward Eggleston, and others. There were the many solid monthlies and quarterlies that found ready audiences for heavy wares, which would doubtless die today. In the light of cold criticism, the popular fiction devoured by schoolboys and swooning maidens was probably no worse, if such standards there be, than that imbibed by the same groups today.

In the sciences it was a remarkable period, producing a number of distinguished philosophers, educators, experimenters, and theologians. Any generation that can boast William James, Charles Peirce, and Josiah Royce need not hang its head in shame. But there were the lesser known figures of equal import such as the men who founded the Johns Hopkins University, other men who renovated the curriculum at Harvard and Yale, the growing scientific faculties at most important schools. Many of the ideas these men set in motion came full circle only later, but as prophets before their time, they were at least free to work and theorize in the Gilded Age. The development of the nation's school system, both public and private, was a great boon to the spread of new ideas, and a gradually expanding and vital curriculum meant better education for life and living.

But granted that this solid foundation of innovation and continuity lie beneath the age's public and historical front, what of the corruption—the Whisky Ring, the Indian Frauds, the Star Routes, the Credit Mobilier—that hangs like a bad odor over the whole period? Was corruption in politics and business as general as it has been depicted? Professor Hoogenboom answers no, pointing out, while not excusing or ignoring these great public scandals, that the attention paid them has obscured the presence of a civil service board under Grant which was not entirely ineffective. It seems unlikely that any substantial portion of the federal civil service was corrupt or inefficient, despite the usual lurid picture of public malfeasance. And while no one denies the presence of governmental and political chicanery, the people of the time were at least aware of it. Few periods have had so articulate a set of reformers with so many organs open to them for disseminating their views; their voice is measured by the degree to which their protests have overemphasized the age's corruption. There is no evidence, furthermore, that the public was more tolerant of corruption than before or after the Gilded Age.

Of all fields of endeavor, none has suffered more from this picture of general corruption than business and finance. Black Friday, the Erie War, "watered stock," all stand in the shadows of such men as Commodore Vanderbilt, "Jubilee Jim" Fisk, "Uncle Dan'l" Drew, the genial Andrew Carnegie, the bloodless Jay Gould, and the grimmest but most potent of all the Robber Barons, John D. Rockefeller. Wresting billions from a complacent and tolerant public, corrupting legislatures, dominating senates and presidents, wasting a nation's resources, pursuing no ethic save self-advancement—such is the standard portrait of their lives and works.

Like most stereotypes, there is enough truth in these assertions to give appeal to the total picture. It is hard to justify in twentieth-century terms the economic development of the nation in this generation. Yet, as Professor Tipple says with felicitous common sense, the generation involved thought relatively little of the antics of the stock exchange and wheat pit. They had always been unregulated and were part of the philosophy of free enterprise and go-getting that supposedly supported the American system. The color and publicity of the corporate jerry-building obscured solid gains and lasting achievements of lesser figures. For every Daniel Drew there was a smaller man in local industry and finance with at least a little more sagacity or less abandon. And, as we often forget, the era's economic opportunists were sometimes considered radicals by their compatriots, attacking as they did the hallowed American institution of competition, revealing a contradiction that most Americans had not seen—individualism devouring itself until further individualism was impossible.

It would be easy to insist that the end result of this economic activity was good, bringing standardization of products, settled prices, less waste, and consolidation that made the economy more sound. But such a conclusion smells of whitewash. Suffice it to say that the stereotype of the Robber Baron is much overdrawn. It must be balanced with a fuller picture, showing the new technology he often brought to his industry, the wealth and resources he developed for the economy in general, the social good he sometimes did with his money, offsetting the bitter fact that he paid little in taxes. Some might argue that the government should have regulated, taxed, and controlled business in more sane channels of development, that it should perhaps have participated in the economy; but this was not at the time a feasible alternative. Moreover, there was amid all the greed and overbuilding, an inevitable if unseen social return on the investments of the Gilded Age. And perhaps the tax favors, gifts of public domain, and government grants to business were not as exorbitant as they seem.

For labor this also had advantages. Most working men could aspire with some shred of logic to emulate Rockefeller and Carnegie, themselves fulfillments of the "rags to riches" myth. They could also feel that in the long run their wages rose, their hours of labor shortened, their working conditions improved, and their general economic security expanded. They would not recognize the benefits their grandchildren enjoy under highly organized labor, but by pre–Civil War standards, there is no doubt that the worker like the businessman advanced during the Gilded Age. Labor's gains do not seem as vivid as those of capital. The worker's story is written too largely, however, in the lurid phrases of strikes and depressions, while the prosaic statistics that record real growth and progress, though apparently slow to a later generation, lie forgotten in the dust of faulty memory.

Henry Adams the man disliked the age's crass materialism and often questionable morality, but he was a prescient observer and, when cast in the role of historian, saw its deeper accomplishments. As the century ended and the whole long process of growth and change fell into some pattern, he could say of these developments: "How much they cost was another matter; if the public is ever driven to its last resources and the usual remedies of chaos, the result will probably cost more." Perhaps the most important development in recent American history has been the peaceful and steady narrowing of the gap between the extreme haves and the have-nots, the very rich and the very poor. There is much irony in realizing that while the men and measures of the Gilded Age seemed to widen this gap by piling fortune upon fortune, they also helped close it. They brought amelioration of the divisive issues of the day in the economy, the political system, and society that would have wrecked a less flexible and optimistic system. The belief in progress, savored with enough evidence to make it compelling to the masses of Americans, and the nation's widespread wealth gave the lie to those who predicted that the arrogance of riches would soon clash bloodily with the resentment of poverty. In this watershed period, it was no small accomplishment to ease those great tensions peacefully, despite periodic flurries of violence in hard times, and to provide safety valves for their future reduction.

And the hard, welcome fact remains that the nation *did* grow stronger in all spheres. The foundations for future expansion as a world power economically second to none were laid during this period. The questionable practices, rapid growth, and waste did not triumph over hard work and common sense. Whatever else may be said of the age, it built. . . .

The Machine as Deity and Demon

ALAN TRACHTENBERG

I

Even before the Civil War, the westward trails were destined to be lined with tracks; the pony express and the covered wagon, like the mounted Plains Indian, would yield to the Iron Horse. For if the West of "myth and symbol" . . . provided one perspective by which Americans might view their society, the machine provided another. The two images fused into a single picture of a progressive civilization fulfilling a providential mission. . . . Many Americans before the Civil War had believed that industrial technology and the factory system would serve as historic instruments of republican values, diffusing civic virtue and enlightenment along with material wealth. Factories, railroads, and telegraph wires seemed the very engines of a democratic future. Ritual celebrations of machinery and fervently optimistic prophecies of abundance continued throughout the Gilded Age, notably at the two great international expositions, in Philadelphia in 1876, and in Chicago in 1893.

The image of the machine, like the image of the West, proved to be a complex symbol, increasingly charged with contradictory meanings and implications. If the machine seemed the prime cause of the abundance of new products changing the character of daily life, it also seemed responsible for newly visible poverty, slums, and an unexpected wretchedness of industrial conditions. While it inspired confidence in some quarters, it also provoked dismay, often arousing hope and gloom in the same minds. For, accompanying the mechanization of industry, of transportation, and of daily existence, were the most severe contrasts yet visible in American society, contrasts between "progress and poverty" (in Henry George's words), which seemed to many a mockery of the republican dream, a haunting paradox. Each act of national celebration seemed to evoke its opposite. The 1877 railroad strike, the first instance of machine smashing and class violence on a national scale, followed the 1876 Centennial Exposition, and the even fiercer Pullman strike of 1894 came fast on the heels of the World's Columbian Exposition of 1893.

It is no wonder that closer examination of popular celebrations discloses bewilderment and fear. . . . In the language of literature, a machine (railroad or steamship) bursting on a peaceful natural setting represented a symbolic version of the trauma inflicted on American society by unexpectedly rapid mechanization. The popular mode of celebration covered over all signs of trauma with expressions of confidence and fulsome praise. But confidence proved difficult to sustain in the face of the evidence.

Current events instilled doubt at the very site of celebration. A period of great economic growth, of steadily rising per capita wealth, and new urban markets feeding an expanding industrial plant, the Gilded Age was also wracked with persisting crises. An international "great depression" from 1873 to 1896 afflicted all industrial nations with chronic overproduction and dramatically falling prices, averaging one-third on all commodities. . . . A perilously uneven business cycle continued for more than twenty years, affecting all sections of the economy: constant market uncertainties and stiffening competition at home and abroad for business; inexplicable surpluses and declining world prices, together with tightening credit for farmers; wage cuts, extended layoffs and irregular employment, and worsening conditions, even starvation, for industrial workers. . . . Thus, even in the shadow of glorious new machines displayed at the fairs, the public sense of crisis deepened.

No wonder modern machinery struck observers, especially those associated with the business community, as in Charles Francis Adams, Jr.'s words, "an incalculable force." The tempo of crisis accelerated in the 1870's. Farmers agitated through Granger clubs and the Greenback Party against the government's policy of supporting business through deflationary hard money and the gold standard. Industrial unrest reached a climax and a momentary catharsis in July 1877, when fears of a new civil war spread across the country during the great railroad strike. Provoked by a 10 percent wage cut announced without warning by the Baltimore and Ohio line, a measure to halt a declining rate of profit, the strike spread like wildfire to other lines, reaching from Baltimore to Pittsburgh, Chicago, St. Louis, Kansas City, and San Francisco. The apparently spontaneous work stoppages met with approval and support from local merchants, farmers, clergy, and politicians, tapping reserves of anger and wrath against the railroad companies. Workers in other industries joined the walkout, and for a short spell it seemed that the United States faced a mass rebellion, a recurrence of the Paris Commune of 1871 on an even vaster scale. In some communities (St. Louis, for example) committees of strikers briefly assumed control of government and railroad services.

The strike turned bloody and destructive, arousing a vehemence of response from big business and the national government even surpassing the wrath vented by strikers against railroad yards and equipment. . . . The newly inaugurated President, Rutherford Hayes, invoked his powers of military intervention and called out federal troops to protect "by force" (as he noted in his diary) the property of the railroad companies, among whose leaders he counted many of his closest friends and supporters. In the end, the strike left more than a hundred dead, millions of dollars of property destroyed, and a toughened company and government stand against unions. Strikers were very often fired and blacklisted, their leaders fined and jailed.

The War Department issued a pamphlet on "riot duty" and constructed for the first time a system of armories in major cities to house a standing "national guard." Industrialization of the state's military force seemed a necessary adjunct to the mechanization of production.

The very extremes of effect lent to the machine an aura of supreme power, as if it were an autonomous force that held human society in its grip. In *The First Century of the Republic,* a book of essays published by *Harper's* magazine in celebration of the nation's centennial in 1876, the economist David Wells observed that "like one of our mighty rivers," mechanization was "beyond control." And indeed the display in Machinery Hall in Philadelphia that summer gave credence to the image of a flood, though without Wells's ominous note. Here, in an exposition of machines removed from their working location, a profusion of mechanisms seduced the eye: power looms, lathes, sewing machines, presses, pumps, toolmaking machines, axles, shafts, wire cables, and locomotives. . . . Alexander Graham Bell here gave the world first notice of the greatest wonder of electrical communication: the telephone. For sheer grandeur and sublimity, however, the mechanisms of communication could not compete with the two most imposing structures in the Hall: the thirty-foot-high Corliss Double Walking-Beam Steam Engine, which powered the entire ensemble from a single source, and its counterpart, a 7,000-pound electrical pendulum clock which governed, to the second, twenty-six lesser "slave" clocks around the building. Unstinted but channeled power, and precisely regulated time: that combination seemed to hold the secret of progress. . . .

II

The idea of an autonomous and omnipotent machine, brooking no resistance against its untold and ineluctable powers, became an article of faith. The image implied a popular social theory: the machine as a "human benefactor," a "great emancipator of man from the bondage of labor." Modern technology was mankind's "civilizing force," driving out superstition, poverty, ignorance. "Better morals, better sanitary conditions, better health, better wages," wrote Carroll D. Wright, chief of the Massachusetts Bureau of Statistics of Labor, in 1882; "these are the practical results of the factory system, as compared with what preceded it, and the results of all these have been a keener intelligence." Wright's paper, originally given as an address before the American Social Science Association, bore the title "The Factory System as an Element in Civilization."

The events of the 1870's and 1880's, however, also elicited less sanguine accounts of what the factory system had wrought. . . . Not surprisingly, a growing number of Americans openly questioned whether industrialization was in fact, in Henry George's words, "an unmixed good." As if in pointed rebuke of Wright's arguments and images, George observed the following year, in *Social Problems* (1883), that so-called labor-saving inventions, the "greater employment of machinery," and "greater division of labor," result in "positive evils" for the working masses, "degrading men into the position of mere feeders of machines.'' Machines employed in production under the present system are ''absolutely injurious,'' ''rendering the workman more dependent; depriving him of skill and of opportunities to acquire it; lessening his control over his own condition and his hope of improving it; cramping his mind, and in many cases distorting and enervating his body.'' . . . George plainly perceived the process of degradation in factory labor as strictly mechanical, experienced as an *effect* of machinery.

. . . George, a native Philadelphian of middle-class birth who had wandered to California in the late 1850's, working as a seaman, printer, newspaperman, failing as a Democratic candidate for office and as the owner of an independent newspaper, wished to arouse the nation to its plight, urging the adoption of a ''single tax'' against land rents as the solution to the paradox whereby ''laborsaving machinery everywhere fails to benefit laborers.'' His *Progress and Poverty,* written in the wake of the destruction, violence, and frustration of the summer of 1877, fuses evangelical fervor with simplified Ricardian economic theory; its simplicity of analysis and solution, its jeremiad rhetoric of righteousness and exhortation, helped the book find a remarkably wide audience. It reached more than 2 million readers by the end of the century. Appealing to a range of political sentiments and economic interests, George evoked a vision of older republican and entrepreneurial values restored through the ''single tax'' in the new corporate industrial world. . . .

George's picture of the failures of the machine and of its potential promise corresponded to the perceptions of a significant section of the society, particularly since he promised a change fundamentally within the existing order, the existing relations of capital and labor. Among representatives of older ruling groups, the picture held less promise. ''It is useless for men to stand in the way of steam-engines,'' wrote Charles Francis Adams, Jr., in 1868. Adams, from one of the oldest Eastern families of property and former political status, would soon join forces with the engine as corporate executive of railroad and other enterprises. His less sanguine brother, Henry Adams, wrote later in *The Education of Henry Adams* (1907), regarding his own ''failure,'' that ''the whole mechanical consolidation of force ruthlessly stamped out the life of the class into which Adams was born.'' Devising a theory of history based on ''forces,'' Adams crystallized the technological determinism implicit in both the popular and academic thought of his time. . . .

. . . The familiarization of American society with machinery represents one of the major cultural processes of these years, even in such simple matters as riding in streetcars and elevators, getting used to packaged processed foods and the style of machine-made clothing, let alone growing accustomed to new harsh sounds and noxious odors near factories and railroad terminals. The proliferation of new machines and machine-made tools for industrial and agricultural production marked an even more drastic upheaval in the forms, rhythms, and patterns of physical labor.

Perhaps more expressive of changing cultural perceptions because of its greater diffusion than serious or ''high'' literature, popular fiction and folklore in these years represented machinery especially in its sheer power and exemption from human vulnerability. In regional folktales and ballads, such figures as the lumberjack Paul Bunyan, the railroad worker John Henry, the locomotive engineer Casey Jones pit their strength and skill and daring against the machine.

Dime-novel Western adventures depict orgies of shootings and killings with every variety of automatic repeating weapons, each named precisely. A magical machine, endowing its owner with ultimate powers of "civilization" against "savagery," the gun not only won the West in such fictions (as it did in fact) but helped make the notion of repeatability, of automation, familiar. Indeed, as recent scholars have remarked, the interchangeability of plots and characters in dime novels parallels the standardization of machine production that became a central feature of factory life in the 1880's. Dime novels also provided a field for technological fantasy; beginning with *The Huge Hunter,* or *The Steam Man of the Prairies* in 1865, these novels included inventors (often boys) as standard fare, along with robots (like the ten-foot steam man), armored flying vessels, electrified wire, and remote-control weapons. The fiction provided vicarious mechanical thrills along with fantasies of control and power. Machines are imagined as exotic instruments of destruction, only obliquely linked to the means of production revolutionizing the industrial system.

The fictive imagination of terror, of technological cataclysm, served as a form of familiarization. The implications of a technologized world and its potential for explosion were not lost on more troubled observers, who felt themselves on a precarious bridge between an earlier America and the present. . . .

. . . Nervousness provoked by modern mechanical life provided the theme of the widely read medical treatise by George M. Beard in 1884. A pioneering work in the study of neurasthenia, *American Nervousness* builds its case through an elaborate mechanical metaphor: the nervous system is like a machine presently under strain in response to the pressures of the machinery of civilized life. Like Thomas Edison's central electric-light generator, wrote Beard (a friend of the inventor), "the nervous system of man is the centre of the nerve-force supplying all the organs of the body." "Modern nervousness," he explains, "is the cry of the system struggling with its environment," with all the pressures exerted on striving Americans by the telegraph and railroad and printing press. Simply to be on time, Beard argues, exacts a toll from the human system. . . .

. . . [Beard] also discloses another source of severe anxiety prevalent among middle- and upper-class Americans, that of impending chaos, the rule of accident, exigency, and rampant city mobs. . . .

The fear of cataclysm implicit here is not so much technological as social: a fear manifest throughout the popular media after 1877 of uprisings and insurrection, of a smoldering volcano under the streets. For David Wells, writing in 1885, such popular disturbances as the agitation for an eight-hour day and talk of socialism "seem full of menace of a mustering of the barbarians from within rather than as of old from without, for an attack on the whole present organization of society, and even the permanency of civilization itself." Henry George, too, concluded *Progress and Poverty* with a picture of potential collapse, of "carnivals of destruction." "Whence shall come the new barbarians," he asked. "Go through the squalid quarters of great cities, and you may see, even now, their gathering hordes! How shall learning perish? Men will cease to read, and books will kindle fires and be turned into cartridges!" The association of social unrest with the imagery of technological violence, of new city crowds with ignorance and contempt for culture (or regression to "savagery"), fired the imagination with a nightmarish narrative of impending apocalypse. . . .

III

. . . Association of machines with violence suggest profound tensions among Americans who . . . otherwise saluted modern technology as a boon to republican ideals. Metaphors of wreckage and self-destruction seem to express unresolved cultural dilemmas, conflicting value systems such as those described by Leo Marx as "machine" and "garden," the values of mechanical progress and those of pastoral harmony in a peaceful landscape. But the coexistence of figures of destruction, of "dark Satanic mills," with those of unbounded Promethean production, also points in the direction of the Promethean effort itself, toward the character of the mechanization process. Subtle interweavings of destruction and creation formed the inner logic of the industrial capitalist system, a logic less conspicuous but nonetheless compelling in its consequences than the more dramatic versions of contradiction evoked by Henry George . . . As analysts here and in Europe had begun to discover, that system possessed a baffling unconscious energy which resulted in recurrent cycles of expansion and contraction, inflation and deflation, confidence and depression. Such aberrations seemed to follow from precisely those increases in productive power which marked the industrial world in these years.

If Americans seemed especially intense in their response to mechanization, especially obsessed with alternating images of mechanical plenitude and devastation, an explanation lies in the special circumstances of native industrialization, its speed, its scale, its thoroughness within a brief period. Suffering fewer social barriers, possessing the largest domestic region convertible to a national market without internal restriction, by the end of the century American industry rapidly surpassed its chief European rivals, England and Germany. Figures of absolute increase signified the triumph: the production of raw steel rising from 13 tons in 1860 to near 5,000 in 1890, and of steel rails multiplying ten times in the same years; total agricultural output tripling between 1870 and 1900. Agriculture showed the most dramatic and immediate evidence. A single mechanized farmer in 1896 was able to reap more wheat than eighteen men working with horses and hand equipment sixty years earlier. . . .

[The American] propensity [for mechanical improvement] characterized the entire industrial world, but it had been a special mark of American manufacturing since its beginnings. With a scarcity of skilled labor, of craftsmen and artisans with accumulated experience in nascent industrial processes such as spinning, weaving, and milling, American circumstances placed a premium on mechanical invention and improvement. Scarcity of skills together with cheapness of land had maintained a relatively high cost of labor in the young United States. . . . Without an inherited aristocratic social order, the new country held out more hope to entrepreneurs for social acceptance as well as material rewards. Many early industrial entrepreneurs had begun their working lives as craftsmen, mechanics with a knack for invention, and had risen to wealth and status as a result of their mechanical skill and entrepreneurial expertise. . . . By the 1850's, the practical Yankee inventor-entrepreneur, the tinkerer with an eye on profit, had come to seem an American type, proof of the republican principle that self-taught men of skill and ingenuity might rise to wealth and social position. . . .

Technological determinism implied that machines demanded their own improvement, that they controlled the forms of production and drove their owners and workers. Americans were taught to view their machines as independent agencies of power, causes of "progress." Machines seemed fixed in shape, definite self-propelled objects in space. In fact, however, machinery underwent constant change in appearance, in function, in design. Machines were working parts of a dynamic system. And the motives for change, the source of industrial dynamism, lay not in the inanimate machine but in the economic necessities perceived by its owners. Higher rates of productivity through economies of scale and velocity, through greater exploitation of machinery and reorganization of both factory labor and corporate structures, were deliberate goals chosen by business leaders out of economic need. . . .

. . . The American fascination with the machine . . . tended to divert attention from the countless small innovations at the work place, changes both in machinery and the design of work. . . . The belief that viewed "progress" as a relation between new machines and old, a matter of replacing the outmoded by the novel, obscured the transformations of labor, of the human relation to production, each mechanical improvement represented. Technological change in these years consisted of a vast interrelated pattern of novelty, developments in metallurgy, mining, chemistry, hydraulics, electricity feeding back into each other. . . . With steam power prevailing in the 1870's, machines grew bigger and faster, and factories resembled jungles of shafts, belts, axles, and gears to transmit power from immense prime movers. . . . Electricity offered new possibilities of conversion of power into heat, light, and motion, and permitted new efficiencies and economics in the design of factories, including decentralization, dispersion of work areas, and assembly lines. In both the transformative (textiles, chemicals, food processing, glass making) and assembling (construction, clothing, shoe, machine making) industries, electricity worked major alterations in the forms of labor. . . .

. . . Unsettled economic conditions made manufacturers obsessed with efficiency, with the breaking of bottlenecks, the logistics of work flow, the standardization of parts, measurements, and human effort. . . . As a result, human effort fell more and more into mechanical categories, as if the laborer might also be conceived as an interchangeable part. Furious efforts to cut labor costs led to the announcement of severe work rules, the replacement of traditional craftsmen by unskilled or semiskilled labor: the effort, that is, to lower the cost of wages by increasing investment in the fixed capital of new machinery. Such developments, . . . set the stage for several of the fiercest labor struggles of the 1880's and 1890's. The process of continual refinement and rationalization of machinery, leading to twentieth-century automation, represented to industrial workers a steady erosion of their autonomy, their control, and their crafts.

In the record, then, of mechanical change lay an intermingling of production and destruction, the scrapping of old machines, old processes, and old human skills. An inevitable wreckage accompanied the "progress in manufacturing" David Wells had described as a "mighty river." That image hinted at unconscious meanings, the figure of speech disclosing more than Wells himself recognized. "Like one of our mighty rivers," he wrote in 1876 about manufacturing, "its movement is beyond control." . . .

IV

. . . In the quest for greater productivity, for more efficient machines, more output per unit of cost, calculation of several kinds played an increasingly significant role. With the enlarged role of the accounting office in decisions relevant to materials and labor, transportation, advertising, and sales, mathematical considerations entered the business world in a major way. . . .

As if called forth by this prime economic motive, Frederick W. Taylor, a foreman at the Midvale Steel Company in Pennsylvania, inaugurated in the 1880's his famous "time-study" experiments, aimed at elimination of waste, inefficiency, and what he called "soldiering" on the part of workers. With his stopwatch—a further encroachment of time on physical movement—Taylor proposed to systematize exactly that process Wells had described as production through destruction: the absolute subordination of "living labor" to the machine. He envisioned a complete renovation of the production process, with standardization of tools and equipment, replanning of factories for greater efficiency, and a "piece-rate" method of payment as incentive for workers. In *The Principles of Scientific Management* (1911), Taylor made explicit the heart of his program: to take possession for management of the "mass of traditional knowledge" once possessed by the workers themselves, "knowledge handed down to them by word of mouth, through the many years in which their trade has been developed from the primitive condition." For Taylor the stopwatch and flowchart were basic instruments whereby management might reduce that knowledge to measurable motions, eradicating their workers' autonomy at one stroke while enhancing their productivity.

Thus, the social distribution of knowledge begins a major shift, a transference (as far as technology and technique are concerned) from bottom to top, in these years of extensive and intensive mechanization. Just as important, and as a symbol of the process, *thought* now appears often in the dumb, mystifying shapes of machines, of standing and moving mechanical objects as incapable of explaining themselves to the unknowing eye as the standing stones of ancient peoples. The momentous event of mechanization, of science and technology coming to perform the labor most significant to the productivity of the system, reproduced itself in ambivalent cultural images of machines and inventors, and in displacements running like waves of shock through the social order.

ꙮ *F U R T H E R   R E A D I N G*

Paul Avrich, *The Haymarket Tragedy* (1984)
Daniel Boorstin, *The Americans: The Democratic Experience* (1973)
Stuart W. Bruchey, *Enterprise: The Dynamic Economy of a Free People* (1990)
Mari Jo Buhle, *Women and American Socialism, 1870–1920* (1983)
Sean Cashman, *America in the Gilded Age* (1984)
S. Giedion, *Mechanization Takes Command* (1948)
Daniel Walker Howe, ed., *Victorian America* (1976)
Christopher Lasch, *The True and Only Heaven: Progress and Its Critics* (1991)
Donald B. Meyer, *The Positive Thinkers* (1985)
John L. Thomas, *Alternative America: Henry George, Edward Bellamy, Henry Demarest Lloyd and the Adversary Tradition* (1983)
Alan Trachtenberg, *The Brooklyn Bridge: The Incorporation of America Culture and Society in the Gilded Age* (1982)
Robert Wiebe, *The Search for Order, 1877–1920* (1967)

The Search for Order in Industrial America

⚜

Though operating at opposite ends of the socioeconomic ladder, industrial workers and factory owners sought to bring order to a volatile and often threatening world. For wage workers, the problem was rooted in both the genie of industrialization, with its march toward a more efficient (that is, cheaper) use of labor and toward the dilution of traditional artisan skills, and the imbalance of power between capitalists and themselves. For company owners, competitive pressures and unpredictable markets made the customary demands of skilled workers and the heavy investments required in capital goods fraught with peril. For labor and capital alike, organization beckoned as a lifeline in a sea of uncertainty.

⚜ D O C U M E N T S

The wide range of contemporary responses to marketplace pressures is evident in the documents that follow. In the first selection, excerpts from testimony before the landmark 1883 U.S. Senate investigation of the relations between labor and capital in Fall River, Massachusetts, mule spinner Thomas O'Donnell describes a workingman's desperate struggle to support his family. In the second document, the distinctive outlook of women cigar makers and typesetters is chronicled by journalist Jennie Cunningham Croly before the same committee. The attempt to make "moral worth," not wealth, the measure of worldly success was the transcendent aim of the Noble and Holy Order of the Knights of Labor, as is revealed in its constitutional preamble (document three). Part trade union, part political movement, and part fraternal order (but with a nearly universal membership that included women and blacks), the Knights articulated broad aims that contrasted with the subsequent emphasis by the trade unions affiliated with the American Federation of Labor on specific workplace-related grievances. In the fourth selection, John Mitchell, first president of the United Mine Workers of America (AF of L), identifies the collective-bargaining contract as the centerpiece of the trade-union program.

Next, Frederick Winslow Taylor, the father of scientific management, describes the training of "Schmidt, the little Dutchman." In this famous passage from his *Scientific Management* (1910), Taylor aimed to rationalize the recruitment and efficiency of hired labor. In the sixth selection, a response to contemporary attacks on "monopoly," Charles M. Schwab, chairman of the board of Bethlehem Steel Corporation, defends big business as a training ground for the application of scientific principles of production and rational labor-management relations. If both Taylorism and business "combination" reflected attempts to bring more predictable control to industry, the Sherman Act of 1890—the basis of antitrust law and subsequent prosecutions of the trusts in the Progressive Era—expressed the contrary pull of the older entrepreneurial ideal, the truly free and competitive marketplace.

Thomas O'Donnell on the Decline of the Factory Artisan, 1883

BOSTON, MASS., *October* 18, 1883

THOMAS O'DONNELL examined.

By the CHAIRMAN:

Question. Where do you live? *Answer.* At Fall River.
Q. How long have you lived in this country? *A.* Eleven years.
Q. Where were you born? *A.* In Ramsbotham, England.
Q. Have you been naturalized here? *A.* No, sir.

Life of a Mule-Spinner

Q. What is your business? *A.* I am a mule-spinner by trade. I have worked at it since I have been in this country—eleven years.

Q. Are you a married man? *A.* Yes, sir; I am a married man; have a wife and two children. I am not very well educated. I went to work when I was young, and have been working ever since in the cotton business; went to work when I was about eight or nine years old. I was going to state how I live. My children get along very well in summer time, on account of not having to buy fuel or shoes or one thing and another. I earn $1.50 a day and can't afford to pay a very big house rent. I pay $1.50 a week for rent, which comes to about $6 a month. . . .

Q. Do you have work right along? *A.* No, sir; since that strike we had down in Fall River about three years ago I have not worked much more than half the time, and that has brought my circumstances down very much.

Q. Why have you not worked more than half the time since then?— *A.* Well, at Fall River if a man has not got a boy to act as "back-boy" it is very hard for him to get along. In a great many cases they discharge men in that work and put in men who have boys.

Q. Men who have boys of their own? *A.* Men who have boys of their own capable enough to work in a mill, to earn 30 or 40 cents a day.

Child Labor Necessary to the Employment of Parents

Q. Is the object of that to enable the boy to earn something for himself? *A.* Well, no; the object is this: They are doing away with a great deal of mule-spinning there and putting in ring-spinning, and for that reason it takes a good deal of small help to run this ring work, and it throws the men out of work because they are doing away with the mules and putting these ring-frames in to take their places. For that reason they get all the small help they can to run these ring-frames. There are so many men in the city to work, and whoever has a boy can have work, and whoever has no boy stands no chance. Probably he may have a few months of work in the summer time, but will be discharged in the fall. That is what leaves me in poor circumstances. Our children, of course, are very often sickly from one cause or another, on account of not having sufficient clothes, or shoes, or food, or something. And also my woman; she never did work in a mill; she was a housekeeper, and for that reason she can't help me to anything at present, as many women do help their husbands down there, by working, like themselves. My wife never did work in a mill, and that leaves me to provide for the whole family. I have two children.

Hardship of Undertakers' and Doctors' Bills upon the Poor

And another thing that helped to keep me down: A year ago this month I buried the oldest boy we had, and that brings things very expensive on a poor man. For instance, it will cost there, to bury a body, about $100. Now, we could have that done in England for about £5; that would not amount to much more than about $20, or something in that neighborhood. That makes a good deal of difference. Doctors' bills are very heavy—about $2 a visit; and if a doctor comes once a day for two or three weeks it is quite a pile for a poor man to pay.

Q. Will not the doctor come for a dollar a day? *A.* You might get a man sometimes, and you sometimes won't, but they generally charge $2 a day.

Q. To operatives? *A.* Oh, all around. You might get one for $1.50 sometimes.

Q. They charge you as much as they charge people of more means? *A.* They charge as much as if I was the richest man in the city, except that some of them might be generous once in a while and put it down a little in the end; but the charge generally is $2. That makes it hard. . . .

Supporting a Family on $133 a Year

. . .

Q. Taking a full year back can you tell how much you have had?—*A.* That would be about fifteen weeks' work. Last winter, as I told you, I got in, and I worked up to about somewhere around Fast Day, or may be New Year's day; anyway, Mr. Howard has it down on his record, if you wish to have an exact answer to that question; he can answer it better than I can, because we have a sort of union there to keep ourselves together.

Q. Do you think you have had $150 within a year? *A.* No, sir.

Q. Have you had $125? *A.* Well, I could figure it up if I had time. The thirteen weeks is all I have had. . . .

Q. That would be somewhere about $133, if you had not lost any time? *A.* Yes, sir.

Q. That is all you have had? *A.* Yes, sir.

Q. To support yourself and wife and two children? *A.* Yes, sir.

Q. Have you had any help from outside? *A.* No, sir.

Q. Do you mean that yourself and wife and two children have had nothing but that for all this time? *A.* That is all. I got a couple dollars' worth of coal last winter, and the wood I picked up myself. I goes around with a shovel and picks up clams and wood.

Digging Clams to Eke out an Existence

Q. What do you do with the clams? *A.* We eat them. I don't get them to sell, but just to eat, for the family. That is the way my brother lives, too, mostly. He lives close by us.

Q. How many live in that way down there? *A.* I could not count them, they are so numerous. I suppose there are one thousand down there.

Q. A thousand that live on $150 a year? *A.* They live on less.

Q. Less than that? *A.* Yes; they live on less than I do.

Q. How long has that been so? *A.* Mostly so since I have been married.

Q. How long is that? *A.* Six years this month.

Too Poor to Go West

Q. Well, I want to know why you do not go out West on a $2,000 farm, or take up a homestead and break it and work it up, and then have it for yourself and family? *A.* I can't see how I could get out West. I have got nothing to go with.

Q. It would not cost you over $1,500. *A.* Well, I never saw over a $20 bill, and that is when I have been getting a month's pay at once. If some one would give me $1,500 I will go. . . .

Q. Are you a good workman? *A.* Yes, sir.

Q. Were you ever turned off because of misconduct or incapacity or unfitness for work? *A.* No, sir.

Q. Or because you did bad work? *A.* No, sir.

Q. Or because you made trouble among the help? *A.* No, sir.

Q. Did you ever have any personal trouble with an employer? *A.* No, sir.

Q. You have not anything now you say? *A.* No, sir.

Q. How old are you? *A.* About thirty.

Q. Is your health good? *A.* Yes, sir.

Q. What would you work for if you could get work right along; if you could be sure to have it for five years, staying right where you are? *A.* Well, if I was where my family could be with me, and I could have work every day I would take $1.50, and be glad to.

Q. One dollar and fifty cents a day, with three hundred days to the year, would make more than you make now in three or four years, would it not?

Only a Dollar's Worth of Coal in Ten Months

A. Well, I would have no opportunity then to pick up clams. I have had no coal except one dollar's worth since last Christmas.

Q. When do the clams give out? *A.* They give out in winter.

Q. You spoke of fuel—what do you have for fuel? *A.* Wood and coal.

Q. Where does the wood come from? *A.* I pick it up around the shore—any old pieces I see around that are not good for anything. There are many more that do the same thing.

Q. Do you get meat to live on much? *A.* Very seldom.

Q. What kinds of meat do you get for your family? *A.* Well, once in a while we gets a piece of pork and some clams and make a clam-chowder. That makes a very good meal. We sometimes get a piece of corn beef or something like that. . . .

Q. . . . . Have you had any beef-steak in your own family, of your own purchase, within a month? *A.* Yes; there was a half a pound, or a pound one Sunday—I think it was.

Q. Have you had only a pound or a half a pound on Sunday? *A.* That is all.

Q. A half pound of pork? *A.* Yes. About two pounds of pork I guess we have had in the month, to make clam-chowder with, and sometimes to fry a bit. . . .

Q. And there are four of you in the family? *A.* Yes, sir. . . .

Q. What other kinds of meat have you had within a year? *A.* Well, we have had corn beef twice I think that I can remember this year—on Sunday, for dinner.

Q. Twice is all that you can remember within a year? *A.* Yes—and some cabbage.

Q. What have you eaten? *A.* Well, bread mostly, when we could get it; we sometimes couldn't make out to get that, and have had to go without a meal.

Q. Has there been any day in the year that you have had to go without anything to eat? *A.* Yes, sir, several days.

Q. More than one day at a time? *A.* No.

Q. How about the children and your wife—did they go without anything to eat too?

The Children Crying for Food

A. My wife went out this morning and went to a neighbor's and got a loaf of bread and fetched it home, and when she got home the children were crying for something to eat.

Q. Have the children had anything to eat to-day except that, do you think? *A.* They had that loaf of bread—I don't know what they have had since then, if they have had anything.

Q. Did you leave any money at home? *A.* No, sir.

Q. If that loaf is gone, is there anything in the house? *A.* No, sir; unless my wife goes out and gets something; and I don't know who would mind the children while she goes out.

Q. Has she any money to get anything with? *A*. No, sir.

Q. Have the children gone without a meal at any time during the year? *A*. They have gone without bread some days, but we have sometimes got meal and made porridge of it.

Q. What kind of meal? *A*. Sometimes Indian meal, and sometimes oatmeal.

Q. Meal stirred up in hot water? *A*. Yes, sir.

Q. Is it cold weather down there now? *A*. It is very cold now.

Scant Clothing in Cold Weather

Q. What have the children got on in the way of clothing? *A*. They have got along very nicely all summer, but now they are beginning to feel quite sickly. One has one shoe on, a very poor one, and a slipper, that was picked up somewhere. The other has two odd shoes on, with the heel out. He has got cold and is sickly now.

Q. Have they any stockings? *A*. He had got stockings, but his feet comes through them, for there is a hole in the bottom of the shoe. . . .

Q. Is there anything else that you want to say to the committee? *A*. Well, as regards debts; it costs us so much for funeral expenses and doctors' expenses; I wanted to mention that.

The CHAIRMAN. You have stated that. It is clear that nobody can afford either to get sick or to die there.

The WITNESS. Well, there are plenty of them down there that are in very poor health, but I am in good health and my children generally are in fair health, but the children can't pick up anything and only get what I bring to them.

Q. Are you in debt? *A*. Yes, sir.

Q. How much? *A*. I am in debt for those funeral expenses now $15—since a year ago.

Q. Have you paid the rest? *A*. Yes, sir.

Q. You live in a hired tenement? *A*. Yes; but of course I can't pay a big rent. My rent is $6 a month. The man I am living under would come and put me right out and give me no notice either if I didn't pay my rent. He is a sheriff and auctioneer man. I don't know whether he has any authority to do it or not, but he does it with people.

Q. Do you see any way out of your troubles—what are you going to do for a living—or do you expect to have to stay right there? *A*. Yes, I can't run around with my family.

Q. You have nowhere to go to, and no way of getting there if there was any place to go to? *A*. No, sir; I have no means nor anything, so I am obliged to remain there and try to pick up something as I can.

Q. Do the children go to school? *A*. No, sir; they are not old enough; the oldest child is only three and a half; the youngest one is one and a half years old.

Q. Is there anything else you wanted to say? *A*. Nothing further, except that I would like some remedy to be got to help us poor people down there in some way. Excepting the Government decides to do something with us we have a poor show. We are all, or mostly all, in good health; that is, as far as the men who are at work go. . . . I am looking for work in a mill. The way they do there is this: There are about twelve or thirteen men that go into a mill every morning, and they have to stand their chance, looking for work. The man who has a boy with him he stands the best chance, and then, if it is my turn or a neighbor's turn who has no boy, if another man comes in who has a boy he is taken right in, and we are left out. I said to the boss once it was my turn to go in, and now you have taken on that man; what am I to do; I have got two little boys at home, one of them three years and a half and the other one year and a half old, and how am I to find something for them to eat; I can't get my turn when I come here.

He said he could not do anything for me. I says, "Have I got to starve; ain't I to have any work?" They are forcing these young boys into the mills that should not be in mills at all; forcing them in because they are throwing the mules out and putting on ring-frames. They are doing everything of that kind that they possibly can to crush down the poor people—the poor operatives there.

Jennie Cunningham Croly Relates the Story of a Working Girl, 1883

Story of a Working Girl

An intelligent cigar girl, recently on strike, said that of all the girls she knew, who had grown up with her and worked with her, the worst off were those who had married, for they had, almost invariably, to support the family, and suffer abuse and ill-treatment besides. This young woman is perhaps twenty-five or twenty-six years of age; she is by no means ill-looking, and is one of the most sensible and thoughtful of her class. She has always, as she says, had a comfortable home. Her father was an honest, industrious man; her mother a kindly, home-loving Englishwoman, who cooked, and washed, and ironed, and took the best care of her family. When the husband died she took in sewing and washing, and kept the children together, with their help, till a son and daughter married, and then the mother and only remaining daughter lived together, the daughter supporting the mother, and the mother taking care of the daughter, doing the little housework and all of the sewing, and occasionally helping by doing something in the way of sewing or taking care of children for a neighbor. "I never knew what it was to hear an unkind word," said the girl, when she related to me this little history, "and mother was never tired of doing anything she could to give me pleasure. I would far rather have had to support her than not all my days, and since she has been gone I still live alone and keep house, for I can't bear to part with her bits of things, and I feel more independent like in my own room, where I can come and go just as I please."

Cost of Her Support

"How much does it cost you to support yourself in your room?" I asked. "Well," she replied, "I have two little rooms in a rear house, but it's clean, and one of them has a window as looks out where it is quite fresh and pleasant. For these I pay $6 a month, and my living, I reckon, costs me, what with coal and wood and light, about $4 a week." Your washing, then, I remarked, would bring your weekly expenses, without extra fare, clothing, and the like up to $6 per week. "I do my washing and ironing myself," she said, "on Saturday afternoons, but you may count it $6 all the same, for it comes to about that."

Her Earnings

"How much are you able to earn, then, at cigar-making," I inquired. "Well, cigar-making used to be a pretty good business for first hands," she replied, with a pleasant look, at the thought of those old times. "I've seen the time when I could make $12 and $13 a week at cigar-making; but you can't do it now, and that was the reason why we struck; it was not for a rise; it was to have the superintendent back as was good to us, and give the girls some chance as well as the bosses."

Difficulties of Her Work

"How did the change of superintendents affect your interest," was asked. "Well, you see, we had been getting 80 cents a thousand, and a smart worker can make 2,000 cigars a day, counting a day from 7 o'clock in the morning till half past five in the afternoon, with half an hour for dinner, which is a regular ten-hours day. But sometimes, when we are very busy, like now, we'd have to work till 9 o'clock at night, and then we'd make 2,500, may be, and earn $2 in a day; but that would only be for a little while, and we could not do it for long. Besides, we never get the full count; if there is the least little flaw the inspector throws it out, and these do not count at all; but they always go through another sorting, and more than half of those that have been thrown out and are not counted in the girl's work are counted in as good all the same. Our superintendent and his inspector were very good to us; they didn't throw out unless there *was* a flaw; and they looked out that the tobacco was in good condition for rolling, neither too dry or too damp, for this makes a great difference in the doing of the work; so they made up their minds that this superintendent was too good and too much of a gentleman, and they discharged him and put a regular rough in his place, a man who bullied the girls and never spoke a civil word in giving an order, but just swore at them; and when he found how much the best hands could earn he cut the prices down from 80 to 65 cents a thousand and threw out at such a rate that the loss of pay went up from $1 to $2 a week; you see $1 a week out of each girl's wages, where 500 girls are employed, mounts up to $500, and is an item, but it cuts the wages of the girls down to a little over half what they used to be, and a good many of the best girls have given up the business. I think I'll give it up myself, for I can't earn enough to keep myself in a home of my own, and I don't like boarding."

The Manners of Rough Working Girls

Subsequently I asked her how it had happened that she had not married since her mother's death. Her reply was characteristic. She said, "Men was too sassy." She wouldn't mind so much supporting a man for company, but she didn't want to be abused for it. A good deal of the slang among the rougher girls, who work with men, is the same as that commonly used by the rudest men; but it would give a bystander, who might be shocked by it, a very false impression, if it were supposed that they were moral delinquents, and not abundantly able to "take care of themselves." They pride themselves on being "tough" able to "give as good as they get," but it is the universal testimony of men themselves who work in these shops that it is not these apparently rude and aggressive girls who fall; it is more frequently the gentle and timid, who crave affection and companionship, and must take them in any form in which they can get them. The manner of the majority of the girls is derived from their often dreadful associates and surroundings. Even correctness of language would be looked upon as "airs," and punished accordingly. Yet that appreciation, and even ambition for a different life exists in common with rough habits, and almost brutal surroundings, there is sufficient evidence. In one of the worst neighborhoods in the lower part of this city there live in two rooms three girls. Dens of wickedness are on either side of them and over the way, and the girls themselves would perhaps be taken by a superficial observer for specimens of the lowest order. For they can swagger, and even swear, and "talk back," but if rude words proceed beyond their limit they would not perhaps hesitate to hit back, and hit "straight," for no man who knows them in or out of the shop but respects them for all their free talk, and is well aware that they "don't stand no nonsense," and that they "know how to take care of themselves." The girls work in a type-foundry, and earn from $5 to $7, and $8 per week. Their father died in a drunken fight; their mother, as soon as they were old enough to do regular work, they relieved from outside labor, keeping her at home, "like a lady" and maintaining also a brother at school. Upon this brother their hopes and ambitions rest, and they are devoting all their young lives to him. Their mother died, but they retain their home, such as it is, and, inside, it is home to them, after all, and they have educated their brother at a high preparatory school and now at a medical college, for he is to be a professional man and a gentleman, and he is to be made so by their labor and sacrifices. . . .

The Purposes and Program of the Knights of Labor, 1878

The recent alarming development and aggression of aggregated wealth, which, unless checked, will inevitably lead to the pauperization and hopeless degradation of the toiling masses, render it imperative, if we desire to enjoy the blessings of life, that a check should be placed upon its power and upon unjust accumulation, and a system adopted which will secure to the laborer the fruits of his toil; and as this much-desired object can only be accomplished by the thorough unification of labor, and the united efforts of those who obey the divine injunction that "in the sweat of thy brow shalt thou eat bread," we have formed the [*name of local assembly*] with a view to securing the organization and direction, by co-operative effort, of the power of the industrial classes; and we submit to the world the objects sought to be accomplished by our organization, calling upon all who believe in securing "the greatest good to the greatest number" to aid and assist us.

Objectives

I. To bring within the folds of organization every department of productive industry, making knowledge a standpoint for action, and industrial, moral worth, not wealth, the true standard of individual and national greatness.

II. To secure to the toilers a proper share of the wealth that they create; more of the leisure that rightfully belongs to them; more [social] advantages, more of the benefits, privileges, and emoluments of the world; in a word, all those rights and privileges necessary to make them capable of enjoying, appreciating, defending, and perpetuating the blessings of good government.

III. To arrive at the true condition of the producing masses in their educational, moral, and financial condition, by demanding from the various governments the establishment of bureaus of Labor Statistics.

IV. The establishment of co-operative institutions, productive and distributive.

V. The reserving of the public lands—the heritage of the people—for the actual settler. Not another acre [is to be allocated] for railroads or speculators.

VI. The abrogation of all laws that do not bear equally upon capital and labor, the removal of unjust technicalities, delays, and discriminations in the administration of justice, and the adopting of measures providing for the health and safety of those engaged in mining, manufacturing, or building pursuits.

VII. The enactment of laws to compel chartered corporations to pay their employees weekly, in full, for labor performed during the preceding week, in the lawful money of the country.

VIII. The enactment of laws giving mechanics and laborers a first lien on their work for their full wages.

IX. The abolishment of the contract system on national, state, and municipal work.

X. The substitution of arbitration for strikes, whenever and wherever employers and employees are willing to meet on equitable grounds.

XI. The prohibition of the employment of children in workshops, mines and factories before attaining their fourteenth year.

XII. To abolish the system of letting out by contract the labor of convicts in our prisons and reformatory institutions.

XIII. To secure for both sexes equal pay for equal work.

XIV. The reduction of the hours of labor to eight per day, so that the laborers may have more time for social enjoyment and intellectual improvement, and be enabled to reap the advantages conferred by the labor-saving machinery which their brains have created.

XV. To prevail upon governments to establish a purely national circulating medium, based upon the faith and resources of the nation, and issued directly to the people, without the intervention of any system of banking corporations, which money shall be a legal tender in payment of all debts, public or private.

John Mitchell on the Need for Collective Bargaining, 1914

Mr. Mitchell . . . In my judgment there can be no permanent prosperity to the workingmen, there can be no permanent industrial peace, until the principle is firmly and fully established that in industrial life the settlements of wages, hours of labor, and all the important conditions of work, are made between the employers and the workingmen collectively and not between employers and working men individually. The individual workman theoretically bargains with his employer as to the wages to be paid by his employer; but practically there is no bargaining. The individual workman must accept the wages and conditions of employment that are offered to him by his employer. It is a matter of no concern at all to an employer if one workingman refuses employment. He thinks nothing about it, because there is another workingman ready to take the job.

As a consequence of this system of individual bargaining, which is really nonunionism, the conditions of the best men in the industry are brought down, practically, to a level with those of the weakest men in the industry. Collective bargaining, of course, means that there shall be a uniform and minimum standard of wages and that there shall be uniform hours of labor. . . .

I know that in the industry with which I am best acquainted, the coal industry, collective bargaining has not only increased tremendously the earnings of the mine workers, but what is perhaps of more importance it has given the whole mining population a different and a better view of life. That is, instead of being, as they once were, a hopeless, despondent people, whose labor brought them less than that upon which they could live decently, they have become a hopeful people; they have got a different outlook; they regard this as "our country," a country in which they feel an interest, a country that means something to them.

Now, it has given them that feeling of justifiable independence; it has made them better men, better citizens, better fathers, given them better homes; it has meant education for their children, and it has meant, in most cases, a provision for their old age. . . .

Mr. Thompson. Do the conditions which exist in the contract field exist also in the fields where the union does not exist, and where there are no contracts; or what, in general, is the difference between the two fields, if you know?

Mr. Mitchell. No; the conditions are not at all similar in the districts and States where the union is not established, and of course there is no contractual relation; I mean there is no collective bargaining in the nonunion fields. For instance, in nearly all the state of West Virginia, which is now the second coal-producing state in the United States, the men work under terms that are fixed by mine owners absolutely, and that is true of a great many of the Southern states—of Alabama, parts of Tennessee, and parts of Kentucky— the mine owners fix the terms of employment as they do in most parts of Colorado and Utah and New Mexico, and in parts of Pennsylvania there is what we call the Westmoreland County, Pennsylvania, district, and in western Maryland the terms are entirely fixed by the mine owners. The wages in all of these districts that I speak of are much lower than they are in the fields where trade agreements are made, and the hours of labor are longer in the nonunion fields. . . .

It seems to me, gentlemen, I repeat, that there can be no permanent industrial peace until workingmen have the right and exercise the right to collectively bargain with their employers for the sale of their labor. It does not matter that the head of some great corporation may be generous, that he may desire to improve the conditions of the working people. The working people are not satisfied with those gifts and benefactions which are given to them by their employers. What they want is not gifts; they want independence; they want security in their jobs—that reasonable security that makes them feel they may not be dismissed from their employment without good cause, and that they can not have in the absence of united action.

F. W. Taylor on the Ideal Worker, 1910

Our first step was the scientific selection of the workman. In dealing with workmen under this type of management, it is an inflexible rule to talk to and deal with only one man at a time, since each workman has his own special abilities and limitations, and since we are not dealing with men in masses, but are trying to develop each individual man to his highest state of efficiency and prosperity. Our first step was to find the proper workman to begin with. We therefore carefully watched and studied these 75 men for three or four days, at the end of which time we had picked out four men who appeared to be physically able to handle pig iron at the rate of 47 tons [as opposed to the customary $12\frac{1}{2}$ tons] per day. A careful study was then made of each of these men. We looked up their history as far back as practicable and thorough inquiries were made as to the character, habits, and the ambition of each of them. Finally we selected one from among the four as the most likely man to start with. He was a little Pennsylvania Dutchman who had been observed to trot back home for a mile or so after his work in the evening about as fresh as he was when he came trotting down to work in the morning. We found that upon wages of $1.15 a day he had succeeded in buying a small plot of ground, and that he was engaged in putting up the walls of a little house for himself in the morning before starting to work and at night after leaving. He also had the reputation of being exceedingly "close," that is, of placing a very high value on a dollar. As one man whom we talked to about him said, "A penny looks about the size of a cart-wheel to him." This man we will call Schmidt.

The task before us, then, narrowed itself down to getting Schmidt to handle 47 tons of pig iron per day and making him glad to do it. This was done as follows. Schmidt was called out from among the gang of pig-iron handlers and talked to somewhat in this way:

"Schmidt, are you a high-priced man?"

"Vell, I don't know vat you mean."

"Oh yes, you do. What I want to know is whether you are a high-priced man or not."

"Vell, I don't know vat you mean."

"Oh, come now, you answer my questions. What I want to find out is whether you are a high-priced man or one of these cheap fellows here. What I want to find out is whether you want to earn $1.85 a day or whether you are satisfied with $1.15, just the same as all those cheap fellows are getting."

"Did I vant $1.85 a day? Vas dot a high-priced man? Vell, yes, I vas a high-priced man."

"Oh, you're aggravating me. Of course you want $1.85 a day—every one wants it! You know perfectly well that that has very little to do with your being a high-priced man. For goodness' sake answer my questions, and don't waste any more of my time. Now come over here. You see that pile of pig iron?"

"Yes."

"You see that car?"

"Yes."

"Well, if you are a high-priced man, you will load that pig iron on that car to-morrow for $1.85. Now do wake up and answer my question. Tell me whether you are a high-priced man or not."

"Vell—did I got $1.85 for loading dot pig iron on dot car to-morrow?"

"Yes, of course you do, and you get $1.85 for loading a pile like that every day right through the year. That is what a high-priced man does, and you know it just as well as I do."

"Vell, dot's all right. I could load dot pig iron on the car to-morrow for $1.85, and I get it every day, don't I?"

"Certainly you do—certainly you do."

"Vell, den, I vas a high-priced man."

"Now, hold on, hold on. You know just as well as I do that a high-priced man has to do exactly as he's told from morning till night. You have seen this man here before, haven't you?"

"No, I never saw him."

"Well, if you are a high-priced man, you will do exactly as this man tells you to-morrow, from morning till night. When he tells you to pick up a pig and walk, you pick it up and you walk, and when he tells you to sit down and rest, you sit down. You do that right straight through the day. And what's more, no back talk. Now a high-priced man does just what he's told to do, and no back talk. Do you understand that? When this man tells you to walk, you walk; when he tells you to sit down, you sit down, and you don't talk back at him. Now you come on to work here to-morrow morning and I'll know before night whether you are really a high-priced man or not.''

This seems to be rather rough talk. And indeed it would be if applied to an educated mechanic, or even an intelligent laborer. With a man of the mentally sluggish type of Schmidt it is appropriate and not unkind, since it is effective in fixing his attention on the high wages which he wants and away from what, if it were called to his attention, he probably would consider impossibly hard work. . . .

Schmidt started to work, and all day long, and at regular intervals, was told by the man who stood over him with a watch, "Now pick up a pig and walk. Now sit down and rest. Now walk—now rest," etc. He worked when he was told to work, and rested when he was told to rest, and at half-past five in the afternoon had his $47\frac{1}{2}$ tons loaded on the car. And he practically never failed to work at this pace and do the task that was set him during the three years that the writer was at Bethlehem. And throughout this time he averaged a little more than $1.85 per day, whereas before he had never received over $1.15 per day, which was the ruling rate of wages at that time in Bethlehem. That is, he received 60 percent higher wages than were paid to other men who were not working on task work. One man after another was picked out and trained to handle pig iron at the rate of $47\frac{1}{2}$ tons per day until all of the pig iron was handled at this rate, and the men were receiving 60 percent more wages than other workmen around them.

The writer has given above a brief description of three of the four elements which constitute the essence of scientific management: first, the careful selection of the workman, and, second and third, the method of first inducing and then training and helping the workman to work according to the scientific method. Nothing has as yet been said about the science of handling pig iron. The writer trusts, however, that before leaving this illustration the reader will be thoroughly convinced that there is a science of handling pig iron, and further that this science amounts to so much that the man who is suited to handle pig iron cannot possibly understand it, nor even work in accordance with the laws of this science, without the help of those who are over him. . . .

Charles M. Schwab Defends Big Business, 1926

Big business has been charged with seeking a return on excessive capitalisation, with stamping out competition by ruthless and unscrupulous methods, and with oppressing labour. That these abuses of power have often occurred may be admitted; on the other hand they are by no means as

Reprinted with permission from ''Some Reflections on Big Business'' in *The Historians' History of the World* © 1926 by Encyclopaedia Britannica, Inc.

frequent as they used to be, and it can be shown that they are not necessary accompaniments to the conduct of large corporations. It would be easy to cite a great many important industries of which such charges would be utterly untrue. But the public is primarily interested in the question of prices; and it seems to be very generally the opinion among the uninformed that big business should be blamed for a large share of the increase in the cost of living. Now it is very true that where combination has replaced cut-throat competition, prices have been raised, but no one believes that prices could be indefinitely maintained at a level below the cost of production. Large corporations have naturally sought to avoid losses and to make a profit, and some have undoubtedly made exorbitant profits, but it could easily be demonstrated that on the whole, American big business has actually kept prices below what they would have been if combination had been effectually prevented. The profits of large corporations have largely come from the economies that have been effected; and where these have been very high, the natural result has been to attract new capital and effective competition into the field. It may be considered axiomatic that no combination can be strong enough to eliminate the possibility of effective competition; and this factor affords the consumer a very real protection against exploitation.

In recent years, moreover, rigid legislation has served to remedy the worst evils that used to be regarded as typical of the American "trusts." These laws provide for more effective scrutiny of methods of incorporation, and enlarge the responsibility of directors to stockholders and the public. Public opinion has also had its influence, and the typical "captain of industry" of to-day regards his position more as a public trust than as a mere opportunity for private gain.

The United States is not the only country that has witnessed the growth of big business, though it is unquestionably the most prominent one. In Great Britain combinations in a great many trades have been formed, though the tendency originally was to organise "selling combinations" rather than one large corporation. In late years many large industries have been united into single corporations maintaining a virtual monopoly. These consolidations have not aroused the hostility that similar combinations once did in America, nor has the Government sought to restore competition by legal interference.

In Germany, before the war, the tendency toward consolidation was often favoured rather than opposed by the Government. This was undoubtedly due in part to the superior advantage of large corporations in developing foreign trade, especially where a long period of "missionary" work is required to make the new market profitable. Early combinations in Germany were largely in the form of cartels, involving contracts among independent establishments. These contracts were designed to regulate the output of each concern, and in certain cases to fix prices. Very often, too, a central selling bureau for all the members of the combination was maintained. In Germany, too, are seen the most noteworthy examples of the so-called "vertical trust." The "vertical trust," it is hardly necessary to say, is one in which control is sought not so much in a single product, or allied products, but in all the things that go to make up the finished product from the source to the end. Many

American firms have extended their operations in like manner, though usually for the purpose of obtaining cheap and sufficient raw materials.

This is an age of science, and no man more than the engineer is applying the lessons of science to the promotion of the well-being and the happiness of mankind. The achievements of the American engineer are among the wonders of the modern world. The Panama Canal, the railways, the New York subways, the sky-scrapers, the great aqueduct tunnels, to say nothing of the stupendous manufacturing enterprises—these are among the most spectacular achievements which have yet come from the mind of man.

But there is one respect not so often talked about in which engineers are to-day taking the lead, and that is in the development of human engineering. We may build great buildings, dig deep tunnels, span rivers with stupendous bridges, erect great factories and lay uncounted miles of railway, but unless the men who must do the ordinary routine work of operation are imbued with the right spirit and have a healthy orientation toward their work, there can be no success. And so in recent years the engineers—and I use the term engineers in the broadest sense—have directed their energies not alone toward great mechanical achievements but toward the promotion of sound and amicable relations with labour.

The people who labour are not and cannot be treated like dumb, driven cattle; they are human beings, with feelings and sentiments, hopes and aspirations, and the fundamental problem of all industry is so to relate the human elements in the men who do the work, to the machines which they operate, that the men themselves shall be happy and healthy, and so that they shall thus be able to operate their machines with spirit and efficiency.

Few things in our modern world are more wonderful than the great enterprise which Henry Ford has developed. Mr. Ford has taught many new lessons in the handling of machinery and large-scale production. But all of Mr. Ford's machinery and plans would have amounted to little had he not been able to build upon the foundation of satisfied and happy employees. When during the World War I was placed at the head of Emergency Fleet Corporation, I realised that the need was not so much for machinery, or more machinery, as to put spirit and power into the hearts, minds and muscles of the rank and file of the men who were doing the work. To build great plants, to erect huge machines, would take time, and the war would not wait. To put new life and spirit into the men who were doing the job could be accomplished in a very short time. I paid, therefore, little attention to the mechanical and material end of the business. I devoted my time to going among the men, both the superintendents and the rank and file, and seeking to promote in them a spirit which would enable them to get almost miraculous results with the materials at their command.

Many people conceived the relationship between capital and labour as one of stress and struggle. They talk as though the interest of the two were different. My experience is that there can be no success in industry unless there is at least a measurable appreciation of what is so fundamentally true, namely, that the interests of labour and capital are identical. Perhaps the division of the effort of industry as between labour and capital is not always equitable, but the effort of all engaged in industry should be to make that division ever more equitable. And that is the direction which human engineering is taking to-day.

There is a distinct movement among industries all over the world toward giving the men a greater voice in the management, towards securing for the employees representation with the management in the consideration of problems of mutual interest. There is a sincere effort being made to give every man the benefit of the economies and the improvements which his efforts make possible, and great progress is being realised in making the men understand that their interest and the interest of the corporations for whom they work are the same.

As an illustration of the possibilities in this direction, the Bethlehem Steel Corporation is enabling and assisting its employees to purchase the preferred stock of the Company in order to create interest on the part of the employees in the activities of the Company. Another and similar instance of importance in securing cooperation between management and employees is being worked out in the Pennsylvania Railroad.

There are many other organisations, many groups of men, engaged in this movement for the perfection of human engineering. It is not only a movement which will promote the material well-being of our civilisation and continue to produce *big things,* but it is also a movement in which American engineers can well take greater pride, because it will produce *great men.*

The Sherman Anti-Trust Act, 1890

An ACT To protect trade and commerce against unlawful restraints and monopolies. . . .

Be it enacted

SEC. 1. Every contract, combination in the form of trust or otherwise, or conspiracy, in restraint of trade or commerce among the several States, or with foreign nations, is hereby declared to be illegal. Every person who shall make any such contract or engage in any such combination or conspiracy, shall be deemed guilty of a misdemeanor, and, on conviction thereof, shall be punished by fine not exceeding five thousand dollars, or by imprisonment not exceeding one year, or by both said punishments, in the discretion of the court.

SEC. 2. Every person who shall monopolize, or attempt to monopolize, or combine or conspire with any other person or persons, to monopolize any part of the trade or commerce among the several States, or with foreign nations, shall be deemed guilty of a misdemeanor, and, on conviction thereof, shall be punished by fine not exceeding five thousand dollars, or by imprisonment not exceeding one year, or by both said punishments, in the discretion of the court.

SEC. 3. Every contract, combination in form of trust or otherwise, or conspiracy, in restraint of trade or commerce in any Territory of the United

States or of the District of Columbia, or in restraint of trade or commerce between any such Territory and another, or between any such Territory or Territories and any State or States or the District of Columbia, or with foreign nations, or between the District of Columbia and any State or States or foreign nations, is hereby declared illegal. Every person who shall make any such contract or engage in any such combination or conspiracy, shall be deemed guilty of a misdemeanor, and, on conviction thereof, shall be punished by fine not exceeding five thousand dollars, or by imprisonment not exceeding one year, or by both said punishments, in the discretion of the court.

SEC. 4. The several circuit courts of the United States are hereby invested with jurisdiction to prevent and restrain violations of this act; and it shall be the duty of the several district attorneys of the United States, in their respective districts, under the direction of the Attorney-General, to institute proceedings in equity to prevent and restrain such violations. Such proceedings may be by way of petition setting forth the case and praying that such violation shall be enjoined or otherwise prohibited. When the parties complained of shall have been duly notified of such petition the courts shall proceed, as soon as may be, to the hearing and determination of the case; and pending such petition and before final decrees, the court may at any time make such temporary restraining order or prohibition as shall be deemed just in the premises.

SEC. 5. Whenever it shall appear to the court before which any proceeding under Section four of this act may be pending, that the ends of justice require that other parties should be brought before the court, the court may cause them to be summoned, whether they reside in the district in which the court is held or not; and subpoenas to that end may be served in any district by the marshal thereof.

SEC. 6. Any property owned under any contract or by any combination, or pursuant to any conspiracy (and being the subject thereof) mentioned in section one of this act, and being in the course of transportation from one State to another, or to a foreign country, shall be forfeited to the United States, and may be seized and condemned by like proceedings as those provided by law for the forfeiture, seizure, and condemnation of property imported into the United States contrary to law.

SEC. 7. Any person who shall be injured in his business or property by any other person or corporation by reason of anything forbidden or declared to be unlawful by this act, may sue therefor in any circuit court of the United States in the district in which the defendant resides or is found, without respect to the amount in controversy, and shall recover threefold the damages by him sustained, and the costs of suit, including a reasonable attorney's fee.

SEC. 8. That the word "person," or "persons," wherever used in this act shall be deemed to include corporations and associations existing under or authorized by the laws of either the United States, the laws of any of the Territories, the laws of any State, or the laws of any foreign country.

ɔʊ *E S S A Y S*

A key issue affecting industrial workers and owners at the turn of the century concerned who would control the productive process on the shop floor. In the first essay, a classic piece of labor history, historian David Montgomery of Yale University describes the skilled worker's elaborate contest for job control, ranging from the customary, informal rights of the trade to examples of highly organized interunion solidarity in the face of managerial initiatives. At another level, the tug-of-war in American industry raged within the business community itself, this time between the great corporations and the "little" men trying to scratch out an independent piece of industrial turf. George Rice's epic contest with the Standard Oil trust is the subject of business historian C. Joseph Pusateri's illuminating narrative in the second essay.

The Workers' Code of Ethics

DAVID MONTGOMERY

"In an industrial establishment which employs say from 500 to 1000 work-men, there will be found in many cases at least twenty to thirty different trades," wrote Frederick Winslow Taylor in his famous critique of the practices of industrial management which were then in vogue.

> The workmen in each of these trades have had their knowledge handed down to them by word of mouth. . . . This mass of rule-of-thumb or traditional knowl-edge may be said to be the principle asset or possession of every tradesman. . . . [The] foremen and superintendents [who comprise the management] know, bet-ter than anyone else, that their own knowledge and personal skill falls far short of the combined knowledge and dexterity of all the workmen under them. . . . They recognize the task before them as that of inducing each workman to use his best endeavors, his hardest work, all his traditional knowledge, his skill, his ingenuity, and his good-will–in a word, his "initiative," so as to yield the largest possible return to his employer."

Big Bill Haywood put the same point somewhat more pungently, when he declared: "The manager's brains are under the workman's cap."

Both Taylor and Haywood were describing the power which certain groups of workers exercised over the direction of production processes at the end of the nineteenth century, a power which the scientific management movement strove to abolish, and which the Industrial Workers of the World wished to enlarge and extend to all workers. It is important to note that both men found the basis of workers' power in the superiority of their knowledge over that of the factory owners. It is even more important to note that they

David Montgomery, "The Workers' Code of Ethics," in "Workers' Control of Machine Produc-tion in the Nineteenth Century," *Labor History*, vol. 17 (Fall 1976), pp. 486–509. Reprinted by permission of *Labor History*.

were referring not to "pre-industrial" work practices, but to the factory itself. . . .

My concern here . . . is . . . with the patterns of behavior which took shape in the second and third generations of industrial experience, largely among workers whose world had been fashioned from their youngest days by smoky mills, congested streets, recreation as a week-end affair and toil at the times and the pace dictated by the clock (except when a more or less lengthy layoff meant no work at all). It was such workers, the veterans, if you will, of industrial life, with whom Taylor was preoccupied. They had internalized the industrial sense of time, they were highly disciplined in both individual and collective behavior, and they regarded both an extensive division of labor and machine production as their natural environments. But they had often fashioned from these attributes neither the docile obedience of automatons, nor the individualism of the "upwardly mobile," but a form of control of productive processes which became increasingly collective, deliberate and aggressive, until American employers launched a partially successful counterattack under the banners of scientific management and the open shop drive.

Workers' control of production, however, was not a condition or state of affairs which existed at any point in time, but a struggle, a chronic battle in industrial life which assumed a variety of forms. Those forms may be treated as successive stages in a pattern of historical evolution, though one must always remember that the stages overlapped each other chronologically in different industries, or even at different localities within the same industry, and that each successive stage incorporated the previous one, rather than replacing it. The three levels of development which appeared in the second half of the nineteenth century were those characterized by 1) the functional autonomy of the craftsman, 2) the union work rule, and 3) mutual support of diverse trades in rule enforcement and sympathetic strikes. Each of these levels will be examined here in turn, then in conclusion some observations will be made on the impact of scientific management and the open shop drive on the patterns of behavior they represented.

The functional autonomy of craftsmen rested on both their superior knowledge, which made them self-directing at their tasks, and the supervision which they gave to one or more helpers. Iron molders, glass blowers, coopers, paper machine tenders, locomotive engineers, mule spinners, boiler makers, pipe fitters, typographers, jiggermen in potteries, coal miners, iron rollers, puddlers and heaters, the operators of McKay or Goodyear stitching machines in shoe factories, and, in many instances, journeymen machinists and fitters in metal works exercised broad discretion in the direction of their own work and that of their helpers. They often hired and fired their own helpers and paid the latter some fixed portion of their own earnings.

James J. Davis, who was to end up as Warren Harding's Secretary of Labor, learned the trade of puddling iron by working as his father's helper in Sharon, Pennsylvania. "None of us ever went to school and learned the chemistry of it from books," he recalled. "We learned the trick by doing it, standing with our faces in the scorching heat while our hands puddled the metal in its glaring bath." His first job, in fact, had come at the age of twelve, when an aged puddler devised a scheme to enable him to continue the physically arduous exertion of the trade by taking on a boy (twelve-year old Davis) to relieve the helper of mundane tasks like stoking the furnace, so that the helper in turn could assume a larger share of the taxing work of stirring the iron as it "came to nature." By the time Davis felt he had learned enough to master his own furnace, he had to leave Sharon, because furnaces passed from father to son, and Davis' father was not yet ready to step down. As late as 1900, when Davis was living at home while attending business college after having been elected to public office, he took over his father's furnace every afternoon, through an arrangement the two had worked out between themselves.

The iron rollers of the Columbus Iron Works, in Ohio, have left us a clear record of how they managed their trade in the minute books of their local union from 1873 to 1876. The three twelve-man rolling teams, which constituted the union, negotiated a single tonnage rate with the company for each specific rolling job the company undertook. The workers then decided collectively, among themselves, what portion of that rate should go to each of them (and the shares were far from equal, ranging from $19\frac{1}{4}$ cents, out of the negotiated $1.13 a ton, for the roller, to 5 cents for the runout hooker), how work should be allocated among them, how many rounds on the rolls should be undertaken per day, what special arrangements should be made for the fiercely hot labors of the hookers during the summer, and how members should be hired and progress through the various ranks of the gang. To put it another way, all the boss did was to buy the equipment and raw materials and sell the finished product. . . .

Three aspects of the moral code, in which the craftsmen's autonomy was protectively enmeshed, deserve close attention. First, on most jobs there was a stint, an output quota fixed by the workers themselves. As the laments of scientific management's apostles about workers "soldiering" and the remarkable 1904 survey by the Commissioner of Labor, *Regulation and Restriction of Output,* made clear, stints flourished as widely without unions as with them. Abram Hewitt testified in 1867 that his puddlers in New Jersey, who were not unionized, worked 11 turns per week (5 $\frac{1}{2}$ days), made three heats per turn, and put 450 pounds of iron in each charge, all by arrangement among themselves. Thirty-five years later a stint still governed the trade, though a dramatic improvement in puddling furnaces was reflected in union rules which specified 11 turns with five heats per turn and 550 pounds per charge (a 104% improvement in productivity), while some nonunion mill workers followed the same routine but boiled bigger charges.

Stints were always under pressure from the employers, and were often stretched over the course of time by the combined force of competition among employers and improving technology. In this instance, productivity under union rules expanded more than three percent annually over three and half decades. But workers clung doggedly to the practice, and used their superior knowledge both to determine how much they should do and to outwit employers' efforts to wring more production out of them. In a farm equipment factory studied in 1902, for example, the machine shop, polishing department, fitting department and blacksmith shop all had fixed stints, which made each group of workers average very similar earnings despite the fact that all departments were on piecework. In the blacksmith shop, which unlike the others had no union rule fining those who earned too much, workers held down the pace by refusing to replace each part they removed from the heaters with a cold one. They emptied the heaters entirely, before refilling them and then waited for the new parts to heat up. Similarly, Taylor's colleague Carl Barth discovered a planer operator who avoided exceeding the stint while always looking busy, by simply removing the cutting tool from his machine from time to time, while letting it run merrily on.

"There is in every workroom a fashion, a habit of work," wrote efficiency consultant Henry Gantt, "and the new worker follows that fashion, for it isn't respectable not to." A quiver full of epithets awaited the deviant: 'hog,' 'hogger-in,' 'leader,' 'rooter,' 'chaser,' 'rusher,' 'runner,' 'swift,' 'boss's pet,' to mention some politer versions. And when a whole factory gained a reputation for feverish work, disdainful craftsmen would describe its occupants, as one did of the Gisholt turret lathe works, as comprised half "of farmers, and the other half, with few exceptions, of horse thieves." On the other hand, those who held fast to the carefully measured stint, despite the curses of their employers and the lure of higher earnings, depicted themselves as sober and trustworthy masters of their trades. Unlimited output led to slashed piece rates, irregular employment, drink and debauchery, they argued. Rationally restricted output, however, reflected "unselfish brotherhood," personal dignity, and "cultivation of the mind."

Second, as this language vividly suggests, the craftsmen's ethical code demanded a "manly" bearing toward the boss. Few words enjoyed more popularity in the nineteenth century than this honorific, with all its connotations of dignity, respectability, defiant egalitarianism, and patriarchal male supremacy. The worker who merited it refused to cower before the foreman's glares—in fact, often would not work at all when a boss was watching. When confronted with indignities, he was expected to respond like the machinist in Lowell, who found regulations posted in his shop in 1867 requiring all employees to be at their posts in their work clothes when the first bell rang, to remain there until the last bell, and to be prevented from leaving the works between those times by locked doors:

Not having been brought up under such a system of slavery, [he recalled,] I took my things and went out, followed in a few hours by the rest of the men. Thinking perhaps that it might be of some benefit to the rest, I remained with them on the strike. They went back to work with the understanding that the new rules should not apply except in regard to the doors being locked. A few days after I went for my pay and it was politely handed me without the trouble of asking for it.

Finally, "manliness" toward one's fellow workers was as important as it was toward the owners. "Undermining or conniving" at a brother's job was a form of hoggish behavior as objectionable as running more than one machine, or otherwise doing the work that belonged to two men. Union rules commanded the expulsion of members who performed such "dirty work," in order to secure employment or advancement for themselves. When the members of the Iron Heaters and Rollers Union at a Philadelphia mill learned in 1875 that one of their brothers had been fired "for dissatisfaction in regard to his management of the mill," and that another member had "undermined" the first with the superintendent and been promised his rolls, the delinquent was expelled from the lodge, along with a lodge member who defended him, and everyone went on strike to demand the immediate discharge of both excommunicants by the firm.

In short, a simple technological explanation for the control exercised by nineteenth-century craftsmen will not suffice. Technical knowledge acquired on the job was embedded in a mutualistic ethical code, also acquired on the job, and together these attributes provided skilled workers with considerable autonomy at their work and powers of resistance to the wishes of their employers. On the other hand, it was technologically possible for the worker's autonomy to be used in individualistic ways, which might promote his own mobility and identify his interests with those of the owner. The ubiquitous practice of subcontracting encouraged this tendency. In the needle trades, the long established custom of a tailor's taking work home to his family was transformed by his employment of other piece workers into the iniquitous "sweat shop" system. Among iron molders, the "berkshire" system expanded rapidly after 1850, as individual molders hired whole teams of helpers to assist them in producing a multitude of castings. Carpenters and bricklayers were lured into piece work systems of petty exploitation, and other forms of subcontracting flourished in stone quarrying, iron mining, anthracite mining, and even in railroad locomotive works, where entire units of an engine's construction were let out to the machinist who filed the lowest bid, and who then hired a crew to assist him in making and fitting the parts.

Subcontracting practices readily undermined both stints and the mutualistic ethic (though contractors were known to fix stints for their own protection in both garment and locomotive works), and they tended to flood many trades with trained, or semi-trained, workers who undercut wages and work standards. Their spread encouraged many craftsmen to move beyond reliance on their functional autonomy to the next higher level of craft control, the enactment and enforcement of union work rules. In one respect, union rules simply codified the autonomy I have already described. In fact, because they were often written down and enforced by joint action, union rules have a visibility to historians, which has made me resort to them already for evidence in the discussion of autonomy per se. But this intimate historical relationship between customary workers' autonomy and the union rule should not blind us to the fact that the latter represents a significant new stage of development.

The work rules of unions were referred to by their members as "legislation." The phrase denotes a shift from spontaneous to deliberate collective action, from a group ethical code to formal rules and sanctions, and from resistance to employers' pretensions to control over them. In some unions the rules were rather simple. The International Association of Machinists, for example, like its predecessors the Machinists and Blacksmiths' International Union and the many machinists' local assemblies of the Knights of Labor, simply specified a fixed term of apprenticeship for any prospective journeyman, established a standard wage for the trade, prohibited helpers or handymen from performing journeymen's work, and forbade any member from running more than one machine at a time or accepting any form of piece work payment.

Other unions had much more detailed and complex rules. There were, for example, sixty-six "Rules for Working" in the by-laws of the window-glass workers' Local Assembly 300 of the Knights of Labor. They specified that full crews had to be present "at each pot setting," that skimming could be done only at the beginning of blowing and at meal time, that blowers and gatherers should not "work faster than at the rate of nine rollers per hour," and that the "standard size of single strength rollers" should "be 40x58 to cut 38x56." No work was to be performed on Thanksgiving Day, Christmas, Decoration Day or Washington's Birthday, and no blower, gatherer or cutter could work between June 15 and September 15. In other words, during the summer months the union ruled that the fires were to be out. In 1884 the local assembly waged a long and successful strike to preserve its limit of 48 boxes of glass a week, a rule which its members considered the key to the dignity and welfare of the trade.

Nineteenth-century work rules were not ordinarily negotiated with employers or embodied in a contract. From the 1860's onward it became increasingly common for standard *wages* to be negotiated with employers or their associations, rather than fixed unilaterally as unions had tried earlier, but working rules changed more slowly. They were usually adopted unilaterally by local unions, or by the delegates to a national convention, and enforced by the refusal of the individual member to obey any command from an employer which violated them. Hopefully, the worker's refusal would be supported by the joint action of his shop mates, but if it was not, he was honor bound to pack his tool box and walk out alone, rather than break the union's laws. As Fred Reid put the point so well in his description of nineteenth-century Scottish miner's unionism: "The strength of organised labour was held to depend upon the manliness of the individual workman."

On the other hand, the autonomy of craftsmen which was codified in union rules was clearly not individualistic. Craftsmen were unmistakably and consciously group-made men, who sought to pull themselves upward by their collective boot straps. As unions waxed stronger after 1886, the number of strikes to enforce union rules grew steadily. It was, however, in union legislation against subcontracting that both the practical and ideological aspects of the conflict between group solidarity and upwardly mobile individualism became most evident, for these rules sought to regulate in the first instance not the employers' behavior, but that of the workers themselves. Thus the Iron Molders Union attacked the "berkshire" system by rules forbidding any of its members to employ a helper for any other purpose than "to skim, shake out and to cut sand," or to pay a helper out of his own earnings. In 1867, when

8,615 out of some 10,400 known molders in the country were union members, the national union legislated further that no member was allowed to go to work earlier than seven o'clock in the morning. During the 1880s the Brick Layers' Union checked subcontracting by banning its members from working for any contractor who could not raise enough capital to buy his own bricks. All building trades unions instructed their members not to permit contractors to work with tools along side with them. The United Mine Workers limited the number of helpers a bituminous miner could engage, usually to one, though the employment of several laborers by one miner remained widespread in anthracite mines through the first World War. The Carpenters and the Machinists outlawed piece work altogether, for the same purpose. The Amalgamated Iron and Steel Workers required the companies to pay helpers directly, rather than through the craftsmen, and fixed the share of tonnage rates to which helpers were entitled. All such regulations secured the group welfare of the workers involved by sharply rejecting society's enticements to become petty entrepreneurs, clarifying and intensifying the division of labor at the work place, and sharpening the line between employer and employee.

Where a trade was well unionized, a committee in each shop supervised the enforcement in that plant of the rules and standard wage which the union had adopted for the trade as a whole. The craft union and the craft local assembly of the Knights of Labor were forms of organization well adapted to such regulatory activities. The members were legislating, on matters on which they were unchallenged experts, rules which only their courage and solidarity could enforce. On one hand, the craft form of organization linked their personal interests to those of the trade, rather than those of the company in which they worked, while, on the other hand, their efforts to enforce the same rules on all of their employers, where they were successful, created at least a few islands of order in the nineteenth-century's economic ocean of anarchic competition.

Labor organizations of the late nineteenth century struggled persistently to transform workers' struggles to manage their own work from spontaneous to deliberate actions, just as they tried to subject wage strikes and efforts to shorten the working day to their conscious regulation. "The trade union movement is one of reason, one of deliberation, depending entirely upon the voluntary and sovereign actions of its members," declared the executive Council of the AFL [American Federation of Labor]. Only through "thorough organization," to use a favorite phrase of the day, was it possible to enforce a trade's work rules throughout a factory, mine, or construction site. Despite the growing number of strikes over union rules and union recognition in the late 1880s, the enforcement of workers' standards of control spread more often through the daily self-assertion of craftsmen on the job than through large and dramatic strikes. . . .

The third level of control struggles emerged when different trades lent each other support in their battles to enforce union rules and recognition. An examination of the strike statistics gathered by the U.S. Commissioner of Labor for the period 1881–1905 reveals the basic patterns of this development. Although there had been a steady increase in both the number and size of strikes between 1881 and 1886, the following 12 years saw a reversal of that growth, as stoppages became both smaller and increasingly confined to skilled crafts (except in 1894). With that change came three important and interrelated trends. First, the proportion of strikes called by unions rose sharply in comparison to spontaneous strikes. Nearly half of all strikes between 1881 and 1886 had occurred without union sanction or aid. In the seven years beginning with 1887 more than two-thirds of each year's strikes were deliberately called by a union, and in 1891 almost 75 percent of the strikes were official.

Secondly, as strikes became more deliberate and unionized, the proportion of strikes which dealt mainly with wages fell abruptly. Strikes to enforce union rules, enforce recognition of the union, and protect its members grew from 10 percent of the total or less before 1885 to the level of 19–20 percent between 1891 and 1893. Spontaneous strikes and strikes of laborers and factory operatives had almost invariably been aimed at increasing wages or preventing wage reductions, with the partial exception of 1886 when 20 percent of all strikes had been over hours. The more highly craftsmen became organized, however, the more often they struck and were locked out over work rules.

Third, unionization of workers grew on the whole faster than strike participation. The ratio of strike participants to membership in labor organizations fell almost smoothly from 109 in 1881 to 24 in 1888, rose abruptly in 1890 and 1891 (to 71 and 86 respectively), then resumed its downward trend to 36 in 1898, interrupted, of course, by a leap to 182 in 1894. In a word, calculation and organization were the dominant tendencies in strike activity, just as they were in the evolution of work rules during the nineteenth century. But the assertion of deliberate control through formal organization was sustained not only by high levels of militancy (a persistently high propensity to strike), but also by remarkably aggressive mutual support, which sometimes took the form of the unionization of all grades of workers within a single industry, but more often appeared in the form of sympathetic strikes involving members of different trade unions.

Joint organization of all grades of workers seemed most likely to flourish where no single craft clearly dominated the life of the workplace, in the way iron molders, brick layers, or iron puddlers did where they worked. It was also most likely to appear at the crest of the waves of strike activity among unskilled workers and operatives, as is hardly surprising, and to offer evidence of the organizational impulse in their ranks. In Philadelphia's shoe industry between 1884 and 1887, for example, the Knights of Labor successfully organized eleven local assemblies, ranging in size from 55 to 1000 members, each of which represented a different craft or cluster of related occupations, and formulated wage demands and work rules for its own members. Each assembly sent three delegates to District Assembly 70, the highest governing body of the Knights for the industry, which in turn selected seven representatives to meet in a city-wide arbitration committee with an equal number of employers' representatives. Within each factory a "shop union" elected by the workers in that plant handled grievances and enforced the rules of the local assemblies, aided by one male and one female "statistician," who kept track of the complex piece rates.

There is no evidence that local assemblies of unskilled workers or of semi-skilled operatives ever attempted to regulate production processes themselves in the way assemblies of glass blowers and other craftsmen did. They did try to restrict hiring to members of the Knights and sometimes regulated layoffs by seniority clauses. For the most part, however, assemblies of operatives and laborers confined their attention to wages and to protection of their members against arbitrary treatment by supervisors. On the other hand, the mere fact that such workers had been organized made it difficult for employers to grant concessions to their craftsmen at the expense of helpers and laborers. Consequently, the owners were faced simultaneously with higher wage bills and a reduction of their control in a domain where they had been accustomed to exercise unlimited authority.

Moreover, workers who directed important production processes were themselves at times reluctant to see their own underlings organized, and frequently sought to dominate the larger organization to which their helpers belonged. A case in point was offered by the experience of the Knights of Labor in the garment industry, where contractors were organized into local assemblies of their own, supposedly to cooperate with those of cutters, pressers, tailors, and sewing machine operators. Contractors were often charged with disrupting the unionization of their own employees, in order to promote their personal competitive advantages. Above all, they tried to discourage women from joining the operators' assemblies. As the secretary of a St. Louis tailors' local assembly revealed, contractors who were his fellow Knights were telling the parents of operators that "no dissent [*sic*] girl belong to an assembly."

On the other hand, the experience of the Knights in both the shoe and garment industries suggests that effective unionization of women operatives was likely to have a remarkably radicalizing impact on the organization. It closed the door decisively both on employers who wished to compensate for higher wages paid to craftsmen by exacting more from the unskilled, and on craftsmen who were tempted to advance themselves by sweating others. In Philadelphia, Toronto, Cincinnati, Beverly, and Lynn both the resistance of the manufacturers to unionism and the level of mutuality exhibited by the workers leapt upward noticeably when the women shoe workers organized along with the men. Furthermore, the sense of total organization made all shoe workers more exacting in their demands and less patient with the protracted arbitration procedures employed by the Knights. Quickie strikes became increasingly frequent as more and more shoe workers enrolled in the Order. Conversely, the shoe manufacturers banded tightly together to destroy the Knights of Labor.

In short, the organization of all grades of workers in any industry propelled craftsmen's collective rule making into a more aggressive relationship with the employers, even where it left existing styles of work substantially unchanged. The other form of joint action, sympathetic strikes, most often involved the unionized skilled crafts themselves, and consequently was more directly related to questions of control of production processes. When Fred S. Hall wrote in 1898 that sympathetic strikes had "come so much in vogue during the last few years," he was looking back on a period during which organized workers had shown a greater tendency to walk out in support of the struggles of other groups of workers than was the case in any other period in the history of recorded strike data. Only the years between 1901 and 1904 and those between 1917 and 1921 were to see the absolute number of sympathetic strikes approach even *one-half* the levels of 1890 and 1891. . . .

Eugene V. Debs was to extoll this extreme manifestation of mutuality as the "Christ-like virtue of sympathy," and to depict his own Pullman boycott, the epoch's most massive sympathetic action, as an open confrontation between that working-class virtue and a social order which sanctified selfishness. It is true that the mutualistic ethic which supported craftsmen's control was displayed in its highest form by sympathetic strikes. It is equally true, however, that the element of calculation, which was increasingly dominating all strike activity, was particularly evident here. As Fred S. Hall pointed out, sympathetic strikes of this epoch differed sharply from "contagious" strikes, which spread spontaneously like those of 1877, in two respects. First, the sympathetic strikes were called by the workers involved, through formal union procedures. Although figures comparing official with unofficial strikes are not available, two contrasting statistics illustrate Hall's point. The construction industry was always the leading center of sympathetic strikes. In New York more than 70 percent of the establishments shut by sympathetic action between 1890 and 1892 were involved in building construction. On the other hand, over the entire period of federal data (1881–1905) no less than 98.03 percent of the strikes in that industry were called by unions.

Second, as Hall observed, the tendency toward sympathetic strikes was "least in those cases where the dispute concerns conditions of employment such as wages and hours, and [was] greatest in regard to disputes which involve questions of unionism—the employment of only union men, the recognition of the union, etc." The rise of sympathetic strikes, like the rise of strikes over rules and recognition, was part of the struggle for craftsmen's control—its most aggressive and far-reaching manifestation.

It is for this reason that the practice of sympathetic strikes was ardently defended by the AFL in the 1890s. Building trades contracts explicitly provided for sympathetic stoppages. Furthermore, at the Federation's 1895 convention a resolution carried, directing the Executive Council to "convey to the unions, in such way as it thinks proper, not to tie themselves up with contracts so that they cannot help each other when able." The Council itself denied in a report to the same convention that it opposed sympathetic strikes. "On the contrary," it declared, "we were banded together to help one another. The words union, federation, implied it. An organization which held aloof when assistance could be given to a sister organization, was deserving of censure," even though each union had the right to decide its own course of action. . . .

In short, historians have, on the whole, been seriously misled by Norman J. Ware's characterization of the period after the Haymarket Affair as one of

"Sauve qui peut!" As craftsmen unionized, they not only made their struggles for control increasingly collective and deliberate, but also manifested a *growing* consciousness of the dependence of their efforts on those of workers in other crafts. They drew strength in this struggle from their functional autonomy, which was derived from their superior knowledge, exercised through self-direction and their direction of others at work, and both nurtured and in turn was nurtured by a mutualistic ethic, which repudiated important elements of acquisitive individualism. As time passed this autonomy was increasingly often codified in union rules, which were collectively "legislated" and upheld through the commitment of the individual craftsmen and through a swelling number of strikes to enforce them. Organized efforts reached the most aggressive and inclusive level of all in joint action among the various crafts for mutual support. When such actions enlisted all workers in an industry (as happened when women unionized in shoe manufacturing), and when they produced a strong propensity of unionized craftsmen to strike in support of each other's claims, they sharply separated the aggressive from the conservative consequences of craftsmen's autonomy and simultaneously provoked an intense, concerted response from the business community.

In an important sense, the last years of the [1890s] depression represented only a lull in the battle. With the return of prosperity in 1898, both strikes and union organizing quickly resumed their upward spiral, work rules again seized the center of the stage, and sympathetic strikes became increasingly numerous and bitterly fought. Manufacturers' organizations leapt into the fray with the open shop drive, while their spokesmen cited new government surveys to support their denunciations of workers "restriction of output."

On the other hand, important new developments distinguished the first decade of the twentieth century from what had gone before. Trade union officials, who increasingly served long terms in full-time salaried positions, sought to negotiate the terms of work with employers, rather than letting their members "legislate" them. The anxiety of AFL leaders to secure trade agreements and to ally with "friendly employers," like those affiliated with the National Civic Federation, against the open shop drive, prompted them to repudiate the use of sympathetic strikes. The many such strikes which took place were increasingly lacking in union sanction and in any event never reached the level of the early 1890s.

Most important of all, new methods of industrial management undermined the very foundation of craftsmen's functional autonomy. Job analysis through time and motion study allowed management to learn, then to systematize the way the work itself was done. Coupled with systematic supervision and new forms of incentive payment it permitted what Frederick Winslow Taylor called "*enforced* standardization of methods, *enforced* adoption of the best implements and working conditions, and *enforced* cooperation of all the employees under management's detailed direction." Scientific management, in fact, fundamentally disrupted the craftsmen's styles of work, their union rules and standard rates, and their mutualistic ethic, as it transformed American industrial practice between 1900 and 1930. Its basic effect, as Roethlisberger and Dickson discovered in their experiments at Western Electric's Hawthorne Works, was to place the worker "at the bottom level of a highly stratified organization," leaving his "established routines of work, his cultural traditions of craftsmanship, [and] his personal interrelations" all "at the mercy of technical specialists."

Two important attributes of the scientific management movement become evident only against the background of the struggles of nineteenth-century craftsmen to direct their own work in their own collective way. First, the appeal of the new managerial techniques to manufacturers involved more than simply a response to new technology and a new scale of business organization. It also implied a conscious endeavor to uproot those work practices which had been the taproot of whatever strength organized labor enjoyed in the late nineteenth century. A purely technological explanation of the spread of Taylorism is every bit as inadequate as a purely technological explanation of craftsmen's autonomy .

Second, the apostles of scientific management needed not only to abolish older industrial work practices, but also to discredit them in the public eye. Thus Taylor roundly denied that even "the high class mechanic" could "ever thoroughly understand the science of doing his work," and pasted the contemptuous label of "soldiering" over all craft rules, formal and informal alike. Progressive intellectuals seconded his arguments. Louis Brandeis hailed scientific management for "reliev[ing] labor of responsibilities not its own." And John R. Commons considered it "immoral to hold up to this miscellaneous labor, as a class, the hope that it can ever manage industry." If some workers do "shoulder responsibility," he explained, "it is because certain *individuals* succeed, and then those individuals immediately close the doors, and labor, as a class, remains where it was."

It was in this setting that the phrase "workers' control" first entered the vocabulary of the American labor movement. It appeared to express a radical, if often amorphous, set of demands which welled up around the end of World War I among workers in the metal trades, railroading, coal mining, and garment industries. Although those demands represented very new styles of struggle in a unique industrial and political environment, many of the workers who expressed them could remember the recent day when in fact, the manager's brains had been under the workman's cap.

George Rice Tackles the Standard Oil Trust

C. JOSEPH PUSATERI

On the afternoon of October 12, 1898, two men faced each other in the New Amsterdam Hotel in New York City. They had not seen each other in some years and now they found themselves, as they had so often in the past, on

Joseph Pusateri, "Trust and Antitrust: George Rice and the War Against Standard Oil," in *American Business History: Case Studies,* ed. Henry C. Dethloff and C. Joseph Pusateri, pp. 216–26. Copyright © 1987 Harlan Davidson, Inc.

opposite sides in a legal proceeding. The slighter in stature and somewhat younger of the two men approached the other with hand extended in a gesture of friendship.

"How are you, George? We are getting to be gray-haired men now, aren't we? Don't you wish you had taken my advice years ago?"

The older of the two, pointedly ignoring the proffered hand, replied bitterly: "Perhaps it would have been better for me if I had. You have certainly ruined my business, as you said you would."

Surprised at the vehemence of the reply to his greeting, the younger man drew back, denying the charge. The attacker persisted, however: "But I say it is so. You know well that by the power of your great wealth you have ruined my business, and you cannot deny it!"

Seeing no point in continuing what he considered to be a hopeless conversation, the first man turned away, commenting to the small crowd of onlookers as he left the room that there was not one word of truth in the accusations.

The incident was closed only for the moment. Four days later—Sunday, October 16—a description of the encounter was printed, amid a full page article detailing the older man's charge, in one of the nation's most widely read newspapers, *The New York World*. *The World* headlined its account with the banner: "How I Was Ruined by Rockefeller." The author of the story, the angry attacker during the New Amsterdam incident a few days before, was George Rice of Marietta, Ohio. His antagonist was one of the most powerful and feared men in the United States, John Davison Rockefeller, creator of and dominant force in the globe-straddling Standard Oil empire.

The twin stories of Rice and Rockefeller reveal much of the developing history of a key industry in the American economy, an industry that has been marked by controversy from its inception in 1859 until our present-day headlines of Arab oil embargoes and rising energy costs. Yet Rice and Rockefeller also smybolize much more. In many ways they stand as personal embodiments of two converging forces in the evolution of the nation—the concern and the passion to maintain equality of economic opportunity for all Americans on the one hand, and the desire and drive to amass the most stupendous material achievements possible in the most efficient manner available on the other. Opportunity and achievement—two goals between which a choice was often forced because frequently one could not be sought without sacrificing a measure of the other.

For many Americans, freedom itself has come to be defined in primarily economic terms. One contemporary scholar has written that in large part freedom today is "the right to earn a living in the way of one's own choosing, to launch an enterprise, to save and invest, to own property, and, above all, to share in the income and wealth that a progressive economy generates."

For the individual who takes utmost advantage of his or her granted opportunity, there has always been a special kind of popular approval. Fellow citizens have looked upon such persons with particular admiration. They have become legendary heroes—the self-made woman or man. As Irvin G. Wyllie has stated, the self-made man "represents our most cherished conceptions of success, and particularly our belief that any man can achieve fortune through the practice of industry, frugality, and sobriety.''

Such a figure was George Rice. He was born in Swanton Falls, Vermont, just four miles below the Canadian-American border, in 1835. He had entered the infant oil business at a relatively early age, first operating as a producer, owning oil well properties in the Pennsylvania fields in the 1860s. Then in the 1870s he switched the base of his operations to Ohio and took on the additional task of refining the crude oil secured from his wells into kerosene, the principal petroleum product of that era. In 1875, he and Charles Leonard established the Ohio Oil Works on the banks of the Ohio River at Marietta. Two years later, Rice bought Leonard out and operated thereafter as a sole proprietor until he shut the plant down permanently in 1896.

His operations in the refining field were always relatively small scale. He once noted to a Congressional investigating committee that ''The executive part of the business is done altogether by my family. One daughter keeps the books, another daughter does nine-tenths of the correspondence, and my son-in-law is the general manager.'' Rice himself claimed to tend to outside matters, meaning the marketing of his illuminating oil output.

The world of George Rice was not to be a happy one, however. He sought his markets first in the Great Lakes region and later in the Southern states, but in each instance he found himself confronted by a truly formidable enemy— the overmastering competition posed by the operations of Rockefeller's burgeoning Standard Oil organization. Thus the long war between the two men began.

Standard Oil can be regarded as representing the second of the two influences in American economic life mentioned earlier—material achievement. In the two decades after its emergence on the petroleum scene, it transformed an industry marked by chronic excess capacity, instability, and general aimlessness into one of the cutting edges of an enormous American economic expansion. During the Rockefeller years the United States displaced Great Britain as the leading producer of manufactured goods in the world, a position that this country was never again to relinquish.

But one means to reach the end of material achievement lay in combination, the merging and consolidating of ever more and ever larger units of capital, labor, technology, and managerial expertise. Observers simplistically but accurately called the resulting combinations ''big business,'' and a new age was ushered in. While there was little doubting the effectiveness of combination, there was also little doubting that the price that had to be paid lay in the sacrifice of a measure of the equality of opportunity held dear by the Founding Fathers. Gordon S. Wood has noted that the generation of the Declaration of Independence ''who hoped for so much from equality assumed that republican America would be a community where none would be too rich or too poor, and yet at the same time believed that men would readily accede to such distinctions as emerged as long as they were fairly earned.'' It was said by some early writers that what was required was a ''fundamental law, favoring an equal or rather a general distribution of property.'' The very author of the Declaration itself, Thomas Jefferson, had written that an equal division of all inheritance would be the ideal corrective to "overgrown wealth," thereby, in the words of another Founding Father, "giving every citizen an equal chance of being rich and respectable."

But combination implied inequality; it signalled that some would be rich and some would be poor whereas the Revolutionary generation had assumed "that equality of opportunity would necessarily result in a rough equality of station." Nevertheless, and here is where a quandary of policy emerged, combination was also desirable because it allowed firms to attain greater efficiencies, taking advantage of economies of scale available only to the larger enterprises. If the savings were then passed on to customers in the form of lower prices, individual real incomes were thereby increased. Of course, combinations might not pass on those savings to consumers; they might, indeed, find advantage in using their real power to fix prices artificially.

For John Rockefeller, however, the choice was not a difficult one as he unhesitatingly chose the path of combination and defended his choice vigorously all the days of his long life. As he readily admitted: "I have been frank to say that I believe in the spirit of combination and cooperation when properly and fairly conducted in the world of commercial affairs, on the principle that it helps to reduce waste; and waste is a dissipation of power."

Rockefeller's willingness to adopt the strategy of combination, or cooperation as he often preferred to call it, was deeply tied to his own ingrained passion for order. An insight into his motivations can be gained by a brief look at his early life. He was born in western New York state in 1839. His father engaged in a variety of occupations including that of an itinerant patent medicine salesman. Even after his son had become enormously wealthy and a dominant force in a major industry, the father continued traveling a circuit of western towns, billing himself as "Dr. William Rockefeller, the Celebrated Cancer Cure Specialist." He was a flamboyant figure, powerful of physique, jovial in manner, aggressive in style, characteristics which, with the exception of the last, were not to be shared by his eldest son. The mother of the family, on the other hand, was a startling contrast. Infected with a deep puritan piety, she was frugal in her habits, strait-laced in her behavior, and a firm believer in stern discipline. The personality of the son closely resembled that of his mother though the vision and business shrewdness of his father were obviously not lost upon him.

Significantly, the uncertainties of John Rockefeller's early home life, frequent changes of residence and long paternal absences while "Doctor" Rockefeller rode the circuit, created in the young man a distaste for uncertainty, a relishing of order and security, and a zeal for structuring each situation he might encounter. Most of all, he abhorred waste. His mother's favorite maxim, "willful waste makes woeful want," repeated endlessly it seemed, was not without its effect on her children.

The Rockefeller family moved to Ohio in 1853, and it was in Cleveland two years later that John secured his first full-time employment, as an assistant bookkeeper for a local commission merchant. He threw himself into the new-found world of business with unbridled enthusiasm. He found his work place "delightful to me—all the method and system of the office."

Four years later—the same year that saw the birth of the petroleum industry with Edwin Drake's successful well in Titusville, Pennsylvania—Rockefeller went into business for himself, forming a partnership to operate as a commission merchant in agricultural products and other miscellaneous goods. The firm, Clark and Rockefeller, was successful from the start and generated sufficient profits to allow the partners to look for other areas of potential investment. Petroleum offered such a possibility.

Eschewing the wildly speculative drilling and production phase of the petroleum industry, Rockefeller chose to invest in a refinery transforming the Pennsylvania crude oil into kerosene for illumination and a then small number of by-products. Refining required only a moderate amount of capital in order to begin operations, the demand for kerosene was expanding, and Cleveland, by virtue of its location on several rail lines and Lake Erie, was well suited to tap most western and many eastern markets. By 1863, when Cleveland boasted twenty refineries and was fast becoming the center of the rapidly developing industry, Rockefeller and Clark accepted the proposition of Samuel Andrews, an experienced and talented refiner, that together they build a plant. The first two men were to provide the necessary capital and Andrews the technical ability. By 1867, Rockefeller had dissolved the commission business and was concentrating completely on refining in a new partnership styled Rockefeller, Andrews, and Flagler, the immediate predecessor of the Standard Oil Company.

The history of Standard Oil in its Rockefeller years fell into three general, overlapping phases. The first of these, that of "combination," lasted from the inception of the corporation in 1870 until the end of the decade. The impetus for this phase stemmed from the then current conditions in the refining industry. With little capital required for entry into the petroleum industry, unrestrained competition was the rule. Prices fluctuated wildly; failures among producers and refiners alarmingly increased during the 1860s, and waste was everywhere. "Lack of balance between functions was chronic: first production would outrun the throughput by refiners; then manufacturing capacity would exceed both current production of raw materials and the rate of consumption of finished products. Oilmen knew from bitter experience that their business was wasteful, risky, hazardous, and unstable."

The response of the Standard Oil Company management, headed by Rockefeller, was in accord with the maternal dictum: willful waste makes woeful want. Following what its chief executive officer called "our plan," Standard Oil's policy was to eliminate the "wasteful" competition by "convincing" other manufacturers to either cease operations or to join the Rockefeller group in a loose alliance. Standard Oil possessed two substantial advantages in working its will on its competitors. It was the most efficient producer, and it had developed close ties with the railroads it utilized for its freight shipments. In order to reduce unit costs, the firm had begun to engage in a variety of auxiliary enterprises including the provision of its own chemicals, barrels, and transportation equipment. Further, the railroads proved quite willing to grant discounts or "rebates" on freight charges to an expanding operation like Standard Oil's, and such advantages could prove decisive in a competitive struggle.

Critics of the Rockefeller organization castigated it severely for its use of the rebate weapon. George Rice himself railed continually against "the combined hosts of the Standard Oil Company and its co-conspirators, the railroads," who refused to allow him "the same rates, advantages, and facilities, in all respects, that the most favored or larger shipper has, in order that we may be able to compete in the general markets." But what was called "the utterly unscrupulous manipulation of railroad rates by the Rockefellers and their associates in order to destroy competition" was seen in a quite different light by Standard Oil executives.

Rockefeller denied the charges of unfair competition. He claimed: "The profits of the Standard Oil Company did not come from advantages given by railroads. The railroads, rather, were the ones who profited by the traffic of the Standard Oil Company, and whatever advantage it received in its constant efforts to reduce rates of freight was only one of the many elements of lessening cost to the consumer which enabled us to increase our volume of business the world over because we could reduce the selling price."

By 1879, Standard's combination effort had proved so successful that its alliance of companies controlled 90 percent of the refined petroleum sold in the United States. As important, "they showed a profound faith in the permanence of the industry, a belief not generally held in years when the petroleum business was characterized by instability, rapid exhaustion of producing fields, and doubts about the appearance of new ones."

In the second phase of its history, that of "consolidation," Standard Oil welded its loose alliance of companies into a tight amalgam, centrally controlled and rationally organized and administered. The device utilized to bring about the consolidation was the "trust," a system whereby Standard stock as well as that of other allied companies was placed in the hands of nine trustees who thus wielded a control over the combine which was complete and unquestionable. And with the control of the Standard Oil Trust, as the new structure was called, came control over the industry as a whole. Never before had Americans witnessed such an enormity of power centralized in so few hands.

Consolidation was completed with the perfection of the trust agreement in 1882. But even prior to that date, Rockefeller and his associates had begun a third phase of the organization's development—"vertical integration." In actual fact, Standard Oil had been emphasizing vertical integration since before its chartering as a corporation in 1870. As early as 1864, at Rockefeller's urging, it had begun making its own barrels and even purchasing its own tracts of land to provide the timber. In 1866 Rockefeller had recruited his younger brother William into the organization to set up a New York office specializing in the marketing of petroleum products for the export trade. In the years after the establishment of the Trust, Standard Oil faced a series of challenges from both foreign and domestic sources, challenges which led it to speed the process of integration. The bulk of Standard's market lay overseas, and the development of Russian oil competition prompted the creation of tanker fleets and foreign subsidiaries to meet the Russian threat in Europe and in Asia. In the United States the continual discovery of new crude oil fields and the appearance of independent refiners led Standard Oil, for the first time, into crude production on a massive scale and to control over a network of trunk pipelines linking the fields to the refineries. By the close of the 1890s, Standard Oil had completed the fashioning of a vast, vertically integrated structure involved in every aspect of its industry.

The achievements of the petroleum industry in its Rockefeller years were indeed impressive. From a production of only a few barrels in 1859, output had soared to nearly sixty million barrels yearly by the turn of the century. The bulk of this crude oil production was refined into kerosene, the world's first inexpensive illuminant. As one historian of the industry has noted: "Few products associated with America have had so extensive an influence as kerosene on the daily living habits of so large a proportion of the world's population." But illumination was not the sole application for petroleum. By 1900 some two hundred by-products accounted for at least half of the industry's sales, and numbered among them were the lubricating oils essential to the development of industrialization. Moreover, this expansion of output was being achieved while prices to consumers were being reduced. The wholesale price of kerosene, for example, declined from 45¢ a gallon in 1863 to about 6¢ by 1895, a decline faster than any other drop in the general wholesale price level of commodities.

Petroleum men had every right to feel proud of themselves; theirs was a truly impressive material accomplishment. Yet, they found the public reaction to their record contained as much wrath as it did admiration. Many Americans argued strongly that the social cost of economic progress had been too great; that this progress had required the rise of big business as embodied in the giant corporation, and that that instrumentality was destroying America's traditional role as a land of opportunity. Very often the persons who joined the fight against big business were those whose jobs or businesses had been directly and adversely affected by the economic transformation.

A small manufacturer such as George Rice, determined to maintain his independence in the face of a galloping combination movement, would speak out against the phenomenon in cataclysmic tones. Of Standard Oil he wrote: "History proves that there is no crime in the calendar—save possibly murder—of which it is not guilty or capable. It is the blue-ribbon enemy of eveything moral and religious, although it includes within its corporation canting hypocrites who occupy front seats beneath the altar in churches that are desecrated by their presence." And harkening back to the example of the American colonists and their revolt against George III, he warned: "The last resort is for the people to retake into their own hands the power that has been delegated and abused. Vigilance Committees have more than once had a purifying influence. There may be conditions which will again render them a necessity. There is a limit to human forbearance. Has the limit yet been reached?"

After 1880 more and more of the attention of concerned Americans focused upon the industrial corporations, especially those that had by the process of combination come to dominate a key industry. In March 1881 a young Chicago journalist, Henry Demarest Lloyd, fired what might be regarded as the starting gun in the race by the public and its representatives to check the accelerating power of industrial enterprise. In that month Lloyd published in the *Atlantic Monthly* an article titled, "The Story of a Great Monopoly," dealing with the success of the Standard Oil Company. The article, so popular that the issue had to be reprinted six times, brought to the attention of most Americans for the first time the fact that the petroleum industry had come to be dominated by a single organization. From that point on, the glare of the spotlight was never shifted from the oil giant and its officials. Pamphlets, speeches, articles, books, state and federal investigations remained dramatically focused upon the operations of Standard Oil. It came for most Americans to particularly typify their new and uncertain industrialized society, and when in 1890 in reponse to a tidal wave of public pressure, Congress placed upon the statute books the Sherman Antitrust Act, it could be said with only slight exaggeration that the law had been passed with Standard Oil primarily in mind.

But enacting an antitrust law, it soon became clear, was not the same as solving the problem of monopoly power in the United States. During the decade of the 1890s, a combination of lukewarm presidential interest in antitrust prosecutions, inadequate financing by the Congress of a miniscule Justice Department, and unfavorable judicial interpretations of key sections of the act resulted in little progress in the campaign against the trusts. The Standard Oil Company had itself apparently made government action against it more uncertain by abandoning the old trust framework and adopting instead, in the late 1890s, a holding company structure.

The Standard Oil Company (New Jersey) now became the parent corporation for the family of firms that formerly operated within the trust umbrella. Thus despite the passage of the Sherman Act specifically outlawing the trust device as a means of controlling an industry, the oil trust continued in existence under the guise of a new legal form. No wonder that George Rice could write his friend, Henry Demarest Lloyd, in 1897 that "surely the devil is at the helm to guide the Standard Oil Trust in all its devilish work, and there seems to be no overruling providence to demur or stop them, and laws are of no account, and our national emblem becomes a fraud and a farce."

The 1890s had been busy years for Rice. He continually besieged the Justice Department with requests for antitrust action against Standard Oil. The Department did not respond favorably to his call, however, and during the McKinley years it even informed Rice that the "alleged combination against which you complained," was "not of an interstate character."

More sympathetic to Rice's aims was Frank Monnett, an ambitious and energetic Ohio Attorney-General. Acting upon evidence and even funds supplied by Rice, Monnett instituted a suit against the Standard Oil Company of Ohio in 1898 seeking a forfeiture of its corporate charter. Despite a considerable body of sensational testimony and even the face-to-face New Amsterdam Hotel confrontation between Rice and Rockefeller described earlier, the Supreme Court of Ohio dismissed the suit in December, 1900. For Frank Monnett the decision had become academic as his Republican party had denied him renomination as Attorney-General in 1899 in punishment for his aggressive activities in the antitrust field. Rice thus lost an influential ally.

Three years later, in 1902, Rice was supplying a fresh ally, Ida Tarbell, with the facts of his oil industry experiences, details which would shortly appear in her *History of the Standard Oil Company* series for *McClure's Magazine*. Rice was portrayed in that work as a dogged and embattled defender of American free enterprise against the onslaughts of concentrated economic power.

At the same time, not entirely through with the judicial process, Rice had returned to the courts. In between testifying in antitrust actions in states ranging from Nebraska to Texas, he also filed suit in the United States Court of Appeals in Trenton, New Jersey, charging the Standard Oil combination with violation of the Sherman Act and asking for triple damages totalling three million dollars. It was his contention that Standard Oil had destroyed his Marietta business. The suit was still pending at the time of his death on February 28, 1905, and was later dismissed by the Court on technical grounds.

In his obituary, the *New York Times* stated that Rice's life "had been spent in his fight for what he considered the right, and he often declared that he would rather be right than rich." *The Petroleum Gazette* added: "It is within the facts to say that no other single individual has been so instrumental as Mr. Rice was in forcing revelations of the inner workings of the Standard Oil Company." The comments of other reform journals echoed a similar tone.

Rice was to receive a posthumous vindication of sorts as Standard Oil soon faced what appeared to be a final collision with the federal government. A 1905 Congressional resolution mandated an investigation of the petroleum situation by the recently established Bureau of Corporations. Unfortunately for Standard Oil, the commissioner of the Bureau, James R. Garfield, had lately been taken to task by the press for a report on the meat industry that the public regarded as insufficiently critical, given the current popularity of Upton Sinclair's graphic novel, *The Jungle*. Garfield, therefore, apparently resolved that the Bureau's oil report would not suffer the same fate. Its release in May 1906 was a body blow to the officials of Standard Oil, who had cooperated fully with the investigating agency.

Garfield supported many of the allegations leveled at Rockefeller's organization over the years and thereby set in motion further actions by Washington. On November 15, of the same year, the Justice Department, with the encouragement of an increasingly progressive Theodore Roosevelt, filed suit in the U.S. Circuit Court for the Eastern District of Missouri against the Standard Oil Company (New Jersey) and the other corporations of the combination. It was the government's contention that Standard Oil, by its past conduct and present stance in the petroleum industry, stood in violation of the Sherman Antitrust Act. Hearings on the suit began in the fall of 1907 and continued for fifteen months.

Despite a vigorous defense, a four-judge circuit court rendered a unanimous decision unfavorable to the Standard Companies. On November 20, 1909, that court found Jersey Standard and most of its subsidiary corporations to be in violation of the Sherman Act as an illegal monopoly. Not surprisingly, the ruling was quickly appealed to the U.S. Supreme Court. There arguments and briefs were again presented by both sides with a final decision not rendered until May 15, 1911.

When it was announced, it merited banner headlines in every newspaper in the land. The Supreme Court, upholding the verdict of the lower circuit court, ordered the oil giant dismembered. Thirty-three companies were to be severed from the parentage of Jersey Standard, including 16 of its 20 largest affiliates.

Ironically, the Court's holding that Standard Oil did constitute a monopoly was reached at the very moment that the organization was losing rather than retaining control over its industry. With Rockefeller himself in retirement from the active management for over ten years, Standard's share of the market in 1911 was the smallest it had been for decades. The opening of new crude fields even faster than it could expand operations to keep pace; the rise of aggressive, integrated competitors such as Pure Oil, Gulf, Texaco; a reduced demand for kerosene, Standard's staple, and a new demand for fuel oil, gasoline, and other products; and a top management in the Jersey structure marked by increasing age and conservatism, all contributed to reducing its share of the nation's refining capacity to just over 60 percent by 1911.

But it would not have been to George Rice's pleasure to have known that the Standard organization, or at least the stockholders of its various companies, seemed to have actually benefited from the Court-ordered separation. All Jersey Standard shareholders received their ratable proportion of stock in the subsidiaries of which the holding company was forced to divest itself. They found themselves in many instances sharing, figuratively, in multiple gold mines rather than a single lode. Dividends of the individual companies generally increased in the following year, and stock prices in a number of instances more than doubled after the dissolution. The investing public, through the information disseminated during the lengthy legal struggle, gauged for the first time the enormous real worth of the various Standard entities and began to bid for the stock accordingly. The principals holding the greatest interests in those companies, and most notably John Rockefeller, found that the Supreme Court of the United States had made them even wealthier than they had been before!

☙ F U R T H E R   R E A D I N G

David Brody, *Steelworkers in America: The Nonunion Era* (1960)

Alfred D. Chandler, Jr., *The Visible Hand: The Managerial Revolution in American Business* (1977)

Leon Fink, *Workingmen's Democracy: The Knights of Labor and American Politics* (1983)

Herbert G. Gutman, *Work, Culture, and Society in Industrializing America* (1976)

Edward C. Kirkland, *Dream and Thought in the Business Community, 1860–1900* (1956)

Naomi R. Lamoreaux, *The Great Merger Movement in American Business, 1895–1904* (1985)

Susan Levine, *Labor's True Woman* (1984)

Harold C. Livesay, *American Made: Men Who Shaped the American Economy* (1979)
———, *Andrew Carnegie and the Rise of Big Business* (1975)
David Montgomery, *The Fall of the House of Labor* (1987)
Daniel Nelson, *Managers and Workers: Origins of the New Factory System in the United States, 1850–1920* (1975)
David F. Noble, *America by Design: Science, Technology, and the Rise of Corporate Capitalism* (1977)
Richard J. Oestreicher, *Solidarity and Fragmentation: Working People and Class Consciousness in Detroit, 1875–1900* (1986)
C. Joseph Pusateri, *A History of American Business* (1988)
Daniel T. Rodgers, *The Work Ethic in Industrial America, 1850–1920* (1974)

C H A P T E R
3

"Civilizing" the Wild West

*For many easterners in the late nineteenth century, the spectacle of the Wild West
served as a kind of antidote to the increasing routinization and bureaucratization
of industrial culture. For years—indeed, in a pattern reaffirmed as recently as the
1980s by the man-on-horseback-as-president—the trials of frontier life, the violent
dramas of cowboys and Indians, the irreverence of the mining camps, and the
legion stories of wild men and loose women have exercised a continuing attraction
for those living more confined lives. However, the western tableau in fact
represented a projection of the same forces of development that were simultaneously
reshaping the more densely settled areas of the country: industrialization,
migration, immigration, acculturation, and race, class, and gender conflict. These
themes were as indigenous to the West as a good horse and a six-shooter. When
"civilization" overtook the Wild West, in short, it introduced the same tensions (if
sometimes in different forms) between new productive processes and older ideals
that gripped the larger culture. The one social feature of the trans-Mississippi West
that made the conflicts there most distinct was the concentrated presence of Native
American peoples. Here, in the inevitable extension of Euro-American settlement,
the drama of "Americanization" took a peculiarly ironic and unheroic twist.*

✿ D O C U M E N T S

The "civilizing" process in the West is replete with ironies. In the first document,
a buffalo hunter unself-consciously depicts the arrival of modernity to the Great
Plains as a weapon of mass destruction. Attempting to surmount the failure of past
Indian removals and the backwardness of reservation life, President Chester
Arthur (1881–1885), in the second selection, anticipates the reformist themes of
the Dawes Act (1887), proposing the radical cultural surgery of breaking up
commonly held Indian lands into individually functioning homesteads.

Next, three examples of the real-life extension of the homesteading ideal to
the plains are presented. A German-American farmer builds a sod house in
Kansas, a Montana woman finds unexpected cooperation from neighboring
cattlemen, and John Stands-in-Timber recalls the rigors of reservation farming
among the Cheyenne in Oklahoma and Montana. In the eyes of a few,
"civilization" was less a product of Anglo-American settlement than of its already

established inhabitants. In the sixth document, Walt Whitman offers a tribute to the West's Hispanic and Indian heritage; the occasion was the anniversary celebration of the settlement of Sante Fe in 1883. In the final selection, excerpted from a famous paper read before the American Historical Association in 1893, historian Frederick Jackson Turner defines the moving boundary of Western settlement as the caldron of American democratic character. The passing of the frontier, he suggests, carries ominous implications.

On Killing Buffalo, c. 1875

About this time the hunt had grown to such an enormous business that J. R. Lobenstein [Loganstein], a capitalist of that time, and ram rodder of the buffalo hunt, . . . furnished the capital and contracts were sub-let for robe hides, dry hides, bull hides, etc. Merchants were furnished supplies, equipments, etc., [and] they in turn furnished smaller men, who kept up with hunters ready to supply them. An enormous amount of this business was done on time. As they had begun to make money out of it, they would supply any hunter who had a team and wagon. Now all this while the hunter was pegging away and it was not until afterwards that they got it down to a system to make it profitable over a scant living.

There was several methods to kill [buffaloes] and each [hunter] adopted his own course and plan. They would get together and while one gained a point from another, he, in turn, would gain a point from him. One method was to run beside them, shooting them as they ran. Another was to shoot from the rear, what was termed tail shooting: [always shooting] the hindmost buffalo and when a day's hunt was done, they would be strung on the ground for a mile or more, from ten to fifteen yards apart, and in this way the skinner had so much territory to go over he couldn't make wages.

We first noticed that the buffaloes always went around a ravine or gulch, unless going for water straight down a bluff; and as the buffalo always followed these trails a man on foot by a mere cut-off of a hundred yards could cut him off. That is why they was so far apart in tail-hunting, as it was called.

Hunting this way, the skinner and his wagon and team would have to travel to get in a day's work to make it profitable. Another method was to start out in the morning, which was most generally daylight both winter and summer. The hunter would start on horseback and when he came to a high place he would find out the direction of the wind, . . . and would then know which way to approach them. He would then proceed until he came to a bunch of buffalo, and if there was no ravine to get near, he would dismount, hobble or lariat his horse or turn him loose—whatever method he was used to—and proceed to crawl on his stomach so as to get near enough to shoot into the main herd. They would then run off two or three hundred yards, stopping to look back; if they happened to get wind of him at the second shot, they would not halt for a mile, and sometimes not for five. Sometimes the

"The Buffalo Hunt," in Rex W. Strickland, ed., "The Recollections of W. S. Glenn, Buffalo Hunter," *Panhandle-Plains Historical Review* no. 22 (1949), pp. 20–26. Approved by the Board of Trustees, Panhandle-Plains Historical Society.

whole herd running would be moving for miles and in this way making his rounds [he] would often run or walk some twenty-five or thirty miles and come into camp from the opposite direction from which he had left his horse and would have to walk after him. This system was afterwards dubbed "tenderfoot" hunting and did not often pay expenses for either hunter or skinner.

Another method of hunting was to leave your horse out of sight after you had determined the direction and course of the wind, and then get as near as possible. If the herd was lying at rest, he would pick out some buffalo that was standing up on watch and shoot his ball in the side of him so that it would not go through, but would lodge in the flesh; as on many times it had been proven by men [who were] well hid and the wind taking the sound of the gun and the whizz of the bullet off, [that] if a ball passed through a buffalo the herd would stampede and run for miles. A buffalo shot in this manner would merely hump up his back as if he had the colic and commence to mill round and round in a slow walk. The other buffalo sniffing the blood and following would not be watching the hunter, and he would continue to shoot the outside cow buffalo; if there were old cows they would take them as there would be some two or three offsprings following her. If she would hump up, he would know that he had the range, and in this way hold the herd as long as they acted in this way as well as the well trained cowpuncher would hold his herd, only the hunter would use his gun. This was termed mesmerising the buffalo so that we could hold them on what we termed a stand, which afterwards proved to be the most successful way of killing the buffalo.

It was not always the best shot but the best hunter that succeeded, that is, the man who piled his buffalo in a pile so as to be more convenient for the skinner to get at and not have to run all over the country. . . .

The hunter was hired by the piece: if robe hides were worth $3.00, [he was] given twenty-five cents for every one that he killed and was brought in by the skinners—was tallied up at camp. It was the camp rustler's business to keep tally of the number of hides killed each day. If the hides were worth $2.50, he [the hunter] got 20 cents; $2.00, he got 15 cents; $1.50, he got 10 cents; and $1.00, he got 5 cents. . . .

. . . . At the Doby Walls fight [the Adobe Walls, June 27, 1874], the hunters [used] all classes of guns, such as the Spencer, Springfield, Winchester and six-shooters, also all classes of buffalo guns, including a new sample 45, which Sharp had just sent out, . . . [Billy Dixon's famous long shot, so Glenn says, was made with the new 45-caliber Sharp.] Still some were not satisfied, so went outside and stepped off a 150 yards and commenced to pile dry bull hides ten in a bunch, and began to shoot with all four guns—as they went through so easily, they added more and continued to add until they had shot through 32 [hides] and one bullet stook in the thirty-third one and it proved to be the new gun. All had to have a shot with the new gun and as it gave entire satisfaction, they sent word back that this was the gun for the buffalo, and all of them ordered a gun. Sharp began to manufacture these rifles as fast as he could in various lengths and this gun, as it afterwards proved, was the cause of the extermination of the buffalo, as before this they had increased faster than killed out as it took too many shots to get a buffalo.

[Mean] while the hunter would be looking over his dead and wounded and cutting out the tongue, hump, and sometimes the tallow, it being the hunter's business to take these out while the buffalo was fresh, throwing them on some tree or rock where the wolves could not get them. In some instances if the hunter did good work the skinner could not keep up with him. Where the buffalo would be killed one day and skinned the next, [they] would be called stinkers. A buffalo left with his hide on will sour even in freezing weather, if skinned right after killing, would not smell for months if his entrails were removed.

I have seen their bodies so thick after being skinned, that they would look like logs where a hurricane had passed through a forrest [sic]. If they were lying on a hillside, the rays of the sun would make it look like a hundred glass windows. These buffalo would lie in this way until warm weather, drying up, and I have seen them piled fifty or sixty in a pile where the hunter had made a stand. As the skinner commenced on the edge, he would have to roll it out of the way to have room to skin the next, and when finished they would be rolled up as thick as saw logs around a mill. In this way a man could ride over a field and pick out the camps that were making the most money out of the hunt. . . .

We will now describe a camp outfit. They would range from six to a dozen men, there being one hunter who killed the buffalo and took out the tongues, also the tallow. As the tallow was of an oily nature, it was equal to butter; [it was used] for lubricating our guns and we loaded our own shells. Each shell had to be lubricated and [it] was used also for greasing wagons and also for lights in camp. Often chunks as large as an ear of corn were thrown on the fire to make heat. This [the removal of the tallow] had to be done while the meat was fresh, the hunter throwing it into a tree to wind dry; if the skinner forgot it, it would often stay there all winter and still be good to eat in the spring and better to eat after hanging there in the wind a few days.

We will return to the wagon man. [There were] generally two men to the wagon and their business was to follow up the hunter, if they were not in sight after the hunter had made a killing, he would proceed in their direction until he had met them, and when they would see him, he would signal with his hat where the killing was. If they got to the buffalo when they were fresh, their duty was to take out all the humps, tongues and tallow from the best buffalo. The hunter would then hunt more if they did not have hides enough to make a load or finish their day's work.

A remarkable good hunter would kill seventy-five to a hundred in a day, an average hunter about fifty, and a common one twenty-five, some hardly enough to run a camp. It was just like in any other business. A good skinner would skin from sixty to seventy-five, and average man from thirty to forty, and a common one from fifteen to twenty-five. These skinners were also paid by the hide, about five cents less than the hunter was getting for killing, being furnished with a grind stone, knives and steel and a team and wagon. The men were furnished with some kind of a gun, not as valuable as Sharp's rifle, to kill cripples with, also kips and calves that were standing around. In several incidents [instances?] it has been known to happen while the skinner was busy, they would slip up and knock him over. Toward the latter part of the hunt, when all the big ones were killed, I have seen as many as five hundred up to a thousand in a bunch, nothing but calves and have ridden right up to them, if the wind was right. . . .

President Chester A. Arthur Aims to Turn Indians into U.S. Citizens, 1881

Prominent among the matters which challenge the attention of Congress at its present session is the management of our Indian affairs. While this question has been a cause of trouble and embarrassment from the infancy of the Government, it is but recently that any effort has been made for its solution at once serious, determined, consistent, and promising success.

It has been easier to resort to convenient makeshifts for tiding over temporary difficulties than to grapple with the great permanent problem, and accordingly the easier course has almost invariably been pursued.

It was natural, at a time when the national territory seemed almost illimitable and contained many millions of acres far outside the bounds of civilized settlements, that a policy should have been initiated which more than aught else has been the fruitful source of our Indian complications.

I refer, of course, to the policy of dealing with the various Indian tribes as separate nationalities, of relegating them by treaty stipulations to the occupancy of immense reservations in the West, and of encouraging them to live a savage life, undisturbed by any earnest and well-directed efforts to bring them under the influences of civilization.

The unsatisfactory results which have sprung from this policy are becoming apparent to all.

As the white settlements have crowded the borders of the reservations, the Indians, sometimes contentedly and sometimes against their will, have been transferred to other hunting grounds, from which they have again been dislodged whenever their new-found homes have been desired by the adventurous settlers.

These removals and the frontier collisions by which they have often been preceded have led to frequent and disastrous conflicts between the races.

It is profitless to discuss here which of them has been chiefly responsible for the disturbances whose recital occupies so large a space upon the pages of our history.

We have to deal with the appalling fact that though thousands of lives have been sacrificed and hundreds of millions of dollars expended in the attempt to solve the Indian problem, it has until within the past few years seemed scarcely nearer a solution than it was half a century ago. But the Government has of late been cautiously but steadily feeling its way to the adoption of a policy which has already produced gratifying results, and which, in my judgment, is likely, if Congress and the Executive accord in its support, to relieve us ere long from the difficulties which have hitherto beset us.

For the success of the efforts now making to introduce among the Indians the customs and pursuits of civilized life and gradually to absorb them into the mass of our citizens, sharing their rights and holden to their responsibilities, there is imperative need for legislative action.

My suggestions in that regard will be chiefly such as have been already called to the attention of Congress and have received to some extent its consideration.

First. I recommend the passage of an act making the laws of the various States and Territories applicable to the Indian reservations within their borders and extending the laws of the State of Arkansas to the portion of the Indian Territory not occupied by the Five Civilized Tribes.

The Indian should receive the protection of the law. He should be allowed to maintain in court his rights of person and property. He has repeatedly begged for this privilege. Its exercise would be very valuable to him in his progress toward civilization.

Second. Of even greater importance is a measure which has been frequently recommended by my predecessors in office, and in furtherance of which several bills have been from time to time introduced in both Houses of Congress. The enactment of a general law permitting the allotment in severalty, to such Indians, at least, as desire it, of a reasonable quantity of land secured to them by patent, and for their own protection made inalienable for twenty or twenty-five years, is demanded for their present welfare and their permanent advancement.

In return for such considerate action on the part of the Government, there is reason to believe that the Indians in large numbers would be persuaded to sever their tribal relations and to engage at once in agricultural pursuits. Many of them realize the fact that their hunting days are over and that it is now for their best interests to conform their manner of life to the new order of things. By no greater inducement than the assurance of permanent title to the soil can they be led to engage in the occupation of tilling it.

The well-attested reports of their increasing interest in husbandry justify the hope and belief that the enactment of such a statute as I recommend would be at once attended with gratifying results. A resort to the allotment system would have a direct and powerful influence in dissolving the tribal bond, which is so prominent a feature of savage life, and which tends so strongly to perpetuate it.

Third. I advise a liberal appropriation for the support of Indian schools, because of my confident belief that such a course is consistent with the wisest economy. . . .

A Kansas Farmer Stakes His Claim, 1877

We got home about noon, and between 2 and 3 we three started for Squire Walrond's office to make application for land. We took out homesteads directly. We might have "filed" on the land, and that filing would have been

---

Howard Ruede, from *Sod-House Days,* pp. 19–20, 28–29, 30–31, 91–92, ed. John Ise (Columbia University Press, New York). Used by permission.

good for 30 months, at the end of which time (or before) we could have bought the land or put a homestead on it. As it is, we must live on it five years. The first two years we live "off and on"—that is, we must sleep on it once in a while and make some improvements on it within 6 months, or it will be forfeited. It is to be our home, but we can hire out by the day or month as we like. A man here has three rights—homestead, filing and timber filing. By taking land under the first he must live on it five years, and at the end of five years of actual residence can "prove up" and get a deed. The second right I explained above. The timber filing requires a man to break 10 acres the first year, which he must plant with trees 12 feet apart the second year, besides breaking an additional 10 acres. The third year he must plant these 10, and break 20, which must be planted the fourth year. Then he is entitled to an additional 160 acres. It is a hard thing to live up to the law on a timber filing because young trees are hard to get, and when you have them, the question is whether they will grow. The application and affidavit cost us $16—50 cents cheaper than if we had gone at separate times. If we had gone to the land office at Kirwin it would have cost but $15 but then we would have had the expenses to and from Kirwin, besides our meals there. We were recommended by Mr. Schweitzer to go to Walrond. . . .

Perhaps you will be interested in the way a sod house is built. Sod is the most available material, in fact, the only material the homesteader has at hand, unless he happens to be one of the fortunates who secured a creek claim with timber suitable for house logs.

Occasionally a new comer has a "bee," and the neighbors for miles around gather at his claim and put up his house in a day. Of course there is no charge for labor in such cases. The women come too, and while the men lay up the sod walls, they prepare dinner for the crowd, and have a very sociable hour at noon. A house put up in this way is very likely to settle and get out of shape, but it is seldom deserted for that reason.

The builder usually "cords up" the sods, though sometimes he crosses the layers, making the walls about two feet thick, but a little experience shows that the extra thick walls are of no real advantage. When the prairie is thoroughly soaked by rain or snow is the best time for breaking sod for building. The regulation thickness is $2\frac{1}{2}$ inches, buffalo sod preferred on account of its superior toughness. The furrow slices are laid flat and as straight as a steady-walking team can be driven. These furrow slices, 12 inches wide, are cut with a sharp spade into 18-inch lengths, and carefully handled as they are laid in the wall, one length reaching across the wall, which rises rapidly even when the builders are green hands. Care must be taken to break joints and bind the corners of the house. "Seven feet to the square" is the rule, as the wall is likely to settle a good deal, especially if the sod is very wet when laid. The door and window frames are set in place first and the wall built around them. Building such a house is hard work. . . .

The people who live in sod houses, and, in fact, all who live under a dirt roof, are pestered with swarms of bed bugs. . . . The vermin were not brought here by the immigrants; they grew on the trees along the river and creeks before the first settlers arrived. The bugs infest the log and sod chicken coops, too, in countless thousands, or, if you wish to measure them in a spoon, you can gather them up in that way from between the sods in the wall. I have heard chicken raisers complain that their fowls are killed by the bugs getting into their ears. Whether or not that is the cause of the fowls dying, the bugs are blamed. Where the sod houses are plastered the bed bugs are not such a nuisance.

You don't have to keep a dog in order to have plenty of fleas, for they are natives too and do their best to drive out the intruding settlers. Just have a dirt floor and you have fleas, sure. They seem to spring from the dust of the earth. Coal oil and water are sometimes used to sprinkle the floor, but that abates the pest only for a short time, and oil costs 35 cents a gallon. People who have board floors are not bothered so much with these fleas.

Another nuisance here is what people call "Kansas itch," which attacks nearly everybody within a short time after arrival here; few are immune. Not all are affected alike; some scratch a few days, other are affected for months. It is not contagious—at least not all who come in contact with those suffering with it take the disease. There is only one way in which a sufferer can get relief—scratching; and that aggravates the itching and sometimes produces raw sore spots. But those are easier to heal than it is to get the disease out of your system. Change of water is sometimes given as the cause; bed bugs and fleas are sometimes blamed, but it seems as if the itch has to run its course in every case. It disappears as mysteriously as it came.

Catharine Calk McCarty Meets Her Cattlemen
Neighbors, 1916

My homestead home, a log house, on the side of a hill on the open range with its dirt floor and dirt roof, seemed a haven that next summer when the hot winds, parching the land as well as the face, seemed never to end. At the back of the house, where the shadows were longest, a hole in the ground, about two feet deep and four feet in diameter served as the "icebox." The water, carried up the hill from my brother's well, and kept covered in the icebox, seemed very cool. . . .

My brother was not on the homestead that summer. Colonel, my dog, followed Tramp and me wherever we went. The old saying, a horse and a dog are man's best friends, I found was true.

As the hot days of July, 1916, neared their end, the wheat as well as the oats were turning yellow. One morning I was awakened by Colonel barking as though something was wrong. Opening the door, stepping out into the morning sun just coming over the hill, I saw a large herd of range cattle pushing against the wire fence around the crop.

This is serious—in a day our crop will be gone and all the feed for winter, I thought. Saddling Tramp and taking my revolver I attempted to round up the cattle. I was not very adept at this. The cattle sensed it. In despair, I shot into the air; this really got them going, and with Colonel helping, the cattle were driven what seemed a long ways away, and I hoped they would not find their way back. Hurrying home, I fed Colonel and Tramp, ate my breakfast, dinner and supper in one.

The next day, at daylight the cattle were back. This continued for several days. Shooting in the air and the dog barking seemed to be the only way I could get them moving.

One day when my three-meals-in-one was over, two strange men rode up, came to the door, introduced themselves, and said, "We are representatives of the local stock association. Are you the lady shooting cattle?"

"No," I replied, "I am not shooting cattle. I am just driving them away from that little crop. Every day I think they will lose their way but every morning, there they are."

"Aren't you shooting at them? That's illegal. The stockmen cannot put up with that. The sheriff will serve notice on you if you don't stop."

"I cannot drive them; the only way I can get them away is to shoot in the air."

"You can't do that," they cried. "We are a committee to notify you that this will have to stop."

"Fine," I said, "if I stop shooting at your cattle, you'll have to help." By that time, they were drinking some coffee. "I'm just a forlorn homesteader trying to protect a little crop while my brother is away. You both have mowers, haven't you, and men, and horses? Well, how about coming here, cutting the crop, and putting up a corral?"

They looked at me.

"If you don't want me to run your cattle, you'll have to cut the crop," I laughed.

They looked at each other. Finally one of them said, "By golly, maybe we could do that."

I said, "Well, if you do that, I'll cook the best dinner I can. You'll have to come early, as those cattle will push in the fence and one hundred head of cattle can do a lot of eating."

We talked awhile about the cattle business, what luck they were having, and how the range had been taken up; and if I were going to shoot and run their cattle, they would not weigh anything in the fall. "They will be nothing but drags if we ever get them to market," they cried.

I listened very attentively, wondering, "Will they really do this? Will they be here tomorrow?" They left with a grin.

Sure enough, next morning, at daylight they were back with a mower and hay rake. There were two men, one mowing, one raking, and two others putting up a corral, taking the wire and posts from the fence. "How wonderful of them," I kept saying to myself.

I cooked everything I had on hand. Making some lemon pies, with lemons and eggs taken from the "icebox" at the back of the cabin, hot biscuits, and the last of some ham and beans, jam, and anything else I could find. I got them filled up. I tried to show them what good sports I thought they were, and how much I appreciated their help, telling them that they were not at all like stockmen who hate honyockers, as homesteaders were called.

They left with mower, hay rake, horses, and bid me a very friendly farewell. I looked at the hay in the corral and the herd having a good feed on the stubble left on the field. That night I slept soundly, way into the next day. No more riding at daybreak, shooting, running cattle. Those days were over.

Shortly I had word from Mr. Hetherington, who seemed to be head of the local stockmen and dominated the association. He wanted to see me. I was afraid that he would want pay for the men who worked and for his rake and mower. I heard he was crippled with rheumatism and I decided to face the lion in his den. I found the way to his home, one day after a long ride. When I knocked at the door, Mrs. Hetherington opened it, and I introduced myself.

"Oh yes," she greeted me, "Mr. Hetherington thought you would be coming one of these days." She brought me into the room where a large man, with shaggy greying hair and heavy eyebrows, sat on a chair.

"Did you want to see me?" I meekly asked.

He fairly shouted, "I sent for you, didn't I? I wanted to see the red-headed girl who rides around shooting cattle."

"But, Mr. Hetherington," I began.

"No, I know. When the local association sent two men to order you to stop shooting and running cattle, what did the weak fools do? Nothing to make you stop, but you talked them into bringing our machinery, horses, and men, cutting your crop, and even building a corral for that handful of hay."

"Did you want to see me?" I began again.

"Yes, I wanted to see what you looked like," he bellowed. Then he threw back his head and laughed and laughed. "This is the best joke on us I ever heard, stockmen cutting honyocker's hay. If it gets around, we'll be the laughing stock of the country."

I laughed, too. Mrs. Hetherington came in with coffee and cake, and we talked and talked. I told him what fine men I thought stockmen are, not at all like homesteaders pictured them, and that my brother hopes in the future to join their crowd.

We parted friends. During that summer, some of the stockmen now and then rode by the house to see how everything was. I thought that the resentment they bore to homesteaders was highly exaggerated.

John Stands-in-Timber Recalls Reservation Farming (1877–1900), 1900

The government started the Indians raising gardens as soon as they surrendered. Some had gardens of corn and other crops at Fort Keogh. They had forgotten how, though they all used to garden in the old days before they hunted buffalo. Now they were learning about new crops as well, things

"John Stands-in-Timber Recalls Reservation Farming, 1877–1900," *Cheyenne Memories,* by John Stands-in-Timber and Margot Liberty, pp. 276–78 (New Haven: Yale University Press, 1967). Used by permission.

they had never seen before. The Dull Knife people got to Oklahoma in 1877 about the time the watermelons ripened, and when the Southern Cheyennes gave them some they cut them up and boiled them like squash. They did not know you could eat them raw. But later when they planted their own they put sugar with the seeds. They said it would make them sweeter when they grew.

When they reached Tongue River every man was supposed to have a garden of his own. A government farmer went around to teach them. And many of them worked hard, even carrying buckets of water from the river by hand. One man, Black White Man, wanted to raise cotton. He had seen it in Oklahoma. He plowed a piece of ground and smoothed it up, and when it was ready he took his wife's quilt and made little pieces from the inside and planted them with a garden hoe. When his wife missed the quilt, she got after him. He was afraid to tell her, but finally he said, ''I got it and took out the cotton and planted it. We will have more quilts than we need, as soon as it grows.''

When they first learned to plow in Oklahoma the farmer told them to get ready and come to a certain place and he would show them. They did not understand. They thought ''Get ready'' meant fancy costumes and not their new pants and shirts. So everybody had feathers on their heads and necklaces and leggings and fancy moccasins. It looked like a dance, not a farming lesson. And all the women and children went along to see them.

The farmer told one man to grab the handles while he started ahead with the team. But the plow jumped out of the ground and turned over, and the Indian fell down. But he tried again, and by the time they got back around he was doing pretty well. Then they all tried. At last they came to one man who had been watching closely. When he started off the dirt rolled right over and he went clear around that way, and the criers started announcing, ''Ha-aah! See that man!'' The women made war cries and everybody hollered just as if he had counted coup.

Another time when they practiced plowing down there, one man plowed up a bull snake and the next man plowed up a rattlesnake, and after that they were all afraid to go.

In Montana they began to help each other. The government issued plows to quite a few men, and in Birney the Fox Military Society used to plow together as soon as the frost was out. They would all gather at the farthest place up the river and work together until that was done, and then move to the next. They had seven or eight plows and it went faster that way. Besides, it was more fun.

One year they decided to finish every garden in ten days, and any member who did not show up would be punished. Everything was fine for several days, until they got to Black Eagle's place. And Looks Behind never came. The rest of them finished plowing for Black Eagle and Medicine Top and Broken Jaw. Then they all got on their horses, and us kids followed them to the Medicine Bull place on Tie Creek and there was Looks Behind, fixing his fence.

They all yelled and fired their guns, and galloped by and hit him with their quirts. There were twenty or thirty of them. Looks Behind had a shovel and at first he was going to fight, but he took it. Afterwards he could hardly talk. They made him get on his horse and go back and start plowing right away.

Walt Whitman Salutes the Indo-Hispanic Contribution to America, 1883

Dear Sirs:

Your kind invitation to visit you and deliver a poem for the 333d Anniversary of founding Santa Fé has reach'd me so late that I have to decline, with sincere regret. But I will say a few words off hand.

We Americans have yet to really learn our own antecedents, and sort them, to unify them. They will be found ampler than has been supposed, and in widely different sources. Thus far, impress'd by New England writers and schoolmasters, we tacitly abandon ourselves to the notion that our United States have been fashion'd from the British Islands only, and essentially form a second England only—which is a very great mistake. Many leading traits for our future national personality, and some of the best ones, will certainly prove to have originated from other than British stock. As it is, the British and German, valuable as they are in the concrete, already threaten excess. Or rather, I should say, they have certainly reach'd that excess. To-day, something outside of them, and to counterbalance them, is seriously needed.

The seething materialistic and business vortices of the United States, in their present devouring relations, controlling and belittling everything else, are, in my opinion, but a vast and indispensable stage in the new world's development, and are certainly to be follow'd by something entirely different—at least by immense modifications. Character, literature, a society worthy the name, are yet to be establish'd, through a nationality of noblest spiritual, heroic and democratic attributes—not one of which at present definitely exists—entirely different from the past, though unerringly founded on it, and to justify it.

To that composite American identity of the future, Spanish character will supply some of the most needed parts. No stock shows a grander historic retrospect—grander in religiousness and loyalty, or for patriotism, courage, decorum, gravity and honor. (It is time to dismiss utterly the illusion-compound, half raw-head-and-bloody-bones and half Mysteries-of-Udolpho, inherited from the English writers of the past two hundred years. It is time to realize—for it is certainly true—that there will not be found any more cruelty, tyranny, superstition, &c., in the *résumé* of past Spanish history than in the corresponding *résumé* of Anglo-Norman history. Nay, I think there will not be found so much.)

Then another point, relating to American ethnology, past and to come, I will here touch upon at a venture. As to our aboriginal or Indian population— the Aztec in the South, and many a tribe in the North and West—I know it seems to be agreed that they must gradually dwindle as time rolls on, and in a few generations more leave only a reminiscence, a blank. But I am not at all clear about that. As America, from its many far-back sources and current supplies, develops, adapts, entwines, faithfully identifies its own—are we to see it cheerfully accepting and using all the contributions of foreign lands from the whole outside globe—and then rejecting the only ones distinctively its own—the autochthonic ones?

As to the Spanish stock of our Southwest, it is certain to me that we do not begin to appreciate the splendor and sterling value of its race element. Who knows but that element, like the course of some subterranean river, dipping invisibly for a hundred or two years, is now to emerge in broadest flow and permanent action?

If I might assume to do so, I would like to send you the most cordial, heartfelt congratulations of your American fellow-country-men here. You have more friends in the Northern and Atlantic regions than you suppose, and they are deeply interested in the development of the great Southwestern interior, and in what your festival would arouse to public attention.

Very respectfully, &c.,
WALT WHITMAN

Frederick Jackson Turner on the Frontier as the Source of American Democracy, 1893

In a recent bulletin of the Superintendent of the Census for 1890 appear these significant words: "Up to and including 1880 the country had a frontier of settlement, but at present the unsettled area has been so broken into by isolated bodies of settlement that there can hardly be said to be a frontier line. In the discussion of its extent, its westward movement, etc., it can not, therefore, any longer have a place in the census reports." This brief official statement marks the closing of a great historic movement. . . .

From the conditions of frontier life came intellectual traits of profound importance. The works of travelers along each frontier from colonial days onward describe certain common traits, and these traits have, while softening down, still persisted as survivals in the place of their origin, even when a higher social organization succeeded. The result is that to the frontier the American intellect owes its striking characteristics. That coarseness and strength combined with acuteness and inquisitiveness; that practical, inventive turn of mind, quick to find expedients; that masterful grasp of material things, lacking in the artistic but powerful to effect great ends; that restless, nervous energy; that dominant individualism, working for good and for evil, and withal that buoyancy and exuberance which comes with freedom—these are traits of the frontier, or traits called out elsewhere because of the existence of the frontier. Since the days when the fleet of Columbus sailed into the waters of the New World, America has been another name for opportunity, and the people of the United States have taken their tone from the incessant expansion which has not only been open but has even been forced upon them. He would be a rash prophet who should assert that the expansive character of American life has now entirely ceased. Movement has been its dominant fact, and, unless this training has no effect upon a people, the American energy will continually demand a wider field for its exercise. But never again will such gifts of free land offer themselves. For a moment, at the frontier, the bonds of custom are broken and unrestraint is triumphant. There is not *tabula rasa*. The stubborn American environment is there with its imperious summons to accept its conditions; the inherited ways of doing things are also there; and yet, in spite of environment, and in spite of custom, each frontier did indeed furnish a new field of opportunity, a gate of escape from the bondage of the past; and freshness, and confidence, and scorn of older society, impatience of its restraints and its ideas, and indifference to its lessons, have accompanied the frontier. What the Mediterranean Sea was to the Greeks, breaking the bond of custom, offering new experiences, calling out new institutions and activities, that, and more, the ever retreating frontier has been to the United States directly, and to the nations of Europe more remotely. And now, four centuries from the discovery of America, at the end of a hundred years of life under the Constitution, the frontier has gone, and with its going has closed the first period of American history.

❧ E S S A Y S

The following essays treat two related aspects of the "civilizing" process in the West. In the first, historian Robert L. Griswold of the University of Oklahoma examines the spread of domestic ideology from its secure eastern perches to the wilder settings of western communities. This "cultural system"—particularly its set of expectations for and limitations on women's behavior—drew strength, suggests Griswold, not only because of the direct transferal of dominant thinking westward but also because women were able to manipulate the terms of domestic idealism to meet immediate needs.

An equally complicated manifestation of the domestication of the West was the federal government's attempts to turn Indian nations into communities of landowning farm families. In exploring the troubled legacy of the Dawes Act (1887) on the Cheyenne-Arapaho reservation, the second essay, by historian Donald J. Berthrong of Purdue University, clarifies the difference between an ideology (or worldview) lived and breathed within a community and one utterly imposed from the outside on a subject people. In the latter case, at least as we see it among the Cheyennes and Arapahoes, the arrival of the Yankee work ethic proved an unmitigated disaster.

Western Women and the Uses of Domestic Ideology

ROBERT L. GRISWOLD

When nineteenth-century Anglo women left their homes in New England, the South, or the Midwest to live in the West, they took with them more than the material items necessary for survival. They also took a set of values, assumptions, and ideals that enabled them to make sense of their lives. Although the

Robert L. Griswold, "Anglo Women and Domestic Ideology in the American West in the Nineteenth and Early Twentieth Centuries," in *Western Women: Their Land, Their Lives*, eds. Lillian Schlissel, Vicki L. Ruiz, and Janice Monk (Albuquerque: University of New Mexico Press, 1988), pp. 15–29. Used by permission of the author.

content of this ideological baggage is not altogether clear, very likely these women subscribed to some variant of domestic ideology. Most undoubtedly believed that women's chief responsibilities were homemaking and child rearing, that females represented the moral foundation of the family and society, and that a commitment to family preceded and took precedence over a commitment to self. As a corollary, they also likely believed that women deserved respect and consideration commensurate with their high moral influence both inside and outside the home.

Yet, the key word is variant. Much of the confusion about women's roles and self-perceptions in the West stems from an overly rigid conception of domestic ideology: as a consequence, the historical debate too often turns on whether or not women slavishly adhered to a narrowly conceived conception of domesticity. Were or were not women submissive, pure, domestic, and pious? Did they or did they not subscribe to the cult of true womanhood? But if ideology is understood less narrowly, if ideology is perceived as a cultural system and not as a cult, such questions disappear and a more complex picture emerges of western Anglo women who were both brave and timid, resourceful and dependent, aggressive and retiring. In short, domestic ideology in the West was less a rigid set of assumptions than a supple perspective about gender ideals, less a well-defined "cult of true womanhood" than a way common women made sense of everyday existence. . . .

This less rigid definition of ideology allows suspension of the debate on whether or not western Anglo women actually adhered to eastern moralists' conceptions of ideal womanhood. This is not the issue. . . . As Elizabeth Jameson has suggested, "We need to approach western women's history not through the filters of prescriptive literature or concepts of frontier liberation and oppression, but through the experiences of the people who lived the history." Western Anglo women inherited an ideology that arose in the East, but it was an ideology that was fluid, elastic, and complex: women explained their own action by its assumptions, sometimes wrestled to align behavior with diverse perceptions of its tenets, and modified it to meet changing realities. In so doing, these migrants became creators as well as preservers of ideology.

The fact that domesticity arose in the East as part of the complex shift from a corporate household economy to a nascent urban, industrial economy would suggest that domestic ideology might have had trouble establishing firm roots in the West; moreover, eastern domesticity arose in conjunction with the separation of men's and women's worlds into two separate spheres, a separation that was virtually impossible to establish on the plains and in the mining towns of the West. Yet domestic ideology—in particular the valorization of motherhood and the emphasis on women's moral responsibilities to their families and communities—was central to the world view of Anglo women in the West. Although the spheres may have overlapped, the cultural values of domestic ideology had a powerful appeal to female settlers: they gave meaning to women's domestic work, made the blurring of sex roles culturally intelligible, helped confirm women's self-worth, offered a sense of stability in an inherently unstable world, and fostered bonds of friendship with other women. Domestic ideology, furthermore, legitimated women's efforts to "civilize" the West and provided a vocabulary with which to redefine the nature of manhood.

Domesticity for western Anglo women cannot be divorced from the productive labor they performed within the home. . . . The lives of all but wealthy women were characterized by hard work, work given cultural meaning by the ideology of domesticity. After all, the physical and moral well-being of the family stood at the core of nineteenth-century domestic social theory, and while a few privileged women could concentrate exclusively on the latter, most nineteenth-century wives, especially western wives, had to direct much of their energies to the former. But domesticity was never a theory of idleness: it always underscored the importance of productive labor, hence Catharine Beecher's efforts to increase the productivity and efficiency of housewives. And though western women, like their eastern counterparts, observed a gender-based division of labor, the spheres overlapped as women often performed labor generally reserved for men and as men occasionally did the reverse.

The labor of farm wives, for example, was indispensable to the success of the family venture. With her labor she produced the goods necessary for survival and often earned what little cash the family could claim by selling produce. Miners' wives likewise performed a seemingly endless number of tasks essential for their families' survival: they cooked, cleaned, hauled water, gardened, cared for livestock, chopped wood, sewed, canned, slaughtered, cured meat, made candles and soap and, if poor, washed, sewed, and cooked for single men. Despite this numbing work load, "the underlying social ideology of the Victorian era," writes Elliot West, "survived largely intact among Western miners' wives." A virtuous woman used her labor and talents to establish and maintain a proper home; a sphere that would be a refuge for her husband "and a school of strength and virtue for her children." To be successful, West concluded, women had to be assertive, resourceful, dynamic and skillful. This variant of domesticity had no room for passivity. To what extent such economic indispensability translated into power within the family is unclear, but the variety of work done by women both stretched and confirmed the fundamental belief that women's first responsibilities were to her family and home. When a wife made clothes, took in laundry, slaughtered livestock, mended fences, or harvested wheat, she did so because her family needed her labor.

The private writings of western women reveal that domestic tasks and the ideology that made cultural sense of these tasks validated women's self-worth. Frontier women described their first homes with affection and wrote with pride of their own innovativeness and resourcefulness in maintaining a home. One Iowa frontierswoman could not contain her pride or excitement as she and her family prepared to move into their new home: "It seems real nice to have the whole control of my house; can say I am monarch of all I survey and none to dispute my right." So, too, miners' wives improvised to make their homes comport with Victorian standards of taste and often moved a few cherished belongings from mine to mine in an effort to secure symbolically the domestic stability their peripatetic lives so clearly lacked. Many women seemed to gain an artisan's satisfaction from their domestic duties and regarded their work as a craft. Women took understandable pride in pies well-baked, shirts well-made, and children well-tended. Here was a healthy, instrumental, republican brand of domesticity free of the ornamental parasitism that allegedly plagued elite urban women.

Although the satisfaction women gained from their domestic work should not be overestimated—after all, many women also complained of the drudgery of their lives—work within the home may have also seemed relatively desirable given the alternatives outside the home. In other words, just as factory work confirmed conventional life expectations for eastern women at the turn of the century, the even more narrow job choices for western women likely did the same thing. In light of their high cultural status, wifehood and motherhood were very appealing in comparison to life as an unmarried domestic, seamstress, or laundress. Teaching was probably the most appealing occupation, in part because teachers combined aspects of domestic ideology with some prospects of autonomy and advancement, but in most towns, life as a teacher required life without marriage and children. That was a sacrifice few women willingly made. Finally, the slow development of industrialization in the West left women there with even fewer job possibilities than in the East.

Given the low level of industrialization, women in far western cities worked primarily in domestic service. For young single working women, this universally despised occupation undoubtedly helped propel them into marriage. The fact that most single working women lived at home also made marriage seem inviting: it was a way to chart an independent course from parents, no matter how illusory the independence might actually be. Thus, for every adventuresome, single, female homesteader, there were scores of overworked and underpaid domestics, sales clerks, and non-industrial manufacturers for whom marriage and family represented a genuine hope for a better life.

The significance of domesticity, of course, went far beyond the nature of the work itself. Domesticity represented ties with community, and migration disrupted those ties. Most wives dutifully followed their husbands on the arduous and dangerous trail west. En route, women encountered the sickness and death, hardship and heartache that accompanied almost every overland expedition. But though a woman might have to leave her home, she did not leave behind the thoughts that filled that home. Domestic ideology was a tie to the past, a way one connected new surroundings to older roots. Amidst the uncertainties and upheavals characteristic of life in a new land, domesticity offered a familiar way to describe one's basic attitudes and hopes. Mothers were especially concerned that their daughters receive the lessons of domesticity, thereby validating the mothers' past and providing a sense of continuity between the two generations. External conditions might change without altering, so mothers hoped, the great lessons of life. The bonds of womanhood between mother and daughter, the complex web of obedience and obligation inherent in that relationship, served to mitigate the upheaval beyond the home.

A shared set of ideas about woman's place also bound non-related women to each other. Frontier women missed the company of other women, urged friends from home to migrate, promised repeatedly to visit female friends in the East, and made determined efforts to establish new friendships as quickly as possible. The cement of these bonds was comprised, in part, of a shared belief about women's duties, responsibilities, and prerogatives. Thus, women sought out other virtuous women for company and shunned those who violated the principles of nineteenth-century womanhood. Whether or not domestic ideology was prevalent among working-class women is debatable—evidence from Mormon women, black women, California divorcees, and miners' wives suggest that it was not restricted to the white middle-class—but domestic ideology strengthened the bonds of sisterhood among women. It did so by offering women a cultural system of social rules, conventions, and values . . . that gave meaning to their daily behavior and to their friendships with other women.

Domestic ideology brought western Anglo women together in another way as well. Fired by the moral message of domesticity, women united to "civilize" the West. This effort should not be confused with the influence of ethereal "madonnas in sunbonnets" or bloodless "gentle tamers" who allegedly worked wonders by the sheer force of their pious, self-sacrificing example. These images of western women are useless stereotypes that obscure the real relations between men and women and blind us to women's prolonged battle over what the West was to become, a battle that often brought women into conflict with entrenched male interests. If women were civilizers, they civilized for their families, for themselves, and for their gender: their quest was not to establish a lofty, other-worldly abstraction called *civilization* but to create the institutions—the schools, churches, charity associations, reforms—that would check male inspired disorder, assist the victims and losers of the male dominated society, and secure a social order within which domestic virtues and family life could flourish.

Sexual struggle was at the core of this quest, a struggle predicated on the fact that western men and women had different conceptions of social order. Where womenless men dominated the West, prostitution and drinking were not only tolerated but were integral parts of the service structure of the community. Men without families in mining camps and cowtowns had little interest in schools and even less in charity associations, benevolent societies, temperance reforms, and churches. "Competitive opportunism" underlay their enterprise, a search for individual gain that often led to sharp clashes and factionalization within the Western communities. This male-inspired, competitive, acquisitive ethos created an inhospitable climate for social reform. Most western mining camps, for example, were places of brief but intense economic exploitation occupied by highly transient males who showed open disdain for the domestic morality of the East. These men came for money, not for righteousness, and the laws they passed generally focused on economic matters and practical needs. Only with the arrival of families did

the more stable western mining towns witness the emergence of the appurtenances of civilization. . . .

To the farmers and merchants who succeeded the cowboy, brothels,
saloons, and gambling dens were open affronts to middle-class economic
order based upon hard work and self-restraint: such evils hurt business, or at
least the kinds of businesses middle-class entrepreneurs hoped to establish.
Brothels and saloons might appeal to lonely cowboys, rowdy cattlemen, and
hard luck miners, but the future of the towns lay with solid farmers,
craftsmen, merchants, and their families. Thus, law, order, morality, and
economic prosperity stood lined against the get-rich-quick immorality of the
booming cowtowns and mining camps. Men's support for reform, then,
stemmed from a conception of morality inextricably linked to bourgeois
economic respectability, rather than from a sense that men were primarily
responsible for the moral purity of their communities or that frontier vices
subverted their ability to rear proper children: hence men's willingness to
compromise and to allow other men to pursue their fortunes and pleasures.

The wives of these men, however, likely had a different perception of
social order. Entrusted with primary child-rearing responsibilities, intent on
protecting and enhancing the morality of their families, women's opposition
to frontier vice had roots deep within their own perceptions of self, family,
and society. To protect morality, to build churches and schools, to see that
sons and daughters grew up morally straight, these were important goals of
many, if not most, Anglo western women. For them, compromise with
vice—with the sinful indulgences of men—was unacceptable. Building a
decent society required the efforts of both men and women, but women had
the greater moral leverage to accomplish the needed reforms. They were the
gender entrusted with the moral welfare of their home and community, and to
protect their homes, middle-class women had to weave domestic morality
into the fabric of society. After all, a pious, peaceful, domestic sphere might
somehow survive amidst immoral conditions but would flourish only in an
environment suffused with Christian morality. Thus women's diaries and
letters record their efforts to establish schools, churches, Sunday school
classes, benevolent associations, and charities. Some single females, in fact,
came to the West intent on rescuing the region from barbarity: hundreds of
unmarried female teachers from New England and upper New York state, for
example, tried with mixed success to redeem the West with a blend of pietism
and pedagogy. . . .

Civilizing the West meant, above all, civilizing men, and nowhere was
the clash between male and female cultures more vivid than in the western
settlements. To change male behavior and to define the nature of disorder and
moral impropriety, women turned to the assumptions of domesticity. They
did so not only because the domestic ideal elevated women's status within the
family but because it also legitimated the call for a new style of masculine
behavior both inside and outside the family. Thus, in building schools,
churches, and charities, women recreated eastern civilization and checked a
certain style of western masculinity that tolerated drinking, violence, gambling, and whoring. With the arrival of mothers and daughters, a struggle

between women and men over masculine identity ensued, a struggle involving the sexual double standard, religious commitment, temperance, gambling, men's psychological commitment to their wives and children, and male and female prerogatives within the family. Domesticity's reforming power lay in its ability to dramatize the social importance of a home-inspired morality and to insist that men and women adhere to a single standard of conduct, and a feminine one at that.

For women the choice was clear: either descend to the level of a male culture that tolerated vice—an unthinkable prospect—or align with righteous women and men and destroy these appurtenances of undomesticated masculinity. Thus, it was women who dominated the ranks of those opposed to drink, gambling, and prostitution. Antiprostitution, temperance, and reform campaigns in Kansas illustrate the reform process at work. In the early booming years of the cowtowns, for example, local newspapers viewed prostitution with amused tolerance, and ordinances against the practice simply served to fill the town coffers with collected fines. Local authorities considered prostitution a necessary social service. The arrival of families, however, challenged this vision of prostitution. With the advent of more even sex ratios, a sharp increase in the number of children, and the rise of respectable, middle-class occupations, women (and some men) called for the strict regulation or abolition of brothels. After all, prostitution was an affront to women's moral sensibilities and to Victorian ideas about sexual exclusivity, emotional intimacy, the sanctity of motherhood, and the importance of domestic life. To virtuous women, prostitution degraded men and women and threatened the sexual integrity of husbands and sons.

Nor did Kansas women limit themselves to antiprostitution campaigns. Helped by connections with eastern organizations (a Lawrence, Kansas, study club, for example, evolved directly from a group in Quincy, Illinois) Kansas women settlers in the late nineteenth century established a host of organizations to civilize the new state. Within a year of settlement, both Wichita and Dodge City witnessed the birth of women's benevolent societies. Organizations like the Woman's Relief Corps, the American Association of University Women, the PEO, the Kansas Federation of Women's Clubs, and the Woman's Christian Temperance Union "affirmed the women's sense of the validity and importance of their own values." The meetings helped break down the isolation many women undoubtedly felt, created complex networks among women reformers, offered women useful instruction on frontier living, and, perhaps most importantly, provided a way for women to translate the moral lessons of domesticity into direct social action. One women's club, for example, ran a successful day nursery for working mothers; another group founded the Home for Friendless Women in Leavenworth; a third helped to start what became the Girls' Industrial School in Beloit. Still other women tried to help prostitutes, poor older women and widows, or concentrated on school reforms, including scholarships for poor girls and an end to gender-based teacher pay inequities. Whether fighting for these reforms or for temperance legislation, the right of wives to refuse intercourse with drunken husbands, or protection and relief for female victims of a male-run economy, the women's groups of Kansas offered an implicit and sometimes explicit critique of a social order dominated by men.

Women's efforts at church formation and temperance, antiprostitution, and gambling reforms were public efforts that protected women's families and fostered in women a collective sense of identity and accomplishment. But the female effort to change male behavior also reverberated within the private lives of western women. Here, too, a battle of sorts was being waged. Domestic ideology made sense to Anglo women not only because it offered a moral basis for social reform but because it gave wives, within the privacy of the home, the right to expect, even demand, behavior from husbands commensurate with women's moral position within the family. Thus, a paradox emerges: domesticity was an ideology of social order, a "cultural rationalization for a specific social ordering of the relations between men and women" that helped legitimate male monopolization of economic, political, educational, and legal life. Yet, domestic ideology contained within it elements of a powerful critique of male behavior and prerogatives that could, if pursued far enough, break up the family, the very foundation of Victorian social order. Civilizing men included civilizing the man who headed the household, and if he could not be reconstructed, increasing numbers of western women simply filed for divorce.

Evidence from California divorce courts from 1850 to 1890 suggests that domestic ideology, however vague and imperfectly realized, shaped the ongoing debate on gender by providing a language that checked traditional male prerogatives and called for both intimacy and mutual respect within the family. Helped by California's wide ranging grounds for divorce and expansive interpretations of marital cruelty by the state supreme court, female divorce seekers could use the leverage afforded by domestic ideology to break free of ties with cold, aloof, insensitive, and domineering husbands. Wives took pains to describe their own allegiance to the domestic ideal and to show how their husbands' cruel behavior made the establishment of peaceful, respectable homes impossible. As home guardians and moral exemplars, women deserved better treatment. Thus, a wife might complain about an overbearing husband "who treated me as a slave" or about one who insisted that his wife follow his every command. Other wives demanded respect and complained of husbands' selfishness and of husbands who tried to restrict their wives' contacts outside the home; wives also criticized husbands who meddled in their personal correspondence, who ignored them with a "brutal silence," who unfairly denied them credit with local merchants, or who ignored their physical limitations. While such male behavior might have been objectionable in the first half of the nineteenth century, only in the second half do such complaints by women gain standing in divorce suits. Although these particular complaints might not bring a divorce in and of themselves—California law demanded proof of extreme cruelty—they did bolster cruelty complaints and helped to prove that a man's general behavior did not comport with social expectations for husbands. . . .

If the divorce rate is an accurate barometer of rising material expectations, women's claims on men were clearly rising in the second half of the nineteenth century. Women brought almost 70 percent of the suits, and courts showed little inclination to stem the tide of divorce. These trends were especially pronounced in the West, the region with the highest divorce rate, the most expansive statutes, and the most liberal judicial interpretations of matrimonial cruelty in the nation. In fact, California was a leader in this regard—from 1867 to 1906, over seven thousand California wives sued successfully for divorce on the ground of cruelty—and in the late nineteenth century, California courts redefined the nature of marital cruelty to include mental anguish, a definition with far more latitude than traditional interpretations had permitted.

Why western courts adopted such expansive positions is not altogether clear: perhaps women's claims had special appeal in the West where an overwhelmingly male culture (at least initially) met with female demands for a different cultural ethos. This clash of men's and women's conceptions of social order may have lent considerable weight to women's desires to break free of cruel husbands. Far from home and kin and bereft of familiar institutions, harshly treated women likely made strong claims on the sensibility of middle-class jurists. Thus, judges in rural California listened sympathetically to wives who complained about husbands' brutish sexual demands or about husbands who ignored their sick or pregnant wives, who spent too much time away from the domestic hearth, or who were heartless toward the children. With such behavior, husbands stood opposed to women's civilizing influence, thereby threatening to stop the moral progress so necessary to middle-class perceptions of settlement in the West. By their actions, they lost their right to be husbands. The moral leverage of domesticity asked men to reshape their behavior and to treat the opposite sex with more respect, and when men failed to do so, women increasingly turned to divorce courts for relief. . . .

Despite its origins in the East, domestic ideology established a powerful hold on the lives of western Anglo women. En route, and once settled, women kept alive the basic assumptions of domesticity, helped, no doubt, by frontier schoolbooks, newspapers, and magazines that underscored women's duties as child-rearers, housewives, and moral guardians of family and community. The advice was general and vague but also ubiquitous and constant, and the effect was to preempt competing visions of womanhood. A woman who opposed domestic ideology for whatever reasons likely lacked even the language to express alternative views.

Moreover, the very suppleness of the concepts, the fact that domestic ideology was less a cult or a rigid orthodoxy and more a flexible vocabulary about gender ideals, meant that most Anglo women could turn to its values to make sense of their own lives. For most women, western migration was a family enterprise, and their commitment to their families defined their sense of self. What gave cultural meaning to these family responsibilities was the ideology of domesticity, an elastic and resilient set of ideas which supplied a much needed sense of stability, community, and generational continuity in a new region and provided an effective critique of immoral, undomesticated men. The last point is especially important. Given the masculine ethos of the early West, domesticity may have been especially appealing to western Anglo women who found in the ideology a powerful counterpoint to male assumptions about family and community life.

Indians into Citizens: The Tragedy of the Dawes Act

DONALD J. BERTHRONG

During the Progressive Era, the ideals of nineteenth-century Christian reformers continued to influence the Indian policy of the United States. Assimilation of Native Americans into the mainstream of American life remained the principal goal. However, in implementing the larger outlines of Indian policy, both reformers and government officials invariably encountered obstacles. One of the major obstacles that blocked progress was the leasing of Indian allotments. The Dawes Act of 1887 had made allotments to tribesmen who instead of starting small farms had leased their land and soon were drawing a substantial income from farmers and ranchers. Reformers, imbued with the work ethic, pronounced this arrangement an evil and reasoned that if the Indians owned less land, they would be forced to gain a livelihood directly from farming or some other employment. If allotted land were sold, the money obtained could be used to buy farm machinery, provide houses, and generally assist an Indian begin farming. To achieve such a program, Congress enacted legislation between 1902 and 1910 which permitted the sale of all Indian lands allotted under the Dawes Act. Poorly administered by misguided bureaucrats, these statutes created myriad opportunities for whites to defraud Indians of their land and property. By 1921 more than one half of the individuals within tribes affected by the Dawes Act were landless, rural, and economically devastated people. The impact of this national disgrace was vividly illustrated by the alienation of Indian lands on the Cheyenne-Arapaho Reservation in Oklahoma during these years.

Christian reformers and humanitarians, allied with government officials, believed by 1900 that the "Indian question" would soon be solved. Their naive assumption resulted from the anticipated efficacy of the General Allotment (Dawes) Act of 1887. Key features of the act provided for the allotment of reservation land, the eventual sale of non-alloted land to whites, and citizenship for all Indian allottees. Allotted land would remain in trust for twenty-five years. . . . The benefits of private property and citizenship would be supplemented by vocational education emphasizing farming, stock raising, and manual skills, and by religious instruction stressing individualism over tribalism. In a generation, it was assumed, Indians would possess all the requisites for full participation in American society. Labor, thrift, and the

Donald J. Berthrong, "Legacies of the Dawes Act" in *Arizona and the West* 21 (Winter 1979), pp. 335–51, 353–54. Used by permission of the *Journal of the Southwest.*

accumulation of private property would swiftly transform tribesmen into self-supporting farmers and stockmen who would have no need for federal paternalism.

Congress, responding to Western land demands, had enacted legislation to implement the intent of the Dawes Act. A clause in the Indian Appropriation Act passed in March of 1889 authorized the appointment of a commission to negotiate with various tribes for lands in central and western Indian Territory. The Unassigned (Oklahoma) District was opened on April 22, 1889, and quickly occupied by land seekers. A year later, on May 2, 1890, Congress created the Territory of Oklahoma and immediately sought to expand the new political unit by opening land on adjoining Indian domains. To accomplish this objective, a three-man commission chaired by David H. Jerome in June initiated talks to implement the allotment program and purchase unoccupied reservation land.

The Jerome Commission met with the Southern Cheyennes and Arapahoes during July and October of 1890. Hard bargaining, threats, deception, and bribery were employed to break down the resistance of several Cheyenne and Arapaho chiefs to the concept of allotment and loss of unused land. When the cession agreement was worked out, every Cheyenne and Arapaho listed on the 1891 tribal roll would be allotted a one hundred sixty acre homestead—eighty acres each of crop and grazing land—and the surplus land would be sold to the government. In time, when the allotting process was completed, 3,294 Cheyennes and Arapahoes had acquired a total of 529,682 acres of land, out of slightly more than four million on the reservation, to be held in trust for twenty-five years by the government. . . .

Even before the Cheyennes and Arapahoes had accepted the allotment program, Congress began modifying the Dawes Act. The modification was necessary because, in setting aside allotments, the 1887 statute made every conveyance or contract touching trust lands "absolutely null and void" during the trust period. On March 10, 1890, Senator Henry L. Dawes, the sponsor of the original act, introduced a bill to authorize Indians, subject to the approval of the Secretary of Interior, to lease their allotments. . . . Congress broadened the leasing criteria in 1894 by amending the defining phrase to read, "by reason of age, disability or inability," and by extending the lease periods.

With these modifications, Indian agents began arranging leases. By 1900 approximately 1,100 leases had been signed for the Cheyennes and Arapahoes, who realized $42,120.83 for the 1899–1900 fiscal year. These leases, which covered approximately one third of their allotted land, increased Cheyenne-Arapaho income by slightly more than 40 percent. Leasing of allotments was more prevalent at the Cheyenne-Arapaho Agency than in other jurisdictions in 1900, when it was estimated that 13 percent of land allotted to all tribes was leased.

The Dawes Act, however, did not eliminate tribalism. Allotted Indians continued to live together in extended families and small villages, resisting the white man's education, Christianity, family structure, and concept of private property. Furthermore, marginal soil fertility and rainfall, minimal capacity to operate agricultural machinery, and deep aversion to agricultural labor prevented most tribesmen from becoming farmers. A Cheyenne-Arapaho Indian agent reported that eight years after allotment only 15 to 18 percent of the adult male population was "actually occupying and cultivating their own lands." . . . Commissioner William A. Jones complained in 1900 that the widespread practice of leasing Indian allotments undermined the goals of the Dawes Act. "The Indian," wrote Jones, "is allotted and then allowed to turn over his land to whites and go on his aimless way." Leases not only fostered "indolence with its train of attendant vices," but also provided white settlers and realtors an effective means to exploit Indian lands. When an allottee became discouraged by unsuccessful efforts to farm, he usually leased his land and returned to camp life.

. . . If lease income permitted Indians to live without engaging in physical labor, then legislation amending the Dawes Act was necessary. . . . If this land could be removed from a trust status and opened for sale, Indians would have less land to lease. Indians could use the money derived from the sale of whole or partial allotments to aid in building houses, barns, and fences; buying draft animals, cattle, and swine; and providing the necessities of life while bringing smaller and more manageable acreage into cultivation. Congress would also be relieved of approving larger appropriations to support Indians.

Westerners also wanted to see Indian allotments sold to whites. The editor of a newspaper in Watonga, the seat of Blaine County, Oklahoma Territory, alleged that 69 percent of the original Cheyenne and Arapaho allottees were dead and their land was idle and unproductive. Nothing, the editor argued, could benefit Blaine County more than to have those allotments belonging to "dead Indians" owned and cultivated by white farmers.

In 1902 the Dawes Act was modified to free inherited allotments from trust status. According to the act, when an allottee died his homestead would be held in trust for his heir or heirs for the remainder of the twenty-five-year trust period. However, tucked obscurely into the Indian Appropriation Act of 1902 was a little-discussed provision which altered this requirement. Section 7 stated that adult heirs "of any deceased Indian to whom a trust . . . has been . . . issued for lands allotted to him may sell and convey lands inherited from such decedent."

Congress also responded to pressure from Western townsite promoters to approve alienation of allotted land. . . . [Some Cheyenne allotments] had become extremely valuable because [they] lay adjacent to the intersection of four railroads, including branch lines of the Rock Island and Frisco railroads. Despite the provisions of the Dawes Act, Congress was prevailed upon to vote under Section 9 of the Indian Appropriation Act to free 320 acres of allotted land belonging to . . . four Cheyennes from all "restrictions as to the sale, encumbrance or taxation" of the specified tracts. The Indians received $6,200 for their tracts. When divided into town lots, the land was sold for more than $150,000. . . . Congress willingly had set aside provisions of the Dawes Act to satisfy the economic ambitions of Western entrepreneurs.

When Congress began debating the need for a major modification of the Dawes Act, reformers, legislators, and Western residents expressed differing . . . goals. Reformers saw no harm in issuing fee patents for allotments to those Indians who by reason of education, intelligence, industry, and thrift appeared competent to manage their own economic affairs without supervision of the Bureau of Indian Affairs (BIA). Legislators hoped that Indians who received fee patents would drift away from their people and into white society, so that congressional appropriations supporting Indian affairs could be reduced. Westerners knew that few allotted Indians, regardless of competency criteria, would be sufficiently adroit in business matters to protect their unrestricted property.

The Burke Act of May 8, 1906, significantly modified the Dawes Act. Under this legislation, competent Indians, at the discretion of the Secretary of Interior, could be issued fee patents freeing their allotments from [most] restrictions "as to sale, encumbrance or taxation. . . ." The new law also stipulated that thereafter citizenship would be granted only to Indians who received fee patents for their allotments. Those allottees with restricted property still . . . remained "subject to the exclusive jurisdiction of the United States" until they were issued a fee patent. . . .

Thus, two decades after the passage of the Dawes Act, every square inch of land used and occupied by Indians was subject to alienation. How much land Indians would retain depended upon the rapidity with which the Dawes Act and its modifying legislation would be applied administratively to Indian tribes or individuals.

In part, the land base of Indians diminished because reformers and government officials were blinded by their ideologies. They tied the destiny and lives of Indians to white institutions, regardless of the Indians' ability or desire to adapt to a new way of life. It was disturbing to see Indians living on reservations or allotments without labor. . . . Albert K. Smiley, long influential in the Lake Mohonk Conference and on the Board of Indian Commissioners, . . . wrote in 1905: ". . . work is the saving thing for the Indians. We have coddled them too much. . . . Put them on their mettle; make them struggle, then we will have some good Indians." Reformers and government officials agreed that assimilation and termination must be the goals of Indian policy, even though many Indians would suffer, "fall by the wayside and be trodden underfoot."

Although some Indian Service field personnel were cautious in stripping land from Indians, pressures grew for the sale of Indian land. Old or incapacitated Indians needed money for life's necessities, young heirs of original allottees required money for education, Indians attempting to farm needed homes, teams, machinery, and barns. Policy changes by the BIA, meanwhile, made alienation easier, and agency administrators who were indifferent to the Indians' interests or who profited by corrupt acts willingly acquiesced to white pressure for the sale of valuable allotments.

Since land was the only significant capital resource the Indians possessed, its retention was imperative. Unlike white Americans, Indians could not replenish their capital resources for a number of reasons: limited employ-ment opportunities; inadequate and inappropriate education; a high incidence of debilitating diseases; an inability to protect property through legal actions; a hostile white population that preyed upon their property; and a tenacious Indian adherence to traditional social and cultural customs. The Cheyennes and Arapahoes of Oklahoma, for example, were systematically impoverished as the Dawes Act and subsequent legislation affected young and old, healthy and infirm, competent and non-competent tribal members alike. Once the act was applied to tribal lands, the allotted land base continued to decrease until many tribal members became landless and indigent. Would the reformers have insisted upon their legislative program if they had known its conse-quences? If Albert K. Smiley's 1905 judgment reflected the opinion of other like-minded reformers, the answer, deplorably, would have been yes!

Beginning in 1908, Cheyenne and Arapaho chiefs protested the sale of allotments. Cloud Chief, Little Bear, and Big Wolf, Cheyenne chiefs from the Darlington Agency, insisted that "it isn't right for old Indians and young ones to draw patents in fee, it makes [them] worse and poor." According to Indian customs, complained the chiefs, "those who have secured patents to their land, sold them and wasted the proceeds, are without home and food . . . [and] the burden of their existence would fall upon those who have held their lands." . . . In May of 1909 tribal representatives presented their objections to Washington bureaucrats. . . . The land question was of greatest concern, especially to the older, uneducated chiefs. Mower, a Dog Soldier chief from the Cantonment Agency, best expressed the attitudes of the traditional chiefs when he asked Acting Commissioner R. G. Valentine to tighten rather than remove restrictions "because we don't know how to use our money, and speculators take money from us. . . . They are standing ready to grab our land and money the moment it is in our possession."

Arapaho spokesmen stated that some tribesmen desired increased land sales to relieve existing hardships for their families. . . . Cleaver Warden, a Carlisle-educated Arapaho and peyote leader, favored increased land sales to alleviate poverty among families that could not live upon lease income and distributions from the sale of inherited land. Warden argued that an Indian should be "treated like a white man and let him suffer the consequences if he does make a mistake." . . .

Regardless of educational status, all Cheyenne and Arapaho delegates insisted that their people needed more money in order to buy the necessities of life. Families could not subsist on the ten-dollar disbursements each month from the restricted Individual Indian Accounts. Little Raven, an Arapaho chief, informed Commissioner Valentine that Indians without money signed promissory notes to cover the costs of food and clothing purchases. When the notes could not be redeemed, merchants foreclosed on the Indians' non-trust property. To increase the amount of money available, all Cheyenne and Arapaho delegates advocated that more Indians be allowed to lease their land and receive the income directly from the lessee. Negotiating leases and expending their own money, it was suggested, would enhance the Indians' ability to deal with the white community.

Leasing of land independent of governmental supervision would not have solved the economic problems of the Cheyennes and Arapahoes. Even if lease and other incomes were maximized, the average annual per capita income for all Cheyennes and Arapahoes at this time would have been approximately $160. Only a few fortunate individuals, or families with multiple inherited allotments, lived far above subsistence level. Since Congress accepted the reformers' view that lease income hindered the inculcation of steady work habits and agreed that Indians should support themselves, the sale of original or inherited allotments was the only means of preventing starvation. But the amount of allotted land was finite, and land sales merely postponed the day of permanent poverty and deprivation.

The May 1909 conference prompted the Indian Office to send Indian Inspector Edgar A. Allen to investigate how Indian policy was affecting the welfare of the Cheyennes and Arapahoes. Allen's report, confined to the Darlington Agency, was shocking. He found that ninety-seven fee patents had been issued to the "most promising allottees" to test their capacity to manage their property, and at the time of his report in November all but two of the patentees had sold their land—in most instances, at far below market value. Futhermore, they had signed over title to cancel debts or in exchange for horses, buggies, and other merchandise at inflated prices, and had received little cash for their land. None of the property acquired remained in their possession, and few permanent improvements were visible on their remaining lands. . . .

Many Cheyennes and Arapahoes were in dire need by November of 1909, despite the sale of almost 22 percent of all inherited and original allotments and extensive land leasing. Without funds or credit, Indians had "nothing to tide them over during the cold weather." Even Indian farmers were in straits. Corn crops, for example, for the 1909 season produced only from five to twenty bushels per acre because of hot, dry weather. . . .

The lack of agricultural progress by the Cheyennes and Arapahoes disturbed Valentine. At the Cantonment Agency he noted that only 2,587 acres were cultivated out of a total of 92,859 acres of trust land, while 80,320 acres were leased to non-Indians. He encouraged Superintendent Walter G. West to expedite the sale of inherited land to provide agency Indians with funds to improve their farming operations. Even if a family had not inherited land, portions of original allotments should be sold to buy farming equipment.

Such recommendations reflected Valentine's bureaucratic blindness. The Cheyennes and Arapahoes of Cantonment were the least likely groups of the two tribes to adapt to agriculture. After two decades of BIA efforts to implant the work ethic in these tribesmen through agricultural pursuits, their per capita cultivated acreage in 1912 was 3.38 acres. Agricultural machinery purchased for them would be abandoned, stolen, sold, or mortgaged, despite laws which prohibited the disposal of trust property. Therefore, if their agricultural land was sold, lease money would diminish and the Indians would be forced to work, thereby fulfilling the reformers' ideals, or starve.

Superintendent West hoped that younger Cheyennes and Arapahoes would become productive citizens after they were provided with farming machinery. More than 50 percent of the tribal population at the Cantonment Agency still lived in tipis and in camps consisting of from two to fifteen families. Some would fail to earn a living after their lands were sold, but West rationalized that "in any case, the Government will have done its part and the Indians will be no worse off than he [sic] would otherwise be . . . [and] will be benefited by the experience afforded them." Toward the older people, West was more compassionate. He optimistically predicted that the government could "conserve their health and make them as comfortable and happy as possible during the remainder of their days." When lease income of an elderly person was insufficient, West suggested the use of tribal shares and the sale of trust lands, reserving only enough land for the elderly to live on and to raise a garden.

During the administration of Woodrow Wilson, the onslaught against allotted lands increased. No new legislation was necessary; the reformers had provided all administrative statutory authority required to strip land and property from allotted Indians. This power was seized by Franklin K. Lane, a Californian, and Cato Sells, a Texan, who as President Wilson's Secretary of Interior and Commissioner of Indian Affairs, respectively, viewed Indian affairs from a pro-Western perspective. Arable land in the public domain was becoming less plentiful immediately before and during World War I, making unused Indian allotments attractive to non-Indian land speculators, farmers, and ranchers. The policies of the Theodore Roosevelt and William Howard Taft administrations of selling Indian allotments required only different emphases to decimate further the land base of many allotted tribes.

Cheyenne and Arapaho chiefs and spokesmen quickly perceived that more of their people were receiving fee patents and selling trust land. They were also worried that tribal restrictions would not be renewed in 1917, when their twenty-five-year trust period expired. When Wolf Chief, an uneducated Cheyenne chief from the Seger Agency, heard in 1914 that Commissioner Sells intended to turn the Cheyennes and Arapahoes "loose to be civilized," he began "to moan aloud" and traveled to Washington to protest Sell's proposal. To Assistant Commissioner E. B. Meritt, Wolf Chief insisted that his people were not prepared to be severed from governmental supervision. "I am kind of afraid," Wolf Chief explained, "to take the white man's ways yet—I don't know how to write, I don't know how to manage my affairs the white man's way . . . when I look around amongst my tribe, my people, my school children—none of them are able to work like the white man, none of them can be doctors, none lawyers, none clerks in stores, and other work like that—they are too far behind yet." . . .

Evidence abounds that few Cheyennes and Arapahoes were prepared to be declared competent under the 1906 Burke Act. During a 1916 inspection tour of the Concho Agency, Supervisor H. G. Wilson learned that none of the 173 persons who had been issued fee patents since 1906 retained any of their allotted land. Only one patentee had invested his money by purchasing other land and buying good livestock. The others had sold their allotments for less than market value and spent the money for unneeded merchandise. Wilson recommended that the Cheyenne and Arapaho land "be held in trust for them for many years to come."

Ignoring information received from field personnel, Commissioner Sells in January of 1917 sent a competency board to the four Cheyenne-Arapaho agencies to prepare a list of Indians to whom fee patents should be issued. While the board members were en route to Oklahoma, a Cheyenne-Arapaho delegation made a futile appeal to Commissioner Meritt to have the board's proceedings delayed. Victor Bushyhead, a Haskell-educated Cheyenne, explained that even the younger educated people were not able to assume control of their land and money. "We young people," Bushyhead declared, "are always tempted to fall back and adopt the customs of the older people. We realize that if we were given . . . the right of conducting our own business affairs and our land turned over to us, that then all of our property and money would fall into the hands of grafters. We are not ready to prepare ourselves to compete with civilized people in a business way." Commissioner Sells made no concessions to the delegation, indicating only that he would recommend a ten-year extension of the trust period for those judged non-competent. The younger people and mixed-bloods would have to take their chances with white merchants, bankers, and lawyers.

On January 19, 1917, the competency board began hearings on the "business competency" of the Cheyennes and Arapahoes. The board was concerned primarily with the level of education, the amount and value of trust land, the degree of Indian blood, employment, the number of dependents, marital status, and the ability of the Indians to read, write, and speak English. At the conclusion of the hearings, the board recommended that 177 Cheyennes and Arapahoes be issued fee patents. By executive order on April 4, 1917, President Wilson directed that 167 patents be issued from the list the board submitted.

The allottees recommended as competent had attained at least a fourth or fifth grade education. A significant fraction had attended programs at non-reservation schools such as Carlisle, Haskell, Chilocco, and Hampton. Of the individuals recommended for fee patents, 26.5 percent were of mixed Indian, white, black, or Mexican ancestry, and 73.5 percent were full-blood Indians.

The board's criteria of business competency were unclear. A few Indians recommended for fee patents worked as laborers, store clerks, held agency positions, or were craftsmen. A large majority of the younger people, however, pursued no vocation and lived on lease money. . . . Of the 167 whose restrictions on land were removed, 76.5 percent were between the ages of twenty-one and thirty-nine. Regardless of age, 58.2 percent refused to sign applications for the removal of restrictions from their land. As the board's journal and recommendations indicate, little consideration was given to the allottee's previous record of handling his or her money and property.

The fears of the Cheyenne and Arapaho chiefs and spokesmen soon became realities. Land thieves, grafters, merchants, bankers, lawyers, and realtors prepared to profit handsomely from land which the Cheyennes and Arapahoes would be free to sell. An estimated $660,000 worth of land was available for plundering. Superintendent J. W. Smith of the Seger Agency warned Commissioner Sells that many younger Indians had purchased automobiles, giving the dealers undated mortgages on their lands which could be recorded after the fee patents had been received. If the "reckless disposition" of the money affected only the young men, Smith complained, he would not protest so vigorously. But in many instances the Indians were the "father[s] of several children and most often have wives who do as much as they can to discourage such practices." W. W. Scott, superintendent at Concho and a competency board member . . . had learned that many Indians had "pledged" or mortgaged their allotments in anticipation of receiving a fee patent. In a matter of a few weeks after the patents had been received, Superintendent Smith claimed that all patented land had been sold. The Indians rarely acquired full value for their land. . . .

On April 17, 1917, Commissioner Sells announced a new Indian policy. Among all allotted tribes, any individual of one-half or more white ancestry, every Indian twenty-one years of age or older who had completed a full course of instruction in a government school, and all other Indians judged to be as competent as the "average whiteman" would be given "full control of his property and have all his lands and money turned over to him, after which he will no longer be a ward of the government." . . . The depletion of the Indian land base quickened even more when Indians who escaped the judgments of competency boards had trust restrictions removed from their property and money. Although Sells described his program as the "beginning of the end of the Indian problem," the reverse was correct. Once the land sales closed and the money received was expended, allotted Indians and their dependents faced lives of endless poverty.

Wherever allotted Indians lived, whites schemed to defraud them of their holdings. One center of white conspirators was the small community of Watonga, around which hundreds of Cheyenne and Arapaho allotments were concentrated in Blaine and adjacent counties. . . . At the heart of the ring of land thieves was Ed Baker, a Blaine County lawyer and judge, who was assisted by livestock dealers, merchants, bankers, county officials, four or five Cheyennes and Arapahoes, and at least one agency superintendent. Baker ingratiated himself with Cheyennes and Arapahoes by acting as their attorney for moderate fees in criminal and civil suits before local courts. He also loaned money at ten percent interest to Indians whom he believed would be granted fee patents, keeping complete records of their indebtedness to him.

Baker never loaned Indians more than one half of the value of the land for which a fee patent would be issued. When Indians first obtained money from him, the attorney secured their signatures on undated mortgages which were recorded against their land and dated at a later time. The Indian spent the borrowed money for horses and merchandise (at highly inflated prices), feasts for his friends, and trips to visit relatives in Wyoming or Montana. When the mortgage fell due and Baker demanded repayment, the Indian had run through all of the money and could not borrow more from any source. Threatening foreclosure, Baker obtained the individual's signature to a deed to the patented land for a small additional sum. Merchants who cooperated with Baker sold the Indians horses, buggies, wagons, and other goods valued higher than the amount borrowed from Baker, obtaining a promissory note for the difference. When a note fell due and the Indian was unable to redeem it, the merchant foreclosed and seized the chattel property before a cooperative county court. . . . Although [eventually] judgments were rendered against Baker for his crimes, the lawyer never repaid one cent of the money he had defrauded from over one hundred Cheyennes and Arapahoes.

The economic potential of the Cheyennes and Arapahoes was severely crippled during Cato Sells's administration. A total of 181,500 acres, or 34.3 percent, of all their allotted land was alienated. By adding land sold during the Roosevelt and Taft administrations, 297,214 acres, or 56.3 percent of all land allotted to the tribes, had passed from their possession. . . . What happened to the Cheyennes and Arapahoes, unfortunately, also occurred at other Western agencies. With less land to sell and reduced demand during the 1920s, allotted land sales declined sharply. Because much of the productive agricultural land had been sold, income from leases and crops decreased at the Cheyenne and Arapaho agencies. And since Individual Indian Accounts were depleted even before Sells left office in 1921, the economic future of the tribesmen was bleak.

The attempt to transform the Cheyennes and Arapahoes into self-sufficient farmers and stock raisers during the Progressive Era had been a failure. The Dawes Act and its modifications led directly to the destruction of a viable land base for the two tribes, and bureaucrats wasted little sympathy on Indians when their land and money slipped away. Horace G. Wilson, supervisor of farming, commented with remarkable callousness in early 1919 that some Cheyennes and Arapahoes were "probably better off now than they were before, as they made little or no use of their lands, and now that the land is gone and they receive no rentals, they are compelled to go to work." Land thieves such as Ed Baker, ready to defraud the Indians, profited from the blind adherence of reformers and bureaucrats to the work ethic. Misguided idealism, crippling legislation, destructive Indian policy and BIA regulations, hostile or indifferent courts, and white greed sapped the economic vitality of the Cheyenne and Arapaho peoples. That they have survived and multiplied in the twentieth century in spite of the policies of reformers and bureaucrats is a singular testament to their inner strength and a way of life based upon time-honored customs and spiritualism.

☙ *F U R T H E R   R E A D I N G*

Robert F. Berkhofer, Jr., *The White Man's Indian* (1978)
Allen G. Bogue, *From Prairie to Corn Belt* (1963)
Albert Camarillo, *Chicanos in a Changing Society* (1979)
Harry Sinclair Drago, *The Great Range Wars* (1985)
Philip Durham and Everett L. Jones, *The Negro Cowboys* (1965)
Robert R. Dykstra, *The Cattle Towns* (1968)
John M. Faragher, *Women and Men on the Overland Trail* (1979)

Robert V. Hine, *Community on the American Frontier* (1980)

Paul Andrew Hutton, "From Little Bighorn to Little Big Man: The Changing Image of Western Hero in a Popular Culture," *Western Historical Quarterly* 7 (January 1976), 19–44

Sandra L. Myres, *Westering Women and the Frontier Experience, 1800–1915* (1982)

Robert J. Rosenbaum, *Mexicano Resistance in the Southwest* (1981)

Lillian Schlissel et al., eds., *Western Women: Their Land, Their Lives* (1988)

Richard Slotkin, *The Fatal Environment* (1985)

Richard White, *The Roots of Dependency: Subsistence, Environment, and Social Change Among the Choctaws, Pawnees, and Navajos* (1983)

CHAPTER
4

New South Image
Versus New South Reality

❧

With the withdrawal of the last federal troops from the reconstructed South in 1876, the region's white leaders predicted a new era of economic, social, and political progress. Yet the ghosts of endemic problems and older conflicts would not be quickly banished. Economically, the difficulties were rooted in the South's cotton-centered agriculture, which was mired in postwar debt and, by the 1880s, faced plunging world cotton prices. The squeeze on cotton financing rippled down through factors, bankers, and merchants to landowners, sharecroppers, and tenant farmers operating under the crop-lien system of pledging a future crop against a current loan. For the sharecroppers and tenant farmers, black and white alike, the situation verged on catastrophe.

It was out of this gloomy milieu that the dream of a "new" South emerged. An idealized version of the northern urban-industrial revolution gripped the imaginations of many southern boosters, including a number of newspaper editors. They initially pinned their hopes on the cotton mill, or more precisely the recruitment of the textile industry from its traditional New England base to the labor-rich, low-cost South. They got their way but not entirely with the results they expected.

"New South" industrialization blossomed, however, as a white-only affair, and black communities struggled to develop against great odds. Carrying the legal claim to freedom and citizenship, southern blacks found their entry to economic advancement cut off at every turn. Whether massed in Black Belt regions along the Mississippi without land of their own or drifting to and within southern cities— where they were denied entry to skilled trades—the freed people and their children were thrown back on their own resources. In this situation the development of widespread black education proved a significant accomplishment.

❧ D O C U M E N T S

Contending at once with severe economic disadvantages and with political opinions still largely divided by bitter wartime memories, post-Reconstruction southern leaders appealed, of necessity, to northern goodwill and northern pocketbooks. No gesture in this direction was more effective than *Atlanta Constitution* editor Henry W. Grady's appeal for national reconciliation, excerpted in the first document. Appearing before the New England Society of New York City on December 21, 1886, Grady sings a song of an industrious New South that was music to northern businessmen's ears. Looking back in the second document on the cotton-mill campaign that was a cornerstone of New South development, Broadus Mitchell, a young economic historian of the day, accepts the entrepreneurs' view that civic benevolence, as much as self-interest, underlay mill development. By way of contrast, in the third document, the legendary labor organizer "Mother" Jones portrays the mill village as a feudal barony populated by tyrannical overseers and half-starved millworkers.

In the same period, with characteristic outspokenness, former slave Frederick Douglass, speaking before the Louisville National Convention of Colored People in 1883, describes the utter recalcitrance and naked intimidation with which white America was turning back blacks' claims to full citizenship. Next, with equal eloquence and wit, Harvard-trained sociologist W. E. B. Du Bois places the enigma of the "lazy" field hand in a political and economic context. In the final selection, a black Alabama schoolteacher and two of his pupils reflect an earnest striving for group improvement in their testimony before an inquiring Senate Committee on Labor and Education.

Henry W. Grady Heralds the New South, 1886

"There was a South of slavery and secession—that South is dead. There is a South of union and freedom—that South, thank God, is living, breathing, growing every hour." These words, delivered from the immortal lips of Benjamin H. Hill, at Tammany Hall, in 1866, true then and truer now, I shall make my text to-night. . . .

. . . The soldier stepped from the trenches into the furrow; horses that had charged federal guns marched before the plow, and fields that ran red with human blood in April were green with the harvest in June; women reared in luxury cut up their dresses and made breeches for their husbands, and, with a patience and heroism that fit women always as a garment, gave their hands to work. There was little bitterness in all this. Cheerfulness and frankness prevailed. "Bill Arp" struck the keynote when he said, "Well, I killed as many of them as they did of me, and now I'm going to work." So did the soldier returning home after defeat and roasting some corn on the roadside who made the remark to his comrades, "You may leave the South if you want to, but I'm going to Sandersville, kiss my wife, and raise a crop, and if the Yankees fool with me any more, I'll whip 'em again." . . .

But what is the sum of our work? We have found out that in the summing up the free negro counts more than he did as a slave. We have planted the schoolhouse on the hilltop and made it free to white and black. We have sown towns and cities in the place of theories, and put business above politics. We have challenged your spinners in Massachusetts and your ironmakers in Pennsylvania. We have learned that the $400,000,000 annually received from our cotton crop will make us rich when the supplies that make it are home-raised. We have reduced the commercial rate of interest from 24 to 6 per cent, and are floating 4 per cent bonds. We have learned that one Northern immigrant is worth fifty foreigners, and have smoothed the path to Southward, wiped out the place where Mason and Dixon's line used to be, and hung out the latch-string to you and yours.

We have reached the point that marks perfect harmony in every household, when the husband confesses that the pies which his wife cooks are as good as those his mother used to bake; and we admit that the sun shines as brightly and the moon as softly as it did before the war. We have established thrift in city and country. We have fallen in love with work. We have restored comfort to homes from which culture and elegance never departed. We have let economy take root and spread among us as rank as the crab-grass which sprung from Sherman's cavalry camps, until we are ready to lay odds on the Georgia Yankee as he manufactures relics of the battlefield in a one-story shanty and squeezes pure olive oil out of his cotton seed, against any downeaster that ever swapped wooden nutmegs for flannel sausage in the valleys of Vermont. Above all, we know that we have achieved in these "piping times of peace" a fuller independence for the South than that which our fathers sought to win in the forum by their eloquence or compel in the field by their swords.

It is a rare privilege, sir, to have had part, however humble, in this work. Never was nobler duty confided to human hands than the uplifting and upbuilding of the prostrate and bleeding South—misguided, perhaps, but beautiful in her suffering, and honest, brave, and generous always. In the record of her social, industrial, and political illustration we await with confidence the verdict of the world.

But what of the negro? Have we solved the problem he presents or progressed in honor and equity toward solution? Let the record speak to the point. No section shows a more prosperous laboring population than the negroes of the South, none in fuller sympathy with the employing and landowning class. He shares our school fund, has the fullest protection of our laws, and the friendship of our people. Self-interest, as well as honor, demand that he should have this. Our future, our very existence, depend upon our working out this problem in full and exact justice. We understand that when Lincoln signed the Emancipation Proclamation, your victory was assured, for he then committed you to the cause of human liberty, against which the arms of man cannot prevail—while those of our statesmen who trusted to make slavery the corner stone of the Confederacy doomed us to defeat as far as they could, committing us to a cause that reason could not defend or the sword maintain in sight of advancing civilization. . . .

To liberty and enfranchisement is as far as law can carry the negro. The rest must be left to conscience and common sense. It must be left to those among whom his lot is cast, with whom he is indissolubly connected, and whose prosperity depends upon their possessing his intelligent sympathy and confidence. Faith has been kept with him, in spite of calumnious assertions to the contrary by those who assume to speak for us or by frank opponents. Faith will be kept with him in the future, if the South holds her reason and integrity. . . .

The old South rested everything on slavery and agriculture, unconscious that these could neither give nor maintain healthy growth. The new South presents a perfect democracy, the oligarchs leading in the popular movement; a social system compact and closely knitted, less splendid on the surface, but stronger at the core; a hundred farms for every plantation, fifty homes for every palace; and a diversified industry that meets the complex needs of this complex age.

The new South is enamored of her new work. Her soul is stirred with the breath of a new life. The light of a grander day is falling fair on her face. She is thrilling with the consciousness of growing power and prosperity. As she stands upright, full-statured and equal among the people of the earth, breathing the keen air and looking out upon the expanded horizon, she understands that her emancipation came because, through the inscrutable wisdom of God, her honest purpose was crossed and her brave armies were beaten.

This is said in no spirit of time-serving or apology. The South has nothing for which to apologize. She believes that the late struggle between the States was war and not rebellion, revolution and not conspiracy, and that her convictions were as honest as yours. I should be unjust to the dauntless spirit of the South and to my own convictions if I did not make this plain in this presence. The South has nothing to take back.

In my native town of Athens is a monument that crowns its central hill—a plain, white shaft. Deep cut into its shining side is a name dear to me above the names of men—that of a brave and simple man who died in brave and simple faith. Not for all the glories of New England, from Plymouth Rock all the way, would I exchange the heritage he left me in his soldier's death. To the foot of that shaft I shall send my children's children to reverence him who ennobled their name with his heroic blood. But, sir, speaking from the shadow of that memory which I honor as I do nothing else on earth, I say that the cause in which he suffered and for which he gave his life was adjudged by a higher and fuller wisdom than his or mine, and I am glad that the omniscient God held the balance of battle in His Almighty hand, and that human slavery was swept forever from American soil—that the American Union was saved from the wreck of war.

This message, Mr. President, comes to you from consecrated ground. Every foot of soil about the city in which I live is sacred as a battle ground of the Republic. Every hill that invests it is hallowed to you by the blood of your brothers who died for your victory, and doubly hallowed to us by the blood of those who died hopeless, but undaunted, in defeat—sacred soil to all of us, rich with memories that make us purer and stronger and better, silent but stanch witnesses in its red desolation of the matchless valor of American hearts and the deathless glory of American arms, speaking an eloquent witness in its white peace and prosperity to the indissoluble union of American States and the imperishable brotherhood of the American people.

Now, what answer has New England to this message? Will she permit the prejudice of war to remain in the hearts of the conquerors, when it has died in the hearts of the conquered? Will she transmit this prejudice to the next generation, that in their hearts, which never felt the generous ardor of conflict, it may perpetuate itself? Will she withhold, save in strained courtesy, the hand which straight from his soldier's heart Grant offered to Lee at Appomattox? Will she make the vision of a restored and happy people, which gathered above the couch of your dying captain, filling his heart with grace, touching his lips with praise, and glorifying his path to the grave—will she make the vision, on which the last sigh of his expiring soul breathed a benediction, a cheat and delusion?

If she does, the South, never abject in asking for comradeship, must accept with dignity its refusal; but if she does not refuse to accept in frankness and sincerity this message of good will and friendship, then will the prophecy of Webster, delivered in this very society forty years ago amid tremendous applause, be verified in its fullest sense, when he said: "Standing hand to hand and clasping hands, we should remain united as we have been for sixty years, citizens of the same country, members of the same government, united, all united now and united forever. . . .

Broadus Mitchell Describes a Benevolent Cotton-Mill Campaign, 1921

One cannot view the passion with which [the New South] revival was undertaken without realizing how pointed were the lessons taught the South in the war and its aftermath. Convinced of old errors, the remaking of the South was emphatically in response to a moral stimulus, not less real because not always outwardly apparent. "A man who has been in the whirl of New York or in any of the brand new cities of the great West coming into Charleston might easily enough come to the conclusion that the old city was in a sad state of decadence—but our own people who have been accustomed to its quiet way of doing business, if they have their eyes open (or hearts open would perhaps be the better expression) could not fail to see manifest improvement—progress even, if you like the word better."

As the movement proceeded from introspection, the very genius of "Real Reconstruction" was self-help. It took courage to begin, but confidence rallied about every sign of genuine performance. Thus it was said that "Every true South Carolinian must rejoice at the . . . energy exhibited by the citizens of Columbia in their management of the Cotton-Mill Campaign. For years they have appeared to depend on somebody else to help them. The Legislature made liberal concessions. No effort was spared to interest Northern capitalists in the splendid water power. . . . But nothing was done. Tired of waiting a number of business men in Columbia took up the matter themselves. They soon found that the citizens generally would sustain them. . . . The city is full of life again. A handsome sum of money has been subscribed already to the capital stock of the Cotton Mill Company. . . . It will be a happy day for the whole State when the hum of a myriad spindles is heard on the banks of the historic Canal." . . .

Understanding the straits of the South at the opening of the cotton mill era, the readiness of Southern men to realize and assume responsibility in public matters, and the spirit of social service which characterized the awakening to a program of "Real Reconstruction," one accepts as natural the fact that cotton manufactories were frequently motivated by the desire to help a community to its feet. Often this wish was joined, and very properly so, with usual commercial promptings, but sometimes it controlled alone. . . .

No undertaking was born more emphatically in the impulse to furnish work than the Salisbury Cotton Mills. All the circumstances of the founding of this factory were singularly in keeping with the philanthropic prompting. The town of Salisbury, North Carolina, in 1887 had done nothing to recover from the war. It was full of saloons, wretched, unkempt. It happened that an evangelistic campaign was conducted; Mr. Pearson, remembered as a lean, intense Tennesseean, preached powerfully. A tabernacle was erected for the meeting, which lasted a month and, being undenominational, drew from the whole town and countryside. The evangelist declared that the great morality in Salisbury was to go to work, and that corruption, idleness and misery could not be dispelled until the poor people were given an opportunity to become productive. The establishment of a cotton mill would be the most Christian act his hearers could perform. "He gave Salisbury a moral dredging which made the people feel their responsibilities as they had not before, and made them do something for these folks. There had been little talk of manufacturing before Pearson came; there had been some tobacco factories in the town, but they had failed. The Salisbury Cotton Mills grew out of a moral movement to help the lower classes, largely inspired by this campaign. Without the moral issue, the financial interest would have come out in the long run, but the moral considerations brought the matter to a focus."

Mother Jones Compares Southern Mill Life to Serfdom, 1901

The miners and railroad boys of Birmingham, Ala., entertained me one evening some months ago with a graphic description of the conditions among the slaves of the Southern cotton mills. While I imagined that these must be something of a modern Siberia, I concluded that the boys were overdrawing the picture and made up my mind to see for myself the conditions described. Accordingly I got a job and mingled with the workers in the mill and in their homes. I found that children of six and seven years of age were dragged out of bed at half-past 4 in the morning when the task-master's whistle blew. They eat their scanty meal of black coffee and corn bread mixed with cottonseed oil in place of butter, and then off trots the whole army of serfs, big and little. By 5:30 they are all behind the factory walls, where amid the whir of machinery they grind their young lives out for fourteen long hours each day. As one looks on this brood of helpless human souls one could almost hear their voices cry out, "Be still a moment, O you iron wheels of capitalistic greed, and let us hear each other's voices, and let us feel for a moment that this is not all of life."

We stopped at 12 for a scanty lunch and a half-hour's rest. At 12:30 we were at it again with never a stop until 7. Then a dreary march home, where we swallowed our scanty supper, talked for a few minutes of our misery and then dropped down upon a pallet of straw, to lie until the whistle should once more awaken us, summoning babes and all alike to another round of toil and misery.

I have seen mothers take their babes and slap cold water in their face to wake the poor little things. I have watched them all day long tending the dangerous machinery. I have seen their helpless limbs torn off, and then when they were disabled and of no more use to their master, thrown out to die. I must give the company credit for having hired a Sunday school teacher to tell the little things that "Jesus put it into the heart of Mr.——————to build that factory so they would have work with which to earn a little money to enable them to put a nickel in the box for the poor little heathen Chinese babies."

The Rope Factory

I visited the factory in Tuscaloosa, Ala., at 10 o'clock at night. The superintendent, not knowing my mission, gave me the entire freedom of the factory and I made good use of it. Standing by a siding that contained 155 spindles were two little girls. I asked a man standing near if the children were his, and he replied that they were. "How old are they?" I asked. "This one is 9, the other 10," he replied. "How many hours do they work?" "Twelve," was the answer. "How much do they get a night?" "We all three together get 60 cents. They get 10 cents each and I 40."

I watched them as they left their slave-pen in the morning and saw them gather their rags around their frail forms to hide them from the wintry blast. Half-fed, half-clothed, half-housed, they toil on, while the poodle dogs of their masters are petted and coddled and sleep on pillows of down, and the capitalistic judges jail the agitators that would dare to help these helpless ones to better their condition.

Gibson is another of those little sections of hell with which the South is covered. The weaving of gingham is the principal work. The town is owned by a banker who possesses both people and mills. One of his slaves told me she had received one dollar for her labor for one year. Every weekly pay day her employer gave her a dollar. On Monday she deposited that dollar in the "pluck-me" store to secure food enough to last until the next pay day, and so on week after week.

There was once a law on the statute books of Alabama prohibiting the employment of children under twelve years of age more than eight hours each day. The Gadston Company would not build their mill until they were promised that this law should be repealed.

When the repeal came up for the final reading I find by an examination of the records of the House that there were sixty members present. Of these, fifty-seven voted for the repeal and but three against. . . .

I asked one member of the House why he voted to murder the children, and he replied that he did not think they could earn enough to support themselves if they only worked eight hours. These are the kind of tools the intelligent workingmen put in office. . . .

Almost every one of my shop-mates in these mills was a victim of some disease or other. All are worked to the limit of existence. The weavers are expected to weave so many yards of cloth each working day. To come short of this estimate jeopardizes their job. The factory operator loses all energy either of body or of mind. The brain is so crushed as to be incapable of thinking, and one who mingles with these people soon discovers that their minds like their bodies are wrecked. Loss of sleep and loss of rest gives rise to abnormal appetites, indigestion, shrinkage of stature, bent backs and aching hearts.

Such a factory system is one of torture and murder as dreadful as a long-drawn-out Turkish massacre, and is a disgrace to any race or age. As the picture rises before me I shudder for the future of a nation that is building up a moneyed artistocracy out of the life-blood of the children of the proletariat. It seems as if our flag is a funeral bandage splotched with blood. The whole picture is one of the most horrible avarice, selfishness and cruelty and is fraught with present horror and promise of future degeneration. The mother, over-worked and under-fed, gives birth to tired and worn-out human beings.

I can see no way out save in a complete overthrow of the capitalistic system, and . . . I will work . . . and pray for the coming of that better day.

Frederick Douglass Describes a Legacy of Race Hatred, 1883

Born on American soil in common with yourselves, deriving our bodies and our minds from its dust, centuries having passed away since our ancestors were torn from the shores of Africa, we, like yourselves, hold ourselves to be in every sense Americans, and that we may, therefore, venture to speak to you in a tone not lower than that which becomes earnest men and American citizens. Having watered your soil with our tears, enriched it with our blood, performed its roughest labor in time of peace, defended it against enemies in time of war, and at all times been loyal and true to its best interests, we deem it no arrogance or presumption to manifest now a common concern with you for its welfare, prosperity, honor and glory. . . .

It is our lot to live among a people whose laws, traditions, and prejudices have been against us for centuries, and from these they are not yet free. To assume that they are free from these evils simply because they have changed their laws is to assume what is utterly unreasonable and contrary to facts. Large bodies move slowly. Individuals may be converted on the instant and change their whole course of life. Nations never. Time and events are required for the conversion of nations. Not even the character of a great political organization can be changed by a new platform. It will be the same old snake though in a new skin. Though we have had war, reconstruction and abolition as a nation, we still linger in the shadow and blight of an extinct institution. Though the colored man is no longer subject to be bought and sold, he is still surrounded by an adverse sentiment which fetters all his movements. In his downward course he meets with no resistance, but his course upward is resented and resisted at every step of his progress. If he comes in ignorance, rags, and wretchedness, he conforms to the popular belief of his character, and in that character he is welcome. But if he shall come as a gentleman, a scholar, and a statesman, he is hailed as a contradiction to the national faith concerning his race, and his coming is resented as impudence. In the one case he may provoke contempt and derision, but in the other he is an affront to pride, and provokes malice. Let him do what he will, there is at present, therefore, no escape for him. The color line meets him everywhere, and in a measure shuts him out from all respectable and profitable trades and callings. In spite of all your religion and laws he is a rejected man.

He is rejected by trade unions, of every trade, and refused work while he lives, and burial when he dies, and yet he is asked to forget his color, and forget that which everybody else remembers. If he offers himself to a builder as a mechanic, to a client as a lawyer, to a patient as a physician, to a college as a professor, to a firm as a clerk, to a Government Department as an agent, or an officer, he is sternly met on the color line, and his claim to consideration in some way is disputed on the ground of color.

Not even our churches, whose members profess to follow the despised Nazarene, whose home, when on earth, was among the lowly and despised, have yet conquered this feeling of color madness, and what is true of our churches is also true of our courts of law. Neither is free from this all-pervading atmosphere of color hate. The one describes the Deity as impartial, no respecter of persons, and the other the Goddess of Justice as blindfolded, with sword by her side and scales in her hand held evenly between high and low, rich and low, white and black, but both are the images of American imagination, rather than American practices.

Taking advantage of the general disposition in this country to impute crime to color, white men *color* their faces to commit crime and wash off the hated color to escape punishment. In many places where the commission of crime is alleged against one of our color, the ordinary processes of law are set aside as too slow for the impetuous justice of the infuriated populace. They take the law into their own bloody hands and proceed to whip, stab, shoot, hang, or burn the alleged culprit, without the intervention of courts, counsel, judges, juries, or witnesses. . . . Every one knows that what is called Lynch law is peculiarly the law for colored people and for nobody else. If there were no other grievance than this horrible and barbarous Lynch law custom, we should be justified in assembling, as we have now done, to expose and denounce it. But this is not all. Even now, after twenty years of so-called emancipation, we are subject to lawless raids of midnight riders, who, with blackened faces, invade our homes and perpetrate the foulest of crimes upon us and our families. This condition of things is too flagrant and notorious to require specifications or proof. Thus in all the relations of life and death we are met by the color line. We cannot ignore it if we would, and ought not if we could. It hunts us at midnight, it denies us accommodation in hotels and justice in the courts; excludes our children from schools, refuses our sons the chance to learn trades, and compels us to pursue only such labor as will bring the least reward. While we recognize the color line as a hurtful force, a mountain barrier to our progress, wounding our bleeding feet with its flinty rocks at every step, we do not despair. We are a hopeful people. . . .

W. E. B. Du Bois Explains Black Belt Backwardness, 1903

Thus it is that in the country districts of the South, by written or unwritten law, peonage, hindrances to the migration of labor, and a system of white patronage exists over large areas. Besides this, the chance for lawless oppression and illegal exactions is vastly greater in the country than in the city, and nearly all the more serious race disturbances of the last decade have arisen from disputes in the country between master and man. . . . As a result of such a situation, there arose, first, the Black Belt; and, second, the Migration to Town. The Black Belt was not, as many assumed, a movement toward fields of labor under more genial climatic conditions; it was primarily a huddling for self-protection—a massing of the black population for mutual defence in order to secure the peace and tranquillity necessary to economic advance. This movement took place between Emancipation and 1880, and only partially accomplished the desired results. The rush to town since 1880 is the countermovement of men disappointed in the economic opportunities of the Black Belt.

In Dougherty County, Georgia, one can see easily the results of this experiment in huddling for protection. Only ten percent of the adult population was born in the county, and yet the blacks outnumber the whites four or five to one. There is undoubtedly a security to the blacks in their very numbers,—a personal freedom from arbitrary treatment, which makes hundreds of laborers cling to Dougherty in spite of low wages and economic distress. But a change is coming, and slowly but surely even here the agricultural laborers are drifting to town and leaving the broad acres behind. Why is this? Why do not the Negroes become land-owners, and build up the black landed peasantry, which has for a generation and more been the dream of philanthropist and statesman?

To the car-window sociologist, to the man who seeks to understand and know the South by devoting the few leisure hours of a holiday trip to unravelling the snarl of centuries,—to such men very often the whole trouble with the black field-hand may be summed up by Aunt Ophelia's word, "Shiftless!" They have noted repeatedly scenes like one I saw last summer. We were riding along the highroad to town at the close of a long hot day. A couple of young black fellows passed us in a mule-team, with several bushels of loose corn in the ear. One was driving, listlessly bent forward, his elbows on his knees,—a happy-go-lucky, careless picture of irresponsibility. The other was fast asleep in the bottom of the wagon. As we passed we noticed an ear of corn fall from the wagon. They never saw it,—not they. A rod farther on we noted another ear on the ground; and between that creeping mule and town we counted twenty-six ears of corn. Shiftless? Yes, the personification of shiftlessness. And yet follow those boys: they are not lazy; to-morrow morning they'll be up with the sun; they work hard when they do work, and they work willingly. They have no sordid, selfish, money-getting ways, but rather a fine disdain for mere cash. They'll loaf before your face and work behind your back with good-natured honesty. They'll steal a watermelon, and hand you back your lost purse intact. Their great defect as laborers lies in their lack of incentive to work beyond the mere pleasure of physical exertion. They are careless because they have not found that it pays to be careful; they are improvident because the improvident ones of their acquaintance get on about as well as the provident. Above all, they cannot see why they should take unusual pains to make the white man's land better, or to fatten his mule, or save his corn. On the other hand, the white land-owner argues that any attempt to improve these laborers by increased responsibility, or higher wages, or better homes, or land of their own, would be sure to result in failure. He shows his Northern visitor the scarred and wretched land; the ruined mansions, the worn-out soil and mortgaged acres, and says, This is Negro freedom!

Now it happens that both master and man have just enough argument on their respective sides to make it difficult for them to understand each other. The Negro dimly personifies in the white man all his ills and misfortunes; if he is poor, it is because the white man seizes the fruit of his toil; if he is ignorant, it is because the white man gives him neither time nor facilities to learn; and, indeed, if any misfortune happens to him, it is because of some hidden machinations of "white folks." On the other hand, the masters and the masters' sons have never been able to see why the Negro, instead of settling down to be day-laborers for bread and clothes, are infected with a silly desire to rise in the world, and why they are sulky, dissatisfied, and careless, where their fathers were happy and dumb and faithful. "Why, you niggers have an easier time than I do," said a puzzled Albany merchant to his black customer. "Yes," he replied, "and so does yo' hogs." . . .

A Teacher and Two Pupils Outline the Problems of a "Colored" School, 1883

OPELIKA, ALA., *November* 22, 1883.

C. S. GIDDENS sworn and examined.

By the CHAIRMAN:

Question. You teach this colored school? *Answer.* Yes, sir.

Q. How many scholars do you have? *A.* There are one hundred and sixty-five enrolled in this school.

Q. How long have you taught this school? *A.* Six years, right along, all the time.

Q. Are you hired by the parents of the children, or are you paid by the State? *A.* Just now I am paid by the State. I am paid by the State for about seven months every year, and the balance of the time by the parents.

Q. What wages do you get, or do teachers generally get? *A*. I get in this school $40 a month.

Q. Is there any other colored school in Opelika? *A*. Yes, sir; there is school No. 2. This is school No. 1.

Q. This, I suppose, is a larger and more advanced school? *A*. Yes, sir.

Q. About how many scholars have you present this morning? *A*. There are about twenty-nine present this morning.

Q. I suppose there will be more in during the day? *A*. Yes, sir.

Q. How do your schools compare with the white schools in the town? *A*. The board of trustees think they compare very well.

Q. Are the members of the board white men? *A*. They are all white.

Q. There are no white teachers of colored schools in this part of the country, I suppose? *A*. No, sir.

Q. And no colored teachers of white schools? *A*. No, sir.

Q. You think that your colored scholars do you as much credit as the white scholars do their teachers? *A*. Yes, sir; I think so. . . .

Q. If the Government would allow you to have some money for your schools that would be a good thing, wouldn't it? *A*. Oh, yes.

Q. I suppose you colored people do not pay much attention to politics now? *A*. No, sir; we do not pay much attention to those things now.

Q. You are trying to make money and let politics alone? *A*. Yes, sir.

Q. I suppose the colored people have talked that over among themselves, and have come to the conclusion that they had better turn their attention to making money and let politics go for one or two generations? *A*. Yes, sir.

Q. Is that so generally? *A*. No, sir. In Montgomery County the colored people take an active part, and also down in Coffee and Dale, they take an active part, because they are more able.

Q. I think it is the best way for you colored people to stick right to work and to try to get some education and to get some property, and that you say is the general idea of the colored people? *A*. Yes, sir; I think so. I took a census of the town and sent it to the superintendent of education, so that he should know how to make appropriations for the children, and I find that we have here about seven hundred children of the legal school age, from seven to twenty-one. That is in this district. We call this the Opelika district. Between the two schools No. 1 and No. 2, we would have about three hundred scholars.

Q. How old are those three women that I see over there studying their lessons? *A*. All of those three are married ladies.

Q. About what age do you take the oldest to be? *A*. About forty-seven or forty-eight.

Q. Have they children? *A*. Only one of them.

Q. Are they learning to read? *A*. Yes, sir; very well.

Q. Which is the oldest one? *A*. The one sitting on the left.

Q. What is their object in learning to read at their age? *A*. Well, their object is just to learn to read and write, so that they can act for themselves.

Q. How long have they attended school here? *A*. About seven months.

Q. How much longer will they attend? *A*. They will attend probably three or four months longer. . . .

BONNEY DRAKE, one of the pupils, was questioned as follows:

By the CHAIRMAN:

Q. How old are you? *A*. I am ten years old.

Q. How long have you been at school? *A*. I do not know.

Q. Let us hear you read. (The boy read a few sentences from an elementary reader.)

Q. What State is this? *A*. Opelika.

Q. Which is the larger, a State or a town? *A*. A State.

Q. Do you know the name of this State? (No answer.)

Q. Do any of these little people know the name of this State? *A*. (By one of the girls.) Alabama.

Q. Which is larger, Opelika or Alabama? *A*. Alabama.

Q. Did you ever hear of Montgomery? *A*. Yes, sir.

Q. What is Montgomery? *A*. Alabama.

Q. Montgomery is in Alabama, just as Opelika is; but what is Montgomery? *A*. A town.

Q. Yes; Montgomery is a city, and a good many people live there. You have never been there, have you? *A*. Yes, sir.

Q. It is a good deal larger place than this, is it not? *A*. Yes, sir.

Q. They call it the capital, don't they? *A*. Yes, sir.

Q. It is the place where the people live who govern the State, is it not? *A*. Yes, sir.

(The three adult pupils referred to in the testimony of the teacher were questioned by the Chairman. As they gave no names, they are here designated as Nos. 1, 2, and 3.)

No. 1 was questioned, and answered as follows:

Question. What is your age? *Answer*. I am thirty-six years old.

Q. Why are you at school? *A*. I taken a notion I want to learn, after waitin' so long. I been workin' a good deal and lost my health, and I thought I would learn to read and write, and may be it would be more intelligence to me and fetch on to other business to make a livin'.

Q. You are a married lady? *A*. Yes, sir.

No. 2 was questioned as follows:

Question. How old are you? *Answer*. Thirty-five.

Q. How long have you been attending school? *A*. Not quite three weeks.

Q. What success do you have in learning? *A*. Well, not much.

Q. Nobody learns much in three weeks. You must stick to it. Some of the greatest men in the history of the world did not begin certain studies until they were sixty or seventy or eighty years old. You are not discouraged, are you? *A*. No, sir. I hope I will improve.

The following is the examination of No. 3:

Question. How old are you? *Answer*. Thirty-eight.

Q. Are you a married lady? *A*. Yes, sir.

Q. Have you any family? *A*. One child.

Q. How long have you been learning to read? *A*. A month or more.

Q. You are going to stick to it until you learn to read, I suppose? *A*. Yes, sir; that is my aim.

Q. What do you want to learn to read and write for? *A*. I find there is a great advantage in readin' and writin'.

Q. You find that people who can read and write get on best? *A*. Yes, sir.

Q. Are most of the colored people taking pains to teach their children? *A*. Yes, sir.

❧ E S S A Y S

In the following essays, several historians contrast the myths with the realities of the New South. First, Paul M. Gaston of the University of Virginia sets the problems and limitations of southern economic development against the unqualified expectations of commercial and editorial boosters. In the second essay, Jacqueline Dowd Hall, Robert Korstad, and James Leloudis of the University of North Carolina at Chapel Hill challenge the portrait of the paternal mill owner surrounded by powerless millhands, replacing it with a more complex image of informal worker influence, mill-community cohesion, and sophisticated managerial innovations.

The Myth of the New South

PAUL M. GASTON

Allegiance to both the myth of the Old South and the dream of a New South was but one of several contradictions imbedded in the New South creed. There were many others: an institutional explanation of industrial backwardness in the Old South coupled with the faith that natural resources could not help but assure industrialization in the New; an elaborate propaganda campaign to attract immigrants into the region negated by hostility to the immigration pool easiest to tap; a gospel of economic interdependence and reconciliation with the North as part of a campaign for independence and domination; a lauding of freedom for the Negro in a politics of white supremacy; dreams of equal treatment of allegedly unequal races in separate societies devoted to mutual progress—these are among the most obvious.

Rich in paradoxes, the New South creed also had an ironic outcome. Designed to lead the region out of poverty, it made converts by the thousands in all parts of the country of men who looked forward confidently to a South of abundance. Instead, the expectations were unrealized and the South remained the poorest and economically least progressive section of the nation. The plans for regional and personal success, the restoration of self-confidence, and a position of influence and respect in the nation likewise fired the imagination and gained legions of adherents, but they too were largely unfulfilled and at the end of the New South crusade the region found itself in the uncomfortable, if familiar, role of a colonial dependent. Rid of many of the humiliating frustrations of the early postwar years, it was saddled with new ones that had greater staying power. Finally, the dream of a just and practical solution to the race question appealed to former abolitionists and radicals as well as to long-time racists because it promised that justice and practicality could be balanced, that Southerners themselves could do what Yankee reformers had failed to do, and that a harmonious biracial society would emerge and permit Americans to forget about injustice to the black man. Instead, violence increased in the 'eighties, and disfranchisement and rigid segregation followed later as the Negro reached the nadir of his history as a free man.

Unable to bequeath to the next generation of Southerners a legacy of solid achievement, the New South spokesmen gave them instead a solidly propounded and widely spread image of its success, a mythic view of their own times that was as removed from objective reality as the myth of the Old South. In creating the myth of the New South, they compounded all of the contradictions originally built into their creed, added others, and crowned their professions of realism with a flight of fantasy. . . .

In 1880 Atticus G. Haygood declared that the New South meant, above all, that a time would come when "the words 'the South' will have only a geographical significance." He foresaw the end of sectionalism and the integration of the South into the mainstream of American progress. Much remained to be done, Haygood felt, and he predicted that it would take at least twenty years for the New South program to succeed. By 1886, however, [Henry] Grady was rapturous and confident in declaring to his New York audience that the South had "wiped out the place where Mason and Dixon's line used to be." Elsewhere in the same address, and increasingly in the statements of Grady and other New South prophets, their program began to assume the solidity of accomplished fact. Almost imperceptibly at first the promotional strategy changed from the original emphasis on the gap separating accomplishment from ambition to a parade of "facts" that proved the rapidity with which the gap was being closed. As the strategy changed, a bewildering mixture of fact and fancy, wish and reality, emerged. Writing early in 1887, Wilbur Fisk Tillett, a theologian from Vanderbilt, declared "that such a marvelous advance has been made in the South in the last ten years as has rarely been made in any country or in any part of any country in an equally limited period in the history of the world." The New South, which had first "showed itself in 1880," had by 1886 "proved its name by evidences so powerful and convincing that only the blindest can fail to see them." . . .

With the end of prejudice and discord and with the advent of industrial might came the sense of power and achievement that was the ultimate goal of the New South movement. "Above all," Grady said in New York, "we known that we have achieved in these 'piping times of peace' a fuller independence for the South than that which our fathers sought to win in the forum by their eloquence or compel in the field by their swords." In response to a critic's suggestion that Northern financial and industrial interests were decisive in the movement and that perhaps the South was not quite as independent as he believed, Grady replied confidently that such charges were completely erroneous. Citing Fulton County, Georgia—the "capital" of the New South—as typical of the region, he stated that only 774 Northerners were numbered in a total population of 47,588. More to the point, Grady would believe, was the analysis of [William Dorrah] Kelley, who wrote in 1888 that the magnificent progress taking place in the South could "justly be regarded as the work of Titans." And as others looked on the scene later they declared that these titans had brought into existence a South that was everywhere blessed with "plenty and prosperity"; that the South, at last, had risen "victorious in peace from the desolation of war." The metamorphosis was now complete. During the years of conception—the 'seventies—"New South" meant an idea, a program, a goal; by the end of the 'eighties it denoted a whole region that had acted upon the idea, followed the program, and achieved the goal.

Walter Hines Page was the only one of the notable New South spokesmen who believed that failures outnumbered the successes of the movement. A persistent critic of the defects in Southern society, Page participated in one crusade after another to save his native region; in the 'eighties he was at one with Grady and Edmonds in looking to industrialization for the answer to the region's problems; in the later 'nineties he joined the education crusade, hoping that a new enlightenment would bring salvation; still later he put his hopes in elimination of the hookworm and for a while appeared to think that the South could be saved only when the ill health which plagued so many of her people disappeared. More cosmopolitan and sensitive than the other New South spokesmen, Page was always suspicious of the extravagant claims made by Southerners. In his autobiographical novel, for example, he recalled his experiences as a schoolboy and wrote that "nobody tells the whole truth about institutions. They prefer to accept traditions and to repeat respectful formulas." By the 'nineties the New South claims had become "respectful formulas" and Page was losing faith with them. Touring the region in 1899, he had hoped to see a South that would justify the optimistic statistics he read in the *Manufacturers' Record,* a journal of which he was the second largest stockholder. Instead, he saw a land that appeared to him to be "listless, discouraged, poverty-stricken, and backward-looking," and he returned from his journey "infinitely sad."

Ten years earlier, Lewis H. Blair, a native Virginian and former Confederate soldier, had been similarly disillusioned by the contrast between what he called the "real South" and what he read in the New South propaganda sheets. "Judging by the glowing reports in the newspapers for the past three years," Blair wrote, "we must conclude that the South is enjoying a veritable deluge of prosperity." According to the propaganda, the South was "surpassing even the Eastern States," and had become a place "where poverty is unknown and where everybody is industriously and successfully laying up wealth." The irate Virginian traced the source of this "mischievous and misleading" information to the "so-called Manufacturers' Records" that had become so popular in the 'eighties. Commenting on their objectivity, he wrote:

> Such journals proceed on the same plan as would the Superintendent of the Census in 1890, should he, instead of actually enumerating the people, start with the population of 1880, and add thereto not only all the births, but also all the stillbirths, all the miscarriages, and all the abortions since that year, and deduct nothing for deaths in the meanwhile.

It was the habit of these journals, Blair claimed, to arrive at figures of total aggregate manufacturing capital in the South by including in their estimates not only established firms but those that were merely in the planning stage as well. Failures and bankruptcies were seldom recorded; the inevitable trend had to be upwards.

[Richard Hathaway] Edmonds [, editor of the *Manufacturers' Record*] was a natural target of such criticisms and, though not named, it was probably he in particular whom Blair had in mind. Edmonds was accustomed to such charges and occasionally reprinted them in the *Record* to provide a springboard from which to launch an optimistic picture of Southern achievements. In 1887 the Newberry, South Carolina, *Observer* commented that the statistics in Edmonds's journal "make a fine showing." But the ordinary Southerner "feels something like the penniless boy who stands out on the sidewalk and gazes wistfully through plate-glass windows at the beautiful display of toys and candies within!" Edmonds replied that the boy was penniless because he spent too much time gazing; wealth was there for those who wished to work. On another occasion the Baltimore *Sun* described what it considered to be "The Real Condition of the South" in gloomy terms. Edmonds countered with a long statistical table which he believed proved that "none can question" the industrial advance of the region. Even more pointed was an editorial comment in the Chattanooga *Times* that passed off one of Edmonds's statistical surveys as "about three-fourths moonshine and wind." Edmonds characterized this attack on his veracity as "the insolent snarls of envious curs," the product of an editor who was a "disreputable falsifier . . . moved by enmity and spite." With this background, Blair did not exaggerate when he declared that "to doubt the current charming presentations of Southern growth and prosperity is to bring down anathemas upon one's head. What! the South not prosperous. Impossible, they cry; and the individual who questions is an idiot."

Risking the anathemas, Blair wrote a penetrating analysis of the economic and racial problems of the South. His thesis was that the prosperity of the region depended upon the elevation, not the degradation, of the Negro; and because Negroes were not being elevated and Southern economic advance not planned intelligently, the region sustained one setback after another. "We are," he feared, "making an Ireland of the South, and are digging broad and deep graves in which to bury prosperity and all its untold advantages." To support this view he attacked not only the statistics but the integrity of the New South spokesmen. He also pointedly began his analysis with Georgia—"as she has been held up as a model to all the other States"— and, with what he called reliable statistics, he concluded that "the people of Georgia had not added materially to their wealth during the twenty years preceding 1886." Clearly, this was not Henry Grady's doctrine.

Blair and Page had perhaps let their disappointment cause them to underestimate the material advances that were evident in the South, for it is obvious that impressive forward strides had been taken since the end of the war. Factories had been built where there were none before, boom towns dotted the region, railroad mileage increased substantially, and investors, both foreign and domestic, were genuinely impressed by the future prospects of Southern development. Moreover, there was a romantic quality to the New South quest for riches and power that stirred the souls of observers in all parts of the country. Recognizing all of these factors, however, nothing can gainsay the fact that Blair and Page came closer to describing actuality than Grady and Edmonds did or that the New South writings were that fuzzy medley of strong belief and personal experience out of which social myth emerges.

In his general history of the post-Reconstruction South, C. Vann Woodward shows the gap that separated South from North by using per capita wealth figures. In 1880, when the New South movement was just taking hold, the per capita wealth of the Southern states was $376 and the national average was $870. By 1900 the figure for the South had increased to $509 while the national average had risen to $1,165. Expressed in percentages, the per capita wealth of the Southern states in 1880 was 56.8 percent below the national average. In 1900 it was 56.3 percent below. The very slight gain on the North which is reflected in these data is misleading, however, because the figures include valuations of Southern railroads, mines, mortgages, and other properties owned by "outside interests." Estimates of per capita income show a similar pattern. In 1880 the per capita income in the South was $88; the national average was $175. By 1900 the South's per capita income had risen to $102 while the national average had moved to $203. Expressed in percentages, the per capita income of the South in 1880 was 49.7 percent below the national average; in 1900 it was 49.8 percent below.

These figures show that the per capita wealth of the South increased by 13.5 percent between 1880 and 1900 and that per capita income increased by 15.9 percent in the same period. The gains are significant, of course, and they provided just enough substance to make the myth of the New South credible to many persons. But in truth the industrial evolution of the postwar years was neither extensive enough nor revolutionary enough to make much impact on the standard of living of the great mass of Southerners. In the first place, the movement was extremely limited. In 1900, as in 1880, the overwhelming majority of the population was engaged in the extractive industries of agriculture, forestry, fisheries, and mining. With 67.3 percent of its labor force employed in these occupations in 1900 the South was a unique section of the country. The comparable figure for New England, the New South spokesmen's primary model, was 17.6 percent. Only 6.3 percent of the Southern labor force was employed in manufacturing in 1900, which reflects but a modest rise from the 4.6 percent that was claimed by manufacturing twenty years earlier. Remaining an essentially raw-material economy, the South suffered "the attendant penalties of low wages, lack of opportunity, and poverty."

In addition to the limited extent of industrial development, the industries that did emerge and expand were largely of the low-wage variety. This was particularly true in the case of the cotton-textile industry, which became to many New South spokesmen the symbol of their movement. The low wages paid by Southern factories were further entrenched by the exploitative nature of the early industrial movement. Dependence on child labor and, for a good period of time, on convict labor as well, scarcely validated the happy images woven into the picture of the New South. William H. Nicholls, an economist who has brooded over the Southern past, sums up the failures of the period by writing that "the rate of industrialization in the South during the post-bellum years of the nineteenth century, while no inconsiderable achievement, was hardly sufficient to make more than a small dent in the low-income problems of its overwhelmingly rural-agricultural population."

As reality failed to bear out the New South dream of opulence so, too, did it fail to record success in the campaign for power and independence. With a few notable exceptions, the New South program produced no real Southern Rockefellers and Carnegies, but only a large number of their liveried servants. It was by adopting the ways of Northern industry—by putting business above politics and sowing towns and cities in the place of theories—that the new power and independence were meant to have been gained. But as the industrial pattern deviated from the Northern model the achievement of these goals became impossible. Instead, as of old, the South remained saddled with the burdens of a colonial economy.

Her railway system fell under the control of Northern financial tycoons like J. P. Morgan and her iron and steel industries, during and after the depression of 1893, succumbed to the control of outsiders, culminating in 1907 when United States Steel achieved effective domination of the Tennessee Coal and Iron Company. Even the proud mills, so many of which were built with local money raised in patriotic subscription campaigns, fell into the colonial pattern. Their chief products were often sent North for final processing and their dependence on Northern capital and Northern commission houses belied the claims of self-determination. Finally, many of the South's natural resources—the most celebrated guarantee of industrial progress and power—came to be controlled by men from outside the region. As Woodward writes, the South's "rich mineral deposits . . . were 'Southern' monopolies only in the sense that the sulphur of Sicily, owned by a British syndicate, was once a 'Sicilian' monopoly. Protected by patent laws, franchises, options, or outright possession of mineral lands, the Mellons, Rockefellers, Du Ponts, and other capitalists monopolized 'Southern monopolies.' "

To explain why the New South movement failed to produce the blessings it promised is a task well beyond the scope of this study, but a few observations on the nature of the problem may help to cast light on other questions which are of primary concern. To begin with, the persistent optimism of the New South spokesmen was grounded in an unrealistic conception of the industrial process. Repeatedly they claimed that the region's rich endowment of natural resources was a sure guarantee of industrialization. The falsity of this assumption requires no elaboration. As David M. Potter has observed, "a vital distinction separates mere abundance—the copious supply of natural resources—and actual abundance—the availability to society of a generous quota of goods ready for use." The two are related, of course, but the history of the modern world—including the history of the Old South—shows that the potential does not automatically lead to the actual and that "environmental riches" in fact occupy "a relatively small place in the explanation of economic growth." Much more important are institutional and human factors which increase the capacity of society to produce.

It is probably true that the New South dream of rapid industrialization and urbanization, with the attendant benefits of power and prestige for the region, was an unrealistic one to begin with because of the plethora of both economic and non-economic obstacles which had to be surmounted. Among economic factors which militated against success was the relative lateness of the Southern industrial movement. Beginning after industrialism was well advanced in other parts of the country, the South had a critical shortage of entrepreneurial talent, skilled workers, "and other external economies whose presence in the already industrially established North tended to make industrialization there self-generating." The lack of these advantages in the South, as Nicholls observes, meant that "it was the old agrarian pattern— only slightly modified by the development of such low-skill manufactures as textiles—which tended to be self-generating." In addition to these economic problems, cultural, intellectual, and social patterns in the region also militated against rapid industrialization on the Northern model. Loyalty to an agrarian past and determination to preserve the value system produced by it as well as an essentially romantic and static conception of history, class, and race were not compatible with swift industrialization and urbanization.

The New South spokesmen were aware of some of these problems and it would be unfair to say that they did not try to face up to some of those that they saw. One is especially impressed by their attempt to revise attitudes toward the industrial society and its principal ideological appurtenances. But more striking are their several failures: they straddled fences, arguing that the peculiar sense of honor and personal identification of the slave regime could be maintained and fulfilled in an industrial age; they rejoiced in the wealth of natural resources, but were prevented by race and class biases from developing a program to utilize adequately the human resources; they knew they lacked capital, but their plan for getting it encouraged a colonial relationship that tended to drain the region of its wealth; and, finally, their retreat into mythmaking—the most pervasive feature of the New South movement after the mid-'eighties—betrays the absence of the kind of single-minded realism which they correctly said the situation required but so signally failed to embody in their leadership. . . .

Cotton-Mill People, 1880–1940

JACQUELYN DOWD HALL, ROBERT KORSTAD, AND JAMES LELOUDIS

Textile mills built the New South. Beginning in the 1880s, business and professional men tied their hopes for prosperity to the whirring of spindles and the beating of looms. Small-town boosterism supplied the rhetoric of the mill-building campaign, but the impoverishment of farmers was industrialization's driving force. The post–Civil War rise of sharecropping, tenantry, and the crop lien ensnared freedmen, then eroded yeoman society. Farmers of both races fought for survival by clinging to subsistence strategies and habits of sharing even as they planted cash crops and succumbed to tenantry. Meanwhile, merchants who had accumulated capital through the crop lien invested in cotton mills. As the industry took off in an era of intensifying segregation, blacks were relegated to the land, and white farmers turned to yet another strategy for coping with economic change. They had sold their cotton to the merchant; now they supplied him with the human commodity needed to run his mills. This homegrown industry was soon attracting outside capital and underselling northern competitors. By the end of the Great Depression, the Southeast replaced New England as the world's leading producer of cotton cloth, and the industrializing Piedmont replaced the rural Coastal Plain as pacesetter for the region.

Despite the lasting imprint of textile manufacturing on regional development and labor relations, we have no modern survey of the industry's evolution. Nor has the outpouring of research on working-class history been much concerned with factory workers in the New South. To be sure, recent studies have uncovered sporadic, and sometimes violent, contention over the shape of the industrial South. But those findings have done little to shake the prevailing wisdom: The South's mill villages supposedly bred a "social type" compounded of irrationality, individualism, and fatalism. Unable to unite in their own interests, textile workers remained "silent, incoherent, with no agency to express their needs."

We have reached different conclusions. Our research began with a collaborative oral history project aimed at discovering how working people made sense of their own experience. We did not view memory as a direct window on the past. But we did presume the moral and intellectual value of listening to those who lacked access to power and, thus, the means of affecting historical debate. Our effort was repaid in two major ways. Oral autobiographies dissolved static images, replacing them with portrayals of mill village culture drawn by the men and women who helped create it. Workers' narra-

Jacquelyn Dowd Hall, Robert Korstad, and James Leloudis, "Cotton Mill People: Work, Community and Protest in the Textile South, 1880–1940" in *American Historical Review* 91 (April 1986), pp. 245–55, 257–66, 285. Reprinted by permission of the authors.

tives also steered as away from psychological interpretations and toward patterns of resistance, cultural creativity, and structural evolution. Later we turned to the trade press, particularly the *Southern Textile Bulletin*. Published by David Clark in Charlotte, North Carolina, the *Bulletin* spoke for factory owners at the cutting edge of industrial innovation. . . . Together, retrospective and contemporary evidence revealed the social logic that underlay daily practices and suggested an analysis that distinguished one epoch from another in a broad process of technological, managerial, and cultural change.

Nothing better symbolized the new industrial order than the mill villages that dotted the Piedmont landscape. Individual families and small groups of local investors built and owned most of the early mills. Run by water wheels, factories flanked the streams that fell rapidly from the mountains toward the Coastal Plain. Of necessity, owners provided housing where none had been before. But the setting, scale, and structure of the mill village reflected rural expectations as well as practical considerations. Typically, a three-story brick mill, a company store, and a superintendent's house were clustered at one end of the village. Three- and four-room frame houses, owned by the company but built in a vernacular style familiar in the countryside, stood on lots that offered individual garden space, often supplemented by communal pastures and hog pens. A church, a company store, and a modest schoolhouse completed the scene. By 1910 steam power and electricity had freed the mills from their dependence on water power, and factories sprang up on the outskirts of towns along the route of the Southern Railway. Nevertheless, the urban mill village retained its original rural design. Company-owned villages survived in part because they fostered management control. Unincorporated "mill hills" that surrounded towns such as Charlotte and Burlington, North Carolina, and Greenville, South Carolina, enabled owners to avoid taxes and excluded workers from municipal government. But the mill village also reflected the workers' heritage and served their needs.

Like the design of the mill village, the family labor system helped smooth the path from field to factory. On farms women and children had always provided essential labor, and mill owners took advantage of these traditional roles. They promoted factory work as a refuge for impoverished women and children from the countryside, hired family units rather than individuals, and required the labor of at least one worker per room as a condition for residence in a mill-owned house. But this labor system also dovetailed with family strategies. The first to arrive in the mills were those least essential to farming and most vulnerable to the hazards of commercial agriculture: widows, female heads of households, single women, and itinerant laborers. By the turn of the century, families headed by men also lost their hold on the land. Turning to the mills, they sought not a "family wage" that would enable a man to support his dependents but an arena in which parents and children could work together as they had always done. ,

The deployment of family labor also helped maintain permeable boundaries between farm and mill. The people we interviewed moved with remark-

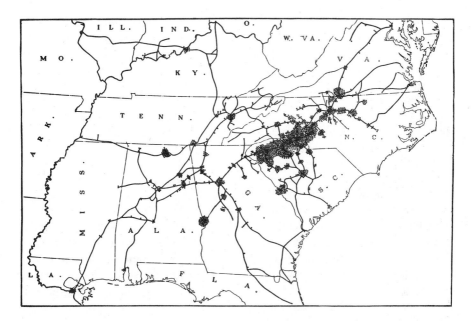

Cotton Mills in the South, 1925. This map shows the geographical distribution of the textile industry in territory served by the Southern Railway System, 1925. This distribution represents 75% of the 17,359,420 cotton spindles in the cotton-growing states. Each dot represents 10,000 spindles.

able ease from farming to mill work and back again or split their family's time between the two. James Pharis's father raised tobacco in the Leaksville-Spray area of North Carolina until most of his six children were old enough to obtain mill jobs. The family moved to a mill village in the 1890s because the elder Pharis "felt that all we had to do when we come to town was to reach up and pull the money off of the trees." From the farm Pharis saved his most valuable possession: his team of horses. While the children worked in the mill, he raised vegatables on a plot of rented ground and used his team to do "hauling around for people." . . .

This ability to move from farming to factory work—or combine the two—postponed a sharp break with rural life. It also gave mill workers a firm sense of alternative identity and leverage against a boss's demands. Lee Workman recalled his father's steadfast independence. In 1918 the superintendent of a nearby cotton mill came to the Workmans' farm in search of workers to help him meet the demand for cloth during World War I. The elder Workman sold his mules and cow but, contrary to the superintendent's advice, held on to his land. Each spring he returned to shoe his neighbors' horses, repair their wagons and plows, and fashion the cradles they used to harvest grain. "He'd tell the superintendent, 'You can just get somebody else, because I'm going back to make cradles for my friends.' Then he'd come back in the wintertime and work in the mill.'' This type of freedom did not sit well with the mill superintendent, but the elder Workman had the upper hand. '' 'Well,' he told them, 'if you don't want to do that, I'll move back to the country and take the family.' ''

Although Lee Workman's father periodically retreated to the farm, his sons and daughters, along with thousands of others, eventually came to the mills to stay. There they confronted an authority more intrusive than anything country folk had experienced before. In Bynum, North Carolina, the mill owner supervised the Sunday School and kept tabs on residents' private lives. "If you stubbed your toe they'd fire you. They'd fire them here for not putting out the lights late at night. Old Mr. Bynum used to go around over the hill at nine o'clock and see who was up. And, if you were up, he'd knock on the door and tell you to cut the lights out and get into bed.'' Along with surveillance came entanglement with the company store. Mill hands all too familiar with the crop lien once again found themselves in endless debt. Don Faucette's father often talked about it. "Said if you worked at the mill they'd just take your wages and put it in the company store and you didn't get nothing. For years and years they didn't get no money, just working for the house they lived in and what they got at the company store. They just kept them in the hole all the time.''

The mill village undeniably served management's interests, but it also nurtured a unique workers' culture. When Piedmont farmers left the land and took a cotton mill job, they did not abandon old habits and customs. Instead, they fashioned familiar ways of thinking and acting into a distinctively new way of life. This adaptation occurred at no single moment in time; rather, it evolved, shaped and reshaped by successive waves of migration off the farm as well as the movement of workers from mill to mill. Village life was based on family ties. Kinship networks facilitated migration to the mill and continued to play a powerful integrative role. Children of the first generation off the land married newcomers of the second and third, linking households into broad networks of obligation, responsibility, and concern. . . . Mill folk commonly used a family metaphor to describe village life. Hoyle McCorkle remembered the Highland Park mill village in Charlotte as a single household knit together by real and fictive kin: "It was kind of one big family; it was a 200-house family.'' . . .

Under these conditions, necessity and habit fostered rural traditions of mutual aid. Although each family claimed a small plot of land, villagers shared what they grew and "live[d] in common.'' In late summer and early fall, they gathered for the familiar rituals of harvest and hog killing. Paul and Don Faucette remembered how it was done in Glencoe, North Carolina. "We'd kill our hogs this time, and a month later we'd kill yours. Well, you can give us some, and we can give you some. They'd have women get together down in the church basement. They'd have a quilting bee, and they'd go down and they'd all quilt. They'd have a good crop of cabbage, [and] they'd get together and all make kraut.'' Villagers helped one another, not with an expectation of immediate return but with the assurance of community support in meeting their individual needs. "They'd just visit around and work voluntarily. They all done it, and nobody owed nobody nothing."

Cooperation provided a buffer against misery and want at a time when state welfare services were limited and industrialists often refused to assume responsibility for job-related sickness and injury. It bound people together and reduced their dependence on the mill owners' charity. When someone fell ill, neighbors were quick to give the stricken family a "pounding." "They'd all get together and help. They'd cook food and carry it to them—all kinds of food—fruits, vegetables, canned goods." Villagers also aided sick neighbors by taking up a "love offering" in the mill. Edna Hargett organized such collections in the weave room at the Chadwick-Hoskins Mill in Charlotte. "When the neighbors got paid they'd come and pay us, and we'd take their money and give it to [the family of the weaver who was ill], and they'd be so proud of it, because they didn't have any wage coming in." To the people we interviewed, the village was "just one big community and one big family" whose members "all kind of hung together and survived."

Community solidarity did not come without a price. Neighborliness could shade into policing; it could repress as well as sustain. Divorced women and children born out of wedlock might be ostracized, and kinship ties could give mill supervisors an intelligence network that reached into every corner of the village. Alice Evitt of Charlotte remarked that "people then couldn't do like they do now. They was talked about. My daddy would never allow us to be with people that was talked about. This was the nicest mill hill I ever lived on. If anybody done anything wrong and you reported them, they had to move." A Bynum proverb summed up the double-edged quality of village life. "If you went along, they'd tend to their business and yours, too, if you let them, your neighbors would. Tend to your business and theirs, too. And the old saying here, you know, 'Bynum's red mud. If you stick to Bynum, it'll stick to you when it rains.' "

Given such tensions, we were struck by how little ambivalence surfaced in descriptions of mill village life. Recollections of factory work were something else again, but the village—red mud and all—was remembered with affection. The reasons are not hard to find. A commitment to family and friends represented a realistic appraisal of working people's prospects in the late nineteenth- and early twentieth-century South. Only after World War II, with the expansion of service industries, did the Piedmont offer alternatives to low-wage factory work to more than a lucky few. Until then, casting one's lot with others offered more promise and certainly more security than the slim hope of individual gain. To be sure, mill people understood the power of money; they struggled against dependency and claimed an economic competence as their due. Nevertheless, they had "their own ideas . . . about what constitute[d] the 'good life.' " Communal values, embodied in everyday behavior, distanced mill folk from the acquisitiveness that characterized middle-class life in New South towns.

This is not to say that mill village culture destroyed individuality. On the contrary, it conferred status and dignity that the workplace could seldom afford. Although mill ways encouraged group welfare at the expense of personal ambition, they did support individual accomplishment of a different sort. The practice of medicine provides one example, music another.

Folk medicine formed an important part of workers' "live-at-home" culture. Until well into the twentieth century, mill hands simply could not afford medical fees; besides, they viewed doctors with distrust and fear. In emergencies, the village turned to its own specialists. Among the earliest of these in Bynum was Louise Jones's mother, Madlena Riggsbee. "She was what you'd say was a midwife. She could just hold up under anything. Unless they were bound and compelled to have the doctor, they'd usually get her to go." In the 1920s and 1930s, the company retained the services of a physician, paid for with funds withheld from workers' checks. But in the eyes of the villagers, he was a partner—indeed a junior partner—to Ida Jane Smith, a healer and midwife who was one of the most respected figures in the community. "Lord, she was a good woman," Carrie Gerringer recalled. "She knowed more about younguns than any doctor."

If the midwife was the most prestigious member of the female community, the musician held that place among men. String bands had been a mainstay of country gatherings, and they multiplied in the mill villages where musicians lived closer together and had more occasions to play. Mastery of an instrument brought a man fame as the local "banjo king" or expert guitar picker. Musicians sometimes played simply for their own enjoyment. Paul Faucette and a small group of friends and kinfolk used "to get together on the porch on Saturday night and just have a big time." On other occasions, they performed for house dances and community celebrations. Harvey Ellington remembered that on Saturday night "you'd have a dance in somebody's house—they'd take the beds and all out, and then we'd just play." . . .

Special talents won Harvey Ellington and Madlena Riggsbee places of honor in their neighbors' memories. But most villagers never achieved such distinction. They lived in quiet anonymity, often guided and strengthened by religious faith. Most textile workers were evangelical Protestants, and many worshipped in churches built and financed by factory owners. On one level, these churches proved helpful, maybe even essential, to the mills. Like their counterparts in other industrializing societies, they inculcated the moral and social discipline demanded by factory life. Still, there was another side to evangelical religion, one that empowered the weak, bound them together, and brought them close to God. At springtime revivals, faith turned to ecstasy. "People got happy and they shouted. They'd sing and hug each other—men and women both." When the Holy Spirit moved individuals to confessions of sin, the entire body of worshippers joined in thanksgiving for God's saving grace.

. . . In mills throughout the Piedmont, manufacturers endeavored to shape the southern yeomanry into a tractable industrial workforce. Workers' attitudes toward factory labor, like those toward village life, owed much to the cycles and traditions of the countryside. Owners, on the other hand, sought to substitute for cooperation and task orientation a labor system controlled from the top down and paced by the regular rhythms of the machine. Barring adverse market conditions, work in the mills varied little from day to day and season to season. Workers rose early in the morning, still tired from the day before, and readied themselves for more of the same. For ten, eleven, and twelve hours they walked, stretched, leaned, and pulled at their machines. Noise, heat, and humidity engulfed them. The lint that settled on their hair and skin marked them as mill workers to the outside world. The cotton dust that silently entered their lungs could also kill them.

Owners enforced this new pattern of labor with the assistance of a small coterie of supervisors. As a rule, manufacturers delegated responsibility for organizing work and disciplining the help to a superintendent and his overseers and second hands. . . . Supervision was a highly personal affair; there were as many different approaches to its problems as there were second hands and overseers. As one observer explained, "There was nothing that could be identified as a general pattern of supervisory practice."

At times, discipline could be harsh, erratic, and arbitrary. This was particularly true before 1905, when most workers in southern mills were women and children. Even supervisors writing in the *Southern Textile Bulletin* admitted that "some overseers, second hands, and section men have a disposition to abuse the help. Whoop, holler, curse, and jerk the children around." James Pharis remembered that "you used to work for the supervisor because you were scared. I seen a time when I'd walk across the road to keep from meeting my supervisor. They was the hat-stomping kind. If you done anything, they'd throw their hat on the floor and stomp it and raise hell."

In the absence of either state regulation or trade unions, management's power seemed limitless, but there were, in fact, social and structural constraints. Although manufacturers relinquished day-to-day authority to underlings, they were ever-present figures, touring the mill, making decisions on wages and production quotas, and checking up on the help. These visits were, in part, attempts to maintain the appearance of paternalism and inspire hard work and company loyalty. At the same time, they divided power in the mill. Workers had direct access to the owner and sometimes saw him as a buffer between themselves and supervisors, a "force that could bring an arbitrary and unreasonable [overseer] back into line." . . .

Authority on the shop floor was further complicated by social relations in the mill village. Before the introduction of industrial engineers and college-trained foremen in the 1920s and 1930s, most supervisors worked their way up through the ranks. Personal and occupational life were inseparable; supervisors knew the mill, and the various jobs, and the ways of the workers. Edgar Moore, superintendent of the Bynum mill from 1904 to 1955, was carefully picked and groomed for his job. Relatives recalled how he attained his position. "They told Edgar, 'Now if you'll come down there and work through the mill, start at the first, just learn the machinery, when you get through with it, I'll put you overseer.' They seen something in him. And he was a brilliant fellow. The company helped him, and he worked through the mill and got to be superintendent."

As time went on, Moore became known for his threats to fire workers at the least provocation, but he seldom acted on his words. He was involved both inside and outside the mill in relationships other than that of worker and manager. Like the rest of the villagers, Moore relied on the healing skill of Ida Jane Smith. He also played in the village string band, where he took a back seat to a drifter who was Bynum's best musician. Most important, Moore's brothers and sisters, nieces and nephews, had married established Bynum residents and newcomers from other mills. Those kinship ties gave him access to details of workers' private lives, but they also meant that blatant injustice on his part might have repercussions on his own family. In their daily lives, managers whose interests were tied to those of owners had to meet the pressures of a community to which the owners did not belong. As a result, overseers were sometimes as loyal to the workers as to the company. Eva Hopkins's father, an overseer in the Mercury mill in Charlotte, "worked with the help. He didn't work against them. He didn't work just for the company, he worked with the people." . . .

A personal style of labor management posed but one obstacle to the imposition of strict discipline. Mill owners also faced the limitations of existing technology. The small size of most mills before World War I made it difficult to coordinate production in a way that kept all hands constantly at work. The people we interviewed remembered long breaks while they waited for their machines to finish a production cycle. Weavers and spinners had time to sit down and rest or visit neighbors in the mill, while doffers, most of whom were children, could play outdoors. Workers who had spare time also helped others so that all could share a few moments away from the job. Mamie Shue offered one example. "All the boys that doffed in the spinning room, they'd bring me my bobbins and then, when they got caught up, they come out there and helped me spool. When I'd catch up, we'd go out behind the mill, sit in the grass, and stay out there about two hours. We'd come down to North Charlotte and get watermelons. Carry them back up there behind the mill and sit down. Then we'd come back in and do that all over."

Most prewar mills had central power systems in which a water wheel, steam engine, or single electric motor drove the machinery through an elaborate network of belts, shafts, and pulleys. At certain times of the year water-powered mills were prone to frequent stoppages. Ethel Faucette explained that, "when the water'd get low, maybe they'd stop off for an hour or two. That was in the summertime. Well, this gang of boys would get their instruments and get out there in front of the mill, and they would sing and pick the guitar and the banjo and play different kinds of string music. And maybe they'd stand an hour or two, and the water'd gain up, and they'd start back up."

The introduction of steam power and electricity at the turn of the century reduced the irregularities of production, but mills remained susceptible to the problems caused by belt-driven machinery. Paul Cline of Greenville remembered that "back in them days they had that old machinery that run by belt drives and things. They couldn't run [too fast]. Them belts'd slip off, and they'd have to stop to put the belts back on. It'd break, and they'd have to get somebody to fix the belts." Such breakdowns could stop work on a single machine or in an entire section of the mill, sometimes sending workers home for the remainder of the day.

Mill owners and workers alike had to accommodate themselves to a work environment not entirely of their own choosing. Factory labor did not allow the independence and flexibility of labor on the farm, but neither did it meet the standards of rigor and regularity desired by owners. An informal compromise governed the shop floor. "We worked longer then in the mill than they do now," explained Naomi Trammell, "and made less, too. But we didn't work hard. I done all my playing in the mill."

This tradeoff between a relatively relaxed work pace on the one hand and long hours and low wages on the other was tenuous at best. Despite manufacturers' efforts to create a secure world in the mill and village, there were recurrent symptoms of unrest. During the 1880s and 1890s, southern mill hands turned first to the Knights of Labor and then to the National Union of Textile Workers (NUTW) to defend their "freedom and liberty." In 1900 an intense conflict led by the NUTW flared in Alamance County, center of textile manufacturing in North Carolina, when an overseer at the Haw River Mill fired a female weaver for leaving her loom unattended. The next day, September 28, union members "threw up" their machines, defending the woman's right to "go when she pleased and where she pleased." By mid-October, workers at other mills throughout the county had joined in a sympathy strike.

The mill owners, conveniently overstocked with surplus goods, posted armed guards around their factories, declared they would employ only non-union labor, and threatened to evict union members from company-owned houses. Undeterred, the workers resolved to stand together as "free men and free women"; five thousand strong, they brought production in Alamance mills virtually to a halt. But by the end of November evictions had overwhelmed the NUTW's relief fund, and the Alamance mill hands were forced to accept a settlement on management's terms.

The Haw River strike capped more than two decades of unrest. During those years, Populists and factory laborers challenged the power of planters, merchants, and industrialists. Between 1895 and 1902, southern Democrats turned to race baiting, fraud, and intimidation to destroy this interracial movement. The passage of state constitutional amendments disfranchising blacks and many poor whites, accompanied by a flurry of Jim Crow laws, restructured the political system, narrowing the terms of public discourse, discouraging lower-class political participation, and making it impossible for opposition movements to survive.

As prospects for collective protest diminished, Piedmont mill hands opted for a personal strategy as old as the industry itself—relocation. In Alamance County alone, more than three hundred workers left to find new jobs in South Carolina and Georgia. "Among them," reported the *Alamance Gleaner*, "are a great many excellent people who prefer to go elsewhere rather than surrender rights and privileges which they as citizens deem they should own and enjoy." . . . Until the end of World War I, quitting was textile workers' most effective alternative to public protest or acquiescence. One student of the southern textile industry declared that a mill hand's "ability to move at a moment's notice was his Magna Carta, Declaration of Independence, and Communist Manifesto." . . .

In these ways, the Piedmont became what journalist Arthur W. Page described in 1907 as "one long mill village." Individual communities were woven together—through kinship, shared occupational experiences, and popular culture—into an elaborate regional fabric. According to Lacy Wright, who worked at Greensboro's White Oak Mill, "We had a pretty fair picture, generally speaking, of what you might say was a 200-mile radius of Greensboro. News traveled by word of mouth faster than any other way in those days, because that's the only way we had. In other words, if something would happen at White Oak this week, you could go over to Danville, Virginia, by the weekend and they'd done heard about it. It looked like it always worked out that there would be somebody or another that would carry that information all around." Rooted in a regional mill village culture, workers like Wright took the entire Piedmont as their frame of reference.

Owners and workers understood that the ability to move in search of more satisfying employment could serve as a check on mill management. After a tour of North and South Carolina mills in 1906, a superintendent vented his frustrations in the pages of the *Southern and Western Textile Excelsior*. "Unfortunately," he lamented, "the help have come to think that they and not the mill owners control the situation." . . . Blaine Wofford, a Charlotte mill hand, explained. "The drawback on the mill was that a whole family would get mad and quit; if one would get mad, all would quit. That kind of put the mill behind the eight ball. There'd be all those jobs and nobody on them. I guess back then the overseers had to walk lightly with them."

Through the end of World War I, mill workers' "roving disposition" not only posed serious problems for shop floor discipline but also aggravated a chronic labor shortage. As early as 1906, manufacturers worried openly that labor turnover was leaving machines idle and shrinking profits. They had unwittingly contributed to these problems by taking part in a building boom at the turn of the century that dramatically increased the demand for labor. As jobs became more plentiful, mill hands were free to move more frequently. Workers remembered that "it wasn't no job at all to get a job then." By 1907 the annual labor turnover rate in the southern textile industry had reached 176 percent, and various mill owners estimated that anywhere from 20 to 40 percent of their employees belonged to the "floating" population. Mill worker Paul Cline summed it up in one vivid image. "My daddy had an old rooster—when he seen the wagon coming, he'd just lay down and cross his legs; he knowed it was time to move."

Owners first responded to the problems of labor scarcity and control by competing more fiercely with one another. In hopes of attracting and keeping reliable workers, many mill owners raised wages. Between 1902 and 1907 the earnings of male weavers in South Carolina rose by 58 percent, those of female weavers by 65 percent, and those of spinners by 138 percent, while the cost of living increased by only 9 percent. But, if owners sought stability, they did not achieve it with wage competition. As one superintendent complained, "The more the help can earn, the less they work. . . . The prices paid at present have gotten to be so high that an average family, or individual, can make in four days what it once took a full week to earn, and the result is in most instances, such help work only four-sixths of their time. The average mill hand is inclined to care only for enough to live on and when they have made that, they rest the balance of the week."

A more drastic response to the competition for workers was labor pirating. Mill owners throughout the Piedmont hired recruiters to circulate through other mill villages and induce workers to leave their jobs. "In some instances," reported the *Southern Textile Bulletin,* "men are sent to other towns to mix with the people on Saturday night, display rolls of money, and tell remarkable stories of how much they earn at this or that mill." Owners paid moving expenses and offered free housing and groceries to lure workers into their mills. But those practices, like wage increases, only exacerbated the problems they were intended to resolve. The *Southern and Western Textile Excelsior* warned mill owners that "the scarcity of help among the cotton mills is aggravated by the pernicious practice of furnishing transportation and enticing help from one mill to another. . . . You furnish transportation from another mill to yours, and another man furnishes transportation from your mill to his, and so the game goes on and maybe there are enough operatives on the trains all the time going from place to place to operate all the idle spindles in the South."

Manufacturers took such warnings to heart, realizing that the solution to their problems lay not in fighting among themselves but in rethinking their relations to one another and the nature of mill management. Joining forces in 1908, they turned to their own advantage the efforts of overseers and second hands to organize a supervisor's union. Although uninvited, David Clark and representatives from the state's leading mills attended an overseers' meeting in Spray, North Carolina, and convinced those present that their interests would best be served by allying themselves with mill owners rather than seeking a separate voice. In October of that year, Clark presided over the formation of the Southern Textile Association, which offered membership to all superintendents, overseers, master mechanics, electricians, engineers, editors of textile publications, and instructors at textile schools. The association subsequently played a major role in the industry's development, serving as a conduit for the introduction of new theories of personnel management and industrial relations.

The manufacturers' most ambitious undertaking in the prewar years was the implementation of company-sponsored "welfare work." Taking their cue from the National Civic Federation and major northern corporations, southern mill owners embarked on a campaign to beautify their villages and provide new social services for their employees. Urged on by industry publicists such as Clark, they began substituting professional intermediaries—social workers, nurses, and teachers—for the direct surveillance of workers' lives. Welfare work was expensive and therefore gained only a limited following among small-scale manufacturers. But the Piedmont's largest mills embraced the new approach to labor-management relations with enthusiasm.

Writing in the *Southern Textile Bulletin,* manufacturers made clear the relationship between welfare work and labor mobility. One mill president explained that he and others undertook welfare work "to secure an attachment for the village to decrease the migratory tendency." . . .

But how could such mundane activities as garden clubs and organized recreation accomplish mill owners' goals? Above all, welfare programs tried to redefine the neighborhood as a physical extension of the mill rather than a network of human relations. Manufacturers awarded prizes for the best flower gardens in their villages and set aside specific plots of land for the vegetable gardens workers had always tilled. They also took over many of the activities that bound workers together. They established "domestic science" classes in which girls learned the arts of housekeeping and cooking not from their mothers and grandmothers but from a professional social worker, and company nurseries replaced informal, family-based child care. Mills financed workers' "pick-up" baseball teams and organized factory leagues in an effort to transform community games into a sport sponsored by and identified with the company. They formed brass bands to take the place of village string bands and built YMCAs to structure workers' leisure. On occasion, owners outlawed the collection of "love offerings" and, in the 1920s, began to offer minimal insurance programs instead. Promotional literature for these programs promised to "eliminate passing the hat in the mill" and enable the employer "to assist the community in meeting some of its welfare problems."

Welfare programs also aimed at stimulating desires for consumer goods that would compel mill hands to work regularly. Here domestic science classes did double duty. As we have already seen, workers' nonacquisitiveness could decrease productivity by promoting absenteeism and "loafing." To combat the problem, professional social workers taught mill women to make fashionable clothes, cook elaborate meals, and keep neat homes furnished with upholstered sofas and chairs. The *Southern and Western Textile Excelsior* voiced owners' confidence that, if these measures did not change the present generation of mill workers, they would at least influence their children. "Their needs must be increased to equal the rise in wages to get them to work steadily," one mill president candidly explained. "The people are not sufficiently ambitious to care to work all the time, but as we are throwing about them elevating influences their needs are growing greater and the next generation will be all right."

Despite promises that welfare work would bring "the employer and the employee into closer touch and . . . eliminate industrial unrest," results were disappointing. . . . As an economic depression settled over the textile industry in the years after World War I, manufacturers became convinced that the results of welfare work did not justify the expense. Only a handful of mills initiated new programs after 1920, and many abandoned their welfare activities altogether.

World War I marked a turning point in the development of the southern textile industry. Stimulated by wartime demand, new mills sprang up, old ones operated around the clock, wages rose, and profits soared. But, when peace came, overexpanded businesses went into a tailspin. The situation worsened when tariff policies and the advent of textile manufacturing in other parts of the world cut into the southern industry's lucrative foreign markets. A sudden change in clothing styles added to manufacturers' troubles. Young women in the 1920s hiked their skirts six inches above the ankle, then all the way to the knee, causing consternation among their elders and panic in the textile industry. All in all, the depression that hit the rest of the country in 1929 began for textile manufacturers in the immediate postwar years.

Mill officials greeted the armistice with a rollback of workers' wages. But, to the owners' surprise mill hands refused to abandon small but cherished advances in their standard of living. When wage cuts were announced in 1919, thousands of workers joined the American Federation of Labor's United Textile Workers (UTW). "They are in deadly earnest," reported the Raleigh *News and Observer,* "and almost religiously serious in their belief in the union." Manufacturers were equally determined not to employ union members, and in many cases they simply shut their factory gates to all workers. As the conflict dragged on, threats of violence mounted. Armed strikers patrolled the mill villages, intent on enforcing community and union solidarity. Manufacturers eventually agreed to a settlement but insisted that "the adjustment . . . shall not be construed as a recognition by the mills of collective bargaining." Similar confrontations occurred throughout the Piedmont until 1921, when a severe business downturn crippled union locals and gave management the upper hand. But workers had made their message clear: mill owners would no longer be able to shore up profits simply by cutting wages. . . .

Thus was a world of cotton mill people made and unmade. Pushed off the land, white farmers created a mill village culture that sustained their personal lives and public protest. They suffered poverty and exploitation, but they did not live in a closed society that stripped them of independence, hope, and dignity. On the contrary, the manufacturers' authority was hedged about by technological and social constraints. . . .

❧ *F U R T H E R　　R E A D I N G*

David Carlton, *Mill and Town in South Carolina, 1880–1920* (1982)
Wilbur J. Cash, *The Mind of the South* (1941)
Don H. Doyle, *New Men, New Cities, New South: Atlanta, Nashville, Charleston, Mobile, 1860–1910* (1989)
Paul M. Gaston, *The New South Creed: A Study in Southern Mythmaking* (1976)
Jacquelyn D. Hall et al., *Like a Family: The Making of a Southern Cotton Mill World* (1987)
Howard N. Rabinowitz, *Race Relations in the Urban South, 1865–1890* (1978)
Peter Rachleff, *Black Labor in the South* (1984)
Roger L. Ransom and Richard Sutch, *One Kind of Freedom: The Economic Consequences of Emancipation* (1977)

CHAPTER
5

City and Suburb:
New Vistas, New Walls

꙰

The industrial revolution, as we have seen, reached into the frontier West and the agrarian South, but the classic site of nineteenth-century economic development was the industrial city. Indeed, America's rise to industrial preeminence—from fourth-largest (in dollar value) producer of manufactured goods in 1860 to world leader by 1894—was intimately linked to the massing of labor resources in the cities. In 1860 only 13 percent of the population lived in urban areas; by 1900 the figure had jumped to 40 percent, and by 1920 cities and towns were home to a majority of Americans. In the 1880s alone, when manufacturing overtook agricultural production in value, one hundred cities more than doubled their size, and the manufacturing centers of New York, Philadelphia, and Chicago all topped 1 million in population. American cities and their polyglot laboring populations, it is fair to say, supplanted England in this period as the "workshop of the world."

While taking stock of the physical growth of the cities and their surrounding suburbs, we concern ourselves here with their cultural significance. What did contemporaries themselves make of the urban explosion? How did they perceive the promises and perils of the city? And did the expanding metropolis offer Americans a way out or merely provide a new environment for a continuation of older social problems?

꙰ *D O C U M E N T S*

The following selections at once highlight the remarkable physical transformation of urban-industrial life and accent the social and political problems thus engendered. The first document, a table drawn from census data, reveals the dramatic rise in urban population by region from 1870 to 1920. Englishman Rudyard Kipling's encounter with Chicago in the second selection translates statistics into an emotional response—in this case, repulsion. A more sympathetic, although no less gritty, view of the city emerges in the third selection in Carl Sandburg's Chicago poems. In the fourth document, Boston clergyman and author Edward Everett Hale expresses hope in 1888 that the early, physically

Population Growth in Select U.S. Cities, 1870–1920

	1870	1880	1890	1900	1910	1920
New England						
Boston	250,526	362,839	448,477	560,892	670,585	748,060
Lowell	40,928	59,475	77,696	94,969	106,294	112,759
Providence	68,904	104,857	132,146	175,597	224,326	237,595
New Haven	50,840	62,882	86,045	108,027	133,605	162,537
Worcester	41,105	58,291	84,655	118,421	145,986	179,754
Middle Atlantic						
New York	942,292	1,164,673	1,441,216	3,437,202	4,766,883	5,620,048
Brooklyn	419,921	599,495	838,547	In N.Y.C.	In N.Y.C.	In N.Y.C.
Rochester	62,386	89,366	133,896	162,608	218,149	295,750
Buffalo	117,714	155,134	255,664	352,387	423,715	506,775
Newark	105,059	136,508	181,830	246,070	347,469	414,524
Jersey City	82,546	120,722	163,003	206,433	267,779	298,103
Philadelphia	674,022	847,170	1,046,964	1,293,697	1,549,008	1,823,779
Pittsburgh	139,256	235,071	343,904	451,512	533,905	588,343
South Atlantic						
Baltimore	267,354	332,313	434,439	508,957	558,485	733,826
Washington	109,199	147,293	188,932	278,718	331,069	437,571
Richmond	51,038	63,600	81,388	85,050	127,628	171,667
Durham, N.C.	—	2,041	5,485	6,679	18,241	21,719
Charlotte, N.C.	4,473	7,094	11,557	18,091	34,014	46,338
Charleston	48,956	49,984	54,955	55,807	58,833	67,957
Savannah	28,235	30,709	43,189	54,244	65,064	83,252
Atlanta	21,789	37,409	65,533	89,872	154,839	200,616

North Central					
Cincinnati	216,239	255,139	296,908	325,902	401,247
Cleveland	92,829	160,146	261,353	381,768	796,841
Detroit	79,577	116,340	205,876	285,704	993,678
Milwaukee	71,440	115,587	204,468	285,315	457,147
Chicago	298,977	503,185	1,099,850	1,698,575	2,701,705
St. Louis	310,864	350,518	451,770	575,238	772,897
Kansas City, Mo.	32,260	55,785	132,716	163,752	324,410
Wichita, Kans.	—	4,911	23,853	24,671	72,217
Omaha	16,083	30,518	140,452	102,555	191,601
Minneapolis	13,066	46,887	164,738	202,718	380,582
South Central					
Mobile	32,034	29,132	31,076	38,469	60,777
Birmingham	—	3,086	26,178	38,415	178,806
New Orleans	191,418	216,090	242,039	287,104	387,219
Memphis	40,226	33,592	64,495	102,320	162,351
Nashville	25,865	43,350	76,168	80,865	118,342
Louisville	100,753	123,758	161,129	204,731	234,891
Houston	9,382	16,513	27,557	44,633	138,276
Dallas		10,358	38,067	42,638	158,976
Mountain					
Denver	4,759	35,629	106,713	133,859	256,491
Salt Lake City	12,854	20,768	44,843	53,531	118,110
Pacific					
Los Angeles	5,728	11,183	50,395	102,479	576,673
San Francisco	149,473	233,959	298,997	342,782	506,676
Portland, Ore.	8,293	17,577	46,385	90,426	258,288
Seattle	1,107	3,533	42,837	80,671	315,312

Bayrd Still, *Urban America: A History with Documents* (Boston: Little Brown, 1974), pp. 210–211. Reprinted by permission of Little, Brown and Company.

unimpressive "railroad suburbs" might eventually attract a more respectable, more settled population. Already by 1902, in document five, Howard A. Bridgeman, managing editor of *The Congregationalist,* is offering a paean to the tastefully balanced life-style of the middle-class "suburbanite." But many of those just moving to the cities with hopes for a better life found disappointing prospects. In the conclusion to his classic study *The Philadelphia Negro* (1899), sociologist W. E. B. Du Bois presents a balanced and unadorned checklist of obstacles that urban blacks faced solely on account of their skin color.

Rudyard Kipling Gives a Visitor's View of Chicago, 1899

I have struck a city,—a real city,—and they call it Chicago. The other places do not count. San Francisco was a pleasure-resort as well as a city, and Salt Lake City was a phenomenon. This place is the first American city I have encountered. It holds rather more than a million people with bodies, and stands on the same sort of soil as Calcutta. Having seen it, I urgently desire never to see it again. It is inhabited by savages. Its water is the water of the Hugli, and its air is dirt. Also it says that it is the 'boss' town of America.

I do not believe that it has anything to do with this country. They told me to go to the Palmer House, which is a gilded and mirrored rabbit-warren, and there I found a huge hall of tessellated marble, crammed with people talking about money and spitting about everywhere. Other barbarians charged in and out of this inferno with letters and telegrams in their hands, and yet others shouted at each other. A man who had drunk quite as much as was good for him told me that this was 'the finest hotel in the finest city on God Almighty's earth.' By the way, when an American wishes to indicate the next county or State he says, 'God A'mighty's earth.' This prevents discussion and flatters his vanity.

Then I went out into the streets, which are long and flat and without end. And verily it is not a good thing to live in the East for any length of time. Your ideas grow to clash with those held by every right-thinking white man. I looked down interminable vistas flanked with nine-, ten-, and fifteen-storeyed houses, and crowded with men and women, and the show impressed me with a great horror. Except in London—and I have forgotten what London is like—I had never seen so many white people together, and never such a collection of miserables. There was no colour in the street and no beauty— only a maze of wire ropes overhead and dirty stone flagging underfoot. A cab-driver volunteered to show me the glory of the town for so much an hour, and with him I wandered far. He conceived that all this turmoil and squash was a thing to be reverently admired; that it was good to huddle men together in fifteen layers, one atop of the other, and to dig holes in the ground for offices. He said that Chicago was a live town, and that all the creatures hurrying by me were engaged in business. That is to say, they were trying to make some money, that they might not die through lack of food to put into their bellies. He took me to canals, black as ink, and filled with untold abominations, and bade me watch the stream of traffic across the bridges. He then took me into a saloon, and, while I drank, made me note that the floor was covered with coins sunk into cement. A Hottentot would not have been guilty of this sort of barbarism. The coins made an effect pretty enough, but the man who put them there had no thought to beauty, and therefore he was a savage. Then my cab-driver showed me business-blocks, gay with signs and studded with fantastic and absurd advertisements of goods, and looking down the long street so adorned it was as though each vendor stood at his door howling: 'For the sake of money, employ or buy of me and me only!' Have you ever seen a crowd at our famine-relief distributions? You know then how men leap into the air, stretching out their arms above the crowd in the hope of being seen; while the women dolorously slap the stomachs of their children and whimper. I had sooner watch famine-relief than the white man engaged in what he calls legitimate competition. The one I understand. The other makes me ill. And the cabman said that these things were the proof of progress; and by that I knew he had been reading his newspaper, as every intelligent American should. The papers tell their readers in language fitted to their comprehension that the snarling together of telegraph wires, the heaving up of houses, and the making of money is progress.

I spent ten hours in that huge wilderness, wandering through scores of miles of these terrible streets, and jostling some few hundred thousand of these terrible people who talked money through their noses. The cabman left me: but after a while I picked up another man who was full of figures, and into my ears he poured them as occasion required or the big blank factories suggested. Here they turned out so many hundred thousand dollars' worth of such-and-such an article; there so many million other things; this house was worth so many million dollars; that one so many million more or less. It was like listening to a child babbling of its hoard of shells. It was like watching a fool playing with buttons. But I was expected to do more than listen or watch. He demanded that I should admire; and the utmost that I could say was: 'Are these things so? Then I am very sorry for you.' That made him angry, and he said that insular envy made me unresponsive. So you see I could not make him understand. . . .

Carl Sandburg: Chicago Poems

Chicago

Hog Butcher for the World,
Tool Maker, Stacker of Wheat,
Player with Railroads and the Nation's Freight Handler;
Stormy, husky, brawling,
City of the Big Shoulders:

They tell me you are wicked and I believe them, for I
   have seen your painted women under the gas lamps
   luring the farm boys.

And they tell me you are crooked and I answer: Yes, it
is true I have seen the gunman kill and go free to
kill again.
And they tell me you are brutal and my reply is: On the
faces of women and children I have seen the marks
of wanton hunger.
And having answered so I turn once more to those who
sneer at this my city, and I give them back the sneer
and say to them:
Come and show me another city with lifted head singing
so proud to be alive and coarse and strong and cunning.
Flinging magnetic curses amid the toil of piling job on
job, here is a tall bold slugger set vivid against the
little soft cities;
Fierce as a dog with tongue lapping for action, cunning
as a savage pitted against the wilderness,
    Bareheaded,
    Shoveling,
    Wrecking,
    Planning,
    Building, breaking, rebuilding,
Under the smoke, dust all over his mouth, laughing with
white teeth,
Under the terrible burden of destiny laughing as a young
man laughs,
Laughing even as an ignorant fighter laughs who has
never lost a battle,
Bragging and laughing that under his wrist is the pulse,
and under his ribs the heart of the people,
    Laughing!
Laughing the stormy, husky, brawling laughter of
Youth, half-naked, sweating, proud to be Hog
Butcher, Tool Maker, Stacker of Wheat, Player with
Railroads and Freight Handler to the Nation.

Happiness

I asked professors who teach the meaning of life to tell
me what is happiness.
And I went to famous executives who boss the work of
thousands of men.
They all shook their heads and gave me a smile as
though I was trying to fool with them.
And then one Sunday afternoon I wandered out along
the Desplaines river
And I saw a crowd of Hungarians under the trees with
their women and children and a keg of beer and an
accordion.

Muckers

Twenty men stand watching the muckers.
  Stabbing the sides of the ditch
  Where clay gleams yellow,
  Driving the blades of their shovels
  Deeper and deeper for the new gas mains,
  Wiping sweat off their faces
    With red bandanas.
The muckers work on . . . pausing . . . to pull
Their boots out of suckholes where they slosh.

  Of the twenty looking on
Ten murmur, "O, it's a hell of a job,"
Ten others, "Jesus, I wish I had the job."

Edward Everett Hale on the Lure of the Suburbs, 1888

The summer exodus from the cities is very suggestive [of the desire to escape the city's congestion], and is certainly teaching a lesson and working out conclusions which lie in the right direction. . . . Many a man now takes his family into the country for several months, whose father, doing the same business and living in the same social grade, would never have thought of doing so fifty years ago. It is quite possible to carry this same relief very much farther, so as to benefit the artisan and even the day-laborer. In Massachusetts the law now compels every railway company which runs into Boston to maintain what used to be called a "laborers' train," which shall reach Boston before seven in the morning, and which shall leave Boston after six at night, with rates so low as to meet the needs of men who receive the lower grades of wages. . . . The result is that not only merchants and their clerks, whose work begins at eight or nine in the morning, have their country residences outside of Boston, but also that those workmen live in the country whose daily work in the city begins at seven in the morning. . . .

And the result is that in the last thirty years the population of Boston proper has scarcely increased. The warehouses and shops and places of manufacture have increased, in the change which has raised the population of the whole city, including the environs. . . . But the population of the working wards is about the same as it was. For the people who do the work live, in many instances, fifteen miles away from the places of their daily duty. The result . . . has been the growth of a large number of villages where workingmen can live with their families in homes of their own, where the children can have the advantages of country life, or out-of-door life, while the workman himself goes into the town for his day's work and returns in the evening. . . .

Suburban life at the present moment has a bad name. This comes from the rather curious fact that the people who first undertake the development of a suburb are people who look at their problem from the lowest point of view.

They have "lots" to sell, and they are apt to wish to give the impression that their suburb is not a suburb, but that it is a part of the city, with blocks of houses, asphalt pavements and curb-stones, lamp-posts and other physical arrangements, in which they imitate, as well as they can, the dreariness of the place from which they would lure their customers away. Undoubtedly they have their reward, or they would not continue in this course. But there is arising . . . another class of speculators, who . . . see that men who leave towns want to retain the charm of the country as far as possible, while they still cling to the real conveniences of city life. Thus, the railway company which gives us a pretty garden around the station, and makes the station itself comfortable—a club-room, in fact, for the people who gather there—does its part toward luring into the suburb the men and women whom it wishes to have as regular passengers. . . . Let [the railroad manager] make his short trips quick, comfortable, and cheap, and he will have ten passengers out from the city and in again where he now has one. He has a new bonanza waiting for his pick when he really relieves the present congestion of the cities.

Howard A. Bridgeman on the Emergence of the Suburbanite, 1902

A generation ago debating societies about once in so often threshed over the question of the relative advantages of city and of country life. There were then two distinct human types—the city man and the country man. To them has been added in comparatively recent years a third—the suburbanite. He emerges into view not only at great world centers like London and New York, but in a hundred lesser cities in Europe and America. . . . The suburbanite is a recent growth, because cheap and rapid transportation is a modern affair. . . .

The cities, it is true, are still the goal of the average American heart. . . . As the city man walks briskly to his office in the morning . . . he may be pardoned for being proudly conscious of the fact that his daily course is not hedged about with threatening time-tables; that he has easy access to the best that the rich, resourceful city offers in the way of music, and theaters, and lectures, and preaching, and libraries. . . . But on the other hand, Mr. Suburbanite . . . puts in his claim to be heard. "It's all well enough for bachelors and elderly couples and people who like crowds, to reside in town, but if you want to bring up a family, to prolong your days, to cultivate the neighborly feeling, . . . leave your city block and become like me. It may be a little more difficult for us to attend the opera, but the robin in my elm tree struck a higher note and a sweeter one yesterday than any *prima donna* ever reached." . . .

We are sure to get in America, through the rise of numerous little colonies of people who plant themselves five, ten or fifteen miles from town, a renaissance of the old, beautiful neighborhood life that characterized this nation before the rush to the cities began. . . . There is a Villagers' Club in one of Boston's best known suburbs, composed of prominent business and professional men of the city, that for years has maintained high intellectual standards, and in its fortnightly meetings through the winter has given serious attention to large subjects in the realm of politics, literature and religion. . . .

. . . The great danger is that the self-complacent suburbanite will ignore his obligations to the city in which he spends his working hours and earns his daily bread. These obligations continue, even tho he is no longer a citizen of the metropolis. If he evades them he exposes himself to what Rev. Dr. Horton, of London, strikingly calls the "Curse of Suburbanity." . . . What attitude, then, shall the suburbanite take to the city of which he is by necessity still a part? Shall he look upon it simply as . . . a place that he is well rid of when night comes? Shall he hurry by the slum section and never notice the bundles of rags and misery that now and then disfigure the street? Shall he consider it no concern of his whether or not the city which furnishes him and his children with a living be well governed, whether its streets are clean and its parks large enough for the thousands of people who are crowded into the tenement districts? Because he has become a suburbanite shall he cast off responsibility for the city? . . .

Our ideal suburbanite is yet in the process of evolution. When he emerges he will blend the best traits of the pure city man and the pure country man. . . . Subjected daily to the influences of both city and country, their constant play upon him will make him broad, symmetrical, responsive to life on all sides and alive to all life's obligations. His suburban home . . . will strengthen him for the daily grapple with the problems that await him yonder in the noisy town. And every evening as he returns from toil he will bring to his family and his neighborhood much of the city's inspiration, so that they, too, will feel its thrill of life, and its call to strenuous labor while the day lasts.

W. E. B. Du Bois on Racial Prejudice in Philadelphia, 1899

Incidentally throughout this study the prejudice against the Negro has been again and again mentioned. It is time now to reduce this somewhat indefinite term to something tangible. Everybody speaks of the matter, everybody knows that it exists, but in just what form it shows itself or how influential it is few agree. In the Negro's mind, color prejudice in Philadelphia is that widespread feeling of dislike for his blood, which keeps him and his children out of decent employment, from certain public conveniences and amusements, from hiring houses in many sections, and in general, from being recognized as a man. Negroes regard this prejudice as the chief cause of their present unfortunate condition. On the other hand most white people are quite unconscious of any such powerful and vindictive feeling; they regard color prejudice as the easily explicable feeling that intimate social intercourse with a lower race is not only undesirable but impracticable if our present standards of culture are to be maintained; and although they are aware that some people feel the aversion more intensely than others, they cannot see how such a feeling has much influence on the real situation, or alters the social condition of the mass of Negroes.

As a matter of fact, color prejudice in this city is something between these two extreme views: it is not to-day responsible for all, or perhaps the greater part of the Negro problems, or of the disabilities under which the race labors; on the other hand it is a far more powerful social force than most Philadelphians realize. The practical results of the attitude of most of the inhabitants of Philadelphia toward persons of Negro descent are as follows:

1. As to getting work:

No matter how well trained a Negro may be, or how fitted for work of any kind, he cannot in the ordinary course of competition hope to be much more than a menial servant.

He cannot get clerical or supervisory work to do save in exceptional cases.

He cannot teach save in a few of the remaining Negro schools.

He cannot become a mechanic except for small transient jobs, and cannot join a trades union.

A Negro woman has but three careers open to her in this city: domestic service, sewing, or married life.

2. As to keeping work:

The Negro suffers in competition more severely than white men.

Change in fashion is causing him to be replaced by whites in the better paid positions of domestic service.

Whim and accident will cause him to lose a hard-earned place more quickly than the same things would affect a white man.

Being few in number compared with the whites the crime or carelessness of a few of his race is easily imputed to all, and the reputation of the good, industrious and reliable suffer thereby.

Because Negro workmen may not often work side by side with white workmen, the individual black workman is rated not by his own efficiency, but by the efficiency of a whole group of black fellow workmen which may often be low.

Because of these difficulties which virtually increase competition in his case, he is forced to take lower wages for the same work than white workmen.

3. As to entering new lines of work:

Men are used to seeing Negroes in inferior positions; when, therefore, by any chance a Negro gets in a better position, most men immediately conclude that he is not fitted for it, even before he has a chance to show his fitness.

If, therefore, he set up a store, men will not patronize him.

If he is put into public position men will complain.

If he gain a position in the commercial world, men will quietly secure his dismissal or see that a white man succeeds him.

4. As to his expenditure:

The comparative smallness of the patronage of the Negro, and the dislike of other customers makes it usual to increase the charges or difficulties in certain directions in which a Negro must spend money.

He must pay more house-rent for worse houses than most white people pay.

He is sometimes liable to insult or reluctant service in some restaurants, hotels and stores, at public resorts, theatres and places of recreation; and at nearly all barber-shops.

5. As to his children:

The Negro finds it extremely difficult to rear children in such an atmosphere and not have them either cringing or impudent: if he impresses upon them patience with their lot, they may grow up satisfied with their condition; if he inspires them with ambition to rise, they may grow to despise their own people, hate the whites and become embittered with the world.

His children are discriminated against, often in public schools.

They are advised when seeking employment to become waiters and maids.

They are liable to species of insult and temptation peculiarly trying to children.

6. As to social intercourse:

In all walks of life the Negro is liable to meet some objection to his presence or some discourteous treatment; and the ties of friendship or memory seldom are strong enough to hold across the color line.

If an invitation is issued to the public for any occasion, the Negro can never know whether he would be welcomed or not; if he goes he is liable to have his feelings hurt and get into unpleasant altercation; if he stays away, he is blamed for indifference.

If he meet a lifelong white friend on the street, he is in a dilemma; if he does not greet the friend he is put down as boorish and impolite; if he does greet the friend he is liable to be flatly snubbed.

If by chance he is introduced to a white woman or man, he expects to be ignored on the next meeting, and usually is.

White friends may call on him, but he is scarcely expected to call on them, save for strictly business matters.

If he gain the affections of a white woman and marry her he may invariably expect that slurs will be thrown on her reputation and on his, and that both his and her race will shun their company.

When he dies he cannot be buried beside white corpses.

7. The result:

Any one of these things happening now and then would not be remarkable or call for especial comment; but when one group of people suffer all these little differences of treatment and discriminations and insults continually, the result is either discouragement, or bitterness, or over-sensitiveness, or recklessness. And a people feeling thus cannot do their best. . . .

❧ *E S S A Y S*

Urban America grew up within both technological and cultural specifications. It is to the promise and limits of urban physical design that we turn in this chapter's essays. In the first selection, historians Maury Klein of the

University of Rhode Island and Harvey A. Kantor of New York University suggest an interlocking pattern of problem solution and problem creation at the heart of urban technological innovation. Then historian Robert Fishman of Rutgers University at Camden explores the cultural contradictions of the "classic" middle-class suburb in the second essay. Focusing on Philadelphia, he argues that suburban design expressed both middle-class confidence and middle-class fears about urban civilization. In the final essay, historian William M. Tuttle, Jr., of the University of Kansas describes a hoary case of cultural resistance overwhelming the physical promise of urban development. Drawn cityward by the labor needs of the war industries, beginning in 1915, as well as by dreams of escaping the misery of the southern countryside, more than three hundred thousand blacks had migrated to northern cities by 1920. Although this development, in the long run, would energize both individual artistic creation and collective political power, in the short run the mass migration heightened racial tensions over neighborhood turf (as well as employment), kindling a conflict that would mushroom into a conflagration in 1919.

Technology and the Treadmill of Urban Progress

MAURY KLEIN AND HARVEY A. KANTOR

To the modern urbanite the industrial city seems a quaint, almost primitive place. Its sights and smells bear a strong flavor of nostalgia: streets lit by gas lamps and filled with carriages, drays, and streetcars; sidewalks bustling with gentlemen in tall hats or derbies, wearing high, starched collars; ladies in long dresses with parasols resting on their shoulders; workmen dressed in cheap drab shirts and pants, brightened by gaudy bandanas tied about their neck or head; messenger boys dashing from one office building to another; deliverymen straining beneath their blocks of ice, kegs of beer, or racks of clothing; sidestreets filled with peddlers' carts loaded with wares of every kind, their cries intermingling in a cacophony of confusion; sidewalk markets bulging with fresh fruit and produce, tiers of fish or slabs of meat, all picked over by swarms of shoppers; strolling policemen with bright brass buttons and fat nightsticks; and ragged newsboys trumpeting the day's headlines above the din of the street traffic.

The wistful flavor of this scene is deceptive. While its pace and tumult may appear tame to people in a high-speed, computerized, automated society, contemporaries regarded the city as an engine of progress in which everything seemed constantly on the move. In this feeling, that generation was no less correct than our own; the difference lay largely in the level of technology achieved by each era. To an amazing degree advances in technol-

From *Prisoners of Progress: American Industrial Cities, 1850–1920* by Maury Klein and Harvey A. Kantor, pp. 144–51, 154–60, 163–74. Copyright © 1976 by Macmillan Publishing Company, reprinted by permission.

ogy shaped the growth, appearance, and pace of the industrial city. Then as now, cities could expand only by discovering new techniques for moving people, goods, and information. New machines, materials, and designs revamped the city's face and accelerated its inner rhythms. Urban growth was therefore both a function of technology and a reflection of its pervasive influence.

Yet technology, even in its most imaginative forms, did not solve problems so much as recast them. Rapid growth strained the city's ability to perform such elementary functions as transporting, feeding, and housing people, protecting them from fire and crime, educating their children, and providing a healthy, attractive environment in which to live. It complicated every aspect of urban life and fragmented urban society. Almost every industrial city endured a phase of madcap expansion during which its distended social system threatened to collapse beneath the weight of increased demands for services and accumulated social tensions.

To solve the physical problems created by rapid growth, most cities resorted to sophisticated technology and techniques. But every "solution" unmasked a tangle of new problems which in turn called for still more sophisticated hardware. Thus the electric trolley and elevated railway moved more people at greater speed than the omnibus, but both presented problems unforeseen in the heyday of the horse and buggy. The result was a vicious circle, a kind of "Catch-22" in which every new stage of technological advance proved less a gateway into some new golden age than a harbinger of fresh difficulties.

Nor was this all. The vicious circle traced by the interaction between technology and growth uncovered a deeper contradiction in the American notion of progress. Americans had always tended to equate progress with growth. During the industrial era, progress came increasingly to be defined in material and mechanical terms. This faith in the notion that "bigger is better" assumed that quantitative growth would improve the quality of life. Since technology was a primary instrument in quantitative growth, Americans logically turned to it as a means for resolving the perplexities of industrial society.

Urban growth especially fed upon advances in technology. In quantitative terms, that growth proceeded at breakneck pace and reached gigantic proportions. But the industrial city turned out to be something less than the promised land. For all the splendors of its swelling statistics, it never became a pleasant or even decent place in which to live for a majority of its inhabitants. Too late city-dwellers discovered that their faith in technology had been misplaced; that mere quantitative growth did not automatically bring qualitative improvement. In their quest for a better life, urbanites had created not a road to utopia but a treadmill which they labeled "progress."

Just as the railroad affected the locations and functions of cities on a national scale, the street railway shaped their internal growth. From its crude beginnings with horse-drawn omnibuses to steam-power trolleys and later the electrified lines, mass transit moved urbanites faster and more efficiently.

Every advance in transportation technology quickly outmoded its predecessor only to create new problems in construction, congestion, and pollution.

The most important effect of mass transit was its expanding the physical limits of the city. The street railway destroyed the compact "walking city" of colonial and preindustrial towns. Prior to about 1850 most towns were still intimate locales where street congestion involved nothing more than people on foot, on horseback, or in carriages. Most people lived near their place of work and could reach nearly any spot in the city in a thirty-minute walk. Few towns extended farther than two miles from their core, which usually nestled against some waterway.

During the 1820s the omnibus emerged as the first urban passenger carrier. Initially little more than enlarged hackney coaches, these wagons later resembled boxes on wheels with two lengthwise seats holding twelve to twenty people. They appeared first in the larger cities—New York, Boston, Philadelphia, New Orleans, Washington. . . .

. . . Even though the fare was too steep for the masses, omnibuses drew heavy patronage from small businessmen and clerks, many of whom still went home for lunch. By the 1840s Boston had eighteen omnibus lines, of which twelve extended to outlying suburban communities. Despite its limitations, the omnibus speeded up the tempo of life, regularized transportation patterns, and launched the outward migration of wealthier people from the center of the city to the suburbs.

The era of the omnibus lasted scarcely a generation before the horse railway surpassed it in the 1850s. The horse railway, too, resembled a stagecoach, but utilized flanged wheels operating on iron tracks. . . . By the 1850s [New York,] Boston, Philadelphia, Chicago, Baltimore, St. Louis, Cincinnati, Newark, and Pittsburgh all had laid horsecar tracks and were extending their boundaries. Iron rails allowed horsecars to reach speeds of six to eight miles per hour, about one-third more than the omnibus could muster. Reduced friction did more than add speed. It provided a smoother ride and increased the number of passengers that could be hauled.

Iron rails also increased costs. Inevitably the horsecar companies required a greater capital investment than the omnibus lines. As expenses mounted, financing became more feasible through incorporation rather than individual ownership. . . . Ownership of transit facilities fell increasingly into the hands of outside entrepreneurs who neither knew the local scene nor cared about how cities developed. Each phase of technological innovation made urban transportation a bigger business than it had been. By the end of the nineteenth century, transit or "traction" enterprises held the nexus of political and economic power in most major cities. . . .

The horsecar had another unsavory effect upon the urban landscape: it added to the piles of horse manure littering the streets. Lest we forget that pollution comes in many forms, it is well to heed Joel Tarr's reminder that the automobile was once hailed as the savior of the city from animal waste. "In a city like Milwaukee in 1907," he wrote, ". . . with a human population of 350,000 and a horse population of 12,500, this meant 133 tons of manure a day, for a daily average of nearly three-quarters of a pound of manure for each resident.'' For New York and Brooklyn in the 1880s, with a total horse population of around 150,000, the problem was much worse. Carcasses of dead horses sprawled in the streets added to the sanitation nightmare.

This contemporary image of mass transit as a crowded, unsafe, unpleasant, and polluting form of transportation sounds hauntingly familiar to the modern ear. Moreover, the horsecar had inherent limitations as a form of transportation: it could go no faster than the horse pulling it and could not increase its passenger load without adding more horses, which posed other difficulties. To growing cities, these became intolerable drawbacks. The obvious solution was to devise a transit system that utilized mechanical rather than muscle power. By the 1860s the search for alternatives was well underway. Louis Ransom of Akron, Ohio, advocated adopting his Ransom Steamer to iron rails. George Clark of Cincinnati promoted a system of compressed-air cars, while a New Orleans firm experimented with a car propelled by ammonia gas. . . .

No innovation in urban mass transit rivaled the application of electrical power. Oddly enough, the pioneer projects developed in the least urbanized area of the nation. James A. Gaboury, the owner of an animal traction line in Montgomery, Alabama, witnessed a demonstration of an electrical car at the Toronto Agricultural Fair in 1885 and determined to adopt the method to his system. In 1886 Montgomery's Court Street line became the first in the country to offer a citywide system of electric transportation. Several years later, Frank J. Sprague, a naval engineer who had worked for Thomas Edison, formed his own company and secured a contract to build a line in Richmond, Virginia. The success of his project spurred the construction of electrical transit lines elsewhere.

The electric cars moved along iron tracks in the street, drawing current from a central power source passed to the trains through overhead wires. The effect of a wire leading a car resembled that of a ''troller''; soon the corruption of the word became universal and the new vehicles were dubbed ''trolleys.'' Trolleys displaced horses so rapidly that by 1900 only 2 percent of the lines were horse-drawn, compared to 70 percent a decade earlier. By 1895, 850 lines embraced over 10,000 miles of electrified track. The new trolleys speeded up travel service to about twelve miles per hour and more in less congested areas. Their overhead wires cluttered the streetscapes of American cities and wreaked havoc during high winds and storms.

Frank Sprague made a second major contribution to transportation systems. He designed an electrical multiple-unit control system which allowed each car to be independently powered, lighted, heated, and braked. These cars did not require a locomotive since they possessed their own power source; yet they could be controlled by a master switch located in any one of them. At one stroke Sprague removed the major obstacles to constructing underground railways. Automated electric cars could operate without the accumulation of smoke, gas, and dirt discharged by steam-powered cars. Between 1895 and 1897 Boston built a mile-and-a-half subway at a cost of $4,000,000. Immediately after the turn of the century, New York constructed a route from downtown City Hall to 145th Street. . . . The popularity of the subway, coupled with the city's extreme congestion, led New York to take the lead in underground transportation. Moreover, its hard-rock geological formation could support the construction of tall buildings above ground and tunnels below.

All these achievements in the technology of transportation affected the physical growth of cities. The rural ideal retained its hold upon Americans even in the city, where its influence drove people toward the suburbs. Prior to the advent of mass transit lines, however, only the wealthy could maintain houses on the outskirts of the city. Once the pedestrian confines were broken in the 1850s, an outward migration commenced. [Samuel Bass] Warner has painstakingly traced the development of Roxbury, West Roxbury, and Dorchester as bedroom satellites of Boston. Every stage of suburban development expanded the physical limits of Boston to house wealthy, middle-class, and lower middle-class expatriates from the city. Since all of the transit lines were privately built, the new suburbs alongside their tracks were the product of individual decision-making rather than coordinated social policy. . . .

Traction entrepreneurs enthusiastically promoted the flight to the suburbs. They found support among those who regarded the exodus as a boon for relieving congestion in the city's inner core. Adna Weber, the leading student of American cities in the nineteenth century, stated flatly, "it is clear that we are now in the sight of a solution of the problem of concentration of population." Weber advocated the extension of electrified transit lines and cheap fares because he saw in the rise of the suburbs "the solid basis of a hope that the evils of city life, so far as they result from overcrowding, may be in large part removed."

Unhappily, things did not work out that way. While upper- and middle-class urbanites left for greener pastures, the poor remained packed together in the central city, where they shared space with businesses and industries. Mass transit promoted this pattern of segregation within the city. More than any other factor, it transformed the diversified walking city into a central urban core of poor people and businesses surrounded by successive rings of suburban neighborhoods.

In fact, mass transit failed even to relieve population congestion. Transit lines did not scatter people about so much as cluster them in dense communities wherever transportation was available. New housing developments pursued every new construction or extension and quickly overflowed its service. As one alert observer wrote in an 1896 *Harper's Weekly,* "the trolleys seem to have created a new patronage of their own. Travel has been stimulated rather than diverted." Instead of thinning out settlement, mass transit created corridors of dense groupings alongside their lines. This magnetic pull pleased the traction promoters immensely. It was great for business; its effect upon the city's already strained social structure was quite another matter.

Technology extended the city's boundaries in another important way. Innovations in bridge-building made it possible for the first time to span the widest rivers. The implications of this breakthrough for urban growth were enormous: waterways ceased to be an obstacle to physical expansion. More important, it allowed traffic to flow in and out of the city with ease. Just as railroads dissolved limitations upon land travel, so the new bridges banished the fickle vagaries of waterways. Small wonder that to many Americans the Brooklyn Bridge and other mighty spans became the supreme symbol of American civilization. . . .

As mass transit and great bridges expanded the city's outer limits, innovations in building forms lifted its inner face. Like bridge-building, the new age of construction dawned with the shift from wood to iron and steel. Preindustrial cities were filled with two- or three-story buildings, shops, warehouses, and row houses made of timber. Government buildings, merchant exchanges, and athenaeums comprised the major public buildings; the church spire still dominated the skyline.

The industrial city presented a radically different scene. Multi-story buildings filled with corporate and professional offices stretched high into the sky. Cast-iron and sash-steel factories housed long ranks of machines whose operators lived in tall brick tenements. New kinds of buildings—railroad terminals, department stores, theaters, apartments—ornamented the urban landscape. The transition from church spire to skyscraper signified a revolution in construction techniques and in the way city-dwellers identified with their surroundings.

Great movements often hinge upon small details. In construction it was the lowly nail that boomed residential building and urban expansion. Prior to the 1820s home-building in America copied the English method of using heavy beams shaped at the ends to fit into slots in adjoining beams. If there was tension on the two beams, a hole was augured and a wooden peg fitted into place to hold the stress. This mortise-and-tenon method required skilled craftsmen. Houses built in this manner were sturdy but expensive.

The mass production of iron nails in the 1820s liberated builders from the English method. With these inexpensive joining devices, houses could be built in the skeleton form still common today. The "balloon frame," as it was called, consisted of thin plates and studs usually 2" × 4") "nailed together in such a way that every strain went in the direction of the wood (i.e. against the grain)." The first balloon-frame building appeared in Chicago, where in 1833 a carpenter named Augustine Deodat Taylor built the city's first Catholic church in three months at a cost of only $400.

With that simple edifice, Chicago commenced its long career as a pioneer in urban design. Balloon-frame structures sprang up all over the city, and the popularity of skeleton construction survived even the Great Fire of 1871. Other young western towns like San Francisco, Denver, and Seattle adopted the balloon-frame form, as did the more established cities of the East. Although attacked by contemporaries as shoddy and tasteless, the balloon frame proved irresistible to the urban market with its insatiable appetite for cheap housing. Once transit lines made commuting feasible, developers and speculators bought large tracts of farmland adjacent to the city, carved them into lots, and threw up whole neighborhoods of houses modeled upon a common design.

Like another simple innovation, Eli Whitney's cotton gin, the balloon frame energized an entire industry. It put single-unit dwellings within the reach of many people once unable to afford such a luxury. Home construction soared in every major industrial city and fueled the exodus to the suburbs. Once this pattern of settlement emerged, most cities hastened to annex the new subdivisions that dotted their perimeters. Urban boundaries marched steadily into the surrounding countryside in random fashion, and new towns sprang up everywhere. As Carl W. Condit noted, "Within a generation the balloon frame dominated the West. . . . Without it the towns of the prairies could never have been built in the short time that saw the establishment of rural and urban society in the region."

Commercial buildings underwent no less drastic changes in design and construction techniques. Preindustrial cities utilized wood or bulky masonry for all their buildings. In downtown areas, where buildings were packed closely together, the inhabitants lived in constant fear of fire. The search for stronger, less inflammable materials began as early as the 1820s when two American architects—John Haviland and William Strickland—experimented with iron supports on some of their buildings. . . .

[In the 1850s] James Bogardus, an imaginative mechanic and inventor, . . . constructed the first wholly cast-iron building in New York at the corner of Centre and Duane Streets. The cast-iron design . . . eliminated the thick, space-consuming masonry columns in the interiors, thereby offering more room to economy-minded occupants. Iron buildings went up quickly and could be disassembled quickly if the need arose. For two decades cast-iron dominated the construction of warehouses, department stores, and office buildings in American cities. . . . The ability of cast iron to reproduce elaborate details as decorations at low cost gave five- or six-story buildings a unique flavor of elegance in the 1850s and 1860s.

Yet cast iron's primacy lasted only two decades before steel replaced it as the leading construction material. Steel was more durable and stronger for both tension and compression and, unlike cast iron, did not melt when fire reached it. It allowed architects and engineers to raise their structures higher, a compelling feature at a time when downtown land values were soaring. By the 1890s steel framing had converted most major architects through its ability to provide added height and more flexible interior space. The mass production of plate glass gave architects a material for large windows strong enough to withstand wind and stress at high altitudes. This combination of steel framing and plate glass laid the foundation for skyscraper construction in the twentieth century. . . .

The skyscraper mania was not without its detractors. In 1896 the New York Chamber of Commerce declared that tall buildings were "not consistent with public health and that the interests of the majority of our citizens require that the height should be limited." That same year *The New York Times* warned that "the time is evidently near when it will be necessary to proceed in the public interest against the excesses of selfishness." The major complaints were that the tall buildings exacerbated the already crowded conditions of most downtown areas, cut off sunlight to adjacent structures and sidewalks, and were basically unsafe. Completion of the Woolworth Building sparked the drive to limit building heights. In 1916 New York City adopted its comprehensive zoning law which included a restriction on height. But architects deftly circumvented the provision by utilizing the "wedding cake" design and skyscrapers continued their upward spiral.*. . .

The physical strain wrought by urban growth involved more than land and buildings. Expanding populations required not only housing but water, gas, electricity, and sewer lines. Better and wider streets were needed to handle the city's heavier traffic. Small cities suddenly grown large found themselves called upon to provide more utilities and services than ever before. Once again municipalities sought refuge in new technology and techniques, and once again every solution gave rise to new problems. As with mass transit, "progress" brought fewer benefits to the public than to the corporate interests that owned the utilities and charged exorbitant rates for their services. Utility franchises, paving contracts, street cleaning, garbage hauling, and maintenance work all reaped financial windfalls for the contractors and politicians in charge of dispensing contracts or fulfilling them.

The importance of streets to urban growth and commerce is so obvious that it needs no elaboration. Yet the history of their construction and care is a dismal chapter in the conflict between public and private interest. Streets in most American cities took a terrific pounding and most were in wretched condition. Any city-dweller who ventured beyond his front door understood that fact only too well. When civic-minded individuals complained about the scandalous condition of their town's thoroughfares, the lament usually fell upon deaf ears. A first-rate street system required a large capital investment, which meant higher taxes. Many other services were also clamoring for more funds even while urbanites protested against more taxes. The result was a pattern of benign neglect in which streets got a relatively low priority in the municipal budget. On one hand, few cities allocated sufficient funds for street construction and care; on the other, graft, inefficiency, and lack of planning sapped the effectiveness of the funds that were allocated.

When it came to paving, for example, most city governments agreed to it only as a last resort, and then tried to do the job as cheaply as possible. Streets were extended long before money was available to pave them. When they were finally paved, the contractor concentrated on the surface rather than the foundation. As a result, few streets enjoyed a long or happy life. Repairs were frequent and recurring. . . . But if this "pound-foolish" economy did not serve the public well, it proved a boon to politicians and their friends who discovered that paving contracts were lucrative plums for "friendly" contractors. . . .

---

* The "wedding cake" design involved setting each five or ten stories back from those beneath it. The effect resembled the layers of a wedding cake. . . .

The erratic surfaces of most American streets provoked much consternation as traffic increased. In the 1880s Washington, Buffalo, and Philadelphia adopted the European practice of paving with asphalt. Although it refracted the heat and tended to be slippery, asphalt did provide a quiet surface. Usually it was laid in the suburbs and new sections of town. For the central business district, which required a stronger material, bricks became common in the 1880s, particularly in cities like Philadelphia, Des Moines, Columbus, and Cleveland, which manufactured them.

But American streets did not improve appreciably until builders got beneath the surface of the problem. A substantial and well-drained foundation reduced the amount of surface material used and provided a longer-lasting road. Once cities and their contractors took the trouble to prepare the roadbed, macadam soared in popularity. Cheap stones crushed and mixed with oil, then placed in a well-laid foundation, became the standard paving practice in many cities during the 1880s and 1890s. . . .

If street care often languished from neglect, it also suffered from spurts of municipal zeal. Technological innovations never operate in a vacuum. Progress toward solution of one problem often had unfortunate repercussions elsewhere. In this case, cities found it necessary to rip up their streets to install pipes, tubing, or cables for utility services. Sewer lines especially took their toll on streets because, once in widespread use, they went down in nearly every neighborhood. Growing cities produced a mountain of human, animal, and industrial waste, the disposal of which defied the capacities of government and private citizen alike. Few problems dogged the industrial city so persistently or outran new solutions so rapidly. Nor has the modern city improved much upon this legacy of failure.

Most cities handled the problem by simply dumping their waste in the nearest body of water. New York, Boston, and Chicago, which in 1856 built the first comprehensive sewer system, installed underground conduits to carry wastes into the nearby sea. By 1916 New York City alone was dumping close to 500,000,000 gallons of raw sewage a day into her rivers. Smaller towns relied upon village depositing techniques which held little value for the congested city. . . . The inadequacy of this ancient arrangement impressed itself upon the eyes and nostrils of every city-dweller. One citizen echoed a familiar complaint of the era when he reported that in Philadelphia and "numerous other cities of eastern Pennsylvania the pedestrian along the streets was continually stepping over a little stream of soapy water flowing in channels across the sidewalk from the house to the street gutters."

Discontent brought action but little relief. . . . Chicago's experience offers the most instructive example of the waste-disposal treadmill. Realizing even in the 1870s that the city's waste was ruining Lake Michigan, city officials struck upon an audacious plan to reroute the flow of deposits: they would reverse the flow of the Chicago River away from Lake Michigan and allow the river to carry waste downstream where ultimately it would reach the Mississippi River. After considerable effort and the expenditure of $80,000,000, which included the construction of six pumping stations to keep the flow moving, this was accomplished.

To its chagrin, Chicago discovered that it had not solved the problem so much as compounded it. The new system inflicted Chicago's wastes upon distant rivers where it spoiled the water of downstream towns. Moreover, the drainage system backed up into Chicago and Lake Michigan during heavy rains. The waterways around Chicago and heavily industrialized Gary went on accumulating waste, and regional pollution continued to run rampant. . . .

The use of technology to increase the supply of pure water illustrates again the manner in which technology failed to satisfy the appetites of its recipients and merely stimulated the demand it was intended to quell. As Lewis Mumford put it, "the most characteristic technical achievements of the big city are those that further congestion; and the first of these is the canalization of water into storage in reservoirs, its transmission through vast mains, tubular rivers, from the open country to the heart of the city.". . .

Most cities in the 1870s and 1880s constructed major waterworks but the inability to keep up with spiraling demand caused many places to experience "water famines." And the water that did come was virtually untreated. In 1870 no city had a filtration system, and by 1900 only 6 percent of the urban population received filtered water. Pittsburgh, which deposited its industrial waste into and drew its drinking water from the Allegheny River, waited until its death rate from typhoid fever reached four times the national average before constructing a filter system. Between 1908 and 1914, the city installed pumping stations along the Allegheny to filter the water through sediment, whereupon the death rate promptly dropped. Yet even after the improvements, the city's typhoid death rate, although only about half the American average, remained twice that of major European centers.

By 1920 a majority of large American cities possessed filtration and treatment plants. Jersey City pioneered in chemical treatment with a plant built in 1908. But everywhere the surge of population growth pressed hard upon the ingenuity of engineers and resources of municipal governments. The passing decades have brought no solution to the water dilemma; on the contrary, it has reached crisis proportions in many modern cities. Even a century ago it often seemed that in the complex urban environment the most basic needs were the hardest to fulfill satisfactorily.

Technology had another curious effect upon the urban environment: it transformed innovations into necessities of life. The advent of electric energy illustrates the process by which technological breakthroughs generate on a colossal scale demands which had never before existed. Electricity touched every aspect of the city's life—it powered machinery, ran trains, lifted elevators, and lighted streets and homes. To some extent, electricity merely replaced other sources of power and performed old functions in a new way. But once its versatility was recognized, new inventions utilized it for an incredible variety of purposes which urbanites by 1920 accepted as indispensable to their life-style. No one grasped the impact of the dynamo, the means for converting mechanical energy into electric energy, more surely than Henry Adams. "Among the thousand symbols of ultimate energy," he concluded, "the dynamo was not so human as some, but it was the most expressive.". . .

Even more than gas lamps, electric lighting transformed the city into a twenty-four-hour place. The pace of urban activities livened as nightlife entertainment was extended, people were able to get around more freely and safely, and the evening hours began to attract rather than discourage walkers. Merchants extended their hours, and some industrialists kept their factories running longer. New lighting inspired aesthetic adornments for the city like well-designed lampposts and illuminated monuments, statues, and fountains. The whole atmosphere of city streets seemed cleaner and whiter, a bit like the "Great White City" of the Chicago Fair which had impressed visitors so deeply. It was as if someone, by turning on these electric wonders, had caused urbanites to take a closer look at their cities, and to extract from the shadows a new sense of the degree to which the magic of technology had altered their lives.

As new inventions changed the outward appearance of the industrial city, so did they improve its inner efficiency. . . .

Edison's mimeograph machine (1876), along with the cash register (1876), the stenotype (1876), the adding machine (1888), and the spring-weighing scale (1895), combined with the telephone and typewriter to indicate how far business operations had come from the quill pen, letter book, musty ledger, messenger boy, and hand copyist of an earlier era. Yet none of these equaled another instrument as the supreme symbol of the industrial order: the mass-produced watch.

The hand watch embodied both the genius of American inventiveness and the spirit of the age of mechanization. Fittingly enough, machine watch-making developed during the 1850s, the same decade in which the preindustrial walking city was giving way to the industrial city. Aaron Dennison's factory in Roxbury, Massachusetts, was the first to manufacture a watch with interchangeable parts in large quantities. Dennison removed his factory to Waltham, Massachusetts, and with Edward Howard formed the American Watch Company which anticipated Henry Ford's assembly line production by fifty years.

Waltham quickly emerged as the center of America's watchmaking industry. By 1900 the factories there averaged 250 watches a year per worker, while Swiss watchmakers could manage only 40. . . . By the late 1870s watchmakers in Waterbury, Connecticut, were producing timepieces at a price the masses could afford. In 1900 a mass-produced watch, complete with a year's guarantee, sold for a dollar. The dollar watch offered tangible benefits and some intangible liabilities. On one hand, the workingman owned a fine timepiece to slide in and out of his pocket; on the other hand, he could no longer plead ignorance or poverty as an excuse for being late to work. . . .

. . . The clock vastly transcended its immediate function of telling time. It symbolized the concerted attempt to harness the raw material of labor to the iron regimen of American work habits. Workmen predictably resisted the efforts as best they could, but the odds turned against them. As immigration swelled the labor force, it created a surplus which heightened the competition for jobs, especially in hard times. However distasteful the factory routine, it was preferable—even inviting—when starvation seemed the only alternative. [Herbert] Gutman cites a verse by Yiddish poet Morris Rosenfeld which vividly portrays the clock as oppressor:

> The Clock in the workshop,—it rests not a moment;
> It points on, and ticks on: eternity—time;
> Once someone told me the clock had a meaning,—
> In pointing and ticking had reason and rhyme. . . .
> At times, when I listen, I hear the clock plainly;—
> The reason of old—the old meaning—is gone!
> The maddening pendulum urges me forward
> To labor and still labor on.
> The tick of the clock is the boss in his anger.
> The face of the clock has the eyes of the foe.
> The clock—I shudder—Dost hear how it draws me?
> It calls me "Machine" and it cries [to] me "Sew"!

As urban man grew more apart from his rural cousin with every passing year, nothing separated them more than the clock. While the farmer measured his life by the organic rhythms of seasonal change, of sunrise and sunset, the urbanite chained himself to the "tyranny of time." Trains ran on schedule and were expected to be "on time"; work proceeded with "clockwork efficiency"; mechanical processes were geared "according to the clock"; novels gave way to "periodicals"; and when electricity was mated with the clock in plants, workers had to "clock in.". . .

Technology powered the city, expanded it upward and outward, provided its water, lighted it, carried its wastes, and organized its work patterns. It did much of this crudely, inefficiently, and at great human sacrifice, but Americans had always been slow to reckon the social cost of "progress." More important, it fixed the destiny of the industrial city. Future change or improvement would center upon more sophisticated technology, more prudently applied. No amount of daydreaming or wishful thinking could banish or reverse the technological presence.

The industrial revolution changed the physical city into a larger, more congested, more polluted place. But it had done so under man's guidance. Blind faith in mechanical progress as human progress and the unfettered power of the profit system left little room for pondering the larger ramifications of success. By World War I the industrial city was the dominant urban form which the legacy of unbridled technology willed to the twentieth century.

The Railroad Suburb as Middle-Class Utopia

ROBERT FISHMAN

In the history of the middle-class residential suburb, the late nineteenth century railroad suburb represents the classic form, the era in which suburbia most closely approached the bourgeois monument and the bourgeois utopia.

It exemplified the central meaning and contradiction of suburbia: a natural world of greenery and family life that appeared to be wholly separate from the great city yet was in fact wholly dependent on it.

Inevitably, this classic stage of suburbia coincided with the classic stage of the industrial metropolis itself. At the close of the nineteenth century great cities reached their most dominant phase in the world economy. They were, in H. G. Wells's word, whirlpools whose vortices sucked in both population and industry from farms and from smaller regions. Not only was the agrarian population of Europe and North America drawn with tremendous force out of the countryside and into great cities—often crossing the Atlantic in their migrations—but the most advanced industries deserted the countryside and the small towns to find in the booming inner city that surrounded the metropolitan core the most profitable location for growth.

Finally, the great cities were the inevitable setting for large scale organizations: the public and private bureaucracies that were coming to dominate the modern world. And the large cities saw the largest growth in the "service" sector of the economy. The consumer culture of the late nineteenth century was almost entirely an urban phenomenon; only in the great cities did the bright lights shine. The unprecedented crowding of humanity in these cities, far from limiting their appeal, seemed to double it, drawing more and more people and industries.

In this context the middle-class suburb was at once the conquering outer edge of urban expansion and a kind of protest against that expansion. Suburbia expressed both the increasing concentration of people and resources in the inhumanely crowded, man-made world of the great cities and kept alive an alternative image of the relationship of man and nature. If suburbia was the bourgeois utopia, it existed in an inevitable tension with the bourgeois hell—the teeming world of the urban slum—from which suburbia could never wholly escape because the crowded city was the source of its prosperity.

If the classic suburb of the late nineteenth century was built ultimately on these general contradictions in bourgeois civilization, its actual form depended on a highly specific piece of industrial technology: the railroad. Although to the late twentieth century mind suburbia is inevitably associated with the automobile, this association is a mistake. The automobile, when it came, helped to destroy the basic conditions for classic suburbanization; the true suburban means of transportation has been the commuter rail line.

We tend to think of transportation and suburbanization in terms of access: a transportation system makes suburbanization possible by providing convenient access from the center to the periphery. Yet, in the history of suburbia, inaccessibility has usually been at least as important as accessibility. The relatively cheap land at the urban outskirts inevitably draws poor people and noisome industries unless that land is relatively hard to reach. This difficulty confines the bulk of people and factories to the core, while only the well-to-do have the time and resources to take the trouble to reach the outskirts.

Thus relatively inconvenient transportation facilities characterized suburbs until the late nineteenth century. Both London and Manchester suburbs made do with slow and expensive omnibus lines (or private carriages). Often new roads were resisted, as were attempts by the early railroad lines that ran through suburban areas to place their stations in such fashionable areas as Hampstead near London. Such accessibility, it was feared, would lower the tone of an area.

Only in the second half of the nineteenth century did developers and residents grasp the potential of rail lines for suburbanization. For the rail system—especially the steam railroad—combined to a unique degree accessibility and inaccessibility. It provided remarkably rapid access to the center, yet its relatively high cost insulated the bourgeois peripheries from lower-class invasion. The structure of the rail system in a late nineteenth century metropolis—or rail systems, because they soon included not only steam railroads but electric trolleys, streetcars, elevated lines, and subways—came to resemble a diagram of the class structure. Each income group was distributed along the system according to how far it could afford to travel from the center and which line it could afford to take.

The rail system limited accessibility in another important way. Development necessarily proceeded along the rail lines; in the usual rule of thumb, commuters could rarely live more than a fifteen minute walk from the rail station, so development was drawn into certain coherent nodes organized around the station. It inevitably created a kind of railroad village—a community with its own identity, limited in space, and surrounded by open countryside—and gave a unity of design even to railroad suburbs that had been developed piecemeal. . . . Finally, the rail system was almost always a radial one. Its many lines were organized as spokes from a hub, focusing the many suburban communities on a single "downtown" center.

"Suburbanites," wrote Agnes Repplier in the 1920s, "are traitors to the city." This statement is at best a half truth with regard to the railroad suburbs. Precisely because they excluded so much of the city in their quest to escape from it, they remained wholly dependent on it. Downtown was a daily destination for men and an almost equally frequent destination for women. There could be found not only the jobs that supported the suburban economy, but also those urban monuments of consumption: department stores, concert halls, clubs, restaurants, theaters, and cultural centers.

Suburbanization in the railroad era thus strengthened the city, especially the downtown area. Every suburban house meant greater demand for office space, stores, and other facilities patronized by the middle class. Indeed, the urban core was the only possible place for those central institutions like the department store or the teaching hospital, which drew their clientele from all the peripheral locations. This functional unity of city and suburb was more important than whether a particular suburb was located within or outside the boundaries of the central city. For a brief moment, the railroad tracks held city and suburb in precarious equilibrium. . . .

I have chosen the suburbs of Philadelphia to exemplify this era in the history of suburbia. Philadelphia not only has an urban heritage that goes back to the seventeenth century; it also became a major industrial power in the course of the nineteenth century. With the dynamism of the post–Civil

War American economy, Philadelphia became a textile center rivaling Manchester, a shipbuilding center rivaling the Clydeside shipyards of Glasgow, an iron and steel center rivaling Sheffield, and finally a center of such new industries as electrical goods and food processing. A major railroad terminus, home to both the Pennsylvania Railroad and the Baldwin Locomotive Works, Philadelphia was reshaped by the steam locomotive and the electric trolley. Middle-class suburbanization transformed the wealth created by the enterprises of the inner city into a bourgeois utopia at the outskirts.

Philadelphia began with a kind of suburban vision. When in 1683 William Penn laid out the checkerboard pattern of streets between the Delaware and Schuylkill rivers that still forms the basic pattern of the city, he envisioned Philadelphia as a "green country town." The citizens, he hoped, would spread their dwellings over the whole area of the city, leaving ample space for a city composed of detached dwellings interspersed with yards, fields, and orchards. . . .

Penn, however, was premature. Even in the vast spaces of the New World, the Old World notion of a city prevailed. People crowded close to the port on the Delaware, and Philadelphia evolved into a city based on the ubiquitous row house with substantial dwellings fronting on the major streets and alley dwellings for the poor crowded in behind. In this space intensive manner, the city advanced slowly as a solid mass from the Delaware to the Schuylkill, advancing from east to west much the way contemporaneous New York City building was advancing from south to north along Manhattan Island. Only in the 1840s did the city reach the "Center Square" that Penn had laid out as the midpoint of his decentralized city of the 1680s.

As early as the 1820s and 1830s the middle class showed some tendencies to separate work and residence, with workplaces remaining close to the older districts near the port and homes moving to the peripheries. Nevertheless, this movement could hardly be called suburban. The bourgeois residence remained a row house on a solid street of houses; most builders even retained the alleyways for the poor as part of their projects. The city maintained its separation from the countryside, advancing in stately rows toward the west. . . .

The 1840s . . . saw the beginnings of both rapid industrialization and—in the anti-Catholic riots—social conflict. Perhaps not coincidentally, the patrician elite was displaced from its mastery of the city's government during these years, which lessened its attachment to the old center. . . . By the mid nineteenth century the balance had shifted to genuine suburban development. For the expansion of Philadelphia was no longer the advance of a solid city into the countryside. It was genuinely suburban in that it sought by design to incorporate natural elements permanently into a domestic landscape. At first the models were all English, or at least English as filtered through the sensibility of Andrew Jackson Downing. Powelton Village, a suburban West Philadelphian settlement beloved by the Quaker elite, was identical to the London suburbs built by Evangelicals twenty-five years earlier.

These first suburbs were located at the old "gateways" of the city and were easily reached by horse drawn omnibus or tram. But the incessant growth of the city was forever threatening to overwhelm them. By the nineteenth century, Philadelphia was already a low density city based on individual row houses even for the working class. The Quaker sense of thrift had inspired the creation of building societies, which put the purchase of a modest row house within the grasp of most regularly employed workers. Their houses spread out rapidly from the factory districts just beyond the urban core.

The need to put some distance between bourgeois suburbia and the expanding industrial city inspired the shift to the railroad suburb. The early attempts to forge a rail connection between Philadelphia and the eastern Pennsylvania coal fields had by the 1840s led to several lines that ran north from the city through a hilly area called Germantown. Settled by German religious refugees in William Penn's time, Germantown was still a quiet agricultural village only five miles from Independence Hall. Its picturesque heights had already attracted a number of bourgeois villas; the railroad connections provided the spur that turned the area into a true suburb. . . .

Among the early residents of Germantown was Henry Howard Houston, a prominent executive with the Pennsylvania Railroad. In the late 1870s he conceived the idea of turning some 3,000 acres of hilly farmland just beyond the settled part of Germantown into an exclusive suburb. This land, eleven miles northwest of the commercial center of Philadelphia, was part of the village of Chestnut Hill which had been annexed by Philadelphia in 1854 but which in the 1870s still retained its near-rural quiet and isolation.

As a railroad executive, [Houston] grasped a basic point, which held true not only in the railroad era but also in the highway era that followed it: the ultimate purpose of suburban transportation lines is not to move people; it is to increase the value of the land through which it passes. The best suburban land developer must also be a rail developer, so he can direct his lines through land he already owns, and retain the bulk of the increased value for himself.

Houston did not own the Pennsylvania Railroad, but he was sufficiently influential to persuade the line to build a special branch line with stops along his property ending in the village of Chestnut Hill. Suddenly his land was within thirty minutes of the center of Philadelphia. It was also surrounded by land that remained relatively inconvenient, land that was unlikely to be developed rapidly and which thus remained as an agricultural buffer around his village.

The rail line, however, was not in itself sufficient. There were many lines leading out of Philadelphia, and more land available within commuting distance than there were prosperous families to purchase it. The next step was a street plan for his land in Chestnut Hill that would distinguish it from its rivals. . . .

Houston and [his architects, G. W. and W. D. Hewitt] had grasped the essentials: the balance of public and private land secured through large houses set well back on substantial landscaped plots ranging from one to three acres. More important than the design, moreover, were the institutions that Houston founded for Chestnut Hill or persuaded to locate there. First came a grand resort hotel, the Wissahickon Inn; then a country club, the Philadelphia Cricket Club; and finally an Episcopal church called St. Martin-in-the-Fields.

The hotel came first because it established immediately the social tone of the community. Its presence points to the close relation between the resort and the suburb in this period. In the 1880s a resort could still be located only eleven miles from the city center; it served as a summer retreat for those still living in townhouses in the urban core. As such it was a natural point of transition between urban living and a suburban residence near the hotel. . . .

The country club and the Episcopal church completed the trio of Chestnut Hill institutions founded by Houston. However their earthly purposes may have diverged, socially they stood for the same thing. Physically, the church, designed by the Hewitts in an English Gothic style, adjoined the neo-Georgian cricket club (which, in fact, soon devoted itself to tennis and golf). The membership of these two institutions defined exactly that bourgeois class which Houston was trying to attract.

The extravagantly English tone of both institutions was also significant. It was the sign of an American Protestant elite attempting to detach itself from a metropolis whose Catholic, Jewish, and fundamentalist Protestant populations were rapidly growing. It reveals, moreover, the odd anomaly between these ''traditions'' and real history. Philadelphia had been established and first settled by men and women who had attempted to escape the oppression of the Anglican church and the English establishment. Just as the Manchester manufacturers had seized upon the trappings of a hated aristocracy to justify their authority, so the Philadelphia gentlemen of the late nineteenth century revived the styles of their ancestors' oppressors in order to buttress their position in the industrial metropolis.

The distinguishing feature of Chestnut Hill and other classic suburbs, however, was not such community institutions as churches or country clubs but the landscape. The pattern of tree shaded streets, broad open lawns, substantial houses set back from the sidewalks was a pattern of prosperity, family life, and union with nature that represents the culmination of the suburban style.

This style is difficult to describe because it could be neither the creation of the original planners nor that of the individual householders. Nor could it be created immediately; it required decades of patience before the foliage and shrubbery could achieve its intended effect. It is, rather, a genuinely communal creation, a style created by the bourgeoisie for itself. The suburban landscape, not the individual house, is the true monument. . . .

The front lawn is not family space, and family members rarely venture out into it except to maintain it. It belongs, rather, to the community. The lawns, in conjunction with the roadside trees, create the illusion of a park. Their greenery transforms an urban street into a country lane. The lawn is the owner's principal contribution to the suburban landscape—the piece of the "park" he keeps up himself. At the same time the lawn is also private space, which no casual sidewalk passerby can make his own. It insulates the house while helping to create the green world of the landscape. Not surprisingly, lawn maintenance is considered a civic duty at least as important as any other form of morality. The lawn thus maintains that balance of the public and the private which is the essence of the mature suburban style. . . .

The culmination of the lawn culture was the country club, with its carefully tended golf course. It represents the suburban equivalent of the urban park, the railroad suburb's closest approach to genuine public space. Golf and suburbia have been intimately connected since the late nineteenth century. St. Andrew's, the first American golf club, was founded in 1889 in Yonkers, New York, and the institution spread to all the other bourgeois suburbs. . . .

Yet these institutions were of course *clubs,* institutionalized means to define the social boundaries of suburbia. The result is an apt symbol of "public space" in the railroad suburb. The most impressive spaces are the most strictly private; and "nature" itself (as controlled by the country club) becomes the instrument of social snobbery and of racial and religious prejudice. . . .

. . . The railroad suburb itself remained an increasingly defensive enclave. Even as the city expanded, its lavish use of space set it off from the working class and (more pertinently) from the aspiring members of the lower middle class. Surprisingly close to Germantown and Chestnut Hill were the spinning mills and other industries from which many of the most prosperous suburbanites derived their incomes. A subtle but deep division kept the factory workers' row houses from straying too close to the bourgeois utopia. This division did not correspond to any political boundary; it reflected instead the power of property, as reflected in the restrictive covenants that prohibited division of lots for smaller houses or their use for multifamily dwellings. The typical covenant set a minimum value for a house; prohibited any commercial or industrial use; and frequently barred Jews and blacks.

A different kind of segregation kept out the lower middle class. The steam railroads carried the bourgeoisie to their suburban retreats. The trolley lines of the 1890s and 1900s brought the rest of the middle class to different destinations. "Streetcar magnates" such as Peter A. B. Widener and William Elkins followed Henry Howard Houston's lead in joining transportation and real estate speculation. Their new lines carefully followed the map of their property holdings. On each new tract opened up to trolley commutation they built solid blocks of row houses, substantial structures with large back yards, all built essentially to the same plan. Land was too expensive to attempt to imitate the detached houses of bourgeois suburbia.

As the lower middle class pressed in from one direction, a new upper class moved out in the other. Encouraged by the success of the Chestnut Hill line, the Pennsylvania Railroad took the initiative in developing the quiet farm villages that lay ten to fifteen miles outside Philadelphia on its main line to Harrisburg and Pittsburgh. The beautiful countryside attracted the very rich, who built mansions on estates that covered hundreds of acres. The merely affluent soon followed, along with their country clubs and Episcopal churches.

In the industrial metropolis every social stratum thus grouped itself along the all important rail lines that organized the region. Yet, in spite of all the growth at the periphery, the center still held. Only the historic core, where all the rail lines converged, could offer a prime commercial location. So Wanamaker's Department Store expanded their already massive headquarters across from City Hall into a palazzo to dwarf any that Michelangelo ever saw; skyscrapers vied for space with new theaters and hotels; the downtown area attained its own kind of monumentality.

Similarly, the factory districts adjacent to the core gained what seemed to be an ever increasing advantage over their counterparts in small towns or the countryside. They had not only the best transportation facilities and the largest pool of skilled workers; they also had a virtual monopoly on flexibility and innovation. The multitude of firms closely packed together gave each one the crucial personal contacts that made it possible to profit from each tiny shift in rapidly changing markets. Innovation, too, seemed to be an urban monopoly, as the largest cities gained an advantage in the most advanced techniques.

The metropolis seemed to be an unbreakable growth machine, and the railroad suburb reflected this confidence and prosperity. Its solid houses were built to last, and they have lasted. The factories whose profits built these suburbs have closed or moved; the downtown area has entered a permanent crisis of rebuilding and renewal; the railroads themselves have long been bankrupt. Yet the classic railroad suburb remains a sought-after monument.

It has been suggested that monuments rarely exactly coincide with the high point of confidence of the class that built them. When confidence and power are unshakable, there is no need to build monuments. It is only when confidence begins to wane that people feel the need for the reassurance that a solid embodiment of their beliefs can bring. According to this argument, the cathedrals were less the outward sign of an unquestioned age of faith than a desperate attempt to hold onto faith when inner belief was slipping. The classic suburb is one such ambivalent symbol. Its appearance of solid confidence conceals a deep anxiety over the reality of its values. It stands for the prosperity of a bourgeois elite, yet that elite could not conceal from itself the fragility of the economic system that supported it. . . .

The tension closest to the surface was that between the implied confidence that suburbia represented the natural leadership of the city and the nation, and the fear that the city was now under the control of "alien" elements. This fear led to the portrayal of the city as a dumping ground of Europe's refuse, inferior people incapable of understanding the American values, which survived only in suburban isolation. Owen Wister, the patrician Philadelphian who wrote the cowboy story *The Virginian* to celebrate true Anglo-Saxon virtue against "Poles or Huns or Russian Jews," captured the hysterical tone of these fears when he wrote of America in 1891: "No rood of modern ground is more debased and mongrel with its hordes of encroaching alien vermin, that turn our cities into Babels and our citizenship into a hybrid farce, who degrade our commonwealth from a nation into something half-pawnshop, half broker's office.''

As Wister's references to pawnshops and broker's offices imply, the main target of this hysteria was usually the Jews. An anti-Semitism that ranged from the genteel to the vicious was endemic in these suburbs and still has its bastions even today. Yet the habit of mind that distinguished between the pure, American suburb and the ''debased and mongrel'' city has survived the particular targets of Wister's fears to enter into our national sub-conscious.

The classic suburb has thus left a dual legacy. It is first a monument to bourgeois civilization at its most prosperous and self-confident, an aesthetic achievement in both landscape and domestic architecture that commands respect; but it is also a testimony to bourgeois anxieties, to deeply buried fears that translate into a contempt or hatred for the ''others'' who inhabit the city. Both elements have left their mark on American culture in the twentieth century.

Building a Race Riot, 1919

WILLIAM M. TUTTLE, JR.

''The eighteenth birthday party given by Mrs. Richard B. Harrison in honor of her daughter,'' the *Chicago Defender* reported in the late autumn of 1918, was ''one of the social events of the season among the younger smart set. . . .'' Held at Ogden Grove pavilion, the party featured an orchestra and a grand march. A half-year later, however, in May 1919, there was sadness in the Harrison family, as the front porch of their house on Grand Boulevard lay smoking in ruins, its windows shattered, the victim of a bombing.

Best known for his role of ''de Lawd'' in *The Green Pastures* in the 1930's, Richard B. Harrison was a black actor whose forte in 1919 was Shakespeare and readings from the poetry of Paul Laurence Dunbar. During World War I he was frequently on the road entertaining, part of the time at Liberty Loan rallies, and as a result his family was alone in the new house he and his wife had purchased. Mrs. Harrison heard rumors shortly after moving to Grand Boulevard in March that the ''colored lady's house would be bombed.'' Warned by a black janitor that there was a plot to destroy her home, Mrs. Harrison telephoned the police, who casually rebuffed her and characterized her fears as ''idle talk.'' The following evening, a Saturday, the bomber struck. At 11 o'clock, a Yellow Cab pulled up to the curb in front of the Harrison house, the door sprang open, and a man jumped out and ran to the front porch. There he deposited a package before dashing back to the taxicab. An explosion rocked the house just minutes after the taxicab sped away. Anger swept the black community. ''This recent explosion could have been easily prevented by the police,'' exclaimed the *Defender*. But not only

Excerpted with the permission of Atheneum Publishers, an imprint of Macmillan Publishing Company from *Race Riot* by William M. Tuttle, Jr., pp. 156–69, 171–76, 178–83. Copyright © 1970 by William M. Tuttle, Jr.

did the police seem to be uninterested in protecting the property of blacks; they appeared to the newspaper to have been "giving aid and comfort to a certain element of violators of the law." The police belatedly detailed a squad to protect the family, but the very next night the bombers lobbed explosives from a vacant flat next door onto the roof of the Harrison house. The skylight was destroyed and more windows were shattered. Someone had unlocked the flat to admit the bombers and had locked it afterward, but the police did not question the occupants of the adjacent building or those leaving it after the explosion. "Neighbors Planned Bombing," charged the *Defender*. "The people in the block appeared to have information as to the exact time the explosion would occur."

Nor was this the end of the story. The Harrisons had bought the property from a white realtor, William B. Austin, a man who apparently was sympathetic to giving blacks and whites equal access to adequate housing. Anonymous letters began to arrive in Austin's mail after the two bombings, assuring him that police guards would be useless and promising that the bombing campaign had only commenced. The Harrisons moved from Grand Boulevard in mid-June 1919, just a couple weeks after "a man on a bicycle" had ridden by Austin's Lake Shore Drive home and hurled a bomb at it on the way past.

The Harrison and Austin bombings were not isolated occurrences. From July 1917 to the eruption of the Chicago race riot in late July 1919, no fewer than twenty-six bombs were exploded at isolated black residences in once all-white neighborhoods and at the offices of certain realtors who had sold to blacks. Over half of these bombs were exploded during the tense six months leading up to the riot. According to the virulent denunciations by the black press of both the bombers and the police who failed to apprehend them, the single most important cause of the riot was housing. Out of the interracial conflict over housing there arose in the black community a marked lack of faith in the willingness and ability of the police to provide impartial protection. This sentiment, in some cases based on actualities and in others unfounded, led blacks to depend more and more on their own resources for protection. Furthermore, participation in the war, a recently realized and potent political voice in Chicago's affairs, and the self-respect of a courted wage earner had kindled a "New Negro" attitude. The "New Negro" was resolved to defend his family and home with militance.

The housing crisis also stimulated the formation of property owners' associations avowedly hostile to blacks. The threats of these organizations and the bombings accentuated the blacks' racial solidarity, thus retarding even further the possibility of interracial accord through mutual interchange.

It is ironic, in light of the strident contention of numerous white property owners that blacks were alien to Chicago's institutions, that the city's first resident was apparently Jean Baptiste Point du Saible, a San Dominican Negro who built a trading post at the mouth of the Chicago River in 1779 and lived there for sixteen years. Despite this beginning, only a few blacks trickled into Chicago before the Civil War, largely because of laws excluding blacks, slave and free, from the state. From 1860 to 1870, however, Chicago's black population rose 285 per cent, although nationwide the race's increase was 9.9 per cent. Most of the new arrivals obtained domestic employment; and, although there was no one black settlement, concentrations of black servants evolved in vicinities near their wealthy white employers. After the Great Fire of 1871, a second fire in 1874, and the dispersal of blacks as well as whites to the undamaged areas, the concentration of blacks and their social institutions on the South Side took vague shape. Chicago was expanding with such rapidity after 1870 that the black influx, though large, little more than kept pace with the flood of white immigrants. New residential districts emerged, but, as these were often segregated, the black arrivals gravitated to their increasingly dense settlements, especially the major concentration on the South Side. Although at the turn of the century blacks' residences were scattered throughout the city, a black man studying in Chicago reported that "no large Northern city shows a greater degree of segregation."

As evidenced by several incidents in the 1890's and the first few years of the twentieth century, the most effective enforcer of residential segregation in Chicago was organized white resistance. In 1897, for example, Woodlawn property owners met and "declared war" against the small colony of blacks living in the neighborhood. Owners who rented to blacks were angrily denounced as "enemies" who "should be tarred and feathered." Intimidated by threats of violence, blacks often chose to move. Five years later, whites in Woodlawn succeeded in having construction terminated on an apartment house that was being remodeled for black occupancy. Celia Parker Woolley, the founder of a black settlement house, noted at this time that she could not obtain property for the venture. Realtors "were not averse to Negroes living on the premises if they were servants," she reported, "but so soon as they heard that the Negroes were to be considered on a par with white people they refused to lease the property."

By 1906, well over one half of Chicago's black people lived in the South Side black belt, between 12th and 57th Streets, and Wentworth and Cottage Grove Avenues. And while blacks, as one of their leaders wrote in 1905, did "not occupy all the worst streets and live in all the unsanitary houses in Chicago, what is known as the 'Black Belt' is altogether forbidding and demoralizing.". . . "In no other part" of the city, wrote S. P. Breckenridge of the University of Chicago, "was there found a neighborhood so conspicuously dilapidated as the black belt on the South Side. No other group," she added, "suffered so much from decaying buildings, leaking roofs, doors without hinges, broken windows, insanitary plumbing, rotting floors, and a general lack of repairs." This was the deplorable state of black housing in 1912, several years before the migration more than doubled the city's black population. . . .

Numerous blacks naturally wanted to escape these surroundings. The black belt was dilapidated, decaying, and overcrowded, and its landlords were obdurate in their refusal to make needed repairs. It was also a breeder of disease and the city's officially sanctioned receptacle for vice. Chicago's medical authorities boasted of the city's low death rate, pointing to statistics which indicated that it was the lowest of any city in the world with a population of over one million. Their statistics told another story as well, however, and it was that Chicago's blacks had a death rate which was twice that of whites. The stillbirth rate was also twice as high; the death rate from tuberculosis and syphilis was six times as high; and from pneumonia and nephritis it was well over three times as high. The death rate for the entire city was indeed commendable, but the statistics indicated that the death rate for Chicago's blacks was comparable to that of Bombay, India. . . .

The directions in which the black belt could expand were few; it was in "the zone of transition—the interstitial region between residence and industry." To the north were many of the city's light factories and businesses. Although the district was rundown, prices were far beyond the reach of the ordinary househunter because of the industrial potential of the property. To the west, across Wentworth Avenue, were the Irish, whose hostility excluded blacks from that market. This hostility was so intense that the population in one Irish-dominated neighborhood bordering on Wentworth would tolerate only twenty-nine blacks out of 3,762 residents, while in the neighborhood just on the other side of Wentworth, 1,722 out of 3,711 residents were black. To the east the blacks could move into the limited area between Wabash Avenue and Lake Michigan. But as soon as they occupied this, the only direction for sizable expansion was southward—to the neighborhood of Hyde Park and Kenwood.

Being immediately adjacent to the black belt, Hyde Park was the inevitable destination of numerous blacks. Also important, Hyde Park was a deteriorating neighborhood, one whose homes blacks could afford. Of the over 900 black property owners there in 1920, scarcely ten could have purchased their properties at the original prices. For twenty to thirty years property values had declined because of the odors of the stockyards, the smoke and soot of the Illinois Central trains, the conversion of large homes into apartment buildings and flats, and the fear of an "invasion" of blacks from nearby areas. The residents of Hyde Park had moved away from the neighborhood to escape further depreciation, and in 1916, just as the migration from the South was gaining momentum, an estimated 25 per cent of the buildings in the district stood vacant. The earlier black inhabitants and the few migrants who brought money with them or united with others to purchase properties at the prevailing low prices streamed into Hyde Park to join the few blacks who had moved in earlier, almost unnoticed. Other blacks rented in the neighborhood. This process of expansion continued for nearly two years.

During the war residential construction largely ceased in Chicago as elsewhere. In the early months of 1918 the first effects of a housing shortage, which was soon to be acute, were felt. The demands of whites for dwellings began to exceed the supply. Ugly interracial competition for homes broke out, as enterprising realtors touched off artificial panics with rumors that the blacks were "invading," and then proceeded to buy the properties of whites at less than their values and to sell to blacks at sizable profits. Many whites soon blamed blacks for the perplexities of property values, the scarcity of housing, and urban decay.

Although blacks seemed to blight the neighborhoods they inhabited, these neighborhoods were generally run-down before their arrival. It was natural, moreover, that black tenants should exhibit a lack of respect for properties upon which their landlords bestowed few improvements, actually allowing them to deteriorate further. In addition, because of excessive rents and exclusion from adjoining vicinities, blacks overcrowded both their abodes and their districts. . . .

Several white property owners' associations, most of which had organized initially for responsible community projects and beautification, now focused their efforts on forcing out the blacks already residing in their neighborhoods and on insuring that no others entered. The activities of these associations were conspicuous in the contested districts lying between 39th and 59th Streets, and State Street and Lake Michigan, and they consisted both of mass meetings to arouse the neighborhood residents against the blacks and of the publication in white journals of scathing denunciations of the race. . . .

Two obstacles blocked the possibility of legislatively quarantining the blacks. In order for the Chicago City Council to enact zoning legislation, racial or otherwise, it first had to obtain an enabling act from the Illinois General Assembly, which was dominated by representatives from southern Illinois whose antagonism for Chicago was renowned. The second roadblock was a decision which the United States Supreme Court delivered in 1917. In *Buchanan* v. *Warley,* the court invalidated a Louisville, Kentucky, racial zoning ordinance. As a direct result of this ruling, restrictive covenants came into being, but these efficacious instruments of segregation did not gain currency in Chicago until the mid-1920's. Lacking the voluntary or legal means to isolate the blacks, whites resorted to extralegal or illegal methods—intimidation and bombs.

In November 1917, just days after the Supreme Court handed down the *Buchanan* v. *Warley* decision, the Chicago Real Estate Board reaffirmed the need of founding property owners' associations. The Board resolved to "start a propaganda through its individual members to recommend owners' societies in every white block for the purpose of mutual defense." Of these organizations, the Hyde Park–Kenwood Property Owners' Association, which first gained notice in the fall of 1918 for its agitation to "make Hyde Park white," was perhaps the largest and undoubtedly the most vocal. "WE want you to join our organization," began the organization's letter of solicitation. "Hyde Park is the finest residential district in Chicago," and in spite of "the weak-kneed [who] think it is too late . . . WE are going to keep it that way." Joining this "red-blooded organization," the letter continued, would put "big money in your pocket besides preserving our homes for ourselves and children.". . .

As a solution to the black "invasion," bombing might have been viewed as a last resort, but it was attempted early. The first of the bombs arrived in July 1917, when one crashed into the vestibule of the home of Mrs. S. P. Motley near 53rd Street on the South Side. Mrs. Motley and her family had moved into the house in 1913, the first black family on the block, and they had lived there for four years before violence struck. She had purchased the property from a Mrs. Hughes, who, blacks charged, was a "nigger hater" and "an ardent supporter" of the Hyde Park–Kenwood Association. What seemed particularly to rankle Mrs. Hughes, in addition to her hatred of blacks, was that a white agent had negotiated the transaction for Mrs. Motley, and she had not discovered that blacks had been the buyers until the Motleys moved in. When several other black families joined the Motleys on the block in 1917, the white neighbors denounced Mrs. Motley for enticing them there and for operating a rooming house. Fortunately, the bomb claimed no victims, but a family residing in a first-floor flat barely escaped injury when the bomb was detonated, showering plaster, blowing out part of the parlor wall, and demolishing the vestibule and porch.

After an eight-month hiatus, during which the black expansion continued, the bombers returned in earnest. From March 1918 to the outbreak of the riot, twenty-five bombs rocked the homes of blacks and the homes and offices of realtors of both races. Of the eleven bombings in 1918, four were of properties merely held by black real estate agents, while the other seven were of black-inhabited dwellings. Moreover, mobs brandishing brickbats and other weapons and missiles stoned buildings, and intimidation and threats of further violence burgeoned as well. "Look out; you're next for hell," read a "black hand notice." Another was addressed to the black tenants on Vincennes Avenue: "We are going to BLOW these FLATS TO HELL and if you don't want to go with them you had better move at once.". . .

Whether or not the realtors of the Hyde Park–Kenwood Association conspired to bomb out the blacks, two facts were evident: that the bombings usually occurred shortly after the speakers at the association's meetings had denounced the blacks in vitriolic language (four bombs succeeded the organization's May 5 meeting); and that these denunciations were becoming decidedly more vitriolic in the summer of 1919.

"PREVENT FURTHER INCURSION BY UNDESIRABLES," proclaimed a poster announcing the June 6 meeting of the Hyde Park–Kenwood Association. No doubt the association would have been shocked to discover that blacks, among them the white-skinned, blue-eyed Walter F. White of the NAACP, had infiltrated the meetings, and that White would attend on June 6. White's descriptions of the meeting's "inflammatory and incendiary remarks" were corroborated by Mrs. Meta Harvey, a black who attended the June 20 and 27 gatherings. When she entered the June 20 meeting, which was convened at a bank, she heard the speaker outlining a plan for removing a black hospital from the South Side within the next two months. A voice from the floor interrupted to demand action, not talk; and there were other references to the need for "pep" in forcing the hospital's removal within thirty rather than sixty days. Mayor William H. Thompson and the city's health commissioner were castigated for "their favorable attitude" toward blacks and for "assenting to the location of the hospital where it was." Some voices urged caution, but their advice was ignored. Blacks had armed, said one man; they had bought 800 rifles and buckets full of ammunition at a local department store; there would be bloodshed "if they went at the matter the way they were talking about."

"Bloodshed, nothing!" another man shouted in anger. "Let them step on my corns and I'll show them what I'll do." "If we can't get them out any other way," agreed a voice in the rear, "we are going to put them in with the bolsheviki and bomb them out." Throughout the evening, speakers referred to blacks as "niggers" and "undesirables." One speaker told what he had done to three blacks "hanging around his place." He had put a "bolt" in his fist and knocked one down; "that's the way to treat the niggers," he added. The association's officers, practically all of whom were local realtors and officials of the Chicago Real Estate Board, reported that any real estate agent who did not refuse to rent or sell to blacks would be blacklisted; that block captains had been selected to report any attempts by blacks to move into the district; and, finally, that three hotels in the neighborhood had agreed to cooperate in a plan whereby black employees who did not consent to vacate their residences in the district would be discharged. With these announcements, the meeting was adjourned.

And, in turn, blacks advocated arming themselves in the summer of 1919. The police's flagrant negligence and misperformance of duty had convinced them that they would have to provide their own protection against the property owners' associations and the bombers. Even when blacks reported bomb threats, and the police staked out the dwellings beforehand, no arrests were made after the outrages occurred. A delegation twice attempted to file a complaint with Mayor Thompson in June 1919, but the mayor's secretary refused to permit the blacks to see him. The *Defender* expressed the consensus of the black community when it protested: "Police activity has been so deliberate and brazenly neglectful that one might construe that they are working in harmony with the bomb throwers." The following week the *Defender* offered the only practicable solution it saw to such one-sided law enforcement when it asked: "Why do these things go on unchecked and the perpetrators not apprehended? . . . Something must be done, and something will be done. If we must protect ourselves we shall do it with a vengeance. . . . This is nature's first law.". . .

ꙮ *F U R T H E R   R E A D I N G*

Gunther Barth, *City People* (1980)
Charles W. Cheape, *Moving the Masses* (1980)
Michael H. Ebner and Eugene M. Tobin, eds., *The Age of Urban Reform* (1977)
Robert Fishman, *Bourgeois Utopias: The Rise and Fall of Suburbia* (1987)
Kenneth T. Jackson, *Crabgrass Frontier: The Suburbanization of the United States* (1985)
Maury Klein and Harvey A. Kantor, *Prisoners of Progress: American Industrial Cities, 1850–1920* (1976)
Margaret Marsh, "Suburban Men and Masculine Domesticity, 1870–1915," *American Quarterly* 40 (June 1988), 165–86

Zane Miller, *Boss Cox's Cincinnati* (1968)

Raymond A. Mohl, *The New City: Urban America in the Industrial Age, 1860–1920* (1985)

Gilbert Osofsky, *Harlem* (1971)

Harold L. Platt, *The Electric City: Energy and the Growth of the Chicago Area* (1991)

Jon C. Teaford, *The Unheralded Triumph: City Government in America, 1870–1900* (1984)

Sam Bass Warner, Jr., *Streetcar Suburbs* (1974)

Gwendolyn Wright, *Building the Dream: A Social History of Housing in America* (1981)

CHAPTER
6

Power in the Gilded Age:
Political Parties and
Social Movements

Of all the elements of late-nineteenth-century America, perhaps the most colorfully notorious has been the political order. How did the nation's public institutions respond to the era's cascade of new wealth, explosive growth, and unprecedented challenges? Not too well, most twentieth-century analysts have concluded. In fact, national politics was undergoing a wrenching, and fascinating, period of transition in the 1880s and 1890s from the popular, if ritualistic, politics of the past toward the more bureaucratic, organizational models of the future. As organized through the two major parties, electoral turnout reached a record 77 percent, an astonishing level by today's standards. But to latter-day eyes, the fierce partisanship of the major political contests, often playing on older ethnogeographic divisions among the populace, appeared to ignore the country's substantive social changes.

Beneath the surface of electoral results, however, one sees a host of new issues and political constituencies invading the traditional political turf. Especially evident in politicized groups of workers and farmers and among women's rights and temperance advocates, these issue-oriented social movements pressed hard against the old parties with new demands and even alternative electoral formations. The high point of insurgency came in the formation of the People's party in 1892. This Populist challenge, centered on an alliance of ailing southern cotton growers and western wheat farmers, crested in the presidential election of 1896 with the crushing defeat of the fusion Populist-Democratic ticket led by William Jennings Bryan. Yet if the frontal assault on the status quo was turned back, the restructuring issues raised in the Gilded Age would return with renewed vigor in the Progressive Era.

175

❧ *D O C U M E N T S*

The following selections offer a good sampling of the Gilded Age political furor. Partisan political culture is reflected in the first selection, featuring three cartoons. In the first, from *Harper's Weekly,* Thomas Nast attacks the Democrats as the party of Tammany Hall and the Confederacy; in the second cartoon, amateur caricaturist Watson Heston targets parties and their corporate patrons for the proto-populist (pro–Union Labor party) *American Non-Conformist and Kansas Industrial Liberator* in 1888; and the third cartoon, from the brilliantly satirical *Puck,* conservative Democratic in its politics and a defender of the gold standard, takes aim at William Jennings Bryan and the "popocrats" in 1896.

The passions—and eloquence—of the period never ran higher than in the critical presidential election of 1896. The second selection, Bryan's "Cross of Gold" address, the most famous speech of perhaps the nation's greatest orator of all time, was delivered in support of a free-silver plank in the party platform at the Democratic national convention in Chicago on July 9, 1896. The third document, excerpted from the last political address of the celebrated Republican orator and free-thinker Robert G. Ingersoll, attacked Bryan. It was delivered before tens of thousands of listeners in Chicago and New York City in October 1896. Swayed by Ingersoll's combination of gushing sentimentality and piercing sarcasm, the crowd, according to one witness, "cheered till they seemed hypnotized by their own voices."

The building blocks of politicized social movements are exemplified in the concluding documents. These include the People's party platform, adopted at Omaha, Nebraska, in 1892; two appeals on behalf of women's rights—the first from suffrage matriarch Elizabeth Cady Stanton, delivered before a Senate committee in 1892, and the second a letter from a black Virginia activist in 1880; and two prohibitionist poems from 1910. In each case, specific political demands are tinged with passionate regard for the larger morality of the nation's public life. As manifested in this group of documents, what are the main conflicts among contemporary political contestants? What qualities connect, or disconnect, their political culture to or from our own?

William Jennings Bryan Scorns Advocates of the Gold Standard: The "Cross of Gold" Speech, 1896

And now, my friends, let me come to the paramount issue. If they ask us why it is that we say more on the money question than we say upon the tariff question, I reply that, if protection has slain its thousands, the gold standard has slain its tens of thousands. If they ask us why we do not employ in our platform all the things that we believe in, we reply that when we have restored the money of the Constitution all other necessary reforms will be possible; but that until this is done there is no other reform that can be accomplished.

Why is it that within three months such a change has come over the country? Three months ago, when it was confidently asserted that those who believe in the gold standard would frame our platform and nominate our candidates, even the advocates of the gold standard did not think that we could elect a president. And they had good reason for their doubt, because there is scarcely a State here today asking for the gold standard which is not in

Three Cartoonists Interpret the Political Scene, 1880, 1888, 1896

Thomas Nast Attacks the Democrats, 1880

AS SOLID AND DEFIANT AS EVER.

In this vintage example of "waving the bloody shirt," German-born staunch Republican cartoonist Thomas Nast invokes powerful symbols of good and evil to elevate the significance of late-nineteenth-century partisanship. With what counter-imagery might the Democrats have responded?

Watson Heston Lampoons Parties and Their Corporate Patrons, 1888

How the Voting Cattle Obey the Will of the "Powers that Be."--(*Will show the "Powers That Be" in our Next.*)

Heston's critique of the two-party system reflected a common viewpoint among the economically and politically disaffected in the late 1880s and early 1890s. Who might be so alienated and why? What options did they have?

the absolute control of the Republican party. But note the change. Mr. McKinley was nominated at St. Louis upon a platform which declared for the maintenance of the gold standard until it can be changed into bimetallism by international agreement. Mr. McKinley was the most popular man among the Republicans, and three months ago everybody in the Republican party prophesied his election. How is [it] today? Why, the man who was once pleased to think that he looked like Napoleon—that man shudders today when he remembers that he was nominated on the anniversary of the battle of Waterloo. Not only that, but as he listens he can hear with ever-increasing distinctness the sound of the waves as they beat upon the lonely shores of St. Helena.

Why this change? Ah, my friends, is not the reason for the change evident to any one who will look at the matter? No private character, however pure, no personal popularity, however great, can protect from the avenging wrath of an indignant people a man who will declare that he is in favor of fastening the gold standard upon this country, or who is willing to surrender the right of self-government and place the legislative control of our affairs in the hands of foreign potentates and powers. . . .

Puck *Assails William Jennings Bryan and the "Popocrats," 1896*

IN BATTLE ARRAY,—AND THERE'S NOT MUCH DOUBT ABOUT THE RESULT.

To the nation's political establishment, the Populist coalition gathered around Bryan in 1896 represented an unholy conspiracy to undermine the foundations of domestic peace and security. Judging from the symbols invoked by the cartoonist, what was so threatening?

Mr. Carlisle said in 1878 that this was a struggle between "the idle holders of idle capital" and "the struggling masses, who produce the wealth and pay the taxes of the country;" and, my friends, the question we are to decide is: Upon which side will the Democratic party fight; upon the side of "the idle holders of idle capital" or upon the side of "the struggling masses?" That is the question which the party must answer first, and then it must be answered by each individual hereafter. The sympathies of the Democratic party, as shown by the platform, are on the side of the struggling masses who have ever been the foundation of the Democratic party. There are two ideas of government. There are those who believe that, if you will only legislate to make the well-to-do prosperous, their prosperity will leak through on those below. The Democratic idea, however, has been that if you legislate to make the masses prosperous, their prosperity will find its way up through every class which rests upon them.

You come to us and tell us that the great cities are in favor of the gold standard; we reply that the great cities rest upon our broad and fertile prairies. Burn down your cities and leave our farms, and your cities will spring up again as if by magic; but destroy our farms and the grass will grow in the streets of every city in the country.

My friends, we declare that this nation is able to legislate for its own people on every question, without waiting for the aid or consent of any other nation on earth; and upon that issue we expect to carry every State in the Union. I shall not slander the inhabitants of the fair State of Massachusetts nor the inhabitants of the State of New York by saying that, when they are confronted with the proposition, they will declare that this nation is not able to attend to its own business. It is the issue of 1776 over again. Our ancestors, when but three millions in number, had the courage to declare their political independence of every other nation; shall we, their descendants, when we have grown to seventy milions, declare that we are less independent than our forefathers? No, my friends, that will never be the verdict of our people. Therefore, we care not upon what lines the battle is fought. If they say bimetallism is good, but that we cannot have it until other nations help us, we reply that, instead of having a gold standard because England has, we will restore bimetallism, and then let England have bimetallism because the United States has it. If they dare to come out in the open field and defend the gold standard as a good thing, we will fight them to the uttermost. Having behind us the producing masses of this nation and the world, supported by the commercial interests, the laboring interests, and the toilers everywhere, we will answer their demand for a gold standard by saying to them: You shall not press down upon the brow of labor this crown of thorns, you shall not crucify mankind upon a cross of gold.

Robert G. Ingersoll Waves the Bloody Shirt, 1896

The gentleman now running for the presidency—a tireless talker—oh, if he had a brain equal to his vocal chords, what a man! And yet when I read his speeches it seems to me as though he stood on his head and thought with his feet. This man is endeavoring to excite class against class, to excite the poor against the rich. Let me tell you something. We have no classes in the United States. There are no permanent classes here. The millionaire may be a mendicant, the mendicant may be a millionaire. The man now working for the millionaire may employ that millionaire's sons to work for him. There is a chance for us all. Sometimes a numskull is born in the mansion, and a genius rises from the gutter. Old Mother Nature has a queer way of taking care of her children. You cannot tell. You cannot tell. Here we have a free open field of competition, and if a man passes me in the race I say: "Good luck. Get ahead of me if you can, you are welcome.". . .

And why should we hate the successful? Why? We cannot all be first. The race is a vast procession; a great many hundred milions are back of the center, and in front there is only one human being; that is all. Shall we wait for the other fellows to catch up? Shall the procession stop? I say, help the fallen, assist the weak, help the poor, bind up the wounds, but do not stop the procession.

Why should we envy the successful? Why should we hate them? And why should we array class against class? It is all wrong. For instance, here is a young man, and he is industrious. He is in love with a girl around the corner.

She is in his brain all day—in his heart all night, and while he is working he is thinking. He gets a little ahead, they get married. He is an honest man, he gets credit, and the first thing you know he has a good business of his own and he gets rich; educates his children, and his old age is filled with content and love. Good! His companions bask in the sunshine of idleness. They have wasted their time, wasted their wages in dissipation, and when the winter of life comes, when the snow falls on the barren fields of the wasted days, then shivering with cold, pinched with hunger, they curse the man who has succeeded. Thereupon they all vote for Bryan. . . .

Now, the next question is, or the next thing is, you have to choose between men. Shall Mr. Bryan be the next President or shall McKinley occupy that chair? Who is Mr. Bryan? He is not a tried man. If he had the capacity to reason, if he had logic, if he could spread the wings of imagination, if there were in his heart the divine flower called pity, he might be an orator, but lacking all these, he is as he is.

When Major McKinley was fighting under the flag, Bryan was in his mother's arms, and judging from his speeches he ought to be there still. What is he? He is a Populist. He voted for General Weaver. Only a little while ago he denied being a Democrat. His mind is filled with vagaries. A fiat money man. His brain is an insane asylum without a keeper.

Imagine that man President. Whom would he call about him? Upon whom would he rely? Probably for Secretary of State he would choose Ignatius Donnelly of Minnesota; for Secretary of the Interior, Henry George; for Secretary of War, Tillman with his pitchforks; for Postmaster-General, Peffer of Kansas. Once somebody said: "If you believe in fiat money, why don't you believe in fiat hay, and you can make enough hay out of Peffer's whiskers to feed all the cattle in the country." For Secretary of the Treasury, Coin Harvey. For Secretary of the Navy, Coxey, and then he could keep off the grass. And then would come the millennium. The great cryptogram and the Bacon cipher; the single tax, State saloons, fiat money, free silver, destruction of banks and credit, bondholders and creditors mobbed, courts closed, debts repudiated and the rest of the folks made rich by law. . . .

Then you have to make another choice. You have to choose between parties, between the new Democratic and the old Republican. And I want to tell you the new Democratic is worse than the old, and that is a good deal for me to say. In 1861 hundreds and hundreds of thousands of Democrats thought more of country than of party. Hundreds and hundreds of thousands shouldered their muskets, rushed to the rescue of the Republic, and sustained the administration of Abraham Lincoln. With their help the Rebellion was crushed, and now hundreds and hundreds of thousands of Democrats will hold country above party and will join with the Republicans in saving the honor, the reputation, of the United States; and I want to say to all the National Democrats who feel that they cannot vote for Bryan, I want to say to you, vote for McKinley. This is no war for blank cartridges. Your gun makes as much noise, but it does not do as much execution. . . .

. . . The new Democratic party, with its allies, the Populists and Socialists and Free Silverites, represents the follies, the mistakes, and the absurdities of a thousand years. They are in favor of everything that cannot be done. Whatever is, is wrong. They think creditors are swindlers, and debtors who refuse to pay their debts are honest men. Good money is bad and poor money is good. A promise is better than a performance. They desire to abolish facts, punish success, and reward failure. They are worse than the old. And yet I want to be honest. I am like the old Dutchman who made a speech in Arkansas. He said: "Ladies and Gentlemen, I must tell you the truth. There are good and bad in all parties except the Democratic party, and in the Democratic party there are bad and worse." The new Democratic party, a party that believes in repudiation, a party that would put the stain of dishonesty on every American brow and that would make this Government subject to the mob. . . .

I had an old friend down in Woodford County, Charley Mulidore. He won a coffin on Lincoln's election. He took it home and every birthday he called in his friends. They had a little game of "sixty-six" on the coffin lid. When the game was over they opened the coffin and took out the things to eat and drink and had a festival, and the minister in the little town, hearing of it, was scandalized, and he went to Charley Mulidore and he said: "Mr. Mulidore, how can you make light of such awful things?" "What things?" "Why," he said, "Mr. Mulidore, what did you do with that coffin? In a little while you die, and then you come to the day of judgment." "Well, Mr. Preacher, when I come to that day of judgment they will say, 'What is your name?' I will tell them, 'Charley Mulidore.' And they will say, 'Mr. Mulidore, are you a Christian?' 'No, sir, I was a Republican, and the coffin I got out of this morning I won on Abraham Lincoln's election.' And then they will say, 'Walk in, Mr. Mulidore, walk in, walk in; here is your halo and there is your harp.' ". . .

Populist Principles: The Omaha Platform, 1892

Assembled upon the 116th anniversary of the Declaration of Independence, the People's Party of America, in their first national convention, invoking upon their action the blessing of Almighty God, puts forth, in the name and on behalf of the people of this country, the following preamble and declaration of principles:—

The conditions which surround us best justify our cooperation: we meet in the midst of a nation brought to the verge of moral, political, and material ruin. Corruption dominates the ballot-box, the legislatures, the Congress, and touches even the ermine of the bench. The people are demoralized; most of the States have been compelled to isolate the voters at the polling-places to prevent universal intimidation or bribery. The newspapers are largely subsidized or muzzled; public opinion silenced; business prostrated; our homes covered with mortgages; labor impoverished; and the land concentrating in the hands of the capitalists. The urban workmen are denied the right of organization for self-protection; imported pauperized labor beats down their wages; a hireling standing army, unrecognized by our laws, is established to shoot them down, and they are rapidly degenerating into European conditions. The fruits of the toil of millions are boldly stolen to build up colossal fortunes for a few, unprecedented in the history of mankind; and the possessors of these, in turn, despise the republic and endanger liberty. From the same prolific womb of governmental injustice we breed the two great classes—tramps and millionaires.

The national power to create money is appropriated to enrich bondholders; a vast public debt, payable in legal tender currency, has been funded into gold-bearing bonds, thereby adding millions to the burdens of the people. Silver, which has been accepted as coin since the dawn of history, has been demonetized to add to the purchasing power of gold by decreasing the value of all forms of property as well as human labor; and the supply of currency is purposely abridged to fatten usurers, bankrupt enterprise, and enslave industry. A vast conspiracy against mankind has been organized on two continents, and it is rapidly taking possession of the world. If not met and overthrown at once, it forebodes terrible social convulsions, the destruction of civilization, or the establishment of an absolute despotism.

We have witnessed for more than a quarter of a century the struggles of the two great political parties for power and plunder, while grievous wrongs have been inflicted upon the suffering people. We charge that the controlling influences dominating both these parties have permitted the existing dreadful conditions to develop without serious effort to prevent or restrain them. Neither do they now promise us any substantial reform. They have agreed together to ignore in the coming campaign every issue but one. They propose to drown the outcries of a plundered people with the uproar of a sham battle over the tariff, so that capitalists, corporations, national banks, rings, trusts, watered stock, the demonetization of silver, and the oppressions of the usurers may all be lost sight of. They propose to sacrifice our homes, lives and children on the altar of mammon; to destroy the multitude in order to secure corruption funds from the millionaires.

Assembled on the anniversary of the birthday of the nation, and filled with the spirit of the grand general and chieftain who established our independence, we seek to restore the government of the Republic to the hands of "the plain people," with whose class it originated. We assert our purposes to be identical with the purposes of the National Constitution, "to form a more perfect union and establish justice, insure domestic tranquillity, provide for the common defence, promote the general welfare, and secure the blessings of liberty for ourselves and our posterity." We declare that this republic can only endure as a free government while built upon the love of the whole people for each other and for the nation; that it cannot be pinned together by bayonets; that the civil war is over, and that every passion and resentment which grew out of it must die with it; and that we must be in fact, as we are in name, one united brotherhood of freemen.

Our country finds itself confronted by conditions for which there is no precedent in the history of the world; our annual agricultural productions amount to billions of dollars in value, which must, within a few weeks or months, be exchanged for billions of dollars of commodities consumed in their production; the existing currency supply is wholly inadequate to make this exchange; the results are falling prices, the formation of combines and rings, the impoverishment of the producing class. We pledge ourselves, if given power, we will labor to correct these evils by wise and reasonable legislation, in accordance with the terms of our platform. We believe that the powers of government—in other words, of the people—should be expanded (as in the case of the postal service) as rapidly and as far as the good sense of an intelligent people and the teachings of experience shall justify, to the end that oppression, injustice, and poverty shall eventually cease in the land.

While our sympathies as a party of reform are naturally upon the side of every proposition which will tend to make men intelligent, virtuous, and temperate, we nevertheless regard these questions—important as they are—as secondary to the great issues now pressing for solution, and upon which not only our individual prosperity but the very existence of free institutions depends; and we ask all men to first help us to determine whether we are to have a republic to administer before we differ as to the conditions upon which it is to be administered; believing that the forces of reform this day organized will never cease to move forward until every wrong is remedied, and equal rights and equal privileges securely established for all the men and women of this country.

We declare, therefore,—

First. That the union of the labor forces of the United States this day consummated shall be permanent and perpetual; may its spirit enter all hearts for the salvation of the republic and the uplifting of mankind!

Second. Wealth belongs to him who creates it, and every dollar taken from industry without an equivalent is robbery. "If any will not work, neither shall he eat." The interests of rural and civic labor are the same; their enemies are identical.

Third. We believe that the time has come when the railroad corporations will either own the people or the people must own the railroads; and, should the government enter upon the work of owning and managing all railroads, we should favor an amendment to the Constitution by which all persons engaged in the government service shall be placed under a civil service regulation of the most rigid character, so as to prevent the increase of the power of the national administration by the use of such additional government employees.

First, *Money.* We demand a national currency, safe, sound, and flexible, issued by the general government only, a full legal tender for all debts, public and private, and that, without the use of banking corporations, a just, equitable, and efficient means of distribution direct to the people, at a tax not to exceed two per cent per annum, to be provided as set forth in the sub-treasury plan of the Farmers' Alliance, or a better system; also, by payments in discharge of its obligations for public improvements.

(a) We demand free and unlimited coinage of silver and gold at the present legal ratio of sixteen to one.

(b) We demand that the amount of circulating medium be speedily increased to not less than fifty dollars per capita.

(c) We demand a graduated income tax.

(d) We believe that the money of the country should be kept as much as possible in the hands of the people, and hence we demand that all state and national revenues shall be limited to the necessary expenses of the government economically and honestly administered.

(e) We demand that postal savings banks be established by the government for the safe deposit of the earnings of the people and to facilitate exchange.

Second, *Transportation.* Transportation being a means of exchange and a public necessity, the government should own and operate the railroads in the interest of the people.

(a) The telegraph and telephone, like the post-office system, being a necessity for the transmission of news, should be owned and operated by the government in the interest of the people.

Third, *Land.* The land, including all the natural sources of wealth, is the heritage of the people, and should not be monopolized for speculative purposes, and alien ownership of land should be prohibited. All land now held by railroads and other corporations in excess of their actual needs, and all lands now owned by aliens, should be reclaimed by the government and held for actual settlers only. . . .

Elizabeth Cady Stanton Demands Suffrage as the Protection of Selfhood, 1892

The point I wish plainly to bring before you on this occasion is the individuality of each human soul—our Protestant idea, the right of individual conscience and judgment—our republican idea, individual citizenship. In discussing the rights of woman, we are to consider, first, what belongs to her as an individual, in a world of her own, the arbiter of her own destiny, an imaginary Robinson Crusoe with her woman Friday on a solitary island. Her rights under such circumstances are to use all her faculties for her own safety and happiness. . . .

The isolation of every human soul and the necessity of self-dependence must give each individual the right to choose his own surroundings. The strongest reason for giving woman all the opportunities for higher education, for the full development of her faculties, her forces of mind and body; for giving her the most enlarged freedom of thought and action; a complete emancipation from all forms of bondage, of custom, dependence, superstition; from all the crippling influences of fear—is the solitude and personal responsibility of her own individual life. The strongest reason why we ask for woman a voice in the government under which she lives; in the religion she is asked to believe; equality in social life, where she is the chief factor; a place in the trades and professions, where she may earn her bread, is because of her birthright to self-sovereignty; because, as an individual, she must rely on herself. . . .

To throw obstacles in the way of a complete education is like putting out the eyes; to deny the rights of property is like cutting off the hands. To refuse political equality is to rob the ostracized of all self-respect, of credit in the market place, of recompense in the world of work, of a voice in choosing those who make and administer the law, a choice in the jury before whom they are tried, and in the judge who decides their punishment. Shakespeare's play of Titus and Andronicus contains a terrible satire on woman's position in the nineteenth century—"Rude men seized the king's daughter, cut out her tongue, cut off her hands, and then bade her go call for water and wash her hands." What a picture of woman's position! Robbed of her natural rights, handicapped by law and custom at every turn, yet compelled to fight her own battles, and in the emergencies of life to fall back on herself for protection. . . .

How the little courtesies of life on the surface of society, deemed so important from man towards woman, fade into utter insignificance in view of the deeper tragedies in which she must play her part alone, where no human aid is possible! . . .

Is it, then, consistent to hold the developed woman of this day within the same narrow political limits as the dame with the spinning wheel and knitting needle occupied in the past? No, no! Machinery has taken the labors of woman as well as man on its tireless shoulders; the loom and the spinning wheel are but dreams of the past; the pen, the brush, the easel, the chisel, have taken their places, while the hopes and ambitions of women are essentially changed.

We see reason sufficient in the outer conditions of human beings for individual liberty and development, but when we consider the self-dependence of every human soul, we see the need of courage, judgment and the exercise of every faculty of mind and body, strengthened and developed by use, in woman as well as man. . . .

Live Pryor Seeks Help for Her Downtrodden Black Sisters, 1880

A Letter to Susan B. Anthony

[I read] Your Call for all woman of These United States to sign a petition . . . to be sent to you, from Your Mass Meeting to be sent to the Republican Presidential Convention asking them to extend to us Woman some recognition of our rights. We are your Sister though Colored still we feel in our Bosom and want of Faternal love from our White Sister of the Country. Our White men of this State of Virginia, who rule us with a rod of iron, and show themselves on every occasion the same Crule Task Master, as ever, have introduce on the Statute books right to wipp woman for any poor Discretion, that she might be guilt of. During the early part of febuary a poor weak colored Woman who was in the Extremes wants, stole a Over skirt Value fifty Cent, for which the presiding Magistrate Named J. J. Gruchfield, Did order the poor creature 72 lashes to be well laid on. 36 lashes at the time the Other 36 in a week time and the man or, brute, went himself and saw the whipping was executed. Captain Scott a Col man became indignant went to the jail to see the poor Creature, was refused admission at first but succeed at Last. O My God, what a sight he then saw. the poor Woman Breast was Cut wide open by the lash, her poor back cut to pieces I call some woman together went to the Governor and stated the Case. he forbid the further lashing of the poor woman because the Dr. Beal said she could not live to receive further whipping. Yet the woman still have to remain in jail 12 month for stealing one over skirt Value fifty Cent and have since then been enable to enroll quite a number of Woman to gather form a Club. Our Object is to petition Lecture and to do all things wich shall so soffen the heart of Mankind that they will see and must grant and respect our rights. Would and pray that the Mass Meeting may endorse or demand of the Republican Convention to be Held in Chicigo the rights of Woman to put an Amendment to the Constitution a Cumpulsory Education of Every state of this Union.

    Pardon me for this long letter i must i feel let my feeling go out, so to you Dear Madam have i address you on Behalf of your Down Trodden Colored Sisters of Virginia.

LIVE PRYOR, Richmond, Virginia
President, Ladies Enterprise Club

If you have any papers or book that is of no use to you our society would feel grateful to receive them as we wish to form a library.

Two Prohibition Poems, 1910

Vote It Down

IDA M. BUDD

There's a demon in the glass,
   Vote it down!
You can bring the thing to pass;
   Vote it down!
Oh! my brothers, do you know
You can turn to joy its woe,
And its tyranny o'erthrow?
   Vote it down!

How it fills our souls with dread!
   Vote it down!
As it rears its serpent head,
   Vote it down!
Oh! so subtle has it been
Dare not close your eyes and say
It has left its trail of sin,
   Vote it down!

It is growing all the time,
   Vote it down!
To protect it is a crime,
   Vote it down!
Dare not close your eyes and say
"There must be some other way,"
Lest your own the demon slay,
   Vote it down!

In your manliness arise,
　　Vote it down!
Throw aside old party ties,
　　Vote it down!
If you love our native land,
Smite this blighting, cursing hand
With your ballot's magic wand,
　　Vote it down!

Christian man, we call on you,
　　Vote it down!
Are you honest? are you true?
　　Vote it down!
Christ, your Saviour crucified,
Then, as though he stood beside,
　　Vote it down!

Ladies' Entrance

OLIVER ALLSTORM

"Ladies' entrance." Ah, yes.
You've all seen the sign.
It leads to the pit
Of whiskey and wine.
It leads to the room
With the little closed door,
From which there's no exit
For purity more;
An hour for a song
And another for drink,
And some mother's girl
Is beginning to sink.

"Ladies' entrance." Of course,
'Tis the side door, too
For shame never cared
To be open to view.
They slip and they trip
In their haste to get in,
Lest someone might see
They are sporting with sin;
The shadows are falling,
There's no escort now,
Save strangers who drink
To the curl on her brow.
Home, mother, and honor
Are lost in the whirl,
And the river of vice
Claims some mother's girl.

"Ladies' entrance." Ah, yes.
Now boldly they go
Through the little side entrance
So bitter with woe.
Corrupt in their morals
And deep in disgrace,
They blush not to enter,
Nor falter a pace.
Half dead to Life's meaning,
Half dead to its care,
They drift through wild
    pleasure
Right into despair.

"Ladies Entrance." To where?
Ah, finish the sign—
Mark plainly the rest,—
To the end of the line.
To the serpent that charms,
And passions that rave,
To torment that plunges
One into the grave.
If live ones would hear,
And if dead ones could tell,
The sign would read on,
"Ladies' Entrance to HELL."

❧ *E S S A Y S*

The following selections explore three distinct aspects of Gilded Age political culture. In the first essay, the late historian Richard Hofstadter of Columbia University delivers a classic verdict on mainstream politics and ideology. Bruce Palmer, a historian at the University of Houston, Clear Lake, offers a sympathetic but not uncritical reading of the southern Farmers Alliance and its political instrument, the People's Party, in the second essay. Finally, historian Estelle Freedman of Stanford University comments on the unexpected benefits for political action and institution building of a separate cultural space for women. Ironically, her argument suggests, the very rhetoric of equality associated with the suffrage amendment of 1920 actually weakened women's political capacities.

Politics in a Cynical Age

RICHARD HOFSTADTER

The parties of the period after the post–Civil War were based on patronage, not principle; they divided over spoils, not issues. Although American political parties are never celebrated for having sharp differences of principle, the great age of the spoilsmen was notable for elevating crass hunger for office to the level of a common credo. "The American parties now continue to exist, because they have existed," wrote Lord Bryce in *The American Commonwealth*. An eminent journalist observed to him as late as 1908 "that the two parties were like two bottles. Each bore a label denoting the kind of liquor it contained, but each was empty." In 1879 young Woodrow Wilson expressed in eight words his disgust with the degradation of American politics: "No leaders, no principles; no principles, no parties."

The Republicans were distinguished from the Democrats chiefly by being successful. From the war and Reconstruction onwards, when it sought actively to strengthen its social base by espousing the policies of American industrialists, the Republican Party existed in an unholy and often mutually hostile conjunction with the capitalistic interests. Capitalists, seeking land grants, tariffs, bounties, favorable currency policies, freedom from regulatory legislation and economic reform, supplied campaign funds, fees, and bribes and plied politicians with investment opportunities. Seward had said that "a party is in one sense a joint stock company in which those who contribute the most, direct the action and management of the concern." The interests owned important shares in both parties, but they occasionally grew restive under what they considered the excessive demands of the politicians. Until the 1880's, in fact, the machines depended very heavily upon the contributions of their office-holders to party treasuries, and it was not until businessmen, feeling their power, began to go into politics themselves on a more considerable scale that the parties came more fully under their sway. Before business learned to buy statesmen at wholesale, it had to buy privileges at retail. Fabulous sums were spent. A disgruntled Congressman from Ohio declared in 1873 that "the House of Representatives was like an auction room where more valuable considerations were disposed of under the speaker's hammer than in any other place on earth." Between 1866 and 1872, for example, the Union Pacific spent $400,000 on bribes; between 1875 and 1885 graft cost the Central Pacific as much as $500,000 annually. Little wonder that an honest Republican of the old school like Walter Q. Gresham could describe his party as "an internally corrupt concern," or that Senator Grimes of Iowa, once an important leader, could say in 1870: "I believe it is to-day the most corrupt and debauched political party that ever existed." "One might search the whole list of Congress, Judiciary, and Executive during the twenty-five years 1870 to 1895," concluded Henry Adams, "and find little but damaged reputation.". . .

There were, of course, untainted politicians, and they were esteemed. Grant was happy to have Hamilton Fish in his Cabinet, a man of conspicuous rectitude who adorned the group like a jewel in the head of a toad. The impeccable Carl Schurz became Secretary of the Interior under President Hayes. Hayes and Harrison, two of the five Republican Presidents of the period, had tolerable reputations; but these two were as innocent of distinction as they were of corruption and they have become famous in American annals chiefly for their obscurity. Their relation to underlying political realities is expressed in the retort of Boss Matt Quay to Harrison's remark upon his election in the close campaign of 1888. "Providence," breathed the aristocratic Harrison solemnly, "has given us the victory." "Think of the man," snorted Quay. "He ought to know that Providence hadn't a damn thing to do with it." Harrison would never know, he added, "how close a number of men were compelled to approach the gates of the penitentiary to make him President." Harrison found out soon enough what his role was expected to be. "When I came into power," he once lamented in Theodore Roosevelt's presence, "I found that the party managers had taken it all to themselves. I could not name my own Cabinet. They had sold out every place to pay the election expenses."

Of the remaining three presidents not much need be said. Grant's administrations are notorious for their corruption. Hayes's successor, the sanctimonious Garfield, although essentially an honest and worthy soul, was tainted by a few minor scandals. Garfield's successor by virtue of assassination, Chester A. Arthur, had been before his vice-presidential nomination the major domo of Conkling's notorious New York Customhouse machine, a spoilsman's spoilsman. ("My God! Chet Arthur in the White House!" a friend was reported to have exclaimed.) Nevertheless Arthur, trying to rise to his office, sought conscientiously but ineffectually to promote a few reforms; ironically, his signature made the Pendleton Civil Service Act a law.

It was not the presidents who gave the machine its dynamic force, but the factional leaders and bosses of the Republican Party, men like Roscoe Conkling and James G. Blaine. In spite of their violent mutual animosity, these two seem now to have had much in common. Above all, both looked upon life as an amusing and rather profitable game of wits. . . .

Conkling had come from a well-to-do New York family; it was characteristic that as a lawyer he tried and won his first case before his father, a judge who sat in the United States District Court. Well born and well married, he could indulge his fancies without resorting to personal corruption; he is not known to have accepted graft, but graft was the milieu in which he lived. One of Grant's most powerful supporters, master of the rich patronage of the New York Customhouse, he was a machine product par excellence, flagrantly contemptuous of reformers who tried to challenge orthodox politics. Of course a party was a machine run by machine methods, and how else did the proprietors of ladies' magazines propose to manage them?

> We are told the Republican party is a machine. Yes. A government is a machine; a church is a machine; an army is a machine . . . the common-school system of the State of New York is a machine; a political party is a machine.

. . .

The magnetic Blaine was the most popular Republican of his time. Only once, in 1884, was he nominated by his party for the presidency, but in all other conventions from 1876 to 1892 he was a formidable possibility. His popularity persisted long after his spotty financial record became an open story to those who cared to read it; and while his little sins were a handicap that may have cost him the presidency, they never ruled him out of consideration. . . .

Blaine has been accounted by both contemporaries and historians as a man of unusual intellectual faculties for a politician. His major intellectual effort, a massive two-volume history, *Twenty Years of Congress,* is still of some use; but its governing conception is simply that the Republic was safe only in the hands of the Republican Party, and it can be judged as well by what it omits as by what it includes. Blaine saw fit, for example, to say nothing at all of the corruptions and scandals of the Grant administrations. And this was characteristic: so much of his life was spent in obscuring the truth that falsehood and evasion blanket even his historical prose. By common testimony he was a man of intense personal charm, warm and tender in his private relationships, facile, clever, and winning in his public role. Yet he left behind him not a single constructive achievement, hardly even a constructive suggestion; his chief contribution to American politics was to lower its tone. Roscoe Conkling, when asked to campaign for him in 1884, snarled, out of his morbid hatred: "No thank you, I don't engage in criminal practice"; and for once Conkling was right: harmless as a private citizen, Blaine was an antisocial being in his public capacity. "When I want a thing," the Plumed Knight once said to his wife, "I want it dreadfully." It might have been the motto of a whole generation of Americans who wanted things dreadfully, and took them.

The isolation of the reformers was as characteristic as the cynicism and corruption of the regulars. Party warhorses, who tended to identify rapacity with manliness, looked upon "good" men in politics as dudes, freaks, immune to the spirit of their time not out of virtue but perversity—"man milliners," as Conkling said in his famous diatribe. Blaine referred to them in a letter to Garfield as "upstarts, conceited, foolish, vain . . . noisy but not numerous, pharisaical but not practical, ambitious but not wise, pretentious but not powerful." The tart Senator John J. Ingalls of Kansas, who believed that purity in politics is "an irridescent dream," described them as

> effeminate without being either masculine or feminine; unable to beget or to bear; possessing neither fecundity nor virility; endowed with the contempt of men and the derision of women, and doomed to sterility, isolation, and extinction.

This was savage, but it had some truth: in politics the reformers were both isolated and sterile. Intellectuals, obsessed with the abstract ideal of public service, businessmen tired of the cost of graft, patricians worried about the need of honesty in government, they did not know the people, and the people with good reason did not know them. While reformers were concerned with public uplift, farmers and workers were trying to stave off private downfall. The steady deflationary movement of prices was ruinous to farmers, whose history in this period was one of economic tragedies and largely futile struggles against money and monopoly. Industrialism brought down upon the working class that pall of oppression and misery which is found in every chronicle of the Industrial Revolution, and it was unrelieved by fitful and brutal labor struggles. Violent business fluctuations, the great depressions of the seventies and nineties, and the sharp crisis of the mid-eighties spread poverty and insecurity.

It is not surprising, therefore, that reformers who concentrated upon a Civil Service Act, the tariff, or exposing the peccadilloes of politicians did not excite mass enthusiasm. Single-minded concern for honesty in public service is a luxury of the middle and upper classes. The masses do not care deeply about the honesty of public servants unless it promises to lead to some human fruition, some measurable easing of the difficulties of life. If a choice is necessary, the populace of an American city will choose kindness over honesty, as the nation's enduring Tammanys attest. The rural masses look for statesmen of the cheap dollar. . . .

The fate of political reform was paralleled by the failure of economic reform. During the first Cleveland administration the Cullom committee, which had been investigating railroads, concluded that "upon no public question are the people nearly so unanimous" as that Congress should regulate interstate commerce. Congress accordingly gave "the people" the Interstate Commerce Act. But as Senator Nelson W. Aldrich, already the watchdog of the corporations, said, the act was "a delusion and a sham . . . an empty menace to the great interests, made to answer the clamor of the ignorant and the unreasoning"; Senator Cullom, the act's sponsor, described it as "conservative legislation" passed in the guise of a reform measure. Railroads were soon circumventing regulation by the Interstate Commerce Commission with ease. Six years after the law was passed, Richard Olney, Cleveland's Attorney General, advised the president of the Chicago, Burlington & Quincy that to ask for its repeal would be unwise:

The Commission, as its functions have now been limited by the courts, is, or can be made, of great use to the railroads. It satisfies the popular clamor for government supervision of the railroads at the same time that that supervision is almost entirely nominal. Further, the older such a commission gets to be, the more inclined it will be found to take the business and railroad view of things. It thus becomes a sort of barrier between the railroads and the people and a sort of protection against hasty and crude legislation hostile to railroad interests.

The second economic reform, the Sherman Anti-Trust Act, passed during the election year of 1890, likewise in response to public clamor against monopolists, was equally cynical in design. Republican Senator Orville Platt of Connecticut charged during the Sherman bill debate:

The conduct of the Senate . . . has not been in the line of the honest preparation of a bill to prohibit and punish trusts. It has been in the line of getting some bill with that title that we might go to the country with. The questions of whether the bill would be operative, or how it would operate . . . have been whistled down the wind in this Senate as idle talk, and the whole effort has been to get some bill headed: ''A Bill to Punish Trusts'' with which to go to the country.

The best defense of the two-party system is the argument that while it permits the majority party to govern, as it should, it also centralizes the opposition in a single minority group, thus preventing the dissipation of minority energy in sectarian disputes and checking any tyrannical tendencies on the part of the ''ins.'' This argument has seldom fitted the facts of American life, where party differences have rarely been profound and party structure has been so rigid that minorities, instead of being focused in either major party when it was out, have rather had to sunder their traditional party ties and—in most cases—drown alone in the political seas.

The first post–Civil War victory of the Democrats, in 1884 (when they had the estimable assistance of the Mugwump Republicans), is one of the few exceptions to this American story of party loyalty; but the subsequent Democratic administration only confirmed the profound uniformity between Republican and Democratic principles. In Grover Cleveland, however, the Democrats at least had a man who stood out, if only for honesty and independence, as the sole reasonable facsimile of a major president between Lincoln and Theodore Roosevelt.

Grover Cleveland's father, Richard Falley Cleveland, was a poor, studious Presbyterian parson of modest abilities who raised a family of nine children on the niggardly salaries of his village pastorates, never taxed himself to rise in the ministry, and died at forty-nine, when Grover was sixteen. The son took on his father's moral imperatives and accepted his lack of ambition as normal. In him the balance between the call of duty, as he saw it, and the call of ambition was heavily weighted in favor of duty. Simple, sentimental, and unimaginative, he worked for security and comfort and expected little more. On the night of his election to the governorship of New York, at the age of forty-five, he wrote to his brother: ''Do you know that if Mother were alive I should feel so much safer? I have always thought her prayers had much to do with my success.''

The hardship of being thrown on his own resources at an early age made Cleveland neither bitter nor rebellious. A tinge of what psychologists call moral masochism may have made it easier for him to carry his early burdens and, in his later years, to bear the odium that fell upon him. Writing reminiscently about his first years in Buffalo as an underpaid law student and clerk, he declared that he ''had adversity in abundance . . . actually enjoyed his adversities.'' His working habits were irregular: spurts of incredible energy and self-punishing conscientiousness were followed by spells of the easygoing laxity of bachelorhood. Corpulent, rugged, and amiable, falling quickly into the social tone of Buffalo, a thriving city with a large, *gemütlich* German population, Cleveland joined what Professor Allan Nevins aptly calls ''the hotel lobby and barroom set.''

Cleveland's rise to power was rapid and freakish. In the spring of 1881 he was a well-established Buffalo lawyer with a comfortable livelihood and a brief history of conscientious and unaspiring tenure in two minor political offices. In the spring of 1885 he was in Washington, taking the oath of office as President of the United States. A series of chance events catapulted him upward. In 1881 a particularly flagrant Republican boodler was nominated for the mayoralty of Buffalo; the Democrats, searching for an aggressively honest opponent and remembering Cleveland's past services as sheriff, offered him a nomination, which he accepted without enthusiasm. The new Mayor dealt roughly with local grafters, winning himself a good reputation throughout New York Democracy just on the eve of a gubernatorial contest. Circumstances in the state happened to be favorable: New York County delegates who were revolting against Tammany and seeking a suitable candidate threw the nomination to Cleveland after a brief deadlock between two more prominent men. An equally fortuitous split in the New York State Republican Party between the followers of Governor Cornell and those of Conkling made Cleveland's election a certainty. The physical decline of Tilden and the impoverished state of Democratic leadership made Cleveland a logical choice for his party in 1884. His campaign opponent, Blaine, damaged by old sins, the defection of the Mugwumps, and the incredible "Rum, Romanism, and Rebellion" speech of the Rev. Samuel Burchard, lost to Cleveland by the slimmest margin: a change of some 600 votes in New York State could have swung the election the other way. It was through a series of improbabilities that a man of Cleveland's caliber became President in the Gilded Age. . . .

Yet it was hardly a mistake for conservatives of the East to regard Cleveland as their own man or for many normally Republican businessmen to support him even as early as 1884. One of his most notable acts as Governor had been to veto a bill reducing elevated-railway fares in New York City from ten to five cents, in spite of the obvious popularity of the bill among the people of the city. Such acts had given Andrew D. White cause to exult that Cleveland had overcome his "sympathies for the working people" and to praise him for having "not the slightest germs of demagogism." After his first election Cleveland received from Jay Gould the telegraphic message: "I feel . . . that the vast business interests of the country will be entirely safe in your hands.". . .

Cleveland regarded the duties of public office in the most serious light. "It seems to me," he wrote to an old friend in June 1885, "that I am as much consecrated to a service as the religionist who secludes himself from all that is joyous in life and devotes himself to a sacred mission." Vetoes had made him famous as Mayor and Governor, and from the very first he conceived of his presidential task as a negative one: he was the righteous executive; his assignment was to *police* other politicians, to prevent them from giving favors or taking graft. The key to his mind was his dislike of "paternalism" in government. The people, he believed, were entitled to economy, purity, and justice in their government, and should expect no more. "A fair field and no favor.". . .

Cleveland's philosophy of laissez-faire, like the classic theory, was dependent upon one grand assumption: things must work out smoothly without government action, or the whole system, coherent enough in theory, would fall from the weakness of its premises. That these were unrealistic Cleveland had to recognize by the time of his fourth annual message to Congress, written in December 1888, after his defeat by Harrison. This message rumbled with protests that might have been written by a Populist:

> . . . we find the wealth and luxury of our cities mingled with poverty and wretchedness and unremunerative toil. A crowded and constantly increasing urban population suggests the impoverishment of rural sections, and discontent with agricultural pursuits. . . .
>
> We discover that the fortunes realized by our manufacturers are no longer solely the reward of sturdy industry and enlightened foresight, but that they result from the discriminating favor of the government, and are largely built upon undue exactions from the masses of our people. The gulf between employers and the employed is constantly widening, and classes are rapidly forming, one comprising the very rich and powerful, while in another are found the toiling poor.
>
> . . . We discover the existence of trusts, combinations, and monopolies, while the citizen is struggling far in the rear, or is trampled to death beneath an iron heel. Corporations, which should be carefully restrained creatures of the law and the servants of the people, are fast becoming the people's masters.

Nevertheless, Cleveland held to the view that the government could do little to check the forces that brought such results. His only recourse was to appeal to businessmen to improve their morals and become trustees of the public. "Must we always," he asked pathetically of the Philadelphia Commercial Exchange in 1887, "must we always look for the political opinions of our business men precisely where they suppose their immediate pecuniary advantage to be found?" Businessmen should be "guided by better motives than purely selfish and exclusive benefit."

Lacking a more positive conception of social action, Cleveland fell quietly and naturally into an implicit partnership with the interests during the crisis of the nineties. The man who thought that tariffs and bounties were an unwarranted boon to business and a gross violation of justice and equity thought nothing of sending federal troops to break the Pullman strike in 1894, or of putting them substantially under the charge of a railroad attorney. Years later he asserted that he and others of responsibility in the strike were to be "congratulated" for the part they played. He was equally resolute in rebuffing the farmers over the silver question. One did not have to be a plutocrat, of course, to be a rigid adherent of the gold standard; but an equally rigid adherence to laissez-faire required Cleveland to deny the responsibility of the government to produce any alternative to free silver as a remedy for agrarian distress. Few men would have the blunt solidity to do what Cleveland did—or rather to fail to do what he failed to do. It demanded his far from nimble mind to display all the imbecile impartiality of a philosophy that lumped together both the tariff racketeers and the poor bedeviled farmers as illegitimate petitioners of the government. It has been said to Cleveland's credit that he was strong enough to resist popular pressures that no other man could have withstood; it can also be said that he turned his back on distress more acute than any other president would have had the *sang-froid* to ignore.

Cleveland, in short, had made a defect of his merits. He was not a cruel man, but he was dogmatic, obtuse, and insensitive. Making whatever allowance one will, there is something odd about a president's writing during a year of popular agony like 1895 to the man who acted as his broker: "You know rich investors like me have to keep an account of income in these days." The intended note of jocularity rings false. "I find," he writes soon again, "I am developing quite a strong desire to make money"—and curiously, "and I think this is a good time to indulge in that propensity." One is reminded of Carnegie's thoughtful words: "The man who has money during a panic is the wise and valuable citizen."

Certainly this is the spirit of the faithful bourgeois. And Cleveland, this product of good conscience and self-help, with his stern ideas of purity, efficiency, and service, was a taxpayer's dream, the ideal bourgeois statesman for his time: out of heartfelt conviction he gave to the interests what many a lesser politician might have sold them for a price. He was the flower of American political culture in the Gilded Age.

The Southern Populist Creed

BRUCE PALMER

For all the Southern Populists, financial reformers and antimonopoly greenbackers alike, the proper society bore a great resemblance to the rural, agricultural communities in which most of them lived or had grown up. Farmers, or at least producers, formed its center, and nearly all its members earned their living by producing or facilitating the production and distribution of some form of tangible wealth. While individual economic competition and the market system for the most part went unchallenged, personal relationships and moral and religious precept more importantly than Adam Smith's invisible hand and the local police force appeared to delineate and guide the social and economic life of the community. The Southerners distrusted institutions and persons who dealt with intangible things such as credit, interest, and some kinds of written law, and suspected those with whom they had impersonal relationships.

The Southern Populists' ways of thinking and writing about the world they found around them, and its ideal alternative, were not only the heritage of the community in which they lived or had been raised but also reflected it. The Jeffersonian-Jacksonian metaphors dealt with and described a relatively homogeneous and harmonious rural society which knew little of railroad corporations, Andrew Carnegie, Standard Oil, or an industrial proletariat. Their religious and moral metaphors and imagery were premised on and

Reprinted, by permission of the author and publisher, from *"Man over Money": The Southern Populist Critique of American Capitalism* by Bruce Palmer, pp. 199–221. Copyright © 1980 The University of North Carolina Press.

reflected the assumption that society was best organized and governed on a personal and moral basis. The producerite metaphor . . . described a society whose most important function was the production of tangible wealth and in which the physical labor involved in producing that wealth was the most valuable and virtuous activity one could undertake. The Southern Populists used these metaphors and images which so well described their experience in a southern, rural, evangelical Protestant community to criticize another world they found developing around them—an impersonal, amoral, urban-centered, nonsouthern, industrial society—and to project their reform plans for a new social order. . . .

. . . Populists . . . shared the critique of financial and industrial capitalist society which provided the impetus for their varying reform demands. All the Southern Populists, for instance, frequently and vigorously attacked cities, the home of this new society. Bringing to bear on the city the Jeffersonian, the producerite, and the religious and moral metaphors and imagery, the reformers found a number of discrepancies between it and the society they wanted. Kid-gloved, silk-hatted men lived in the city and ran politics. They did no hard work, produced no wealth, yet controlled the country. The town's dominance of the countryside, like the nonproducer's dominance of the producer, stood the proper order of society on its head because the town ultimately depended on the countryside for survival. Some Southern Populists held the failure of existing society to reflect this truth responsible for many of America's problems. An Alabama Populist pointed out that the huge land holdings of aliens and American corporations, having "driven thousands of people out of the country into towns and cities to compete with skilled labor and caused strikes, lock outs, riots, and bloodshed, and caused our nation to be filled with tramps and paupers," brought not only the decline of the countryside but unrest in the cities.

While they muted the sharp accents of class conflict in their rhetoric and analysis as 1896 approached and most of the southern state parties moderated their reform programs to appeal to the new southern town and city middle class, moral condemnation of city life remained a constant theme. Conditions unique to urban areas prevented the development of good citizens. Like Jefferson, the editor of the *Progressive Farmer* felt something in the relationship of people to each other in cities destroyed character. Their dependence on their employers for a livelihood made clerks and tradesmen slaves to their master's politics. "Stay in the country," the editor advised his readers; "be free to think and act."

Other Populists, like W. J. Peele of North Carolina, expanded on the tone if not the substance of Jefferson's indictment. "Cancers upon the body politic," in them originated the "schemes of plunder" which destroyed the moral fiber and virtue necessary to hold America together. A Texas Populist in 1894 warned that it was "from the cities, with their brothels, their low-down groceries, their sweatshops, from districts where dirt, and disease, and rats, and hunger, and despair blot out all that is god-like in man and makes him a ravening beast, that the red hand of anarchy is raised, and it is from the cities that the hosts of old partyism are brought forth." Only the country, most Southern Populists felt, produced the character and morality necessary to save the nation and run it properly. Speaking for most of his brethren, a North Carolina reformer in late 1891 admonished farmers who did not know the cities' sorrows and vices to "feel proud of your mission; honor your calling; for from behind many a plow there has [*sic*] gone forth the leaders of nations. . . . The plow is the power behind the throne in this land."

In combination with their almost complete lack of immediate experience with it, the lack of an analytical framework which dealt with urbanization made the Southern Populists' rejection of the city nearly complete. But their critique of industrial capitalist society usually was not so parochially hostile, although it grew from the same roots from which the attack on the cities sprouted. Many reformers, for instance, noted angrily that money spoke louder than personal virtue and morality, and the many without it went unconsidered, regardless of their worth or ability. . . . This idea usually accompanied the Southern Populists' concern with the decline within the new industrial, urban society of older personal relationships and moral codes of behavior. [Georgia Populist leader Tom] Watson deplored the trend in some large urban churches toward celebrating communion from individual cups rather than a common one. It seemed to him "that religion in the great cities is trying . . . to abolish the simple ways and brotherly teachings of Christ."

The whole tone of modern life bothered Watson even more. "Move on" had become the watchword of civilization. The policeman said it to the tramp, the law to the vagrant, society "to the soldier in the battle of life. . . . [T]o stop is to be run over." Under much of the new haste and impersonality Watson saw an accelerating race for wealth that seemed to dominate all social life, with no respect for human beings or their needs. He continually objected to opening the Chicago World's Fair on Sunday, not for religious reasons but because a country "threatened with a heartless, tireless, pitiless race for wealth such as the world never saw before" needed a day of rest. . . . America was becoming a state of constant personal warfare for a larger share of the spoils. . . . At least some saw these traits for what they were, products of the business culture created by American capitalism. "It is an age of greed. Don't forget that fact," a North Carolina editor reminded his readers. "There are men who would coin the bones of their dead mothers into gold, if they could, and they form the most aggressive business class."

Part of this hostility toward a new urban society obviously reflected the attitude of a farming population which accurately perceived a relative, and often absolute, decline of its wealth and social status. . . . The growing tempo of life in an increasingly impersonal and amoral industrial society was no fiction. In fact, for the Southern Populists the most serious consequence of this was not the decline of rural society but the human toll it took. The exploitation involved in nineteenth-century industrial capitalism appalled them. "A low estimate," wrote the editor of the *Texas Advance* in 1894, "places the enforced paupers of the country at one million." The system that caused this created "thousands of women surrendering their lives to greed, stitch by stitch, fifteen hours a day." It set thousands of unemployed laboring men to tramping the country in search of work, "depending for life on the charity of the people," "all of their pride and manhood" slowly being ground to dust in "this plutocratic mill.". . .

Measured in terms of human destruction, many Southern Populists, radical and moderate, questioned whether the existing social order had any claim to civilization. A North Carolina reformer found it strange that a Brazilian man who ate human flesh shocked the "civilized world." Where, he asked, lay the difference between "this ignorant depraved man, who ate human beings because he had no other way of satisfying his hunger," and "the thousands of educated, wealthy, and in many cases personally refined employers in this country who willfully and intentionally take advantage of the necessities of their employees to grind their wages down to the lowest possible point that will keep soul and body together? Both the cannibal and the grinding employer are living on human flesh, the ignorant one devouring it outright and the intelligent one wearing it out for his benefit, and of the two which is the greatest sinner? Can there be a doubt? We think not."

Charity offered no solution to the suffering; the problem lay with the system. "When plutocracy defrauds the people of this nation out of a billion dollars of value a year through the law, it is business," observed a North Carolinian. When they established soup kitchens, "it is charity." The idea of charity outraged the editor of the *Southern Mercury*. Charity, he wrote in 1895, was "the crust the robber gives back to the man he has robbed. Charity is an apology for justice, and apology will not pay the wages of the toiler, nor feed the hungry in comfort." . . . The Southern Populists often felt, in fact, that American industrial society depended on the destruction, or at least the complete degradation, of the large mass of people. It had to be reorganized and governed so that it served not just a few but the many. "If civilization is worth anything to humanity," maintained another Georgia editor, "its blessings should be extended to all . . . in proportion to their honest, earnest efforts to attain them. This is not so now." The Southern Populists could not accept industrial development at the cost of millions of poor.

The rule of thumb for correcting these abuses cut straight to the heart of the problem. As an Alabama editor wrote, "any nation that holds property rights above human rights is barbarian." A society in which the rush for gain and property exceeded acceptable limits and included the destruction of human rights the Southern Populists felt was neither proper nor decent. "Our people should be greater than our money, our commerce, or anything else in our America." So not only the limitations of their analysis but also the power of their critique flowed from the Southern Populists' evangelical Protestant past, their Jeffersonian and Jacksonian heritage, and their rural experience. . . . "Life," wrote the radical antimonopoly greenbacker W. S. Morgan, "is more sacred than property always and everywhere if the two are in peril, life should be saved if property perish. Capitalism places property above life, thereby declaring war upon humanity. This war must not cease until capitalism is vanquished and property becomes the servant, not the master of man."

The Southern Populists also revealed their recognition of the enemy in their demand that society protect the weak from the strong. It provided a focus for both their critique and their desire for a new social order. . . . Every person had "a right to the means of comfortable existence, the right to the condition that produce [sic] happiness. . . . Society commits a grave fault when it honors the strong and intelligent who have grown rich by robbing the weak and ignorant." "Man generally knows," maintained a Georgia Populist in mid-1894, "that we are bound together in families, communities, states and nations for mutual protection and material happiness and not for self-aggrandizement or the survival of the fittest.". . . Not only an inhuman way to organize society, this method also worked badly. "Hundreds of millions of misguided energies are wasted each year. The energies of the people are not half utilized." The social order needed a fundamental change.

When they limited themselves to a discussion of the ideal system of production and exchange between individuals, the Southern Populists often lamented the decline of competition. Almost all of them, however, opposed using competition as a guide for humanity's wider social life and development. "Under a system where every man is for himself," wrote an Arkansas Populist, "the devil will get most of them.". . . "Free competition," argued a Virginia Alliance editor, "is the great principle of Anglo-Saxon development, and we have all been nurtured on that principle since infancy, and yet it is clearly responsible for the present distressing inequalities of society. . . . The principle "guarantees to every citizen an equal right to compete for the possession of wealth, but it is powerless to prevent the strong from taking the share of the weak.". . . The southern reformers agreed with the Texas Populist who wrote that the "Darwinian theory of the survival of the strongest" could no longer coexist with "the Christian theory of the survival of all," especially since the new industrial developments of the generation following the Civil War had made the effects of competition on society worse.

Obviously human need demanded a change in the system, but what would replace it? For the answer the Southern Populists drew on their Alliance heritage and expanded it to include the whole of society. "Competition forces the employer to cut down wages; he must do so or go under," reasoned an Alabama editor. "Those employers who are guided by feelings of humanity are forced out of business by competition. The system is rotten, and we toss our hat and exclaim, all hail the co-operative commonwealth!" Cooperation would once again value decency above destruction, human beings above money or property. "Each for All and All for Each" ran the motto of the *Virginia Sun*. Cooperation would end strikes, the "war between capital and labor," wrote a Georgia Populist, because "the motive and cause for them would be removed. Co-operative industry means that all wealth will belong to him who creates it." . . . The competitive system had outlived its usefulness, both as a device for increasing production and economic growth and as a means of improving the lot of all. The future would see no slowdown in economic and social development as a result of the cooperative system, but the human wastage caused by competition would disappear. . . .

. . . Southern Populists . . . did not . . . question the fundamental tenets of the American economic system as they understood them—the market, supply and demand, private ownership and profit, and the beneficence of economic competition between small economic units. . . . Almost all . . . Southern Populists rejected . . . radical [Socialist] demand for change, although in practice they sometimes criticized the existing system more harshly than [the Socialists did]. They did not follow through on the implications of their demand that American society replace economic competition with cooperation, the "cooperative commonwealth." They identified themselves as independent producers, or aspiring independent producers, within a simple market society, where economically independent individuals competed with each other while everyone, through a democratic government, owned cooperatively the major elements of distribution.

Part of the reason the Southern Populists stopped short of an attack on the market system lay in the sources to which they turned for a justification of this cooperative order. They measured the existing social order by its human refuse; they measured their cooperative society by its promise of brotherhood. . . .

The main roots of the metaphor lay in the evangelical Protestant experience of the Southern Populists. In the idea of cooperative effort, wrote the editor of the *Virginia Sun* in early 1892, "is contained the secret to all true life and progress—the grand emancipating principle of brotherhood. A man, living to himself alone, can achieve but little. But once let him free himself from his narrow selfishness, and boldly throw himself into work for the good of all, and his share of the good of all shall be returned to him—a hundredfold more than his puny effort could ever have yielded. Thus does the spiritual law find its economic counterpart—if a man would save his life, he must first lose it.". . . To defeat their opponents, the producers and laboring people "must make up their minds to enter an organization whose fundamental principles are the universal fatherhood of God and the brotherhood of man and recognize the great truth that the interest of one is the interest of all—and walk to the ballot box in a solid phalanx and there redress every wrong." Reform ultimately rested on the brotherhood of all producers, employed laborers or independent farmers. . . .

American society's inhumanity to most of its members seemed to the Southern Populists the most compelling reason for a change toward a new society regulated by the principle of cooperative brotherhood, where every person would be responsible for every other. The responsibility was personal, the compulsion to it moral. It was a responsibility which the Southern Populists accused the new urban industrial America of ignoring and destroying. Their Jeffersonian and Jacksonian heritage stressed the equality of all people in a relatively homogeneous, producer-oriented society; their rural experience emphasized the personal, moral connections of each person to every other; their religious background insisted on the essential equality of all people before God. All of these underlined the need for personal responsibility. . . . It was not to be everyone for themselves but all for each other.

The irony was, of course, that they saw no particular conflict between this and the retention of a market society based on private ownership and profit, the same base on which rested the industrial and financial capitalist society they opposed. None of their sources for the ideal of brotherhood and responsibility in a cooperative society suggested any problem. And when their experience did, the Southern Populists proposed as a solution a simple market society within a cooperative national economy. This resolution became untenable only when they turned to dealing with the benefits of America's existing industrial structure, benefits they wished to retain.

By no means did the Southern Populists reject industrial society. Their exposure to some aspects of it in America, particularly the social suffering it caused, resulted in only an apparent repudiation; they actually responded far differently. They disliked not industrial development but its impact on American society. The New South and railroads attracted them precisely because they promised economic improvement and even industrial expansion. The editor of the *Progressive Farmer* in August 1893 criticized the gold standard because by reducing the money supply, it would stop all trains, shut every factory in the land, and put three-quarters of the merchants and bankers in the country out of business. Few newspapers could be published, and telegraph and communications would remain only between large cities. "In short, the progress we have made in the past hundred years will be forgotten as we get poorer and progress backward." This reformer and others conceived of Populist reform as a way to save America's complex industrial society before the social effects attending its organization destroyed it.

For this task, however, what had worked in the past would not necessarily work in the future. Times had changed. . . . The tenets of the People's party were "identical with the true teachings of Jefferson modernized and made applicable to the changed condition of this country." Others felt more change might be necessary. . . . "Is it reasonable," asked a North Carolina editor, "to say that our forefathers who lived a century ago, could have enacted perfect laws to suit this age and generation?" They had known nothing of the "gigantic trusts, greedy monopolists and soulless corporations" that the masses had to contend with in the 1890s. . . . The people's response had to be as radical and as new as the conditions which threatened them.

While the Southern Populists . . . often called for a restoration of Jeffersonian and Jacksonian politics, they consciously designed their specific reforms to meet the needs of a new society. The allusions to older forms most often referred only to general principles of government. America needed to return to earlier forms, maintained a North Carolina Allianceman, to regain a government which protected all Americans rather than a special few, a government "founded upon the principle of justice and equality to the whole people," a government "restored to its primitive parity." Neither Jeffersonian nor Jacksonian politics produced specific demands for a subtreasury, for legal tender irredeemable fiat paper money, for government ownership of the railroads, for an increase in the effort of the national government to guarantee the well-being of all the members of society. . . . Like any thoughtful and creative reform group, they tried to make use of their heritage without allowing themselves to be limited by it. . . .

. . . Populists . . . intended the specific planks in their platforms, among other things, to further industrial development. "The sub-treasury," a North Carolina Populist contended, "will bring Manchester to the South." [R]ailroads are a public necessity," wrote a Texas Populist, "and ought to be more and more perfected and extended. . . . [H]e is a fool who expects that the third part of the stars in the firmament of science and civilization should be blotted out by crippling and killing railroads. They are intended by divine providence to be, and can be made, grand, solid blessings." The Southern Populists proposed their reforms not to end industrial development but to stimulate it while making its benefits available to a much greater number. . . . Their acceptance of the fruits of the new order and its physical manifestations—railroads, factories, steam and electric power—testified to the effect of contemporary experience. So did their attitude toward self-sufficient farming, which directly contradicted important elements in their Jeffersonian heritage.

Their opponents constantly told the Southern Populists that they could solve all their economic problems by diversifying their agriculture and raising on the farm all of what they needed. Some Southern Populists did admit that until social and economic conditions improved a degree of self-sufficiency might be warranted. But self-sufficiency as an ideal they rejected almost completely. In an editorial entitled "Progressing Backwards," the editor of the Gracewood, Georgia, *Wool Hat* maintained that while excessive railroad rates might force farmers to diversify their crops, as a rule of thumb such a policy was "a wrong system. . . . It will result in a farmer living more at home, that acme of rural independence which the aforesaid asses [the Democratic press] prate so much about, but it will also result in less trade, less transportation, less business and less progress." Two months earlier Marion Butler's paper advised farmers, given hard times, to try to raise more of their own food "not because it is right that they should live this way, but because it is necessary." To accept it as right and proper "requires the farmer to step out of the line of progress, to refuse to avail themselves [*sic*] of the industrial improvements of the nineteenth century, turn back the wheels of civilization three thousand years, become a hermit and have nothing to do with the outside world." With the proper reforms "the farmers can make that which he [*sic*] can produce best, turn it into money and buy the products of another man's labor, who can produce another article better than he can." The problem of the farmer, and society, lay not with regional agricultural specialization but with distribution, a social, not a natural problem.

A few blamed the failure of regional specialization on the railroad system. Only government ownership of the railroads could ensure an exchange of goods at cost. More Southern Populists felt that the financial system prevented successful regional specialization. The nineteenth century, contended a North Carolina Populist, was an age of economic development. "True wisdom does not sanction a retrograde movement . . . [to] 'hog and hominy.' " Progress demanded regional specialization, but the existing financial conditions made prices so low that people could not exchange goods. A faulty monetary system brought prices so poor that farmers had to burn corn for fuel while people starved and sell cotton below production cost while people froze.

A system of regional interchange also complemented the Southern Populists' ideas for a simple market society within a cooperative rather than a competitive national social and economic system. When each section, because of transportation at cost, could produce what its soil grew best and exchange it for things other sections could produce more cheaply, posited James Murdock, the whole nation would become "like one vast community making their exchanges to an advantage." No panics could occur and no one suffer biting poverty. With people freezing and starving, a policy of economic self-sufficiency for the farmer made no sense. Besides being against all notions of economic and social progress, a policy of "hog and hominy" also would reduce the quality of life for the farmers and all those whom their products benefited. This perception took into account changes from an earlier society and economy and accepted their significance and value while rejecting the use to which they had so far been put. . . .

Almost all of the southern reformers had enough experience with industrial society to realize the great potential of machines for improving human life. They turned to machine images and metaphors because those they had inherited—Jeffersonian, producerite, and religious and moral—proved inadequate for describing and interpreting a modern industrial society. They lacked enough experience, however, to realize the implications of what they did. Except for perhaps the editor of the *Southern Mercury,* they had no idea of how the very impersonality, inhumanity, and amorality of the industrial and financial capitalism at which they aimed their severest criticisms could creep into their thinking anyway, a product of their increased experience with the manifestations of that society and their requirement that its material benefits be retained along with the essentials of the economic system in which it grew. Their class position made it impossible for them to understand that in the very process of accepting, either from ignorance or necessity, some of the adjuncts to industrial development in a market-oriented, private enterprise, capitalist economy, they paved the way for a vitiation of their criticism of that society, a criticism which they based on their personal and moral judgment of the needs of a decent and humane America.

Once again, as in the case of how much equality ought to be granted the blacks, as in the case of how far reform of the economic structure of the country should go, as in the case of the degree to which the government should be involved in the social and economic life of the country, . . . the Southern Populists ran afoul of contradictions within their own beliefs and demands. They wanted black support without relinquishing white dominance. They wanted to prohibit really large-scale landholding and speculation without threatening their position as landlords or potential landlords. They wanted the subtreasury system and government ownership of the railroad, telegraph, and telephone systems while retaining a small economical government. They wanted to eliminate harmful competition and spread the benefits of industrialization more widely, but do it while preserving in the form of a simple market society the very competitive, private ownership, profit-oriented market economy and social order which they criticized for seriously breaking down. They wanted a personal, moral society while retaining the industrial system which bred an America characterized by the very opposite of these qualities. An inadequate understanding of the operation of an industrial capitalist society led to an ineffective effort to reform it. . . .

The Southern Populists did not generally come from nor speak much for the mudsill of their society, the tenant farmers black and white, although they obviously, and with good reason, feared their decline into it. They did number, however, among those who suffered from and helped pay for, economically and socially, the expansion of American industrial capitalism in the thirty-five years following the Civil War. They were only the last in a line of rural movements protesting this situation.

Their ambiguous position in their own community, neither top nor bottom but losing ground rapidly, very probably had a great deal to do with the peculiar duality of much of their response to a new America. Their acceptance and rejection of the new order, their acceptance and rejection of their own experience and past, accounted for much of the complexity of their thought. On balance, however, the ideal social order which the Southern Populists wanted to create, and even more the critique they made of the existing order, came out of their experience living in a personal, intimate, relatively simple, tangible, homogeneous, and moral community. This world was supported and described by their inherited ways of interpreting and understanding the world around them—the producerite, Jeffersonian-Jacksonian, religious and moral metaphors and images. They found themselves in the 1880s and 1890s increasingly threatened by collapse into economic servitude and social dependency while a world of cities, vast industrial developments, a complicated and stratified social organization, a world of impersonality, important intangibles, complexity and distance, and amoral in the traditional, personal sense of morality, destroyed the community and values they knew and understood and in which they believed. . . .

In response to the threat this new social and economic order posed to their personal lives and the community they knew, the Southern Populists set out to create a society which was both relatively homogeneous and simple yet enjoyed the benefits of the new industrial expansion, in which the relations of people to each other remained relatively personal and the laws of personal morality and responsibility guided a society which contained giant railroads and industry. But the Populists failed to convince enough Americans that the reforms they wanted would retain that new society's benefits. They lacked the analytical tools which experience might have given them and which they needed to construct such a program, although they were picking them up. Even if they had succeeded in acquiring this kind of analytical sophistication, however, their class position as landowners, or aspiring landowners, would have betrayed them. Although they questioned such things more thoroughly than most of their contemporaries, almost all the Southern Populists remained ultimately unwilling to surrender the fundamental premises of a capitalist society—the market system, competition, and private property and profit. A more adequate and complete understanding of American industrial and financial capitalism may well have come, as it had already started to do, only at the expense of the powerful and human critique they had forged from the best and most workable elements in their inheritance from Jeffersonian and Jacksonian thought and their experience as rural, evangelical Protestant southern farmers. They did not understand enough.

So the Southern Populist lost in 1896, but so did a whole range of values which produced a distinctive and valid criticism of American industrial and financial capitalism based on that society's inability to serve all the members of the community. For all their provincialism, narrow-mindedness, and confusion, the Southern Populists, at their best and from their own particular standpoint, realized that a social order which set every person against every other, each group or class in society against every other, the Devil taking the hindmost, represented only exploitation to most of its members and would very likely destroy itself eventually. They never denied the benefits of industrial development, but unless these could be attained within the context of a more decent, responsible, and human social order, in which all benefited according to their contribution, this development could not be considered progress, or even very worthwhile by most of the people it affected. . . .

The Advantages of Female Separatism

ESTELLE FREEDMAN

I would like to argue through historical analysis for the . . . strategy of creating a strong, public female sphere. A number of feminist historians have recently explored the value of the separate, though not necessarily public, female sphere for enriching women's historical experience. Carroll Smith-Rosenberg's research has shown how close personal relationships enhanced the private lives of women in the nineteenth century. At the same time, private "sisterhoods," Nancy Cott has suggested, may have been a precondition for the emergence of feminist consciousness. In the late nineteenth and early twentieth centuries, intimate friendships provided support systems for politically active women, as demonstrated by the work of both Blanche Cook and Nancy Sahli. However, the women's culture of the past—personal networks, rituals, and relationships—did not automatically constitute a political strategy. As loving and supportive as women's networks may have been they could keep women content with a status which was inferior to that of men.

I do not accept the argument that female networks and feminist politics were incompatible. Rather, in the following synthesis of recent scholarship in American women's history, I want to show how the women's movement in

This article is reprinted from *Feminist Studies*, volume 5, number 3 (Fall 1979), pp. 512–529, by permission of the publisher, *Feminist Studies*, Inc., c/o Women's Studies Program, University of Maryland, College Park, MD 20742.

the late nineteenth and early twentieth centuries provides an example of the [strategy of creating a separate women's public sphere]. The creation of a separate, public female sphere helped mobilize women and gained political leverage in the larger society. A separatist political strategy, which I refer to as "female institution building," emerged from the middle-class women's culture of the nineteenth century. Its history suggests that in our own time, as well, women's culture can be integral to feminist politics.

What Happened to Feminism?

My desire to restore historical consciousness about female separatism has both a personal and an intellectual motivation. As a feminist working within male-dominated academic institutions, I have realized that I could not survive without access to the feminist culture and politics that flourish outside of mixed institutions. How, I have wondered, could women in the past work for change within a men's world without having this alternative culture? This thought led me to the more academic questions. Perhaps they could not survive when those supports were not available; and perhaps this insight can help explain one of the most intriguing questions in American women's history: What happened to feminism after the suffrage victory in 1920?

Most explanations of the decline of women's political strength focus on either inherent weaknesses in suffragist ideology or on external pressures from a pervasively sexist society. But when I survey the women's movement before suffrage passed, I am struck by the hypothesis that a major strength of American feminism prior to 1920 was the separate female community that helped sustain women's participation in both social reform and political activism. Although the women's movement of the late nineteenth century contributed to the transformation of women's social roles, it did not reject a separate, unique female identity. Most feminists did not adopt the radical demands for equal status with men that originated at the Seneca Falls Convention of 1848. Rather, they preferred to retain membership in a separate female sphere, one which they did not believe to be inferior to men's sphere and one in which women could be free to create their own forms of personal, social, and political relationships. The achievements of feminism at the turn of the century came less through gaining access to the male domains of politics and the professions than in the tangible form of building separate female institutions.

The self-consciously female community began to disintegrate in the 1920s just as "new women" were attempting to assimilate into male-dominated institutions. At work, in social life, and in politics, I will argue, middle-class women hoped to become equals by adopting men's values and integrating into their institutions. A younger generation of women learned to smoke, drink, and value heterosexual relationships over female friendships in their personal lives. At the same time, women's political activity epitomized the process of rejecting women's culture in favor of men's promises of equality. The gradual decline of female separatism in social and political life precluded the emergence of a strong women's political bloc which might have protected and expanded the gains made by the earlier women's movement. Thus the erosion of women's culture may help account for the decline of public feminism in the decades after 1920. Without a constituency a movement cannot survive. The old feminist leaders lost their following when a new generation opted for assimilation in the naive hope of becoming men's equals overnight.

To explore this hypothesis, I shall illustrate episodes of cultural and political separatism within American feminism in three periods: its historical roots prior to 1870; the institution building of the late nineteenth century; and the aftermath of suffrage in the 1920s.

Historical Roots of Separatism

In nineteenth-century America, commercial and industrial growth intensified the sexual division of labor, encouraging the separation of men's and women's spheres. While white males entered the public world of wage labor, business, the professions and politics, most white middle-class women remained at home where they provided the domestic, maternal, and spiritual care for their families and the nation. These women underwent intensive socialization into their roles as "true women." Combined with the restrictions on women which denied them access to the public sphere, this training gave American women an identity quite separate from men's. Women shared unique life experiences as daughters, wives, childbearers, childrearers, and moral guardians. They passed on their values and traditions to their female kin. They created what Smith-Rosenberg has called "The Female World of Love and Ritual," a world of homosocial networks that helped these women transcend the alienation of domestic life.

The ideology of "true womanhood" was so deeply ingrained and so useful for preserving social stability in a time of flux that those few women who explicitly rejected its inequalities could find little support for their views. The feminists of the early women's rights movement were certainly justified in their grievances and demands for equal opportunity with men. The Seneca Falls Declaration of Sentiments of 1848, which called for access to education, property ownership, and political rights, has inspired many feminists since then, while the ridicule and denial of these demands have inspired our rage. But the equal rights arguments of the 1850s were apparently too radical for their own times. Men would not accept women's entry into the public sphere, but more importantly, most women were not interested in rejecting their deeply rooted female identities. Both men and women feared the demise of the female sphere and the valuable functions it performed. The feminists, however, still hoped to reduce the limitations on women within their own sphere, as well as to gain the right of choice—of autonomy—for those women who opted for public rather than private roles.

Radical feminists such as Elizabeth Cady Stanton and Susan B. Anthony recognized the importance of maintaining the virtues of the female world while eliminating discrimination against women in public. As their political analysis developed at mid-century, they drew upon the concepts of female moral superiority and sisterhood, and they affirmed the separate nature of woman. At the same time, their disillusionment with even the more enlightened men of the times reinforced the belief that women had to create their own movement to achieve independence. The bitterness that resulted when most male abolitionists refused to support women's rights in the 1860s, and when they failed to include Woman Suffrage in the Fifteenth Amendment (as well as the inclusion of the term "male citizen" in the Fourteenth Amendment) alienated many women reformers. When Frederick Douglass proclaimed in defense that "This is the Negro's Hour," the more radical women's rights advocates followed Stanton and Anthony in withdrawing from the reform coalition and creating a separatist organization. Their National Woman Suffrage Association had women members and officers; supported a broad range of reforms, including changes in marriage and divorce laws; and published the short-lived journal, *The Revolution.* The radical path proved difficult, however, and the National Woman Suffrage Association merged in 1890 with the more moderate American Woman Suffrage Association. Looking back on their disappointment after the Civil War, Stanton and Anthony wrote prophetically in 1881:

> . . . Our liberal men counselled us to silence during the war, and we were silent on our own wrongs; they counselled us to silence in Kansas and New York (in the suffrage referenda), lest we should defeat "Negro Suffrage," and threatened if we were not, we might fight the battle alone. We chose the latter, and were defeated. But standing alone we learned our power: we repudiated man's counsels forevermore; and solemnly vowed that there should never be another season of silence until woman had the same rights everywhere on this green earth, as man. . . .
>
> We would warn the young women of the coming generation against man's advice as to their best interests. . . . Woman must lead the way to her own enfranchisement. . . . She must not put her trust in man in this transition period, since while regarded as his subject, his inferior, his slave, their interests must be antagonistic.

Female Institution Building

The "transition period" that Stanton and Anthony invoked lasted from the 1870s to the 1920s. It was an era of separate female organization and institution building, the result on the one hand, of the negative push of discrimination in the public, male sphere, and on the other hand, of the positive attraction of the female world of close, personal relationships and domestic institutional structures. These dual origins characterized, for instance, one of the largest manifestations of "social feminism" in the late nineteenth century—the women's club movement.

The club movement illustrated the politicization of women's institutions as well as the limitations of their politics. The exclusion of women reporters from the New York Press Club in 1868 inspired the founding of the first women's club, Sorosis. The movement then blossomed in dozens and later hundreds of localities, until a General Federation of Women's Clubs formed in 1890. By 1910, it claimed over one million members. Although club social and literary activities at first appealed to traditional women who simply wanted to gather with friends and neighbors, by the turn of the century women's clubs had launched civic reform programs. Their activities served to politicize traditional women by forcing them to define themselves as citizens, not simply as wives and mothers. The clubs reflected the societal racism of the time, however, and the black women who founded the National Association of Colored Women in 1896 turned their attention to the social and legal problems that confronted both black women and men.

The Women's Christian Temperance Union had roots in the social feminist tradition of separate institution building. As Ellen DuBois has argued, the WCTU appealed to late nineteenth-century women because it was grounded in the private sphere—the home—and attempted to correct the private abuses against women, namely, intemperance and the sexual double standard. Significantly, though, the WCTU, under Frances Willard's leadership, became a strong prosuffrage organization, committed to righting all wrongs against women, through any means, including the vote.

The women's colleges that opened in these same decades further attest to the importance of separate female institutions during this "transition period." Originally conceived as training grounds of piety, purity, and domesticity, the antebellum women's seminaries, such as Mary Lyon's Mt. Holyoke and Emma Willard's Troy Female Academy, laid the groundwork for the new collegiate institutions of the postwar era. When elite male institutions refused to educate women, the sister colleges of the East, like their counterparts elsewhere, took on the task themselves. In the process they encouraged intimate friendships and professional networks among educated women. At the same time, liberal arts and science training provided tools for women's further development, and by their examples, female teachers inspired students to use their skills creatively. As Barbara Welter noted when she first described the "Cult of True Womanhood," submissiveness was always its weakest link. Like other women's institutions, the colleges could help subvert that element of the Cult by encouraging independence in their students.

The most famous example of the impact of women's colleges may be Jane Addams's description of her experience at Rockford Seminary where she and other students were imbued with the mission of bringing their female values to bear on the entire society. While Addams later questioned the usefulness of her intellectual training in meeting the challenges of the real world, other women did build upon academic foundations when increasingly, as reformers, teachers, doctors, social workers, and in other capacities they left the home to enter public or quasi-public work. Between 1890 and 1920, the number of professional degrees granted to women increased 226 percent, at three times the rate of increase for men. Some of these professionals had attended separate female institutions such as the women's medical colleges in Philadelphia, New York, and Boston. The new female professionals often served women and children clients, in part because of the discrimination against their encroachment on men's domains, but also because they sincerely wanted to work with the traditional objects of their concern. As their skills and roles expanded, these women would demand the right to choose for themselves where and with whom they could work. This first generation of educated professional women became supporters of the suffrage movement in the early twentieth century, calling for full citizenship for women.

The process of redefining womanhood by the extension, rather than by the rejection, of the female sphere may be best illustrated by the settlement house movement. Although both men and women resided in and supported these quasi-public institutions, the high proportion of female participants and leaders (approximately three-fifths of the total), as well as the domestic structure and emphasis on service to women and children, qualify the settlements as female institutions. Mary P. Ryan has captured the link which these ventures provided between "true womanhood" and "new womanhood" in a particularly fitting metaphor: "Within the settlement houses, maternal sediments were further sifted and leavened until they became an entirely new variety of social reform." Thus did Jane Addams learn the techniques of the political world through her efforts to keep the neighborhood clean. So too did Florence Kelley of Hull House welcome appointment as chief factory inspector of Illinois, to protect women and children workers; and Julia Lathrop, another Hull House resident, entered the public sphere as director of the United States Children's Bureau; while one-time settlement resident Katherine Bement Davis moved from the superintendency of the Bedford Hills reformatory for women to become in 1914 the first female commissioner of corrections in New York City. Each of these women, and other settlement workers who moved on to professional and public office, eventually joined and often led branches of the National American Woman Suffrage Association. They drew upon the networks of personal friends and professional allies that grew within separate female institutions when they waged their campaigns for social reform and for suffrage.

Separate female organizations were not limited to middle-class women. Recent histories have shown that groups hoping to bridge class lines between women existed within working-class or radical movements. In both the Women's Trade Union League and the National Consumers League, middle-class reformers strived for cooperation, rather than condescension, in their relationships with working women. Although in neither organization were they entirely successful, the Women's Trade Union League did provide valuable services in organizing women workers, many of whom were significant in its leadership. The efforts of the Consumers League, led by Florence Kelley, to improve working conditions through the use of middle-class women's buying power were probably less effective, but efforts to enact protective legislation for women workers did succeed. Members of both organizations turned to suffrage as one solution to the problems workers faced. Meanwhile, both in leftist organizations and in unions, women formed separate female organizations. Feminists within the Socialist Party met in women's groups in the early twentieth century, while within the clothing trades, women workers formed separate local unions which survived until the mid-1920s. . . .

The Political Legacy

The separate institution building of the late nineteenth century rested on a belief in women's unique identity which had roots in the private female sphere of the early nineteenth century. Increasingly, however, as its participants entered a public female world, they adopted the more radical stance of feminists such as Stanton and Anthony who had long called for an end to political discrimination against women.

The generation that achieved suffrage, then, stood on the border of two worlds, each of which contributed to its ideology and politics. Suffragists argued that women needed the vote to perform their traditional tasks—to protect themselves as mothers and to exert their moral force on society. Yet they also argued for full citizenship and waged a successful, female-controlled political campaign to achieve it.

The suffrage movement succeeded by appealing to a broad constituency—mothers, workers, professionals, reformers—with the vision of the common concerns of womanhood. The movement failed, however, by not extending fully the political strengths of woman bonding. For one thing, the leadership allowed some members to exploit popular racist and nativist sentiments in their prosuffrage arguments, thus excluding most black and immigrant women from a potential feminist coalition. They also failed to recognize that the bonds that held the constituency together were not "natural," but social and political. The belief that women would automatically use the vote to the advantage of their sex overlooked both the class and racial lines that separated women. It underestimated the need for continued political organization so that their interests might be united and realized.

Unfortunately, the rhetoric of equality that became popular among men and women (with the exception of the National Woman's Party) just after the passage of the Suffrage Amendment in 1920 subverted the women's movement by denying the need for continued feminist organization. Of course, external factors significantly affected the movement's future, including the new Freudian views of women; the growth of a consumer economy that increasingly exploited women's sexuality; and the repression of radicalism and reform in general after World War I. But at the same time, many women, seemingly oblivious that these pressures necessitated further separate organizing, insisted on striving for integration into a male world—sexually, professionally, and politically.

Examples of this integrationist approach can be found in the universities, the workplace, and politics. In contrast to an earlier generation, the women who participated in the New York World's Fair of 1937 had no separate building. Woman, the Fair Bulletin explained, "will not sit upon a pedestal, not be segregated, isolated; she will fit into the life of the Exposition as she does into life itself—never apart, always a part." The part in this World's Fair, however, consisted primarily of fashion, food, and vanity fair. In the universities, the success of the first generation of female academics did not survive past the 1920s, not only because of men's resistance, but as Rosalind

Rosenberg has explained, "Success isolated women from their culture of origin and placed them in an alien and often hostile community." Many academics who cut off their ties to other women "lost their old feminine supports but had no other supports to replace them."

The lessons of women's politics in the 1920s are illustrated by the life of one woman, Emily Newell Blair, who learned first hand the pitfalls of rejecting a separatist basis for feminism. Blair's life exemplified the transformation of women's roles at the turn of the century. Educated at a woman's college, Goucher, this Missouri born, middle-class woman returned to her hometown to help support her family until she married and created her own home. Between 1900 and 1910 she bore two children, supported her husband's career, and joined in local women's club activities. In her spare time, Blair began writing short stories for ladies' magazines. Because she found the work, and particularly the income, satisfying, she became a free lance writer. At this point, the suffrage movement revived in Missouri, and Blair took over state publicity, editing the magazine *Missouri Woman* and doing public relations. Then, in World War I, she expanded her professional activities further by serving on the Women's Council of the U.S. Council of National Defense. These years of training in writing, feminist organizing, and public speaking served Blair well when suffrage passed and she entered politics.

In 1920, women faced three major political choices: they could become a separate feminist political force through the National Woman's Party, which few did; they could follow the moderates of the NAWSA into the newly formed, nonpartisan League of Women Voters, concentrating on citizen education and good government; or they could join the mainstream political parties. Emily Newell Blair chose the last, and rose through the Democratic Party organization to become national vice-chairman of the party in the 1920s.

Blair built her political life and her following on the belief that the vote had made women the political equals of men. Thus, the surest path to furthering women's goals was through participation in the party structure. Having helped to found the League of Women Voters, Blair then rejected nonpartisanship, while she urged women not to vote as women but as citizens. In a 1922 lecture on "What Women May Do with the Ballot," Blair argued that "reactions to political issues are not decided by sex but by intellect and emotion. . . ." Although she believed that lack of political experience and social training made women differ from men temporarily, she expected those differences to be eliminated after a few years of political activity. To hasten women's integration into the mainstream of party politics, Blair set up thirty "schools of democracy" to train the new voters during the early twenties, as well as over one thousand women's clubs. Her philosophy, she claimed, was one of "Boring from Within." Blair rejected the "sex conscious feminists" of the Woman's Party and those who wanted "woman cohesiveness." Although she favored the election of women, she wanted them to be chosen not as women but as politicians. "Give women time," she often repeated, and they would become the equals of men in politics.

By the late 1920s, however, women had not gained acceptance as men's political equals, and Blair's views changed significantly. Once she had claimed that the parties did not discriminate against women, as shown by her own powerful position. After she retired from party office in 1928, however, Blair acknowledged that the treatment of women by the parties had deteriorated since the years immediately after suffrage passed. As soon as male politicians realized that there was no strong female voting bloc or political organization, they refused to appoint or elect powerful women, and a "strong masculine prejudice against women in politics" surfaced. Now they chose women for party office who seemed easiest to manage or who were the wives of male officeholders.

By 1931, Blair's former optimism had turned to disillusionment. She felt herself "ineffective in politics as a feminist," a term that she began to use positively. Blair realized that women could not command political power and the respect of their male colleagues unless, like the suffrage leaders, they had a visible, vocal following. "Unfortunately for feminism," she confessed, "it was agreed to drop the sex line in politics. And it was dropped by the women." In the pages of the *Woman's Journal,* Blair called for a revival of feminism in the form of a new politics that would seek to put more women into office. Reversing her former stance, she claimed that *women* voters should back *women* candidates, and use a *women's* organization to do so. They could remain in the parties, but should form "a new organization of feminists devoted to the task of getting women into politics."

The development of Emily Newell Blair's feminist consciousness may have been unique for her time, but it is a familiar process among educated and professional women today. Having gained access to formerly male institutions, but still commmitted to furthering women's struggles, today's "new women" are faced with political choices not dissimilar to the generation that achieved suffrage. The bitterness of Stanton and Anthony in their advice to the younger generation in 1881, and the strategy that Emily Newell Blair presented in 1931, may serve as lessons for the present. . . .

❧ F U R T H E R   R E A D I N G

Peter H. Argersinger, "New Perspectives on Election Fraud in the Gilded Age," *Political Science Quarterly* 100 (Winter 1985–1986), 669–687

Paula Baker, *The Moral Frameworks of Public Life: Gender, Politics, and the State in Rural New York, 1870–1930* (1991)

Sean Dennis Cashman, *America in the Gilded Age* (1984)

Vincent P. De Santis, *The Shaping of Modern America, 1877–1916* (1976)

Leon Fink, *Workingmen's Democracy* (1983)

Lawrence Goodwyn, *Democratic Promise: The Populist Movement in America* (1976)

Steven Hahn, *The Roots of Southern Populism* (1983)

Morton Keller, *Affairs of State: Public Life in Nineteenth Century America* (1977)

Aileen S. Kraditor, *The Ideas of the Women's Suffrage Movement, 1890–1915* (1963)

Michael McGerr, *The Decline of Popular Politics* (1986)

African-American Politics Under Jim Crow

ॐ

While high hopes and faith in an ever-expanding order of progress marked most Americans at the turn of the century, the situation was different in the black community, in the North as well as the South. In the eyes of many postslavery historians, this period represented the nadir of African-American influence in U.S. public life. In the South the de facto reinstatement of one-party white rule was accompanied by a sharp rise in lynchings of blacks, the general exclusion of African-Americans from active citizenship via disfranchisement statutes, and the erection of a virtual caste system of institutional segregation, called Jim Crow after the name of an old blackfaced vaudeville character. By 1900 the principle of segregation extended into every area of southern life, including street railways, hotels, hospitals, restaurants, recreational facilities, and the workplace. Discrimination was the norm in the North as well, but there it was enforced less by specific legislation than by restrictive real-estate zoning, employment practices (on behalf of both employers and many trade unions), and popular racism. The very density of such ghettoized northern black neighborhoods as Harlem in New York and Chicago's Back o' the Yards, however, offered a creative, self-governing cultural space, which by the 1920s suggested new possibilities for a mass politics.

Even the black educated elite found early-twentieth-century America a tough world to negotiate, for the strategic maneuvering room for black advancement as a whole was severely limited. Nevertheless, the realities of Jim Crow elicited a wide range of responses. The conservative strategy, associated most closely with Booker T. Washington at Tuskegee, Alabama, recognized the impossibility of frontal resistance to white racial norms and opted instead for politically inoffensive self-improvement efforts that might win not only white acceptance but even financial endowment. The more radical course, advocated by sociologist W. E. B. Du Bois and a tiny minority of northern professionals, counseled a direct challenge to the legal, political, and ideological props of Jim Crow. Most contemporary black leaders fell somewhere between these two poles, struggling to gain a foothold amidst an outrushing tide.

In the first selection, from *Plessy* v. *Ferguson,* a case involving the forced separation of blacks on railroad cars, the U.S. Supreme Court set an important precedent on behalf of legalized segregation. Equally significant, the lone dissent of Justice John Harlan of Kentucky foreshadowed the wisdom of a later age. If the court, in *Plessy,* chose to defend segregation laws on rather narrow and technical grounds, the more assertive, unapologetic voice of Jim Crow is reflected in the second document, in the political oratory of Congressman Frank Clark of Florida, supporting an amendment introduced by Congressman J. Thomas Heflin of Alabama to segregate streetcars in Washington, D.C.

Contemporary African-American political opinion is in turn represented in the next three selections. In the third document, Booker T. Washington offers a classic version of his collective self-help philosophy before an admiring white audience at the Atlantic Exposition in 1895. W. E. B. Du Bois, who shortly thereafter led the Niagara group of black intellectuals into the National Association for the Advancement of Colored People (NAACP), answers Washington with bitter sarcasm. In the final commentary, Mary Church Terrell, an Oberlin graduate and the cofounder of the Colored Women's League Clubs, speaks of the painful travail of even the most ambitious and ''respectable'' black families in trying to pursue the education of their children.

The U.S. Supreme Court Upholds Segregation:
Plessy v. *Ferguson,* 1896

Justice Brown The constitutionality of this act is attacked upon the ground that it conflicts both with the 13th Amendment of the Constitution, abolishing slavery, and the 14th Amendment, which prohibits certain restrictive legislation on the part of the states.

1. That it does not conflict with the 13th Amendment, which abolished slavery and involuntary servitude, except as a punishment for crime, is too clear for argument. . . .

A statute which implies merely a legal distinction between the white and colored races—a distinction which is founded in the color of the two races, and which must always exist so long as white men are distinguished from the other race by color—has no tendency to destroy the legal equality of the two races, or re-establish a state of involuntary servitude. . . .

The object of the [14th] amendment was undoubtedly to enforce the absolute equality of the two races before the law, but in the nature of things it could not have been intended to abolish distinctions based upon color, or to enforce social, as distinguished from political, equality, or a commingling of the two races upon terms unsatisfactory to either. Laws permitting, and even requiring their separation in places where they are liable to be brought into contact do not necessarily imply the inferiority of either race to the other, and have been generally, if not universally, recognized as within the competency of the state legislatures in the exercise of their police power. The most common instance of this is connected with the establishment of separate schools for white and colored children, which have been held to be a valid exercise of the legislative power even by courts of states where the political rights of the colored race have been longest and most earnestly enforced. . . .

So far, then, as a conflict with the 14th Amendment is concerned, the case reduces itself to the question whether the statute of Louisiana is a reasonable regulation, and with respect to this there must necessarily be a large discretion on the part of the legislature. In determining the question of reasonableness it is at liberty to act with reference to the established usages, customs, and traditions of the people, and with a view to the promotion of their comfort, and the preservation of the public peace and good order. Gauged by this standard, we cannot say that a law which authorizes or even requires the separation of the two races in public conveyances is unreasonable or more obnoxious to the 14th Amendment than the acts of Congress requiring separate schools for colored children in the District of Columbia, the constitutionality of which does not seem to have been questioned, or the corresponding acts of state legislatures.

We consider the underlying fallacy of the plaintiff's argument to consist in the assumption that the enforced separation of the two races stamps the colored race with a badge of inferiority. If this be so, it is not by reason of anything found in the act, but solely because the colored race chooses to put that construction upon it. The argument necessarily assumes that if, as has been more than once the case, and is not unlikely to be so again, the colored race should become the dominant power in the state legislature, and should enact a law in precisely similar terms, it would thereby relegate the white race to an inferior position. We imagine that the white race, at least, would not acquiesce in this assumption. The argument also assumes that social prejudice may be overcome by legislation, and that equal rights cannot be secured to the Negro except by an enforced commingling of the two races. We cannot accept this proposition. If the two races are to meet on terms of social equality, it must be the result of natural affinities, a mutual appreciation of each other's merits and a voluntary consent of individuals. . . . Legislation is powerless to eradicate racial instincts or to abolish distinctions based upon physical differences, and the attempt to do so can only result in accentuating the difficulties of the present situation. If the civil and political right of both races be equal, one cannot be inferior . . . to the other civilly or politically. If one race be inferior to the other socially, the Constitution of the United States cannot put them upon the same plane.

Justice Harlan, dissenting. . . . In respect of civil rights, common to all citizens, the Constitution of the United States does not, I think, permit any public authority to know the race of those entitled to be protected in the enjoyment of such rights. Every true man has pride of race, and under appropriate circumstances, when the rights of others, his equals before the law, are not to be affected, it is his privilege to express such pride and to take such action based upon it as to him seems proper. But I deny that any legislative body or judicial tribunal may have regard to the race of citizens when the civil rights of those citizens are involved. Indeed such legislation as that here in question is inconsistent, not only with that equality of rights which pertains to citizenship, national and state, but with the personal liberty enjoyed by every one within the United States. . . .

In my opinion, the judgment this day rendered will, in time, prove to be quite as pernicious as the decision made by this tribunal in the Dred Scott Case. It was adjudged in that case that the descendants of Africans who were imported into this country and sold as slaves were not included nor intended to be included under the word "citizens" in the Constitution, and could not claim any of the rights and privileges which that instrument provided for and secured to citizens of the United States; that at the time of the adoption of the Constitution they were "considered as a subordinate and inferior class of beings, who had been subjugated by the dominant race, and, whether emancipated or not, yet remained subject to their authority, and had no rights or privileges but such as those who held the power and the government might choose to grant them." The recent amendments of the Constitution, it was supposed, had eradicated these principles from our institutions. But it seems that we have yet, in some of the states, a dominant race, a superior class of citizens, which assumes to regulate the enjoyment of civil rights, common to all citizens, upon the basis of race. The present decision, it may well be apprehended, will not only stimulate aggressions, more or less brutal and irritating, upon the admitted rights of colored citizens, but will encourage the belief that it is possible, by means of state enactments, to defeat the beneficent purposes which the people of the United States had in view when they adopted the recent amendments of the Constitution, by one of which the blacks of this country were made citizens of the United States and of the states in which they respectively reside and whose privileges and immunities, as citizens, the states are forbidden to abridge. Sixty millions of whites are in no danger from the presence here of eight millions of blacks. The destinies of the two races in this country are indissolubly linked together, and the interests of both require that the common government of all shall not permit the seeds of race hate to be planted under the sanction of law. What can more certainly arouse race hate, what more certainly create and perpetuate a feeling of distrust between these races, than state enactments which in fact proceed on the ground that colored citizens are so inferior and degraded that they cannot be allowed to sit in public coaches occupied by white citizens? That, as all will admit, is the real meaning of such legislation as was enacted in Louisiana. . . .

If evils will result from the commingling of the two races upon public highways established for the benefit of all, they will be infinitely less than those that will surely come from state legislation regulating the enjoyment of civil rights upon the basis of race. We boast of the freedom enjoyed by our people above all other peoples. But it is difficult to reconcile that boast with a state of the law which, practically, puts the brand of servitude and degradation upon a large class of our fellow citizens, our equals before the law. The thin disguise of "equal" accommodations for passengers in railroad coaches will not mislead anyone, or atone for the wrong this day done. . . .

I am of opinion that the statute of Louisiana is inconsistent with the personal liberty of citizens, white and black, in that state, and hostile to both the spirit and letter of the Constitution of the United States. If laws of like character should be enacted in the several states of the Union, the effect would be in the highest degree mischievous. Slavery as an institution tolerated by law would, it is true, have disappeared from our country, but there would remain a power in the states, by sinister legislation, to interfere with the full enjoyment of the blessings of freedom; to regulate civil rights, common to all citizens, upon the basis of race; and to place in a condition of legal inferiority a large body of American citizens, now constituting a part of the political community, called the people of the United States, for whom and by whom, through representatives, our government is administered. Such a system is inconsistent with the guarantee given by the Constitution to each state of a republican form of government, and may be stricken down by Congressional action, or by the courts in the discharge of their solemn duty to maintain the supreme law of the land, anything in the Constitution or laws of any state to the contrary notwithstanding.

For the reasons stated, I am constrained to withhold my assent from the opinion and judgment of the majority.

Congressman Frank Clark Praises Segregation, 1908

On last Sunday afternoon an old negro man living in this city came to my office and spent the afternoon with my wife and myself, and I have not spent a more pleasant afternoon for years. [Applause] He belonged to my father, and he was the first human being that ever carried me out in the yard after my birth. [Applause on the Democratic side.] . . . I love that old negro man [applause], and . . . in a contest between him and others, in a physical contest, I would be found by his side protecting and defending him. [Renewed applause.] . . .

Mr. Chairman, the question raised by the amendment [to segregate street cars in Washington, D.C.] offered by the gentleman from Alabama [Cong. Heflin] is purely a question of disposing of a situation in such manner as will lessen the friction between the races. The adoption of that amendment will not discriminate against the negro race, nor will it inure to the advantage of the white race alone. It will inure to the benefit of both races. It is not intended by the gentleman from Alabama as an attack upon the negro, nor is it an attempt by that gentleman, or by any of us who support it, to deprive the negro of a single right which he has under the law of the land. On its very face it provides equal accommodation for both races on the street cars in the Capital City of this Republic. . . . It is idle to call this amendment a discrimination against the negro. Wherein is the discrimination? The amendment itself contains no discrimination. The language used contains no hint of discrimination, yet gentlemen seize upon it as an excuse to arraign the people of an entire section of this country for alleged wrongs to the negro race. Is this fair? Do gentlemen imagine that even the negro, who has been the willing dupe of the Republican party for all these long years, can be longer deceived by these loud quadrennial protestations of affectionate regard for him? . . .

While on this phase of the subject, Mr. Speaker, I desire to refer to the unsupported, bald declarations of gentlemen that negroes are not supplied with accommodations equal to those furnished to white people upon railroads in the South. Why gentlemen will persist in these statements I can not understand. Let me suggest something here that in all probability these gentlemen have never thought of. On our Florida railroads–and I presume it is the same in other Southern States–the cars furnished for negro passengers are just as good as those furnished for white passengers. I am free to admit, however, that they do not long remain as good, as comfortable, and as clean as do those set apart for white passengers. You will not have to search long for the reason of this change. The average negro is perfectly happy when he finds himself eating a watermelon or going on a railroad excursion. The railroad companies in the South cater to this weakness of the negro for riding on trains, and scarcely a week passes in the summer time that a negro excursion is not "pulled off" in every neighborhood. They flock to these excursion trains by thousands and of course the cars set apart for the negroes on the regular passenger trains are used for negro excursions.

Imagine a nice, new passenger coach, packed with dirty, greasy, filthy negroes, down South, in midsummer, and you can readily understand why that car does not long remain as good, as clean, and as desirable as a similar car occupied exclusively by white travelers. It is said of Sam Jones, the great Georgia revivalist, that on one occasion a certain Northern gentleman asked him if there was very much difference in the instincts of a "nigger" and a white man. Sam replied that he didn't know as to that, but of one thing he was absolutely sure, and that was that there was a vast difference in the *"out stinks"* of the two.

For more than forty years, Mr. Chairman, the white people of the South have been taxing themselves to educate negro children, have been building churches for them, and in every conceivable way, with a patience and forbearance never excelled in any age, have struggled along with the stupendous task of elevating and fitting for the duties of citizenship this black mass of ignorant, vicious, and incapable freedmen. I am not wise enough to foretell the end of the problem confronting us. Mr. Lincoln said that this nation could not exist "half slave and half free." I think it is equally true that this nation can not exist *half white* and *half black*. I am very sure that no country having within its borders two distinct races, alien to each other in every essential respect, can long exist with any degree of harmony between the two upon the beautiful theory of perfect equality of all before the law.

The position which we of the South occupy on this question is not one of hostility to the negro. It is one of patriotic love for our own race. We would not destroy the negro, but we would preserve the Caucasian. We will do the black man no harm, and we will not allow him to harm the white man. Members of Congress who are dependent upon a few negro votes in order to retain their seats in this body, a few long-haired negrophilists in various sections of the country, and a lot of short-haired white women who disgrace both their race and sex, may rant of injustice and wrong to the end of time, but they had as well realize now as at any other time that, no matter what the cost or how great the sacrifice, we shall under any and all circumstances maintain the integrity of our race and preserve our civilization.

If God Almighty had intended these two races to be equal, He would have so created them. He made the Caucasian of handsome figure, straight hair, regular features, high brow, and superior intellect. He created the negro, giving him a black skin, kinky hair, thick lips, flat nose, low brow, low order of intelligence, and repulsive features. I do not believe that these differences were the result of either accident or mistake on the part of the Creator. I believe He knew what He was doing, and I believe He did just what He wanted to do.

We believe in God, and we are willing to accept His work just as it fell from His hands. But these people who profess to believe that "a white man may be as good as a negro if the white man behaves himself" are not satisfied with God's work in this regard. They are quite sure that they can make a better job of it than did the Creator, hence we find them attempting to remove the black man from the menial sphere for which he was created, and where he may be useful, to a higher circle for which he is entirely unfitted and where he is perfectly useless. . . .

The gentleman from New York [Cong. Driscoll] says that we have been allowed to have our own way down South with this question for so long that we have grown "bold" enough to come on the floor of this House and make demands for this kind of legislation. The gentleman uses that word "bold" as though he thought we did not have the right to come here and make demands. We do demand, and we have the right to demand. The blood of the "heroes of the Revolution" flows through our veins; from the Revolution to the present day no foreign foe has ever engaged this Republic in battle that Southern blood has not consecrated every place of conflict; in all our history no foreign foe has ever threatened the flag that we did not rally to its defense. In these emergencies we volunteer, and do not have to be drafted. Yes; we have the right to demand. This is our country, as it was the country of our fathers. The country of the white man, not the home of the mongrel. It will always be the white man's country. If the black man and the yellow man each desire to remain with us, occupying the sphere in life for which God Almighty intended each, let them do so. If not content with that, then let them go elsewhere. . . .

Booker T. Washington Advocates Self-Help, 1895

A ship lost at sea for many days suddenly sighted a friendly vessel. From the mast of the unfortunate vessel was seen a signal, "Water, water; we die of thirst!" The answer from the friendly vessel at once came back, "Cast down your bucket where you are." A second time the signal, "Water, water; send us water!" ran up from the distressed vessel, and was answered, "Cast down your bucket where you are." And a third and fourth signal for water was answered, "Cast down your bucket where you are." The captain of the distressed vessel, at last heeding the injunction, cast down his bucket, and it came up full of fresh, sparkling water from the mouth of the Amazon River. To those of my race who depend on bettering their condition in a foreign land or who underestimate the importance of cultivating friendly relations with the Southern white man, who is their next-door neighbour, I would say: "Cast down your bucket where you are"—cast it down in making friends in every manly way of the people of all races by whom we are surrounded.

Cast it down in agriculture, mechanics, in commerce, in domestic service, and in the professions. And in this connection it is well to bear in mind that whatever other sins the South may be called to bear, when it comes to business, pure and simple, it is in the South that the Negro is given a man's chance in the commercial world, and in nothing is this Exposition more eloquent than in emphasizing this chance. Our greatest danger is that in the great leap from slavery to freedom we may overlook the fact that the masses of us are to live by the productions of our hands, and fail to keep in mind that we shall prosper in proportion as we learn to dignify and glorify common labour and put brains and skill into the common occupations of life; shall prosper in proportion as we learn to draw the line between the superficial and the substantial, the ornamental gewgaws of life and the useful. No race can prosper till it learns that there is as much dignity in tilling a field as in writing a poem. It is at the bottom of life we must begin, and not at the top. Nor should we permit our grievances to overshadow our opportunities.

To those of the white race who look to the incoming of those of foreign birth and strange tongue and habits for the prosperity of the South, were I permitted I would repeat what I say to my own race, "Cast down your bucket where you are." Cast it down among the eight millions of Negroes whose habits you know, whose fidelity and love you have tested in days when to have proved treacherous meant the ruin of your firesides. Cast down your bucket among these people who have, without strikes and labour wars, tilled your fields, cleared your forests, builded your railroads and cities, and brought forth treasures from the bowels of the earth, and helped make possible this magnificent representation of the progress of the South. Casting down your bucket among my people, helping and encouraging them as you are doing on these grounds, and to education of head, hand, and heart, you will find that they will buy your surplus land, make blossom the waste places in your fields, and run your factories. While doing this, you can be sure in the future, as in the past, that you and your families will be surrounded by the most patient, faithful, law-abiding, and unresentful people that the world has seen. As we have proved our loyalty to you in the past, in nursing your children, watching by the sick-bed of your mothers and fathers, and often following them with tear-dimmed eyes to their graves, so in the future, in our humble way, we shall stand by you with a devotion that no foreigner can approach, ready to lay down our lives, if need be, in defence of yours, interlacing our industrial, commercial, civil, and religious life with yours in a way that shall make the interests of both races one. In all things that are purely social we can be as separate as the fingers, yet one as the hand in all things essential to mutual progress. . . .

The wisest among my race understand that the agitation of questions of social equality is the extremest folly, and that progress in the enjoyment of all the privileges that will come to us must be the result of severe and constant struggle rather than of artificial forcing. No race that has anything to contribute to the markets of the world is long in any degree ostracized. It is important and right that all privileges of the law be ours, but it is vastly more important that we be prepared for the exercises of these privileges. The opportunity to earn a dollar in a factory just now is worth infinitely more than the opportunity to spend a dollar in an opera-house.

In conclusion, may I repeat that nothing in thirty years has given us more hope and encouragement, and drawn us so near to you of the white race, as this opportunity [to participate in] the Exposition; and here bending, as it were, over the altar that represents the results of the struggles of your race and mine, both starting practically empty-handed three decades ago, I pledge that in your effort to work out the great and intricate problem which God has laid at the doors of the South, you shall have at all times the patient, sympathetic help of my race; only let this be constantly in mind, that, while from representations in these buildings of the product of field, of forest, of mine, of factory, letters, and art, much good will come, yet far above and beyond material benefits will be that higher good, that, let us pray God, will come, in a blotting out of sectional differences and racial animosities and suspicions, in a determination to administer absolute justice, in a willing obedience among all classes to the mandates of law. This, this, coupled with our material prosperity, will bring into our beloved South a new heaven and a new earth. . . .

W. E. B. Du Bois Rejects Washington's Strategy of Accommodation, 1903

Mr. Washington represents in Negro thought the old attitude of adjustment and submission; but adjustment at such a peculiar time as to make his programme unique. This is an age of unusual economic development, and Mr. Washington's programme naturally takes an economic cast, becoming a gospel of Work and Money to such an extent as apparently almost completely to overshadow the higher aims of life. Moreover, this is an age when the more advanced races are coming in closer contact with the less developed races, and the race-feeling is therefore intensified; and Mr. Washington's programme practically accepts the alleged inferiority of the Negro races. Again, in our own land, the reaction from the sentiment of war time has given impetus to race-prejudice against Negroes, and Mr. Washington withdraws many of the high demands of Negroes as men and American citizens. In other periods of intensified prejudice all the Negro's tendency to self-assertion has been called forth; at this period a policy of submission is advocated. In the history of nearly all other races and peoples the doctrine preached at such crises has been that manly self-respect is worth more than lands and houses, and that a people who voluntarily surrender such respect, or cease striving for it, are not worth civilizing.

In answer to this, it has been claimed that the Negro can survive only through submission. Mr. Washington distinctly asks that black people give up, at least for the present, three things,—

First, political power,

Second, insistence on civil rights,

Third, higher education of Negro youth,—

and concentrate all their energies on industrial education, the accumulation of wealth, and the conciliation of the South. This policy has been courageously and insistently advocated for over fifteen years, and has been triumphant for perhaps ten years. As a result of this tender of the palm-branch, what has been the return? In these years there have occurred:

1. The disfranchisement of the Negro.
2. The legal creation of a distinct status of civil inferiority for the Negro.
3. The steady withdrawal of aid from institutions for the higher training of the Negro.

These movements are not, to be sure, direct results of Mr. Washington's teachings; but his propaganda has, without a shadow of doubt, helped their speedier accomplishment. The question then comes: Is it possible, and probable, that nine millions of men can make effective progress in economic lines if they are deprived of political rights, made a servile caste, and allowed only the most meagre chance for developing their exceptional men? If history and reason give any distinct answer to these questions, it is an emphatic *No*. And Mr. Washington thus faces the triple paradox of his career:

1. He is striving nobly to make Negro artisans business men and property-owners; but it is utterly impossible, under modern competitive methods, for workingmen and property-owners to defend their rights and exist without the right of suffrage.

2. He insists on thrift and self-respect, but at the same time counsels a silent submission to civic inferiority such as is bound to sap the manhood of any race in the long run.

3. He advocates common-school and industrial training, and depreciates institutions of higher learning; but neither the Negro common-schools, nor Tuskegee itself, could remain open a day were it not for teachers trained in Negro colleges, or trained by their graduates. . . .

[Critics of Washington] do not expect that the free right to vote, to enjoy civic rights, and to be educated, will come in a moment; they do not expect to see the bias and prejudices of years disappear at the blast of a trumpet; but they are absolutely certain that the way for a people to gain their reasonable rights is not by voluntarily throwing them away and insisting that they do not want them; that the way for a people to gain respect is not by continually belittling and ridiculing themselves; that, on the contrary, Negroes must insist continually, in season and out of season, that voting is necessary to modern manhood, that color discrimination is barbarism, and that black boys need education as well as white boys. . . .

. . . On the whole the distinct impression left by Mr. Washington's propaganda is, first, that the South is justified in its present attitude toward the Negro because of the Negro's degradation; secondly, that the prime cause of the Negro's failure to rise more quickly is his wrong education in the past; and, thirdly, that his future rise depends primarily on his own efforts. Each of these propositions is a dangerous half-truth. The supplementary truths must never be lost sight of: first, slavery and race-prejudice are potent if not sufficient causes of the Negro's position; second, industrial and common-school training were necessarily slow in planting because they had to await the black teachers trained by higher institutions, . . . and, third, while it is a great truth to say that the Negro must strive and strive mightily to help himself, it is equally true that unless his striving be not simply seconded, but rather aroused and encouraged, by the initiative of the richer and wiser environing group, he cannot hope for great success.

In his failure to realize and impress this last point, Mr. Washington is especially to be criticised. His doctrine has tended to make the whites, North and South, shift the burden of the Negro problem to the Negro's shoulders and stand aside as critical and rather pessimistic spectators; when in fact the burden belongs to the nation. . . .

The South ought to be led, by candid and honest criticism, to assert her better self and do her full duty to the race she has cruelly wronged and is still wronging. The North—her co-partner in guilt—cannot salve her conscience by plastering it with gold. We cannot settle this problem by diplomacy and suaveness, by "policy" alone. If worse come to worst, can the moral fibre of this country survive the slow throttling and murder of nine millions of men?

The black men of America have a duty to perform, a duty stern and delicate,—a forward movement to oppose a part of the work of their greatest leader. So far as Mr. Washington preaches Thrift, Patience, and Industrial Training for the masses, we must hold up his hands and strive with him, rejoicing in his honors and glorying in the strength of this Joshua called of God and of man to lead the headless host. But so far as Mr. Washington apologizes for injustice, North or South, does not rightly value the privilege and duty of voting, belittles the emasculating effects of caste distinctions, and opposes the higher training and ambition of our brighter minds,—so far as he, the South, or the Nation, does this,—we must unceasingly and firmly oppose them. By every civilized and peaceful method we must strive for the rights which the world accords to men, clinging unwaveringly to those great words which the sons of the Fathers would fain forget: "We hold these truths to be self-evident: That all men are created equal; that they are endowed by their Creator with certain unalienable rights; that among these are life, liberty, and the pursuit of happiness."

Mary Church Terrell on Racial Exclusion in Northern Academies, 1940

A young girl of whom I was very fond and with whose family I had been closely associated for years decided to prepare herself for college in a large fitting school in the West—quite near Chicago, to be exact. But there followed such a series of cold rebuffs and positive refusals from the principal to whom the application was sent that even those of us who thoroughly understand prejudice against colored people in the United States, and who have ourselves tasted its bitterness to the very dregs, were shocked.

The young woman to whom I shall refer as Ruth lived in a southern city in which there was no high school for colored youth at that time. At a family council, therefore, it was decided to make the necessary sacrifice to enable Ruth to go to the fitting school. A letter was written to the principal and a favorable reply was received. "We have a room large enough for two girls which we can allow Miss R to occupy alone at the rate of $115 a quarter," read the letter. "We can hold the room till you have time to reply. I very much hope that you will decide to send Miss R to us. . . . I will hope to hear from you very early next week."

While the letter was being written in which to send the required deposit, it occurred to us that it might be wise to say that Ruth had a drop of African blood in her veins. Some of us did not think it necessary to supply that information, since the young woman was to room alone. We insisted upon that arrangement and were perfectly willing to pay for the privilege. At that time we took it for granted that all first class institutions in the North admitted colored students. My own husband had prepared for college at Groton Academy in Massachusetts. It did not occur to us, therefore, that high grade academies for girls would be an exception to this rule. In referring to Ruth's nationality it was explicitly stated that, although she had a speck of African blood in her veins, she was so fair that nobody unaware of the fact could possibly suspect or detect it. Stating that a colored person was fair, so as to induce those with power to grant him the privilege to which he was entitled, has always seemed to me an unfortunate concession to race prejudice.

Replying to this letter the principal wrote:

My dear Madam: I am in receipt of yours of December 3 and we make no objection to receiving Miss R and on receipt of the deposit required in all cases we will hold a room for her. I do not anticipate any difficulty and we will do our best to make Miss R's stay with us a pleasant one.

Upon reading this reassuring letter, we sent the deposit, and Ruth's trunk was packed right away. But within forty-eight hours the following letter was received:

My dear Madam: I regret exceedingly that a close study of the situation here makes it clear to us that we cannot be sure that Miss R could be comfortable here, and I therefore feel that it is better that the engagement of the room be canceled. I return herewith the deposit and hope the delay may cause you no inconvenience.

This letter greatly shocked us all. Ruth had set her heart on going to this particular school, had told her friends about her plans, and now her application for admission was rejected because she was colored. I resolved to save the girl from this bitter disappointment and keen humiliation if I could. So I wrote the principal a courteous letter, telling him how much his decision embarrassed us, how it wounded Ruth's feelings, appealed to his sense of justice, implored him to reconsider his action and admit her to his school. He replied:

> My dear Madam: I regret exceedingly that my first decision was made without sufficient study of the situation. I can only say, however, that I must repeat what I said in my first letter. I would add, however, this—that the University of Chicago is in no way responsible for my decision.

The principal probably felt it his duty to exonerate the University of Chicago because his fitting school made a specialty of preparing girls to enter that institution. When Ruth was finally told she had been denied admission to the school a look of despair and pain came into the girl's face which I cannot forget.

Then Ruth's family, determined to carry out its plans, looked toward the East and made arrangements for Ruth to attend a fitting school near Philadelphia. Remembering their experience with the western school, the family decided to say nothing about Ruth's nationality. I accompanied her to the school myself. No placard of racial classifications was attached to either one of us and we let our faces speak for themselves. But a few months after Ruth had been attending school the following letter was received:

> My dear Madam: I regret very much the necessity that compels me to broach a matter that must prove a wrong done one of us and not pleasant to either. There is a conviction growing up among the members of our student body that Miss R bears other than Caucasian blood. If this be true, her presence here would be contrary to our precedent and would be received by our alumnae and corporation with disfavor. Miss R is a quiet, studious young woman, and while her schoolmates do not approve of race intermingling, they have suspended judgment in her case, and she is treated with due respect. Should what we fear prove true, the school would, of course, refund all money paid in after deducting for her room and tuition while here. If we are mistaken in this matter I shall be very sorry to have caused you this annoyance and will take steps to set the matter right before all concerned. Awaiting your early reply, I am very truly yours.

This letter was unexpected. I myself had taken Ruth to this school, feeling certain that the authorities would know that I had "other than Caucasian blood," as soon as they saw me. . . .

The family feared Ruth was being treated like an outcast by the pupils. . . . They asked me to go to Philadelphia as quickly as I could. The principal and I had a lengthy interview in which he told me he had no idea of my racial identity because I seemed to be highly educated and spoke correct English. He had never seen an educated colored woman before, he said.

"There are some southern girls here," he told me, "and the sight of a colored girl to southern pupils throws them into fits." According to the catalog, there were only five out of a total of 300. What a fine thing it would be if the North were as loyal to what it claims to be its principles as the South is to its views. . . .

The mother of one of the southern girls visited the school, said the principal, and admired Ruth very much. Learning her name, however, and the town she came from, the southern woman grew very excited. She declared Ruth's family was well known and she was sure she was colored. "I denied it," said the principal, "but I promised to write for the facts, which explains my letter to you. Once before, we admitted a colored girl into the school by mistake—a fine young woman who sang divinely—but when we discovered she was not white we asked her to leave."

"But she was white, was she not?" I inquired. "Well, yes," was the quick reply, "white to the eye, but she had African blood in her veins, so we could not have her here."

That afternoon Ruth and I took the train for her home. She had been very finely treated by a few of the girls, she said—by all of them, in fact, till the mother of the southern girl had circulated the report that she was colored and then her trials began. She had made it a rule not to seek the companionship of any of the girls. She let them make all the advances to her, she said. But she did not repel those who showed a disposition to be friendly.

In a burst of confidence the girl who liked Ruth best told her that some of the girls had tried to make fun of her. "I hope you won't feel bad, Ruth, if I tell you what they say. They say you are a nigger. I told them I didn't care if you were a Hottentot, you were far better bred and more congenial to me than they were."

Ruth's family were more determined than ever that the girl should enjoy the advantages she craved and for which they were able to pay. Suddenly I thought of a man who is a well-known author living in a Massachusetts college town where there is a fine fitting school for girls. We attended Oberlin College together. He and his wife once came to hear me speak, invited me to visit them and we spent several pleasant days together. Knowing how broad and just he was, I wrote him to ask the school officials to admit Ruth, feeling that a request from such a man would have its effect. He gave a cheerful assent. . . .

. . . My author friend went personally to see the principal of the fitting school in Ruth's behalf. Then one day I received the following letter:

I have been to see Miss Caswell of the Caswell-Brewster School (this is not the real name of either the teacher or the school) and I dare say I have nothing to add to your wisdom or experience in such matters. It is the same old story—modified in this case as in many others—by good wishes and regrets and a real desire to have things different. But they are not different and the world moves slowly. Miss Caswell says Miss R would have a very unhappy time at her school and nothing but harm, as things are at present, could come on both sides by her joining it. . . .

I shall not try to describe how this letter affected Ruth.

Then a friend told me of another academy in Massachusetts which is one of the oldest in the country. "It is a very expensive school," she said, "but a few colored girls from well-to-do families have attended it nevertheless." We felt that the problem of finding a school for Ruth had been solved at last. Colored girls had actually attended the school. There was no doubt about that. I went to make arrangements with the principal and gave several personal references which I felt sure would enable her to classify me with ease, even if her eyesight were poor. She courteously showed me the really luxurious apartments occupied by the girls and was anxious to have Ruth's family send her at once. . . .

The dormitory was arranged in suites of three rooms—two bedrooms opposite each other which were separated by a sitting room that was shared by the two girls. "Are you quite sure," asked Ruth, when I explained the arrangement to her, "that colored girls who have attended the academy have shared a sitting room with a white girl?" That set me to thinking. . . . I decided that whatever else happened there should be no misunderstanding. Ruth should not be humiliated again if I could prevent it. I wrote the principal that while Ruth was as fair as the average white girl and fairer than many, she was colored. I had not mentioned that when I talked to her, I wrote, because I took it for granted she could see I am a colored woman, and because I had heard on reliable authority that three or four colored girls had already attended the school.

The reply to this letter read as follows:

I was greatly surprised at receiving your letter this morning. I had not the slightest suspicion that Miss R had any colored blood. Blessing Academy has always been friendly to the colored race and to all races. I have no reason to think that any one would object to Miss R's presence as a student. But we have just one vacancy in the building, and the student who takes this place will be put in the same suite of rooms with another student. You can easily see the embarrassment we might have been caused if Miss R had come here and had gone into a room with a white girl.

Certainly it would have made a great deal of trouble, as soon as her roommate discovered that Miss R had colored blood and all the talk and the widespread criticism resulting would have reacted most unfavorably upon our school as well as upon Miss R and her race. Hence it is most fortunate that you wrote me as plainly as you did about the matter. We have three or four single rooms in the building, but they are all occupied. Hence it will be utterly impossible for us to admit Miss R at this time. I am very sorry and I want to repeat that it is not because she belongs to the colored race, but because we cannot give her a room.

Sincerely yours.

. . .

There were good high schools in the North and good institutions for colored youth at which Ruth might have prepared for college. But since she had been a small child, her family had told her they were going to send her to a northern academy to prepare for college. She and the rest of us had set our hearts on it. But I am sorry we were all so ignorant about conditions in the North. Our experience caused us many heartaches.

✌ E S S A Y S

The eminent historian of the South C. Vann Woodward of Yale University, in the first essay, outlines the logic and basic parameters of legalized segregation at the turn of the century. In the second selection, historian Louis Harlan of the University of Maryland offers a revisionist defense of the political strategy and tactics practiced by Booker T. Washington. Finally, writer Paula Giddings, currently scholar-in-residence at Spelman College, compares two styles of political activism through the careers of Mary Church Terrell and journalist Ida B. Wells.

The Heyday of Jim Crow

C. VANN WOODWARD

Up to the year 1898 South Carolina had resisted the Jim Crow car movement which had swept the western states of the South completely by that time. In that year, however, after several attempts, the proponents of the Jim Crow law were on the eve of victory. The Charleston *News and Courier,* the oldest newspaper in the South and a consistent spokesman of conservatism, fired a final broadside against extremists in behalf of the conservative creed of race policy.

'As we have got on fairly well for a third of a century, including a long period of reconstruction, without such a measure,' wrote the editor, 'we can probably get on as well hereafter without it, and certainly so extreme a measure should not be adopted and enforced without added and urgent cause.' He then called attention to what he considered the absurd consequences to which such a law might lead once the principle of the thing were conceded. 'If there must be Jim Crow cars on the railroads, there should be Jim Crow cars on the street railways. Also on all passenger boats. . . . If there are to be Jim Crow cars, moreover, there should be Jim Crow waiting saloons at all stations, and Jim Crow eating houses. . . . There should be Jim Crow sections of the jury box, and a separate Jim Crow dock and witness stand in every court—and a Jim Crow Bible for colored witnesses to kiss. It would be advisable also to have a Jim Crow section in county auditors' and treasurers' offices for the accommodation of colored taxpayers. The two races are dreadfully mixed in these offices for weeks every year, especially about Christmas. . . . There should be a Jim Crow department for making returns and paying for the privileges and blessings of citizenship. Perhaps, the best plan would be, after all, to take the short cut to the general end . . . by establishing two or three Jim Crow counties at once, and turning them over to our colored citizens for their special and exclusive accommodation.'

In resorting to the tactics of *reductio ad absurdum* the editor doubtless believed that he had dealt the Jim Crow principle a telling blow with his heavy irony. But there is now apparent to us an irony in his argument of which the author was unconscious. For what he intended as a *reductio ad absurdum* and obviously regarded as an absurdity became in a very short time a reality, and not only that but a reality that was regarded as the only sensible solution to a vexing problem, a solution having the sanction of tradition and long usage. Apart from the Jim Crow counties and Jim Crow witness stand, all the improbable applications of the principle suggested by the editor in derision had been put into practice—down to and including the Jim Crow Bible.

The South's adoption of extreme racism was due not so much to a conversion as it was to a relaxation of the opposition. All the elements of fear, jealousy, proscription, hatred, and fanaticism had long been present, as they are present in various degrees of intensity in any society. What enabled them to rise to dominance was not so much cleverness or ingenuity as it was a general weakening and discrediting of the numerous forces that had hitherto kept them in check. The restraining forces included not only Northern liberal opinion in the press, the courts, and the government, but also internal checks imposed by the prestige and influence of the Southern conservatives, as well as by the idealism and zeal of the Southern radicals. What happened toward the end of the century was an almost simultaneous—and sometimes not unrelated—decline in the effectiveness of restraint that had been exercised by all three forces: Northern liberalism, Southern conservatism, and Southern radicalism.

1

The acquiescence of Northern liberalism in the Compromise of 1877 defined the beginning, but not the ultimate extent, of the liberal retreat on the race issue. The Compromise merely left the freedman to the custody of the conservative Redeemers upon their pledge that they would protect him in his constitutional rights. But as these pledges were forgotten or violated and the South veered toward proscription and extremism, Northern opinion shifted to the right, keeping pace with the South, conceding point after point, so that at no time were the sections very far apart on race policy. The failure of the liberals to resist this trend was due in part to political factors. Since reactionary politicians and their cause were identified with the bloody-shirt issue and the demagogic exploitation of sectional animosities, the liberals naturally felt themselves strongly drawn toward the cause of sectional reconciliation. And since the Negro was the symbol of sectional strife, the liberals joined in deprecating further agitation of his cause and in defending the Southern view of race in its less extreme forms. It was quite common in the 'eighties and 'nineties to find in the *Nation, Harper's Weekly,* the *North American Review,* or the *Atlantic Monthly* Northern liberals and former abolitionists mouthing the shibboleths of white supremacy regarding the Negro's innate inferiority, shiftlessness, and hopeless unfitness for full participation in the white man's civilization. Such expressions doubtless did much to add to the reconciliation of North and South, but they did so at the expense of the Negro. Just as the Negro gained his emancipation and new rights through a falling out between white men, he now stood to lose his rights through the reconciliation of white men.

The cumulative weakening of resistance to racism was expressed also in a succession of decisions by the United States Supreme Court between 1873 and 1898 that require no review here. In the *Slaughter House Cases* of 1873 and in *United States* v. *Reese* and *United States* v. *Cruikshank* in 1876, the court drastically curtailed the privileges and immunities recognized as being under federal protection. It continued the trend in its decision on the *Civil Rights Cases* of 1883 by virtually nullifying the restrictive parts of the Civil Rights Act. By a species of what Justice Harlan in his dissent described as 'subtle and ingenious verbal criticism,' the court held that the Fourteenth Amendment gave Congress power to restrain states but not individuals from acts of racial discrimination and segregation. The court, like the liberals, was engaged in a bit of reconciliation—reconciliation between federal and state jurisdiction, as well as between North and South, reconciliation also achieved at the Negro's expense. Having ruled in a previous case (*Hall* v. *de Cuir,* 1877) that a state could not *prohibit* segregation on a common carrier, the Court in 1890 (*Louisville, New Orleans, and Texas Railroad* v. *Mississippi*) ruled that a state could constitutionally *require* segregation on carriers. In *Plessy* v. *Ferguson,* decided in 1896, the Court subscribed to the doctrine that 'legislation is powerless to eradicate racial instincts' and laid down the 'separate but equal' rule for the justification of segregation. Two years later, in 1898, in *Williams* v. *Mississippi* the Court completed the opening of the legal road to proscription, segregation, and disfranchisement by approving the Mississippi plan for depriving Negroes of the franchise.

For a short time after the Supreme Court decision of 1883 that held the restrictive parts of the Civil Rights Act unconstitutional, Northern legislatures showed a disposition to protect the rights of Negroes by state action. In the mid-'eighties thirteen states adopted civil rights laws of this sort. In Indiana, however, a study by Emma Lou Thornbrough finds that 'In practice the law proved to be ineffectual in accomplishing its state purpose, and racial patterns [of segregation] remained unchanged by its passage.' The same historian goes further to say that 'Throughout the North there was not only acquiescence among the white population in the 'Southern Way' of solving the race problem but a tendency to imitate it in practice.'

Then, in the year 1898, the United States plunged into imperialistic adventures overseas under the leadership of the Republican party. These adventures in the Pacific and the Caribbean suddenly brought under the jurisdiction of the United States some eight million people of the colored races, 'a varied assortment of inferior races,' as the *Nation* described them, 'which, of course, could not be allowed to vote.' As America shouldered the White Man's Burden, she took up at the same time many Southern attitudes on the subject of race. 'If the stronger and cleverer race,' said the editor of the *Atlantic Monthly,* 'is free to impose its will upon "new-caught, sullen peoples" on the other side of the globe, why not in South Carolina and Mississippi?'' The doctrines of Anglo-Saxon superiority by which Professor John W. Burgess of Columbia University, Captain Alfred T. Mahan of the United States Navy, and Senator Albert Beveridge of Indiana justified and rationalized American imperialism in the Philippines, Hawaii, and Cuba differed in no essentials from the race theories by which Senator Benjamin R. Tillman of South Carolina and Senator James K. Vardaman of Mississippi justified white supremacy in the South. The Boston *Evening Transcript* of 14 January 1899, admitted that Southern race policy was 'now the policy of the Administration of the very party which carried the country into and through a civil war to free the slave.' And *The New York Times* of 10 May 1900 reported editorially that 'Northern men . . . no longer denounce the suppression of the Negro vote [in the South] as it used to be denounced in the reconstruction days. The necessity of it under the supreme law of self-preservation is candidly recognized.' . . .

2

If the psychologists are correct in their hypothesis that aggression is always the result of frustration, then the South toward the end of the 'nineties was the perfect cultural seedbed for aggression against the minority race. Economic, political, and social frustrations had pyramided to a climax of social tensions. No real relief was in sight from the long cyclical depression of the 'nineties, an acute period of suffering that had only intensified the distress of the much longer agricultural depression. Hopes for reform and the political means employed in defiance of tradition and at great cost to emotional attachments to effect reform had likewise met with cruel disappointments and frustration. There had to be a scapegoat. And all along the line signals were going up to indicate that the Negro was an approved object of aggression. These 'permissions-to-hate' came from sources that had formerly denied such permission. They came from the federal courts in numerous opinions, from Northern liberals eager to conciliate the South, from Southern conservatives who had abandoned their race policy of moderation in their struggle against the Populists, from the Populists in their mood of disillusionment with their former Negro allies, and from a national temper suddenly expressed by imperialistic adventures and aggressions against colored peoples in distant lands.

The resistance of the Negro himself had long ceased to be an important deterrent to white aggression. But a new and popular spokesman of the race, its acknowledged leader by the late 'nineties, came forward with a submissive philosophy for the Negro that to some whites must have appeared an invitation to further aggression. It is quite certain that Booker T. Washington did not intend his so-called 'Atlanta Compromise' address of 1895 to constitute such an invitation. But in proposing the virtual retirement of the mass of Negroes from the political life of the South and in stressing the humble and menial role that the race was to play, he would seem unwittingly to have smoothed the path to proscription.

3

Having served as the national scapegoat in the reconciliation and reunion of North and South, the Negro was now pressed into service as a sectional scapegoat in the reconciliation of estranged white classes and the reunion of the Solid South. The bitter violence and blood-letting recrimination of the campaigns between white conservatives and white radicals in the 'nineties had opened wounds that could not be healed by ordinary political nostrums and free-silver slogans. The only formula powerful enough to accomplish that was the magical formula of white supremacy, applied without stint and without any of the old conservative reservations of paternalism, without deference to any lingering resistance of Northern liberalism, or any fear of further check from a defunct Southern Populism.

The first step in applying the formula was the total disfranchisement of the Negro. In part this was presented as a guarantee that in the future neither of the white factions would violate the white man's peace by rallying the Negro's support against the other. In part disfranchisement was also presented as a progressive reform, the sure means of purging Southern elections of the corruption that disgraced them. The disgrace and public shame of this corruption were more widely and keenly appreciated than the circuitous and paradoxical nature of the proposed reform. To one Virginian, however, it did seem that disfranchising the Negroes 'to prevent the Democratic election officials from stealing their votes' would be 'to punish the man who has been injured'—a topsy-turvy justice at best. In no mood for paradoxes, Southerners generally accepted Negro disfranchisement as a reform, without taking second thought.

The standard devices for accomplishing disfranchisement on a racial basis and evading the restrictions of the Constitution were invented by Mississippi, a pioneer of the movement and the only state that resorted to it before the Populist revolt took the form of political rebellion. Other states elaborated the original scheme and added devices of their own contriving, though there was a great deal of borrowing and interchange of ideas throughout the South. First of all, the plan set up certain barriers such as property or literacy qualifications for voting, and then cut certain loopholes in the barrier through which only white men could squeeze. The loopholes to appease (though not invariably accommodate) the underprivileged whites were the 'understanding clause,' the 'grandfather clause,' or the 'good character clause.' Some variation of the scheme was incorporated into the constitutions of South Carolina in 1895, Louisiana in 1898, North Carolina in 1900, Alabama in 1901, Virginia in 1902, Georgia in 1908, and Oklahoma in 1910. The restrictions imposed by these devices were enormously effective in decimating the Negro vote, but in addition all these states as well as the remaining members of the old Confederacy—Florida, Tennessee, Arkansas, and Texas—adopted the poll tax. With its cumulative features and procedures artfully devised to discourage payment, the poll tax was esteemed at first by some of its proponents as the most reliable means of curtailing the franchise—not only among the Negroes but among objectionable whites as well.

But if the Negroes did learn to read, or acquire sufficient property, and remember to pay the poll tax and to keep the receipt on file, they could even then be tripped by the final hurdle devised for them—the white primary. Another of the fateful paradoxes that seemed to dog the history of the progressive movement in the South, the primary system was undoubtedly an improvement over the old convention system and did much to democratize nominations and party control. But along with the progressively inspired primary system were adopted the oppositely inspired party rules, local regulations, and in some cases state laws excluding the minority race from participation and converting the primary into a white man's club. This perverse 'reform' usually followed hard upon, though sometimes preceded, the disfranchisement 'reform.' . . .

5

Within this context of growing pessimism, mounting tension, and unleashed phobias the structure of segregation and discrimination was extended by the adoption of a great number of the Jim Crow type of laws. Up to 1900 the only law of this type adopted by the majority of Southern states was that applying to passengers aboard trains. And South Carolina did not adopt that until 1898, North Carolina in 1899, and Virginia, the last, in 1900. Only three states had required or authorized the Jim Crow waiting room in railway stations before 1899, but in the next decade nearly all of the other Southern states fell in line. The adoption of laws applying to new subjects tended to take place in waves of popularity. Street cars had been common in Southern cities since the 'eighties, but only Georgia had a segregation law applying to them before the end of the century. Then in quick succession North Carolina and Virginia adopted such a law in 1901, Louisiana in 1902, Arkansas, South Carolina, and Tennessee in 1903, Mississippi and Maryland in 1904, Florida in 1905, and Oklahoma in 1907. These laws referred to separation within cars, but a Montgomery city ordinance of 1906 was the first to require a completely separate Jim Crow street car. During these years the older seaboard states of the South also extended the segregation laws to steamboats.

The mushroom growth of discriminatory and segregation laws during the first two decades of this century piled up a huge bulk of legislation. Much of the code was contributed by city ordinances or by local regulations and rules enforced without the formality of laws. Only a sampling is possible here. For up and down the avenues and byways of Southern life appeared with increasing profusion the little signs: 'Whites Only' or 'Colored.' Sometimes the law prescribed their dimensions in inches, and in one case the kind and color of paint. Many appeared without requirement by law—over entrances and exits, at theaters and boarding houses, toilets and water fountains, waiting rooms and ticket windows.

A large body of law grew up concerned with the segregation of employees and their working conditions. The South Carolina code of 1915, with subsequent elaborations, prohibited textile factories from permitting laborers of different races from working together in the same room, or using the same entrances, pay windows, exits, doorways, stairways, 'or windows [*sic*]' at the same time, or the same 'lavatories, toilets, drinking water buckets, pails, cups, dippers or glasses' at any time. Exceptions were made of firemen, floor scrubbers, and repair men, who were permitted association with the white proletarian elite on an emergency basis. In most instances segregation in employment was established without the aid of statute. And in many crafts and trades the written or unwritten policies of Jim Crow unionism made segregation superfluous by excluding Negroes from employment.

State institutions for the care of the dependent or incapacitated were naturally the subject of more legislation than private institutions of the same sort, but ordinarily the latter followed pretty closely the segregation practices of the public institutions. Both types had usually made it a practice all along. The fact that only Mississippi and South Carolina specifically provided by law for general segregation in hospitals does not indicate that non-segregation was the rule in the hospitals of other states. The two states named also required Negro nurses for Negro patients, and Alabama prohibited white female nurses from attending Negro male patients. Thirteen Southern and border states required the separation of patients by races in mental hospitals, and ten states specified segregation of inmates in penal institutions. Some of the latter went into detail regarding the chaining, transportation, feeding, and working of the prisoners on a segregated basis. Segregation of the races in homes for the aged, the indigent, the orphans, the blind, the deaf, and the dumb was the subject of numerous state laws.

Much ingenuity and effort went into the separation of the races in their amusements, diversions, recreations, and sports. The Separate Park Law of Georgia, adopted in 1905, appears to have been the first venture of a state legislature into this field, though city ordinances and local custom were quite active in pushing the Negro out of the public parks. Circuses and tent shows, including side shows, fell under a law adopted by Louisiana in 1914, which required separate entrances, exits, ticket windows, and ticket sellers that would be kept at least twenty-five feet apart. The city of Birmingham applied the principle to 'any room, hall, theatre, picture house, auditorium, yard, court, ball park, or other indoor or outdoor place' and specified that the races be 'distinctly separated . . . by well defined physical barriers.' North Carolina and Virginia interdicted all fraternal orders or societies that permitted members of both races to address each other as brother.

Residential segregation in cities, still rare in the older seaboard towns, developed along five different patterns in the second decade of the century. The type originating in Baltimore in 1910 designated all-white and all-Negro blocks in areas occupied by both races. This experiment was imitated in Atlanta and Greenville. Virginia sought to legalize segregation by a state law that authorized city councils to divide territories into segregated districts and to prohibit either race from living in the other's district, a method adopted by Roanoke and Portsmouth, Virginia. The third method, invented by Richmond, designated blocks throughout the city black or white according to the majority of the residents and forbade any person to live in any block 'where the majority of residents on such streets are occupied by those with whom said person is forbidden to intermarry.' This one was later copied by Ashland, Virginia, and Winston-Salem, North Carolina. A still more complicated law originated in Norfolk, which applied to both mixed and unmixed blocks and fixed the color status by ownership as well as occupancy. And finally New Orleans developed a law requiring a person of either race to secure consent of the majority of persons living in an area before establishing a residence therein. After these devices were frustrated by a Supreme Court decision in 1917, attempts continued to be made to circumvent the decision. Probably the most effective of these was the restrictive covenant, a private contract limiting the sale of property in an area to purchasers of the favored race.

The most prevalent and widespread segregation of living areas was accomplished without need for legal sanction. The black ghettos of the 'Darktown' slums in every Southern city were the consequence mainly of the Negro's economic status, his relegation to the lowest rung of the ladder. Smaller towns sometimes excluded Negro residents completely simply by letting it be known in forceful ways that their presence would not be tolerated. In 1914 there were six such towns in Texas, five in Oklahoma, and two in Alabama. On the other hand there were by that time some thirty towns in the South, besides a number of unincorporated settlements, inhabited exclusively by Negroes. In August 1913, Clarence Poe, editor of the *Progressive Farmer,* secured the unanimous endorsement of a convention of the North Carolina Farmer's Union for a movement to segregate the races in rural districts.

The extremes to which caste penalties and separation were carried in parts of the South could hardly find a counterpart short of the latitudes of India and South Africa. In 1909 Mobile passed a curfew law applying exclusively to Negroes and requiring them to be off the streets by 10 P.M. The Oklahoma legislature in 1915 authorized its Corporation Commission to require telephone companies 'to maintain separate booths for white and colored patrons.' North Carolina and Florida required that textbooks used by the public-school children of one race be kept separate from those used by the other, and the Florida law specified separation even while the books were in storage. South Carolina for a time segregated a third caste by establishing separate schools for mulatto as well as for white and Negro children. A New Orleans ordinance segregated white and Negro prostitutes in separate districts. Ray Stannard Baker found Jim Crow Bibles for Negro witnesses in Atlanta courts and Jim Crow elevators for Negro passengers in Atlanta buildings.

6

A search of the statute books fails to disclose any state law or city ordinance specifying separate Bibles and separate elevators. Right here it is well to admit, and even to emphasize, that *laws are not an adequate index of the extent and prevalence of segregation and discriminatory practices in the South.* The practices often anticipated and sometimes exceeded the laws. It may be confidently assumed—and it could be verified by present observation—that there is more Jim Crowism practiced in the South than there are Jim Crow laws on the books. . . .

Booker T. Washington and the Politics of Accommodation

LOUIS HARLAN

It is ironic that Booker T. Washington, the most powerful black American of his time and perhaps of all time, should be the black leader whose claim to the title is most often dismissed by the lay public. Blacks often question his legitimacy because of the role that favor by whites played in Washington's assumption of power, and whites often remember him only as an educator or, confusing him with George Washington Carver, as "that great Negro scientist." This irony is something that Washington will have to live with in history, for he himself deliberately created the ambiguity about his role and purposes that has haunted his image. And yet, Washington was a genuine black leader, with a substantial black following and with virtually the same long-range goals for Afro-Americans as his rivals. This presentation is concerned with Washington's social philosophy, such as it was, but it also addresses his methods of leadership, both his Delphic public utterances that meant one thing to whites and another to blacks and his adroit private movements through the brier patch of American race relations. It does not try to solve the ultimate riddle of his character.

Washington's own view of himself was that he was the Negro of the hour, whose career and racial program epitomized what blacks needed to maintain themselves against white encroachments and to make progress toward equality in America. The facts of his life certainly fitted his self-image. He was the last of the major black leaders to be born in slavery, on a small farm in western Virginia in 1856. Growing up during the Reconstruction era in West Virginia, he believed that one of the lessons he learned was that the Reconstruction experiment in racial democracy failed because it began at the wrong end, emphasizing political means and civil rights acts rather than economic means and self-determination. Washington learned this lesson not so much through experience as a child worker in the salt works and coal mines as by what he was taught as a houseboy for the leading family of Malden, West Virginia, and later as a student at Hampton Institute in Virginia. . . .

After teaching school in his home town, Washington briefly studied in a Baptist seminary and in a lawyer's office. But he soon abandoned these alternative careers, perhaps sensing that disfranchisement and the secularization of society would weaken these occupations as bases for racial leadership. He returned to Hampton Institute as a teacher for two years and then founded Tuskegee Normal and Industrial Institute in Alabama in 1881. Over the next quarter of a century, . . . Washington built up Tuskegee Institute to be an equal of Hampton.

From *Black Leaders of the Twentieth Century* by Louis Harlan, pp. 2–18. Copyright © 1982, reprinted by permission of the University of Illinois Press and the author.

Washington's bid for leadership went beyond education and institution-building, however. Symbolic of his fresh approach to black-white relations were a speech he gave in 1895 before a commercial exposition, known as the Atlanta Compromise Address, and his autobiography, *Up from Slavery* (1901). As Washington saw it, blacks were toiling upward from slavery by their own efforts into the American middle class and needed chiefly social peace to continue in this steady social evolution. Thus, in the Atlanta Compromise he sought to disarm the white South by declaring agitation of the social equality question "the merest folly" and proclaiming that in "purely social" matters "we can be as separate as the fingers, yet one as the hand in all things essential to mutual progress." These concessions came to haunt Washington as southerners used segregation as a means of systematizing discrimination, and northerners followed suit. And they did not stop at the "purely social."

Washington's concessions to the white South, however, were only half of a bargain. In return for downgrading civil and political rights in the black list of priorities, Washington asked whites to place no barriers to black economic advancement and even to become partners of their black neighbors "in all things essential to mutual progress." Washington saw his own role as the axis between the races, the only leader who could negotiate and keep the peace by holding extremists on both sides in check. . . .

Washington sought to influence whites, but he never forgot that it was the blacks that he undertook to lead. He offered blacks not the empty promises of the demagogue but a solid program of economic and educational progress through struggle. It was less important "just now," he said, for a black person to seek admission to an opera house than to have the money for the ticket. Mediating diplomacy with whites was only half of Washington's strategy; the other half was black solidarity, mutual aid, and institution-building. He thought outspoken complaint against injustice was necessary but insufficient, and he thought factional dissent among black leaders was self-defeating and should be suppressed.

Washington brought to his role as a black leader the talents and outlook of a machine boss. He made Tuskegee Institute the largest and best-supported black educational institution of his day, and it spawned a large network of other industrial schools. . . . It was an all-black school with an all-black faculty at a time when most black colleges were still run by white missionaries. Tuskegee taught self-determination. It also taught trades designed for economic independence in a region dominated by sharecrop agriculture. At the same time, by verbal juggling tricks, Washington convinced the southern whites that Tuskegee was not educating black youth away from the farms. Tuskegee also functioned as a model black community, not only by acquainting its students with a middle-class way of life, but by buying up the surrounding farmland and selling it at low rates of interest to create a community of small landowners and homeowners. The Institute became larger than the town.

Washington built a regional constituency of farmers, artisans, country teachers, and small businessmen; he expanded the Tuskegee Machine nationwide. . . . His first northern black ally was T. Thomas Fortune, editor of the militant and influential New York *Age* and founder of the Afro-American Council, the leading forum of black thought at the time. . . . Seeking more direct allies, Washington founded in 1900 the National Negro Business League, of which he was president for life. The league was important not so much for what it did for black business, which was little, but because the local branch of the league was a stronghold of Washington men in every substantial black population center.

Other classes of influential blacks did not agree with Washington's stated philosophy but were beholden to him for the favors he did them or offered to do for them. He was not called the Wizard for nothing. White philanthropists who approved of him for their own reasons gave him the money to help black colleges by providing for a Carnegie library here, a dormitory there. Through Washington Andrew Carnegie alone gave buildings to twenty-nine black schools. Not only college administrators owed him for favors, but so did church leaders, YMCA directors, and many others. Though never much of a joiner, he became a power in the Baptist church, and he schemed through lieutenants to control the secret black fraternal orders and make his friends the high potentates of the Pythians, Odd Fellows, and so on. Like any boss, he turned every favor into a bond of obligation.

It was in politics, however, that Washington built the most elaborate tentacle of the octopus-like Tuskegee Machine. In politics as in everything else, Washington cultivated ambiguity. He downgraded politics as a solution of black problems, did not recommend politics to the ambitious young black man, and never held office. But when Theodore Roosevelt became president in 1901 and asked for Washington's advice on black and southern appointments, Washington consented with alacrity. He became the chief black adviser of both Presidents Roosevelt and William Howard Taft. He failed in his efforts to liberalize Republican policy on voting rights, lynching, and racial discrimination, however, and relations between the Republican party and black voters reached a low ebb.

In patronage politics, however, Washington found his opportunity. For a man who minimized the importance of politics, Washington devoted an inordinate amount of his time and tremendous energy to securing federal jobs for his machine lieutenants. These men played a certain role in the politics of the period, but their first obligation was to the Tuskegean. . . .

Washington also used high political office in the North to win the loyalty of key figures in the legal profession whose ideology and natural bent were usually in the direction of more outspoken protest. A notable example was William H. Lewis of Boston, a graduate of Amherst College and Harvard University Law School, who had been an outspoken critic of Washington. . . . When Washington began talking of raising the quality of the black civil service, Roosevelt brought up Lewis. Washington was skeptical, but as soon as possible he met with Lewis and made a deal with him. As Lewis wrote, there were "many things about which we might differ, but that we had the same aims and the same end in view." Lewis became, with Washington's blessing, the assistant U.S. district attorney in Boston, and a few years later

Taft appointed him assistant attorney general of the United States, the highest appointive federal post held by a black man up to that time—and for decades afterward. . . .

Washington's outright critics and enemies were called "radicals" because they challenged Washington's conservatism and bossism, though their tactics of verbal protest would seem moderate indeed to a later generation of activists. They were the college-educated blacks, engaged in professional pursuits, and proud of their membership in an elite class—what one of them called the Talented Tenth. The strongholds of the radicals were the northern cities and southern black colleges. They stood for full political and civil rights, liberal education, free expression, and aspiration. They dreamed of a better world and believed Booker T. Washington was a menace to its achievement.

The first to challenge Washington and all his works was a young Harvard graduate, William Monroe Trotter, who founded in 1900 a newspaper, the Boston *Guardian*. Trotter not only differed with the Tuskegean on every conceivable subject but engaged in personal abuse. He spoke of Washington's "crime of race ridicule and belittlement." He called him Pope Washington, the Black Boss, . . . the Great Traitor, and the Great Divider. In reporting a speech by Washington in Boston in 1902 Trotter described him thus: "His features were harsh in the extreme. His vast leonine jaws into which vast mastiff-like rows of teeth were set clinched together like a vise. His forehead shot up to a great cone; his chin was massive and square; his eyes were dull and absolutely characterless. . . . In Trotter's vendetta against Washington no charge, true or false, was too big or too petty to use.

Trotter seized the chance to confront Washington directly when the black leader spoke at a Boston church in 1903 under sponsorship of the local branch of the National Negro Business League. Trotter stood on a chair to interrupt Washington's speech with nine questions that were actually challenges. Quoting from a Washington speech, for example, Trotter asked: "When you said: 'It was not so important whether the Negro was in the inferior car as whether there was in that car a superior man not a beast,' did you not minimize the outrage of the insulting Jim-crow car discimination and justify it by the 'bestiality' of the Negro?" The final provocative question was: "Are the rope and the torch all the race is to get under your leadership?"

. . . The incident appeared next day in all the newspapers as the Boston Riot, penetrating Washington's news screen to show that not all blacks approved of Washington's leadership. Washington publicly ignored the affair, but his Boston lieutenants made a martyr of Trotter by vigorous prosecution of his case, forcing him to serve thirty days in jail. . . .

The following year, Du Bois and Trotter formed their own organization, the Niagara Movement, dedicated to "persistent manly agitation" for civil rights, voting rights, job opportunities, equal educational opportunities, and human rights in general. . . . This small band of intellectuals, hurling their manifestos, was no match for the political skill and marshaled power of the Wizard of Tuskegee. They themselves limited their membership to the small black professional class, insisted on an ideological "likemindedness" that few could achieve, and had no white allies. By contrast, Washington had a broader base and a commoner touch. Though Washington proposed the leadership of another elite class, the black businessmen, he kept in close touch with the black masses and directed his program to their immediate needs. Furthermore, he fished for allies wherever he could find them, among whites and even among the professional men who would ordinarily be expected in the Niagara Movement. He cared little about the ideology of a lieutenant, as long as the man did what Washington wanted done.

The Niagara Movement called Washington, in effect, a puppet of the whites, who thrust him into prominence because he did not challenge their wrongdoing. According to the Niagarites, . . . Washington was a half-educated southerner whose control over black affairs was stifling an emergent black educated elite, the Talented Tenth, the logical leaders. Because of his own class orientation he was trying to change the social position of blacks through the acquisitive propensities and the leadership of businessmen instead of through political and civil rights agitation, which the Niagara men saw as the need of the hour. . . .

Washington dismissed his black critics by questioning their motives, their claim to superior wisdom, and—the politician's ultimate argument—their numbers. Washington understood, if his critics did not, that his leadership of the black community largely depended on his recognition by whites as the black leader. If he did not meet some minimal standards of satisfactoriness to whites, another Washington would be created. He obviously could not lead the whites; he could not even divide the whites. He could only, in a limited way, exploit the class divisions that whites created among themselves. . . .

While Washington recognized the centrality of black-white relations in his efforts to lead blacks, he [operated in] an age of polarization of black and white. The overheated atmosphere of the South at the turn of the century resembled that of a crisis center on the eve of war. Lynching became a more than weekly occurrence; discrimination and humiliation of blacks were constant and pervasive and bred a whole literature and behavioral science of self-justification. Race riots terrorized blacks in many cities, and not only in the South. It would have required not courage but foolhardiness for Washington, standing with both feet in Alabama, to have challenged this raging white aggression openly and directly. Even unqualified verbal protest would have brought him little support from either southern blacks or white well-wishers. Du Bois took higher ground and perhaps a better vision of the future when he urged forthright protest against every white injustice, on the assumption that whites were rational beings and would respond dialectically to black protest. But few white racists of the early twentieth century cared anything for the facts. And when Du Bois in his Atlanta years undertook to implement his protest with action, he was driven to the negative means of refusing to pay his poll tax or refusing to ride segregated streetcars and elevators.

Instead of . . . confronting all of white America, . . . Washington simply met each day as it came, pragmatically, seeking what white allies he could against avowed white enemies. A serious fault of this policy was that

Washington usually appealed for white support on a basis of a vaguely conceived mutual interest rather than on ideological agreement. For example, in both the South and the North Washington allied himself with the white upper class against the masses. In the South he joined with the planter class and when possible with the coal barons and railroad officials against the Populists and other small white farmer groups who seemed to him to harbor the most virulent anti-black attitudes born of labor competition. Similarly, in the North, Washington admired and bargained with the big business class. The bigger the businessman, the more Washington admired him, as the avatar and arbiter of American society. At the pinnacle in his measure of men were the industrialists Carnegie, John D. Rockefeller, and Henry H. Rogers and the merchant princes Robert C. Ogden and Julius Rosenwald. . . .

Washington made constructive use of his philanthropic allies to aid not only Tuskegee but black education and black society as a whole. He guided the generous impulse of a Quaker millionairess into the Anna T. Jeanes Foundation to improve the teaching in black public schools. He persuaded the Jewish philanthropist Julius Rosenwald to begin a program that lasted for decades for building more adequate black schoolhouses all over the South. . . . There were limits, however, to his power to advance black interests through philanthropy. When his northern benefactors became involved in the Southern Education Board to improve the southern public school systems, for example, he worked repeatedly but without success to get this board to redress the imbalance of public expenditures or even to halt the rapid increase of discrimination against black schools and black children. He had to shrug off his failure and get from these so-called philanthropists whatever they were willing to give.

Having committed himself to the business elite, Washington took a dim view of the leaders of the working class. Immigrants represented to him, as to many blacks, labor competitors; Jews were the exception here, as he held them up to ambitious blacks as models of the work-ethic and group solidarity. He claimed in his autobiography that his disillusionment with labor unions went back to his youthful membership in the Knights of Labor and stemmed from observation of their disruption of the natural laws of economics. . . . There is no evidence that Washington ever actively supported black strikebreaking, but his refusal to intervene in behalf of all-white unions is understandable. It was more often white employees rather than employers who excluded blacks, or so Washington believed. He worked hard to introduce black labor into the non-union, white-only cotton mills in the South, even to the extent of interesting northern capitalists in investing in black cotton mills and similar enterprises.

Washington was a conservative by just about any measure. Though he flourished in the Progressive era it was not he, but his opponents who were the men of good hope, full of reform proposals and faith in the common man. Washington's vision of the common man included the southern poor white full of rancor against blacks, the foreign-born anarchist ready to pull down the temple of American business, and the black sharecropper unqualified by education or economic freedom for the ballot. Though Washington opposed the grandfather clause and every other southern device to exclude the black man from voting solely on account of his color, Washington did not favor universal suffrage. He believed in literacy and property tests, fairly enforced. He was no democrat. And he did not believe in woman suffrage, either. . . .

. . . Washington did have a remarkable capacity to convince whites as well as blacks that he not only understood them but agreed with them. It is one of Washington's intangible qualities as a black leader that he could influence, if not lead, so many whites. The agreement that whites sensed in him was more in his manner than in his program or goals, which always included human rights as well as material advancement for blacks.

In his constant effort to influence public opinion, Washington relied on the uncertain instruments of the press and the public platform. A flood of books and articles appeared over his name, largely written by his private secretary and a stable of ghostwriters, because he was too busy to do much writing. . . . So for the crucial twenty years after 1895, Washington's writings showed no fresh creativity or real response to events, only a steady flood of platitudes. Washington's speeches generally suffered from an opposite handicap, that he was the only one who could deliver them. . . . But everywhere he went, North, South, or West, he drew large crowds ready to hear or rehear his platitudes.

Washington did try to change his world by other means. Some forms of racial injustice, such as lynching, disfranchisement, and unequal facilities in education and transportation, Washington dealt with publicly and directly. Early in his career as a leader he tried to sidestep the lynching question by saying that, deplorable though it was, he was too busy working for the education of black youth to divide his energies by dealing with other public questions. Friends and critics alike sharply told him that if he proposed to be a leader of blacks, he was going to have to deal with this subject. So he began an annual letter on lynching that he sent to all the southern white dailies, and he made Tuskegee Institute the center of statistical and news information on lynching. He always took a moderate tone, deplored rape and crime by blacks, but always denied that the crime blacks committed was either the cause of or justification for the crime of lynching. He tried to make up for his moderation by persistence, factual accuracy, and persuasive logic. Disfranchisement of black voters swept through the South from Texas to Virginia during Washington's day. He publicly protested in letters to the constitutional conventions and legislatures in Alabama, Georgia, and Louisiana and aided similar efforts in several other states. He failed to stop lynching, to prevent the loss of voting rights, and to clean up the Jim Crow cars or bring about even minimal standards of fairness in the public schools. But he did try. . . .

What Washington could not do publicly to achieve equal rights, he sought to accomplish secretly. He spent four years in cooperation with the Afro-American Council on a court case to test the constitutionality of the Louisiana grandfather clause, providing funds from his own pocket and from northern white liberal friends. In his own state of Alabama, Washington secretly directed the efforts of his personal lawyer to carry two grandfather-clause cases all the way to the U.S. Supreme Court, where they were lost on technicalities. He took the extra precaution of using code names in all the correspondence on the Alabama cases. Through private pressure on railroad officials and congressmen, Washington tried to bring about improvement in the Jim Crow cars and railroad waiting rooms. He had more success in the Dan Rogers case, which overturned a criminal verdict against a black man because blacks were excluded from the jury. He also secretly collaborated with two southern white attorneys to defend Alonzo Bailey, a farm laborer held in peonage for debt; the outcome here was also successful, for the Alabama peonage law was declared unconstitutional. These and other secret actions were certainly not enough to tear down the legal structure of white supremacy, but they show that Washington's role in Afro-American history was not always that of the accommodationist "heavy." He was working, at several levels and in imaginative ways, and always with vigor, toward goals similar to those of his critics. If his methods did not work, the same could be said of theirs. . . .

There was another, uglier side of Washington's secret behavior, however—his ruthless spying and sabotage against his leading black critics. . . .

Espionage became an important instrument of Washington's black leadership—or bossism—a few days before the Boston Riot in 1903, when he hired a young black man, Melvin J. Chisum, to infiltrate the inner councils of Trotter's anti-Washington organization in Boston. Chisum later spied on the Niagara Movement's Brooklyn branch, arranged to bribe an opposition newspaper editor in Washington, D.C., and reported these and other clandestine actions to the Wizard on a park bench in New York City. Washington also used Pinkerton detectives and other paid and unpaid secret agents on a variety of errands, to infiltrate the inner councils of the Niagara Movement, to repress newspaper reporting of Niagara meetings, to find out if Trotter's wife worked as a domestic, to research the tax records of Atlanta to get evidence that Du Bois, a champion of black political action, had not paid his poll tax. When a young black magazine editor, J. Max Barber, began to criticize him, Washington tried to muzzle Barber through his publisher and advertisers, then hounded Barber not only out of his magazine but out of job after job until Barber retired from race work to become a dentist. Even the white liberals who joined with the Niagara Movement to form the interracial National Association for the Advancement of Colored People in 1909 were not immune from Washington's secret attacks. Washington arranged with the racially biased New York newspaper reporters to cover—in a sensational fashion—a dinner meeting of the Cosmopolitan Club, an interracial social group to which a number of the NAACP leaders belonged. Even they never guessed that Washington had done this in collusion with white racists. . . .

Du Bois spent much of his long life puzzling over the phenomenon of Washington, a man who did not seem to have an abstraction about him. But toward the end of his life, in 1954 in an oral history memoir at Columbia University, Du Bois said of his old rival dead almost forty years: "Oh, Washington was a politician. He was a man who believed that we should get what we could get." Du Bois, who himself found the political part of his race work the least agreeable, went on to say of Washington: "It wasn't a matter of ideals or anything of that sort. . . . With everybody that Washington met, he evidently had the idea: 'Now, what's your racket? What are you out for?' " Du Bois was a shrewd observer, but what he saw in Washington as a lack—of ideals, of principles, of vision—was his great and almost unique gift as a black political leader. Washington could almost immediately, intuitively, and without formal questioning see through the masks and intellectual super-structure of men to the mainsprings of their behavior. Then he imaginatively sought to bend their purposes to his own. . . .

Washington's program was not consensus politics, for he always sought change, and there was always vocal opposition to him on both sides that he never tried to mollify. Denounced on the one hand by the Niagara Movement and the NAACP for not protesting enough, he was also distrusted and de-nounced by white supremacists for bringing the wooden horse within the walls of Troy. All of the racist demagogues of his time—Benjamin Tillman, James Vardaman, Theodore Bilbo, Thomas Dixon, and J. Thomas Heflin, to name a few—called Washington their insidious enemy. One descriptive label for Washington might be centrist coalition politics. The Tuskegee Machine had the middle and undecided majority of white and black people behind it. Washington was a rallying point for the southern moderates, the northern publicists and makers of opinion, and the thousands who read his autobiogra-phy or crowded into halls to hear him. Among blacks he had the businessmen solidly behind him, and even . . . a majority of the Talented Tenth of profes-sional men, so great was his power to reward and punish, to make or break careers. He had access to the wellsprings of philanthropy, political prefer-ment, and other white sources of black opportunity. For blacks at the bottom of the ladder, Washington's program offered education, a self-help formula, and, importantly for a group demoralized by the white aggression of that period, a social philosophy that gave dignity and purpose to lives of daily toil. . . .

To the charge that he accomplished nothing, it can only be imagined what Washington would have answered, since he did not have the years of hind-sight and self-justification that some of his critics enjoyed. He would probably have stressed how much worse the southern racial reaction would have been without his coalition of moderates, his soothing syrup, and his practical message to blacks of self-improvement and progress along the lines of least resistance. . . . But even today, in a very different society, Washington's autobiography is still in print. It still has some impalpable power to bridge the racial gap, to move new readers to take the first steps across the color line. Many of his ideas of self-help and racial solidarity still have currency in the black community. But he was an important leader because, like Frederick Douglass before him and Martin Luther King after him, he had the program and strategy and skill to influence the behavior of not only the Afro-American one-tenth, but the white nine-tenths of the American people. He was a political realist.

Mary Church Terrell, Ida B. Wells, and the Crusade Against Lynching

PAULA GIDDINGS

Before they took his life, they asked Thomas Moss if he had anything to say. "Tell my people to go west," he told his abductors. "There is no justice for them here." With those final words, Thomas Moss and two of his friends, Calvin McDowell and Henry Stewart, were lynched a mile outside of Memphis, Tennessee. A newspaper account of the mob-murder pointed out that the men did not die without a struggle. McDowell had tried to wrestle a gun from the hands of one of the killers. When the Black man's body was recovered, the fingers of his right hand had been shot to pieces; his eyes were gouged out.

The lynching of March 9, 1892, was the climax of ugly events in Memphis. From the time the three Black men had gone into business for themselves, their People's Grocery, as it was called, had been the target of White resentment. The store, which sold food and miscellaneous items and became a gathering place for Memphis Blacks, represented, after all, a desire for economic independence. The start-up capital for the grocery had been provided by Moss, a postman who was the city's first Black to hold a federal position. He worked in the store evenings, while his partners worked there during the day.

For Whites the most galling thing about the People's Grocery was that it took away business from a White store owner who had long been used to a monopoly of Black trade. The White proprietor initiated against the Black businessmen a series of provocations that culminated in an attack of armed thugs sent to raze the grocery. The attack came on a Saturday night, when the store was full of Black men—armed Black men—who repelled the invaders and shot three Whites in the process. In short order Moss, McDowell, and Stewart were arrested along with one hundred other Blacks charged with conspiracy.

The White press in Memphis whipped the community into a frenzy over the incident. The Black men were painted as "brutes" and "criminals" who victimized "innocent" Whites. If the wounded men died, Blacks were warned, there was going to be a bloodletting. The threat hung heavy in the air. Whites were permitted to enter the jail where the Blacks were interned to "look them over." Outside, Blacks stood vigil to discourage the possibility of mob violence.

The vigil ended when it was reported that the Whites would recover from their gunshot wounds—for the Blacks thought their friends would now be safe. They were wrong. In a predawn raid, Moss, McDowell, and Stewart were taken from their cells, put on the switch engine of a train headed out of

From *When and Where I Enter: The Impact of Black Women on Race and Sex in America* by Paula Giddings, pp. 17–31. Copyright © 1984 by Paula Giddings. Reprinted by permission of William Morrow & Co., Inc.

the city, and lynched. In the angry aftermath of the killing, a judge issued an order for the sheriff to shoot any Black demonstrator who seemed to be "causing trouble," and prohibited the sale of guns to Blacks. Emboldened by the order, and unappeased by the death of the three men, armed Whites converged upon the People's Grocery, helped themselves to food and drink, then destroyed most of what they couldn't consume or steal. Creditors auctioned the brutalized remnants and the store was closed down on an ominous note of finality.

If the incident had occurred in any other time or place, it might have been set down as just another dreary statistic. Lynching (legally defined as murder committed by a mob of three or more persons) of Blacks had been on the rise for the last decade. In 1892, the year of the Memphis murders, there had been 255 lynchings, more than in any previous year. But the deaths of Moss, McDowell, and Stewart would open a new chapter in the racial struggle, for they spurred two women to dedicate their lives to the fight against lynching and the malevolent impulses that underlined it. Two women named Mary Church Terrell and Ida B. Wells.

Terrell was living in Washington, D.C., when she heard the terrible news. Born Mary Church in Memphis, Tennessee, she had been a friend of Thomas Moss since childhood. Terrell had seen him less than a year before in Memphis, at her wedding. That had been such a happy time. She had just returned from two years of study in Europe, and it was so good to see her Memphis friends again—especially Moss. For a wedding present he gave her a set of elegant silver oyster forks.

Moss's death was particularly unsettling for Terrell at this time in her life. She was twenty-nine and, though expecting her first child, had not found peace of mind in domestic tranquility. That she always wanted to work had been a point of contention between Mary and her father since her graduation from Oberlin eight years before. A former slave who became one of the wealthiest Blacks in the country, Robert Church wanted his daughter to live the life of a gentlewoman. Ladies didn't work, he always told her. But Mary continually defied that notion. She taught at Wilberforce University and later at Washington Colored High School, despite her father's threats to disinherit her. In D.C. she met Robert Terrell, principal of the highly touted Black public school. She married him and settled in Washington, where the future of her husband—a Harvard graduate and lawyer bound for a municipal judgeship—was assured. The marriage and difficult pregnancy had almost persuaded Terrell to try to live the life of a "lady," as her father would put it. But then came the news about Thomas Moss.

She sought out an old family friend, the abolitionist Frederick Douglass, and together they secured an appointment with President Benjamin Harrison at the White House. They implored him to condemn lynching in his annual address before Congress. Douglass's plea was especially eloquent, Terrell later wrote, but like every President before Franklin Roosevelt, Harrison refused to take a public stand against lynching.

For Terrell, though, the lynching of her friend, followed not long after by the death of her newborn infant in a segregated, poorly equipped hospital, erased forever any idea of leading the traditional life of a lady. She plunged headlong into work, embarking upon a vibrant activism that would continue until her death, sixty-two years later. In a short span of time, she served as president of the country's most prominent Black cultural organization, the Bethel Literary and Historical Society; was appointed to the Washington, D.C., Board of Education, becoming the first Black woman to serve on a citywide board; and co-founded the Washington Colored Women's League.

The implications of Moss's death were seared into Terrell's memory by an editorial in the Black Memphis newspaper *Free Speech*. "The city of Memphis has demonstrated that neither character nor standing avails the Negro if he dares to protect himself against the white man or become his rival," it said in part. The words were written by Ida B. Wells, columnist and co-owner of the paper. She had been so stunned by the lynching that she had had to force herself to write a cogent editorial for her readers. In her ten years as a journalist, and in the nearly half-century of writing that followed, her columns on the Moss lynching were the most painful. A woman who never made friends easily, Wells considered Thomas Moss and his wife, Betty, her very closest friends. She was godmother to their little girl, Maurine; Betty, she knew, was pregnant with her second child.

As a widely respected journalist, Wells's words were taken to heart by the beleaguered Black community. Her first editorials suggested that Blacks, vulnerable to the whims of White lawlessness, should take Moss's advice to "save our money and leave a town which will neither protect our lives and property, nor give us a fair trial in the courts, but takes us out and murders us in cold blood. . . ." Those residents who could, did just that. Hundreds of Blacks began leaving Memphis for Kansas, Oklahoma, and points west. Ministers escorted whole congregations; entire families began their exodus to unknown territories, taking only what they could carry. Betty Moss stayed in Memphis until her child was born, and then moved to Indiana.

So many Blacks took the advice of Wells that the White business community began to panic. "Business was practically at a standstill," Wells recalled in her autobiography, "for the Negro was famous then, as now, for spending his money for fine clothes, furniture, jewelry, and pianos and other musical instruments, to say nothing of good things to eat. Music houses had more musical instruments, sold on the installment plan, thrown back on their hands than they could find storage for." Wells also helped instigate a Black boycott of the city's trolleys, causing the transportation company to join the list of businesses beginning to teeter on the edge of bankruptcy.

Ida B. Wells didn't believe in the ultimate efficacy of passive resistance, however. She purchased a pistol, determined to "sell my life as dearly as possible," and suggested that other Blacks do the same. "A Winchester rifle should have a place of honor in every home," Wells told her community. "When the white man . . . knows he runs as great a risk of biting the dust every time his Afro-American victim does, he will have greater respect for Afro-American life."

But Wells would go beyond these responses to the Moss lynching. What had occurred in Memphis was only a part of a larger phenomenon that threatened Blacks throughout the country. Her entire life, it seemed, had prepared her not only to understand but to confront the broader issue head on—despite the consequences.

Her life paralleled Mary Church Terrell's in many ways. The two women were born a year apart, and both were daughters of former slaves. Their fathers were sons of their former masters; both were men who filled their daughters with racial pride—and the spirit of defiance.

Settling in Memphis after the Civil War, Robert Church was the owner of a saloon which was ransacked in the Memphis riot of 1866. He was shot in the head and left to die, but miraculously survived. The threat of continued violence did not stop him from testifying against the men in a federal inquiry, or from being politically active in the community thereafter. He was a "race man," as one would have been called then.

James Wells, Ida's father, was also a race man, in Holly Springs, Mississippi, where Ida was born. He, too, was a man who refused to be intimidated. A carpenter who worked for the town's leading contractor, Wells refused entreaties to "sell" his newly won vote. The refusal cost him his job, and without hesitation—or regret—he moved his family and went into business for himself. It was a lesson not lost on his oldest daughter. The fathers of both Wells and Terrell married energetic and determined women. Louisa Church established a fashionable hair salon in Memphis which provided the family with their first home and carriage. Elizabeth Wells thrust most of her energies into the rearing of six children, making sure they understood discipline and the need for education, both secular and religious. "Our job," Ida, the firstborn, wrote, "was to learn all we could." Like so many freedmen and women, the Wellses believed deeply in the sanctity of family life. James and Elizabeth were among the many who, though married as slaves, renewed their vows "officially" as persons of free will. Their ideals made the event of 1878 all the more tragic.

That year was a turning point for both families. A yellow fever epidemic raged through the Mississippi Valley leaving death in its wake. Both of Ida's parents were consumed by the disease within twenty-four hours of each other, and their nine-month-old baby died as well. Friends tried to help out, offering to take the children in. But Ida Wells refused to have her five surviving brothers and sisters separated; her parents would "turn over in their graves," she felt, especially since one of her sisters, crippled from a spinal disease, would have been put into an institution. So at the age of sixteen, Wells ended her childhood to become the sole support of her young family. She left Rust College and, lying about her age, got a teaching position in a rural school. For two years Wells maintained a grueling schedule of riding a mule to the school each week and returning on weekends to take care of the domestic needs of her siblings, until at last relatives in Memphis could take the family in.

The epidemic changed the lives of the Churches too, but in another way. Robert Church sent his wife and daughter to New York but remained in Memphis, where residents were deserting their properties or selling them at depressed prices. Church, speculating that the city would eventually recover, bought up all the property he could. The gamble paid off in handsome dividends. Church reputedly became the first Black millionaire in the South.

Both women lived in Memphis in the 1880's. Wells attended LeMoyne Institute and received a license to teach elementary school. During summer vacations she took teachers' training courses at Fisk University. Although never a close friend of the Churches she had brief associations with both Mary and her father. Once, in dire need of funds, Wells wrote Robert Church, asking him for a loan. She was in California and did not have the fare to return to Memphis in time for the opening of the school semester. In the letter Wells assured him that she would repay the loan, with interest, and that she was a woman of reputable character. She wrote to him, Wells said, because he was "the only man of my race I knew could lend me that much money [$150] and wait for me to repay it." Robert Church sent her the needed fare.

Wells also met Mary Church briefly, probably just before the latter went to Oberlin. On Ida Wells, who was serious-minded and disdained social frivolities, the meeting left a lasting impression. Mary Church was "the first woman of my age who is similarly inspired with the same desires, hopes and ambitions," she observed. "I only wish I had known her long ago." At the time, Wells hardly realized that their lives would diverge, only to intersect periodically, sometimes contentiously, for the remainder of their lives. Both had distinct roles in the struggle ahead, roles shaped by the contrasting resonances of their young adult years.

While Mary Church was studying the "Gentleman's Course" at Oberlin—a curriculum that included classical Latin and Greek—Wells underwent a different sort of education. It was 1884, and Ida B. Wells took her accustomed seat in the "Ladies' Coach" of a train bound for Memphis from Woodstock, Tennessee. But by that year, customs in the South were changing. A conductor demanded that Wells leave the first-class section for the smoking car. When she refused, the conductor attempted to force her from her seat—a mistake, he quickly realized when he felt a vicelike bite on the back of his hand. He called more conductors to his aid, and to the standing cheers of the White passengers on the train, the three men dragged the petite Black passenger out of the car.

A humiliated and angry Wells returned to Memphis and immediately engaged the sole Black lawyer in the city to bring suit against the railroad. The attorney seemed to dawdle on the case, and Wells suspected that he had been bought off by the authorities. She got a White lawyer and had her day in court. Before a judge who was an ex-Union officer, the determined Wells won the decision. . . .

Needless to say, Wells was ecstatic about the victory. Inaugurating her journalistic career, she wrote an article in a Baptist weekly called the *Living Way*. If Blacks stood up for their rights, she said, those rights, granted in

Reconstruction legislation, would be preserved. But what she would come painfully to realize was that Reconstruction, in more ways than one, was in rapid eclipse. . . . The institutionalization of "legal" disenfranchisement, segregation, and White terror tactics had not yet congealed, but it was hardening.

The Chesapeake & Ohio Railway appealed to a higher court. Company officials offered Wells more money than the damages previously awarded, if she would agree not to contest the case. Of course she refused the money, on principle, but it was not until much later that she realized the full import of the case. Wells was the first Afro-American to challenge the 1883 nullification of the Civil Rights Bill passed during Reconstruction. Her victory would have set a significant precedent—a fact not lost on the Tennessee Supreme Court, which reversed the lower court's decision.

Wells was devastated. For her, it wasn't just the loss of the case, but the loss of faith that justice would ultimately prevail. "I feel shorn of that belief and utterly discouraged, . . ." she wrote in her diary. In hindsight, her despondency seems naive, but as late as the 1880's most Blacks still believed that racial injustice was the handiwork of the lowly, an aberration that could be successfully challenged. It was their faith in the "system" that steeled their determination to be worthy citizens despite the bitter experience of slavery and discrimination. With that faith, Afro-Americans—and not just the most privileged ones—were making substantial economic gains after the war. They were attending school in droves: All in all, more than a quarter million Blacks attended more than four thousand schools established by the Freedmen's Bureau. Afro-Americans were also making extraordinary efforts to organize their family life in the wake of a turbulent slave system. But as the twentieth century drew nearer, that deeply rooted faith in justice began to be shaken.

For Wells, the court decision brought a focus to her brooding concerns, a focus that would be expressed through journalism. She began writing a column for the *Living Way* on a regular basis, and her articles, about everything from compelling national issues to local community ones, became so popular that they were picked up by other Black newspapers throughout the country. The evolution of her career would parallel that of the Black press nationally. In the 1880's almost two hundred Black newspapers were being published every week, and the best of them—including the Detroit *Plaindealer,* the *New York Age,* and the *Indianapolis Freeman*—carried her columns under the pen name of "Iola." Wells's bold style, combined with her physical attractiveness, elicited a great deal of attention—especially from her male colleagues. . . .

The careers of Wells and Church continued on divergent paths in the late 1880's and 1890's. In 1889, while Mary Church was studying in Europe, Wells was elected as the first woman secretary of the National Afro-American Press Association. . . .

Although Wells, unlike Church, was always strapped for funds, she managed to buy a one-third interest in *Free Speech* that year, and none too soon, it turned out. In 1891, the year that Church married an upwardly mobile young lawyer, Wells was fired from her teaching position as a result of an exposé on the Memphis school system. Her lack of sympathy with "humbug" obviously applied as much to the Black community as to the White. Teaching, frankly, bored her anyway, but the dismissal did pose a financial problem. For all of her fame as a journalist (she was even called "Princess of the Press") it didn't pay the rent. But her new circumstances forced her to turn a passionate avocation into a full-time job. So she took to the road, traveling through Arkansas, Mississippi, and Tennessee to increase the paper's circulation. Within nine months after her school dismissal, *Free Speech* subscriptions increased from 1,500 to 3,500, and within a year she was earning the same income she had as a teacher. Wells was in Natchez on one of those business trips when she heard about the lynching of Thomas Moss.

While Terrell agonized over the incident from afar—in Washington—Wells was forced to return to a Black Memphis community in shock and despair. "I have no power to describe the feeling of horror that possessed every member of the race in Memphis when the truth dawned upon us that protection of the law was no longer ours," she wrote. Wells must have had a sense of *déjà vu* from her own earlier experiences with the railroad. What she had gotten a glimmer of in 1883 was being vented full-force less than a decade later. Beginning with neighboring Mississippi in 1890, all the southern states were in the process of disenfranchising Blacks by legal means; oppressive Black codes replaced their slave antecedents; segregation was becoming the rule, and violence toward Blacks was on the increase.

Still, Blacks in Memphis, perhaps more than those of any other southern city, were convinced that the blood tides would not reach them. True, Memphis had been the scene of one of the worst postwar riots in the country, when forty-six Black men, women, and children were killed and more than $100,000 worth of Black-owned property was destroyed. Black women had been especially victimized by the violence. Federal inquiries revealed that many of them, living alone, were robbed, beaten, and raped. Cynthia Townsend, a Black woman who testified before federal authorities, told of a neighbor who was attacked by "three or four men," all of whom "had connexion [*sic*] with her in turn around, and then one of them tried to use her mouth." The woman, Townsend told the authorities, "has sometimes become a little deranged since then."

It was widely believed that such racial violence was a perversion, the work of poor Whites who had always resented economic competition from Blacks. But endemic racial violence was a thing of the past, many Blacks believed. In subsequent years, Black businessmen had thrived; Black legislators were elected to state and city government. But the Moss lynching of 1892 dimmed such optimism. And the rude awakening sent Wells and Terrell on a course that changed both their lives. Their approaches were different—symbolized by Wells purchasing a pistol, situated as she was within the belly of the beast, while Terrell, no doubt wearing her accustomed white gloves and expensive strand of pearls, went to the White House. Each would be effective in her own way; but Wells's radical response would have a more immediate impact.

The lynching of Thomas Moss further clarified Wells's perspective: The increasing violence toward Blacks had little to do with their alleged criminal behavior; rather lynching was the tool of the new caste system being imposed by the South. For Thomas Moss, everyone knew, was a good man, a loving husband and father, and a sterling citizen. His only crimes were to succeed at a business of his own, then to defend himself when Whites tried to destroy it. Furthermore, his murder was not at the hands of a few aberrants, but with the entire White establishment as accomplice. "The more I studied the situation," wrote Wells, "the more I was convinced that the Southerner had never gotten over his resentment that the Negro was no longer his plaything, his servant, and his source of income." The resentment was even more intense, she surmised, toward Blacks who were in a position to compete with Whites. Lynching was a direct result of the gains Blacks were making throughout the South.

Thomas Moss was only one of a growing number of Afro-Americans who were planting solid economic stakes into southern soil. At the turn of the century, the National Negro Business League, an organization founded by Booker T. Washington, reported that in a city as small as Montgomery, Alabama, with two thousand Black residents, there were:

> . . . twenty-three Black-owned restaurants, a dry-goods store, thirty shoe-makers, twelve contractors and builders, fifteen blacksmith shops, wood and coal yards, butcher stalls, greengrocers, draymen, insurance and real-estate agents, a lawyer, a dentist, 400 preachers, five physicians, and two undertakers—all doing well.

The same report noted that 187,000 Afro-Americans in the South owned their own farms, several of them more than a thousand acres in size. How such figures could be translated into political power was vividly seen in the Populist movement of the late nineteenth century. The movement was made up of farmers who sought to wrest control from the planter class, and in a number of contests, Blacks held the balance of power in electing Populist candidates in the South. If something weren't done, Blacks could upset the South's long-standing political and economic power base. For Black men now represented a significant portion of the electorate; in some states like Mississippi— whose border lay close to Memphis—there were more Black eligible voters than White. There was no doubt about it: Afro-Americans were a threat and lynching was the means to counteract it. . . .

There was no better candidate to articulate the "danger" for the entire nation than [Philip A.] Bruce. He was a trained historian; the son of a plantation owner who had lorded over five hundred slaves; the brother-in-law of writer Thomas Nelson Page; the nephew of the Confederacy's former secretary of war—and a Harvard graduate. Bruce's thesis, formulated in the 1889 publication *The Plantation Negro as a Freeman,* was that Blacks, "cut off from the spirit of White society," had regressed to a primitive and thus criminal state. Bereft of the master's influence, Blacks were now even closer to the "African type" than the slaves had been.

This sudden outbreak of barbarism included a penchant for rape. Black men, he said, "found something strangely alluring and seductive in the appearance of White women." If any poor Black soul thought he could take refuge from the sweeping charges on the basis of his class, he was sorely mistaken. . . . In fact, as a *Harper's Weekly* article noted, middle-class Blacks were the *greater* threat. For it was they who were "most likely to aim at social equality and to lose the awe with which in slavey times, Black men had learned to respect the woman of the superior race." The magazine called the phenomenon "The New Negro Crime."

The charge was leveled so consistently against Black men, and came from such impeccable sources, that the whole nation seemed to take it for granted. . . . The liberal reformer Jane Addams, though opposed to lynching, nevertheless believed that Black men had a proclivity for rape. Even some Blacks began to wonder. Frederick Douglass had begun to believe that "there was an increasing lasciviousness on the part of Negroes," according to Wells. Wells herself had doubts: "Like many another person who had read of lynching in the South," she wrote, "I had accepted the idea meant to be conveyed—that although lynching was irregular and contrary to law and order , . . perhaps the brute deserved death anyhow and the mob was justified in taking his life."

But Moss and his friends were not guilty of any crime, "new" or otherwise. Perhaps others weren't either. Perhaps, as Wells wrote, "lynching was merely an excuse to get rid of Negroes who were acquiring wealth and property and thus keep the race terrorized and 'keep the nigger down.'" Wells set out to find the truth by investigating every lynching she could. For months, she culled newspaper accounts, went to the scene of lynchings, interviewed eyewitnesses. All in all, she researched the circumstances of 728 lynchings that had taken place during the last decade.

The result was a fastidiously documented report. Only a third of the murdered Blacks were even *accused* of rape, much less guilty of it, Wells discovered. Most were killed for crimes like "incendiarism," "race prejudice," "quarreling with Whites," and "making threats." Furthermore, not only men but women and even children were lynched. "So great is Southern hate and prejudice," Wells wrote, "they legally (?) hung poor little thirteen-year-old Mildrey Brown at Columbia, S.C., Oct. 7th on the circumstantial evidence that she poisoned a white infant. If her guilt had been proven unmistakeable, had she been White," Wells concluded, "Mildrey Brown would never have been hung. The country would have been aroused and South Carolina disgraced forever. . . ."

Had Wells been content to publish these findings, she would have been provocative enough. But she tempted fate even further by exposing the rawest nerve in the South's patriarchal bosom. In the course of her investigations, Wells uncovered a significant number of interracial liaisons. She dared to print not only that such relationships existed, but that in many cases White women had actually taken the initiative. Black men were being killed for being "weak enough," in Wells's words, to "accept" White women's favors. . . .

When two more lynchings occurred while Wells was still conducting her investigations, she wrote the editorial that prompted her permanent banishment from the South. "Nobody in this section of the country believed the threadbare lie that Negro men rape white women," she challenged. "If Southern white men are not careful, they will overreach themselves and public sentiment will have a reaction. A conclusion will then be reached which will be very damaging to the moral reputation of their women."

Fortunately, while the editorial was still being set into type she was on her way to Philadelphia to accept a long-standing invitation from the activist and writer Frances Ellen Harper. . . . By then, the editorial had come out in Memphis and the backlash had been brutal and immediate. Wells's newspaper office was looted and burned to the ground; her co-owners, barely beating the mob, were run out of town; and Wells herself was warned that she would be hanged from a lamppost if she were to return. There were "agents" posted at the train station, she was told, to watch out for her. . . .

"The issue was forced," Wells thought after hearing the reaction to her editorial. She would simply have to fight from "exile." On June 5, 1892, the *New York Age* carried her seven-column article on its front page. Touted as the "first inside story of Negro lynching," it included names, dates, places, and circumstances of hundreds of lynchings for alleged rape. The response to the article was sensational and Fortune published ten thousand copies of the issue; one thousand were sold in the streets of Memphis alone.

Wells . . . wanted to publish her investigative findings in booklet form. But she faced the ever-present problem of insufficient funds to underwrite such an enterprise. In 1892, Black women came to her aid. They planned a testimonial, both in honor of her courageous stand and to raise funds for her booklet, which would be called "Southern Horror: Lynch Law in All Its Phases."

The testimonial, held October 5 in New York City's Lyric Hall, was a historic event: "the greatest demonstration ever attempted by race women for one of their own number," Wells later wrote. Never before had so many leading women of the race come together. Two hundred and fifty Black women came to honor Wells, and the list was a veritable *Who's Who* of the Black eastern establishment. Present was Boston's Josephine St. Pierre Ruffin, a suffragist, activist, and wife of a prominent legislator and judge. Dr. Susan McKinney from Brooklyn was also there. She was the valedictorian graduate of Long Island Medical College and considered the leading woman physician of the race. . . .

The testimonial had all the earmarks of a grand occasion. Wells's pen name, Iola, was spelled out in electric lights across the dais. The printed programs were miniature prototypes of the Memphis *Free Speech*. Soul-stirring music was interspersed with uplifting speeches. Five hundred dollars was collected for the booklet, which Wells dedicated "To the Afro-American women . . . whose race love, earnest zeal and unselfish effort made possible this publication." . . .

But as Wells's investigations had so vividly revealed, all Blacks, regardless of class or achievement, were vulnerable. Also, the nature of Wells's campaign had struck a particular chord in Black women, who had never been thought of as a significant factor in the racial struggle, who remained unprotected, and who were held responsible for the denigration forced upon them. They well knew, as Wells stated publicly, that while Black men were being accused of ravishing White women, "The rape of helpless Negro girls, which began in slavery days, still continues without reproof from church, state or press."

The negative images of Black women had always made them vulnerable to sexual assault, but by the late nineteenth century, that stereotype had even more sweeping consequences. Philip Bruce had included women in his diatribe against the race. They, too, were "morally obtuse" and "openly licentious," he wrote. But because they were women, their regression was seen as much worse than that of men. For it was women who were "responsible" for molding the institution of marriage and a wholesome family life which was the "safeguard against promiscuity." In Bruce's eyes, Black women who saw no "immorality in doing what nature prompts," who did not "foster chastity" among their own daughters, were not only responsible for their own denigration but for that of the *entire race*. Even the Black man's alleged impulse to rape was the Black woman's fault. Historically, the stereotype of the sexually potent Black male was largely based on that of the promiscuous Black female. He would have to be potent, the thinking went, to satisfy such hot-natured women. Now released from the constraints of White masters, the Black man found White women so "alluring" and "seductive" because, according to Bruce, of the "wantonness of the women of his own race."

Wells's campaign, by undermining the stereotype of Black men, also challenged presumptions of the immorality of Black women. And it was the public defense of the integrity of Black women, by Black women, which opened the way for the next stage of their political development. Black women like those at Lyric Hall responded to Ida B. Wells's antilynching campaign as not only a call to arms for the race, but for women specifically as well.

The ideas that drew them into battle were older than the Republic itself—for they were rooted in the European minds that shaped America.

ᏻ *F U R T H E R　　R E A D I N G*

Elizabeth Rauh Bethel, *Promiseland: A Century of Life in a Negro Community* (1981)
Raymond Gavins, "The Meaning of Freedom: Black North Carolinians in the Nadir, 1880–1900," in Jeffrey J. Crow et al., eds., *Race, Class, and Politics in Southern History* (1989)
Paula Giddings, *When and Where I Enter: The Impact of Black Women on Race and Sex in America* (1984)
Louis R. Harlan, *Booker T. Washington: Wizard of Tuskegee, 1901–1915* (1983)
Jacquelyn Jones, *Labor of Love, Labor of Sorrow: Black Women, Work and the Family from Slavery to the Present* (1985)
Charles F. Kellogg, *NAACP: The History of the National Association for the Advancement of Colored People, 1909–1920* (1967)

Neil R. McMillen, *Dark Journey: Black Mississippians in the Age of Jim Crow* (1989)
Wilson Moses, *The Golden Age of Black Nationalism* (1978)
Theodore Rosengarten, *All God's Dangers: The Life of Nate Shaw* (1984)
Elliott M. Rudwick, *W. E. B. Du Bois* (1969)
Herbert Shapiro, *Black Violence and White Response* (1988)
William M. Tuttle, Jr., *Race Riot* (1972)
Joel R. Williamson, *A Rage for Order* (1986)
C. Vann Woodward, *The Strange Career of Jim Crow* (1974)

Americanization on Whose Terms?

☙

The years from 1880 to 1920 witnessed a decisive social transformation in the United States in the form of a massive, unprecedented tide of immigration. Attracted by both the promise of economic opportunity and, for many, anticipated relief from religious and political persecution, the "New Immigrants" effectively redrew the demographic map of American cities and basic industries. At the high-water mark, 1900–1910, the 8.8 million immigrants constituted more than 40 percent of urban newcomers, doubling the natural increase by childbirth of the established population. Representing a shift in the incoming stream from the northern and western rim of Europe to the southern and eastern European heartland, the New Immigrants—Italians, Hungarians, Russians, Slavs, Greeks, Jews, and others (with lesser but regionally significant numbers also arriving from Asia and Latin America)—came overwhelmingly from peasant or working-class backgrounds and spoke in strikingly different accents, both literally and figuratively, from the native-born U.S. population.

The nature of immigrant integration into American society raised serious questions both inside and outside the immigrant communities. For a nation culturally suspended between dreams of social progress and worries about the loss of older virtues, the new immigration to the cities roused nativist fears of racial mongrelization and anarchistic insurrection. Even those who welcomed the immigrants' labor power coded their receptivity with an insistence on "Americanization," or the rapid inculcation of "acceptable" attitudes and behavior. For the immigrants themselves, the issues surrounding Americanization were usually different but no less complicated. The problem of how to "succeed" in material terms while maintaining values rooted in a distinct national and religious culture confronted every arriving group. This issue placed the greatest strain on the basic unit of immigrant survival, the family.

☙ D O C U M E N T S

The first two selections reflect the racialist nature of nativist sentiments. In the first document, New York City lawyer and zoologist Madison Grant bemoans the "passing of the great race" under the weight of what he deemed to be an inferior immigrant gene pool. In the second selection, an 1892 congressional report on immigration, reflecting the paranoia of white workers, singles out Chinese immigrant labor as a particular threat to the American way of life.

The remaining documents offer snapshots of the immigrants' own reactions to the issues of acculturation. In these conceptually related selections, a German labor paper regrets the steady disappearance of the mother tongue; an immigrant girl reports to her parents still in Poland on the tribulations of finding a husband and economic security in the New World; and readers of the Yiddish-language *Jewish Daily Forward* seek guidance in negotiating some of the most poignant moments of cultural dissonance.

Madison Grant on the New Immigrants as Survival of the Unfit, 1918

The prosperity that followed the war [World War I] attracted hordes of newcomers who were welcomed by the native Americans to operate factories, build railroads and fill up the waste spaces—"developing the country" it was called.

These new immigrants were no longer exclusively members of the Nordic race as were the earlier ones who came of their own impulse to improve their social conditions. The transportation lines advertised America as a land flowing with milk and honey and the European governments took the opportunity to unload upon careless, wealthy and hospitable America the sweepings of their jails and asylums. The result was that the new immigration, while it still included many strong elements from the north of Europe, contained a large and increasing number of the weak, the broken and the mentally crippled of all races drawn from the lowest stratum of the Mediterranean basin and the Balkans, together with hordes of the wretched, submerged populations of the Polish Ghettos. Our jails, insane asylums and almshouses are filled with this human flotsam and the whole tone of American life, social, moral and political has been lowered and vulgarized by them.

With a pathetic and fatuous belief in the efficacy of American institutions and environment to reverse or obliterate immemorial hereditary tendencies, these newcomers were welcomed and given a share in our land and prosperity. The American taxed himself to sanitate and educate these poor helots and as soon as they could speak English, encouraged them to enter into the political life, first of municipalities and then of the nation.

The native Americans are splendid raw material, but have as yet only an imperfectly developed national consciousness. They lack the instinct of self-preservation in a racial sense. Unless such an instinct develops their race will perish, as do all organisms which disregard this primary law of nature. Nature had granted to the Americans of a century ago the greatest opportunity in recorded history to produce in the isolation of a continent a powerful and racially homogeneous people and had provided for the experiment a pure race of one of the most gifted and vigorous stocks on earth, a stock free from the diseases, physical and moral, which have again and again sapped the vigor of the older lands. Our grandfathers threw away this opportunity in the blissful ignorance of national childhood and inexperience.

The result of unlimited immigration is showing plainly in the rapid decline in the birth rate of native Americans because the poorer classes of Colonial stock, where they still exist, will not bring children into the world to compete in the labor market with the Slovak, the Italian, the Syrian and the Jew. The native American is too proud to mix socially with them and is gradually withdrawing from the scene, abandoning to these aliens the land which he conquered and developed. The man of the old stock is being crowded out of many country districts by these foreigners just as he is to-day being literally driven off the streets of New York City by the swarms of Polish Jews. These immigrants adopt the language of the native American, they wear his clothes, they steal his name and they are beginning to take his women, but they seldom adopt his religion or understand his ideals and while he is being elbowed out of his own home the American looks calmly abroad and urges on others the suicidal ethics which are exterminating his own race.

When the test of actual battle comes, it will, of course, be the native American who will do the fighting and suffer the losses. With him will stand the immigrants of Nordic blood, but there will be numbers of these foreigners in the large cities who will prove to be physically unfit for military duty.

As to what the future mixture will be it is evident that in large sections of the country the native American will entirely disappear. He will not inter-marry with inferior races and he cannot compete in the sweat shop and in the street trench with the newcomers. Large cities from the days of Rome, Alexandria, and Byzantium have always been gathering points of diverse races, but New York is becoming a *cloaca gentium* which will produce many amazing racial hybrids and some ethnic horrors that will be beyond the powers of future anthropologists to unravel.

One thing is certain: in any such mixture, the surviving traits will be determined by competition between the lowest and most primitive elements and the specialized traits of Nordic man; his stature, his light colored eyes, his fair skin and light colored hair, his straight nose and his splendid fighting and moral qualities, will have little part in the resultant mixture.

The "survival of the fittest" means the survival of the type best adapted to existing conditions of environment, which to-day are the tenement and factory, as in Colonial times they were the clearing of forests, fighting In-dians, farming the fields and sailing the Seven Seas. From the point of view of race it were better described as the "survival of the unfit." . . .

Success in colonization depends on the selection of new lands and clima-tic conditions in harmony with the immemorial requirements of the incoming race. The adjustment of each race to its own peculiar habitat is based on thousands of years of rigid selection which cannot be safely ignored. A certain isolation and freedom from competition with other races, for some centuries at least, is also important, so that the colonists may become habitu-ated to their new surroundings.

The Americans have not been on the continent long enough to acquire this adjustment and consequently do not present as effective a resistance to competition with immigrants as did, let us say, the Italians when overrun by northern barbarians. As soon as a group of men migrate to new surroundings, climatic, social or industrial, a new form of selection arises and those not fitted to the new conditions die off at a greater rate than in their original home. This form of differential selection plays a large part in modern industrial centres and in large cities, where unsanitary conditions bear more heavily on the children of Nordics than on those of Alpines or Mediterraneans.

Congress Takes Aim at the "Chinese Menace," 1892

There is urgent necessity for prompt legislation on the subject of Chinese immigration. The exclusion act approved May 6, 1882, and its supplement expires by limitation of time on May 6, 1892, and after that time there will be no law to prevent the Chinese hordes from invading our country in number so vast, as soon to outnumber the present population of our flourishing States on the Pacific slope. . . .

The popular demand for legislation excluding the Chinese from this country is urgent and imperative and almost universal. Their presence here is inimical to our institutions and is deemed injurious and a source of danger. They are a distinct race, saving from their earnings a few hundred dollars and returning to China. This they succeed in doing in from five to ten years by living in the most miserable manner, when in cities and towns in crowded tenement houses, surrounded by dirt, filth, corruption, pollution, and prostitution; and gambling houses and opium joints abound. When used as cooks, farm-hands, servants, and gardeners, they are more cleanly in habits and manners. They, as a rule, have no families here; all are men, save a few women, usually prostitutes. They have no attachment to our country, its laws or its institutions, nor are they interested in its prosperity. They never assimilate with our people, our manners, tastes, religion, or ideas. With us they have nothing in common.

Living on the cheapest diet (mostly vegetable), wearing the poorest clothing, with no family to support, they enter the field of labor in competition with the American workman. In San Francisco, and in fact throughout the whole Pacific slope, we learn from the testimony heretofore alluded to, that the Chinamen have invaded almost every branch of industry; manufacturers of cigars, cigar boxes, brooms, tailors, laundrymen, cooks, servants, farm-hands, fishermen, miners and all departments of manual labor, for wages and prices at which white men and women could not support themselves and those dependent upon them. Recently this was a new country, and the Chinese may have been a necessity at one time, but now our own people are fast filling up and developing this rich and highly favored land, and American citizens will not and can not afford to stand idly by and see this undesirable race carry away the fruits of the labor which justly belongs to them. A war of races would soon be inaugurated; several times it has broken out, and bloodshed has followed. The town of Tacoma, in 1887, banished some 3,000 Chinamen on twenty-four hours' notice, and no Chinaman has ever been permitted to return.

Our people are willing, however, that those now here may remain, protected by the laws which they do not appreciate or obey, provided strong provision be made that no more shall be allowed to come, and that the smuggling of Chinese across the frontiers be scrupulously guarded against, so that gradually, by voluntary departures, death by sickness, accident, or old age, this race may be eliminated from this country, and the white race fill their places without inconvenience to our own people or to the Chinese, and thus a desirable change be happily and peacefully accomplished. It was thought that the exclusion act of 1882 would bring about this result; but it now appears that although at San Francisco the departures largely exceed the arrivals, yet the business of smuggling Chinese persons across the lines from the British Possessions and Mexico has so greatly increased that the number of arrivals now exceed the departures. This must be effectually stopped.

A German Newspaper Laments the Decline of the German Language in America, 1894

The following is an excerpt from an article which appeared in the "Frankfurter Zeitung" about the way Germans living in the United States care for the German language: "I've already barked [gebellt] three times, and nobody's answered." That's the way a German-American addressed me last summer when, having completed a convivial reporter's trip, I finally landed at the door of my host, a busy Milwaukee doctor, at midnight. At first I thought the stranger had been bitten by a mad dog. But his demeanor was too composed for that, so I lay a consoling hand on his shoulder and said: "I'll open up; but—what do you say, as a fellow countryman, would you bark first?" He didn't seem to understand the purpose of this request, but he nevertheless nodded, and, while I waited for him to start barking, he raised his right arm and—rang the doorbell. At the same time, having followed his hand with my eyes, I saw a little plaque inscribed in both German and English: *"Night-bell."* I finally realized what the good man had meant by "barking" ["bellen"].

This little nocturnal adventure is an amusing illustration of the lamentable fact that the large majority of German immigrants in America have neglected their native tongue. It has, in fact, been almost completely cast off, and along with it, all its native peculiarities and customs. And indeed, this happens much quicker among Germans than among other nationalities. It is well known that this fact cannot be denied, and those who are not favorably inclined toward us are extremely pleased to be able to reproach us for it from time to time, as does Max O'rell [sic] in his book, "Brother Jonathan and His Country." After praising the Irish immigrants in America enthusiastically for the fact that their offspring remain Irish to the third and fourth generation, he states: "What a contrast to the Germans one encounters in America! They forget their language, their children never learn it, their fatherland is judged severely. Wherever the German settles, he becomes a native. He doesn't colonize, but rather immediately assumes the customs, faith, and language of his new fatherland; in Africa he becomes a Negro!''

Well bellowed! But just the same, this Frenchman, normally very acute, is going too far. . . . Above all, O'rell is forgetting that the Irish who come to America need not learn a foreign language, and that's why they cannot neglect their own. Though granted, it is true that the Irish in America have much more of a clannish spirit than the Germans. Otherwise, being in a minority, they wouldn't be able to have the say in almost all local administrations, wouldn't be able to govern the country, as it were.

But let's concentrate on the language. Those who emigrate to America to practice a trade must necessarily learn English if they don't want to quickly find themselves at a great disadvantage. This in itself is difficult enough for many Germans, and by the time they've finally learned English, their German is already, to a greater or lesser degree, vulgarized, interspersed with English terms. You won't find a single German-American who says ''Strassenbahnwagen'' instead of *''car,''* because the latter word is much shorter. And then you have immigrants from all over Germany; one person talks in terms of the ''Schlachter,'' another of the ''Metzger,'' yet another of the ''Fleischer'' [regional variations for *butcher*]. To avoid confusion, even when Germans are speaking among themselves, they simply say *''butcher.''* The word *''plumber''* (Bleigiesser, Spengler, Klempner) is used for the same reasons. And there are many more, some of which force their way into written German, too, as a look at German-American newspapers quickly confirms.

The problem is yet augmented when less-educated people attach German endings to English verbs (setteln, mooven, driven, etc.), and—what is even worse—when they mistranslate English words. The word of comparison, for instance, *''like,''* is translated as ''gleich,'' which is correct. But what follows is not correct: ''to *like''* is translated as ''gleichen'' [''to resemble,'' ''to be equal to'']. The German who has come to America for the first time can't believe his ears when he is asked: ''Do you resemble [gleichen] potatoes?'' . . . In Pennsylvania, where the German language has survived for two hundred years, one hears completely different things. There, for instance, a farmer's son addressed his father: ''Der *Ox* is *over* die *Fence* gejumbt und hat's *Corn* verdamnished.'' (The ox jumped over the fence and damaged the corn.)

It would, in fact, be no great loss if this kind of German were to disappear completely; or in any case, it's not worth teaching it to children who have been born in America, especially since they lean more toward English anyway. At best, they struggle along with *''Dutch''* for their parents' sake, and when the latter die, the subscriptions to German-language newspapers are canceled, the German Bible is locked up in the closet with the rest of the family relics, and the process of assimilation is complete.

More-educated people—unless they foolishly renounce their origins and speak only English—keep their German as pure as possible, and see to it that their children learn it before English, letting them more or less pick up English later from contacts with the domestic help, neighbors, and fellow pupils. But once this happens, English can easily supplant German again, and not every immigrant is as impressive when talking to his children about their native language as is the German-American doctor and writer, Friedr. Carl Castelhun—originally from Worms, now living in San Francisco:

> Guard the German language,
> Praise the German phrase;
> Out of which our fathers,
> And their spirits gaze;
> Which the world with so much
> Greatness has instilled,
> Which the heart so often
> With its beauty thrilled.
>
> That which Lessing thought of,
> That which Goethe said,
> Always will be present,
> Always will be read.
> When my thoughts to Schiller,
> Quickens my heart's pace:
> Far too poor's the world
> Schiller to replace!
>
> Value, children, always,
> This land where we live,
> But the German language,
> So much has to give.
> Don't forget the homeland,
> Guard it from distress;
> E'en your great grandchildren
> Shall its charm possess!

A Polish Immigrant Girl Writes Home to Her Family, 1914

Greenburg, Pa., December 8, 1913

Dearest Parents: To your words, "Praised be Jesus Christus," I answer, "For centuries of centuries. Amen."

Dearest parents, I inform you that I received the letter sent by you from which I got information about your health and success also. As to myself, thanks to God the Highest, I am in good health, which I wish also to you from all my heart. As to my success, it is not very good because I have done housework, and have been paid $10 for this month, but I had too heavy work; I was obliged to work too long. Now, dearest parents, I inform you that I have at present no work and I don't know what will be further.

Three letters from Konstancya Walerych in William I. Thomas and Florian Znaniecki, *The Polish Peasant in Europe and America*, 1958, pp. 803–806. Reprinted by permission of Dover Publications Inc.

Dearest parents, you ask to be informed where I have been boarding after coming to America. I was with my sister and now I am with my sister. Dearest parents, don't be angry with me for not sending you anything up to the present, but I inform you that I could not, because when I traveled to America I remained for a week in Antwerp, and when I came to America I had no work for three weeks, and you know well, dearest parents, that I did not come to parents here; in America nothing is to be had without paying.*

Dearest parents, I inform you that I send you meanwhile thirty roubles for Christmas, and by my soul I cannot send you more at present, because I do not work and I need it myself. I have nothing more to write you, only I greet you and send you low salutations, and I wish you a Merry Christmas, and may the Godly Child have you in His care. God grant it. Amen.

Your loving daughter,

Konstancya Walerych

Now, dearest parents, I, your daughter, Frankowska, salute you and greet you heartily and I inform you that I was ill and had two boys born, but they were both dead. Now I [the son-in-law] greet you and salute you, and all our children bow to you and kiss you.

Bronisław Frankowski

Dear Zosia [younger sister], I salute you and write to you that you must go to school and learn well, and next year you will come to America, and then you will write letters.

Konstancya Walerych

January 17, 1914

Dear Parents: . . . I inform you that I married a man from Galicia. Our marriage occurred on the 12th of January; my husband is named Jan Czarnecki. Now, dear parents, I beg you heartily, don't be angry with me for marrying so hastily and a man from so far a country and for not even writing to you about it.† I inform you, dear parents, that I took a husband from so far a country for this reason, that, as you know, the girls who married with us and took husbands from the same village, were most unhappy afterward.‡ And

---

* Allusion to the fact that her sister and brother-in-law take money for board. In the old country they would have given her hospitality at least for some weeks, if not months. The American conditions and customs are considered a justification for not fulfilling the duty of hospitality. The main reason of the change is the fact that here food has to be bought instead of being produced, and thus the economic instead of the social point of view is applied to the question of living.
† The only case in our collection where a girl marries without first asking her parents. Of course it is a complete break of tradition, and a conscious one, since she knows and understands the traditional norms.
‡ The justification of the breach of this custom is interesting, because based upon consideration of utility and personal happiness.

secondly, when I came to America I often wept because I found myself among good people. Dearest parents, I inform you that we had a great wedding, only I was so sad that you were not at my wedding and that you did not even know about it, because I did not write to you.

Dearest parents, I, Jan Czarnecki, your son-in-law, bow to you and greet you heartily, and I beg you not to be angry with me for marrying your daughter, because it is God who gives their fortune to men, and to us also He gave such a fortune and we married in conformity with the will of the Highest. Now, dearest parents, we kiss your hands and we bow to your feet and we ask your parental blessing for this our new life.

Your loving children,

Jan and Konstancya Czarnecki

March 25, 1914

Dearest Parents: . . . We inform you, dearest parents, that we received the letter you sent us, for which we thank you heartily. We thank you for your good hearts, that you sent us your parental blessing. Dearest mother, you think of having sent me to America as if you had sent me to the grave, and you believe that we shall not be able to return to our country; but about this you can be perfectly sure, mother, because if God gives us health and happiness, we can go to our country at any moment.

Now I, your son-in-law, thank you, dear parents, heartily, that you admitted me to the family circle, and at the same time I thank you that you gave your daughter under my care,* and I will endeavor that she may ever be satisfied with me. We inform you, dear parents, that we send you 10 roubles and 2 more, one for grandmother, one to sister Zosia; it makes together 12. We inform you that, thanks to God the Highest, we are in good health, which we wish to you also with our whole heart. We are only sad that you grieve too much, but be calm, because our Lord God gives his fortune to every man, and we married in conformity with God's will.

Now I inform you about my parents. Both my parents are still living and they dwell in Galicia, district Ropczyce, village Czarna, post-station Sędziszów. Father's name is Filip, mother's, Dorota. We are nine brothers— four of us are in America, five in our country—and two sisters.

We have nothing more to write.

Your loving children,

Jan and Konstancya Czarnecki

---

* A good expression of the complex meaning which marriage assumes when it is still a familial matter but has become also an individual matter. There is no place for the idea of putting the girl under the man's care in the familial system, because she remains in the care of the group as a whole; there is no place for the idea of being admitted into the family circle in the individualistic marriage-organization, because the marriage-group becomes then an independent entity.

An Advice Column for Jewish Immigrants, 1906, 1907

Worthy Editor,

We are a small family who recently came to the "Golden Land." My husband, my boy and I are together, and our daughter lives in another city.

I had opened a grocery store here, but soon lost all my money. In Europe we were in business; we had people working for us and paid them well. In short, there we made a good living but here we are badly off.

My husband became a peddler. The "pleasure" of knocking on doors and ringing bells cannot be known by anyone but a peddler. If anybody does buy anything "on time," a lot of the money is lost, because there are some people who never intend to pay. In addition, my husband has trouble because he has a beard, and because of the beard he gets beaten up by the hoodlums.

Also we have problems with our boy, who throws money around. He works every day till late at night in a grocery for three dollars a week. I watch over him and give him the best because I'm sorry that he has to work so hard. But he costs me plenty and he borrows money from everybody. He has many friends and owes them all money. I get more and more worried as he takes here and borrows there. All my talking doesn't help. I am afraid to chase him away from home because he might get worse among strangers. I want to point out that he is well versed in Russian and Hebrew and he is not a child any more, but his behavior is not that of an intelligent adult.

I don't know what to do. My husband argues that he doesn't want to continue peddling. He doesn't want to shave off his beard, and it's not fitting for such a man to do so. The boy wants to go to his sister, but that's a twenty-five-dollar fare. What can I do? I beg you for a suggestion.

Your constant reader,

F.L.

Answer: Since her husband doesn't earn a living anyway, it would be advisable for all three of them to move to the city where the daughter is living. As for the beard, we feel that if the man is religious and the beard is dear to him because the Jewish law does not allow him to shave it off, it's up to him to decide. But if he is not religious, and the beard interferes with his earnings, it should be sacrificed.

Dear Editor,

For a long time I worked in a shop with a Gentile girl, and we began to go out together and fell in love. We agreed that I would remain a Jew and she a Christian. But after we had been married for a year, I realized that it would not work.

I began to notice that whenever one of my Jewish friends comes to the house, she is displeased. Worse yet, when she sees me reading a Jewish newspaper her face changes color. She says nothing, but I can see that she has changed. I feel that she is very unhappy with me, though I know she loves me. She will soon become a mother, and she is more dependent on me than ever.

She used to be quite liberal, but lately she is being drawn back to the Christian religion. She gets up early Sunday mornings, runs to church and comes home with eyes swollen from crying. When we pass a church now and then, she trembles.

Dear Editor, advise me what to do now. I could never convert, and there's no hope for me to keep her from going to church. What can we do now?

Thankfully,

A Reader

Answer: Unfortunately, we often hear of such tragedies, which stem from marriages between people of different worlds. It's possible that if this couple were to move to a Jewish neighborhood, the young man might have more influence on his wife.

Dear Editor,

I, too, want to take advantage of this opportunity to tell about my troubles, and I ask you to answer me.

Eight months ago I brought my girlfriend from Russia to the States. We had been in love for seven years and were married shortly after her arrival. We were very happy together until my wife became ill. She was pregnant and the doctors said her condition was poor. She was taken to the hospital, but after a few days was sent home. At home, she became worse, and there was no one to tend her.

You can hardly imagine our bitter lot. I had to work all day in the shop and my sick wife lay alone at home. Once as I opened the door when I came home at dinnertime, I heard my wife singing with a changed, hoarse voice. I was terror-stricken, and when I ran to her I saw she was out of her head with fever.

Imagine how I felt. My wife was so ill and I was supposed to run back to the shop because the last whistle was about to blow. Everybody was rushing back to work, but I couldn't leave. I knew that my boss would fire me. He had warned me the day before that if I came late again he wouldn't let me in. But how could I think of work now, when my wife was so ill? Yet without the job what would happen? There would not be a penny coming into the house. I stayed at my wife's bedside and didn't move till four o'clock.

Suddenly I jumped up and began to run around the room, in despair. My wife's singing and talking drove me insane. Like a madman I ran to the door and locked it. I leaped to the gas jet, opened the valve, then lay down in the bed near my wife and embraced her. In a few minutes I was nearer death than she.

Suddenly my wife cried out, "Water! water!" I dragged myself from the bed. With my last ounce of strength I crept to the door and opened it, closed the gas valve, and when I came to, gave her milk instead of water. She finished a glassful and wanted more, but there wasn't any more so I brought her some seltzer. I revived myself with water, and both of us slowly recovered.

The next morning they took my wife to the hospital, and after a stay of fourteen days she got well. Now I am happy that we are alive, but I keep thinking of what almost happened to us. Until now I never told anyone about it, but it bothers me. I have no secrets from my wife, and I want to know whether I should now tell her all, or not mention it. I beg you to answer me.

The Newborn

Answer: This letter depicting the sad life of the worker is more powerful than any protest against the inequality between rich and poor. The advice to the writer is that he should not tell his wife that he almost ended both their lives. This secret may be withheld from his beloved wife, since it is clear he keeps it from her out of love.

Worthy Editor,

I am eighteen years old and a machinist by trade. During the past year I suffered a great deal, just because I am a Jew.

It is common knowledge that my trade is run mainly by the Gentiles and, working among the Gentiles, I have seen things that cast a dark shadow on the American labor scene. Just listen:

I worked in a shop in a small town in New Jersey, with twenty Gentiles. There was one other Jew besides me, and both of us endured the greatest hardships. That we were insulted goes without saying. At times we were even beaten up. We work in an area where there are many factories, and once, when we were leaving the shop, a group of workers fell on us like hoodlums and beat us. To top it off, we and one of our attackers were arrested. The hoodlum was let out on bail, but we, beaten and bleeding, had to stay in jail. At the trial, they fined the hoodlum eight dollars and let him go free.

After that I went to work on a job in Brooklyn. As soon as they found out that I was a Jew they began to torment me so that I had to leave the place. I have already worked at many places, and I either have to leave, voluntarily, or they fire me because I am a Jew.

Till now, I was alone and didn't care. At this trade you can make good wages, and I had enough. But now I've brought my parents over, and of course I have to support them.

Lately I've been working on one job for three months and I would be satisfied, but the worm of anti-Semitism is beginning to eat at my bones again. I go to work in the morning as to Gehenna, and I run away at night as from a fire. It's impossible to talk to them because they are common boors, so-called

went forward essentially along two lines: first and most commonly, the general anti-foreign feelings touched off by the internal and international shocks of the late nineteenth century were discharged with special force against these new targets so that each of the southeastern European groups appeared as a particularly insidious representative of the whole foreign menace; secondly and more slowly, a campaign got under way against the new immigration as a unique entity, constituting in its difference from other foreign groups the essence of the nation's peril. The first type of attack was midwife to the second. The new immigrants had the very bad luck to arrive in America en masse at a time when nativism was already running at full tilt, and when neither anarchist nor Jesuit afforded a wholly satisfactory victim for it.

The hostilities which southeastern Europeans faced depended partly on their increasing prominence on the Amercian scene. During the early nineties, peasants and Jews poured out of southern and eastern Europe in ever larger numbers, fleeing from poverty and inhumanity to a new promised land. Cutthroat competition among the transatlantic steamship companies eased their flight; steerage rates on first-class boats dropped to $10 or even less. The depression sharply reduced all immigration, but the new current never fell below one hundred thousand persons per year—a level it had first reached in 1887. More exclusively than most older immigrant groups, the new ones swarmed into the slums, the factories, and the mines. Either urbanites or industrial workers, and usually both, they played a role in American life that lent itself to nativist interpretation. In the crowded places where they made their homes, they lived as a class apart, the least assimilated and most impoverished of the immigrants. Hence, they symbolized vividly the social and economic ills with which nativists identified the immigrants generally. Fears of developing class cleavage could easily center on them; and . . . the problems of depression and unrest could be associated with them. Above all, each of the southern and eastern European nationalities seemed to Americans in some way a disturber of the peace, thereby focalizing the fear of foreign-bred discontent.

On the other hand, the new immigrants, although vulnerable as symbols of a general foreign problem, did not yet stand out readily as a collective entity. Until 1896 the old influx from northern and western Europe surpassed the southern and eastern European current. All in all, at least 80 percent of the European-born population of the United States in the mid-nineties still derived from those accustomed sources—Germany, Great Britain, Scandinavia, France, Switzerland, and the Low Countries. Furthermore, concentration of settlement limited the impact of the new groups. While a few coastal cities and industrial complexes felt their arrival sharply, large parts of the country hardly knew them at all. . . . Most of America was just beginning to learn of their presence, largely at secondhand. Consequently most of the hatred of Italians, Slavs, and Jews consisted of general anti-foreign attitudes refracted through specific national stereotypes.

The Slavic coal miners of Pennsylvania illustrate very well how the new immigration inherited a wider, pre-existing animus. They acquired the immigrant's standard reputation for disorder in an unusually simple, direct form.

The American mind contained, apparently, no distinctive "Slavic" stereotype, comparable to Italian and Jewish stereotypes, which might have individualized the hostile response. Consequently Slavic and Magyar laborers impressed public opinion at large simply as foreigners par excellence: uncivilized, unruly, and dangerous.

The impression fed upon the Slavic coal miners' sporadic but increasing involvement in labor unrest. Ironically, while other workingmen continued to despise them as cheap and docile competitors, the general public fixed its eyes on their lapses from docility. . . . By 1891, when Henry Clay Frick precipitated a strike of fourteen thousand coke workers by posting a new wage scale, Slavic and Magyar nationalities well out-numbered the older immigrants and native Americans in the bituminous fields. Although British and Americans led the strike, it was generally interpreted as an uprising of "Huns," who, in the words of the New York *Tribune*, were "the most dangerous of labor-unionists and strikers. They fill up with liquor and cannot be reasoned with." The company brought in nonunion workers, a step which resulted in riots and vandalism on the part of the strikers. In this tense situation, a crowd of "Huns," returning from a mass meeting, passed a frightened detachment of state militia guarding a company store. Someone fired a shot, the strikers fled, and the militia fired two volleys after them. Ten dead and fifty wounded immigrants littered the road. According to the *Tribune*, the militia's action was "upheld by businessmen and all law-abiding people in the entire region."

Frick finally succeeded in breaking the strike, though he was to face a similar walkout three years later. This time an immigrant mob killed Frick's chief engineer, causing the Pittsburgh *Times* to report that the whole region was "trembling on the brink of an insurrection. Never before were the dangerous foreigners so thoroughly aroused." . . .

The bloodiest episode occurred in 1897. While the United Mine Workers Union was leading the new immigrants to victory in the bituminous fields, an attempt to launch a strike in the anthracite country provoked disaster. About 150 Polish and Hungarian strikers, entirely unarmed, set out from Hazleton, Pennsylvania, toward a nearby town, intent on urging the men there to join the walkout. The sheriff, persuaded by the coal owners that an organized march was illegal, gathered a posse of 102 deputies to intercept it. As the strikers came in sight, the sheriff ordered them to return. Someone struck him, frightening him into commanding the deputies to fire. They poured volley after volley into the surprised and terrorized crowd as it stampeded in flight. They killed twenty-one immigrants and wounded forty more. The sheriff, a former mine foreman, explained that the crowd consisted of "infuriated foreigners . . . like wild beasts." Other mine foremen agreed that if the strikers had been American-born no blood would have flowed.

In the case of the Italians, a rather similar fear of "infuriated foreigners" took a different twist. Anti-foreign sentiment filtered through a specific ethnic stereotype when Italians were involved; for in American eyes they bore the mark of Cain. They suggested the stiletto, the Maffia, the deed of impassioned violence. "The disposition to assassinate in revenge for a fancied wrong,'' declared the Baltimore *News,* ''is a marked trait in the character of this impulsive and inexorable race.'' Every time a simple Italian laborer resorted to his knife, the newspapers stressed the fact of his nationality; the most trival fracas in Mulberry Street caused a headline on ''Italian Vendetta.'' . . .

Time and again, lynching parties struck at Italians charged with murder. In 1891 a wild rumor that drunken Italian laborers had cut the throats of a whole American family in West Virginia set off further rumors of a pitched battle between a sheriff's posse and the assassins. . . . The biggest incident convulsed New Orleans—and then the whole country—at the beginning of the decade. The city combined southern folkways with all of the social problems of the urban North, and as the most southerly of American ports, it was the haven of a large migration from Sicily. In 1891 the superintendent of police was murdered under conditions which pointed to the local Sicilian population. Wholesale arrests followed in an atmosphere of hysteria. The mayor issued a public appeal: ''We must teach these people a lesson that they will not forget for all time.'' The city council appointed a citizens' committee to suggest ways of preventing the influx of European criminals. But when some of the accused were tried, the jury (which may have been suborned) stunned the city by refusing to convict. While officials stood idly by, a mob proceeded ''to remedy the failure of justice'' by lynching eleven Italian suspects. With apparent unanimity local newspapers and business leaders blessed the action.

At that point jingoism intruded upon what had begun as a local, internal episode, transforming it into a nation-wide commotion and a diplomatic crisis. Italy sought redress for the victims' families and punishment of the mob that murdered them. Secretary of State James G. Blaine treated the plea cavalierly, whereupon Italy abruptly recalled her minister in Washington. Internal hatred and external conflict now interacted directly, producing an explosion of feeling against Italy and enormously magnifying the fear of Italian-Americans. A belief that the Italian fleet might suddenly descend on the United States gained fairly wide credence, and patriots flexed their muscles in preparation. Italians within the country now appeared as a potential fifth column; obviously these people could not be depended upon in times of national danger. There were reports of Italian immigrants riddling an American flag with bullets; a rumor circulated that several uniformed corps of Italians were drilling in New York. In Wheeling, West Virginia, miners went on strike because their employer refused to discharge two Italians. . . .

Clearly, as the *Review* pointed out, a revival of Americanism was emerging from the New Orleans incident. Not just Italian immigration but the whole immigration question was dramatized as nothing had dramatized it since the Haymarket Affair. The press, the pulpit, and the magazines rang with demands for stringent restriction. The influential *Nation* concluded that a secure modern state rested on community of language and proposed therefore to limit immigration to English-speaking applicants. This severe idea met considerable favor.

The third major group in the new immigration, the Jews, was also buffeted by the nativism and jingoism of the nineties. They had, of course, their own unique status, fixed by the ancient Shylock stereotype; they stood for chicane rather than crime or revolution. (The American public had heard little as yet about the radical labor movements stirring in the New York ghetto.) But the Jews' supposedly unscrupulous greed now seemed as potentially subversive as the doings of bloodthirsty Italians, "furious Huns," or Irish papists. Hatred, rooted in much the same conditions, lashed them all in rather similar ways.

The Jews felt, too, the violence endemic in that period. Beginning in the late eighties, the first serious anti-Semitic demonstrations in American history occurred in parts of the lower South where Jewish supply merchants were common. In several parishes of Louisiana debt-ridden farmers stormed into town, wrecked Jewish stores, and threatened to kill any Jews who remained in the area. During the worst year, 1893, night-riders burned dozens of farmhouses belonging to Jewish landlords in southern Mississippi, and open threats drove a substantial number of Jewish businessmen from Louisiana. Persecution in northern cities generally took the form of personal taunts and assaults. . . . One serious incident broke out in a New Jersey mill town in 1891. Five hundred tending boys employed in the local glass works went on a rampage when the management hired fourteen young Russian Jews. Three days of riotous demonstrations caused most of the Jewish residents to flee from the area. In one sense the Jews came off a little better than the other minorities; apparently no lives were lost in any of these episodes.

A substantial ideological onslaught accompanied the physical assaults, however. In response to the tensions of the 1890s, the Shylock stereotype—which tended to obscure distinctions between the relatively well-to-do German Jews and the newcomers from eastern Europe—assumed a new potency. To some nativists, the Jews were capable of dominating or ruining American business. Tradition connected Jews with gold, which was becoming one of the major touchstones of internal strife. After 1890 the government's determination to maintain the gold standard excited enormous discontent and defined the great political issue of the period. Since greedy, destructive forces seemed somehow at work in the government and economy, suspicion dawned that a Jewish bid for supremacy was wreaking the havoc America could not control. Agrarian radicals, absorbed in a passionate crusade for free silver, sometimes yielded to this conjecture, but the idea was not theirs alone. The patrician Henry Adams concluded that the United States lay at the mercy of the Jews, and a New York workingman vowed: "The Russian Jews and the other Jews will completely control the finances and Government of this country in ten years, or they will all be dead. . . . The hatred with which they are regarded . . . ought to be a warning to them. The people of this country . . . won't be starved and driven to the wall by Jews who are guilty of all the crimes, tricks and wiles that have hitherto been unknown and unthought of by civilized humanity."

Here too jingoism played a part. It was not enough for jingo-inflamed nativists to see the Jews solely as an internal threat. They were a people without single national home or center of power: an *international* people. Since gold was becoming, in fact, a more and more firmly established international standard, millions of Americans associated their country's troubles with an international medium of exchange and felt themselves in the toils of a world-wide money-power. Did the Jews perhaps have an international loyalty above all governments, a quenchless resolve to rule the world themselves? For at least a few nativists, the new tendency to see America's adversaries operating on a world stage inflated the Jewish peril from one of national subversion to one of world domination. . . . The greatest of the silverites, William Jennings Bryan, bluntly accused President Cleveland of putting the country in the hands of the English Rothschilds. . . .

For understanding late nineteenth century nativism, it is not the latent possibilities of the new anti-Semitism which need emphasis, but rather the common qualities in the assaults on the various new immigrant nationalities. No longer scorned simply for "mere habits of life," each of the major groups from southern and eastern Europe stood forth as a challenge to the nation, either endangering American institutions by unruly behavior or threatening through avarice to possess them. In lashing out at each of these ethnic groups, a distraught society secured a whole set of new adversaries.

On the other hand, the discovery that the miscellaneous Slavs, Jews, and Italians constituted a collective type, a "new immigration," dawned more gradually. The concept of a new immigration would seem to have been largely the work of cultivated minds rather than a simple derivative of popular instincts. Certainly mass opinion in the nineties pictured the Italian, the Slav, and the Jew chiefly within the context of a general foreign peril. The fact of a rising influx of southern Europeans with unusually low living standards had been mentioned as early as 1884 in the discussion of the contract labor bill but did not receive much notice. Occasionally in the late eighties and with increasing frequency after 1890, a few keen observers in the East pointed to the proportional decline of northwestern European entrants. After 1890, as the comfortable belief faded that this was a mere, temporary eddy in the migratory stream, a handful of nativist intellectuals confronted the problem of defining the general threat which the whole movement from southern and eastern Europe raised to the nation's destiny.

Neither of the major traditions of nativist thought quite fitted the problem. The anti-radical theme, with its fears of imported discontent, applied to Europeans as a whole, and surely the new immigrants presented a more docile appearance than did Irish labor leaders or the German anarchists who hanged for the Haymarket Affair. Anti-Catholic nationalism, aside from failing to account for the new Jewish immigration, reeked of religious fanaticism which literate and cultured people now disavowed. On the eve of the A.P.A.'s [American Protective Association] rise to national prominence, a typical nativist intellectual rejoiced that the present movement against immigration would be free from attacks on Catholics. There was, however, a third nativist tradition—weaker than the other two but more adaptable to the purpose at hand. The old idea that America belongs peculiarly to the Anglo-Saxon race would define the special danger of the new immigration if one assumed that northern Europeans were at least first cousins to the Anglo-Saxons.

Eastern patrician intellectuals had been the keepers of the Anglo-Saxon tradition since the Civil War, and in the climate of the nineties it was not difficult for some of them to convert a doctrine that defined their own sense of nationality into censure of an immigrant throng that displayed few common traits except the indubitable fact that it was not Anglo-Saxon. . . .

When [Henry Cabot] Lodge raised the banner of race against the new immigration, it acquired its most dangerous adversary. As Massachusetts' scholar-in-politics, he dominated both the intellectual and legislative phases of nativism. To this dual role, Lodge's own interests and values imperiously summoned him; he embodied in remarkable degree some of the major forces underlying late nineteenth century xenophobia. From his precise Vandyke beard to his clipped Boston accent, Lodge was the model of a patrician. He was steeped in English culture—English to the last fiber of his thought, said Henry Adams—in pride of ancestry, and in nostalgia for New England's past. During the 1870s he had plunged into a study of the Anglo-Saxons; a thesis on early Anglo-Saxon law brought him the first Ph.D. that Harvard conferred in political science. Secondly, connected with Lodge's race consciousness was a morbid sensitivity to the danger of extensive social change. He had a lively repugnance for both the rising plutocracy and the restive mob, and he felt acutely the general nativist response to class conflict. By 1888, as a fledgling Congressman, he was pointing to the diminishing supply of free land in the West and the growth of unrest in the East as reasons for restricting immigration. Finally, while attacking immigration in domestic affairs, Lodge was adopting a belligerent stance in foreign affairs. His campaign against the new immigration during the 1890s interlaced with a jingoist crusade for expansion. Lodge the jingo hated England as much as Lodge the Anglo-Saxon loved the English; accordingly, his diplomatic belligerence took the form of an assertion of American power, his pleas for restriction a defense of the English race. But these and other inconsistencies in the life of the cold, cultivated little Senator were merely logical. They were resolved at another level—in the emotions of nationalism which shaped and guided his career.

Although the Anglo-Saxon tradition in the mid-nineties still swayed few outside of an eastern elite, through Lodge and others around him that elite occupied a position of strategic influence. Both the ideological instrument and the political leadership necessary to bring into a single focus the chaotic resentments against the new immigrant were therefore at hand.

Families Enter America

JOHN BODNAR

Networks of Migration

Throughout the immigrants' homelands families were forced to select emigration as one possible option in confronting the new order of capitalism. But a multitude of practical problems remained once the decision to move was made. How would information of specific jobs be found? Where could living

---

accommodations be located? How in general did individuals enter sprawling new factories and expanding cities? The answers to these pressing issues emerged not from any long and tedious thought process but largely from familiar patterns cultivated over years of dealing with the vagaries of economic systems, social relationships, and human desires. Work, shelter, and order would be secured in industrial America—as they had been in the pre-industrial and proto-industrial homeland—through an intricate web of kin and communal associations. The immigrant would not enter America alone. The intrusion of capitalism in the premigration lands may have raised the alternative of emigration, but it had not destroyed the essential relationship between family and work that most emigrants, regardless of ethnic background, had nurtured. It was a relationship which would enjoy a rejuvenation in the mills and neighborhoods of American industrial cities.

Because families and friends were in close contact even when separated by wide oceans, immigrants seldom left their homelands without knowing exactly where they wanted to go and how to get there. Relatives and friends constantly sent information back regarding locations to live and potential places of employment. Thousands of Poles were brought from Gdansk to Polish Hill in Pittsburgh by aunts, uncles, brothers, and sisters who sent them passage money and instructions of what to bring and where to make steamship and railroad connections. By 1915, as a result of such patterns, investigators could find heavy clusters of families in city neighborhoods. About three-fourths of the Italians and one-half of the Jews who owned property in Providence, Rhode Island, lived in a building with kin at the same address. One Jewish immigrant explained that her father had bought a three-family house with his cousins. Her family lived downstairs, one cousin on the second floor, and another cousin on the top floor. An Italian working for the Scovill Company in Connecticut brought friends who were "big and strong" from Italy. Women brought their sisters or friends into domestic jobs or gave them references of where to go. Chicanos followed each other along railroad lines into Los Angeles and from there throughout southern California. In the early 1920s Chicanos like José Anquiano were arriving in the Chicago area after hearing about openings at the Inland Steel Company and then sending for friends and kin in Texas and in their home villages in Mexico. In fact, relatives and friends were often responsible for movement to second and third locations in America when employment became slack in areas of first settlement. Thus, Italians from southern Illinois moved to the Italian "hill" in St. Louis when coal mining operations were reduced in the 1920s, and Slavs from mines in western Pennsylvania and northern Michigan moved to Detroit's expanding car industry in the same decade.

It was not unheard of for "middlemen" or labor agents to direct large flows of immigrant workers to particular industries or cities in return for modest fees. Such individuals usually shared a common ancestry and language with newcomers and could effectively gather them for shipment to a waiting industry. Oriental workers were channeled in such a fashion into western railroads for a time. . . . Italian "padrones" funneled their fellow countrymen to railroads and public works projects and into labor turmoil as strike-breakers. Ethnic "bankers," such as Luigi Spizziri, advanced passage to individuals in Italy and then found them work in Chicago. . . . In nearly all instances, however, intermediaries functioned only in the early stages of a migration stream. Inevitably the continual and enduring movement of all groups into industrial America would rest on ties and links established in the old world.

Immigrants did not need middlemen in the long run because they received a steady stream of information on labor market conditions and wages from friends and relatives, which allowed them to make reasonably well-informed decisions about where to go and what types of work they could expect to find. Immigrant letters were frequently filled with information on employment prospects, wages, and even the manner in which workers were treated. . . . A Polish steelworker in Pittsburgh wrote to his family in Poland not to keep his younger brother in school much longer; an extended education would be unnecessary for the toil required in the Pittsburgh mills.

Comparative analysis of Italians migrating to Argentina and New York City further revealed the specificity of the information immigrants used to make the decisions to move. In Argentina Italians formed a sizable portion of the economic structure and had access to numerous opportunities to own business and industrial establishments. At the turn of the century 57 percent of the owners of industrial establishments in Buenos Aires were Italian. The New York labor market offered considerably different opportunities for Italians. In the American metropolis they formed a much smaller percentage of the population and were unable to dominate any important economic sector. Because Italians were generally knowledgeable about the divergent opportunity structures in the two cities, different groups selected different destinations. Those from northern Italy, usually more literate, who intended to remain abroad permanently, went to Buenos Aires. Southern Italians, less literate and with less capital, who hoped to return to Italy, tended to move to New York, where they could easily find unskilled, temporary jobs. Indeed, some indications exist that over time, Italians in Argentina when compared to their American counterparts, invested more in business and their children's education than in housing, because they saw a greater chance for success in the future. . . .

Wages alone, however, did not attract immigrants to specific locations. They were frequently concerned about the type of work they would encounter. Italians often sought outdoor employment and were heavily represented in railroad and other forms of outdoor construction in many American cities. In Chicago they shunned meat-packing because they had heard of the intense cold of refrigerated compartments and the sweltering heat and offensive odors of the killing floors. . . . St. Paul, Minnesota, proved attractive to Irish and German women as a second stop in America because of numerous opportunities for domestic work awaiting them. . . . East European Jews moved into garment trades run by German Jews because they found them easier to work with than Gentile employers.

While immigrants clearly had preferences for work and some advance knowledge of wages and opportunities, however, they were not completely free to move into the industrial economy on an individual basis. Throughout the first century of American industrial expansion both workers and employers experimented with techniques of recruitment and job placement, and no method appeared to be as pervasive or as effective as that of informal familial and ethnic networks. The workplace of early industrial capitalism was a relatively accessible place especially during the six or seven decades after 1850, and kinship ties functioned effectively to provide labor, train new members, and effectively offer status and consolation. Poles, relying on relatives and friends, established occupational beachheads in Pittsburgh at the Jones and Laughlin steel plant. . . . As one newcomer recalled, "The only way you got a job was through somebody at work who got you in." . . . Frequently fathers and uncles taught sons and nephews the operation of industrial equipment. At the Amoskeag textile mills in New Hampshire, French-Canadians brought relatives to work, assisted in their placement in the mills, taught them specific work tasks, substituted for them when they were ill, and informally established production quotas. . . . In one New England textile plant nepotism became so widespread in securing employment that workers with familial connections within the plant were actually held in higher esteem than "unattached" employees who were presumed to be more transient.

Kinship not only facilitated the entry of immigrant males into the industrial economy but females as well. A 1930 study of 2,000 foreign-born women revealed that most had secured their initial jobs through relatives and friends. All had worked in either cigar or textile factories, and less than 10 percent had acquired relevant skills for those jobs prior to migrating. Surveys of full-fashioned, hosiery loopers discovered that the majority obtained their positions through acquaintances. . . . A 1924 investigation of Italian females in New York City reported that 75 percent acquired their first jobs through friends or relatives and that these women were "ashamed" to seek employment alone and would quit a job if friends or kin left as well. . . .

The central dynamic, which gradually allowed the industrial workplace to be filled informally by clusters of unskilled immigrants who were usually related, was the quest for greater production. Capitalism in its steady drive toward larger profits and lower costs demanded that goods be produced as quickly and as efficiently as possible. Invariably this imperative required that newer forms of production and technology replace skilled workers. This would not only allow for a faster pace of production but would diminish the influence that skilled workers had exerted over a particular workplace and put more control in the hands of managers and owners. . . .

The most striking result of the decline in skilled jobs was the growing number of immigrant clusters in the nineteenth and twentieth centuries. Nearly one-half of the Philadelphia Irish in 1850 were in unskilled labor, for instance, while 67 percent of the Germans were artisans. In Buffalo, Germans dominated crafts such as masonry, cooperage, and shoemaking while the Irish worked largely as unskilled laborers, domestics, ship carpenters, and teamsters. This early bunching resulted directly from the possession or lack of premigration skills, and newer immigrants after 1880, generally with less skills than the Germans, intensified the pattern of clustering. By 1911 a study of seven urban areas revealed that nearly one-third of all South Italians were categorized as "general laborers" in contrast to only 9 percent of the Poles and 7 percent of the Germans. Fully 65 percent of the Poles were in manufacturing and mechanical pursuits compared to only 28.8 percent of the South Italians. . . . Groups such as the Swedes, Jews, and Germans were considerably underrepresented in "unspecified labor" positions. . . .

Much of this bunching of immigrant workers could be attributed directly to the alteration of skill levels of American workers. As early as the 1840s textile mills in Lowell, Massachusetts, were attempting to improve their productive capacity by switching to spinning mules which could perform more than twice as much work as the older throstle spinners and implement the stretch-out on the assigning of additional looms or spindles to each worker at reduced piece rates. These changes eliminated the homogeneity of the workforce, which was largely native-born, and led directly to an increase in the proportion of immigrants. At one mill, for instance, the foreign-born proportion of the labor force rose from 3.7 percent in 1836 to 61.8 percent by 1860. Thousands of Irish immigrants entered the mills including many women and children who needed the wages and were willing to accept speed-ups and stretch-outs, in part because they were not familiar with an earlier, slower pace. . . .

. . . The substitution of unskilled for skilled labor proceeded rapidly during the final quarter of the nineteenth century. Employers intensified the drive to establish more efficient worker training programs by reducing skill requirements for incoming laborers. Expansion of child, female, and unskilled, foreign-born labor and the decline of apprenticeship programs and of highly skilled operatives underscored the trend. During the early decades of the twentieth century, the number of blacksmiths, machinists, and glassblowers declined substantially. Apprenticeships among brick and stone machinists fell from 39,463 in 1920 to 13,606 a decade later. . . .

The diminution of crafts and skills accelerated after 1900 and had a negative impact upon the older immigrant stocks from northern and western Europe. Germans in nineteenth-century Philadelphia predominated in skilled butchering, tailoring, and shoemaking positions. As these occupations declined, Germans were frequently dislocated and found it more difficult to transfer jobs to their sons. . . .

The blurring of skill distinctions among workers and the implementation of new efficiency schemes were accelerated during the period of the "new immigration." With proletarian protest growing in the late nineteenth century and larger concentrations of workers emerging in urban areas, industrial managers began to impose a bureaucratic structure upon the work force with hierarchical gradations of unskilled and semiskilled operations. This restructuring of work itself resulted in something of a segmentation of the labor market, . . . which created an infinite number of "entry-level" jobs and intensified the process of clustering, while making it extremely unlikely that newcomers could implement any previously acquired skills. The promise of industrial America to immigrant workers was not so much that one could rise as that one could gain access at any number of points of entry. Opportunity was not vertical but horizontal, a fact which tended to blunt any rhetoric of social mobility immediately upon arrival.

If skills were no longer crucial to obtaining work in the expanding sectors of the economy, something else would have to take their place. The alternative would be a random entry of thousands of immigrant workers into the industrial complex. But the widespread existence of clusters suggests that a sense of order in joining newcomers and occupations was operative. In even the most cursory survey of immigrant job acquisition, kinship and ethnic ties invariably emerge as the vital link. . . .

While most newcomers arrived in friendly groups, they were not allowed to function as independently as they might have thought. The industrial economy was certainly accessible but not at every particular point. Frequently, networks of families and relatives could function only where prospective employers allowed them to do so. Owners and managers had distinct impressions regarding the abilities of particular groups, a fact which encouraged group rather than individual movement, and took steps to encourage the hiring of one group at the expense of another. . . . On the Boston and Lowell Railroad in the mid-nineteenth century, only Irishmen were hired as firemen, since it was believed, unlike Yankees, they would not want further promotions. In early Milwaukee, Germans were considered "thrifty, frugal, and industrious" by employers and Poles more industrious than Italians and Greeks. . . . Jewish garment owners sometimes hired only Italians because they were felt to be less amenable to unionization than Jews. On other occasions the owners hired only fellow Jews, hoping that "fraternal instincts" with employers might keep them from unionizing. . . . Scandinavian women were strongly preferred in American homes as domestics, in part because they were Protestants while Irish girls were Catholic. This view caused Finnish women to be in heavy demand in large cities such as New York. The overall preference for western rather than eastern Europeans for better-paying jobs, it has been estimated, cost the "new immigrants" on the average of $1.07 per week in wages.

In the case of Chicanos, employer recruitment and attitude were almost solely responsible for determining where their kinship networks would function. The first significant movement of Mexican workers into the southwest was due to the agitation of agricultural, mining, and railroad companies in the southwest. Restrictions of the 1917 Immigration Law were even waived during World War I. Chicanos could not move into Santa Barbara until the 1880s after inexpensive Chinese labor had been curtailed, and even then they were confined to work in laundries, domestic work, and railroad section gangs. . . . A general assumption existed in the southwest that [Mexicans] were interested in working only a short while and then returning to Mexico, although increasing numbers were settling permanently north of the border after 1880. At El Paso, railroad recruiters considered them "docile, patient, orderly in camp, fairly intelligent under competent supervision, obedient and cheap." . . .

The Rise of a Family Economy

While it is apparent that immigrants were not free to move into the industrial economy wherever they desired, they were able to remain within the confines of small groups and networks, which assisted them tremendously. Such groups could mass around links of friends, villages, or regions but were mostly held together by ties of blood. Kinship formed the stable core of immigrant groups as they flowed into the openings available to them in particular times and places. Ironically, no concept so thoroughly pervaded the older interpretations of the American immigrant experience than the one which linked the growing movement of industrial-urban society to a pattern of family breakdown. This view originated with the belief that the modern capitalist system, especially in its manifestation of the factory system which removed production functions from the traditional family-household unit, simply destroyed the foundation of familial cooperation. Production became compartmentalized in factories and mills and workers began to function as individual components of a factory system and not as integral members of a household. This entire argument rested upon an assumption that families not only became less important in urban-industrial society but that families themselves operated in isolation from the larger economy of industrial capitalism which surrounded them.

The startling discovery of modern historical scholarship, however, has made it quite clear that immigrant families did not wither in their encounter with American capitalism. Immigrant kinship associations not only continued to perform indispensable functions in the industrial city, such as helping to organize the movement of workers into the economy, but actually flourished. At times the relationship between the industrial economy and immigrant families could almost be described as symbiotic, as kinship groups proved very responsive to demands of the workplace, the city, and the individual.

The world the immigrant left had exhibited numerous examples of family, in one form or another, as a central focus of organizing life itself. Families were responsible for socialization patterns, the distribution of land and other resources, and even served as a forum to resolve the question of who should emigrate and why. Because they also performed valuable functions in industrial America meant they were not as much cultural baggage as they were institutions which continued to find a relevant role to play in both societies. Family economies were as much a product of industrial capitalism as they were of subsistence agriculture, for in both systems a mediating institution was necessary to stand between economy and society in order to reconcile individual and group demands.

The manner in which the immigrant family remained functional in two economies was its central and enduring attachment to the value of cooperation. Family members were continually instructed in the necessity of sharing and notions of reciprocity were constantly reinforced. Parents, children, boarders, and others who shared particular households were all assigned a series of duties and obligations. By working together, pooling limited resources, and muting individual inclinations, families attempted to assemble the resources sufficient for economic survival and, occasionally, for an improvement in their standard of living. But the first goal was always the most immediate: cooperate and survive. French-Canadian children in New England recalled how all contributed their savings to their parents. One who was raised in a large family claimed that it stood to reason that everyone was "gonna start working and pitch in." . . .

Another immigrant elaborated on the reciprocal nature of immigrant life. He recalled:

> When you work, you understand, you used to bring your pay home and give it to your parents. And whatever they feel they want to give you, they decide. There was no disagreement. That was their style. And don't you dare talk about paying board, especially in dad's house. If you want to pay board you have to go somewhere else. "This is no boardinghouse. This is a family," my father would say. He said to us to bring our pay home and whatever it was, we would make do.

It was not until the era of postindustrialism after 1940, when kinship ties to the workplace were gradually weakened and success was equated with an individual quest, that the underlying system of familial cooperation would be threatened.

Essentially, family goals came to supersede individual goals, and parents and children both worked vigorously to contribute to familial welfare. Immigrant parents were often able to direct the career paths of their progeny because of the leverage they derived from being able to provide access to industrial jobs or housing in crowded cities. Boys and girls were frequently asked to leave school early and start work either in a mill or in a family business. Girls were often kept at home caring for younger brothers and sisters or performing household chores. Females who wanted to study music were told it was more practical to stay at home and learn cooking, canning, and sewing. One girl wept when forced by her father to leave school after the sixth grade because he felt a woman did not need schooling "to change diapers." Boys were urged to learn a job skill or a business rather than pursue a formal education, as families responded to the nature of the economy during the first century of American capitalism. Often they received such training on the job from fathers or other kin. Interviews with Poles in the Lawrenceville section of Pittsburgh revealed that during the 1920s and 1930s boys worked alongside their fathers in neighborhood foundries and meat-packing plants.

The family economy was not a product of natural evolution, and the effort to insure that children participated directly in the mustering of resources for familial survival was not accomplished without turmoil and tension. . . . Siblings often complained bitterly if one were allowed to stay in school longer than another. And a few resisted parental attempts to send them to work early. Individual plans and dreams were often formulated but reluctantly put aside for family need. Interviews with immigrant children found careers in electrical engineering, bookkeeping, the priesthood, and business relinquished at the insistence of parents. Studies conducted among Polish immigrant girls in the Chicago stockyard areas revealed that many complained if enough of their wages were not "returned" to them by their parents. . . . Not surprisingly, some immigrant children left home, for they saw their parents as obstacles to happiness.

But parents endured difficult tensions as well. In one study of northern New England textile mills, Steven Dubnoff found that Irish fathers lost some influence in the household as their children began to earn more of their own income. . . .

It is not entirely surprising that the cooperative ideal pervaded most immigrant families. These newcomers were not coming from widely disparate sectors of their homeland social structures but from the ranks of middle-class farm owners and tradesmen and the mass of marginal farmers and landless laborers just below them. A sense of hierarchy existed within the total group but all resided somewhere in the middle of society and experienced neither the hopelessness of extreme poverty nor the self-assurance of power and wealth. Surviving together was a constant preoccupation. . . .

Steeped heavily in a tradition of household and familial cooperation as a vehicle for achieving economic stability and finding an economic system in America which frequently encouraged a good deal of group assistance, immigrants who wished to remain found it relatively easy to establish households of their own. Indeed, the decision to do so represented not only a major commitment to remain in industrial society but suggested the means by which economic and emotional stability would be achieved in new circumstances. The creation of a new family often eased the pain of severing familial ties in the premigration society, especially for women who saw motherhood as a means of adjusting to a new life. Financial considerations also prompted many men to seek a companion who would cook, clean, and care for them for no wages at all. Many immigrants were anxious to reunite with wives and children out of fear that continued separation would ultimately lead to complete family disintegration. One scholar has found that southern Italians were quicker to send for their wives than northern Italians because they were sexually jealous and less culturally prepared to establish strong social relations outside the nuclear family.

If no wife existed in the homeland, immigrant males quickly took whatever steps were necessary to find women of similar linguistic and cultural backgrounds with whom they could establish a household. Marriage patterns remained largely within the ethnic group during the first and much of the second generation. Japanese men sought "picture brides" from Japan and initiated unions which stressed the importance of duty and obligation over love and romance. About one of every four Italians who moved to San Francisco actually returned to their native village just for a marriage. Whether they returned to the homeland or found a wife in America the chances were great she would be from the same region or village, a fact which reinforced notions about the manner in which families and households should function. Thus, it is not surprising to learn that among Germans in Wisconsin 86 percent of the first generation and 80 percent of the second married other

Germans. Similar high rates were exhibited by Poles and Russians in the state. . . .

But it would be erroneous to assume that the cooperative family economy grew inevitably out of premigration traditions of collective enterprise or the regional and cultural homogeneity of immigrant streams. Both of these factors . . . would have been insufficient . . . in themselves without the accompanying reality of an industrial workplace which encouraged mutual aid and especially the widespread existence of wages insufficient for even modest standards of living. American industrial wages may have looked attractive to the residents of rural regions undergoing transition, but the available information suggests that the families of most immigrants in this country could not survive on the income of one wage earner. Among Irish millhands in Lowell, Massachusetts, in the 1860s, most fathers could earn only about 54 percent of what was needed to support a family at a minimum level of subsistence. Among packinghouse workers in Chicago in the decade after 1910, the average individual wage earner could earn 38 percent of the minimum needed for a family of four; he could still earn only 48 percent in 1922. . . . Clearly, family income had to be supplemented in some way.

The economic margin of an immigrant family did not usually improve until children reached working age, about fourteen, and began to contribute to family income. In Philadelphia, to illustrate a case, the children of immigrant Irish and German families entered the labor market to a greater degree than did the children from native-born households. . . . Irish children contribut [ed] between 38 and 46 percent of total family labor. . . . The most "vulnerable" economically were those with small children who could not work and who prevented a mother from working. At Amoskeag about 38 percent of all households had members working other than the head or the wife, but for immigrant households the figure was 50 percent. In fact, textile towns, because they offered employment to teenagers, tended to attract families with children of employment age. . . . Families in Chicago's packinghouse district even sent wives and daughters into the packinghouses, a move which ironically helped to keep overall wages low. . . .

While opportunities were sought for adolescent employment, immigrant women, like other women, usually terminated toil outside the household with marriage and focused attention on the roles of wife, mother, and homemaker. By 1920 in urban America, married women accounted for only 21 percent of the female work force. It is true that the percentage of wage earners among foreign-born adult females over the age of sixteen was one-third higher than the percentage for all white women, but this could be attributed to the heavier reliance of the immigrant family on the earnings of their unmarried daughters. Even for immigrant wives the general plan was not leave home for work after marriage. . . . In Chicago in 1900 less than 2 percent of a sample of Polish, Italian, Jewish, German, and Irish wives left the household to toil, while between 52 and 74 percent of the unmarried females over the age of fifteen in these groups left each day for work.

Strong imperatives existed in many immigrant families to prevent [married] women [from leaving] their homes in search of employment. Traditional perspectives on the domestic roles of mothers and wives persisted but were insufficient to account for the pattern by themselves, especially when it was not uncommon for married women to work in the fields of the rural world. Married women also had to raise children, manage the household, and care for boarders because they really had fewer employment opportunities than adult men and adolescents. Restricted opportunity in this case was continually supported by a myriad of cultural preferences. Irish immigrants strongly believed that married women should not work at all. This view was rooted not only in the model family of Irish Catholicism but in a social belief that a working married woman diminished the status of her husband. In Ireland female subservience had reached the point in the 1840s that married women had a shorter life expectancy than fathers and sons because the males were to receive the most nutritious food. . . . Greek families actually considered it a disgrace for a wife, and sometimes a sister, to work outside the house. Whatever the reason for keeping married women at home, the pattern of working-class domesticity was established prior to its celebration by middle-class reformers in urban America. Culture did not simply flow downward from social superiors.

But the immigrant family was never totally insensitive to economic reality, and even married immigrant women could be forced into the labor market. Often their tenure was of short duration or they sought only part-time employment, but nearly always they worked only for familial rather than individual needs as part of a cooperative household. They even found ingenious ways to combine their dual roles as mother and worker. Not all could do as one French-Canadian at Amoskeag who stayed at home and sold sandwiches to girls in the mill who did not bring lunches. Many mothers relied on their skills by entering domestic work, which offered flexible hours. Irish, German, and Scandinavian women were highy prized by American employers for these tasks. By 1900 over 60 percent of the Irish and Scandinavian women worked as domestics, while the figures for Jews, Poles, and Italians was 20 percent or less. . . . Italian women avoided domestic work because they would be without the protection of their men or the companionship of their friends while working. Thus, the Italian female concentration in New York's artificial flower industry seems to have been the result of a desire to work with kin. . . .

Although familial need and economic necessity forced some married women outside the household, traces of individual goals and aspirations were found in their motivation and consciousness. Irish women often delayed marriage to pursue individual jobs of their own. At Amoskeag a few women who started working in their teens continued to do so after marriage because of the social ties they had come to enjoy in the mills. Sometimes the skills women possessed, such as Italian seamstresses or Jewish jewelry makers, caused certain women to be in high demand. Jewish women in several communities loosened traditional ties to the home and organized voluntary associations such as the First Hebrew Ladies Benevolent Society, which met many communal welfare needs. . . . And mothers frequently organized and administered female auxiliary groups to male union locals.

Not only did a few women move outside to assist their families but most of those who remained at home were able to exert considerable influence and power. Too often women have been portrayed as helpless before the demands of household obligations. One representative conclusion by a scholar claimed that because occupational opportunities for women were comparatively limited, females were prevented from broadening their power within the family and thus the "traditional" role segregation of men and women was reinforced. This view is a distortion, however, on several counts. First, a considerable body of evidence exists to suggest that immigrant and other women actually entered into marriage as an act of independence from the original obligations of their household economies. No matter what new responsibilities they were incurring, they viewed the creation of a family of their own as a positive, purposeful act which offered intrinsic rewards rather than simply burdensome obligations. . . . To an immigrant husband who left his parents at a young age, his wife was more than a sex-partner or a co-worker, she could be an adviser and a confidante as well. After all, in nearly every immigrant-household economy, the central manager of financial resources, children's socialization, and the entire operation was the married female. Most immigrant children could share the recollection of one Irish woman that "mother always handled the money; my father never even opened his pay envelope." Because they had such an intimate knowledge of family finances and need, women to a remarkable extent usually made the decision to initiate small, immigrant family business concerns. Among Hungarian newcomers in East Chicago, Indiana, and New Brunswick, New Jersey, it was discovered that the idea of buying a farm or opening a saloon originated with women who had more "energy and ideas." . . . Females in Chinese households strengthened their power at home in America and even determined their children's mate selection at times as men became more tied to workplace concerns. . . .

The immigrant household dominated by female managers usually consisted of only parents and children. To an overwhelming extent, the immigrant family was a nuclear family, although on occasion the household could expand to embrace other kin, boarders, or friends on a temporary basis. The predominance of the nuclear form, however, was clear cut throughout the nineteenth and twentieth centuries in both the premigration lands and in urban America. More complex family forms did tend to exist in eastern than western Europe, but is now clear that nuclearity was not simply a product of the industrial economy, as it was long held. In fact, economic need might dictate that households could use all the wage earners they could get. The pervasive commitments to the nuclear structure, and the tendency to keep boarders only until children could work, suggests that something more than economic pressures explained family structure.

Even a brief survey of household structures among immigrant settlements attests to the hold of the nuclear model. Among Jews and Italians in New York City in 1905 about 95 percent of all households had a nuclear core. Among Germans in the same city in 1850, nine of every ten immigrants lived with kin. . . .

Admittedly, there were stages in the course of familial development which could alter the composition of the household. Boarding was widespread in immigrant homes, as it offered a source of income. But boarders invariably appeared during stages of family life when children were too young to contribute to the household economy or had left to launch households of their own. Seldom were boarders found in the home when a nuclear family could support itself. . . . In Pittsburgh, for instance, the mean number of boarders in Italian and Polish households declined from the "young family" stage when children were too young to work to the "mid-stage" of family life when children entered the work force. . . . Boarders could join the nuclear family in its private space but only for a time.

When most working-class families had their choice, they preferred a private household consisting of parents and children. At times in the life cycle when children were able to work and contribute to finances, they were usually able to obtain their wish. The middle class was not alone in valuing the private household. But economic circumstances, primarily in the form of insufficient wages, forced parents to expand their households at specific times to embrace boarders and others in order to secure additional income.

Conclusion

The predisposition toward doing whatever was necessary to sustain a family-based household was nothing new. It had pervaded the immigrant homelands and received additional support ironically from the new system of industrial capitalism which restructured its labor market in a manner which facilitated the entry of groups of untrained toilers who were often related or at least acquainted with each other. Kin and friends were free to assist each other in entering America by providing access to jobs and homes and supplying important information of labor market conditions. New arrivals were adept at determining where they might enter a very large economy. The immigrant family economy survived and flourished among most newcomers in industrial America because new economic structures actually reinforced traditional ways of ordering life and, consequently, contributed to a supportive "external environment" for capitalism to proceed. In this system, individual inclinations were muted and the household, managed effectively by immigrant females, superseded all other goals and objectives. In the face of a sprawling and complex urban industrial structure, newcomers forged a relatively simple device for establishing order and purpose in their lives. This system would remain predominant among working-class families until the labor market was reshaped again after World War II and credentials and skills regained importance in entering new professional sectors of work. It was a system which would be challenged by outside institutions and values as the stay in America became more permanent.

Finally, it could be argued that not all immigrant families functioned alike and that significant differences existed in religion, cultural background, and particular family strategies. Certainly, this was true. But it was also true that such differences coexisted with a fundamental similarity. Families and households were the predominant form in which all immigrants entered the industrial-urban economy and ordered their lives. Members of nearly all groups received indoctrination in the need to remain loyal to the familial and household unit. The goals of individual households could differ as a result of cultural background or positioning within the economy, and these divergences would come into play over time as separate paths of education, occupation, and mobility were taken. But in the movement to a capitalist world and in the initial decades of settlement, familial and communal networks abounded.

Assembly-Line Americanization

STEPHEN MEYER

> The apperception mass [*sic*] of the immigrant, expressed in the attitudes and values he brings with him from his old life, is the material from which he must build his Americanism. It is also the material we must work with, if we would aid this process. Our tools may be in part American customs and institutions, but the substance we seek to mold into new forms is the product of other centuries in other lands. . . . A wise policy of assimilation, like a wise educational policy, does not seek to destroy the attitudes and memories that are there, but to build on them.
> —Robert E. Park and Herbert A. Miller, 1921

Americanization was the social and cultural assimilation of immigrants into the mainstream of American life. And, it was also a unique, and distinctly American, method for the resolution of a key industrial problem—the problem of work-discipline and of the adaptation of new workers to the factory environment. . . .

The profound paternalism of the Ford [Motor Company's] Profit-sharing Plan captured the Progressive Era's contradictory attitude toward the unskilled immigrant worker. On the one hand, it attempted to assist the worker and to elevate him to a better standard of life. On the other hand, it sought to manipulate or to coerce the worker to match a preconceived ideal of that better life. John R. Commons, the progressive labor historian, noted the double edged character of the Ford program. The Ford plan, he reported, "is just old fashioned industrial autocracy tempered by faith in human nature." A benevolent end—the uplift of the unskilled and unschooled immigrant worker—justified a manipulative and coercive means.

From the very beginning, the Ford Profit-sharing Plan attempted to fit the immigrant worker into its preconceived mold of the ideal American. An early memorandum clarified the objectives of the Ford plan to a branch manager. "It is our aim and object," the home office noted, "to make better men and better American citizens and to bring about a larger degree of comforts, habits, and a higher plane of living among our employees. . . ." Henry Ford

From *The Five Dollar Day: Labor Management and Social Control in the Ford Motor Company, 1908–1921* by Stephen Meyer, pp. 149–62. Copyright © 1981, reprinted by permission of State University of New York Press.

expressed his concern about non-American workers to an interviewer: These men of many nations must be taught American ways, the English language, and the right way to live." He then elaborated on the "right" life for the foreign-born worker. Married men "should not sacrifice family rights, pleasure, and comfort by filling their homes with roomers and boarders." . . . The Ford ideal was to create "a comfortable and cozy domesticity."

. . . A pamphlet pointed toward "right" living conditions:

> Employes should live in clean, well conducted homes, in rooms that are well lighted and ventilated. Avoid congested parts of the city. The company will not approve, as profit sharers, men who herd themselves into overcrowded boarding houses which are menaces to their health. . . .
>
> Do not occupy a room in which one other person sleeps, as the company is anxious to have its employes live comfortably, and under conditions that make for cleanliness, good manhood, and good citizenship.

. . . A clean home reduced the chances for illness and absenteeism. A clean mind provided the sound foundation for the construction of good work habits.

The Ford Sociological Department even extended its interest and attention to the children of immigrant workers. It prescribed a strong dose of Victorian morality for them in order to promote and develop good bodies and souls. "Choose a home," a pamphlet advised:

> where ample room, good wholesome surroundings, will enable the children to get the greatest benefit possible from play, under conditions that will tend to clean helpful ideas, rather than those likely to be formed in the streets and alleys of the city.

Particularly in adolescence, young men and women "should be guarded well, and not allowed to contract habits and vices injurious to their welfare and health."

S. S. Marquis, who headed the Ford Sociological Department, recalled Ford's own reason for this concern about the morality of children. "By underpaying men," Ford told the Episcopalian minister:

> we are bringing up a generation of children undernourished and underdeveloped morally as well as physically; we are breeding a generation of workingmen weak in body and mind, and for that reason bound to prove inefficient when they come to take their places in industry.

The good worker was both physically fit to perform his tasks in the factory and morally fit to perform these tasks diligently.

Often, Ford's paternalistic advice on the care of the home and family contained overt manifestations of middle-class arrogance towards the new immigrant workers. In one instance, a Ford pamphlet advised:

Employees should use plenty of soap and water in the home, and upon their children, bathing frequently. Nothing makes for right living and health so much as cleanliness. Notice that the most advanced people are the cleanest.

Again, the advice cut in two directions. On the one hand, health and cleanliness were important for immigrant workers. On the other hand, the assumption was that lower classes were generally unclean. Indeed, these sentiments typified upper and middle-class American attitudes towards Southern and Eastern European immigrants.

Boris Emmett examined the Ford Profit-sharing Plan for the U.S. Bureau of Labor Statistics. He discovered a class and ethnic bias in the administration of the Ford program. Although the rules and standards of the plan were "strictly applied," he reported that the "rigidity of application" depended on "the specific character of the group of employees concerned." . . . [The company] believed that "the employees of the commercial and clerical occupations, who mostly are native Americans with some education, need not be told how to live decently and respectably." Consequently, the Ford welfare program concerned "chiefly the manual and mechanical workers, many of whom are of foreign birth and unable to speak the English language." . . .

[A] Ford "Human Interest" [story illustrates] how Southern and Eastern European immigrant workers met their good fortune in the form of the Five Dollar Day. [The] story involved a Russian immigrant and his family. . . .

F. W. Andrews, a Ford investigator, wrote his story on Joe, a former peasant, his wife, and their six children. Three years earlier, they left Russia for the United States. "Life was an uphill struggle for Joe since landing in America," Andrews reported. Nevertheless, he had a positive trait—his willingness to work hard. "He was a willing worker and not particular about the kind of employment he secured." In the recent past, he dug sewers and worked as an agricultural laborer. When work ran out, he moved to Detroit with his family. "And here," Andrews noted, "for five long months he tramped with the 'Army of the Unemployed'—always handicapped by his meager knowledge of the English language, and was unable to find anything to do." Consequently, his wife bore the "burden of supporting the family." She "worked at the washtub or with the scrubbing brush when such work could be found."

Fortunately, the tale continued, Joe applied for and received a job at the Ford factory. After the company hired him, Andrews went to Joe's home to determine his eligibility for the Ford Five Dollar Day. The scene could have been from a Dickens novel. He discovered "an old, tumbled down, one and a half story frame house." The family's apartment, Andrews related, "was one half of the attic consisting of three rooms, which were so low that a person of medium height could not stand erect—a filthy, foul-smelling hole." It had virtually no furniture, only "two dirty beds. . . . a ragged filthy rug, a rickety table, and two bottomless chairs (the five children standing up at the table to eat)." The family led a precarious hand-to-mouth existence and ate only when the wife earned enough to purchase food for the evening meal.

They owed money to the landlord, the grocer, and the butcher. The oldest daughter went to a charity hospital a few days earlier. The wife and the other five children "were half clad, pale, and hungry looking."

This scene of poverty and misery set the Sociological Department's paternalistic programs into motion. Through special arrangements, the pay office issued Joe's wages each day instead of every two weeks. The company provided him with an immediate loan from its charity fund for "the family's immediate start toward right living." However, the investigator, and not Joe, took the fifty-dollar loan and paid the bills and rented a cottage. He also purchased inexpensive furniture and kitchen utensils, provisions, and cheap clothes for the wife and children. (Andrews reported that he bought "a liberal amount of soap" and gave the family "instructions to use freely.")

After Andrews arranged for this initial assistance for Joe and his family, a remarkable ritual followed. The Ford investigator:

> had their dirty, old, junk furniture loaded on a dray and under the cover of night moved them to their new home. This load of rubbish was heaped in a pile in the back yard, and a torch was applied and it went up in smoke.
>
> There upon the ashes of what had been their earthly possessions, this Russian peasant and his wife, with tears streaming down their faces, expressed their gratitude to Henry Ford, the FORD MOTOR COMPANY, and all those who had been instrumental in bringing about this marvelous change in their lives. . . .

. . .

In time, the children were well dressed and clean. They attended public school. The wife wore "a smile that 'won't come off.' " Joe soon repaid his loan and expected "to soon have a saving for the inevitable 'rainy day.' "
. . .

Against [this uplifting case], a single and revealing incident demonstrated the nature of the company's concern for the ways in which immigrant traditions affected industrial efficiency. In January 1914, a few days after its impressive gesture—the announcement of the Five Dollar Day—the Ford Motor Company dismissed "between eight and nine hundred Greeks and Russians, who remained away from work on a holiday celebration." The holiday happened to be Christmas. Using the Julian calendar, the Greek and Russian Orthodox Christian workers celebrated Christmas thirteen days later than the rest of the Ford workforce. As justification for this large-scale dismissal, which amounted to about six percent of the Ford workforce, a Ford official stated that "if these men are to make their home in America they should observe American holidays." . . . "It causes too much confusion in the plant," the official concluded, ". . . when nearly a thousand men fail to appear for work."

The Ford English School extended the Ford Americanization program into the classroom. Its exclusive concern was the Americanization of the immigrant worker and his adaptation to the Ford factory and to urban and industrial society. In the English School, as adult immigrant workmen struggled to learn and to comprehend the strange sounds of a new language, they also received the rudiments of American culture. In particular, they learned those habits of life which resulted in good habits of work. In 1916, S. S. Marquis defended the objectives of the Ford educational program before an audience of American educators. The Ford English School, he noted, "was established especially for the immigrants in our employ." It was one part of a total program to adapt men to the new factory system. "The Ford School," he reported, "provides five compulsory courses. There is a course in industry and efficiency, a course in thrift and economy, a course in domestic relations, one in community relations, and one in industrial relations." Later, using the Ford factory as a metaphor for the entire educational program, he added:

> This is the human product we seek to turn out, and as we adapt the machinery in the shop to turning out the kind of automobile we have in mind, so we have constructed our educational system with a view to producing the human product in mind.

The Ford managers and engineers devised a system wherein men were the raw materials which were molded, hammered, and shaped into products which had the proper attitudes and habits for work in the factory.

In April 1914, the Ford Motor Company called upon Peter Roberts, a Young Men's Christian Association educator, to develop a program of English language instruction for immigrant workers in the Highland Park factory. In 1909, as the result of his activities among immigrant coal miners in Pennsylvania, Roberts published a preparatory course of English language instruction, *English for Coming Americans*. This course provided a complete package of materials to teach the basic elements of the English language. The core of the program centered around a domestic, a commercial, and an industrial series of lessons. Each series applied the English language to a different aspect of the immigrant worker's life. . . .

The domestic series provided specific English lessons for the immigrant worker in his role as the head of an "American" family unit. This series, Roberts explained, identified "the experiences common to all peoples reared in the customs of western civilization." The ten lessons included such topics as "Getting Up in the Morning," "Table Utensils," "The Man Washing," and "Welcoming a Visitor."

The commercial series supplied the immigrant worker with the vocabulary to serve in his role as consumer. In particular, it attempted to break the economic power of immigrant bosses, who sold goods and services, who served as employment, travel, and shipping agents, and who functioned as bankers in the immigrant neighborhoods. Moreover, the lessons emphasized and encouraged the virtues of thrift and property ownership, which created stable and reliable citizens. "These lessons," Roberts noted, "describe the acts which foreigners in a strange land daily perform. When they are mastered the pupils will be able to transact their business outside the narrow circle of places controlled by men conversant with their language." The lessons intended to make the immigrant worker a consumer of American goods and services from American merchants. In this series, the subject matter included "Buying and Using Stamps," "Pay Day," "Going to the Bank," "Buying a Lot," "Building a House."

Finally, the industrial series provided flexible lessons to meet the immigrant worker's needs as a producer in the factory. The aim of this series was "to meet the need of thousands who have common experience in industrial life." Here, the lessons included "Beginning the Day's Work," "Shining Shoes," "A Man Looking for Work," and "Finishing the Day's Work."

. . . Each lesson contained specific social and cultural norms for life in urban and industrial America. Ford workers learned the value of time in their personal and working lives. They learned the importance of cleanliness and health. They learned self-discipline through regular habits of saving and work. They learned to invest in and to purchase property and to become responsible citizens. These positive virtues—timeliness, cleanliness, thrift, self-discipline, regularity, and citizenship—represented the Ford, and generally the American middle-class, ideal for remaking former European peasants into reliable and efficient factory workers. The English language was an important means for the adaptation of immigrant workers to the regimen and the discipline of the mechanized factory.

As part of its instructional program, the Ford English School also taught immigrant workers not to offend their social betters in their manner and their behavior. For this reason, table manners and etiquette were important parts of the curriculum. . . . The Ford instructor taught the immigrant worker "the art of eating a meal in a manner that will not interfere with the appetite of the other fellow.". . . Moreover, Ford English instructors expected their students to dress properly for the classes. "A by-product of the classes," a report noted, "was a rise in the 'standard of living' by making men conscious of their personal appearance." Instead of going directly from work to school, the instructors required that "class members first go home, wash, and change clothes." . . .

In 1915, Oliver J. Abell, an industrial journalist, praised Ford's "benevolent paternalism" in industry. He maintained that the "greater must care for the less." Furthermore, he continued, "we provide schools for the child. Instruction and discipline are compulsory, and it is well. But we forget that measured in the great scale of knowledge, there are always children and grownups, pupils and teachers, and age is nothing." Here, Abell captured the essence of Ford paternalism and of the relationship between dominant and subordinate groups in American society. Superiors considered their inferiors—Blacks, servants, women, and even workers—as no more than children. Indeed, the Ford immigrant worker was no more than a child to be socialized, in this case, Americanized, to the reigning social and cultural norms of American society.

S. S. Marquis, the liberal clergyman, explained how the company coerced workers into attending their English lessons. "Attendance," he reported:

is virtually compulsory. If a man declines to go, the advantages of the training are carefully explained to him. If he still hesitates, he is laid off and given uninterrupted meditation and reconsideration. When it comes to promotion, naturally preference is given to the men who have cooperated with us in our work. This, also, has its effect.

. . .

Gregory Mason, a strong advocate of Americanization programs, questioned, "the grotesquely exaggerated patriotism in the Ford plant." In the course of the English lessons, "the pupils are told to 'walk to an American blackboard, take a piece of American chalk, and explain how the American workman walks to his American home and sits down with his American family to their good American dinner.' " "The first thing we teach them to say," Marquis related, "is 'I am a good American,' and then we try to get them to live up to that statement." "It is a very common thing," [Clinton] DeWitt [director of the Ford English School] noted, "to have a fellow born in Austria yell to a teacher passing by, 'We are all good Americans!' " . . . By the end of the First World War, Americanism countered those social and economic philosophies which threatened managerial prerogatives of production, namely Bolshevism, socialism, and even trade unionism.

The mass ritual of graduation was the most spectacular aspect of Americanization in the Ford factory. Ford English School graduates underwent a symbolic ritual which marked the transformation from immigrant to American. DeWitt described the ceremony as:

> a pageant in the form of a melting pot, where all the men descend from a boat scene representing the vessel on which they came over; down the gangway . . . into a pot 15 feet in diameter and $7\frac{1}{2}$ feet high, which represents the Ford English School. Six teachers, three on either side, stir the pot with ten foot ladles representing nine months of teaching in the school. Into the pot 52 nationalities with their foreign clothes and baggage go and out of the pot after vigorous stirring by the teachers comes one nationality, viz, American.

Marquis enriched this image and emphasized the conformity of the one nationality: "Presently, the pot began to boil over and out came the men dressed in their best American clothes and waving American flags."

Following this pageant, teachers and community leaders gave speeches which praised the virtues of American citizenship. When the graduation ceremony ended, all went on "a trip to some park, where American games are played by teachers and students for the rest of the day." . . . At this celebration, DeWitt reported, "the teachers meet with Mr. Ford and other high officials of the company, and a great spirit of one for all and all for one predominates the entire evening."

Americanization in the Ford factory was important for a variety of reasons. First, the Ford programs touched the lives of tens of thousands of Ford workers in its effort to influence those institutions which shaped immigrant working-class culture, particularly the family, the home, the neighborhood, and the factory. From 1915 to 1916, the company reported that some 16,000 workers graduated from the Ford English School. Moreover, Ford statistics indicated that while 35.5 percent of the workforce did not speak English in 1914, only 11.7 percent did not speak the language in 1917.

Second, the Ford Americanization program indirectly captured the American imagination in the prewar years. The Ford program served as the model for a city-wide Americanization campaign in Detroit. And, in 1915, Detroit in turn became the model for the National Americanization Day Committee and its national campaign for the assimilation of immigrants into American society.

Finally, Ford was neither alone nor entirely unique in its attempt to adapt immigrant workers to factory and industrial life. In fact, American industrial leaders and managers developed a new strategy for the management of an immigrant workforce in this period. Whereas the traditional managerial practice divided ethnic groups and played their national and cultural rivalries against one another, the new one emphasized conformity with American social, cultural, and industrial values. During the First World War, as manufacturers and others became increasingly apprehensive about aliens in their midst, they viewed Americanization as a means to remake immigrant workers into their image of the efficient and productive worker. . . . In the postwar labor upsurge, industrial leaders considered Americanization as a cure for the social ills of society. . . .

҉ F U R T H E R   R E A D I N G

John Bodnar, *The Transplanted: A History of Immigrants in Urban America* (1985)
Sarah Deutsch, *No Separate Refuge: Culture, Class, and Gender on an Anglo-Hispanic Frontier in the American Southwest, 1880–1940* (1987)
Elizabeth Ewen, *Immigrant Women in the Land of Dollars* (1985)
Donna R. Gabaccia, *Militants and Migrants: Rural Sicilians Become American Workers* (1988)
John Higham, *Strangers in the Land: Patterns of American Nativism, 1860–1925* (1971)
Irving Howe, *The World of Our Fathers* (1976)
Hartmut Keil, ed., *German Workers in Industrial Chicago, 1850–1920* (1988)
Thomas Kessner, *The Golden Door: Italian and Jewish Immigrant Mobility in New York City, 1880–1915* (1977)
Alan M. Kraut, *The Huddled Masses: The Immigrant in American Society, 1860–1921* (1982)
Stephen Meyer, *The Five Dollar Day: Labor Management and Social Control in the Ford Motor Company, 1908–1921* (1981)
Peggy Pascoe, "Gender Systems in Conflict: The Marriages of Mission-Educated Chinese-American Women, 1874–1939," *Journal of Social History* 22 (Summer 1989), 631–652
Alexander P. Saxton, *The Indispensable Enemy: Labor and the Anti-Chinese Movement in California* (1971)
Judith E. Smith, *Family Connections* (1985)
Ronald T. Takaki, *Iron Cages: Race and Culture in Nineteenth-Century America* (1979)

CHAPTER
9

Progressivism:
The Spirit of Reform

*In the first decade of the twentieth century, a burst of reform activity, deriving
from all social classes but especially notable for initiatives from educated
professionals, commonly adopted the adjective* progressive. *Encompassing
journalistic muckrakers, social workers, enlightened businessmen, and child-
welfare and labor reformers, as well as issue-oriented political activists, the reform
fervor helped transform public opinion as well as public policy in the years before
the Great World War. Indeed, in 1912, when Theodore Roosevelt's third-party
candidacy formally adopted the Progressive party label, three of the four candidates
(Roosevelt, the Democrat Wilson, and the Socialist Debs) openly appealed to the
reform constituency, and the fourth (the Republican Taft) also could claim an
organic connection.*

*Yet for all of its popularity at the time, historiographic debate has swirled ever
since around the pros and cons, and even the basic coherence, of the progressive
vision. On the one hand, progressive thought clearly inherited much of its
antimonopoly impetus from the labor-populist impetus of the 1890s. But its urban,
middle-class character also bent the populist message toward a more optimistic
faith in rational, incremental reform and a new emphasis on social efficiency and
the moral rehabilitation of immigrant slums. Whether progressivism served, on the
whole, to define a necessary agenda for a twentieth-century welfare state or
(perhaps in so doing) established a big-brother role for a new class of ''experts''
remains debatable.*

❧ D O C U M E N T S

The selections in this chapter suggest the far-flung nature of contemporary reform
interests and something of their deeper inspiration. Walter Rauschenbusch, a
Baptist clergyman whose work among German immigrants in New York City led
him to champion the this-worldly doctrines of the social gospel, gives voice in the
first selection to a powerful moral-religious motivation behind the Progressive
critique of industrial individualism. In the second document, Jane Addams,

founder of Hull House, defines the settlement house as an effort to restore a much-needed balance in the lives of the middle class, as well as to redress urban poverty. Then in the third selection, in an excerpt from perhaps the most influential single piece of contemporary muckraking, *The Shame of the Cities*, Lincoln Steffens in 1904 stresses the connections between the supposedly respectable world of business and the sordid world of municipal politics. In direct response to Steffens and other reformers, Tammany Hall boss George Washington Plunkitt (in conversation with jounalist William L. Riordan) openly defends his tried-and-true methods of city government. University of Chicago philospher-educator John Dewey, in the fifth selection, links pedagogical changes within the classroom to a larger democratic transformation without. In the sixth document, dating from 1911, Wisconsin legislator Thomas J. Mahon links workmen's compensation and other labor reforms to the conservation of valuable natural resources. The final selection presents the radical reform demands of the Socialist Party of America in 1912, a presidential election year in which the party of Eugene V. Debs polled almost a million votes and a record 6 percent of the total count.

Walter Rauschenbusch Seeks a Social Christianity, 1912

The chief purpose of the Christian Church in the past has been the salvation of individuals. But the most pressing task of the present is not individualistic. Our business is to make over an antiquated and immoral economic system; to get rid of laws, customs, maxims, and philosophies inherited from an evil and despotic past; to create just and brotherly relations between great groups and classes of society; and thus to lay a social foundation on which modern men individually can live and work in a fashion that will not outrage all the better elements in them. Our inherited Christian faith dealt with individuals; our present task deals with society.

The Christian Church in the past has taught us to do our work with our eyes fixed on another world and a life to come. But the business before us is concerned with refashioning this present world, making this earth clean and sweet and habitable. . . .

Twenty-five years ago the social wealth of the Bible was almost undis-covered to most of us. We used to plow it six inches deep for crops and never dreamed that mines of anthracite were hidden down below. Even Jesus talked like an individualist in those days and seemed to repudiate the social interest when we interrogated him. He said his kingdom was not of this world; the things of God had nothing to do with the things of Caesar; the poor we would always have with us; and his ministers must not be judges and dividers when Labor argued with Capital about the division of the inheritance. To-day he has resumed the spiritual leadership of social Christianity, of which he was the founder. It is a new tribute to his mastership that the social message of Jesus was the first great possession which social Christianity redis-covered. . . .

With true Christian instinct men have turned to the Christian law of love as the key to the situation. If we all loved our neighbor, we should "treat him right," pay him a living wage, give sixteen ounces to the pound, and not charge so much for beef. But this appeal assumes that we are still living in the simple personal relations of the good old times, and that every man can do the right thing when he wants to do it. But suppose a business man would be glad indeed to pay his young women the $12 a week which they need for a decent living, but all his competitors are paying from $7 down to $5. Shall he love himself into bankruptcy? In a time of industrial depression shall he employ men whom he does not need? And if he does, will his five loaves feed the five thousand unemployed that break his heart with their hungry eyes? If a man owns a hundred shares of stock in a great corporation, how can his love influence its wage scale with that puny stick? The old advice of love breaks down before the hugeness of modern relations. We might as well try to start a stranded ocean liner with the oar which poled our old dory from the mud banks many a time. It is indeed love that we want, but it is socialized love. Blessed be the love that holds the cup of water to thirsty lips. We can never do without the plain affection of man to man. But what we most need today is not the love that will break its back drawing water for a growing factory town from a well that was meant to supply a village, but a love so large and intelligent that it will persuade an ignorant people to build a system of waterworks up in the hills, and that will get after the thoughtless farmers who contaminate the brooks with typhoid bacilli, and after the lumber concern that is denuding the watershed of its forests. We want a new avatar of love. . . .

Jane Addams on the Need for Social Settlements, 1892

In a thousand voices singing the Hallelujah Chorus in Handel's "Messiah," it is possible to distinguish the leading voices, but the differences of training and cultivation between them and the voices of the chorus, are lost in the unity of purpose and in the fact that they are all human voices lifted by a high motive. This is a weak illustration of what a Settlement attempts to do. It aims, in a measure, to develop whatever of social life its neighborhood may afford, to focus and give form to that life, to bring to bear upon it the results of cultivation and training; but it receives in exchange for the music of isolated voices the volume and strength of the chorus. It is quite impossible for me to say in what proportion or degree the subjective necessity which led to the opening of Hull-House combined the three trends: first, the desire to interpret democracy in social terms; secondly, the impulse beating at the very source of our lives, urging us to aid in the race progress; and, thirdly, the Christian movement toward humanitarianism. It is difficult to analyze a living thing; the analysis is at best imperfect. Many more motives may blend with the three trends; possibly the desire for a new form of social success due to the nicety of imagination, which refuses worldly pleasures unmixed with the joys of self-sacrifice; possibly a love of approbation, so vast that it is not content with the treble clapping of delicate hands, but wishes also to hear the bass notes from toughened palms, may mingle with these.

The Settlement, then, is an experimental effort to aid in the solution of the social and industrial problems which are engendered by the modern conditions of life in a great city. It insists that these problems are not confined to any one portion of a city. It is an attempt to relieve, at the same time, the overaccumulation at one end of society and the destitution at the other; but it assumes that this overaccumulation and destitution is most sorely felt in the things that pertain to social and educational advantages. From its very nature it can stand for no political or social propaganda. It must, in a sense, give the warm welcome of an inn to all such propaganda, if perchance one of them be found an angel. The one thing to be dreaded in the Settlement is that it lose its flexibility, its power of quick adaptation, its readiness to change its methods as its environment may demand. It must be open to conviction and must have a deep and abiding sense of tolerance. It must be hospitable and ready for experiment. It should demand from its residents a scientific patience in the accumulation of facts and the steady holding of their sympathies as one of the best instruments for that accumulation. It must be grounded in a philosophy whose foundation is on the solidarity of the human race, a philosophy which will not waver when the race happens to be represented by a drunken woman or an idiot boy. Its residents must be emptied of all conceit of opinion and all self-assertion, and ready to arouse and interpret the public opinion of their neighborhood. They must be content to live quietly side by side with their neighbors, until they grow into a sense of relationship and mutual interests. Their neighbors are held apart by differences of race and language which the residents can more easily overcome. They are bound to see the needs of their neighborhood as a whole, to furnish data for legislation, and to use their influence to secure it. In short, residents are pledged to devote themselves to the duties of good citizenship and to the arousing of the social energies which too largely lie dormant in every neighborhood given over to industrialism. They are bound to regard the entire life of their city as organic, to make an effort to unify it, and to protest against its over-differentiation.

It is always easy to make all philosophy point one particular moral and all history adorn one particular tale; but I may be forgiven the reminder that the best speculative philosophy sets forth the solidarity of the human race; that the highest moralists have taught that without the advance and improvement of the whole, no man can hope for any lasting improvement in his own moral or material individual condition; and that the subjective necessity for Social Settlements is therefore identical with that necessity, which urges us on toward social and individual salvation.

Lincoln Steffens Exposes the Corruption of Municipal Politics, 1904

When I set out on my travels, an honest New Yorker told me honestly that I would find that the Irish, the Catholic Irish, were at the bottom of it all everywhere. The first city I went to was St. Louis, a German city. The next was Minneapolis, a Scandinavian city, with a leadership of New Englanders. Then came Pittsburg, Scotch Presbyterian, and that was what my New York friend was. "Ah, but they are all foreign populations," I heard. The next city was Philadelphia, the purest American community of all, and the most hopeless. And after that came Chicago and New York, both mongrel-bred, but the one a triumph of reform, the other the best example of good government that I had seen. The "foreign element" excuse is one of the hypocritical lies that save us from the clear sight of ourselves.

Another such conceit of our egotism is that which deplores our politics and lauds our business. This is the wail of the typical American citizen. Now, the typical American citizen is the business man. The typical business man is a bad citizen; he is busy. If he is a "big business man" and very busy, he does not neglect, he is busy with politics, oh, very busy and very businesslike. I found him buying boodlers in St. Louis, defending grafters in Minneapolis, originating corruption in Pittsburg, sharing with bosses in Philadelphia, deploring reform in Chicago, and beating good government with corruption funds in New York. He is a self-righteous fraud, this big business man. He is the chief source of corruption, and it were a boon if he would neglect politics. But he is not the business man that neglects politics; that worthy is the good citizen, the typical business man. He too is busy, he is the one that has no use and therefore no time for politics. When his neglect has permitted bad government to go so far that he can be stirred to action, he is unhappy, and he looks around for a cure that shall be quick, so that he may hurry back to the shop. Naturally, too, when he talks politics, he talks shop. His patent remedy is quack; it is business.

"Give us a business man," he says ("like me," he means). "Let him introduce business methods into politics and government; then I shall be left alone to attend to my business."

There is hardly an office from United States Senator down to Alderman in any part of the country to which the business man has not been elected; yet politics remains corrupt, government pretty bad, and the selfish citizen has to hold himself in readiness like the old volunteer firemen to rush forth at any hour, in any weather, to prevent the fire; and he goes out sometimes and he puts out the fire (after the damage is done) and he goes back to the shop sighing for the business man in politics. The business man has failed in politics as he has in citizenship. Why?

Because politics is business. That's what's the matter with it. That's what's the matter with everything,—art, literature, religion, journalism, law, medicine,—they're all business, and all—as you see them. Make politics a sport, as they do in England, or a profession, as they do in Germany, and we'll have—well, something else than we have now,—if we want it, which is another question. . . .

But do the people want good government? Tammany says they don't. Are the people honest? Are the people better than Tammany? Are they better than the merchant and the politician? . . .

No, the contemned methods of our despised politics are the master methods of our braggart business, and the corruption that shocks us in public affairs we practice ourselves in our private concerns. There is no essential difference between the pull that gets your wife into society or for your book a favorable review, and that which gets a heeler into office, a thief out of jail, and a rich man's son on the board of directors of a corporation; none between the corruption of a labor union, a bank, and a political machine; none between a dummy director of a trust and the caucus-bound member of a legislature; none between a labor boss like Sam Parks, a boss of banks like John D. Rockefeller, a boss of railroads like J. P. Morgan, and a political boss like Matthew S. Quay. The boss is not a political, he is an American institution, the product of a freed people that have not the spirit to be free.

And it's all a moral weakness; a weakness right where we think we are strongest. Oh, we are good—on Sunday, and we are "fearfully patriotic" on the Fourth of July. But the bribe we pay to the janitor to prefer our interests to the landlord's, is the little brother of the bribe passed to the alderman to sell a city street, and the father of the air-brake stock assigned to the president of a railroad to have this life-saving invention adopted on his road. And as for graft, railroad passes, saloon and bawdy-house blackmail, and watered stock, all these belong to the same family. We are pathetically proud of our democratic institutions and our republican form of government, of our grand Constitution and our just laws. We are a free and sovereign people, we govern ourselves and the government is ours. But that is the point. We are responsible, not our leaders, since we follow them. We *let* them divert our loyalty from the United States to some "party"; we *let* them boss the party and turn our municipal democracies into autocracies and our republican nation into a plutocracy. We cheat our government and we let our leaders loot it, and we let them wheedle and bribe our sovereignty from us. True, they pass for us strict laws, but we are content to let them pass also bad laws, giving away public property in exchange; and our good, and often impossible, laws we allow to be used for oppression and blackmail. And what can we say? We break our own laws and rob our own government, the lady at the custom-house, the lyncher with his rope, and the captain of industry with his bribe and his rebate. The spirit of graft and of lawlessness is the American spirit. . . .

We Americans may have failed. We may be mercenary and selfish. Democracy with us may be impossible and corruption inevitable, but . . . we can stand the truth; that there is pride in the character of American citzenship; and that this pride may be a power in the land. So this little volume [*The Shame of the Cities*], a record of shame and yet of self-respect, a disgraceful confession, yet a declaration of honor, is dedicated, in all good faith, to the accused—to all the citizens of all the cities in the United States.

New York City's Boss Plunkitt Defends "Honest" Graft, 1905

Everybody is talkin' these days about Tammany men growin' rich on graft, but nobody thinks of drawin' the distinction between honest graft and dishonest graft. There's all the difference in the world between the two. Yes, many of our men have grown rich in politics. I have myself. I've made a big fortune out of the game, and I'm gettin' richer every day, but I've not gone in for dishonest graft—blackmailin' gamblers, saloonkeepers, disorderly people, etc.—and neither has any of the men who have made big fortunes in politics.

There's an honest graft, and I'm an example of how it works. I might sum up the whole thing by sayin': "I seen my opportunities and I took 'em."

Just let me explain by examples. My party's in power in the city, and it's goin' to undertake a lot of public improvements. Well, I'm tipped off, say, that they're going to lay out a new park at a certain place.

I see my opportunity and I take it. I go to that place and I buy up all the land I can in the neighborhood. Then the board of this or that makes its plan public, and there is a rush to get my land, which nobody cared particular for before.

Ain't it perfectly honest to charge a good price and make a profit on my investment and foresight? Of course, it is. Well, that's honest graft.

Or supposin' it's a new bridge they're goin' to build. I get tipped off and I buy as much property as I can that has to be taken for approaches. I sell at my own price later on and drop some more money in the bank.

Wouldn't you? It's just like lookin' ahead in Wall Street or in the coffee or cotton market. It's honest graft, and I'm lookin' for it every day in the year. I will tell you frankly that I've got a good lot of it, too.

I'll tell you of one case. They were goin' to fix up a big park, no matter where. I got on to it, and went lookin' about for land in that neighborhood.

I could get nothin' at a bargain but a big piece of swamp, but I took it fast enough and held on to it. What turned out was just what I counted on. They couldn't make the park complete without Plunkitt's swamp, and they had to pay a good price for it. Anything dishonest in that?

Up in the watershed I made some money, too. I bought up several bits of land there some years ago and made a pretty good guess that they would be bought up for water purposes later by the city.

Somehow, I always guessed about right, and shouldn't I enjoy the profit of my foresight? It was rather amusin' when the condemnation commissioners came along and found piece after piece of the land in the name of George Plunkitt of the Fifteenth Assembly District, New York City. They wondered how I knew just what to buy. The answer is—I seen my opportunity and I took it. I haven't confined myself to land; anything that pays is in my line.

For instance, the city is repavin' a street and has several hundred thousand old granite blocks to sell. I am on hand to buy, and I know just what they are worth.

How? Never mind that. I had a sort of monopoly of this business for a while, but once a newspaper tried to do me. It got some outside men to come over from Brooklyn and New Jersey to bid against me.

Was I done? Not much. I went to each of the men and said: "How many of these 250,000 stones do you want?" One said 20,000, and another wanted 15,000, and another wanted 10,000. I said: "All right, let me bid for the lot, and I'll give each of you all you want for nothin."

They agreed, of course. Then the auctioneer yelled: "How much am I bid for these 250,000 fine pavin' stones?"

"Two dollars and fifty cents," says I.

"Two dollars and fifty cents!" screamed the auctioneer. "Oh, that's a joke! Give me a real bid."

He found the bid was real enough. My rivals stood silent. I got the lot for $2.50 and gave them their share. That's how the attempt to do Plunkitt ended, and that's how all such attempts end.

I've told you how I got rich by honest graft. Now, let me tell you that most politicians who are accused of robbin' the city get rich the same way.

They didn't steal a dollar from the city treasury. They just seen their opportunities and took them. That is why, when a reform administration comes in and spends a half million dollars in tryin' to find the public robberies they talked about in the campaign, they don't find them.

The books are always all right. The money in the city treasury is all right. Everything is all right. All they can show is that the Tammany heads of departments looked after their friends, within the law, and gave them what opportunities they could to make honest graft. Now, let me tell you that's never goin' to hurt Tammany with the people. Every good man looks after his friends, and any man who doesn't isn't likely to be popular. If I have a good thing to hand out in private life, I give it to a friend. Why shouldn't I do the same in public life?

Another kind of honest graft. Tammany has raised a good many salaries. There was an awful howl by the reformers, but don't you know that Tammany gains ten votes for every one it lost by salary raisin'?

The Wall Street banker thinks it shameful to raise a department clerk's salary from $1500 to $1800 a year, but every man who draws a salary himself says: "That's all right. I wish it was me." And he feels very much like votin' the Tammany ticket on election day, just out of sympathy.

Tammany was beat in 1901 because the people were deceived into believin' that it worked dishonest graft. They didn't draw a distinction between dishonest and honest graft, but they saw that some Tammany men grew rich, and supposed they had been robbin' the city treasury or levyin' blackmail on disorderly houses, or workin' in with the gamblers and lawbreakers.

As a matter of policy, if nothing else, why should the Tammany leaders go into such dirty business, when there is so much honest graft lyin' around when they are in power? Did you ever consider that?

Now, in conclusion, I want to say that I don't own a dishonest dollar. If my worst enemy was given the job of writin' my epitaph when I'm gone, he couldn't do more than write:

"George W. Plunkitt. He Seen His Opportunities, and He Took 'Em."

John Dewey Advocates a Democratic Schoolroom, 1900

Some few years ago I was looking about the school supply stores in the city, trying to find desks and chairs which seemed thoroughly suitable from all points of view—artistic, hygienic, and educational—to the needs of the children. We had a great deal of difficulty in finding what we needed, and finally one dealer, more intelligent than the rest, made this remark: " I am afraid we have not what you want. You want something at which the children may work; these are all for listening." That tells the story of the traditional education. Just as the biologist can take a bone or two and reconstruct the whole animal, so, if we put before the mind's eye the ordinary schoolroom, with its rows of ugly desks placed in geometrical order, crowded together so that there shall be as little moving room as possible, desks almost all of the same size, with just space enough to hold books, pencils, and paper, and add a table, some chairs, the bare walls, and possibly a few pictures, we can reconstruct the only educational activity that can possibly go on in such a place. It is all made "for listening"—because simply studying lessons out of a book is only another kind of listening; it marks the dependency of one mind upon another. The attitude of listening means, comparatively speaking, passivity, absorption; that there are certain ready-made materials which are there, which have been prepared by the school superintendent, the board, the teacher, and of which the child is to take in as much as possible in the least possible time. . . .

Another thing that is suggested by these schoolrooms, with their set desks, is that everything is arranged for handling as large numbers of children as possible; for dealing with children *en masse,* as an aggregate of units; involving, again, that they be treated passively. The moment children act they individualize themselves; they cease to be a mass and become the intensely distinctive beings that we are acquainted with out of school, in the home, the family, on the playground, and in the neighborhood.

On the same basis is explicable the uniformity of method and curriculum. If everything is on a "listening" basis, you can have uniformity of material and method. The ear, and the book which reflects the ear, constitute the medium which is alike for all. There is next to no opportunity for adjustment to varying capacities and demands. There is a certain amount—a fixed quantity—of ready-made results and accomplishments to be acquired by all children alike in a given time. It is in response to this demand that the curriculum has been developed from the elementary school up through the college. There is just so much desirable knowledge, and there are just so many needed technical accomplishments in the world. Then comes the mathematical problem of dividing this by the six, twelve, or sixteen years of school life. Now give the children every year just the proportionate fraction of the total, and by the time they have finished they will have mastered the whole. By covering so much ground during this hour or day or week or year, everything comes out with perfect evenness at the end—provided the children have not forgotten what they have previously learned. The outcome of all this is Matthew Arnold's report of the statement, proudly made to him by an educational authority in France, that so many thousands of children were studying at a given hour, say eleven o'clock, just such a lesson in geography; and in one of our own western cities this proud boast used to be repeated to successive visitors by its superintendent. . . .

The real child, it hardly need be said, lives in the world of imaginative values and ideas which find only imperfect outward embodiment. We hear much nowadays about the cultivation of the child's "imagination." Then we undo much of our own talk and work by a belief that the imagination is some special part of the child that finds its satisfaction in some one particular direction—generally speaking, that of the unreal and make-believe, of the myth and made-up story. Why are we so hard of heart and so slow to believe? The imagination is the medium in which the child lives. To him there is everywhere and in everything which occupies his mind and activity at all a surplusage of value and significance. The question of the relation of the school to the child's life is at bottom simply this: Shall we ignore this native setting and tendency, dealing, not with the living child at all, but with the dead image we have erected, or shall we give it play and satisfaction? If we once believe in life and in the life of the child, then will all the occupations and uses spoken of, then will all history and science, become instruments of appeal and materials of culture to his imagination, and through that to the richness and the orderliness of his life. Where we now see only the outward doing and the outward product, there, behind all visible results, is the readjustment of mental attitude, the enlarged and sympathetic vision, the sense of growing power, and the willing ability to identify both insight and capacity with the interests of the world and man. Unless culture be a superficial polish, a veneering of mahogany over common wood, it surely is this—the growth of the imagination in flexibility, in scope, and in sympathy, till the life which the individual lives is informed with the life of nature and of society. When nature and society can live in the schoolroom, when the forms and tools of learning are subordinated to the substance of experience, then shall there be an opportunity for this identification, and culture shall be the democratic password.

Thomas J. Mahon on Labor Reform as Human Conservation, 1911

Why not conserve ourselves? If conservation of forests and water-powers and minerals, if conservation of property, is good, why not tackle the question of the conservation of human life? Isn't it of greater importance, doesn't it go to the happiness of the home and through that to the well-being and prosperity of the nation?

A great humane movement is sweeping through the world. It is finding expression even in our legislative bodies. We have felt that the time has come when we must pause for a moment in our commercial and industrial strife and consider the welfare of human beings.

Our Human Foundation

Every nation has flourished only when the physical and mental faculties of its people were developed and preserved to the fullest extent. Perfection of mind and body was the principle that governed the ancient Greeks. To attain perfection of mind and body was the aim of the Romans when the Roman Republic was at its height.

If we are to prosper and progress as a people, we must look to the protection and perfection of the individual. We have the means at hand, the tools with which to work. Why not use them?

Heretofore, legislatures have been working overtime in the giving away of natural resources and franchises, and the enactment of laws to protect rights in property. It is only recently that the idea has crept into our life, both national and state, that, after all, all the wealth which we have in the country is as nothing compared to the main purposes of our existence as a nation—*the protection of the lives, liberty and happiness of the people.*

"Most of Us Are Workers"

If we do not have better opportunities for our workers, safer conditions under which they shall live, better educational opportunities, and if the humane note is not struck in our legislation, then, indeed, our prosperity turns to ashes. After all is said, most of us are workers. The safety of the workers, then, is the safety of us all. How best to secure that safety in employment is the great problem that is strictly "up to us"—up to all of us.

Since we have become the greatest industrial nation of the world, our courts and our legislatures have struggled with the old common law doctrines of "assumption of risk," "contributory negligence" and the "fellow-servant rule"—doctrines borrowed from the dim past. Through the recognition of these principles, the "hazards of industry" have been borne by the employed. For some few years thoughtful men have struggled with the elimination of these archaic rules and the fixing of responsibility for industrial accidents and industrial disease where it rightly belongs—upon the industry itself. The movement for industrial compensation laws is the result.

The Industrial Loss

It is estimated that in the United States thirty to forty thousand wage earners are killed by industrial accidents yearly; five hundred thousand are seriously injured. It is safe to say that double this number of fatalities from industrial accidents would hardly comprehend the number of deaths resulting from occupational diseases—lead poisoning, mercury poisoning, arsenic poisoning, anthrax, compressed air diseases, and the many other industrial diseases that prevail throughout the country. AND THESE ENORMOUS LOSSES OF LIFE AND LIMB ARE LARGELY, IF NOT MOSTLY, PREVENTABLE.

In the last two years we have seen a tremendous movement in favor of workmen's compensation, a more equitable distribution of the burden of accidents incurred in production, and for the prevention of the preventable losses which industry now imposes upon workers—upon us, society. Wisconsin having just passed a Workmen's Compensation Act, the legislature is now considering a measure which aims not merely to improve the rule of compensation or money damages between workers and employers for these industrial losses in human life and limb, but—what is vastly more important—*to prevent these losses.*

Our Labor Laws Ineffective

If we merely compensate at one end, and do not prevent at the other, then we cannot hope to benefit society or even to cheapen the product. For this purpose of prevention the present labor laws are ineffective. They constitute a body of laws ill adapted to the wonderful and changing system of industry under which we live. A law which describes a piece of machinery in detail is hard to draft and still harder to enforce, and after the description has been made as thorough as human ingenuity can make it, there still remains the fact that, with the rapid growth of invention, tomorrow the description may be obsolete and useless. So the manufacturer finds himself unable, even if he really tries to do his best, to readjust conditions to these unequal, misfit and untimely laws.

A factory inspector finds it impossible to enforce laws which are often archaic a year after they are made. To obviate this difficulty, the Industrial Commission Bill has been introduced, proposing a Commission which shall have power to look into the conditions of industry and examine the best safety devices, the best methods which can be used for protection against disease and accident.

The Industrial Commission Idea

Upon a scientific examination of such methods and devices, it is proposed that reasonable standards of safety and health shall be made and enforced by this Commission in the same manner in which reasonable rates and reasonably adequate services and facilities are prescribed and enforced by similar commissions dealing with railroads and public utilities. If we can delegate to a Commission the power to make reasonable rates and require reasonably adequate facilities in transportation, we can delegate to a Commission the power to fix reasonable standards of methods, appliances and conditions to protect health and life in industry.

It will occur at once to the thinker that such a Commission will be the way out of the difficulty of readjusting the law to the rapidly changing economic conditions. It will say to the manufacturer, "Here are certain health and safety devices and methods which we have examined. We have found that they are suitable to the conditions in your factory, and you shall use them."

The well disposed manufacturer will not hesitate to take the advice of a body of experts of this kind, while the man who cares very little about his employees will be compelled to use this reasonable protection to human life. If based upon scientific principles, if common sense is used in working out the problem, then human life will undoubtedly be saved, the conditions of industry will be bettered and life be made more worth living—and saving. Through the workmen's compensation and insurance laws, on the other hand, a just and reasonable compensation for those losses which cannot be forseen and prevented will be spread over industry, and from that to society.

We may hope for the dawn of a new day in labor conditions. We may hope that better and more humane industrial conditions and A GREAT GAIN IN THE SUM TOTAL OF HUMAN WELFARE AND HUMAN HAPPINESS will result from this beneficent and long-desired legislation.

The Socialist Party's Platform, 1912

The Socialist party declares that the capitalist system has outgrown its historical function, and has become utterly incapable of meeting the problems now confronting society. We denounce this outgrown system as incompetent and corrupt and the source of unspeakable misery and suffering to the whole working class.

Under this system the industrial equipment of the nation has passed into the absolute control of a plutocracy which exacts an annual tribute of hundreds of millions of dollars from the producers. Unafraid of any organized resistance, it stretches out its greedy hands over the still undeveloped resources of the nation—the land, the mines, the forests and the water powers of every State of the Union.

In spite of the multiplication of labor-saving machines and improved methods in industry which cheapen the cost of production, the share of the producers grows ever less, and the prices of all the necessities of life steadily increase. The boasted prosperity of this nation is for the owning class alone. To the rest it means only greater hardship and misery. The high cost of living is felt in every home. Millions of wage-workers have seen the purchasing power of their wages decrease until life has become a desperate battle for mere existence.

Multitudes of unemployed walk the streets of our cities or trudge from State to State awaiting the will of the masters to move the wheels of industry.

The farmers in every state are plundered by the increasing prices exacted for tools and machinery and by extortionate rents, freight rates and storage charges.

Capitalist concentration is mercilessly crushing the class of small business men and driving its members into the ranks of propertyless wage-workers. The overwhelming majority of the people of America are being forced under a yoke of bondage by this soulless industrial despotism.

It is this capitalist system that is responsible for the increasing burden of armaments, the poverty, slums, child labor, most of the insanity, crime and prostitution, and much of the disease that afflicts mankind.

Under this system the working class is exposed to poisonous conditions, to frightful and needless perils to life and limb, is walled around with court decisions, injunctions and unjust laws, and is preyed upon incessantly for the benefit of the controlling oligarchy of wealth. Under it also, the children of the working class are doomed to ignorance, drudging toil and darkened lives.

In the face of these evils, so manifest that all thoughtful observers are appalled at them, the legislative representatives of the Republican and Democratic parties remain the faithful servants of the oppressors. . . .

Working Program

As measures calculated to strengthen the working class in its fight for the realization of its ultimate aim, the co-operative commonwealth, and to increase its power against capitalist oppression, we advocate and pledge ourselves and our elected officers to the following program:

Collective Ownership

1. The collective ownership and democratic management of railroads, wire and wireless telegraphs and telephones, express service, steamboat lines, and all other social means of transportation and communication and of all large scale industries.

2. The immediate acquirement by the municipalities, the states or the federal government of all grain elevators, stock yards, storage warehouses, and other distributing agencies, in order to reduce the present extortionate cost of living.

3. The extension of the public domain to include mines, quarries, oil wells, forests and water power.

4. The further conservation and development of natural resources for the use and benefit of all the people: . . .

5. The collective ownership of land wherever practicable, and in cases where such ownership is impracticable, the appropriation by taxation of the annual rental value of all the land held for speculation and exploitation.

6. The collective ownership and democratic management of the banking and currency system.

Unemployment

The immediate government relief of the unemployed by the extension of all useful public works. All persons employed on such works to be engaged directly by the government under a work day of not more than eight hours and at not less than the prevailing union wages. The government also to establish employment bureaus; to lend money to states and municipalities without interest for the purpose of carrying on public works, and to take such other measures within its power as will lessen the widespread misery of the workers caused by the misrule of the capitalist class.

Industrial Demands

The conservation of human resources, particularly of the lives and well-being of the workers and their families:

1. By shortening the work day in keeping with the increased productiveness of machinery.

2. By securing for every worker a rest period of not less than a day and a half in each week.

3. By securing a more effective inspection of workshops, factories and mines.

4. By forbidding the employment of children under sixteen years of age.

5. By the co-operative organization of the industries in the federal penitentiaries for the benefit of the convicts and their dependents.

6. By forbidding the interstate transportation of the products of child labor, of convict labor and of all uninspected factories and mines.

7. By abolishing the profit system in government work and substituting either the direct hire of labor or the awarding of contracts to co-operative groups of workers.

8. By establishing minimum wage scales.

9. By abolishing official charity and substituting a non-contributary system of old age pensions, a general system of insurance by the State of all its members against unemployment and invalidism and a system of compulsory insurance by employers of their workers, without cost to the latter, against industrial diseases, accidents and death.

Political Demands

1. The absolute freedom of press, speech and assemblage.

2. The adoption of a graduated income tax and the extension of inheritance taxes, graduated in proportion to the value of the estate and to nearness of kin—the proceeds of these taxes to be employed in the socialization of industry.

3. The abolition of the monopoly ownership of patents and the substitution of collective ownership, with direct rewards to inventors by premiums or royalties.

4. Unrestricted and equal suffrage for men and women.

5. The adoption of the initiative, referendum and recall and of proportional representation, nationally as well as locally.

6. The abolition of the Senate and of the veto power of the President.

7. The election of the President and Vice-President by direct vote of the people.

8. The abolition of the power usurped by the Supreme Court of the United States to pass upon the constitutionality of the legislation enacted by Congress. National laws to be repealed only by act of Congress or by a referendum vote of the whole people.

9. Abolition of the present restrictions upon the amendment of the constitution, so that instrument may be made amendable by a majority of the voters in a majority of the States.

10. The granting of the right of suffrage in the District of Columbia with representation in Congress and a democratic form of municipal government for purely local affairs.

11. The extension of democratic government to all United States territory.

12. The enactment of further measures for the conservation of health. The creation of an independent bureau of health, with such restrictions as will secure full liberty to all schools of practice.

13. The enactment of further measures for general education and particularly for vocational education in useful pursuits. The Bureau of Education to be made a department.

14. The separation of the present Bureau of Labor from the Department of Commerce and Labor and its elevation to the rank of a department.

15. Abolition of all federal districts courts and the United States circuit court of appeals. State courts to have jurisdiction in all cases arising between citizens of several states and foreign corporations. The election of all judges for short terms.

16. The immediate curbing of the power of the courts to issue injunctions.

17. The free administration of the law.

18. The calling of a convention for the revision of the constitution of the U.S.

Such measures of relief as we may be able to force from capitalism are but a preparation of the workers to seize the whole powers of government, in order that they may thereby lay hold of the whole system of socialized industry and thus come to their rightful inheritance.

❧ E S S A Y S

From different angles, the two essays following treat the ambivalence (and the internal differentiation) of progressive reform. In a sweeping review of progressive historiography, historian Richard L. McCormick of Rutgers University reclaims the social-justice side of progressive reformers from recent preoccupation with their coercive, social-control tendencies. In the second essay, along the same lines, Robert Westbrook, a professor of history at the University of Rochester, contrasts the ethics of Progressive Era documentary photographer Lewis Hine with those of his more manipulative, and socially condescending, contemporaries.

Evaluating the Progressives

RICHARD L. McCORMICK

Convulsive reform movements swept across the American landscape from the 1890s to 1917. Angry farmers demanded better prices for their products, regulation of the railroads, and the destruction of what they thought was the evil power of bankers, middlemen, and corrupt politicians. Urban residents crusaded for better city services, more efficient municipal government, and, sometimes, the control of social groups whose habits they hated and feared. Members of various professions, such as social workers and doctors, tried to improve the dangerous and unhealthy conditions in which many people lived and worked. Businessmen, too, lobbied incessantly for goals which they

From *The Party Period and Public Policy: American Politics from the Age of Jackson to the Progressive Era* by Richard L. McCormick, pp. 263–88. Copyright © 1986 by Richard L. McCormick. Reprinted by permission of Oxford University Press, Inc.

defined as reform. By around 1910, many of these crusading men and women were calling themselves progressives. Ever since, historians have used the term "progressivism" to describe the reform movements of the early twentieth-century United States.

Yet many historians today are no longer very comfortable with the term. David P. Thelen, one of the best scholars working in the field of early twentieth-century reform, recently observed that "progressivism seems basically to have disappeared from historiographical and political discussion." Thelen perhaps exaggerated the point, but this much, at least, is true: there is a malaise among historians about the concept of progressivism and a growing urge to avoid the word itself whenever possible.

Three causes account for this situation. For one, the terms "progressive" and "progressivism" commonly have been invoked in a casual way to denote people and changes that are "good" or "enlightened" or "far-sighted." These are the connotations which the progressives themselves gave to the words. Historians, being naturally wary of such value-laden terms, tend to seek a more neutral language that is better suited to impartial analysis. Such disinclination to use the word "progressivism" has been strengthened by the now-common judgment that early twentieth-century reform was not entirely good or enlightened or farsighted.

Second, the malaise about progressivism reflects a general discouragement with the liberal reform tradition in American history. I refer not simply to the nation's current political conservatism (for relatively few professional historians share the new mood) but more generally to a widespread sense, both within and without academe, that liberalism historically has been characterized by both insincerity and failure. These are the dual criticisms most frequently leveled against the Great Society programs of the 1960s. They were not genuinely intended to uplift the disadvantaged, but rather to assuage guilty liberal consciences. And the devices upon which they relied, namely, expensive governmental bureaucracies, proved conspicuously unequal to the problems at hand.

The same two complaints, of insincerity and failure, underlie most of the contemporary criticism of the early twentieth-century liberals who called themselves progressives. They are said to have used democratic rhetoric only as a cloak for elitist purposes. And they are berated for placing too much confidence in scientific methods and administrative techniques that turned out to possess few of the magical powers which the reformers attributed to them. Almost every major political figure of the era is said to have supported remedies that were grossly inadequate to the observed problems.

Often these two criticisms are conjoined in the notion that the progressives never intended their reforms to succeed, only to appear successful. Thus Richard Hofstadter explained the progressives' attraction to "ceremonial," rather than far-reaching, solutions by observing the reformers' own deep need to feel better about American society and their own status within it. Other historians, including Gabriel Kolko and James Weinstein, have suggested that even more consciously selfish motives—specifically the drive of business elites to turn government to their own ends—lay behind the failure of progressivism to solve the problems of an industrial society.

These alleged evils of progressivism—its dishonest rhetoric and its inadequate methods—bring us to an attribute of liberalism that goes a long way toward explaining the sour reputation it has today. Liberals frequently excel in recognizing—indeed, in dramatizing—the social and economic conflicts of American society, but they quickly cover up those conflicts by declaring them solved through expertise and government. The progressives of the early 1900s did this. Conservatives are at least consistent in affirming that capitalism produces a fundamental "harmony of interests," while radicals, for their part, consider social conflict unremitting and unsolvable, save through revolution. But liberals often seem (and seemed) to occupy the foolish, middle position of alternately recognizing and denying the existence of basic social and economic divisions. I call attention to this pattern because it strikes me as essential to understanding why so many of today's historians appear to have lost respect for progressivism and to avoid the term whenever they can.

The third reason why contemporary historians are dissatisfied with the concept of progressivism is the awful complexity and diversity of early twentieth-century reform. Nothing illustrates this better than the long-standing historiographical debate over the progressives' identity that flourished during the 1950s and 1960s. Farmers, businessmen, professionals, old middle classes, and immigrants all were named by one scholar or another as the key progressives. The historians offering these diverse interpretations were not content with carving out niches within the reform movement for the groups they studied. Rather they tended to claim, at least implicitly, that "their" key progressives placed a distinctive stamp on early twentieth-century reform and to define progressivism narrowly enough to substantiate that claim. We learned a great deal from these studies about how different social and economic groups experienced and responded to the problems of the early 1900s. But obviously all the historians debating the identity question cannot have been right about what progressivism was. For while many groups had a hand in it, none exclusively shaped it.

Of all the answers to the question of who the progressives were, one has exerted an especially pronounced influence upon the field: the so-called "organizational" interpretation. Led by Samuel P. Hays and Robert H. Wiebe, a number of scholars have located the progressive impulse in the drive of newly formed business and professional groups to achieve their goals through cooperation and expertise. Other groups then copied the organizers, whose bureaucratic methods gave progressivism its distinctive character.

Yet while it has influenced dozens of scholars, the organizational model is too limited to encompass much that we know about early twentieth-century reform. Hays's and Wiebe's organized, expert progressives seem too bland, too passionless, and too self-confident to have waged the frantic battles many reformers did. Their interpretations particularly err in downplaying the dramatic events that punctuated the chronology of progressivism, aroused ordinary people, and gave reform its shape and timing: a sensational muckraking article, an amazing political scandal, or a tragic social calamity. Without taking into account how the masses of Americans perceived and responded to such occurrences, progressivism cannot be understood.

More than ten years ago, Peter G. Filene and John D. Buenker published articles recognizing the progressives' diversity and suggesting ways to reorient historical scholarship on the subject. Filene proposed the more drastic response to the complexity of progressivism: abandon the concept of a progressive movement. It had no unity, either of supporters, or purposes, or ideas. Indeed, it "displays a puzzling and irreducible incoherence." Like Filene, Buenker denied there was a unified progressive movement, but he was more optimistic about the meaningfulness of progressivism. Divergent groups, Buenker suggested, came together on one issue and changed alliances on the next. Often, he observed, reformers favored the same measure for different, even opposing, reasons. Only by looking at each reform and the distinctive coalition behind it could progressivism be understood.

Here were two shrewd proposals for coping with the baffling diversity of early twentieth-century reform. Both have been heeded. Filene's pessimism stirred many scholars to abandon the term *progressivism* altogether. Buenker's call for research on individual reforms helped inspire an outpouring of monographic work on discrete aspects of progressivism. Their two responses offer a classic case of the historical profession's effort to cope with the numbing complexity of the past: give up the game or restore coherence through infinite particularizing.

Neither response will do. We cannot avoid the concept of progressivism —or even a progressive movement—because, particularly after 1910, the terms were deeply embedded in the language of reformers and because they considered the words meaningful. We cannot go on merely particularizing because (however valuable many recent monographs have been) it is important to appreciate and understand progressivism as a whole. The "whole" will scarcely turn out to have been unified or simple, but it is unlikely to have been either incoherent or utterly beyond comprehension. The renewed acceptance of the concept of progressivism may have the added benefit of enabling us to regain respect for the reformers—to see why their rhetoric and their true goals sometimes clashed; to understand why they sometimes failed to achieve their purposes; and to grasp how they, like liberals ever since, often were confused over whether the United States was, in the final analysis, a harmonious society or a divided one.

Two lines of analysis seem to me useful in achieving such an understanding of progressivism. The first is to identify the basic characteristics that were common, in varying measure, to many (and probably most) progressive reforms. No one list of progressive characteristics will satisfy every historian, but I think we know enough for a tentative enumeration. The second way to proceed is by distinguishing with care the goals of reform, the reasons publicly given for it, and the actual results. Purposes, rationale, and results are three different things, and the unexamined identification of any one with another is invalid.

Progressivism was characterized, first of all, by a distinctive set of attitudes toward industrialism. By the early 1900s, most Americans seem reluctantly to have accepted the permanence of big business. The progressives shared this attitude. They undertook reforms not to dismantle modern industry and commerce but rather to improve and ameliorate the conditions of industrial life. Yet progressivism was infused with a deep, lingering outrage against many of the worst consequences of industrialism. Outpourings of anger and dismay about corporation wrongdoing and of suspicion for industrial values frequently punctuated the course of reform. Both the acceptance of industrialism and the anger against it were intrinsic to progressivism. This does not mean that the movement was mindless or that it must be considered indefinable. What it suggests is that a powerful irony lay at the heart of progressivism: reforms that gained vitality from a people angry with industrialism ended up by assisting them to accommodate to it.

These ameliorative reforms were distinguished, secondly, by a basic optimism about people's ability to improve their environment through continuous human action. Those hurt by industrialization could be protected and their surroundings made more humane. Progressive intellectuals, as well as popularizers, produced a vast literature denouncing *laissez-faire* and affirming the capacity of men and women to better their conditions. Even reformers with little interest in philosophical questions absorbed the era's optimism and environmentalism. Their reforms reflected this habit of mind.

Improving the environment meant, above all, intervening in people's economic and social affairs to channel natural forces and give them order. This attribute of interventionism, of regulation, and even of coercion, constitutes a third essential characteristic of progressivism, visible in almost every reform of the early 1900s. Intervention could be accomplished through both private and public means. Given a choice, most progressives preferred to work through voluntary associations for noncoercive improvements in economic and social conditions. As time passed, however, more and more of their reforms relied on the hand of government.

Progressive reforms may, then, be characterized as interventions in the environment intended to improve the conditions of industrial life. But such a description says little about the ideals behind progressivism or about its distinctive methods. These must make up part of any account of the character of early twentieth-century reform. Progressivism took its inspiration, as well as much of its substance and technique, from two bodies of belief and knowledge: evangelical Protestantism and the sciences, both natural and social. Each imparted distinctive qualities to the reforms of the age.

Progressivism visibly bore the imprint of the evangelical ethos. Basic to this mentality was the drive to purge the world of sin—such as the sins of slavery and intemperance, against which nineteenth-century reformers had crusaded. Now the progressives carried the struggle into the modern citadels of sin, the teeming industrial cities of the nation. No one can read their moralistic appeals without realizing how deeply many of them felt a Christian duty to right the wrongs that sprang from industrialism. The reforms that followed from such appeals could be generous in spirit, but they also could be intolerant. Some progressive reforms were frankly intended to perpetuate a Protestant social order. Not every progressive shared the evangelical ethos, much less its intolerance, but few of the era's reforms were untouched by the spirit and the techniques of Protestant revivalism.

Science, too, had a pervasive influence on the contents and methods of progressivism. Many of the leading reformers considered themselves social scientists—that is, members of the newer disciplines of economics, sociology, statistics, and psychology that came into being between 1880 and 1910. Sharing the environmentalist and interventionist assumptions of the day, they believed that rational measures could be devised and applied to improve the human condition. Their methods inspired elements common to nearly every reform of the age: the investigation of facts, the application of social-scientific knowledge, the entrusting of trained experts to decide what should be done, and the authorization of governmental officials to take the steps that science suggested.

Dispassionate as these methods sound, they actually were compatible with the moralizing tendencies within progressivism. In its earliest days, American social science was infused by ethical concerns. An essential purpose of economics, sociology, and psychology was to improve and uplift people's lives. Progressives blended science and religion into a view of human behavior that was unique to their generation of Americans: people who had grown up in an age of revivals and come to maturity at the birth of social science.

Finally, progressivism was the first (perhaps the only) reform movement to be experienced by the whole American nation. Widely circulated magazines gave people everywhere the shameful facts of corruption and carried the clamor for reform into every town and city of the country. Almost no one in the United States in, say, 1906 could have been unaware that ten-year-old children worked through the night in dangerous factories or that many United States senators served the big business corporations. Progressivism's national reach and mass base vastly exceeded that of Jacksonian reform several generations before. And its dependence on the people for its shape and timing has no comparison in the later executive-dominated New Deal and Great Society. Wars and depressions had previously engaged the whole nation's attention, but never reform.

These half-dozen attributes of progressivism go a long way toward defining the movement as a whole, but they do not tell us much about who was doing what to whom or about what the reforms accomplished. Most progressive crusades shared in the methods and assumptions enumerated above, but they did so in different measure and with different emphases. Some reflected greater acceptance of industrialism, while others expressed more of the outrage against it. Some intervened to improve the environment through private means; others depended on government. Each reform struck a distinctive balance between the claims of Protestant moralism and scientific rationalism.

To move beyond what are essentially a series of continuums along which diverse reforms ranged, we must distinguish goals from rhetoric from results.

This is a more difficult task than might be supposed. Older interpretations of progressivism implicitly assumed that the rhetoric explained the goals and that if a reform became law the results fulfilled the intentions behind it. Neither assumption is a good one. Writing in 1964, Samuel P. Hays shrewdly exposed the fallacy of equating the reformers' democratic language with their true purposes. The two may have coincided, but the historian has to show that, not take it for granted. The automatic identification of either intentions or rhetoric with results is also invalid, although it is still a common feature of scholarship on progressivism. Only within the last decade or so have historians begun to examine with care the actual achievements of the reformers. To do so is to observe the ironies, complexities, and disappointments that accompanied progressivism. For the reformers by no means always got what they wanted, or what they said they wanted.

If the two lines of analysis sketched out here were systematically applied to early twentieth-century reform, our comprehesion of—and possibly our respect for—progressivism would be substantially enhanced. The existing research and scholarship do not permit that; nor, if they did, is my space here sufficient for it. Instead of being systematic, the following pages are illustrative, taking up, in turn, political reform and social reform. The end in view remains a better understanding of American liberalism and its limits.

Shortly after 1900 many of the basic elements of American politics and government were transformed. New patterns of political participation emerged, while the structure and tasks of government changed, too. Ever since the Jackson period, casting party ballots on election day had formed by far the most important means of political expression and involvement. Sectional, cultural, and historical influences all had contributed to shaping men's party loyalties, and to judge from the available evidence most of them took those loyalties seriously indeed. Only under unusual circumstances did ordinary people turn away from their parties and seek other means of influencing the government, although it is worth observing that nonelectoral methods were the *only* possible avenues of political expression for all women and many blacks. Prior to 1900, however, those nonelectoral avenues were difficult to travel and commonly led to failure.

Beginning in the early twentieth century this older structure of political participation gave way to new patterns. Voter turnout fell, ticket-splitting rose, and relatively fewer voters could be counted upon to support the regular party candidates year after year. In the same period, a great variety of interest groups successfully pioneered new ways of influencing the government and its agencies. By organizing their members, raising money, hiring lobbyists, pressuring officials, and inundating the public with their propaganda, the strongest of these groups managed to compel the government to attend to their demands—not just on election day but whenever their interests were vitally affected.

During the same years, the nature and functions of American government also saw significant changes. To a degree unprecedented in the nineteenth century, public officials became widely involved in monitoring and regulating how people lived and worked. In consequence, both the institutions of government and the content of public policy were decisively altered. Legislatures, which had dominated nineteenth-century governments in both the states and the nation, now lost power to increasingly strong executives and, even more importantly, to the recently created boards and agencies that made up a virtually new branch of government. These new agencies, moreover, carried out policies of a sort only rarely seen before. Where nineteenth-century governmental action had mainly concerned discrete groups and locales (to which governments distributed resources and privileges), public authorities now began to recognize and deal with clashing interests throughout the whole society. Inconsistently at first—but with increasing determination—American governments assumed the responsibility for mitigating social conflicts by taking on such previously neglected functions as regulation, administration, and even planning.

These political and governmental changes were important in themselves, quite apart from what they tell us about progressivism. One might, indeed, be tempted to study them on their own terms, with only passing reference to an upsurge of reform. The changes were, after all, products of those all-powerful, ubiquitous forces in modern American history: industrialization, urbanization, and immigration. Historians accordingly have devoted much of their attention to tracing the twisted pathways leading from economic and social developments to the political and governmental responses. Without progressivism, however, the shape and timing and, above all, the results of the political transformation are impossible to understand.

For in light of the long-term social and economic forces involved, the new patterns of politics and government were established with remarkable speed. In 1900 they were just beginning to make their appearance, but by 1915 they were largely in place. During these years three historic barriers to political and governmental change were significantly weakened: the traditional American devotion to small government, the long-standing unwillingness to enact "class legislation" recognizing the competing needs of different groups, and the intense partisan loyalties of the nineteenth-century electorate. These barriers had largely held throughout the class warfare of the 1880s and the political turmoil of the 1890s. Now they gave way, under assault from a nationwide wave of resentment against bosses and businessmen.

The precipitating crisis came in the form of a series of revelations concerning politico-business corruption. During the two years following Theodore Roosevelt's reelection as president in 1904, while muckraking journalists were trumpeting the details of corruption to a nationwide magazine audience, a remarkable number of cities and states went through wrenching discoveries of how local businessmen bribed legislators, conspired with party leaders, and controlled nominations. . . .

In response, innumerable pent-up proposals for political and governmental reform were enacted. Commonly the progressives presented their plans in moralistic, democratic language, but often the true purposes of many reformers were more complicated. Often, as well, the actual results of reform surprised some of its proponents. On the whole, the anti-boss, anti-business forces that had inspired the outcries of 1905–06 found it difficult to keep control of the complex political developments that followed.

Many new laws redefined the eligible electorate by excluding certain people from voting and including others. Even electors whose eligibility remained unchanged found that the new laws had altered the rules, and even the purposes, of voting. The progressives defended these reforms—together with related measures of direct democracy, including the initiative, referendum, and recall—as efforts to curtail corruption, weaken party bosses, and restore power to ordinary people. But nearly every election-law reform contained fundamental ambiguities, and most brought results that amazed some of their advocates.

A series of laws directed against the party machines provides a case in point. During the years after 1906, most states enacted the direct primary, placing party nominations in the hands of party voters themselves. In practice, this reform eliminated the most blatant abuses of the machine's control over convention nominations, but it left the party leaders substantially in charge of selecting candidates because voter turnout in primary elections tended to be so low. Other progressive measures established stringent governmental regulation of the parties, but in so doing they embedded parties more firmly in the legal machinery of the elections than they had ever been before. In the cities, antimachine elites supported structural reforms, such as commission government, in order to take power from local politicians. But the commissions frequently succumbed to shrewd bosses who learned the new rules of politics. Commission government became the very basis of Frank Hague's rule of Jersey City for three decades.

Governmental policies of economic regulation also were enacted in the aftermath of the exposures of politico-business corruption. Many states established railroad commissions for the first time, while others strengthened their existing boards. Other industries, too, came under effective supervision, not just from state governments but also from the cities and the nation. Yet considerable irony attended the regulatory laws of the early 1900s. Brought forth amidst progressive cries for restraining corrupt corporations and protecting consumers, the new measures usually were opposed by the businesses to be supervised. When it came to shaping the details of regulation, plural, competing interests took a hand in the process and maneuvered to obtain favorable treatment in the law. In actual practice, the regulated corporations often found benefits in the legislation they had initially opposed, although this was not always the case. Perhaps the most significant result of the regulatory revolution of the Progressive era was one that few had expected: the shifting of economic policymaking from the noisy legislative halls to the quiet offices of little-known administrators. There organized interests found a congenial environment for doing their business with the government.

By the end of the Progressive era, the political and governmental system of the United States looked very different than it had in the late nineteenth century. Political parties had been regulated, and the active electorate had become relatively smaller and less enthusiastic. Interest groups had taken over many of the parties' old functions and achieved recognition as legitimate agencies for influencing the now-expanded government. The legislature was less important than before, and the executive more powerful, but many of the government's new roles fell to independent administrative agencies which performed their tasks of investigation and adjustment well outside the public's eye. These changes were not revolutionary, but considering how stable American politics have commonly been (compared, say, with those of Europe) they were changes of great importance.

It would be hard to say whether the new system was more or less democratic than the old one. Voting had become more difficult for many (especially blacks and new immigrants), but for others new avenues of political participation had opened up. The recently created agencies of administrative government often bent to the will of the rich, but so had legislative government in the nineteenth century. Probably we will never have a fully satisfactory answer to the question of whether early twentieth-century American politics became more "progressive" in the casual sense of the word. We can be certain, however, that no one could have anticipated the actual results of political and governmental reform—not the ordinary people whose resentment of bosses and businessmen gave the era its vitality, nor their enemies either.

Progressive social reform, like economic regulation, was based on the recognition of group conflict and on a willingness to intervene in people's lives to mitigate disharmony. Some reformers, inspired by evangelical Protestantism, acted on the basis of a heartfelt desire to alleviate suffering and bring justice. Others sought the professional prestige that went with providing scientific solutions for social problems. Still others craved the power and satisfaction that came to those who imposed what they considered right forms of behavior on the masses. Few of them failed to employ the moralistic rhetoric of altruism; fewer still neglected the needs of their own group or class in determining how to act.

What distinguished the progressive reformers of the early 1900s was their conviction that men and women were social creatures. People who lived in large cities, where social contacts and conflicts were unrelenting, had little choice but to accept their dependence on each other and seek common solutions to problems. Doctors learned that venereal disease and tuberculosis were indices of social conditions; curing them meant stamping out prostitution and eradicating the insanitary conditions that accompanied poverty. Policemen and lawyers saw that crime was most prevalent in certain social circumstances; stopping it depended on improving the environment and rehabilitating the criminal. Many progressives blamed social ills on the habits and practices of the southern and eastern European immigrants who were crowding into the United States; reform thus meant restricting immigration, prohibiting the use of alcoholic beverages, and encouraging the Anglo-Saxon way of life. It might even necessitate preventing unfit people from having children. Whatever changes they advocated, progressives tended to recognize the need for solutions that were citywide, statewide, or even nationwide in scope. Whether tolerant or culturally imperialistic, they saw that everybody was bound up in a common social system. It mattered to everyone how employers treated their employees. It even mattered who was having sexual intercourse with whom.

As the foregoing examples suggest, the progressives sought reforms that would accomplish at least two analytically distinct goals: the establishment of social justice and the imposition of social control. Many reformers focused their efforts on improving the lives of exploited industrial workers and impoverished city dwellers. The progressive campaigns for the abolition of child labor, shorter hours of work and better wages for women, industrial safety and workmen's compensation, improved housing conditions, and the alleviation of poverty were among the leading reforms of this sort. The settlement-house movement was perhaps the most characteristic progressive endeavor for social justice, and Jane Addams of Hull House was the ideal reformer. Traditional scholarship placed predominant emphasis on these progressive campaigns for social justice.

Recent historical writing makes clear that this is too restricted a view. Numerous social reforms of the early twentieth century expressed the progressives' desire to impose uniform living habits on a culturally diverse population whose behavior sometimes seemed to threaten the morality and health of the community. The campaigns for immigration restriction, racial segregation, sterilization of the mentally defective, and mandatory school attendance demonstrated the reformers' passion for social control. The prohibition of alcoholic beverages was perhaps the prototypical reform of this type.

Weighing the relative gains made by progressives for social justice and social control is a significant problem in historical interpretation. But it is equally important to recognize that most reforms and reformers expressed both goals. There was scarcely any social change that was not advocated, often sincerely, as a means of bringing justice. Yet, in practice, almost every progressive reform gave added control to those who implemented it. . . .

Justice and control scarcely meant the same things to all progressives. The settlement-house workers, the reforming professionals, and the advocates of such coercive measures as immigration restriction and racial segregation each gave distinctive interpretations to these goals and placed different emphases upon them. Some progressive controls entailed relatively benign environmental constraints; others mandated recognized "experts" to set standards of behavior within the areas of their supposed competence; still other social controls were frankly racist and repressive.

Whatever meaning they gave to justice and control and whatever balance they struck (or failed to strike) between them, most social progressives adopted roughly similar methods. In time a pattern of social reform became familiar, variations of which were followed by progressives in almost every area. They typically began by organizing a voluntary association, investigating a problem, gathering mounds of relevant social data, and analyzing it according to the precepts of one of the newer social sciences. From such an analysis, a proposed solution would emerge, be popularized through campaigns of education and moral suasion, and—as often as not, if it seemed to work—be taken over by some level of government as a permanent public function. Usually the details of the law were worked out through bargaining among the competing groups interested in the measure.

Certain assumptions guided those who adopted this approach to reform. One concerned the utility of social science in fostering harmony. Progressives knew full well that different groups in American society had competing interests, and they recognized that conflicting social elements often hurt one another. They were not deluded by a belief in a natural harmony of interests. Yet the social sciences, based as they were on a vision of human interdependence, offered the possibility for devising reforms that regulated and harmonized antagonistic social groups. If the facts were gathered and properly understood, solutions could be found that genuinely benefited everyone. Individual reforms might assist one group against another, but a carefully crafted program of reforms would establish a more perfect harmony of interests than ever appeared in nature.

A related progressive assumption held that government could be trusted to carry out broad social reforms. In social policy, just as in the economic area, nineteenth-century American governments had tended to produce haphazard legislative decisions, each having little connection to the next. What Gerald N. Grob has called "clear policy formation and social planning" were largely absent. Most social progressives did not initially set out to expand the limited scope of government. They placed their confidence first in private organization. As time passed, however, the reformers increasingly looked to public agencies to carry out their programs.

Having methods that were largely untried and assumptions that often approximated mere articles of faith, the progressives not surprisingly failed to achieve many of their social purposes. Often they succeeded, however, and their basic approach to social problems has not yet been repudiated in the United States. The foregoing discussion of progressivism has frequently pointed to the differences between the rhetoric, intentions, and results of reform. In every area there were wide gaps between what the progressives said they were doing, what they actually wanted to do, and what they accomplished. It is important to deal explicitly with the reasons for these seeming inconsistencies and to reflect on what they tell us about progressivism.

The failure of reform to fulfill all of the expectations behind it was not, of course, unique to the Progressive era. Jacksonian reform, Reconstruction, and the New Deal all exhibited ironies and disappointments. In each case, the clash between reformers having divergent purposes, the inability to predict how given methods of reform would work in practice, and the ultimate waning of popular zeal for change all contributed to the disjuncture of rationale, purpose, and achievement. Yet the gap between these things seems more noticeable in the Progressive era. So many movements for reform took place in a relatively brief span of time, accompanied by such resounding rhetoric and by such high expectations for improving the American social and political environment. The effort to change so many things at once and the grandiose claims made for the moral and material betterment that would result meant that disappointments were bound to occur.

Yet even the great number of reforms and the uncommonly high expectations behind them cannot fully account for the consistent gaps between the stated purposes, real intentions, and actual results of progressivism. Several additional factors, intrinsic to the nature of early twentieth-century reform, help explain the ironies and contradictions. One of these factors was the progressives' confident reliance on modern methods of reform. Heirs of recent advances in science and social science, they enthusiastically crafted and applied new techniques for improving American government and society. Often their methods worked, but often progressive programs simply did not prove capable of accomplishing what had been expected of them. This was not necessarily the reformers' fault. Making hopeful use of untried methods, they nonetheless lacked a science of society that was equal to all the great problems they perceived. Worse, the progressives' scientific reforms frequently involved the collection of data, making it possible to know just how far short of success their programs sometimes fell. The evidence of their failures was thus more visible than in any previous era of reform. To the progressives' credit, they usually published that evidence—for contemporaries and historians alike to see.

A second aspect of early twentieth-century reform that helps to account for the gaps between aims and achievements was the progressives' deep ambivalence about industrialism and its consequences. Individual reformers were divided, and so was their movement as a whole. Compared with many reformers of the late 1800s, the progressives fundamentally accepted an industrial society and sought mainly to order and ameliorate it. Even reformers who were intellectually committed to socialist doctrines often acted the part of reformers, not radicals. Yet progressivism was infused and vitalized by people truly angry with an industrial society and its conditions. Few of them wished to tear down the modern institutions of business and commerce, but their anger was real, their moralism genuine, and their passions essential to the era's reforms. Progressivism went forward because of their fervor.

Unfortunately, the reform movement never surmounted this ambivalence about industrialism. Much of its rhetoric and popular passion pointed in one direction, while its leaders and their programs went in another. Often the result was confusion and bitterness. Reforms frequently did not measure up to the popular, anti-business expectations for them—and, indeed, never were expected to measure up by those who designed and implemented them.

Perhaps of most significance, progressivism failed to achieve all its goals because, despite their real efforts to do so, the reformers never fully came to terms with the divisions and conflicts in American society. Again and again, they acknowledged the existence of social disharmony more fully and frankly than had nineteenth-century Americans. Nearly every reform of the era was predicated on the progressives' recognition that diverse cultural and occupational groups had conflicting interests and that the responsibility for mitigating and adjusting those differences lay with the whole society, usually the government. Such recognition formed one of the progressives' greatest achievements. Indeed, it stands as one of the most important accomplishments of liberal reform in all of American history. For by accepting social disharmony, the progressives committed the twentieth-century United States to recognizing—and dealing with—the inevitable conflicts within a heterogeneous, industrial society.

Yet significant as it was, the progressives' recognition of diversity was clouded by the methods and institutions they adopted for coping with conflict. Through scientific data-gathering and analysis, they believed that impartial programs could be devised that genuinely benefited every interest. And through expert, administrative government, those programs could be carried out in fairness to all. But science and administration turned out to be less neutral than the progressives expected. No scientific reform could be any more impartial than the experts who gathered the data or than the bureaucrats who implemented the program. In practice, administrative government often succumbed to the domination of special interests.

It would be pointless to blame the reformers for the failure of their new methods and agencies to eliminate the divisions within an industrial society. But it is perhaps fair to ask why the progressives adopted measures which tended to disguise and obscure social conflict almost as soon as they had uncovered it. For one thing, they honestly believed in the almost unlimited potential of science and administration. Our late twentieth-century skepticism of these wonders should not blind us to the sincerity with which the progressives embraced them and imbued them with what now seem magical properties. For another, most progressives were reformers, not radicals. It was one thing to recognize social conflict, but quite another to admit that it was permanent. By and large these men and women were personally and ideologically inclined to believe that America was fundamentally a harmonious society and that such conflicts as existed could be resolved. Finally, the leading progressives' own class and cultural backgrounds often made them insensitive to lower-class immigrant Americans and their cultures. Reducing social divisions sometimes came down to imposing middle-class Protestant ways. Together these factors diminished whatever chance the progressives may have had of eliminating social conflict. Seeing the problem more fully than had their predecessors, the reformers of the early twentieth century nonetheless tended to consider conflicts resolved when, in fact, they had only been disguised by the establishment of scientific policies and the creation of governmental agencies.

Thus progressivism fell short of its rhetoric and intentions. Lest that seem an unfairly critical evaluation, it is important to recall how terribly ambitious were the reformers' stated aims and true goals. They missed some of their marks because they sought to do so much. And despite the shortcomings, they accomplished an enormous part of what they intended to achieve.

The problems with which the progressives struggled have, by and large, occupied Americans ever since. And although the assumptions and techniques of progressivism no longer command the confidence which early twentieth-century Americans placed in them, no equally comprehensive body of reforms has ever been adopted in their place. I have criticized the progressives for having too much faith in their untried methods. Yet if this was a failing, it was also a source of strength, now missing from reform in America. For the essence of progressivism lay in the hopefulness and optimism the reformers brought to the tasks of applying science and administration to the high moral purposes in which they believed. The historical record of their aims and achievements leaves no doubt that in the United States in the early 1900s there lived people who were not afraid to confront the problems of a modern industrial society with vigor and imagination. They of course failed to solve all those problems, but no other generation of Americans has done conspicuously better with the political and social conditions it faced.

Lewis Hine and the Two Faces of Progressive Photography

ROBERT WESTBROOK

No one contributed more to the iconography of American industrialization than Lewis Hine; yet Hine died a penniless and unappreciated artist. Even today, despite the widespread familiarity of his photographs, few people are much aware of who Lewis Hine was or of the ways in which his work reflected a consistent moral vision and engaged some of the central ethical and political issues posed by progressive reform in the United States between 1890 and 1940. In order to grasp the full significance and power of Hine's photographs, they must be seen not only as evidence documenting the lives of those who populate his images but also as important texts in the cultural history of progressivism, less because they reflect the beliefs Hine shared with those in the mainstream of American reform than because they pose a challenge to the benevolent posture at the heart of progressive ideology.

I

In some important respects, Lewis Hine was a *typical* progressive reformer in that he was committed to what historian Richard Hofstadter termed the "business of exposure." Before I turn to an effort to number Hine among those extraordinary progressives who were attuned to the ethical pitfalls of this business, it is perhaps worth recalling Hine's commitment to this widely shared progressive impulse.

Hine's reform credentials were, of course, impeccable. He began his career as a photographer during a brief stint as a teacher in the Ethical Culture School in New York City, an important center of educational experimentation. After abandoning the classroom for a full-time career as a photographer, he signed on as the photographer for Paul Kellogg's pathbreaking 1907 survey of social conditions in Pittsburgh and began his longtime

Text by Robert Westbrook, "Lewis Hine and the Ethics of Progressive Camerawork" *Tikkun* 2 (April/May 1987), pp. 24–29. Reprinted with permission of Tikkun Magazine, a bimonthly Jewish critique of politics, culture, and society based in Oakland, CA.

affiliation with Kellogg's important reform journal, Survey. Around the same time, he began to accept the series of assignments from the national Child Labor Committee that over the next decade would provide the occasion for the photographs of working children that are his finest work. Although in the last decade of his life Hine was excluded from the remarkable photographic project of the Farm Security Administration, which set the standards for documentary expression in the 1930s, he did find some work with the Tennessee Valley Authority, the Works Progress Administration, and other New Deal agencies.

As a reform photographer, Hine shared with many other progressives a belief that his first task was that of providing his fellow citizens with a clear view of the sordid realities of American social life that had been obscured by ignorance and unconcern. As Hofstadter observed, reality for these men and women was:

> a series of unspeakable plots, personal iniquities, moral failures, which, in their totality, had come to govern American society only because the citizen had relaxed his moral diligence. The failures of American society were thus no token of the ultimate nature of man, of the human condition, much less the American condition; they were not to be accepted or merely modified, but fought with the utmost strenuosity at every point. First, reality must in its fullness be exposed, and then it must be made the subject of moral exhortation; and then, when individual citizens in sufficient numbers had stiffened in their determination to effect reform, something could be done.

For these men and women, progressive reform was a politics of revelation. Knowledge of the "inside story" of what American society was "really" like would activate the will of its citizenry to clean up its dirty, hitherto hidden corners.

Hine fully shared this commitment to the business of exposure and urged his fellow reformers to recognize the importance of the camera to their cause. In an important lecture to the National Conference of Charities and Correction in 1909 entitled "Social Photography: How the Camera May Help in the Social Uplift," he argued that "the great social peril is darkness and ignorance" and urged social workers to take their byword from Victor Hugo: "Light! Light in floods!" In the crucial task of opening the eyes of the "great public" the camera was an essential tool. "In this campaign for light," he declared, "we have as our advance agent the light writer—the photograph." The picture was a powerful symbol that "brings one immediately into close touch with reality," for it told "a story packed into the most condensed and vital form." Reformers should not hesitate to take advantage of the heightened realism of these pictures and play upon the widespread belief that "the photograph cannot falsify."

Hine's work for the National Child Labor Committee was a paradigm of the progressive business of exposure. As Alan Trachtenberg has observed, Hine opened to view workplaces that were "fast becoming secret and secretive places, buried in dark corners of tenements, hidden behind imposing brick walls of factories. . . . This secrecy, Hine learned, hid shameful sights . . . and he came to define his task as that of showing the world of consumers exactly what the world of makers was like. This task became a ripping aside of the veil that disguised and mystified the brutal system of production.''

His work entailed as wide a range of humanitarian espionage as reform ideology recommended. Hine was called upon in many of his investigations to act as a progressive spy, passing himself off as a salesman or a photographer of machinery in order to infiltrate mills, fields, and sweatshops brutally exploiting children. Concealing a note pad in his pocket, he recorded the ages and sizes of the children he encountered, many of whom he measured against the buttons on his coat. Like any secret agent he worked under the constant threat of violence: '' I have a number of times been very near getting what has been coming to me from those who do not agree with me on child labor matters.''

II

The naive optimism of reformers like Hine has been an easy target of criticism, and such historians as Hofstadter have attacked progressives for their blind faith in the power of knowledge and the efficacy of good will. This is an important criticism, but it does not get at the most troubling feature of the progressive politics of exposure.

A more penetrating criticism is that advanced by historians who have found in progressive ideology a will to power that seeks to rescue the victims of industrialism from the depredations of evil capitalism only to subject them to the cultural hegemony of the reformers themselves. From this perspective, the overriding aim of the progressive in exposing the exploitation of the immigrant working class was to render these unfortunate people the object of paternal bourgeois benevolence. This, in effect, substituted one form of objectification for another. Critical of unscrupulous factory owners who treated immigrant workers merely as a factor of production, middle-class reformers sought to render them little more than passive beneficiaries of the solicitude and culture of their more fortunate neighbors. The language of middle-class benevolence often betrayed in its metaphors this sense of the ''urban masses'' as inert material upon which reformers might work their will. Addressing an audience of female social workers, for example, one reformer warned that the ''Christian worker'' who went among the ''unchurched masses'' must ''root up weeds of false teaching, dig out rocks of ignorance and prejudice, break up the fallow ground, and be glad if it is given to her to drop a seed of divine truth here and there.''

The critical perspective on this sort of farming for souls has produced an abundant historical literature that treats progressive reform as a species of ''social control.'' This is an argument that is, in many instances, persuasive. What it often overlooks, however, is the presence among progressive reformers of several important figures who were well aware of the troubling ethical implications of paternal benevolence. Lewis Hine, I contend, was among these figures.

Before attempting to support this contention, it is worth considering briefly how this issue was treated in the work of the most important progressive critic of the paternalistic impulse, John Dewey. Although Dewey's own thought and activism, particularly his philosophy of education, has also been targeted (unpersuasively) by the critics of bourgeois hegemony, there is abundant evidence, from the earliest stages of his career forward, of Dewey's deep antipathy to "do-gooders" and to the objectification and antidemocratic consequences of paternalistic benevolence. To cite but one example of this, writing in his *Ethics* (1908), Dewey argued that "regard for the happiness of others means *regard for those conditions and objects which permit others freely to exercise their own powers from their own initiative, reflection, and choice.*" It was precisely in this regard that so many reformers were deficient:

> the vice of the social leader, of the reformer, of the philanthropist and the specialist in every worthy cause of science, or art, of politics, is to seek ends which promote the social welfare in ways which fail to engage the active interest and cooperation of others. The conception of conferring the good upon others, or at least of attaining it for them, which is our inheritance from the aristocratic civilization of the past, is so deeply embodied in religious, political, and charitable institutions and in moral teaching, that it dies hard. Many a man, feeling himself justified by the social character of his ultimate aim (it may be economic, or educational, or political), is genuinely confused or exasperated by the increasing antagonism and resentment which he evokes, because he has not enlisted in his pursuit of the "common" end the freely cooperative activities of others. This cooperation must be the root principle of the morals of democracy.

Surveying the course of reform in his own society, Dewey concluded this cooperative ideal had "as yet made little progress," and "the inherent irony and tragedy of much that passes for a high kind of socialized activity is precisely that it seeks a common good by methods which forbid its being either common or good."

Hine may well have been influenced by Dewey's argument. He studied briefly with the philosopher at the University of Chicago, and they traveled in the same circles in New York after the turn of the century. An even more likely source of Dewey's influence on Hine was Frank Manny, a member of a coterie of undergraduates who gathered around Dewey at the University of Michigan in the 1880s and who were deeply influenced by his moral philosophy. It was Manny who brought Hine to the Ethical Culture School when he became superintendent of that institution in 1901, and the two remained lifelong friends (Hine's only book, *Men at Work,* is dedicated to Manny). In any case, whether or not Dewey's philosophy directly influenced Hine, his camerawork manifested the same sensitivity to the ethical problems of reform.

Perhaps the greatest strength of Hine's work in this regard was its sensitivity to the ways a reform photograph that "exposed" the seamy side of society ran the risk of conveying "knowledge" of its subject as little more than an object of horror or pity. He seems to have perceived the ethical implications in the way reformers *saw* the oppressed and to have recognized that various "ways of seeing" served as a condition of or an obstacle to the development of democratic reform politics that would permit all the members of the society to, as Dewey put it, "exercise the voluntary capacities of a voluntary agent."

In keeping with this Deweyan ethic, Hine approached his subjects with decorum and tact. He rarely took candid shots but rather encouraged eye contact between the camera lens and the subject. As Trachtenberg says, "he learned how to achieve a certain physical distance, corresponding to a psychological distance, that allowed for a free interaction between the eyes of the subject and the camera. . . . he allowed his subjects room for *their* self-expression."

Lewis Hine, "Young Russian Jewess at Ellis Island"

Jacob Riis, "Quarters for the Night"

Lewis Hine, "Breaker Boys in a Coal Chute"

Hine's respectful approach contrasted sharply with that of Jacob Riis, the father of American reform photography, whose expeditions into the dark world, the "other half," were literal attacks on vulnerable working-class targets. Recalling his adventures, Riis remarked that:

> It is not too much to say that our party carried terror wherever it went. The flashlight of those days was contained in cartridges fired from a revolver. The spectacle of half a dozen strange men invading a house in the midnight hour armed with big pistols which they shot off recklessly was hardly reassuring, however sugary our speech . . . and it was not to be wondered at if the tenants bolted through windows and down fire escapes wherever we went. But as no one was murdered, things calmed down after a while, . . . though months after I found the recollection of our visits hanging over a Stanton Street block like a nightmare.

The people Riis fixed with his flashgun were dazed and off-guard. In few of the photographs in his pathbreaking book, *How the Other Half Lives,* do his subjects face the camera on their feet, and many are not only "down" but "out," altogether without consciousness.

Unlike Riis, who regarded the posing of his subjects as a *problem,* Hine welcomed it as an *opportunity* for them to collaborate in their portrait, rendering it less an "exposure" of a life than a revelation and, in part, a self-revelation. Hine's best reform photography is *democratic* in Dewey's sense; it allows its subjects to participate actively in the production of the knowledge others will have of them. His was an ethics of reform camerawork that pointed toward working-class self-portraiture, a conclusion that Hine appears to have recognized. "The greatest advance in social work," he wrote in 1909, "is to be made by the popularizing of camerawork, so that these records can be made by those who are in the thick of the battle." And near the end of his life he wrote a friend that "I have had all along, as you know, a conviction that my demonstration of the value of the photographic appeal can find its real fruition best if it helps the workers realize that they themselves can use it as a lever even though it may not be the mainspring of the works."

As a consequence of his commitment to a democratic ethic and his resistance to benevolent paternalism, Hine's photographs of workers not only opened to view the difficult circumstances of their lives but also revealed their strength and solidarity. The persistent power of Hine's photographs of children also rests, in part, on his refusal to present them simply as one-dimensional victims of industrial capitalism. His children, like his adults, are not thoroughly beaten down into passivity and defeat but retain resources of resistance: They are tough, defiant, and more often than not, they smile. The child labor photographs are moving because we are made aware of the *struggle* that was waged in factories, fields, and sweatshops between the spirit of Hine's children and their exploiters. We face not deadened boys and girls, but are thrust instead into the midst of their deadening, a much more painful prospect. Hine's photographs call upon us not to "do good" for (or to) such children but, as Dewey would say, to establish the conditions that will enable them to actively develop for themselves the powers that peek out from beneath their coal-smudged faces.

III

The contrast I have drawn between the ethics of Hine's progressive camerawork and that of his predecessor can also be drawn between his work and that of many of the younger photographers who documented the trauma of the Great Depression. Hine was frozen out of the greatest documentary project of this decade, the work of the historical section of the Farm Security Administration, by its director Roy Stryker. Stryker claimed that Hine was not employed in the project because he was personally difficult to get along with, but, given the tension between Hine's photographic ethic and that which prevailed in the FSA, it is perhaps worth speculating that the antagonism between Stryker and Hine ran deeper.

As William Stott has demonstrated in his superb book *Documentary Expression and Thirties America* (Oxford, 1973), many of the photographers in the FSA were as anxious to avoid posed photographs and the open participation of their subjects in their "exposure" as Riis. They were after a particular "look"—"half frown, half appeal; a look vacant but despairing; a look that expects rebuff yet *asks* anyway"—and they devised often elaborate strategies to get it. For example, in order to get "the look" in a famous photograph of the wife and child of an Arkansas sharecropper, Arthur Rothstein developed a careful plan of deception. Frustrated because the woman and her child would, on direct approach, give him only "Sunday snapshot

Margaret Bourke-White, "Okefenokee Swamp, Georgia"

Lewis Hine, "Miner's Family"

smiles," Rothstein manipulated them into the "forlorn look" he wanted by getting a local acquaintance of the woman to question her while Rothstein stood unobtrusively in the background, camera ready to hand. Whenever she responded to her neighbor's questions with "anxiety and concern" Rothstein snapped the picture, and this method, he said, "gave me what I wanted, a factual and true scene."

The most aggressive of the thirties photographers in this respect was not, however, Rothstein but Margaret Bourke-White who took the photographs in the decade's most celebrated documentary book, *You Have Seen Their Faces* (Viking, 1937) for which Erskine Caldwell wrote the text. These photographs were a compendium of variations on "the look," accompanied by captions authored by Caldwell and Bourke-White that put words in the mouths of the people portrayed in order to render them as even more conventional icons of despair. "The legends under the picture," Caldwell and Bourke-White wrote, "are intended to express the authors' own conceptions of the sentiments of the individuals portrayed; they do not pretend to reproduce the actual sentiments of these people."

The contrast between the ethic of photographers like Bourke-White and Hine can be seen in a comparison of photographs that each took in the thirties of very similar scenes. In Bourke-White's image of a meager family meal in Georgia, everyone has "the look" (though it looks a bit forced where the children are concerned, and the older boy almost appears to have been *told* to gaze longingly at his brother's more substantial dinner plate). The impression offered is one of wholesale deprivation, despair, and resignation to a lifeboat ethics in which, as the caption reads, "the littlest one gets taken care of." In Hine's photograph of the meal of a miner's family in West Virginia, by contrast, the poverty of a shack papered with newspaper encloses and is in tension with a family gathering that transcends these circumstances and renders its subjects considerably more complex than those forced on the procrustean bed of Bourke-White's benevolent conventions. Here the miner's baby appears to have done something to amuse his older sister, evoking a family bemusement that I have often seen at my own dinner table. While Bourke-White's subjects are objectified as types trapped within a very limited repertoire of feeling, Hine's family betrays a full range of emotions and human capabilities struggling with difficult circumstances.

My speculation that Hine might not have fit in at the FSA takes on a bit of weight in light of Walker Evans's failure to do so, for Evans, fired by Stryker in 1937, is the thirties photographer whose camerawork ethics seem to most closely approximate Hine's. Evans had, as Lionel Trilling observed in an acute review of *Let Us Now Praise Famous Men* (Houghton Mifflin, 1960), "perfect *taste*, taking that word in its largest possible sense to mean tact, delicacy, justness of feeling, complete awareness and perfect respect." In portraits like that of Annie Mae Gudger, Trilling remarked, "the sitter gains in dignity when allowed to defend herself against the lens. The gaze of the

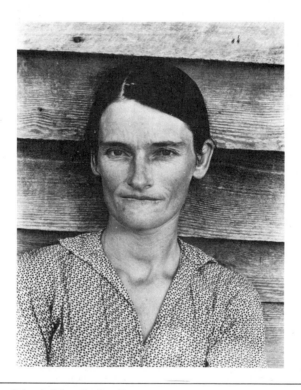

Walker Evans, "Annie Mae Gudger"

woman returning our gaze checks our pity. . . . In this picture, Mrs. Gudger, with all her misery and perhaps with her touch of pity for herself, simply refuses to be an object of your 'social consciousness'; she refuses to be an object at all—everything in the picture proclaims her to be all subject.''

Evans and his collaborator on *Let Us Now Praise Famous Men*, James Agee, were outraged by the success of *You Have Seen Their Faces*. As Evans said, ''we thought it was an evil and immoral thing to do. Not only to cheapen [the tenant farmers] but to profit by them, to exploit them—who had already been so exploited. Not only that but to exploit them without even *knowing* that that was what you were doing.''

This outrage moved Agee to include a savage attack on Bourke-White in an appendix and helped shape *Let Us Now Praise Famous Men* into an extended meditation on the epistemological difficulties and ethical conundrums of documentary expression. Calling for an ''effort to perceive simply the cruel radiance of what is'' while at the same time acknowledging the extraordinary difficulties this task presented, Agee declared that ''the camera seems to me, next to unassisted and weaponless consciousness, the central instrument of our time.'' He felt ''such rage at its misuse; which has spread so nearly a universal corruption of sight that I know of less than a dozen alive whose eyes I can trust even so much as my own.''

Agee's hostility toward Bourke-White and others who corrupted the capacity of the camera ''handled cleanly and literally in its own terms'' to record ''absolute, dry truth'' was contained in a larger skepticism about reform itself and a religious vision that despaired of any cure for suffering short of that provided by ''our father who art in heaven.'' Progressivism, he suggested, could only treat the poor as ''social integers in a criminal economy'' and necessarily obscured the fact that every man and woman was ''a creature which has never in all time existed before and which shall never in all time exist again and which is not quite like any other and which has the grand stature and natural warmth of every other and whose existence is all measured upon a still made and incurable time.''

Hine's camerawork suggests a different vision. It points toward a reform ethic grounded not in pity for downtrodden ''masses'' but in respect for the resilient particularity of individual human lives—not in objectification under the gaze of benevolence but in an empowering dialogue of shared revelation. Such a democratic ethic, as Dewey said, requires a reconstructed conception of ''helping others'' that rests on ''the discovery and promotion of those activities and active relationships in which the capacities of all concerned are effectively evoked, exercised, and put to the test.'' It was the genius of Lewis Hine to recognize that democracy also requires a reconstruction of the very way we see those we would help.

❧ *FURTHER READING*

Paul Boyer, *Urban Masses and Moral Order in America, 1820–1920* (1978)
John D. Buenker, *Urban Liberalism and Progressive Reform* (1973)
Raymond E. Callahan, *Education and the Cult of Efficiency* (1962)

Robert Crunden, Ministers of Reform: The Progressives' Achievement in American Civilization (1982)

Allen F. Davis, Spearheads for Reform: The Social Settlements and the Progressive Movement, 1890–1914 (1967)

Charles Forcey, The Crossroads of Liberalism: Croly, Weyl, Lippmann and the Progressive Era, 1900–1925 (1961)

Jack Temple Kirby, Darkness at Dawning: Race and Reform in the Progressive South (1972)

Gabriel Kolko, The Triumph of Conservatism (1963)

Christopher Lasch, The New Radicalism in America, 1889–1963 (1966)

Richard L. McCormick, Progressivism (1983)

Daniel T. Rodgers, "In Search of Progressivism," Reviews in American History 10 (1982), 113–132

Nick Salvatore, Eugene V. Debs: Citizen and Socialist (1982)

Katherine Kish Sklar, "Hull House in the 1890s: A Community of Women Reformers," Signs 10 (Summer 1985), 658–677

Robert B. Westbrook, John Dewey and American Democracy (1991)

Robert Wiebe, Businessmen and Reform (1962)

Progressivism: Foundations

for a New American State

Progressive reformers made numerous claims on comparatively underdeveloped administrative and regulative functions of the federal government. Beginning in progressive bulwarks like the state of Wisconsin, and later highlighted in the 1912 and 1916 presidential campaigns, political discussion turned increasingly to the construction of a new balance between individual liberties and public responsibilities. While advancing legislative initiatives at both the state and federal levels, however, reformers frequently collided with another peculiarly American governing instrument, the judicial review authority of the U.S. Supreme Court. Despite the pleas of legal reformers for a more flexible, ''sociological'' interpretation of constitutional guidelines, the Court, citing the due-process clause of the Fourteenth Amendment, remained throughout this period a major obstacle to expanded public regulation of the private marketplace. An important exception, nevertheless, emerged in the acceptance of government ''protection'' for those groups (especially women and children) deemed unable to provide for themselves. The result was an ambiguous legacy: a stream of path-breaking regulations governing the hours and conditions of work, which effectively shut women out of many trades and factories.

ಢ *D O C U M E N T S*

The state-building character of progressive action and thought is exemplified in the first three documents. In the opening selection, Wisconsin's legislative librarian, Charles McCarthy, offers a compendium of a rich harvest of legislation, dating from 1909 to 1911, inspired by the state's progressive commander-in-chief, Senator Robert M. La Follette. The second and third documents present the competing attempts of Theodore Roosevelt and Woodrow Wilson, respectively, to offer a justification for government initiatives within a compelling political vision. Roosevelt's ''New Nationalist'' platform is taken from his famous speech delivered in Osawatomie, Kansas, on August 31, 1910. Wilson's inaugural address of 1913 eloquently reaffirms the ''New Freedom'' concept articulated during his campaign.

The section closes with two landmark decisions of the U.S. Supreme Court. In *Lochner* v. *New York* (1905), the majority opinion overturns a New York law limiting bakers' hours to no more than sixty a week or ten a day, even as Justice Oliver Wendell Holmes, Jr., issues a strong dissent. In *Muller* v. *Oregon* (1908), on the other hand, the same Court, impressed with the sociological brief of state counsel Louis Brandeis, lets stand an Oregon law similarly limiting the hours of laundresses and other women factory workers.

Charles McCarthy Inventories
Wisconsin's La Follette–Era Reforms (1909–1911), 1911

The following proposed amendments to the constitution were adopted this year [1911]:

The initiative, referendum.

Providing that the salaries of members of the legislature shall be $600 per annum, instead of $500 for each biennial session.

Permitting cities to acquire lands for park purposes.

Permitting the state to install a system of insurance against sickness, death, accident and invalidity.

Permitting the state to appropriate for internal improvements—"for the purpose of acquiring, preserving and developing the water power resources and forests of the state"; limiting the appropriation therefore to a $\frac{2}{10}$ of a mill tax on the property of the state.

Empowering the legislature to provide for the recall of any public elective officer, except judges.

Declaring "all lanes, mineral rights, water powers and other natural resources of natural wealth within the state which are now or may thereafter become the property of the state, shall remain forever the property of the state and shall not be alienated"; permitting the state to lease or rent such resources; and providing that all mineral rights hitherto reserved in contracts, deeds or instruments conveying real estate are abolished after Jan. 1, 1920, and are declared to inhere to the state except where they have been developed in full or in part prior to Jan. 1, 1920.

The following constitutional amendments were adopted at the 1909 and also the 1911 session and will be submitted to the people at the general election in 1912:—

Permitting municipalities to acquire land within or outside their limits, for park or other public purposes and to plat or sell any part of such land for the purpose of adding to a fund for the maintenance of parks, playgrounds, etc.

Permitting the state legislature to remove the five percent limit upon the public debt of any city, county, town, village or school district, when the debt is incurred for the purpose of purchasing and improving public parks, etc.

The following under the heading "Public health and welfare," show what was accomplished in this line:

Empowering county boards, with the consent of the state board of control, to erect upon grounds of county insane asylums, hospitals for the care of chronic insane affected by pulmonary tuberculosis.—Chapter 461.

Authorizing the secretary of the state board of health to provide biennially for a state conference of health officers and health commissioners of cities and villages.—Chapter 465.

Empowering county boards of supervisors to purchase sites and establish quarters for the treatment of persons suffering from tuberculosis in advanced or secondary stages.—Chapter 457.

Specifying the manner in which the state shall care for dependent, neglected, and delinquent children.—Chapter 460.

Making pandering a felony and providing a penalty therefor.—Chapter 420.

Empowering the state board of health to abate nuisances caused by the pollution of streams and public water supplies.—Chapter 412.

Making it unlawful to store or exhibit fruits, vegetables, or other food products on any sidewalk or outside any place of business, unless covered by glass, wood or metal cases and providing a penalty therefor.—Chapter 379.

Requiring owners or occupants of public or quasi-public institutions to provide cuspidors and cleanse and disinfect same daily.—Chapter 330.

Making it unlawful to abuse, neglect, or illtreat any person confined in a police station or any other place of confinement, and fixing a penalty therefor.—Chapter 375.

Requiring trained nurses to register with the state board of health.—Chapter 346.

Making it unlawful to manufacture, sell, or transport adulterated or misbranded insecticides or fungicides.—Chapter 325.

Prohibiting the manufacturing and sale of certain kinds of firecrackers and fireworks.—Chapter 313.

Making it unlawful for physicians or surgeons to prescribe intoxicating liquor for any person, when unnecessary for the health of such person, and providing a penalty therefor.—Chapter 290.

Empowering common councils to regulate the emission of dense smoke into the open air within the corporate limits of any city, and within one mile therefrom.—Chapter 314.

Making it unlawful to spit or expectorate in any public place.—Chapter 407.

Empowering health officers to take precautions against the spread of dangerous communicable diseases and prescribing the duties of principals of schools and parents, where such diseases are known to exist.—Chapter 44.

Making it a misdemeanor to sell or have in possession, canned goods containing any artificial coloring matter or bleaching compound and fixing the penalty therefor.—Chapter 46.

Prescribing the manner in which explosives may be manufactured and stored within the state.—Chapter 223.

Prescribing the duties of health officers in determining the diagnosis of contagious or infectious diseases.—Chapter 248.

Extending the police authority of agents and superintendents of certain humane societies.—Chapter 258.

Conservation received some attention also:—

Empowering boards of supervisors to lease swamp lands under certain conditions, and conferring the same powers upon the state board of forestry in certain sections of the state.—Chapter 238.

Making it unlawful to waste or maliciously destroy or impair any natural resources and providing a penalty therefor.—Chapter 143.

Making it unlawful to injure, mutilate, cut down, or destroy any shade tree on any street or highway in villages.—Chapter 459.

Requiring all engines operated in, through or near forest, or brush land to be equipped with screen or wire netting between March 1 and December 1 to protect such forest or brush land from fire.—Chapter 494.

Appropriating $50,000 a year for five years for puchase of lands for reforestation.—Chapter 639.

Labor was not ignored in this session as is shown by the following laws:—

Prohibiting the employment of children between the ages of 14 and 16 years unless there is first obtained from the commissioner of labor, state factory inspector or any assistant factory inspector or from a judge of any county, municipal or juvenile court a written permit.—Chapter 479.

Requiring safety appliances and automatic feeding devices on corn shredders.—Chapter 466.

Empowering the state bureau of labor and industrial statistics to investigate contracts between employers and employees and making an appropriation therefor.—Chapter 453.

Increasing the scope of the state employment office located at Milwaukee.—Chapter 419.

Making it the absolute duty of an employer to guard or protect machines or appliances on all premises used for manufacturing purposes and to maintain same after installation.—Chapter 396.

Making it unlawful to employ labor by false representation and providing a penalty therefor.—Chapter 364.

Requiring owners or occupants of all public or quasi-public institutions and factories to keep exit doors unlocked during working hours and requiring all such exit doors to swing outward.—Chapter 378.

Specifying the manner in which indenture and apprenticeship contracts may be made, and providing a penalty for non-compliance therewith.—Chapter 347.

Requiring safety appliances on dangerous machinery and sanitary conditions in factories.—Chapter 470.

Requiring contractors and owners, when constructing buildings in cities, to take proper precautions for the protection of workmen and specifying what precautions are necessary.—Chapter 49.

Requiring owners of factories and manufacturing establishments to provide proper ventilation for same and prescribing a penalty for non-compliance.—Chapter 170.

Limiting the hours of labor on public buildings to eight hours per day and fixing a penalty for non-compliance.—Chapter 171.

Limiting the hours of labor of women to ten a day or fifty-five a week (Chapter 548); and of children under 16 years of age to eight a day and forty-eight a week (Chapter 479).

Theodore Roosevelt on the New Nationalism, 1910

In every wise struggle for human betterment one of the main objects, and often the only object, has been to achieve in large measure equality of opportunity. In the struggle for this great end, nations rise from barbarism to civilization, and through it people press forward from one stage of enlightenment to the next. One of the chief factors in progress is the destruction of special privilege. The essence of any struggle for healthy liberty has always been, and must always be, to take from some one man or class of men the right to enjoy power, or wealth, or position, or immunity, which has not been earned by service to his or their fellows. That is what you fought for in the Civil War, and that is what we strive for now.

At many stages in the advance of humanity, this conflict between the men who possess more than they have earned and the men who have earned more than they possess is the central condition of progress. In our day it appears as the struggle of free men to gain and hold the right of self-government as against the special interests, who twist the methods of free government into machinery for defeating the popular will. At every stage, and under all circumstances, the essence of the struggle is to equalize opportunity, destroy privilege, and give to the life and citizenship of every individual the highest possible value both to himself and to the commonwealth. That is nothing new. . . .

I stand for the square deal. But when I say that I am for the square deal, I mean not merely that I stand for fair play under the present rules of the game, but that I stand for having those rules changed so as to work for a more substantial equality of opportunity and of reward for equally good service. . . .

Now, this means that our government, national and state, must be freed from the sinister influence or control of special interests. Exactly as the special interests of cotton and slavery threatened our political integrity before the Civil War, so now the great special business interests too often control and corrupt the men and methods of government for their own profit. We must drive the special interests out of politics. . . .

The true friend of property, the true conservative, is he who insists that property shall be the servant and not the master of the commonwealth; who insists that the creature of man's making shall be the servant and not the master of the man who made it. The citizens of the United States must effectively control the mighty commercial forces which they have themselves called into being. . . .

Combinations in industry are the result of an imperative economic law which cannot be repealed by political legislation. The effort at prohibiting all combination has substantially failed. The way out lies, not in attempting to prevent such combinations, but in completely controlling them in the interest of the public welfare. For that purpose the Federal Bureau of Corporations is an agency of first importance. Its powers, and, therefore, its efficiency, as well as that of the Interstate Commerce Commission, should be largely increased. We have a right to expect from the Bureau of Corporations and from the Interstate Commerce Commission a very high grade of public service. We should be as sure of the proper conduct of the interstate railways and the proper management of interstate business as we are now sure of the conduct and management of the national banks, and we should have as effective supervision in one case as in the other. . . .

But I think we may go still further. The right to regulate the use of wealth in the public interest is universally admitted. Let us admit also the right to regulate the terms and conditions of labor, which is the chief element of wealth, directly in the interest of the common good. The fundamental thing to do for every man is to give him a chance to reach a place in which he will make the greatest possible contribution to the public welfare. Understand what I say there. Give him a chance, not push him up if he will not be pushed. Help any man who stumbles; if he lies down, it is a poor job to try to carry him; but if he is a worthy man, try your best to see that he gets a chance to show the worth that is in him. No man can be a good citizen unless he has a wage more than sufficient to cover the bare cost of living, and hours of labor short enough so that after his day's work is done he will have time and energy to bear his share in the management of the community, to help in carrying the general load. We keep countless men from being good citizens by the conditions of life with which we surround them. We need comprehensive workmen's compensation acts, both state and national laws to regulate child labor and work for women, and, especially, we need in our common schools not merely education in book learning, but also practical training for daily life and work. . . .

Woodrow Wilson on the New Freedom, 1913

Nowhere else in the world have noble men and women exhibited in more striking forms the beauty and the energy of sympathy and helpfulness and counsel in their efforts to rectify wrong, alleviate suffering, and set the weak in the way of strength and hope. We have built up, moreover, a great system of government, which has stood through a long age as in many respects a model for those who seek to set liberty upon foundations that will endure against fortuitous change, against storm and accident. Our life contains every great thing, and contains it in rich abundance.

But the evil has come with the good, and much fine gold has been corroded. With riches has come inexcusable waste. We have squandered a great part of what we might have used, and have not stopped to conserve the exceeding bounty of nature, without which our genius for enterprise would have been worthless and impotent, scorning to be careful, shamefully prodigal as well as admirably efficient. We have been proud of our industrial achievements, but we have not hitherto stopped thoughtfully enough to count the human cost, the cost of lives snuffed out, of energies overtaxed and broken, the fearful physical and spiritual cost to the men and women and children upon whom the dead weight and burden of it all has fallen pitilessly the years through. The groans and agony of it all had not yet reached our ears, the solemn, moving undertone of our life, coming up out of the mines and factories and out of every home where the struggle had its intimate and familiar seat. With the great Government went many deep secret things which we too long delayed to look into and scrutinize with candid, fearless eyes. The great Government we loved has too often been made use of for private and selfish purposes, and those who used it had forgotten the people.

At last a vision has been vouchsafed us of our life as a whole. We see the bad with the good, the debased and decadent with the sound and vital. With this vision we approach new affairs. Our duty is to cleanse, to reconsider, to restore, to correct the evil without impairing the good, to purify and humanize every process of our common life without weakening or sentimentalizing it. There has been something crude and heartless and unfeeling in our haste to succeed and be great. Our thought has been "Let every man look out for himself, let every generation look out for itself," while we reared giant machinery which made it impossible that any but those who stood at the levers of control should have a chance to look out for themselves. We had not forgotten our morals. We remembered well enough that we had set up a policy which was meant to serve the humblest as well as the most powerful, with an eye single to the standards of justice and fair play, and remembered it with pride. But we were very heedless and in a hurry to be great.

We have come now to the sober second thought. The scales of heedlessness have fallen from our eyes. We have made up our minds to square every process of our national life again with the standards we so proudly set up at the beginning and have always carried at our hearts. Our work is a work of restoration.

We have itemized with some degree of particularity the things that ought to be altered and here are some of the chief items: A tariff which cuts us off from our proper part in the commerce of the world, violates the just principles of taxation, and makes the Government a facile instrument in the hands of private interests; a banking and currency system based upon the necessity of the Government to sell its bonds fifty years ago and perfectly adapted to concentrating cash and restricting credits; an industrial system which, take it on all its sides, financial as well as administrative, holds capital in leading strings, restricts the liberties and limits the opportunities of labor, and exploits without renewing or conserving the natural resources of the country; a body of agricultural activities never yet given the efficiency of great business undertakings or served as it should be through the instrumentality of science taken directly to the farm, or afforded the facilities of credit best suited to its practical needs; water-courses undeveloped, waste places unreclaimed, forests untended, fast disappearing without plan or prospect of renewal, unregarded waste heaps at every mine. We have studied as perhaps no other nation has the most effective means of production, but we have not studied cost or economy as we should either as organizers of industry, as statesmen, or as individuals.

Nor have we studied and perfected the means by which government may be put at the service of humanity, in safeguarding the health of the Nation, the health of its men and its women and its children, as well as their rights in the struggle for existence. This is no sentimental duty. The firm basis of government is justice, not pity. These are matters of justice. There can be no equality of opportunity, the first essential of justice in the body politic, if men and women and children be not shielded in their lives, their very vitality, from the consequences of great industrial and social processes which they can not alter, control, or singly cope with. Society must see to it that it does not itself crush or weaken or damage its own constituent parts. The first duty of law is to keep sound the society it serves. Sanitary laws, pure food laws, and laws determining conditions of labor which individuals are powerless to determine for themselves are intimate parts of the very business of justice and legal efficiency. . . .

And yet it will be no cool process of mere science. The Nation has been deeply stirred, stirred by a solemn passion, stirred by the knowledge of wrong, of ideals lost, of government too often debauched and made an instrument of evil. The feelings with which we face this new age of right and opportunity sweep across our heartstrings like some air out of God's own presence, where justice and mercy are reconciled and the judge and the brother are one. We know our task to be no mere task of politics but a task which shall search us through and through, whether we be able to understand our time and the need of our people, whether we be indeed their spokesmen and interpreters, whether we have the pure heart to comprehend and the rectified will to choose our high course of action.

This is not a day of triumph; it is a day of dedication. Here muster, not the forces of party, but the forces of humanity. Men's hearts wait upon us; men's lives hang in the balance; men's hopes call upon us to say what we will do. Who shall live up to the great trust? Who dares fail to try? I summon all honest men, all patriotic, all forward-looking men, to my side. God helping me, I will not fail them, if they will but counsel and sustain me!

The Supreme Court Rejects Restrictions on Working Men's Hours: *Lochner* v. *New York*, 1904

Mr. Justice Peckham, . . . The statute [the labor law of New York State] necessarily interferes with the right of contract between the employer and employees, concerning the number of hours in which the latter may labor in the bakery of the employer. The general right to make a contract in relation to his business is part of the liberty of the individual protected by the Fourteenth Amendment of the Federal Constitution. Under that provision no State can deprive any person of life, liberty or property without due process of law. The right to purchase or to sell labor is part of the liberty protected by this amendment, unless there are circumstances which exclude the right. There are, however, certain powers, existing in the sovereignty of each State in the Union, somewhat vaguely termed police powers, the exact description and limitation of which have not been attempted by the courts. Those powers, broadly stated and without, at present, any attempt at a more specific limitation, relate to the safety, health, morals and general welfare of the public. . . .

The State, therefore, has power to prevent the individual from making certain kinds of contracts, and in regard to them the Federal Constitution offers no protection. If the contract be one which the State, in the legitimate exercise of its police power, has the right to prohibit, it is not prevented from prohibiting it by the Fourteenth Amendment. Contracts in violation of a statute, either of the Federal or state government, or a contract to let one's property for immoral purposes, or to do any other unlawful act, could obtain no protection from the Federal Constitution, as coming under the liberty of person or of free contract. . . .

It must, of course, be conceded that there is a limit to the valid exercise of the police power by the State. There is no dispute concerning this general proposition. Otherwise the Fourteenth Amendment would have no efficacy and the legislatures of the States would have unbounded power, and it would be enough to say that any piece of legislation was enacted to conserve the morals, the health or the safety of the people; such legislation would be valid, no matter how absolutely without foundation the claim might be. The claim of the police power would be a mere pretext—become another and delusive name for the supreme sovereignty of the State to be exercised free from constitutional restraint. This is not contended for. In every case that comes before this court, therefore, where legislation of this character is concerned and where the protection of the Federal Constitution is sought, the question necessarily arises: Is this a fair, reasonable and appropriate exercise of the police power of the State, or is it an unreasonable, unnecessary and arbitrary interference with the right of the individual to his personal liberty or to enter into those contracts in relation to labor which may seem to him appropriate or necessary for the support of himself and his family? Of course the liberty of contract relating to labor includes both parties to it. The one has as much right to purchase as the other to sell labor.

This is not a question of substituting the judgment of the court for that of the legislature. If the act be within the power of the State it is valid, although the judgment of the court might be totally opposed to the enactment of such a law. But the question would still remain: Is it within the police power of the State? and that question must be answered by the court.

The question whether this act is valid as a labor law, pure and simple, may be dismissed in a few words. There is no reasonable ground for interfering with the liberty of person or the right of free contract, by determining the hours of labor, in the occupation of a baker. There is no contention that bakers as a class are not equal in intelligence and capacity to men in other trades or manual occupations, or that they are not able to assert their rights and care for themselves without the protecting arm of the State, interfering with their independence of judgment and of action. They are in no sense wards of the State. Viewed in the light of a purely labor law, with no reference whatever to the question of health, we think that a law like the one before us involves neither the safety, the morals nor the welfare of the public, and that the interest of the public is not in the slightest degree affected by such an act. The law must be upheld, if at all, as a law pertaining to the health of the individual engaged in the occupation of a baker. It does not affect any other portion of the public than those who are engaged in that occupation. Clean and wholesome bread does not depend upon whether the baker works but ten hours per day or only sixty hours a week. The limitation of the hours of labor does not come within the police power on that ground.

It is a question of which of two powers or rights shall prevail—the power of the State to legislate or the right of the individual to liberty of person and freedom of contract. The mere assertion that the subject relates though but in a remote degree to the public health does not necessarily render the enactment valid. The act must have a more direct relation, as a means to an end, and the end itself must be appropriate and legitimate, before an act can be held to be valid which interferes with the general right of an individual to be free in his person and in his power to contract in relation to his own labor. . . .

We think the limit of the police power has been reached and passed in this case. There is, in our judgment, no reasonable foundation for holding this to be necessary or appropriate as a health law to safeguard the public health or the health of the individuals who are following the trade of a baker. If this statute be valid, and if, therefore, a proper case is made out in which to deny the right of an individual, *sui juris,* as employer or employee, to make contracts for the labor of the latter under the protection of the provisions of the Federal Constitution, there would seem to be no length to which legislation of this nature might not go. . . .

Statutes of the nature of that under review, limiting the hours in which grown and intelligent men may labor to earn their living, are mere meddlesome interferences with the rights of the individual, and they are not saved from condemnation by the claim that they are passed in the exercise of the police power and upon the subject of the health of the individual whose rights are interfered with, unless there be some fair ground, reasonable in and of itself, to say that there is material danger to the public health or to the health of the employees, if the hours of labor are not curtailed. . . .

Mr. Justice Holmes dissenting.

I regret sincerely that I am unable to agree with the judgment in this case, and that I think it my duty to express my dissent.

This case is decided upon an economic theory which a large part of the country does not entertain. If it were a question whether I agreed with that theory, I should desire to study it further and long before making up my mind. But I do not conceive that to be my duty, because I strongly believe that my agreement or disagreement has nothing to do with the right of a majority to embody their opinions in law. It is settled by various decisions of this court that state constitutions and state laws may regulate life in many ways which we as legislators might think as injudicious or if you like as tyrannical as this, and which equally with this interfere with the liberty to contract. Sunday laws and usury laws are ancient examples. A more modern one is the prohibition of lotteries. The liberty of the citizen to do as he likes so long as he does not interfere with the liberty of others to do the same, which has been a shibboleth for some well-known writers, is interfered with by school laws, by the Post Office, by every state or municipal institution which takes his money for purposes thought desirable, whether he likes it or not. The Fourteenth Amendment does not enact Mr. Herbert Spencer's Social Statics. . . . Some of [the previous regulation] laws embody convictions or prejudices which judges are likely to share. Some may not. But a constitution is not intended to embody a particular economic theory, whether of paternalism and the organic relation of the citizen to the State or of *laissez faire*. It is made for people of fundamentally differing views, and the accident of our finding certain opinions natural and familiar or novel and even shocking ought not to conclude our judgment upon the question whether statutes embodying them conflict with the Constitution of the United States. . . .

The Supreme Court Accepts Limits on Working Women's Hours: *Muller* v. *Oregon,* 1908

Justice Brewer. The single question is the constitutionality of the statute under which the defendant was convicted so far as it affects the work of a female in a laundry. . . .

. . . It may not be amiss, in the present case, before examining the constitutional question, to notice the course of legislation as well as expressions of opinion from other than judicial sources. In the brief filed by Mr. Louis D. Brandeis, for the defendant in error, is a very copious collection of all these matters. . . .

The legislation and opinions referred to [in the brief] may not be, technically speaking, authorities, and in them is little or no discussion of the constitutional question presented to us for determination, yet they are significant of a widespread belief that woman's physical structure, and the functions she performs in consequence thereof, justify special legislation restricting or qualifying the conditions under which she should be permitted to toil. . . .

That woman's physical structure and the performance of maternal functions place her at a disadvantage in the struggle for subsistence is obvious. This is especially true when the burdens of motherhood are upon her. Even when they are not, by abundant testimony of the medical fraternity continuance for a long time on her feet at work, repeating this from day to day, tends to injurious effects upon the body, and as healthy mothers are essential to vigorous offspring, the physical well-being of woman becomes an object of public interest and care in order to preserve the strength and vigor of the race. . . .

Differentiated by these matters from the other sex, she is properly placed in a class by herself, and legislation designed for her protection may be sustained, even when like legislation is not necessary for men and could not be sustained. It is impossible to close one's eyes to the fact that she still looks to her brother and depends upon him. Even though all restrictions on political, personal and contractual rights were taken away, and she stood, so far as statutes are concerned, upon an absolutely equal plane with him, it would still be true that she is so constituted that she will rest upon and look to him for protection; that her physical structure and a proper discharge of her maternal functions—having in view not merely her own health, but the well-being of the race—justify legislation to protect her from the greed as well as the passion of man. The limitations which this statute places upon her contractual powers, upon her right to agree with her employer as to the time she shall labor, are not imposed solely for her benefit, but also largely for the benefit of all. Many words cannot make this plainer. The two sexes differ in structure of body, in the functions to be performed by each, in the amount of physical strength, in the capacity for long-continued labor, particularly when done standing, the influence of vigorous health upon the future well-being of the race, the self-reliance which enables one to assert full rights, and in the capacity to maintain the struggle for subsistence. This difference justifies a difference in legislation and upholds that which is designed to compensate for some of the burdens which rest upon her. . . .

For these reasons, and without questioning in any respect the decision in *Lochner* v. *New York,* we are of the opinion that it cannot be adjudged that the act in question is in conflict with the Federal Constitution, so far as it respects the work of a female in a laundry, and the judgment of the Supreme Court of Oregon is

Affirmed.

✺ E S S A Y S

The contributions in this section treat the internal complexities of progressive political culture in two distinct areas. In the first essay, John Milton Cooper, Jr., a professor of history at the University of Wisconsin, compares and contrasts the vision of contending progressives Theodore Roosevelt and Woodrow Wilson in the 1912 presidential campaign. Emphasizing the candidates' differences over trust policy, leadership by personal example, and the role of self-interest, Cooper likens their struggle to one between a latter-day Thomas Jefferson and an Alexander Hamilton. In the second essay, Alice Kessler-Harris, a historian at Rutgers University, probes the passage of protective legislation for women, examining both the ambivalent impact of the new laws and the debate among women activists themselves as to the desirability of the legislation.

The New Nationalism Versus the New Freedom

JOHN MILTON COOPER, JR.

Few people at the time or later asked why such an extraordinary election had produced such an ordinary result. None of the three principal candidates faced the question squarely. Fittingly for a victor, [Woodrow] Wilson looked

Reprinted by permission of the publishers from *The Warrior and the Priest: Woodrow Wilson and Theodore Roosevelt* by John Milton Cooper, pp. 206–21, Cambridge, Mass.: The Belknap Press of Harvard University Press, Copyright © 1983 by the President and Fellows of Harvard College.

to the future. "The result fills me with hope that the thoughtful Progressive forces of the Nation may now at last unite," he announced the day after the election. "It is delightful to see the forces of the Democratic party united," Wilson told [William Jennings] Bryan more realistically, "and their union should now bring fruit of the richest sort." [William] Taft regretted that he had drawn only "the irreducible minimum of the Republican party," but he still hoped that "the incapacity of the Democratic party and their leader will make itself known in a way unmistakable." [Theodore] Roosevelt's crusading fervor cooled again as the returns came in, and he assessed the results with the greatest penetration. "The strength of the old party ties is shown by the fact that, although we carried the primaries two to one against Taft at the polls, about as many Republicans voted for him as for me," he told [Gifford] Pinchot. He also lamented the lack of difference that voters had evidently apprehended between himself and Wilson on critical issues, particularly the trusts.

Roosevelt had touched upon the two major factors that shaped the 1912 results and the main considerations in assessing the significance of his race against Taft and Wilson. The best feeling for how events would go had come from the Republican bosses when they had decided to block Roosevelt even at the cost of likely party defeat. They had bet that the agitation in their own party, in Roosevelt's new party, and among the Democrats would not shake the basic alignment of the electorate in their favor. The results bore out their hopes in three areas: first, the distribution of the votes in a pattern that nearly duplicated the 1908 result; second, the decline of Roosevelt's and other Republican insurgents' support after the convention; and third, the gap between the vote for Roosevelt and for the other Progressives. Further, without a doubt, the Old Guard completely controlled the Republican party.

In the longer view, the Old Guard's reckoning of the most important issues also came close to the mark. Economic concerns related to the tariff, currency, and trusts retained the greatest potency with the bulk of the voters. Roosevelt's troubles with the trust issue, first within his new party and then in the campaign against Wilson, had partially revealed his failure to alter people's overriding material concerns. "We have keyed our note very high," he admitted after the election, "probably too high for the people thoroughly to catch it, at least at first." Yet the outcome of the election augured little better for Wilson. He had done no more than hold on to the minority Democratic constituency that Bryan had built and maintained since 1896, mainly on the three main economic issues. Wilson probably could have won in a two-man race against Taft, but he almost certainly would have lost against Roosevelt alone. He owed his victory to the Republican split. As in the nomination, he won the election because of the peculiar conditions and his opponents' liabilities, not his own strengths. Whether Wilson could change that situation would determine both the success and duration of his presidency and the future prospects of his party.

The other factor that shaped the outcome in 1912, as well as its larger significance, was the electorate's perception of the differences between Roosevelt and Wilson. Most observers have believed that the voters saw little to choose between the two men on major issues. The persistence of the basic party alignments does suggest that in the absence of either a close contest or public perception of clear-cut differences on issues, the voters stuck with their habitual allegiances. Moreover, the increased Socialist vote may have reflected not so much growing radicalism as an undercurrent of dissatisfaction with the two leading candidates. The unevenness of the debate in 1912 probably also diminished public recognition of the differences between Roosevelt and Wilson. In presenting their respective campaign themes, they were like a ukulele and a violin. Roosevelt thumped away forcefully and repetitiously at a few chords, mainly trust regulation and stronger government. Wilson played deftly on a wide range of arguments, from representative government to economic competition to social renewal, with many specific adaptations and variations. Which approach was more effective never received a fair test, since they did not run a two-man race and since Roosevelt's campaign was cut short after he was shot. Under those circumstances many voters may have had understandable difficulty in perceiving differences between the two contenders.

A more important consideration is whether the voters' perceptions were correct. According to the great majority of analysts at the time and later, Roosevelt and Wilson did not differ greatly on the major issues. A classic statement of that view came a few years afterward when William Allen White wrote, "Between the New Nationalism and the New Freedom was that fantastic imaginary gulf that always has existed between tweedle-dum and tweedle-dee." Much evidence supports that view. Both Roosevelt and Wilson strained to accentuate their differences and thereby, albeit often unwittingly, misrepresented each other.

In his attempts to depict Wilson as a bogus progressive, Roosevelt wielded the charges of "toryism" and state rights, both to woo reform Democrats and to stave off insurgent Republican defections. The ease with which Wilson refuted the charges exposed their unfairness. Similarly, aspersions on "Professor Wilson" and his "academic theories" relegated Wilson to the mugwump stereotype Roosevelt had been using for nearly thirty years. Along with fulminations against false "idealism" and dishonest articulateness, such imputations of impracticality and of finickiness bordering on cowardice constituted the arrows most frequently flung against Wilson for the rest of Roosevelt's life. In 1912 Wilson neatly turned the "schoolteacher" charge to his own advantage as he contrasted his view of representative government with Roosevelt's supposedly overbearing ways.

Wilson in turn did Roosevelt and his views three disservices that were somewhat less serious. First, in his criticisms of Roosevelt's trust regulation approach, Wilson perhaps unintentionally reinforced suspicions that his opponent sought to serve big business. The prominence in Progressive councils of such tycoons as George W. Perkins and Frank Munsey lent apparent credence to those suspicions, and many Progressives distrusted those men's influence and motives. Moreover, the fears of Brandeis and others that the regulatory agencies would be subverted by big business did prove to be well founded under the Republican regimes of the 1920s. But to insinuate that Roosevelt believed in anything but the supremacy of government and subordination of business distorted his deepest values. Wilson's second disservice lay in helping to perpetuate notions about Roosevelt's alleged dictatorial tendencies. The ex-president's restraint when he was in power and his renunciation of office had abundantly proven the falsity of those notions. Finally, Wilson cast aspersions on the sincerity of Roosevelt's reform convictions. When he declined to call the Progressives by their chosen name and harped on their lack of support from La Follette and other Republican insurgents, Wilson was also playing the game of trying to steal Roosevelt's supporters. Minimizing the differences between Roosevelt and the Republican Old Guard was as unfair as Roosevelt's tarring him with the state-rights brush.

The distortions by both candidates arose from the heat of the campaign but also in part from the two men's agreement on many specific issues. Roosevelt and Wilson had to play up their differences because on matters of immediate concern, their real differences were few. Their outward differences in style, following, and party spirit lacked substance, even at the outset of the campaign. As the editors of *The Letters of Theodore Roosevelt* have pointed out, despite Roosevelt's denunciations of the Democratic platform, the only differences between it and the Progressive platform were in the Progressives' endorsement of tariff protection and woman suffrage, silence on the trusts, and slightly stronger advocacy of aid to labor, as contrasted with the Democrats' friendlier posture toward farmers. In the course of the campaign Wilson endorsed virtually every specific reform measure Roosevelt favored, with the principal exception of woman suffrage, and he frequently reasserted his partial sympathy for tariff protection. During his first term as president, as Link has observed, Wilson enacted most of the 1912 Progressive platform, including abolition of child labor and legislation favoring organized labor, and he switched to support of woman suffrage in 1915 and 1916.

Their unanimity on current issues extended to their limited concern about two important matters. One was the question on which they parted company in 1912—woman suffrage. In fact, neither man felt strongly about the issue, regarding it as entirely a matter of expediency. Roosevelt probably held more traditional views of women's roles and sex difference, but because he needed the support of such women reformers as Jane Addams, he endorsed nationwide woman suffrage in 1912. Wilson, who had taught in a woman's college and had two suffragette daughters, declined either to support or to oppose the proposition as a federal question, mainly out of deference to antisuffrage Democratic elements in the South and Northeast.

The other issue on which they shared a limited concern was race. Roosevelt qualified as the more self-conscious white racist of the two. He incorporated racial categories into his basic views, and he believed that blacks were decidedly inferior to whites. As president he had made such gestures as inviting Booker T. Washington to dinner at the White House in 1901 and appointing a well-qualified black man, Dr. William D. Crum, to head the Charleston customhouse in 1905. But Roosevelt had also meted out harsh and hasty punishment to the regiment of black troops accused of starting a riot in Brownsville, Texas, in 1906, and he had tried to woo southern whites to the Republicans by loosening party ties to blacks. His search for southern support culminated in 1912 with the Progressives' open renunciation of federal involvement in race relations. As a result, the Progressives' southern efforts gained some ground with Roosevelt placing second in eight of the eleven former Confederate states.

For a white man born and raised in the nineteenth-century South, Wilson held surprisingly mild racial views. As a young man he had defended efforts to educate blacks, and he had spread disquiet among his southern relatives by inviting Booker T. Washington to his inauguration as president of Princeton in 1902. Although he had rarely written or talked much about racial matters, Wilson believed that blacks were not innately inferior to whites and would eventually, probably in two or three centuries, achieve a measure of economic and political, if not social, equality in America. Such views had hardly impelled him to challenge discrimination against or neglect of blacks, however. At Princeton Wilson had maintained the university's long-standing ban on admitting blacks. During the 1912 campaign he did give mild encouragement to a black movement in support of his candidacy led by Bishop Alexander Walters and W. E. B. Du Bois, but he maintained his distance from them. As president, Wilson sanctioned attempts by several of his southern Cabinet members to introduce segregation into federal departments. His administration also witnessed a decline in the percentage of government jobs held by blacks, although the numbers of black jobholders increased somewhat.

The similarities and agreements between Roosevelt's and Wilson's positions did not mean, however, that no important differences separated them. The view expressed in White's "tweedle-dum and tweedle-dee" simile was wrong. During the presidential campaign, clear signs of their ideological divergences surfaced. Further, when one juxtaposes the New Nationalism with the New Freedom, as White did, the differences between them become unmistakable. The 1912 campaign grew so heated not only because of the main contenders' clashing ambitions and ingrained combativeness but also because of their recognition of the ideological gulf between them. Mutual distortions and the requirements of their political situations prevented the two men from exposing the split as clearly as they could have done, but the outlines of their divergence showed up on the two issues they discussed most in 1912—the trusts and leadership.

The trust issue might appear to be another area of agreement masked by each man's misrepresentations of the other's position. Wilson's inconsistency about bigness and Roosevelt's retreat to reaffirmation of the antitrust laws did make it difficult to perceive any great difference between them. Further, Roosevelt never went so far as Croly earlier and Lippmann later in equating bigness in business with efficiency or in portraying big businessmen as quasi-statesmen who were coming to be less and less motivated by profits and more and more by altruism. Similarly, Wilson never consistently adhered to either Brandeis's equation of bigness with inefficiency or his convictions that the overriding concern of businessmen with profits was ineradicable. The Wilson administration later did mount a vigorous antitrust drive, but it was hardly an all-out assault on large corporations. After the United States entered World War I, Wilson presided over the kind of government-business partnership in managing the economy that had earlier been envisioned by apostles of the New Nationalism.

Roosevelt and Wilson were not always consistent when they debated the economic implications of bigness in 1912, yet their arguments reflected economic considerations that pointed to their own deeper concerns. They disagreed over bigness less in the abstract value they put on it than in their interpretations of facts about it. In his strictures against "toryism" and "flint-lock" thinking, Roosevelt implicitly accepted three propositions: that the biggest corporations had for the most part achieved their stature through efficient competition, that large corporations were here to stay, and that present economic conditions represented progress. But for him those were not the most important concerns. When he expounded on such matters as "conduct not size," how businesses treated workers and consumers, and putting "the hand of government" on them, he was voicing his true concern. He believed that the main economic task of government lay in protecting the victims and clients of large-scale enterprise through greatly strengthened regulation and supervision. Some might hold that he was anticipating John Kenneth Galbraith's concept of "countervailing power" between big business and big government. Actually, Roosevelt wanted an overwhelming governmental supremacy that did, in a nonpejorative sense, deserve the designation "paternalism." His vision of public supervision and protection forecast much of the twentieth-century welfare state from a standpoint that resembled approaches taken by his contemporaries among British Liberals, and after World War I by British Conservatives and by various European spokesmen of the center and right, particularly in Italy and Germany. This approach accepted corporate roles and responsibilities in the economy and sought governmental economic management, not so much out of compassion for or identification with the individuals affected, as in the interest of social harmony and national strength. To turn Roosevelt's own epithet nonpejoratively back on himself, this was a "tory" approach to the welfare state. It has remained rare in the United States.

Wilson disagreed on all points. In his distinction between big business and the trusts and in his insistence on restoring competition, he implicitly accepted three opposite economic propositions: that comparatively few of the biggest corporations had achieved their stature through efficient competition, that those corporations were not necessarily here to stay, and that present conditions did not always represent progress over the past. Wilson advanced his side of the argument less clearly than Roosevelt did on those matters. For him, too, the most important concerns lay elsewhere. In his discussion of the trusts Wilson emphasized two considerations. One was governmental regulation of competition. Far from believing in laissez-faire, Wilson maintained that government must intervene actively and continuously in the economy because "unregulated competition" had resulted in the growth of the trusts and the stifling of competition. The other consideration he stressed was the entry of new competitors into the market. Contrary to their public images, Wilson held much more dynamic economic views than

Roosevelt. He believed that the main task of reform was to revitalize the economy through governmental actions to open the market to fresh entrants. Wilson also forecast a central element in the twentieth-century welfare state—public action to promote the economic interests of the less advantaged. This was, in later usage, a "liberal" approach, and it has been at the heart of the major American sources of support for the welfare state.

Roosevelt's and Wilson's concerns behind the trust issue pointed to the basic divergence in their approach to politics—the place of self-interest in the pursuit of social good. This appeared most clearly during the 1912 campaign in their conceptions of leadership. It was fitting that their differences should emerge most sharply there, for at heart each man cared much more about politics than economics. Roosevelt's repeated, sometimes almost savage attacks on Wilson's governmental views indicated that he once more sensed the "unheroic" underpinnings of Wilson's politics. Because he believed so fervently in the need for transcendent national ideals, Roosevelt probably sincerely mistook Wilson's position for a state-rights, limited-government viewpoint. Innocently or not, however, he misrepresented the issue between them. It was not then and never would be the strength or activism of government. Rather, it was the proper method of leadership and, thereby, the true purpose of government.

Wilson grasped and articulated the essential political issue between them much better than Roosevelt. The leadership issue boiled down to inspiration versus education. With his prophetic, evangelical approach Roosevelt sought, in the root sense of the word, to inspire. He wanted to breathe into people a resolve to be better than they were, to instill in them devotion to larger goals and greater effort. With his "schoolmaster" approach to leadership, Wilson similarly sought, in the root sense, to educate. He wished to draw out of people recognition of their own best interests, to let them enlighten their ordinary pursuits. The issue between them over the purposes of government came down to one of the paternalism versus representation. Roosevelt believed that in the right kind of government, leaders inspired by visions of unifying, uplifting national ideals would guide the people. For Wilson, popular interests would be genuinely represented by leaders who listened to the people. Wilson repeatedly urged audiences in the 1912 campaign not to vote for him unless he was expressing their aspirations and beliefs. "I do not wish to be your master," he avowed at one point. "I wish to be your spokesman."

Those arguments infuriated Roosevelt. Besides seeming to suggest that Roosevelt had dictatorial tendencies, Wilson's contentions sounded suspiciously like excuses for governmental inaction. Often labeled laissez-faire, commendations of individual initiative and self-reliance and condemnations of governmental intervention had formed staple political arguments in the United States and Britain for nearly a century. Roosevelt understandably seized upon Wilson's arguments for self-reliance to scorn him as a false progressive. Though plausible, Roosevelt's reasoning was fallacious. Wilson's concern for self-reliance sprang not from any attachment to limited-government views, but from his anticipation of the most telling criticism of the modern welfare state. Both friends and foes of that view have deplored the proposition that governmental promotion of social welfare tends to convert recipients of aid into wards of the state. Wilson perceptively condemned the paternalistic implications in Roosevelt's position.

Wilson's criticisms also exposed a central element in Roosevelt's political approach—his aristocratic assumptions. Although Roosevelt sincerely believed in broad popular participation in politics, he never thought that that offered a cure-all for the problems of a modern industrial society, as many Bryanites, insurgent Republicans, and Progressives did. Roosevelt wanted to preserve the heroic virtues of disinterested service and nonmaterial goals. He continued to seek ways to promote such virtues among citizens whose main concerns were economic. Roosevelt made a noble effort with the Progressives in 1912, but he fell short, as he had before, largely because he lacked the catalyst of a crisis in which to rouse people to higher duties. "Unfortunately, it is not with us," he told a fellow Progressive just after the election, "as it was with the Republicans in [18]56 after their defeat. We have not the clear-cut issues as to which we take one side and our opponents the other side, and as to which the conscience of the people is deeply stirred." From 1910 through 1912 Roosevelt had once more tried and failed to instill a sense of unifying national purpose analogous to the Civil War spirit.

Roosevelt similarly exposed two weaknesses in Wilson's political approach. One was his lack of realism on the trust issue. Roosevelt raised a valid objection when he doubted whether Wilson could succeed with trust-busting any better than Taft or, although he did not say so, himself. When he argued that the size of firms was a less important concern than their social and economic role, particularly as gauged by their treatment of workers and consumers, Roosevelt made an incisive point, although Wilson agreed with him to an extent. Yet Wilson, like Brandeis, did betray an old-fashioned faith that people acting freely in the marketplace would serve the larger good of society. Roosevelt showed greater originality when he questioned the social and economic efficacy of marketplace behavior. His criticisms did not mean that he had a better solution to the trust problem, but he did come closer to recognizing the overriding need to make large-scale private economic power accountable to society through its governmental representatives.

Roosevelt's and Wilson's differences over the trust issue had profounder economic implications than either man probably realized. In common with a few other analysts and some union leaders, such as Samuel Gompers of the American Federation of Labor, Roosevelt appeared willing to cast aside traditional values of individual ownership and management for the sake of higher wages, better working conditions, fairer prices, and more wholesome products. Roosevelt sometimes used the word "collectivism" to describe his arguments. He evidently did accept at least in part the idea of abandoning individual autonomy to collective bodies, not only for corporations but also for unions and government agencies, for the sake of better results from the economic process. Wilson, like Brandeis, though less consistently so, adhered to the older ideal of freedom through individual ownership and management and the argument that individual entrepreneurship remained essential to ensure the inventiveness and initiative that were essential to economic growth and improvement. Wilson's conception of the economy was, therefore, at once more traditional and more dynamic than Roosevelt's.

The second weakness in Wilson's politics that Roosevelt uncovered was his belief in meritocracy. Despite his emphasis on social renewal from below, Wilson admitted that he cared most about upward mobility for the most able people, particularly those from the middle classes. Roosevelt correctly questioned whether such mobility was the most important consideration in a modern industrial society, particularly as opposed to higher wages and safer working conditions for industrial workers and lower prices and better-quality products for consumers. Although Wilson defined the middle classes broadly and favored aid to industrial workers and consumer groups, he did talk in the 1912 campaign as if restored competition and greater upward mobility offered social and economic panaceas. Wilson's comparative lack of economic realism and his meritocratic sympathies sprang from narrowness in apprehending some contemporary problems. Between 1910 and the 1912 election Wilson had shown himself to be a deeper, more insightful political thinker than Roosevelt, but he had not yet matched the ex-president in perceptiveness about current economic and social conditions.

Roosevelt's and Wilson's respective political weaknesses reflected both their personal projections and their social and economic backgrounds. When he continued to uphold heroic virtues, Roosevelt was once more exhorting Americans to emulate him by rising above limitations, renouncing crass commercial goals, and exalting public service. He remained an aristocratic conservative in his views, which accounted for much of the friction with his Progressive followers. Roosevelt had originally fashioned his political viewpoint as part of an effort to preserve a dominant Republican party representing the nation's economically and socially advantaged groups and regions. He had first joined the insurgent Republicans and then bolted with the Progressives in large part because the would-be beneficiaries of his policies had spurned him. Roosevelt often talked about seeking democratic Jeffersonian ends through nationalistic Hamiltonian means. With the Progressives, however, he was pursuing what he regarded as Hamiltonian goals of transcendent nationalism and disinterested leadership through a Jeffersonian following bent on promoting its own interests. The combination spelled trouble for leader and party alike.

Wilson's meritocratic sympathies made a better fit with his partisan and social situation. Despite long residence in the Northeast and his association with Princeton, Wilson had never ceased to identify himself with hardworking, upwardly striving people from the South and West. He was one of them, and when he exalted such people as the indispensable agents of social renewal, he too was urging Americans to emulate him. Wilson fell quickly and easily in step with the Bryanite wing of the Democrats because he could sincerely tell them what they wanted to hear. Despite a lingering aroma of farmer radicalism, those Democrats were mainly people like Wilson; they were aspiring middle-class southerners and westerners, who resented the economic and cultural domination of the Northeast and wanted the same things he wanted. With the Democratic progressives, Wilson had a Jeffersonian following seeking its own interests. Whether he knew it or not, he was also a leader out of the mold of Jefferson, a man who was intellectually and socially detached from his followers but spiritually in tune with them and their aspirations.

To an extent, Roosevelt and Wilson stood as twentieth-century analogues to Hamilton and Jefferson. The passage of time and the changed face of the United States had introduced differences between them and their mentors. Unlike Hamilton and Jefferson, they did not differ over governmental power and centralization, despite Roosevelt's assertions to the contrary. Nor did they laud either manufacturing or agriculture as morally or socially superior to the other. Roosevelt, with his ranching and hunting background, was more of a devotee of rural life, but he also held the more approving view of large-scale industry. Roosevelt likewise departed from Hamilton in despising plutocracy and in wanting to curb and channel the influence of wealth instead of seeking to work through it. But Roosevelt and Wilson did differ fundamentally over the same matters—their conceptions of human nature and the role of self-interest in society—that they believed had separated Hamilton and Jefferson. Roosevelt's New Nationalism and Wilson's New Freedom presented distinct views of how to promote social good, based upon what each man to a degree regarded as Hamiltonian and Jeffersonian conceptions of people's nature and interests.

Roosevelt remained, by his lights, self-consciously Hamiltonian and anti-Jeffersonian in his views. For all his buoyancy and his spirits, Roosevelt was not an optimistic man, and his politics were not based upon an optimistic view of people. He regarded individuals' selfish, private interests as not only barriers to the attainment of public good but also sources of antisocial passion and potential civil conflict. Yet he did not rely mainly on repression and authority, except occasionally during such periods of heightened tension as the mid-1890s and, later, World War I. Rather, he exhorted people to pursue higher national ideals. But at no time did Roosevelt believe that simply letting people have what they wanted or making them happy was a means to social betterment. For him, those ways led to materialist degeneracy, a widening gulf between greedy plutocrats and the envious masses, social revolution, and national doom. As with himself, Roosevelt never fully trusted what he perceived to be other people's basic instincts. He could never relax in the pursuit of self-overcoming virtues, for others as well as himself.

Roosevelt's failure to convert a majority or even a substantial minority of his countrymen to pursuit of higher goals was foreordained. Even if he had gotten the breaks he needed in 1912, he would ultimately have failed to get his insurgent Republican or Progressive followers to renounce thier own interests in favor of national ideals, just as he had failed earlier with the Old Guard. Despite his pessimism about people, Roosevelt indulged in fantastic naiveté in believing that many could be persuaded voluntarily to renounce their interests more than briefly. Further, he never seemed to recognize either that the dominant groups in society would continue to fare better than others under his programs or that it was unjust to ask the disadvantaged to forgo their interests. Despite his frequent preachments about realism and practicality, Roosevelt often was an "idealist" in two pejorative senses of the term—as an impractical visionary and as someone who did not recognize the selfishness in his views.

Roosevelt's misfortune lay in not having a war in which he could act upon his beliefs. His worst time began later, after the outbreak of World War I, which he viewed as a perfect historical occasion for his kind of heroic leadership. He knew he required a great national crisis, like Lincoln's with the Civil War, to practice his politics to the fullest. Only in such a situation could he have succeeded in rousing people and parties to self-sacrificing service and heroic action. Whether or not he could have wrought permanent political changes, Roosevelt would almost certainly have altered the subsequent history of the Republican party. With his heroic virtues and renunciation of materialism, he represented a road not taken for American conservatism.

During the 1912 campaign Wilson came closer than at any other time in his political career to becoming an exponent of what he saw as Jeffersonian views. Although his religious background helped make him cheerfully fatalistic about himself, Wilson's politics were based upon an optimistic view of people. He regarded individuals' selfish interests as not only inescapable facts of life but as instruments that must be used to improve society. Wilson differed from many fellow Democrats in his intellectual detachment, his continuing admiration for Hamilton, and—despite his self-proclaimed scorn for experts—his recognition of the need for trained personnel and specialized knowledge in governing a modern industrial nation. But he agreed with his Bryanite party brethren in seeking to satisfy the desires of a majority of the people. Wilson stressed freedom as the essential means to pursue social betterment because he believed that the continual rising of talent from below would ensure energy, growth, and renewal in society. In the sharpest contrast to Roosevelt, Wilson professed not to fear social conflict, and his nonchalance about the prospects of revolution recalled Jefferson's quip about watering "the tree of liberty . . . with the blood of tyrants."

But Wilson did not offer a total contrast to Roosevelt. If he had been consistent, he would have embraced self-interested competition as the best means to improve society. Wilson continued to eschew class politics and to appeal to elevated national ideals, with the result that he often sounded like Roosevelt. Their apparent similarity was deceptive. Rather than accepting or rejecting self-interested competition, Wilson maintained that people could pursue their own interests and a unifying national purpose at the same time. In a speech in October 1912 Wilson asserted, "We must not settle the war of classes by enabling one class to overcome another, even though it be the bigger class of the two, but we must overcome class prejudice and class warfare by making classes understand one another and that there is a common interest which transcends every particular interest in the United States." Roosevelt would have put it differently, but he pursued the same goal.

Wilson was more realistic than Roosevelt in recognizing that a better society could come only by serving the interests of a majority. He did not entirely renounce service to particular interest groups. He claimed that aid to industrial workers and farmers would help such large and vital segments of society that everyone's interests would be served. Wilson did not yet embrace the proposition that government should foster the interests of less-advantaged groups or regions, but he had gone a long way toward the "broker state," which became the central political concept in support of governmental aid to social welfare and regulation of private economic activity in twentieth-century America. Recurrent debates over the national purpose and outcries against special interests have shown that the greatest weakness of the broker state concept is the point that Roosevelt attacked—the degeneration of interest-group politics into narrow conflicts that strain national cohesion and debase politics into a scramble for favors. Wilson had no answer to Roosevelt's questions about how to promote national unity, except to work through coalitions of interests. His performance at that task played a big part in shaping not only his presidency and the fortunes of his party but also the main course of twentieth-century domestic American politics.

The confrontation between Roosevelt and Wilson did not end with the 1912 election. The two men had taken each other's measure and tested their differences. In a chastened mood following his defeat, Roosevelt temporarily reverted to a milder attitude toward his opponent. Once more he privately called Wilson the Democrats' "strongest man" and a good prospect for presidential success. That mood quickly passed. By late November Roosevelt confided, "I think him a very adroit man; I do not think he has any fixity of conviction." Wilson said little about Roosevelt even in private, but his actions as president soon showed that his predecessor and rival occupied a prominent spot in his mind.

Thus far, foreign affairs, which had been an important element in Roosevelt's break with Taft, had not entered his confrontation with Wilson. Except for two passing allusions by Roosevelt and one by Wilson, neither man mentioned foreign affairs during the 1912 campaign. Shortly before his inauguration, Wilson told a friend in Princeton, "It would be an irony of fate if my administration had to deal with foreign problems, for all my preparation has been in domestic matters." The irony of fate overtook Wilson as soon as he took office, and foreign affairs swiftly furnished a new field of conflict between him and Roosevelt. Once World War I broke out in August 1914, their confrontation rose to a pitch of fury that not only shaped the rest of both men's lives but also affected critical events for the United States and the world.

The Ironies of Protective Labor Legislation

ALICE KESSLER-HARRIS

In various incarnations the search for protection extends over an astonishingly long period of time—longer than the battle for woman suffrage itself. Its origins encompass laws that applied to all workers, male and female, as well

Excerpted from *Out to Work: A History of Wage-Earning Women in the United States*, pp. 180–181, 183–188, 195–198, 205–209, 212–213, by Alice Kessler-Harris. Copyright © 1982 by Alice Kessler-Harris. Used by permission of Oxford University Press, Inc.

as to women and children and to children alone. Legislation based on women's special position derived directly from the search for general protection and was alternately rejected, then supported, then rejected again by the organized women's movement as well as by wage-earning women. Positions fluctuated with the changing meaning of "protection" as well as with changing labor force circumstances. Because the idea of "protection" appeared in different guises at different times, it drew support from new coalitions of supporters on each occasion. It pitted working women against working men, and employers against legislators. Just as often, it aligned unionists with manufacturers and set women in unions against those outside them.

The rubric of protection encompasses a huge variety of laws whose scope differed from state to state. Two intentions emerge clearly. Both rested on a perceived need to redress what labor economist Elizabeth Faulkner Baker called "inequality of bargaining power." The first kind of labor legislation aimed to preserve the worker's independence by providing safe and clean working conditions, minimizing health hazards, putting a floor under wages, shortening hours, and eventually by compensating workers for job-related accidents. The struggle over this so-called regulatory legislation is part of the history of the progressive period. The often arbitrary laws that resulted had long-range consequences for men and women in the labor market. The second kind of labor legislation—restrictive or prohibitive laws—aimed at excluding some workers from certain kinds of jobs altogether. These jobs might be defined by the time and place where they were performed or by the nature of the task. This second series of laws applied almost exclusively to women. Between the two categories, no rigid lines existed. Laws that regulated lighting, seating, and ventilation arrangements under which women could work often served in fact to prevent women from being offered certain kinds of jobs.

By and large, this legislation, because it confirmed changes in the number and kinds of women earning a living and simultaneously regulated their opportunities to work, tended to reflect the prevailing sense of women's proper roles and the tension and the conflict in their work lives. Protective legislation divided workers into those who could and could not perform certain roles. It therefore bears some of the responsibility for successfully institutionalizing women's secondary labor force position. . . .

Even after the Civil War the possibility of justice without gender distinction persisted among working people. When the Knights of Labor introduced demands for the eight-hour day in 1871, its founder, Uriah Stephens, argued the advantages of shorter hours for workers who would "have time for social enjoyment and intellectual improvement, and be enabled to reap the advantages conferred by the Labor-saving machinery which their brains have created." A sprinkling of states responded to such pressure. South Carolina and Maryland passed laws mandating a ten-hour day for all industrial workers. Eleven more states declared eight- or ten-hour "legal" days—but without enacting enforcement machinery. Some states asserted the right to regulate working relations on the most general grounds of health and police power regulation.

But states that tried to legislate working conditions for adult males found their laws unceremoniously struck down in the courts. The New York State Supreme Court decision that voided an 1884 act prohibiting the manufacture of cigars in tenement houses illustrates the point. The court could not see how "the cigarmaker is to be improved in his health or his morals by forcing him from his home and its hallowed associations and beneficent influences to ply his trade elsewhere." It left open the question of whether states had special interest in the health of their citizens, and subsequent legal battles turned on the issue of whether the state's police power could properly be used to protect workers.

The U.S. Supreme Court dealt this doctrine a mortal blow in 1905 when it decided against a New York state law limiting the hours of bakers to ten per day. The issue was not the hours of labor, the Court argued in *Lochner* v. *New York,* but the bread itself. "Clean, and wholesome bread does not depend upon whether a baker works but 10 hours per day," said the Court, concluding that the statute was therefore "an illegal interference with the rights of individuals to make contracts." The decision reflected prevailing opinions. It decisively rejected the idea that a shared sense of justice ought to influence working hours and conditions. Legislators and courts by and large agreed that freely negotiated contracts were necessary to success in a society that offered readily attainable upward mobility.

Under these circumstances only skilled trade unionists managed to achieve significant reductions in hours or to play a role in determining their own work practices. By the 1890s, such groups as cigar makers, builders, and machinists regularly worked only fifty hours a week. But there were precious few women among them. Textile mills, laundries, and the garment industry, all heavily women-employing, still averaged twelve-hour days, and five-and-a-half or six-day weeks.

While the use of state power to limit hours and to regulate work conditions in the interest of the general welfare was still in question, special arguments based on notions of female domesticity began to emerge for restricting women workers. Since the courts rejected the assertion that the general welfare demanded regulation for all workers, proponents moved to the position that women in their capacity as child bearers and rearers served the state's welfare in a special way. The idea that their service to the state entitled women to special protection spread rapidly.

Tactically, the argument grew out of the difficulty in getting any kind of protective legislation past lawmakers and courts. Much of the energy behind attempts to limit the hours of women and children in the 1880s and 1890s came from those who believed that women could be an "opening wedge" in obtaining laws for all the unorganized. Shorter hours for some, they argued, along with adequate factory sanitation and safety devices, would inevitably lead to better conditions for all workers. Economist Elizabeth Brandeis acerbically concluded that Massachusetts workers had decided to "fight the battle behind the women's petticoats." But a substantial amount of pressure for such legislation came from those who genuinely felt that women's peculiarly vulnerable position demanded special protection. When this argument was made by unskilled workers competing with each other for jobs, it carried conviction. Their pressure, for example, encouraged Massachusetts lawmakers in 1874 to limit the labor of women and children to sixty hours per week.

Arguments for special protection for women were marked by sympathy and genuine concern. But there was ideological danger in asserting women's weakness. Originally the organized feminist movement staked its claim to women's rights, including the suffrage, firmly on the conviction that women were more like men than unlike them and were therefore entitled to all human rights. By the 1880s, an important wing of the woman suffrage movement had reversed its position. Woman's special sphere, her special sensibilities nurtured in the home, feminists like Lucy Stone argued, developed unique attributes that required representation in the political process. Reformers like Helen Campbell and Annie McLean held that these same attributes—compassion, nurturance, a better-developed sense of morality—unfitted her for the competitive economic struggle. In the unfortunate event that women were forced into the wage labor force these special sensibilities must be preserved.

The argument provided justification not merely for regulating, but for prohibiting altogether, the work of women in certain occupations. If wage work was necessary it had to be bounded by regulations that would preserve woman's body, mind, and morals for home roles. The argument was implicit in all the official investigations of this period, and became the articulated basis of legislation after 1900. Agitation for protection of wage-earning women now rested squarely on the assumption that all women were homemakers without sufficient skill to compete in the labor market. Proponents of protection did not declare all workers in need of it. Rather, they claimed special privilege for the home and motherhood. . . .

In this climate, legally imposed limitations on the kinds of work women could do took form. . . . In 1881 [the] state [of California] passed a measure denying women the right to work in places that sold alcoholic beverages. The state Supreme Court quickly invalidated it. The state constitution, it ruled, prohibited legislation "either directly or indirectly incapacitating or disabling a woman from entering or pursuing any business, vocation, or profession" open to men. But courts in Ohio and Washington upheld similar statutes as valid exercises of police power, and other forms of prohibition emerged quickly. Most were based on physical and moral grounds. Selling liquor might expose women to lewd men and threaten their innocence. Grinding and polishing metal might clog women's lungs with dust. Work in underground mines (never prevalent in the United States) would coarsen women's gentle natures. Later women were denied work as messengers because Western Union could not guarantee who might open the door to them. Operating elevators, reading meters, becoming letter carriers, and driving taxis were among the erratic series of occupations sporadically denied to women.

A surprising absence of controversy about such legal prohibitions reveals the strength of popular beliefs in women's assigned roles. More often than not, such legislation merely confirmed custom, and courts readily upheld it.

Protests tended to be individual—like those of women who disguised themselves as men in order to obtain jobs—and quickly stifled. When successful, such instances never found their way into the public record. But once caught, women who had tried to pass as men received stiff punishments. One young woman drew six months' imprisonment in New York's Blackwell's Island for dressing like a man. A contemporary noted that "the indictment in her case said that 'she wore men's clothes, she being a woman,' as if the offense she had committed was that of being a woman."

More controversy surrounded legislation that attempted to regulate the conditions under which women could earn wages. Ohio passed the first maximum-hour law for women—a ten-hour day—in 1852. Minnesota, Massachusetts, and Illinois followed after the Civil War. The first legal restrictions against night work for women appeared in Massachusetts in 1890. These were at first isolated instances which state judicial opinion generally upheld. The Pennsylvania Superior Court, in an 1896 decision, the first on the sixty-hour week and twelve-hour day for women, declared: . . . "Adult females are a class as distinct as minors, separated by natural conditions from all other laborers, and are so constituted as to be unable to endure physical exertion and exposure to the extent and degree that is not harmful to adult workers."

In rapid succession, legislators in Nebraska, Washington, and Oregon passed statutes limiting the workday for women. State courts upheld them. Shared assumptions about women's natural weakness underlay their actions. "That which must necessarily affect any great number of women who are the mothers of succeeding generations must necessarily affect the public welfare and morals," argued Washington's Supreme Court in 1902. It was no surprise to many and an enormous relief to proponents when in 1908 the U.S. Supreme Court set its seal on the motherhood argument in response to the famous Brandeis brief in the case of *Muller* v. *Oregon.*

Louis Brandeis and his sister-in-law Josephine Goldmark, working at the time for the National Consumers' League, correctly reasoned that to persuade the court that shorter hours for women were in fact conducive to the general welfare required evidence that long hours were inimical to health and safety. In their carefully prepared argument, presented to the Court in defense of Oregon's ten-hour law, they asserted that woman's "special physical organization," her child-bearing and maternal functions, and the need to prevent "laxity of moral fibre" which "follows physical debility" all required restricting her hours of labor to ten per day. The authors used strong language: "women are fundamentally weaker than men in all that makes for endurance: in muscular strength, in nervous energy, in the powers of persistent attention and application." Quoting extensively from state and federal labor officials, the brief argued: "They must have vacations, and they break down in health rapidly." It cited physicians who asserted "the periodic semi-pathological state of health of women" and their greater predisposition to disease. It dwelt on "pale, crooked, and sickly-looking" women and children who worked sixty or more hours per week. It pointed to women who spent "a good part of their Sundays . . . in bed and recuperating for the next week's demands." Neurasthenia, back troubles, pyrosis, constipation, vertigo, and headaches were the least of the problems identified. Edema, varicose veins, displacement of the uterus, throat and lung diseases were said to follow from excessive work.

The brief thus combined arguments for woman's role with data on her relative lack of physical stamina. And the Court, in affirming Oregon's statute, found this a comfortable resting place. "Women's physical stature and the performance of maternal functions place her at a disadvantage," it declared, and went from affirming woman's essential role in maintaining the "strength and vigor of the race" to accepting the notion that women might legally be wards of the state. . . . But the court did not decide by how much the state could limit women's contractual rights to negotiate their hours of labor. What was a reasonable working day for women? Ten hours? Nine? Eight?

The decision electrified the field of protective legislation, reviving long-dormant restrictive measures. Hours were the first and prime target. Between 1909 and 1917, nineteen states passed laws restricting women's working day. Regulations differed not only from state to state but from industry to industry within each state. Manufacturing and mercantile enterprises were the first statutory targets, with laundries and telegraph and telephone companies running a close second. Hotels, restaurants, and cabarets often escaped regulation entirely. Domestic service and agriculture, still the two leading female occupations and the most arduous, remained untouched. Limits on hours ranged from an eight-hour day and forty-eight-hour week for some industries in Arizona, California, and Washington to ten or twelve hours a day and sixty or more hours a week in most southern states.

By 1914, twenty-seven states had some form of regulation, and three years later, only nine remained without any limitations on hours for women. Six states had an eight-hour day and a forty-eight-hour week for most women. Thirteen states limited the work week to fifty-four hours with no more than nine hours per working day. The remaining states varied maximums from fifty-five to sixty hours per week. By 1924, four more states had enacted such restrictions on hours. Of the five still without restrictions, three—West Virginia, Alabama, and Florida—were in the South. Iowa had virtually no industry to speak of, and Indiana regulated night work, though it did not restrict daytime hours. But some of these restrictions were hardly "protective." North Carolina, for example, forbade women to work more than eleven hours per day, six days per week. Vermont, Tennessee, and New Hampshire had limits of between ten and a quarter and ten and a half hours. Fifteen states, including such heavily women-employing states as Pennsylvania, Connecticut, New Jersey, and Rhode Island, had ten-hour limits.

Even these limits were often evaded. Employers, especially those in small and seasonal businesses, developed a variety of devices for circumventing law enforcement. "Emergency" provisions were built into many laws. Tactics such as stopping clocks and adding time when machinery needed repair protected manufacturers against lost time and enabled employers to extract extra work from women, even in states with stringent laws. For fear of losing their jobs, women often colluded in the evasion, sometimes agreeing to clean machinery on their own time, for example. But the most common form of evasion was simply to build exceptions into the law to serve the interests of special categories of employers. A state might allow women to work a long day where work was seasonal or exempt certain classes of workers from the law altogether. Cannery workers at harvest time, retail clerks at holiday time, night club dancers were routinely exempt from the law's encircling restrictions. . . .

Because limits on hours created an urgent need to address the problem of wages, reform groups like the National Consumers' League and the National Women's Trade Union League began to push as early as 1908 and 1909 for minimum-wage laws that approximated what was popularly known as the "living wage." The Women's Bureau put the problem succinctly in a 1920 pamphlet. Eight-hour days, it argued, were "of questionable value to a worker if to obtain an adequate wage she is obliged to seek supplementary work or to speed up her work in the factory, until, because of her increased efforts, the sum total of her fatigue is as great as under the longer hours." Wages could be increased through organization—a method so far ineffective. Or they could be legislated.

Manufacturers had been known to raise wages to compensate for shorter hours in states where hours for women were reduced. The International Harvester Company granted a two-and-a-half-cent-per-hour wage increase in 1912 when New York State instituted a mandatory fifty-five-hour week. More often employers speeded up the work process, hoping that by driving workers harder they could increase productivity and thus avoid a wage cut. On this basis, Lawrence, Massachusetts, textile owners had maintained weekly wage rates when the state limited women's hours to fifty-six per week in 1910. But when a new fifty-four-hour law was passed in 1912, mill owners refused to raise hourly wages, effectively reducing the take-home pay of operatives already living at the edge of poverty. It took a three-month strike to resolve the issue in favor of wage increases. A 1920 Women's Bureau investigation reported that only half the establishments it studied increased time and piece rates after state-mandated reductions in hours. Some others increased the rates they paid to those who worked by the hour, leaving piece workers to speed up if they wanted to maintain their former wages.

Such evidence heightened demand for minimum-wage legislation. Massachusetts passed the country's first minimum-wage law in 1912. Ohio followed, and within two years ten states had set up mechanisms—usually boards or commissions to determine minimum wages for women and children. But the numbers are deceptive, for as a National Consumers' League study indicated in 1914, up to that date minimum-wage determinations had been "confined with one exception to states whose wealth is concentrated chiefly in man-employing industries." Only Massachusetts, of all the great industrial states, had any legislation on the books by 1920. In effect, states where rural interests far exceeded industrial and mercantile concerns passed such legislation. Others held out. With the notable exception of the

International Ladies' Garment Workers' Union, trade unions that pushed for maximum hours remained ambivalent to or negative about minimum wages.

Even in Massachusetts, the promise held out by such legislation quickly evaporated. That state's Minimum Wage Commission was empowered to recommend "living wages" for women and minors. But its enforcement powers were limited to publishing the names of employers who did not comply. The Commission could create wage panels, specific to each occupation, with a mandate to consider not only the needs of the wage-earning women but "the financial condition of the occupation and the probable effect thereon of any increase in the minimum wage paid, and . . . to determine the minimum wage . . . suitable for a female of ordinary ability." The Commission did not hesitate to exercise its judgment in these matters. After carefully calculating a weekly budget for millinery workers at $11.64 a week, it recommended a wage of $10.00 per week for experienced employees. In explanation the Commission said, "The successful working of the law and justice to the employers do not permit of a higher minimum wage." It set an even lower wage for apprentices ($7.50 per week)—a sum which by its own estimate was not even sufficient for board and lodging; and it declared that "the board does not look with favor upon higher wages for young girls in the millinery trade."

Some of the eight states that passed minimum wage laws in 1913 had stronger provisions. Oregon stated that "it shall be unlawful to employ women in any occupation . . . for wages which are inadequate to supply the necessary cost of living and to maintain them in health." Yet the "necessary cost of living" was to be determined by face-to-face negotiations between employers and employees: a process that left unschooled, unorganized, and easily intimidated young women at a decided disadvantage. Minnesota's Minimum Wage Commission suggested in 1914 that "the idea of getting men employees to represent women might be worth trying." In practice the living wage thus negotiated never rose to a level adequate to provide the necessities of life for a single, self-supporting woman, much less for one with dependent children.

Nor were adequate enforcement provisions built into these state laws. Massachusetts threatened evaders only with adverse publicity, and exempted from compliance all those who could prove that they would be unable to conduct their businesses at a reasonable profit. Rates, even when reasonable to begin with, quickly diminished in the face of inflation, and an endless round of hearings and investigations was required to raise them. Even outright refusal to comply with an order normally produced only the proverbial rap on the knuckles. Laundry owners who were fined $100 and ordered to pay thousands of dollars in back wages appealed the order. Ethel Smith of the WTUL complained:

> The back pay is collectible when the court decision comes if it is favorable, and *if the women individually bring suit,* but aside from the fact that the women are intimidated, it is a well known fact that laundry workers, whose pay is only $4 to $10 a week, are constantly shifting and the employers refuse to keep accurate

records even of their present addresses. In fact, their counsel is advising them not to keep the records which are necessary for the Minimum Wage Board to have in future if the law is sustained. By the time the decision comes the employers may easily have had a complete turnover of force. Their turnover is always high, and in the present season of unemployment they can hire and fire as rapidly as they wish.

Clearly the minimum wage-requirement could not be relied upon to offset income potentially threatened by shorter hours. Although occasional employers acquiesced, they did so only after studies showed that minimum wages soon paid for themselves in improved public opinion and greater productivity. As a representative of the California Consumer's League argued in 1923, by then even employers supported that state's minimum-wage commission.

By then it was too late for such laws. Although a series of state courts had upheld the validity of minimum-wage laws, the U.S. Supreme Court would have none of it. Oregon's Supreme Court had provided the justification accepted by most states. "Women and minors should be protected from conditions of labor which have a pernicious effect on their health and morals," said the court, echoing the rationale for shorter hours, "and inadequate wages have a pernicious effect." The argument underlying the abrogation of a woman's freedom of contract in favor of the state's interest in her health and morals was held to apply to wages as much as to hours. But when the issue got to the Supreme Court, the majority, striking down a District of Columbia law in 1923, declared, "It is quite simply and exclusively a price fixing law, confined to adult women . . . who are legally as capable of contracting for themselves as men." At the same time the freedom that women had to negotiate their wages was not held to extend to their hours, a conclusion reached by such tortuous logic that Chief Justice Taft was moved to dissent. He supported, he said, the view that "a sweating wage has a great and as direct a tendency to bring about an injury to the health and morals of workers, as . . . long hours."

All the largest women's reform groups enthusiastically advocated protective labor legislation—first as a device to entice wage-earning women into the suffrage movement, then as a panacea for their ills. The Women's Trade Union League turned from organizing to legislative action in 1912, and by 1915 legislation was its major priority. The national and state consumers' leagues, whose activities had ranged from providing labels to identify products made by well-treated workers, to compiling "white" lists of stores that sold them, to inspecting factories for health hazards, debated for a year whether its efforts could not better be spent seeking legislation. Finally turning toward restriction in 1918, the National Consumers' League urged its general secretary to "actively oppose everywhere the employment of women under twenty-one years as messengers, letter carriers, elevator or street railroad employees, or as meter readers and bell girls in hotels, restaurants, and men's clubs." The League of Women Voters, successor to the National

American Woman's Suffrage Association, similarly turned to protection as its goal.

All of these groups offered the same double-pronged rationale. Women, they argued first, "were inadequately organized" and therefore had been unable "to obtain the better conditions enjoyed by the men who have obtained them through the power of their labor unions." To prevent women from becoming, in the words of a NWTUL pamphlet, "underbidding competitors" who would "drag down the standards of all industry," they needed labor laws. And, second, women had special need for these laws "to permit efficient motherhood and healthy children."

The continuing paradox of this appeal from women's weakness contributed to splitting feminist ranks. For the organizational energy and skill required to pass protective legislation conflicted with the continuing struggle toward women's equality. In opposition to advocates of legislation, an important group of feminists argued, "If you demand equality, you must accept equality." Led by Alice Paul's National Women's Party, the militant wing of the women's suffrage movement, these women began to urge a constitutional amendment guaranteeing equality—which they finally got submitted to Congress in December 1923. The so-called Lucretia Mott amendment declared, "Men and women shall have equal rights throughout the United States and every place subject to its jurisdiction." It rested, as had the original arguments for women's rights made in 1848, on the assumption that women, who were basically similar to men, were entitled to all human rights.

Consistent with this viewpoint, the NWP insisted that the benefits of industrial legislation extend to all workers and that occupation, not sex, be the basis of legislative restriction. Jane Norman Smith explained the Women's Party's position. "If . . . a law is passed applying to women and not applying to men, it will discriminate against women and handicap them in competing with men in earning their livelihood." She dismissed arguments of moral danger and biological inferiority. "This is a philosophy that would penalize all women because some women are morally frail and physically weak." An Equal Rights Amendment, explained Crystal Eastman, lawyer, writer, and pioneer in developing workmen's compensation laws, would "establish the principle that industrial legislation should apply to all workers, both men and women, in any given occupation and not to women workers alone."

It was, on its face, a reasonable position. It had already been adopted by the International Labor Organization's 1919 International Congress of Working Women, where it was bitterly opposed by Women's Bureau head Mary Anderson. It represented the predominant position of British and Western European feminists. It had been articulated by a variety of women's groups before 1923, and was to emerge again in the early years of the New Deal when optimists believed that protective labor legislation for all workers might yet prevail.

In the United States some of the leading proponents of special legislation in the 1920s had earlier taken a more flexible stance. Lillian Wald and Florence Kelley, veterans of campaigns against child labor and for factory inspection, had believed in 1914 that protective legislation should cover all workers. In a lengthy exchange of letters with Florence Harriman, resident commissioner of the Industrial Relations Commission, they strongly dissented from the Commission's attempts to separate women from men in the legislative arena. "Miss Kelley and I," wrote Lillian Wald, "both hope very much that your Industrial Relations Commission will find it wise to make your recommendations for industry itself, rather than for women and children as distinct from boys and men." An ambiguous reply produced a joint response: ". . . it is becoming more obvious every day that it is unwise to segregate women and children in the field of industrial legislation." In those early days, others had concurred. Mary Van Kleeck, who had headed the Women in Industry Service and was Mary Anderson's good friend, told the first International Congress of Working Women in 1919: "We seek not only the protection of women against the evils of industry, but we seek such a position in industry in relation to its controlling forces as will enable women to remove the evils of industry as they affect either men or women workers." Women, in short, had to mobilize to fight poor industrial conditions for all workers, not only for themselves.

But when, after some vacillation, the National Women's Party chose to pursue a constitutional amendment as the means of achieving equality, reformers feared that the gains of decades of struggle to improve working conditions for women might be lost. National Women's Party officials, floating various versions of a proposed amendment, knew that protective legislation was vulnerable should the amendment pass. Maude Younger, the Party's national legislative chairman, wrote to Ethel Smith of the WTUL agreeing to accept changes in the ERA. "We would be glad to find any other form of wording which would better accomplish the object we have in view, namely the removal of all legal discriminations against women without at the same time injuring the eight hour law and other social legislation in which as you know, I am personally deeply interested." Ethel Smith rejected the olive branch. "I have found no one yet . . . who believes it possible to draft a blanket *Federal* constitutional amendment which would not jeopardize our social legislation." Still the NWP would not give up. Though most legal opinion claimed that minimally an amendment would mean court fights over existing legislation, there were occasional dissenters. Albert Leavitt, one of the amendment's drafters and a professor at the University of North Dakota School of Law, wrote to a Labor Department official: "When it is in final shape, I am of the opinion that it will not jeopardize the legal protection given to women workers. Indeed it is the purpose of the National Women's Party to safeguard protective legislation to the utmost extent."

But unlike the Women's Party most advocates of protection were not willing to risk hard-won legislation for an abstract commitment to equality. Faced with the possibility of seeing all protective labor legislation collapse, Kelley, Wald, and Mary Van Kleeck, among others, became fierce opponents of what they called a blanket amendment. By 1924, Van Kleeck was Mary Anderson's staunchest supporter for special legislation for women, and Crystal Eastman called Florence Kelley "the leading spirit" in opposition to the ERA and "a passionate advocate of protective laws for women and children in industry."

The NWTUL officially called on the NWP to "discontinue its efforts for blanket legislation." The best legal minds in the country, including Felix Frankfurter, agreed. Frankfurter wrote to Ethel Smith in 1921 of his "shock" at learning of the amendment, which "threatens the well-being, even the very life of these millions of wage-earning women." The WTUL pulled out all the stops in its fight. It publicly chastised women who favored the ERA, solicited and published the support of union leaders, and asserted its exclusive right to speak for wage-earning women.

The state and national consumers' leagues also strongly opposed the amendment: the 1922 national board meeting resolved that "since the Board of Directors are advised by counsel that the effect . . . of the amendment proposed by the Women's Party which, in its present form, abolishes all political, civil, and legal disabilities and inequalities on account of sex or marriage, would be to wipe out protective legislation for wage earning women, Mrs. Kelley be directed to inform the protagonists of the proposed amendment that unless its wording is so changed as to safeguard the validity of the legislation for women, such as the NCL had advocated throughout its existence, the NCL would be constrained actively to oppose the amendment."

Male organized labor joined in the attack. Having long since arrived at the position that protective legislation was more effective than organization as a way of keeping women in their place, Gompers, in 1922, came out unequivocally against the ERA. . . .

Of all the potential solutions to the "problem" of wage-earning women, protective legislation satisfied more interests than any other. Widely accepted views of women's primary responsibilities to the home governed its development and guaranteed its acceptance. A world view shared by trade unions and employers alike and acknowledged by most women—wage earners as well as reformers—made protective legislation only the final seal on already accepted behavior patterns. In a period when the notion of equal opportunity for women at work had virtually no popular approval, ameliorating their work conditions seemed wholly to satisfy perceived need. The body of legislation that emerged undertook to help women without violating traditional female roles and in accord with labor market needs and trade union sensibilities. As Mary Anderson put it, "I consider myself a good feminist, but I believe I am a practical one."

In a period when family restrictions and limited availability of jobs perhaps doomed in advance such solutions as cooperatives, education, and training, legislation appeared as the most plausible solution to problems of overwork. It came at the cost of affirming the relative labor force positions of men and women. Protective labor legislation joined with limited labor force opportunities and virtual exclusion from labor unions to institutionalize women's isolation from the mainstream of labor. This translated into special behavior on the part of women workers that isolated them still further from male workers. What was more, legislation ignored the poorest women such as agricultural workers and domestics who had perhaps the most tiring jobs. At the other end of the spectrum, it did not deal with "brain workers," exempting thousands of office workers and professionals from its mandate. These workers were thought to be strong enough to protect themselves. While it acknowledged, by restrictions, the increasing place of women in the work force, legislation attempted to avoid changes in their social roles that more freely available economic opportunities might have permitted. It recognized that women had two jobs, one of which had to be limited if the other was to be performed adequately. By denying that women were full-fledged, equal wage earners, legislation institutionalized social reproduction as women's primary role. It thus extended a version of the ideology of domesticity to working-class people. Since it acknowledged the possibility of wage labor for women, however, it simultaneously loosened the bonds of propriety from around some middle-class women.

As they affected both the work place and the home, protective statutes provided a continuing device for dividing workers along gender lines and stratifying the work force at a time when the number of skilled jobs was declining and the resulting homogenization of the work force threatened to lead to developing class consciousness and thence to class conflict. Neither protagonists nor critics ever lost sight of the possibility that legislation could both ameliorate the worst abuses against women and simultaneously confirm their status as a separate group of workers. . . .

✧ F U R T H E R   R E A D I N G

John Milton Cooper, Jr., *The Warrior and the Priest: Woodrow Wilson and Theodore Roosevelt* (1983)

Samuel P. Hays, "The Politics of Reform in Municipal Government in the Progressive Era," *Pacific Northwest Quarterly* 55 (1964), 154–169

Alice Kessler-Harris, *Out to Work: A History of Wage-Earning Women in the United States* (1982)

Arthur S. Link, *Woodrow Wilson and the Progressive Era* (1963)

Richard L. McCormick, *From Realignment to Reform: Political Change in New York State, 1893–1910* (1981)

———, *Progressivism* (1983)

Edmund Morris, *The Rise of Theodore Roosevelt* (1979)

Bruno Ramirez, *When Workers Fight: The Politics of Industrial Relations in the Progressive Era, 1898–1916* (1978)

John F. Reynolds, *Testing Democracy: Electoral Behavior and Progressive Reform in New Jersey, 1880–1920* (1988)

Bradley R. Rice, *Progressive Cities: The Commission Government Movement in America, 1901–1920* (1977)

Martin J. Schiesl, *The Politics of Efficiency* (1977)

Stephen Skowronek, *Building a New American State* (1982)

David P. Thelen, *Robert La Follette and the Insurgent Spirit* (1976)

Melvin I. Urofsky, *Louis Brandeis and the Progressive Tradition* (1981)

James Weinstein, *The Corporate Ideal in the Liberal State, 1900–1918* (1968)

CHAPTER 11

Sex and the

Construction of Gender

৵

The boundaries of traditional gender relations shifted dramatically at the turn of the century. Among the most noted features of Victorian culture were the norm of a "separate sphere" of women's activities and, culturally akin to the latter, the ideal of "true womanhood." Rooted in domestic labor and child nurture, women's sphere, in theory, offered protection from both the competitive jungle of the marketplace and the "corruption" of the political world. The female sphere had its counterpart in the cultural code for manhood, elaborated in the schoolroom as well as in the workplace and broadcast from the pulpit as well as from the playing field.

A changing economy and job structure, revised child-rearing practices, a growing heterosexual consumer and leisure market, and the political demands of women's rights advocates all contributed to the erosion of older gender certainties in the pre–World War I period. A "cult of manliness" evident in American political and religious rhetoric, in particular, bespoke a preoccupation with reestablishing a solid sense of social function and identity among middle-class men. Although the ratification in 1920 of the Nineteenth Amendment, granting woman's suffrage, marked the most visible breakthrough of these years, more fundamental critiques of the domestic sphere emanated from the birth-control movement and—among anarcho-socialists and radical feminists—from open questioning of the institution of marriage itself.

৵ D O C U M E N T S

A middle-class world of well-ordered gender roles is reflected in the first two documents: excerpts from Mary Sherwood's etiquette book for spinsters and from the instructions of famous Yale football coach Walter Camp—who began the sporting All-America selections—to college athletes. But the contemporary defense of the separate spheres also took on a hard edge. By the mid-nineteenth century, a motley group of medical professionals, vice reformers, and aspiring politicians had fixated on birth control and abortion, as well as illicit sex, as grave threats to the national physical and moral order. Their campaign climaxed in 1873 with the passage of the so-called Comstock Law, named after evangelical crusader Anthony Comstock. This legislation, excerpted in the third document, banned the production and transportation of all pornographic and abortion-related materials. Comstock's coercive prurience was openly challenged in the decision of socialist Margaret Sanger to devote her full attention to the birth-control movement, the subject of the fourth document, and in the free-love preachings of feminist-anarchist Emma Goldman, which are featured in the final selection.

Mary Sherwood's Rules of Etiquette for Spinsters, 1907

The question is sometimes asked, whether a young woman of thirty-five, at the head of her father's house, with no intention of ever marrying, requires a chaperon.

A young lady of thirty-five is sometimes a very attractive person, and does "not look her age." Still, as she is at the head of her father's house, etiquette does yield a point and allow her to judge for herself as to the proprieties which must bend to her. Of course, with every year of a woman's life after twenty-five, she becomes less and less the subject of chaperonage. For one thing, she is better able to judge of the world and its temptations; in the second place, a certain air which may not be less winning, but which is certainly more mature, has replaced the grace of girlhood. She has, with the assumption of years, taken on a dignity which, in its way, is fully the compensation for some lost bloom. Many people prefer it.

But we must say here that she is not yet, in European opinion, entirely emancipated from that guardianship which society dispenses with for the youngest widow. She must have a "companion" if she is a rich woman; and if she is a poor one she should, if possible, join some party of friends when she travels. She can travel abroad with her maid, but in Paris and other Continental cities a woman still young-looking had better not do this. She is not safe from insult nor from injurious suspicion if she signs herself "Miss" Smith, and is without her mother, an elderly friend, a companion, or a party.

In America a woman can go anywhere and do almost anything without fear of insult. But in Europe, where the custom of chaperonage is so universal, she must be more circumspect.

In the matter of paying for tickets, if a lady of thirty-five wishes to allow a gentleman to pay for her admission to picture-galleries and theatres she has an indisputable right to do so. But we are not fighting for a right, only defining a law of etiquette, when we say that it is not generally allowed in the best society, abroad or here. In the case of young girls it is quite unallowable, but in the case of a lady of thirty-five it may be permitted as a sort of *camaraderie,* as one college friend may pay for another. The point is, however, a delicate one. Men, in the freedom of their clubs, recount to one another the clever expedients which many women of society use to extort from them boxes for the opera and suppers at Delmonico's. A woman should remember that it may sometimes be very inconvenient to young men who are invited by her to go to concerts and theatres to pay for these pleasures. Many a poor fellow who has become a defaulter has to thank for it the lady who first asked him to take her to Delmonico's to supper. He was ashamed to tell her that he was poor, and he stole that he might not seem a churl. . . .

Travelling alone with a gentleman escort was at one time allowed in the West. A Kentucky woman of that historic period, "before the war," would not have questioned the propriety of it, and a Western man of to-day still has the desire to pay everything, everywhere, "for a lady."

The increase in the population of the Western States and the growth of a wealthy and fashionable society in the large towns have greatly modified this spirit of unwise chivalry, and such customs are passing away even on the frontier.

"An old maid," may do almost anything without violating etiquette, if she consents to become a chaperon, and takes with her a younger person. Thus an aunt and niece can travel far and wide; the position of an elder sister is always dignified; the youthful head of a house has a right to assert herself— she must do it—therefore etiquette bows to her (as "nice customs courtesy to great kings"). There is very much in the appearance of a woman. It is a part of the injustice of nature that some people look coquettish who are not so. Bad taste in dress, a high color, a natural flow of spirits, or a loud laugh has often caused a very good woman to be misinterpreted. . . . Calm and cold Puritanical people may not be more respectable than the fresh-colored and laughing "old maids" of thirty-five, but they look more so, and in this world women must consult appearances. An elderly girl must even think how she looks. A woman who at a watering-place dresses conspicuously, dyes her hair, or looks as if she did, ties a white blond veil over her locks, and sits on a hotel piazza, showing her feet, may be the best, the most prudent woman in the house, but a superficial observer will not think so. In the mind of every passer-by will lurk the feeling that she lacks the first grace of womanhood, modesty—and in the criticism of a crowd there is strength. . . . If, however, "Miss" Smith were very plain and quiet, and dressed simply and in good taste, or if she sat on the sands looking at the sea, or attended an invalid or a younger friend, then Miss Smith might be as independent as she pleased; she would suffer from no injurious comments. . . .

There are some people who are born with what we call, for want of a better name, a pinchbeck air. Their jewelry never looks like real gold; their manner is always bad; they have the false air of fashion, not the real one. Such people, especially if single, receive many a snub which they do not deserve, and to a woman of this style a companion is almost necessary. . . . In our own country we have almost abolished the idea that a companion is necessary for women of talent who are physicians or artists or musicians; but to those who are still in the trammels of private life we can say that the presence of a companion need not destroy their liberty, and it may add very much to their happiness. There is, no doubt, a great pleasure in the added freedom of life which comes to an elderly girl. "I can wear a velvet dress now," said an exceedingly handsome woman on her thirtieth birthday. . . . So many delightful women are late in loving, so many are true to some buried love, so many are "elderly girls" from choice, and from no neglect of the stronger sex, that to them should be accorded all the respect which is supposed to accrue naturally to the married. "It takes a very superior woman to be an old maid," said Miss Sedgwick.

Walter Camp Instructs the College Athlete, 1893

> Who misses or who wins the prize,
> Go lose or conquer as you can;
> But if you fail or if you rise
> Be each, pray God, a gentleman!

Before taking up the direct plan of this book I want to seize upon the opportunity when, my dear sirs, I find you all together and in such good spirits that you will bear with an old preacher for sermonizing a little. I will not bore you long, but to each of you I have a word to say—to you, my boy, just home from school for the short holidays; to you, young man, whose college years are hastening by; to you, *paterfamilias*, who, relieved for a day of business or professional cares, can spare a moment to look back upon your own school and college days, over which the lapse of years has thrown a glamour that, hiding some of the hard realities, still lends a halo of romance to the incidents. . . .

The field I enter with you, my boy, is the playground, where you go out to meet your school rivals; I want you, collegian, when you are after championships; I want you, sir, when you are talking with your boy about his sports.

"Be each, pray God, a gentleman!" It is an easy word, and a pleasant one. I don't doubt but that you all pronounce it trippingly enough, and have each one his own high ideal of what a gentleman should be. Do you live up to it? Or are you letting it come down a little here and there; so little, perhaps, that you hardly notice it until you make comparison? A gentleman against a gentleman always plays to win. . . . A gentleman does not make his living, however, from his athletic prowess. He does not earn anything by his victories except glory and satisfaction. Perhaps the first falling off in this respect began when the laurel wreath became a mug. So long as the mug was but the emblem, and valueless otherwise, there was no harm. There is still no harm where the mug or trophy hangs in the room of the winner as indicative of his skill; but if the silver mug becomes a silver dollar, either at the hands of the winner or the donor, let us have the laurel back again.

A gentleman never competes for money, directly or indirectly. Make no mistake about this. No matter how winding the road may be that eventually brings the sovereign into the pocket, it is the price of what should be dearer to you than anything else,—your honor. . . .

Now, my young college friend, it is your turn. Remember it is upon you that the eyes of the preparatory school-boy are fixed, . . . and whatever you do in your four years' course, you will see magnified by the boys who come after you. Support your class and your college in every way compatible with your position. Gentlemen are not stingy, nor are they selfish. Play if you can and your class or college needs you. Play if you can afford it, but do not allow a false pride to lead you into subscriptions beyond your means. Don't be ashamed of enthusiasm. A man without it is a man without a purpose.

I remember a little incident of my own college course. I was a freshman, and knew almost no one in college except a certain junior. [I had entered in] a hurdle race. . . . My opponents had all been upper classmen, and received no little encouragement from their friends. I felt very lonely and disgusted with myself and life in general when I got on the mark for the hurdle. I had but two competitors, and both had been cheered when they came to the scratch. Suddenly as we were getting on our marks I heard a voice half-way down the course call out, "You can do 'em," and I saw my junior friend waving his hat to me. It was not a classical remark, but it made me feel better. I was clumsy in getting off, and when we came to the sixth hurdle was nearly five yards behind the other two, but from that time on I could hear my friend roaring out, "Go in!" "You've got 'em yet!" "Now you're over," as I went up each flight. I *did* finish first, and I had hardly touched the tape before he was patting me on the back. I don't suppose it cost him much to yell for a poor freshman, but I know that I always thought of him as one of the best fellows I ever knew, and in after years I have remembered enough of the feeling that was in my heart toward him, to go out and try to make some others feel that even a freshman has friends.

Apropos of this, a word to non-contestants. . . . About the treatment of your rivals. A gentleman is courteous. It is not courtesy upon a ballfield to cheer an error of the opponents. If it is upon your own grounds, it is the worst kind of boorishness. Moreover, if there are remarkable plays made by your rivals you yourselves should cheer; conceal any chagrin you may feel at the loss it may be to your side, but be courteous to appreciate and applaud an exceptional play by the opponents.

After winning a race or a match, there is no reason why a good, healthy lot of young men should not do plenty of cheering, but there is every reason why they should not make their enjoyment depend upon insulting those who have lost. You cannot take your hilarity off into a corner and choke it to death, and no one wants you to; but gratuitous jibes and jeers at the crestfallen mark you as a man who does not know how to bear a victory, a man whose pate is addled by the excitement or whose bringing up has been at fault.

Finally, to non-contestants, I want to say a word regarding "celebrating." Primarily, do not, I beg of you, do anything because it looks smart. Enjoy yourselves, but do not try to "show off." Don't be "tough." A little unusual hilarity, a tendency to believe that everything is expressly for the collegian, can be upon these occasions overlooked and forgiven, but be ready to appreciate the point beyond which it is carried too far; be ready to apologize quickly and instantly where offense is taken. Show that behind the jolly fun there is the instinct and cultivation of a gentleman's son, and that the ebullition of enthusiasm, although it may be a bore to those who fail to kindle at it, has nothing of the vicious element, and is thoroughly innocent of intentional offense to any one. If you find you are losing your head, go home; you will not be sorry for it. . . .

I say that the collegian's standard of purity in his sports should be the highest. The very fact of having the leisure to devote four years to a higher education, should be taken to involve the duty of acquiring a keener perception of right and wrong in matters where right and wrong depend upon a delicacy of honor. Gentlemen do not cheat, nor do they deceive themselves as to what cheating is. If you are elected the captain of a [baseball] nine, team, or crew, read over your rules, and note exactly who are allowed as contestants by those rules, not by the custom of some predecessor, not by what you think some rival will do, but by the rules themselves. . . . It is your duty to know that every one of your men is straight and square. I know what I am talking about when I say that a college captain can, in ninety-nine cases out of a hundred, become possessed of the exact truth regarding any man he thinks of trying. . . .

What if, at the time, your side may be the weaker? Don't be a coward on that account. Face it like a man, and say with your whole heart that you are on the side of the men who want no chance of retreat or escape, only a fair contest and certain victory or defeat at the end of it. . . .

Perhaps if you, sir, the father of these boys, have had patience to listen thus far to me, you will allow me to put in a word. . . . When you see anything in their speech or conduct that betokens a lowering of the high ideal of gentlemanliness, don't hesitate to say so. You don't want your boy "hired" by any one. If he plays, he plays as a gentleman, and not as a professional; he plays for victory, not for money; and whatever bruises he may have in the flesh, his heart is right, and he can look you in the eye as a gentleman should.

Be each, pray God, a gentleman!

"Comstockery" and the Legal Suppression of Birth Control, 1873

Act for the Suppression of Trade in, and Circulation of, Obscene Literature and Articles of Immoral Use, 1873

Tit. 18. Crimes and Criminal Procedure
Ch. 71. Obscenity

SECTION 1461. Mailing obscene or crime inciting matter.

Every obscene, lewd, lascivious, indecent, filthy or vile article, matter, thing, device or substance; and

Every article or thing designed, adapted, or intended for preventing conception or producing abortion, or for any indecent or immoral use; and

Every article, instrument, substance, drug, medicine, or thing which is advertised or described in a manner calculated to lead another to use or apply it for preventing conception or producing abortion, or for any indecent or immoral purpose; and

Every written or printed card, letter, circular, book, pamphlet, advertisement, or notice of any kind giving information, directly or indirectly, where, or how, or from whom, or by what means any of such mentioned matters, articles, or things may be obtained or made, or where or by whom any act or operation of any kind for the procuring or producing of abortion will be done or performed, or how or by what means conception may be prevented or abortion produced, whether sealed or unsealed; and

Every paper, writing, advertisement, or representation what any article, instrument, substance, drug, medicine, or thing may, or can, be used or applied for preventing conception or producing abortion, or for any indecent or immoral purpose; and

Every description calculated to induce or incite a person to so use or apply any such article, instrument, substance, drug, medicine, or thing–

Is declared to be nonmailable matter and shall not be conveyed in the mails or delivered from any post office or by any letter carrier.

Whoever knowingly uses the mail for the mailing, carriage in the mails, or delivery of anything declared by this section to be nonmailable, or knowingly causes to be delivered by mail according to the direction thereon, or at the place at which it is directed to be delivered by the person to whom it is addressed, or knowingly takes any such thing from the mails for the purpose of circulating or disposing thereof, or of aiding in the circulation or disposition thereof, shall be fined not more than $5,000 or imprisoned not more than five years, or both, for the first such offense, and shall be fined not more than $10,000 or imprisoned not more than ten years, or both, for each such offense thereafter.

The term "indecent" as used in this section includes matter of a character tending to incite arson, murder, or assassination.

Margaret Sanger Recalls Her Fight for Birth Control, 1931

Early in the year 1912 I came to a sudden realization that my work as a nurse and my activities in social service were entirely palliative and consequently futile and useless to relieve the misery I saw all about me. . . .

. . . [This] was the day of home nursing, and it gave a trained nurse splendid opportunities to learn social conditions through actual contact with them.

Were it possible for me to depict the revolting conditions existing in the homes of some of the women I attended in that one year, one would find it hard to believe. There was at that time, and doubtless is still today, a substratum of men and women whose lives are absolutely untouched by social agencies. . . .

Margaret Sanger, *My Fight for Birth Control* (New York: Henry Holt and Company, Inc., 1931), pp. 46–53, 56–57. Reprinted by permission of Dr. Grant Sanger.

It is among the mothers here that the most difficult problems arise—the outcasts of society with theft, filth, perjury, cruelty, brutality oozing from beneath.

Ignorance and neglect go on day by day; children born to breathe but a few hours and pass out of life; pregnant women toiling early and late to give food to four or five children, always hungry; boarders taken into homes where there is not sufficient room for the family; little girls eight and ten years of age sleeping in the same room with dirty, foul smelling, loathsome men; women whose weary, pregnant, shapeless bodies refuse to accommodate themselves to the husbands' desires find husbands looking with lustful eyes upon other women, sometimes upon their own little daughters, six and seven years of age.

In this atmosphere abortions and birth become the main theme of conversation. On Saturday nights I have seen groups of fifty to one hundred women going into questionable offices well known in the community for cheap abortions. I asked several women what took place there, and they all gave the same reply: a quick examination, a probe inserted into the uterus and turned a few times to disturb the fertilized ovum, and then the woman was sent home. Usually the flow began the next day and often continued four or five weeks. Sometimes an ambulance carried the victim to the hospital for a curetage, and if she returned home at all she was looked upon as a lucky woman.

This state of things became a nightmare with me. There seemed no sense to it all, no reason for such waste of mother life, no right to exhaust women's vitality and to throw them on the scrap-heap before the age of thirty-five.

Everywhere I looked, misery and fear stalked—men fearful of losing their jobs, women fearful that even worse conditions might come upon them. The menace of another pregnancy hung like a sword over the head of every poor woman I came in contact with that year. The question which met me was always the same: What can I do to keep from it? or, What can I do to get out of this? Sometimes they talked among themselves bitterly.

"It's the rich that know the tricks," they'd say, "while we have all the kids." Then, if the women were Roman Catholics, they talked about "Yankee tricks," and asked me if I knew what the Protestants did to keep their families down. When I said that I didn't believe that the rich knew much more than they did I was laughed at and suspected of holding back information for money. They would nudge each other and say something about paying me before I left the case if I would reveal the "secret.". . .

I heard over and over again of their desperate efforts at bringing themselves "around"—drinking various herb-teas, taking drops of turpentine on sugar, steaming over a chamber of boiling coffee or of turpentine water, rolling down stairs, and finally inserting slippery-elm sticks, or knitting needles, or shoe hooks into the uterus. I used to shudder with horror as I heard the details and, worse yet, learned of the conditions *behind the reason* for such desperate actions. Day after day these stories were poured into my ears. I knew hundreds of these women personally, and knew much of their hopeless, barren, dreary lives. . . .

They claimed my thoughts night and day. One by one these women, with their worried, sad, pensive and ageing faces would marshal themselves before me in my dreams, sometimes appealingly, sometimes accusingly. I could not escape from the facts of their misery, neither was I able to see the way out of their problems and their troubles. Like one walking in a sleep, I kept on.

Finally the thing began to shape itself, to become accumulative during the three weeks I spent in the home of a desperately sick woman living on Grand Street, a lower section of New York's East Side.

Mrs. Sacks was only twenty-eight years old; her husband, an unskilled worker, thirty-two. Three children, aged five, three and one, were none too strong nor sturdy, and it took all the earnings of the father and the ingenuity of the mother to keep them clean, provide them with air and proper food, and give them a chance to grow into decent manhood and womanhood.

Both parents were devoted to these children and to each other. The woman had become pregnant and had taken various drugs and purgatives, as advised by her neighbors. Then, in desperation, she had used some instrument lent to her by a friend. She was found prostrate on the floor amidst the crying children when her husband returned from work. Neighbors advised against the ambulance, and a friendly doctor was called. The husband would not hear of her going to a hospital, and as a little money had been saved in the bank a nurse was called and the battle for that precious life began.

It was in the middle of July. The three-room apartment was turned into a hospital for the dying patient. Never had I worked so fast, never so concentratedly as I did to keep alive that little mother. . . .

At the end of two weeks recovery was in sight, and at the end of three weeks I was preparing to leave the fragile patient to take up the ordinary duties of her life, including those of wifehood and motherhood. . . .

But as the hour for my departure came nearer, her anxiety increased, and finally with trembling voice she said: "Another baby will finish me, I suppose."

"It's too early to talk about that," I said, and resolved that I would turn the question over to the doctor for his advice. When he came I said: "Mrs. Sacks is worried about having another baby."

"She well might be," replied the doctor, and then he stood before her and said: "Any more such capers, young woman, and there will be no need to call me."

"Yes, yes—I know, Doctor," said the patient with trembling voice, "but," and she hesitated as if it took all of her courage to say it, "*what* can I do to prevent getting that way again?"

"Oh ho!" laughed the doctor good naturedly, "You want your cake while you eat it too, do you? Well, it can't be done." Then, familiarly slapping her on the back and picking up his hat and bag to depart, he said: "I'll tell you the only sure thing to do. Tell Jake to sleep on the roof!"

With those words he closed the door and went down the stairs, leaving us both petrified and stunned.

Tears sprang to my eyes, and a lump came in my throat as I looked at that face before me. It was stamped with sheer horror. I thought for a moment she might have gone insane, but she conquered her feelings, whatever they may have been, and turning to me in desperation said: "He can't understand, can he?—he's a man after all—but you do, don't you? You're a woman and you'll tell me the secret and I'll never tell it to a soul."

She clasped her hands as if in prayer, she leaned over and looked straight into my eyes and beseechingly implored me to tell her something—something *I really did not know*. It was like being on a rack and tortured for a crime one had not committed. To plead guilty would stop the agony; otherwise the rack kept turning.

I had to turn away from that imploring face. I could not answer her then. I quieted her as best I could. She saw that I was moved by the tears in my eyes. I promised that I would come back in a few days and tell her what she wanted to know. The few simple means of limiting the family like *coitus interruptus* or the condom were laughed at by the neighboring women when told these were the means used by men in the well-to-do families. That was not believed, and I knew such an answer would be swept aside as useless were I to tell her this at such a time. . . .

There was only one thing to be done: call out, start the alarm, set the heather on fire! Awaken the womanhood of America to free the motherhood of the world! I released from my almost paralyzed hand the nursing bag which unconsciously I had clutched, threw it across the room, tore the uniform from my body, flung it into a corner, and renounced all palliative work forever.

I would never go back again to nurse women's ailing bodies while their miseries were as vast as the stars. I was now finished with superficial cures, with doctors and nurses and social workers who were brought face to face with this overwhelming truth of women's needs and yet turned to pass on the other side. They must be made to see these facts. I resolved that women should have knowledge of contraception. They have every right to know about their own bodies. I would strike out—I would scream from the housetops. I would tell the world what was going on in the lives of these poor women. I *would* be heard. No matter what it should cost. *I would be heard* . . .

I asked doctors what one could do and was told I'd better keep off that subject or Anthony Comstock would get me. I was told that there were laws against that sort of thing. This was the reply from every medical man and woman I approached. . . .

Emma Goldman Critiques Marriage, 1910

The popular notion about marriage and love is that they are synonymous, that they spring from the same motives, and cover the same human needs. Like most popular notions this also rests not on actual facts, but on superstition.

Marriage and love have nothing in common; they are as far apart as the poles; are, in fact, antagonistic to each other. No doubt some marriages have been the result of love. Not, however, because love could assert itself only in marriage; much rather is it because few people can completely outgrow a convention. There are today large numbers of men and women to whom marriage is naught but a farce, but who submit to it for the sake of public opinion. At any rate, while it is true that some marriages are based on love, and while it is equally true that in some cases love continues in married life, I maintain that it does so regardless of marriage, and not because of it.

On the other hand, it is utterly false that love results from marriage. On rare occasions one does hear of a miraculous case of a married couple falling in love after marriage, but on close examination it will be found that it is a mere adjustment to the inevitable. Certainly the growing-used to each other is far away from the spontaneity, the intensity, and beauty of love, without which the intimacy of marriage must prove degrading to both the woman and the man.

Marriage is primarily an economic arrangement, an insurance pact. It differs from the ordinary life-insurance agreement only in that it is more binding, more exacting. Its returns are insignificantly small compared with the investments. In taking out an insurance policy one pays for it in dollars and cents, always at liberty to discontinue payments. If, however, woman's premium is a husband, she pays for it with her name, her privacy, her self-respect, her very life, "until death doth part." Moreover, the marriage insurance condemns her to life-long dependency, to parasitism, to complete uselessness, individual as well as social. Man, too, pays his toll, but as his sphere is wider, marriage does not limit him as much as woman. He feels his chains more in an economic sense.

Thus Dante's motto over Inferno applies with equal force to marriage. "Ye who enter here leave all hope behind."

That marriage is a failure none but the very stupid will deny. One has but to glance over the statistics of divorce to realize how bitter a failure marriage really is. . . .

. . . Scores of writers are discussing the barrenness, the monotony, the sordidness, the inadequacy of marriage as a factor for harmony and understanding.

The thoughtful social student will not content himself with the popular superficial excuse for this phenomenon. He will have to dig down deeper into the very life of the sexes to know why marriage proves so disastrous.

Edward Carpenter says that behind every marriage stands the life-long environment of the two sexes; an environment so different from each other that man and woman must remain strangers. Separated by an insurmountable wall of superstition, custom, and habit, marriage has not the potentiality of developing knowledge of, and respect for, each other, without which every union is doomed to failure.

Henrik Ibsen, the hater of all social shams, was probably the first to realize this great truth. Nora leaves her husband, not—as the stupid critic would have it—because she is tired of her responsibilities or feels the need of woman's rights, but because she has come to know that for eight years she had lived with a stranger and borne him children. Can there be anything more humiliating, more degrading than a life-long proximity between two strangers? No need for the woman to know anything of the man, save his income. As to the knowledge of the woman—what is there to know except that she has a pleasing appearance? We have not yet outgrown the theologic myth that woman has no soul, that she is a mere appendix to man, made out of his rib just for the convenience of the gentleman who was so strong that he was afraid of his own shadow.

Perchance the poor quality of the material whence woman comes is responsible for her inferiority. At any rate, woman has no soul—what is there to know about her? Besides, the less soul a woman has the greater her asset as a wife, the more readily will she absorb herself in her husband. It is this slavish acquiescence to man's superiority that has kept the marriage institution seemingly intact for so long a period. . . .

From infancy, almost, the average girl is told that marriage is her ultimate goal; therefore her training and education must be directed toward that end. Like the mute beast fattened for slaughter, she is prepared for that. Yet, strange to say, she is allowed to know much less about her function as wife and mother than the ordinary artisan of his trade. It is indecent and filthy for a respectable girl to know anything of the marital relation. Oh, for the inconsistency of respectability, that needs the marriage vow to turn something which is filthy into the purest and most sacred arrangement that none dare question or criticize. Yet that is exactly the attitude of the average upholder of marriage. The prospective wife and mother is kept in complete ignorance of her only asset in the competitive field—sex. Thus she enters into life-long relations with a man only to find herself shocked, repelled, outraged beyond measure by the most natural and healthy instinct, sex. It is safe to say that a large percentage of the unhappiness, misery, distress, and physical suffering of matrimony is due to the criminal ignorance in sex matters that is being extolled as a great virtue. . . .

If, however, woman is free and big enough to learn the mystery of sex without the sanction of State or Church, she will stand condemned as utterly unfit to become the wife of a "good" man, his goodness consisting of an empty brain and plenty of money. Can there be anything more outrageous than the idea that a healthy, grown woman, full of life and passion, must deny nature's demand, must subdue her most intense craving, undermine her health and break her spirit, must stunt her vision, abstain from the depth and glory of sex experience until a "good" man comes along to take her unto himself as a wife? That is precisely what marriage means. How can such an arrangement end except in failure? This is one, though not the least important, factor of marriage, which differentiates it from love.

Ours is a practical age. . . . If, on rare occasions, young people allow themselves the luxury of romance, they are taken in care by the elders, drilled and pounded until they become "sensible."

The moral lesson instilled in the girl is not whether the man has aroused her love, but rather is it, "How much?" The important and only God of practical American life: Can the man make a living? Can he support a wife? That is the only thing that justifies marriage. . . .

Doubtless there are people who continue to consider love above dollars and cents. Particularly is this true of that class whom economic necessity has forced to become self-supporting. The tremendous change in woman's position, wrought by that mighty factor, is indeed phenomenal when we reflect that it is but a short time since she has entered the industrial arena. Six million women wage workers; six million women who have the equal right with men to be exploited, to be robbed, to go on strike; aye, to starve even. Anything more, my lord? Yes, six million wage workers in every walk of life, from the highest brain work to the mines and railroad tracks; yes, even detectives and policemen. Surely the emancipation is complete.

Yet with all that, but a very small number of the vast army of women wage workers look upon work as a permanent issue, in the same light as does man. No matter how decrepit the latter, he has been taught to be independent, self-supporting. Oh, I know that no one is really independent in our economic treadmill; still, the poorest specimen of a man hates to be a parasite; to be known as such, at any rate.

The woman considers her position as worker transitory, to be thrown aside for the first bidder. That is why it is infinitely harder to organize women than men. "Why should I join a union? I am going to get married, to have a home." Has she not been taught from infancy to look upon that as her ultimate calling? She learns soon enough that the home, though not so large a prison as the factory, has more solid doors and bars. It has a keeper so faithful that naught can escape him. The most tragic part, however, is that the home no longer frees her from wage slavery; it only increases her task.

According to the latest statistics submitted before a committee "on labor and wages, and congestion of population," 10 percent of the wage workers in New York City alone are married, yet they must continue to work at the most poorly paid labor in the world. Add to this horrible aspect the drudgery of housework, and what remains of the protection and glory of the home? As a matter of fact, even the middle-class girl in marriage cannot speak of her home, since it is the man who creates her sphere. It is not important whether the husband is a brute or a darling. What I wish to prove is that marriage guarantees woman a home only by the grace of her husband. . . .

But the child, how is it to be protected, if not for marriage? After all, is not that the most important consideration? The sham, the hypocrisy of it! Marriage protecting the child, yet thousands of children destitute and homeless. Marriage protecting the child, yet orphan asylums and reformatories overcrowded, the Society for the Prevention of Cruelty to Children keeping busy in rescuing the little victims from "loving" parents, to place them under more loving care, the Gerry Society. Oh, the mockery of it! . . .

As to the protection of the woman,—therein lies the curse of marriage. Not that it really protects her, but the very idea is so revolting, such an outrage and insult on life, so degrading to human dignity, as to forever condemn this parasitic institution.

It is like that other paternal arrangement—capitalism. It robs man of his birthright, stunts his growth, poisons his body, keeps him in ignorance, in poverty, and dependence, and then institutes charities that thrive on the last vestige of man's self-respect.

The institution of marriage makes a parasite of woman, an absolute dependent. It incapacitates her for life's struggle, annihilates her social consciousness, paralyzes her imagination, and then imposes its gracious protection, which is in reality a snare, a travesty on human character.

If motherhood is the highest fulfillment of woman's nature, what other protection does it need, save love and freedom? Marriage but defiles, outrages and corrupts her fulfillment. Does it not say to woman, Only when you follow me shall you bring forth life? Does it not condemn her to the block, does it not degrade and shame her if she refuses to buy her right to motherhood by selling herself? . . .

Love, the strongest and deepest element in all life, the harbinger of hope, of joy, of ecstasy; love, the defier of all laws, of all conventions; love, the freest, the most powerful moulder of human destiny; how can such an all-compelling force be synonymous with that poor little State and Church-begotten weed, marriage? . . .

Love needs no protection; it is its own protection. So long as love begets life no child is deserted, or hungry, or famished for the want of affection. I know this to be true. I know women who became mothers in freedom by the men they loved. Few children in wedlock enjoy the care, the protection, the devotion free motherhood is capable of bestowing.

The defenders of authority dread the advent of a free motherhood, lest it will rob them of their prey. Who would fight wars? Who would create wealth? Who would make the policeman, the jailer, if woman were to refuse the indiscriminate breeding of children? The race, the race! shouts the king, the president, the capitalist, the priest. The race must be preserved, though woman be degraded to a mere machine,—and the marriage institution is our only safety valve against the pernicious sex awakening of woman. But in vain these frantic efforts to maintain a state of bondage. In vain, too, the edicts of the Church, the mad attacks of rulers, in vain even the arm of the law. Woman no longer wants to be a party to the production of a race of sickly, feeble, decrepit, wretched human beings, who have neither the strength nor moral courage to throw off the yoke of poverty and slavery. Instead she desires fewer and better children, begotten and reared in love, and through free choice; not by compulsion, as marriage imposes. Our pseudo moralists have yet to learn the deep sense of responsibility toward the child, that love in freedom has awakened in the breast of woman. Rather would she forego forever the glory of motherhood than bring forth life in an atmosphere that breathes only destruction and death. And if she does become a mother, it is to give to the child the deepest and best her being can yield. To grow with the child is her motto; she knows that in that manner alone can she help build true manhood and womanhood. . . .

In our present pygmy state love is indeed a stranger to most people. . . . Some day, some day men and women will rise, they will reach the mountain peak, they will meet big and strong and free, ready to receive, to partake, and to bask in the golden rays of love. What fancy, what imagination, what poetic genius can foresee even approximately the potentialities of such a force in the life of men and women. If the world is ever to give birth to true companionship and oneness, not marriage, but love will be the parent.

♣ E S S A Y S

The following essays highlight the cultural foundations of the turn-of-the-century gender gap and something of the complexity of sustaining it in changing times. In the first essay, historian Susan Curtis of Purdue University demonstrates how the theology of the social gospel (whose contribution to progressive reform was considered in Chapter 10) responded creatively not only to political imperatives but to a crisis of male gender identity in the period. Writer-activist Margery Davies, in the second selection, pursues the contemporary controversy raised by the entry of growing numbers of women into office work. The expansion of the female labor force, she suggests, did not necessarily breach older notions of women's proper sphere.

The Social Gospel and the Crisis of Victorian Masculinity

SUSAN CURTIS

In many ways, masculinity had become problematic in late-Victorian America. Middle-class culture, grounded in individual ambition and manly achievement earlier in the century, gradually had been transformed by the 1890s and early 1900s in response to a number of key cultural developments. As Ann Douglas has observed, men grew up in a culture that was undergoing "feminization." Women novelists penned novels that chronicled the domestic lives of middle-class women. Ministers softened the stern Calvinism of their elders with a more liberal creed, which they preached to congregations made up largely of women. Together, ministers and their female parishioners articulated a culture based on nurture, sentiment, and indulgence. This feminized culture was intended to bolster Victorian domesticity, but it inadvertently opened doors for women in careers outside the home. Social expectations, women's place in society, and Victorian ideals all were called into question in the years immediately following the Civil War.

What did it mean to be a man in such a society? Boys were advised to aspire to the ideal of the "Christian Gentleman," honest and genteel, yet ambitious and self-reliant. This was consistent with the small shops, farms, and factories of the pre–Civil War economy. It also was supported by evangelical Protestantism. But this ideal was buffeted by an industrializing economy and a feminizing culture in the last third of the nineteenth century. As the new century dawned, a new masculine ideal was beginning to take shape— one based on personality, social involvement, and, in David Riesman's terms, "other-direction."

Some of the young men who helped redefine masculinity were also the authors of a restatement of Protestantism: the social gospel. Social gospelers reacted against the norms of individual responsibility and self-control because as young men, they had failed to live up to these ideals themselves. By

---

the 1880s and 1890s they recognized that it was as difficult to save oneself spiritually and morally as to make a success of oneself in the economy. The feminized version of Protestantism available to them offered some comfort as they struggled to succeed, but it did not satisfy their longing to emulate and surpass their fathers. They incorporated certain aspects of this feminized religion into a gospel that would appeal to men as well as to women. As Josiah Strong put it in 1901, "There is not enough of effort, of struggle, in the typical church life of today to win young men to the church. A flowery bed of ease does not appeal to a fellow who has any manhood in him. The prevailing religion is too utterly comfortable to attract young men who love the heroic." Caught between the frustrating demand for individualism in industrial America and the influence of feminization in religion, social gospelers at the turn of the century hoped to create a religious ideal that nevertheless did justice to their manliness.

With a few exceptions, social gospelers were middle-class Protestant men from rural or small-town America. Inspired by the work of older men like Josiah Strong, Washington Gladden, and Lyman Abbott, they coalesced as a movement in the late 1880s and early 1890s. While they made important overtures to the working class, they spoke mostly to Northern middle-class audiences. The popularity of the social gospel by the early twentieth century suggests that at least parts of their message had wide appeal.

In many respects, the social gospelers were much like other boys. They romped in the fields, read adventure stories with relish, and valued spirited, but fair, play. But their recollections of childhood, recorded decades after the fact in autobiographies, emphasized some aspects of childhood over others. Written in large part to show how and why they had departed from the religion of their elders, the autobiographical accounts were tinged with heightened memories of early religious experiences. Despite these distortions of memory, social gospelers' stories of their youthful quests for faith are worth exploring because they offer a glimpse at some of the important issues that made masculinity so problematic. An examination of the lives of men who became social gospelers further shows how the social gospel helped affirm a changing conception of masculinity.

The young men who eventually became part of the social gospel move-ment remembered most vividly the importance of individualism in their lives. As children they were exposed to an individualistic religion that warned of the tortures of hell for the unrepentant. Harry Emerson Fosdick recalled "weeping at night for fear of going to hell, with my mystified and baffled mother trying to comfort me." He joined his family's church at the age of seven. . . . Shailer Mathews described his "Puritan" training in a pious community where "hell and the devil were very real" and where "the mes-sage from the pulpit was essentially for the individual." He experienced conversion at a revival in 1877 led by George C. Needham. Walter Rau-schenbusch learned from his father, August Rauschenbusch, a scholar at the Rochester Theological Seminary, that there was no salvation for the unrepen-tant. Accordingly, in 1878 young Rauschenbusch accepted responsibility for his own salvation, and declared, "I want to be a man."

As Rauschenbusch's comment suggests, this religious individualism promised to prepare converts for work in life as well as salvation in heaven. Mindful of their fathers' attainments, these young men hoped to succeed as individuals. Rauschenbush assumed he would become the seventh in an unbroken line of ministers in his family and successor to his father, a respected scholar. Charles Macfarland remembered his father's disciplined biblical instruction and his physical labor to erect a monument to the Pilgrims at Plymouth, which eventually cost him his life. . . .

Although they viewed their fathers as exemplars of industry, discipline, and success, many social gospelers were deprived of an effective paternal presence. For many children of the middle class, fathers played a diminishing role in the nineteenth century. The separation of work from home meant that fathers were gone much of the day. No more did they pass along the skills of their craft. Many of the men who became social gospelers experienced this separation more intensely, for their fathers died or were otherwise unavailable before the boys reached adolescence. Charles Macfarland, Charles Stelzle, Francis Greenwood Peabody, and Washington Gladden all lost their fathers as boys. Walter Rauschenbusch and his father were separated by an ocean for many of the boy's formative years. . . . Lyman Abbott's father, who wanted to work in New York City, sent Lyman and his two brothers to various uncles and grandparents when their mother died. Young Abbott remembered his childhood as one of "absolute freedom" from paternal authority.

Those who were separated from their fathers because of death or the demands of work were affected in several ways. They were left with powerful boyish memories of successful fathers up to whose standards they should try to measure. Rauschenbusch and Macfarland both idealized their fathers but admitted in later years that they scarcely knew them. Rauschenbusch, for example, undertook the completion of his father's memoir because he admired him. Yet in *Leben und Wirken* (1901), he noted with surprise, "I myself had little idea how rich and interesting his life was until my father's papers and correspondence revealed it to me." . . .

In these circumstances the influence of their mothers was especially important. Rauschenbusch learned religion at his mother's knee as well as from August Rauschenbusch. He also wanted to emulate one of his older sisters, who married a missionary and lived in India for many years. In his short autobiography, Peabody . . . referred to the second phase of his youth as a period of "congenial companionship" with his mother in their newly found "convenient and agreeable" home. . . . The boys experienced an intense complement of ideals—the rugged individualism of their fathers and the nurture and self-sacrifice of their mothers.

Another problem they faced was a change in the post–Civil War economy that made them think it impossible to attain the individualistic success they longed for as youths. . . . As the century drew to a close, a wide variety of mass-produced goods, a host of public institutions, increasing vacation and leisure, and a longing to escape the monotony and degradation of work all undermined Victorian verities of hard work, self-reliance, delayed gratification, and self-control. These were also the ideals of the young social gospelers.

Shailer Mathews watched his father struggle mightily (and unsuccessfully) to avert business collapse. Young Mathews gave up his elder's individual ideal, and in college experienced the pleasure of teamwork, social organization, and collective enterprise. And he studied religion instead of business. . . . In the 1870s and early 1880s, Gladden left the ministry for magazine work, then returned to the ministry when rewards eluded him at the *Independent* and when his own periodicals, *Sunday Afternoon: A Magazine for the Household* and *Good Company,* failed. Stelzle clung to an individualistic work ethic in his job at a factory until he realized that his ambitious pace drove the piece rate down and productivity quotas up for himself and his fellow workers.

These young men also began to realize that they were not alone. Industrial warfare in the 1870s and 1880s, the cross-country march of Coxey's army in 1894, and urban slums swelling with masses of impoverished working people reinforced their conclusion that hard work and self-control no longer necessarily produced success. As Henry Atkinson put it, many men "tried as hard as possible" but failed to provide "enough bread for the little ones." Gladden saw "multitudes" of "worthy people" in Columbus, Ohio, who worked and saved and prayed, but who did not succeed in "raising themselves." For Gladden this broken equation constituted the "labor question" that haunted him and his colleagues for decades. Charles Sheldon moved in 1890 to Kansas, where he sought to understand the plight of laboring men in Topeka's stagnant economy. For days he searched for work until he began to feel the weight of personal failure. "The getting and holding of a job," he declared, "had come to seem . . . the very apex of success in life." Sheldon's quest revealed to him the crisis faced by manual laborers, and raised fears of softness in himself. He complained that as a minister he felt "isolated" from the "great world of labor."

As Rauschenbusch, Mathews, Macfarland, Sheldon, Peabody, and others came of age in the 1880s, they became dissatisfied with both the religious individualism and the lonely enterprise of their youth. Many began by rejecting the individualism of their religious experiences. Fosdick, for example, harbored a "hidden anger" at the church because of its "wretched play upon my selfish fears and hopes." In 1888 Rauschenbusch looked back at his initial conversion experience and decided "there was a great deal in it that was not really true." At the age of twenty-seven, he underwent a second conversion to "redeem humanity" and to "live over again the life of Christ." . . .

Although these young Protestants opposed the individualism of their youth, they did not reject religious commitment. . . . They proposed a social gospel that would force Christians to address social problems that thwarted individual regeneration. They believed that Christians had an obligation to attack the evils that led to moral ruin. Thus, they posited that the individual and society should share the burden of responsibility for salvation. They attacked the evils of alcohol, prostitution, and gambling, which tempted young men away from upright living. They addressed poverty by providing soup kitchens, bathing facilities, visitng nurses, industrial training for boys, inexpensive used clothing, and assistance for the unemployed. They bolstered the home and tried to provide an alternative to street life by organizing social clubs and by building bowling alleys and gymnasiums on church property. And they showed their sympathy for laboring men and women by evangelizing workers at lunchtime meetings at factories and shops, by providing nurseries for children of working mothers, and by endorsing the right to collective bargaining. In short, they offered a social creed rather than an individualistic one. In order to carry out this ambitious program, social gospelers established reform unions, denominational brotherhood organizations, investigative teams, and social services. Some affiliated with universities, settlement houses, or political parties; others formed organizations that demanded teamwork, and few actually limited their careers to the pulpit. Most were surrounded by men who shared their zeal for social reform, and they enjoyed the newfound sense of community. They also articulated three great laws of the social gospel: service, sacrifice, and love. These feminine virtues associated with Victorian domesticity were important parts of their disavowal of individualism in work and in faith.

The social gospel was not, however, a new expression of feminized religion. The men who came to the movement wrestled with the meaning of manhood and with the legacy of their fathers. They articulated a gospel that transformed the domestic concerns of their reforms into expressions of manly endeavor. Their concerns about manhood were revealed in their portrayals of God and Jesus. Jesus, the son and brother, was central to the social gospel as an example of cooperative, righteous, and manly behavior. Jesus was viewed as a reformer who cared for the downtrodden and worked with others to save humanity. He was thus worthy of emulation. God, the Father, was "indwelling" and "immanent" but not interventionist. In many ways this God resembled the social gospelers' own impressive and distant fathers. Both Jesus and God in the social gospel served as masculine ideals in industrializing America.

The Jesus to which many social gospelers were accustomed as Victorian children was largely the product of sentimental writers. Jesus was neither fully masculine nor fully feminine. Popular depictions featured him in long white gowns with long wavy locks and a soft brown beard. Both madonna and man, Jesus represented a complement of tender nurture and manly endeavor, which helped legitimize the commitment to social service as an acceptable replacement for individual enterprise. Jesus was also a son, which made him a peer instead of an unapproachable figure of authority. But social gospelers did not accept a feminized version of Jesus. Rauschenbusch insisted that "there was nothing mushy, nothing sweetly effeminate about Jesus." Rather, Jesus was a "man's man," who "turned again and again on the snarling pack of His pious enemies and made them slink away." . . . When Macfarland extolled the strength and courage of Jesus in 1912, he confessed, "I know it would have been a great help to me in my boyhood and young manhood had I been led to appreciate the manhood of Jesus."

According to Josiah Strong, interest in Jesus had been growing since midcentury. With the appearance of dozens of scholarly treatments and imaginative reconstructions of the life of Jesus, American Protestants could follow in "the footsteps of the master" from "manger to throne," or they could stand in the "shadow of the cross" and answer the "call of the carpenter." They longed to know what he had said (or might have said), how he appeared to his contemporaries, the condition of his life, and his attitudes on a wide range of social and political questions. . . . Nor was interest in Christ confined to schools of theology. Novels about Jesus proliferated. . . . Protestants in both humble country churches and magnificent urban temples worshiped the carpenter more directly than ever before. . . .

Jesus' humanness and altered outward appearance resulted in a changed demeanor. Instead of sentimentalizing the soft-spoken author of the Beatitudes, social gospelers noted the activism and reforming spirit of this workingman. Jesus the Carpenter particularly appealed to laborers, progressives, and social reformers. A New York settlement-house worker, Bouck White, in *The Call of the Carpenter* (1914) imagined Jesus as a radical populist who believed in a "social gospel." "His ideal is the civic ideal," White declared. "Its goal is 'the holy city descending from God out of heaven.' Therefore the Carpenter-Christ is the fit leader of the multitudinous." At the same time that Jesus sprouted muscles and manlier beard, and showed a passion for justice, he also became more congenial and social-minded. . . .

The Jesus of the social gospel was a reformer whose service, sacrifice, and love did not dissuade him from manly assertion. And although Jesus depended on disciples and followers, he could nonetheless inspire "real" men. Harry Emerson Fosdick reminded readers of *The Manhood of the Master* (1913): "The Master appeals to all that is strongest and most military in you." Jesus performed his manly duties, but he did so in ways different from the individualistic examples offered by the social gospelers' fathers. Jesus affirmed the social ideal and freed men from the unrealistic psychological burden of individual success and salvation, but he was not effeminate. The young men who had struggled unsuccessfully to live up to the ideals of their parents in the 1880s helped to create and endorse a new set of masculine ideals that were more appropriate in the large-scale workplaces of turn-of-the-century America. . . .

There is evidence of a subtle shift in the movement in the 1910s and 1920s. While still dedicated to the social gospel and social reform, many younger social gospelers began to plead for efficiency and businesslike promotion of their ideas. The socially responsible progressive reformer became the basis for the socially responsive man—and Jesus—of the 1920s. Under these changed conditions of the social gospel, images of Jesus underwent some subtle shifts as well. In the 1920s Jesus' charm, glowing good health, and physical strength served him well in his role as an effective leader of men. In 1920 Frederick Anderson discussed "Jesus and his career" and insisted that "the personality of the Man of Nazareth . . . is the power behind Christian history." . . . The ideal Jesus reflected personal traits that were valued by corporate America: charm, youth, personality, and the ability to work with others. Burton Easton's and Charles Fiske's "real Jesus," for example, was "impressive in appearance and of great physical strength." . . . Others, such as Bruce Barton and Walter Denny, emphasized his leadership. His success derived not from his skill as a fisherman, carpenter, or rabbi, and not even from his relationship to God the Father. Rather, it depended on his ability to organize and manipulate men.

God's image underwent no less dramatic a transformation than Jesus'. The God of the social gospelers' youth had been a stern and distant judge, not unlike their fathers. As the boys grew to manhood and came to terms with both their fathers and their faith, they modified this God in their work. As Henry Cope put it in *The Friendly Life* (1909), "God has grown in our thinking from a giant who makes worlds to a heart that suffers with ours, a soul that seeks ours, a being who is man's friend, and who cannot be satisfied until all humanity is embraced in that friendship." In the same year, William Dawson rejected the Old Testament God "of purity, not pity; of majesty, not compassion; of supreme ineffable righteousness and power and wisdom—the God of the roaring sea, and the live lightning, and the tremendous thunder, not the Parent of little children who claim His love and render in return their filial service. The Old Testament pictures God as a King, not God as a Parent." Dawson preferred God as a parent.

One of the consequences of this new portrait, however, was to diminish the importance of the Almighty to his children on earth. Josiah Strong noted in 1910 that in the late nineteenth century God had "gradually and rather unceremoniously bowed out of his universe." God's disappearance was due in part to attempts to authenticate and verify the historical accuracy of biblical events, for God himself eluded verification. Advances in science had offered alternative explanations for the creation and for the genesis of man that challenged God's power. Confidence in their ability to control and exploit the natural world made some men less dependent on and less attracted to the idea of divine intervention. But the judgmental God was also ushered out of his universe because he was too daunting and inaccessible to men who had rejected their fathers' stern individualism in religion and vocation. Lyman Abbott explained his aversion to the domineering God of his youth in *What Christianity Means to Me* (1912): "Suppose that all your life you had dreaded an awful God, or in fear submitted to a fateful God, or hesitated between defying and cringing before a hated God . . . and suddenly the curtain were rent aside and you saw the luminous figure of the living Christ, and over his head were written the words, 'This is thy God, O man.' " Abbott embraced the Son "who is upon earth" and who lived a "life of love, service, and sacrifice." Similarly, Rauschenbusch explained why he rarely wrote about God. "The God of the stellar universe is a God in whom I drown," he wrote. "Christ with the face of Jesus I can comprehend, and love, and assimilate. So I stick to him." . . .

When social gospelers became fathers themselves, they tried to define their relationships with their children in keeping with their ideal of Jesus. Perhaps to prevent the frustration they had felt toward their own fathers, social gospelers befriended their children and urged parents to treat their children as "chums." One social gospeler advised parents to appoint a "captain of the day," whose job would be to discipline siblings. They were loath to demand a standard of behavior that would set them apart from their children. . . . Rauschenbusch told his son Hilmar, "There is no love available to you which is so unvarying and always trustworthy as the love of your mother and father. . . . You must help us make the transition from parenthood to friendship."

This "friendship" changed the nature of the relationship between parents and their children, and it served the younger people well in a society increasingly based on interdependence. Instead of the old model, in which the son's struggle to transcend paternal authority prepared him for the competitive and individualistic workplace, social gospelers conceived of friendlier parental relationships as a means to build a cooperative and egalitarian society. Individualism, and masculinity, now took on meaning only in collective endeavor. This new relationship eased some of the frustration inherent in the masculine identity of Victorian Americans, but it failed to build a society founded on Christian cooperation. Even their children became something of a disappointment. Many chose secular careers and placed their faith in large institutions rather than in religion. Walter Rauschenbusch fretted in his final hours that his children neither loved nor understood him.

Images of Jesus and ideals of manhood evolved between the 1880s and the 1920s in response to one another. Anxieties over their own masculinity prompted social gospelers to look for a manly example, which they now found in Jesus. And as the social gospelers worked through both their identity and their religion, they altered both. The new ideals they created served as important components of an evolving culture from which later generations drew strength. Thus the social gospel had important cultural ramifications in the twentieth century. The definition of masculinity for late-Victorian men was conditioned by cultural expectations, experiences in childhood, and their own redefinition of religion and culture. They helped shift manliness away from an individual standard and toward a social, "other-directed" ideal. By the 1920s their social ideals merged with a capitalistic consumer culture, and identity formation ceased to be dominated by religion.

Women's Place Is at the Typewriter: The Contemporary Debate, 1889–1930

MARGERY DAVIES

When women first started to work in offices, their presence was regarded pretty much as an oddity, and either praised as a courageous experiment or castigated as a ridiculous mistake. For example, an 1875 engraving showed a shocked man entering an office "taken over by ladies." They were preening themselves before a mirror, fixing each other's hair, reading *Harper's Bazaar,* spilling ink on the floor—in short, doing everything but an honest day's work. The engraving made women working in an office seem ludicrous. Only in the 1890s was the question of such work for women debated in earnest. By then female office workers were no longer an oddity, and the sheer weight of their increasing numbers seems to have provoked a debate that was taken dead seriously by its participants.

The controversy over whether or not women should engage in office work took place within the context of the broader debate about whether or not women should work outside the home at all, a debate that endured throughout the period of this study, 1870 to 1930. The more specific question of female office work was still hotly disputed in 1930, forty years after it first surfaced. That this was so seems surprising. After all, fully a quarter of all employees in clerical occupations in 1900 were women and by 1930 they made up half of this workforce. Furthermore, the percentage of women was much greater in certain sectors: in 1880 they constituted 40 percent of all stenographers and typists, exceeded 75 percent in 1900, and made up over 95 percent by 1930. But as long as people were still arguing over whether or not woman's place was exclusively in the home, the question of women as office workers would continue. That it had become moot was irrelevant.

Those opposed to female clerical workers used three arguments: first, that "woman's nature" was not suited to clerical work; second, that women were physically incapable of such work; and third, that women were taking jobs away from men.

"Woman's Nature"

Opponents of female clerical workers maintained that women had been trained to be, and were destined to become, wives and mothers. Domestic concerns, it was argued, were critical to the development of women's character. These had made them the standard-bearers of a higher moral code than existed in the workday world outside the homes, or, as some claimed, had allowed them to become flighty and temperamental, protected as they had been from the mundane necessities of nondomestic life. No matter how it was defined, femininity was an integral part of women's personalities. And, argued opponents of women office workers, that femininity was inappropriate to clerical work or was in danger of being forfeited to the harsh realities of office life. Women simply would not survive as clerical workers; or if they did, it would be at the expense of their precious femininity. Both interpretations led to the same conclusion: women should devote themselves exclusively to that domestic sphere that was their original destiny. . . .

The case for the female office worker rarely challenged this view of woman's nature. In the first place, virtually no one suggested that woman's domestic role was not her most important one. Instead it was argued that office work actually made women better wives and mothers: it provided training in being systematic and well organized, which would be useful in future household management, and it offered an opportunity to experience first-hand the daily problems that their future husbands would face. Second, women's higher moral caliber—on which all agreed—would not be lost in the office. Rather, it would improve the business world. Third, defenders of women office workers tended to deny that women were flighty and temperamental. Finally, they argued that, while women certainly were possessed of femininity, they were in no danger of losing it in the office. They also assumed that, once married, female clerical workers would leave the office, femininity intact, to go off and build their domestic nests. . . .

One of the opening shots fired by the opponents of female employment was Marion Harland's article, "The Incapacity of Business Women," published in 1889. Harland did not equivocate: "it will be taken for granted that men conduct all branches of what is known as business—manufacturing, merchandising, professional, and even educational—more systematically and successfully than women." To prove his point, Harland compared the typical male and female office worker:

The office-boy is ruled up sharply by line and plummet, not only as to work, but deportment. He must be punctual, move quickly and quietly, leave all thought of frolic and out-door companionship behind when he crosses the threshold of his place of business; he must be prompt and respectful in speech to employers, and civil to customer, client, and caller—or he goes! The girl stenographer and typewriter "giggles and makes giggle" with the girl bookkeeper, and has tiffs (audible) with her enemy, the "old-maid" cashier. One and all, when reproved for negligence, breach of rules, or inefficiency, they retort, or sulk, or—most likely—snivel!

The explanation for this state of affairs lay in "the fact that women look forward to marriage as a definite means of support, and hold but loosely that which they may be called upon at any moment to give up." As a remedy for their incapacities, Harland recommended that women "undertake the allotted labor with the forceful purpose of performing it as if it were the one and only object in life." For, he concluded, "the steadfast industry, the discipline of speech and conduct, the concentration of thought and energy upon the matter set before one for accomplishment, that are essential to business prosperity, are the best conceivable preparation for the high and holy sphere of wife, housekeeper, and mother."

Shortly after Harland's article appeared, another writer, Clara Lanza, also took up the subject of the proper "woman's sphere." But this time the argument came down solidly in favor of female clerical workers, "the work of a clerk being admirably adapted to the sex." Lanza asked the head of a large publishing house whether he preferred to hire women or men as clerical workers:

"Women," was the answer, "are much to be preferred for a number of reasons. They are capable and industrious, and, so far as my personal experience goes, absolutely reliable. Besides, a woman is more conscientious about her work. . . . I wouldn't take men in place of these girls in any circumstances. Men are troublesome. . . .

Lanza also claimed that businessmen preferred female stenographers because they were better trusted with business secrets. While admitting that some hired women because their labor was cheaper, she maintained that "efficient women can command as high salaries as men." Lanza found that "the girls make good wives."

> There is nothing in clerical training that detracts from the finest womanly qualities, and men have outgrown their admiration for feminine helplessness and have come to look upon independence as something worth having. Clerical training educates the mind to accuracy in details, punctuality in the daily affairs of life, economy in the adjustment of time and quickness of perception. Perhaps this is the reason why so many men choose a wife amid the deft-fingered clerks in preference to the society misses. . . .

There are several interesting aspects of Lanza's argument. The critique of male clerical employees can be found elsewhere, and virtually word for word, in criticisms of female office workers. Moreover, her support for women in offices was based on "woman's nature," the rationale for Harland's opposition. But since Lanza concluded by noting that many clerical workers eventually married and what good preparation clerical work was for matrimonial life, she left the impression that women's ultimate goal was just what Harland had affirmed: the "high and holy sphere of wife, housekeeper, and mother." Harland and Lanza were at odds on the issue of women office workers, but their assumptions about woman's nature were identical.

One of the qualities ascribed to nineteenth-century women, or at least to those from bourgeois or professional backrounds, was a high level of moral idealism. Their finer moral spirit, it was argued, would be damaged if they entered the dog-eat-dog world of the business office. . . . Notions about woman's nature partly shifted after the 1880s and 1890s, and so did the grounds used in arguing that her nature made woman unsuitable for office work. By the 1920s woman was no longer portrayed as the protectress of higher values. Instead, she was depicted as scatterbrained, unable to concentrate on the business at hand in the office, too temperamental and emotional for the impersonal world of work.

In 1920 an article entitled "The Feminine Failure in Business" depicted the potential female office worker as a well-to-do woman speculating about what she would do if widowed. She would start a business career "modestly enough, private secretary to the president of a big bank or corporation or something of that sort." But her eyes would be fixed on matrimony, and the corporate president would be unable to resist the "pathetic and lonely" sight of his secretary dressed "simply in black and white—half mourning, you know." Another writer cautioned against using women as reception clerks: "It is just as inadvisable to have a girl at the reception desk. Nine out of ten girls are temperamental. On one day they are likely to flirt with every male visitor. On another day they are likely to be flippant. On still another they are likely to be unduly sarcastic. The tenth girl, who possesses the right qualifications for the reception desk, can be utilized in a more responsible position.'' The theme of woman's unstable temperament was still being sounded in 1929. An article on ''The Temperamental Typist'' claimed that certain women regarded ''their inability to get along with their fellows as a special gift from Nature.'' Such pride in moodiness prompted many employers to complain and wonder why their female employees could not ''forget their own personalities for a few hours a day.''

Significantly, critics of women office workers no longer urged women to leave clerical jobs; instead they merely complained about their behavior. Clearly, the number of female clerical workers had grown so large that even their opponents had to accept their presence. Some even admitted that a few women were able to overcome the handicaps inherent in woman's nature. But those who did so were then accused of losing their feminine qualities and becoming ''mannish.'' . . .

Others argued that it was entirely possible for a woman to maintain her femininity in the office. Harriet Brunkhurst cited the case of a woman who carefully distinguished between her positions as worker and woman in the office where she worked alongside her husband: ''I take my share of the office work as a man partner would, no favors and no shirking. It is business, not pretense with us. At the same time, if I forget my umbrella, I would not think of returning for it, nor would I think of going upstairs for something he could get for me. I am his wife, not his business partner, then.'' . . .

The claim that office work did not rob women of the femininity was generally invoked. Rather than defining ''femininity'' in different terms, supporters of women clerical workers were, by and large, content to turn opposing statements on their heads. Some, however, depicted women in terms markedly different from the conventional perspective, suggesting that women were perfectly capable of clear, efficient, rational intelligence: to oppose women entering the office because of some mistaken notion about their ''nature'' was ridiculous. George Gissing's *The Odd Women* is in large part the story of two English women, one of whom, Mary Barfoot, inherited some money and set up a school to give salable skills, particularly stenography and typewriting, to women who had to work. . . .

Barfoot challenged those who argued that women should leave office work because they were displacing men. She did not contend otherwise. Rather she defended women office workers on the ground that women were entitled to develop their potential: ''If woman is no longer to be womanish, but a human being of powers and responsibilities, she must become militant, defiant. She must push her claims to the extremity. . . . I don't care whether we crowd out the men or not. I don't care *what* results, if only women are made strong and self-reliant and nobly independent!'' . . .

Women's Physical Capacities

Although the main argument against female clerical workers was that woman's nature and office work did not mix, and that woman's place was in the home, other objections were also advanced. Women, for example, were considered physically or biologically unsuited to such work. An article of 1920 on "The Feminine Failure in Business" blamed woman's physical inferiority on her menstrual cycle:

> In the case of girls past their adolescent period there are physical obstacles to success in business which every employer of women in offices and shops fully understands. The loss of the services of women employees for several days each month is a serious problem where salaries are paid regularly and the "docking" system for absences is not in practice. The fact that women are less strong, less agile, less enduring under continued mental strain than men, makes it evident that woman in contest with man must be granted something more than a fair field and unrestricted competition.

A male stenographer for the U.S. Congress, who recorded congressional pontifications, offered his opinion on why women were not employed in this occupation: "they haven't the physical endurance. A reporter has to have the constitution of a Missouri mule." In 1929, the author of "The Temperamental Typist" felt that the physical reasons given for women not working in offices had been repeated so often that there was no need for him to do so.

The debate over whether women or men were physically more fit for office work had been going on for quite some time. Even *Scientific American* had examined the question "Are Men Better Typists than Women?" in 1913. It sought an answer in some "interesting scientific tests" done by a certain J. M. Lahy. What emerged was an unintentionally hilarious account of tests measuring muscular sensibility with the "myo-esthesimeter," the strength of the hand with the "Regnier-Cheron dynamometer," the tactile sense with the "Weber compass," and auditory reaction time with the "d'Arsonval chronoscope." After detailed descriptions of these various instruments, with careful attention paid to their degree of accuracy, the results of testing six women and five men, judged to be "strictly comparable" (exactly how they were comparable was not explained), were summarized. "Good women typists," Lahy found, demonstrated "tactile and muscular sensibility," an "excellent memory for letters," and "keen and sustained" attention; but they had a "relative slowness of auditory reaction." For their part, the men "surpass women in rapidity of auditory actions and, consequently, in speed of work, but are inferior to women, perhaps, in power of sustained attention." Lahy ended by acknowledging that his sample was too small to be conclusive and that his results "are merely indications which may be confirmed or invalidated by future researches."

These "indications" provoked a response from C. E. Smith, the author of *Practical Course in Touch Typewriting*, who favored women office workers, arguing that women surpassed men in manual dexterity. He also claimed that a typewriter keyboard was more suited to women than to men, since the latter were often handicapped by their "extremely large and strong fingers." This was "especially the case when all the fingers of the hands are employed in striking the keys, which is the only scientific method of operating a typewriter." . . .

That women did not have the physical endurance to withstand the grueling pace of office work was the biological grounds for opposition to women clerical workers. Their menstrual cycles, presumed to incapacitate them several days out of every month, were also cited. Proponents, however, usually asserted women's greater manual dexterity when calling upon biology to support their position. This emphasis on female manual dexterity was a double-edged sword. For it could justify the contention that woman's place was indeed at the typewriter, but not much higher in the office bureaucracy.

Displacing Men

The third issue that repeatedly cropped up in the office-work debate was that of women displacing male workers. Opponents of female office workers argued that women prevented men from getting good wages. Such deprivation in turn reduced the number of men who were financially able to marry and support their wives. Eleanor Whiting, for instance, affirmed that "sometimes [men's] wages are cut because of the competition of women; sometimes they are displaced altogether by women. The young man who should marry and become the head of a family finds himself displaced at the counter or in the office by a young woman who may be obliged to struggle single-handed with poverty for years because the man who is her social mate cannot afford to marry her."

In 1909 a "successful business woman" wrote a cautionary piece, "Why I Will Not Let My Daughter Go Into Business." The author had been married to a man incapable of sustained, diligent work who moved from job to job, always dissatisfied with something or other about his position. Finally, fed up with what she regarded as her husband's shiftlessness, she took on the work that he had just quit and made a success of it. Meanwhile he stayed home and took care of the house and children. One summer night, when her husband and children were away on a vacation that she could not afford the time to take, the "successful business woman"

> suddenly realized that John was not working at all, or at least just at intervals, earning enough so that he did not ask me to give him carfare or spending money. . . . Lying in the dark that night there came to me the sickening truth; I was supporting a man—a healthy, able-bodied, clear-brained man. . . .
>
> In the gray light of dawn I sent a telegram to my father. He came and said it was quite true. The world agreed with him and with me that I was doing my sons, my fine, straight-limbed lads, a grievous wrong in showing them the example of a father who "lives off" his wife's—a woman's—earnings. How did I expect to make men of them with such a man sitting at the head of the table?
>
> And again I chose the easier way. I secured a divorce!

But she now had to work hard to regain her children's affection, lost through the years of neglect. In the denouement, she learns that her husband had not only remarried, but had at last become a "successful man."

Some said that the shock of divorce and separation from his children had steadied him. Others said he had married money and had taken a fresh start. But I *knew*. He had married a woman who had done that in which I had failed—made a man of him. . . .

If I had grappled with my husband's weakness as I had with the problem of self-support!

It is too easy today for the woman to get into business. It is too easy, I say, for the family life, the domestic purity, the moral standard of our nation.

The message was obvious: for reasons of family stability and emotional health, rather than finance, women should not displace men if they had any choice in the matter. The "successful business woman" directed her advice explicitly at the "woman who does not have to become a wage-earner" and had only pity for those women forced to work for financial reasons.

George Gissing's *The Odd Women* contained the most direct response to the complaint that women were displacing men in office work. Male clerks, Mary Barfoot stated, "doubtless had a grievance. But, in the miserable disorder of our social state, one grievance had to be weighed against another, and . . . there was much more to be urged on behalf of women who invaded what had been exclusively the men's sphere, than on behalf of the men who began to complain of this invasion."

Harriet Brunkhurst, who was a staunch defender of women office workers, also countered the male-displacement argument. In most cases, she pointed out, the woman's wage was very badly needed. . . . In 1917 Brunkhurst advised working women to forgo domestic tasks lest they become overworked and nervous. Implicit in this advice was the assumption that women working in offices did so out of necessity, and that for them to try to fulfill the function of housewife as well was foolhardy. That they displaced men in offices may have been true, but financial need, not choice (as the "successful business woman" had argued), drove them. Instead of looking on them with pity, as that successful woman had done, Brunkhurst was more interested in lessening their burdens.

The Function of the Ideological Debate

Though many clerical jobs had been feminized by 1930, discord over the change continued. As noted earlier, it was only part of a larger and long-enduring debate on the whole subject of whether women should work outside the home at all. This partially explains why critics were still bothering to attack or justify women working in offices long after their employment was well established. The debate had another function, one that its participants were at best only dimly aware of: many of the assertions and conclusions of both sides served as ideological confirmation for the sexual stratification of the office labor force and for the concentration of women in lower-level work.

With the exception of Gissing's heroines and of Harriet Brunkhurst, participants in the debate assumed that woman's ultimate goal was to become a wife and mother. Supporters and opponents of female office workers differed only on whether office work assisted or damaged women in their preparations for matrimony and maternity. The conviction that woman's place was in the home served to justify her restriction to lower-level clerical work. If women eventually were going to stop working to marry and have children, what was the point of promoting them to managerial or even higher-level clerical positions? To do so would be a waste of resources and training. Furthermore, women whose hearts were set on future family life probably did not care that much about their work in the office. Or so the argument went, and thus did it legitimate their segregation in the lower-paid, lower-status jobs.

The manual-dexerity argument was used repeatedly as evidence that women made better typists than men. Since they did, small wonder that such a high percentage of typists were women. The concentration of women in typing jobs was thereby neatly justified.

A comparison of management policies concerning messenger boys and girls provides an interesting example of the way in which the ideological assumptions about men and women buttressed their respective positions and futures in the office. Although their policies were formally stated at about the same time, these companies seem to have been at different stages in the development of a highly stratified office workforce with rigid promotional channels. In 1923 one group of companies still regarded the position of messenger as an excellent springboard to managerial positions, but clearly the reference was to messenger *boys* only: "The Scott Company reports in one of its bulletins the results of a survey made in three nationally known companies of the messenger-boy situation. 'Messenger and office boys are of particular interest because they are so definitely a source of supply for future executive material. Messenger work offers a splendid chance to learn in an intimate way the methods and policies of a company. This is an educational opportunity that should be made available only to those who are capable of taking advantage of it.' " The policy of the Hupp Motor Company, stated two years later by its office manager, was altogether different: "The first radical change [in the messenger department] was the substitution of girls for boys. . . . It was immediately found that girls were more amenable to discipline. . . . A few months serve to tell whether a girl has special adaptability for any line of higher work we have to offer. Some are given the opportunity to practice typewriting during the noon hour. These girls usually take courses in typing at night school. Others seem better fitted for clerical work. Promotions to minor positions in other departments are made in accordance with the capacity of the particular girl." No more talk of "future executive material." A messenger *girl* at the Hupp Motor Company could hope to aspire only to a "minor position," and she was more likely to end up behind a typewriter.

The point here is that different assumptions were made about sex-linked characteristics. When the position of messenger was a training ground for executive positions, boys were characterized as "a natural and logical source of supply for higher positions." But when promotion led at most to a "minor position," boys were said to have a "natural tendency to boyishness and play" and to be less "amenable to discipline" than were girls. Thus the ideological assumptions about the natural characteristics of males and females were made to mesh very neatly with the way in which clerical work was organized. Assumptions about women helped to justify not only a situation in which women were clustered in the lower levels of a work organization, but also the very fact that such positions, devoid of much chance of substantial promotion, existed at all.

❧ F U R T H E R   R E A D I N G

Mark C. Carnes, *Secret Ritual and Manhood in Victorian America* (1989)
Margery Davies, *Woman's Place Is at the Typewriter* (1982)
Sidney Ditzion, *Marriage, Morals and Sex in America* (1953)
Peter Filene, *Him/Herself: Sex Roles in Modern America* (1986)
Linda Gordon, *Woman's Body, Woman's Right: A Social History of Birth Control in America* (1976)
John S. Haller and Robin M. Haller, *The Physician and Sexuality in Victorian America* (1974)
Helen Horowitz, *Alma Mater: Design and Experience in the Women's Colleges* (1984)
John Kasson, *Rudeness and Civility* (1990)
David M. Kennedy, *Birth Control in America* (1970)
J. A. Mangan and James Walvine, eds., *Manliness and Morality* (1987)
Carroll Smith-Rosenberg, *Disorderly Conduct: Visions of Gender in Victorian America* (1985)

CHAPTER

12

Protecting the Natural
and Man-Made Environments

*Environmentalism emerged as an important progressive cause, affecting attitudes
and public policies toward the cities as well as the land. On the one hand, its
emergence indirectly resulted from a general retreat from explanations of social
behavior (especially poverty and social "breakdown") in terms of individual
character and moral purity toward more collective, behaviorist terms of reference.
If "outside" influences significantly conditioned human actions, as social scientists
universally proclaimed, then the "control" of those influences became paramount.
In the cities this basic behaviorist argument could be used on behalf of parks and
playgrounds as well as sanitation campaigns.*

*Better known is the rise of the modern conservationist movement, closely
associated with President Theodore Roosevelt and his chief of the U.S. Forest
Service, Gifford Pinchot. In this form, "conservationism" is distinguished from
"preservationism": the former sought the application of science and engineering to
the responsible development of natural resources; the latter, attracting Sierra Club
founder John Muir, emphasized the aesthetic and spiritual virtues of the unspoiled
wilderness. In 1913 the two positions collided in the fight over the Hetch Hetchy
Dam, a project that would alleviate a water shortage in San Francisco—at the cost
of a section of Yosemite National Park.*

☙ DOCUMENTS

The first document, excerpted from a description by landscape architect par
excellence Frederick Law Olmsted on the benefits of New York City's Central
Park, suggests a connection between the moral reformers of the late nineteenth
century and the urban environmentalists of the Progressive Era. A gritty critique
by one of the latter, Upton Sinclair, is featured in the second document, taken
from *The Jungle,* Sinclair's famous exposé of the depredations of the
slaughterhouse industry.

The remaining selections highlight differences of emphasis within the ranks
of natural environmentalists. The third document, President Roosevelt's

path-breaking address to the Congress in 1907, cogently elaborates the argument for the federal government's conservation of natural resources. Preservationist Enos Mills, a disciple of John Muir, in the fourth document offers a poignant tribute to an ancient pine tree felled by developers. The last document presents congressional testimony concerning the Hetch Hetchy Dam, a project that stirred up a classical confrontation between utilitarian conservationists and wilderness preservationists. The controversy pitted former Chief Forester Gifford Pinchot, together with former San Francisco mayor James D. Phelan, against the Society for the Protection of National Parks, represented by Boston lawyer Edmund A. Whitman and poet Robert Underwood Johnson.

Frederick Law Olmsted Describes the Social Benefits of Central Park, 1870

No men less strong, and no men less confident in their strength than these men—by virtue in part of personal character, in part of the extraordinary powers vested in them by the legislature, and in part by the accident of certain anomalous political circumstances—happened to be, could have carried through a policy and a method which commanded so little immediate public favor. As it was, nothing but personal character, the common impression that after all they were honest, saved them. By barely a sabre's length they kept ahead of their pursuers, and of this you may still see evidence here and there in the park, chiefly where something left to stop a gap for the time being has been suffered to produce lasting defects. At one time nearly four thousand laborers were employed; and for a year at one point, work went on night and day in order to put it as quickly as possible beyond the reach of those who were bent on stopping it. . . .

For practical every-day purposes to the great mass of the people, the Park might as well be a hundred miles away. There are hundreds of thousands who have never seen it, more hundreds of thousands who have seen it only on a Sunday or holiday. The children of the city to whom it should be of the greatest use, can only get to it on holidays or in vacations, and then must pay car-fare both ways.

It must be remembered, also, that the Park is not planned for such use as is now made of it, but with regard to the future use, when it will be in the centre of a population of two millions hemmed in by water at a short distance on all sides; and that much of the work done upon it is, for this reason, as yet quite barren of results.

The question of the relative value of what is called off-hand common sense, and of special, deliberate, business-like study, must be settled in the case of the Central Park, by a comparison of benefit with cost. During the last four years over thirty million visits have been made to the Park by actual count, and many have passed uncounted. From fifty to eighty thousand persons on foot, thirty thousand in carriages, and four to five thousand on horseback, have often entered it in a day.

Among the frequent visitors, I have found all those who, a few years ago, believed it impossible that there should ever be a park in this republican country,—and especially in New York of all places in this country,—which would be a suitable place of resort for "gentlemen." They, their wives and daughters, frequent the Park more than they do the opera or the church.

There are many men of wealth who resort to the Park habitually and regularly, as much so as business men to their places of business. Of course, there is a reason for it, and a reason based upon their experience.

As to the effect on public health, there is no question that it is already great. The testimony of the older physicians of the city will be found unanimous on this point. Says one: "Where I formerly ordered patients of a certain class to give up their business altogether and go out of town, I now often advise simply moderation, and prescribe a ride in the Park before going to their offices, and again a drive with their families before dinner. By simply adopting this course as a habit, men . . . are able to retain an active and controlling influence in an important business, from which they would have otherwise been forced to retire. . . .

The lives of women and children too poor to be sent to the country, can now be saved in thousands of instances, by making them go to the Park. During a hot day in July last, I counted at one time in the Park eighteen separate groups, consisting of mothers with their children, most of whom were under school-age, taking picnic dinners which they had brought from home with them. The practice is increasing under medical advice, especially when summer complaint is rife.

The much greater rapidity with which patients convalesce, and may be returned with safety to their ordinary occupations after severe illness, when they can be sent to the Park for a few hours a day, is beginning to be understood. The addition thus made to the productive labor of the city is not unimportant.

The Park, moreover, has had a very marked effect in making the city attractive to visitors, and in thus increasing its trade, and causing many who have made fortunes elsewhere to take up their residence and become taxpayers in it,—a much greater effect in this way, beyond all question, than all the colleges, schools, libraries, museums, and art-galleries which the city possesses. It has also induced many foreigners who have grown rich in the country, and who would otherwise have gone to Europe to enjoy their wealth, to settle permanently in the city.

And what has become of the great Bugaboo? This is what the "Herald" of later date answers:—

"When one is inclined to despair of the country, let him go to the Central Park on a Saturday, and spend a few hours there in looking at the people, not at those who come in gorgeous carriages, but at those who arrive on foot, or in those exceedingly democratic conveyances, the street-cars;" . . . the effusion winding up thus: "We regret to say that the more brilliant becomes the display of vehicles and toilettes, the more shameful is the display of bad manners on the part of the—extremely fine-looking people who ride in carriages and wear the fine dresses. We must add that the pedestrians always behave well."

Here we touch a fact of more value to social science than any other in the history of the Park; but to fully set it before you would take an evening by itself. The difficulty of preventing ruffianism and disorder in a park to be frequented indiscriminately by such a population as that of New York, was from the first regarded as the greatest of all those which the commission had to meet, and the means of overcoming it cost more study than all other things.

It is, perhaps, too soon to judge of the value of the expedients resorted to, but there are as yet a great many parents who are willing to trust their school-girl daughters to ramble without special protection in the Park, as they would almost nowhere else in New York. One is no more likely to see ruffianism or indecencies in the Park than in the churches, and the arrests for offenses of all classes, including the most venial, which arise simply from the ignorance of country people, have amounted to but twenty in the million of the number of visitors, and of these, an exceedingly small proportion have been of that class which was so confidently expected to take possession of the Park and make it a place unsafe and unfit for decent people. . . .

Jeremy Bentham, in treating of "The Means of Preventing Crimes," remarks that any innocent amusement that the human heart can invent is useful under a double point of view: first, for the pleasure itself which results from it; second, from its tendency to weaken the dangerous inclinations which man derives from his nature.

No one who has closely observed the conduct of the people who visit the Park, can doubt that it exercises a distinctly harmonizing and refining influence upon the most unfortunate and most lawless classes of the city,—an influence favorable to courtesy, self-control, and temperance.

At three or four points in the midst of the Park, beer, wine, and cider are sold with other refreshments to visitors, not at bars, but served at tables where men sit in company with women. Whatever harm may have resulted, it has apparently had the good effect of preventing the establishment of drinking-places on the borders of the Park, these not having increased in number since it was opened, as it was originally supposed they would.

I have never seen or heard of a man or woman the worse for liquor taken at the Park, except in a few instances where visitors had brought it with them, and in which it had been drank secretly and unsocially. The present arrangements for refreshments I should say are makeshift and most discordant with the design.

Every Sunday in summer from thirty to forty thousand persons, on an average, enter the Park on foot, the number on a very fine day being sometimes nearly a hundred thousand. While most of the grog-shops of the city were effectually closed by the police under the Excise Law on Sunday, the number of visitors to the Park was considerably larger than before. There was no similar increase at the churches.

Shortly after the Park first became attractive, and before any serious attempt was made to interfere with the Sunday liquor trade, the head-keeper told me that he saw among the visitors the proprietor of one of the largest "saloons" in the city. He accosted him and expressed some surprise; the man replied, "I came to see what the devil you'd got here that took off so many of my Sunday customers."

Upton Sinclair Depicts Chicago's Garbage Dumps, 1906

Later that afternoon he and Ona went out to take a walk and look about them, to see more of this district which was to be their home. In back of the yards the dreary two-story frame houses were scattered farther apart, and there were great spaces bare—that seemingly had been overlooked by the great sore of a city as it spread itself over the surface of the prairie. These bare places were grown up with dingy, yellow weeds, hiding innumerable tomato-cans; innumerable children played upon them, chasing one another here and there, screaming and fighting. The most uncanny thing about this neighborhood was the number of the children; you thought there must be a school just out, and it was only after long acquaintance that you were able to realize that there was no school, but that these were the children of the neighborhood—that there were so many children to the block in Packingtown that nowhere on its streets could a horse and buggy move faster than a walk!

It could not move faster anyhow, on account of the state of the streets. Those through which Jurgis and Ona were walking resembled streets less than they did a miniature topographical map. The roadway was commonly several feet lower than the level of the houses, which were sometimes joined by high board walks; there were no pavements—there were mountains and valleys and rivers, gullies and ditches, and great hollows full of stinking green water. In these pools the children played, and rolled about in the mud of the streets; here and there one noticed them digging in it, after trophies which they had stumbled on. One wondered about this, as also about the swarms of flies which hung about the scene, literally blackening the air, and the strange, fetid odor which assailed one's nostrils, a ghastly odor, of all the dead things of the universe. It impelled the visitor to questions—and then the residents would explain, quietly, that all this was "made" land, and that it had been "made" by using it as a dumping-ground for the city garbage. After a few years the unpleasant effect of this would pass away, it was said; but meantime, in hot weather—and especially when it rained—the flies were apt to be annoying. Was it not unhealthful? the stranger would ask, and the residents would answer, "Perhaps; but there is no telling."

A little way further on, and Jurgis and Ona, staring open-eyed and wondering, came to the place where this "made" ground was in process of making. Here was a great hole, perhaps two city blocks square, and with long files of garbage wagons creeping into it. The place had an odor for which there are no polite words; and it was sprinkled over with children, who raked in it from dawn till dark. Sometimes visitors from the packing-houses would wander out to see this "dump," and they would stand by and debate as to whether the children were eating the food they got, or merely collecting it for the chickens at home. Apparently none of them ever went down to find out.

Beyond this dump there stood a great brick-yard, with smoking chimneys. First they took out the soil to make bricks, and then they filled it up again with garbage, which seemed to Jurgis and Ona a felicitous arrangement, characteristic of an enterprising country like America. A little way beyond was another great hole, which they had emptied and not yet filled up. This held water, and all summer it stood there, with the near-by soil draining into it, festering and stewing in the sun; and then, when winter came, somebody cut the ice on it, and sold it to the people of the city. This, too, seemed to the newcomers an economical arrangement; for they did not read the newspapers, and their heads were not full of troublesome thoughts about "germs.". . .

President Theodore Roosevelt's Conservation Message, 1907

To the Senate and House of Representatives:

. . . The conservation of our natural resources and their proper use constitute the fundamental problem which underlies almost every other problem of our national life. . . . As a nation we not only enjoy a wonderful measure of present prosperity but if this prosperity is used aright it is an earnest of future success such as no other nation will have. The reward of foresight for this nation is great and easily foretold. But there must be the look ahead, there must be a realization of the fact that to waste, to destroy, our natural resources, to skin and exhaust the land instead of using it so as to increase its usefulness, will result in undermining in the days of our children the very prosperity which we ought by right to hand down to them amplified and developed. For the last few years, through several agencies, the government has been endeavoring to get our people to look ahead and to substitute a planned and orderly development of our resources in place of a haphazard striving for immediate profit. Our great river systems should be developed as national water highways, the Mississippi, with its tributaries, standing first in importance, and the Columbia second, although there are many others of importance on the Pacific, the Atlantic, and the Gulf slopes. The National Government should undertake this work, and I hope a beginning will be made in the present Congress; and the greatest of all our rivers, the Mississippi, should receive special attention. From the Great Lakes to the mouth of the Mississippi there should be a deep waterway, with deep waterways leading from it to the East and the West. Such a waterway would practically mean the extension of our coastline into the very heart of our country. It would be of incalculable benefit to our people. If begun at once it can be carried through in time appreciably to relieve the congestion of our great freight-carrying lines of railroads. The work should be systematically and continuously carried forward in accordance with some well-conceived plan. The main streams should be improved to the highest point of efficiency before the improvement of the branches is attempted; and the work should be kept free from every taint of recklessness or jobbery. The inland waterways which lie just back of the whole Eastern and Southern coasts should likewise be developed. Moreover, the development of our waterways involves many other important water problems, all of which should be considered as part of the same general scheme. The government dams should be used to produce hundreds of thousands of horse-power as an incident to improving navigation; for the annual value of the unused water-power of the United States perhaps exceeds the annual value of the products of all our mines. As an incident to creating the deep waterways down the Mississippi, the government should build along its whole lower length levees which, taken together with the control of the headwaters, will at once and forever put a complete stop to all threat of floods in the immensely fertile delta region. The territory lying adjacent to the Mississippi along its lower course will thereby become one of the most prosperous and populous, as it already is one of the most fertile, farming regions in all the world. I have appointed an inland waterways commission to study and outline a comprehensive scheme of development along all the lines indicated. Later I shall lay its report before the Congress.

Irrigation should be far more extensively developed than at present, not only in the States of the great plains and the Rocky Mountains, but in many others, as, for instance, in large portions of the South Atlantic and Gulf States, where it should go hand in hand with the reclamation of swampland. The Federal Government should seriously devote itself to this task, realizing that utilization of waterways and water-power, forestry, irrigation, and the reclamation of lands threatened with overflow, are all interdependent parts of the same problem. The work of the Reclamation Service in developing the larger opportunities of the Western half of our country for irrigation is more important than almost any other movement. The constant purpose of the government in connection with the Reclamation Service has been to use the water resources of the public lands for the ultimate greatest good of the greatest number; in other words, to put upon the land permanent home-makers, to use and develop it for themselves and for their children and children's children. . . .

Some such legislation as that proposed is essential in order to preserve the great stretches of public grazing-land which are unfit for cultivation under present methods and are valuable only for the forage which they supply. These stretches amount in all to some 30,000,000 acres, and are open to the free grazing of cattle, sheep, horses, and goats, without restriction. Such a system, or lack of system, means that the range is not so much used as wasted by abuse. As the West settles, the range becomes more and more overgrazed. Much of it cannot be used to advantage unless it is fenced; for fencing is the only way by which to keep in check the owners of nomad flocks which roam hither and thither, utterly destroying the pastures and leaving a waste behind so that their presence is incompatible with the presence of home-makers. The existing fences are all illegal. . . . All these fences, those that are hurtful and those that are beneficial, are alike illegal and must come down. But it is an outrage that the law should necessitate such action on the part of the Administration. The unlawful fencing of public lands for private grazing must be stopped, but the necessity which occasioned it must be provided for. The

Federal Government should have control of the range, whether by permit or lease, as local necessities may determine. Such control could secure the great benefit of legitimate fencing, while at the same time securing and promoting the settlement of the country. . . . The government should part with its title only to the actual home-maker, not to the profit-maker who does not care to make a home. Our prime object is to secure the rights and guard the interests of the small ranchman, the man who ploughs and pitches hay for himself. It is this small ranchman, this actual settler and home-maker, who in the long run is most hurt by permitting thefts of the public land in whatever form.

Optimism is a good characteristic, but if carried to an excess it becomes foolishness. We are prone to speak of the resources of this country as inexhaustible; this is not so. The mineral wealth of the country, the coal, iron, oil, gas, and the like, does not reproduce itself, and therefore is certain to be exhausted ultimately; and wastefulness in dealing with it today means that our descendants will feel the exhaustion a generation or two before they otherwise would. But there are certain other forms of waste which could be entirely stopped—the waste of soil by washing, for instance, which is among the most dangerous of all wastes now in progress in the United States, is easily preventable, so that this present enormous loss of fertility is entirely unnecessary. The preservation or replacement of the forests is one of the most important means of preventing this loss . . . We should acquire in the Appalachian and White Mountain regions all the forest-lands that it is possible to acquire for the use of the nation. These lands, because they form a national asset, are as emphatically national as the rivers which they feed, and which flow through so many States before they reach the ocean. . . .

Enos Mills Mourns the Death of a One-Thousand-Year-Old Pine, 1914

I

The peculiar charm and fascination that trees exert over many people I had always felt from childhood, but it was that great nature-lover, John Muir, who first showed me how and where to learn their language. Few trees, however, ever held for me such an attraction as did a gigantic and venerable yellow pine which I discovered one autumn day several years ago while exploring the southern Rockies. It grew within sight of the Cliff-Dwellers' Mesa Verde [Colorado], which stands at the corner of four States, and as I came upon it one evening just as the sun was setting over that mysterious tableland, its character and heroic proportions made an impression upon me that I shall never forget, and which familiar acquaintance only served to deepen while it yet lived and before the axeman came. Many a time I returned to build my camp-fire by it and have a day or a night in its solitary and noble company. I learned afterwards that it had been given the name "Old Pine," and it certainly had an impressiveness quite compatible with the age and dignity which go with a thousand years of life.

When, one day, the sawmill-man at Mancos wrote, "Come, we are about to log your old pine," I started at once, regretting that a thing which seemed to me so human, as well as so noble, must be killed.

I went with the axemen who were to cut the old pine down. . . . Never have I seen so much individuality, so much character, in a tree. Although lightning had given him a bald crown, he was still a healthy giant, and was waving evergreen banners more than one hundred and fifteen feet above the earth. His massive trunk, eight feet in diameter at the level of my breast, was covered with a thick, rough, golden-brown bark which was broken into irregular plates. Several of his arms were bent and broken. Altogether, he presented a timeworn but heroic appearance. . . .

Trees, like people, struggle for existence, and an aged tree, like an aged person, has not only a striking appearance, but an interesting biography. I have read the autobiographies of many century-old trees, and have found their life-stories strange and impressive. The yearly growth, or annual ring of wood with which trees envelop themselves, is embossed with so many of their experiences that this annual ring of growth literally forms an autobiographic diary of the tree's life.

I wanted to read Old Pine's autobiography. A veteran pine that had stood on the southern Rockies and struggled and triumphed through the changing seasons of hundreds of years must contain a rare life-story. . . . Many a wondrous secret he had locked within his tree soul. Yet, although he had not recorded what he had *seen,* I knew that he had kept a fairly accurate diary of his own personal experience. This I knew the saw would reveal, and this I had determined to see. . . .

II

Two loggers swung their axes: at the first blow a Frémont squirrel came out of a hole at the base of a dead limb near the top of the tree and made an aggressive claim of ownership, setting up a vociferous protest against the cutting. . . . From time to time he came out on the top of the limb nearest to us, and, with a wry face, fierce whiskers, and violent gestures, directed a torrent of abuse at the axemen who were delivering death-blows to Old Pine.

The old pine's enormous weight caused him to fall heavily, and he came to earth with tremendous force and struck on an elbow of one of his stocky arms. The force of the fall not only broke the trunk in two, but badly shattered it. The damage to the log was so general that the sawmill-man said it would not pay to saw it into lumber and that it could rot on the spot. . . . Receiving permission to do as I pleased with his remains, I at once began to cut and split both the trunk and the limbs, and to transcribe their strange records. Day after day I worked. I dug up the roots and thoroughly dissected them, and with the aid of a magnifier I studied the trunk, the roots, and the limbs.

I carefully examined the base of his stump, and in it I found ten hundred and forty-seven rings of growth! He had lived through a thousand and forty-seven memorable years. As he was cut down in 1903, his birth probably occurred in 856.

In looking over the rings of growth, I found that a few of them were much thicker than the others; and these thick rings, or coats of wood, tell of favorable seasons. There were also a few extremely thin rings of growth. In places two and even three of these were together. These were the results of unfavorable seasons,—of drought or cold. . . . The somewhat kinked condition of several of the rings of growth, beginning with the twentieth, shows that at the age of twenty he sustained an injury which resulted in a severe curvature of the spine, and that for some years he was somewhat stooped. I was unable to make out from his diary whether this injury was the result of a tree or some object falling upon him and pinning him down, or whether his back had been overweighted and bent by wet, clinging snow. . . . However, after a few years he straightened up with youthful vitality and seemed to outgrow and forget the experience.

A century of tranquil life followed, and during these years the rapid growth tells of good seasons as well as good soil. This rapid growth also shows that there could not have been any crowding neighbors to share the sun and the soil. The tree had grown evenly in all quarters, and the pith of the tree was in the center. . . .

When the old pine was just completing his one hundred and thirty-fifth ring of growth, he met with an accident which I can account for only by assuming that a large tree that grew several yards away blew over, and in falling, stabbed him in the side with two dead limbs. His bark was broken and torn, but this healed in due time. . . .

A year or two later some ants and borers began excavating their deadly winding ways in the old pine. They probably started to work in one of the places injured by the falling tree. . . . Both the borers and the ants succeeded in establishing colonies that threatened injury and possibly death.

Fortunately relief came. One day the chief surgeon of all the Southwestern pineries came along. This surgeon was the Texas woodpecker. . . . After a brief examination, holding his ear to the bark for a moment to get the location of the tree's deadly foe beneath, he was ready to act. He made two successful operations. . . . The wounds finally healed, and only the splitting of the affected parts revealed these records, all filled with pitch and preserved for nearly nine hundred years.

Following this, an even tenor marked his life for nearly three centuries. This quiet existence came to an end in the summer of 1301, when a stroke of lightning tore a limb out of his round top and badly shattered a shoulder. He had barely recovered from this injury when a violent wind tore off several of his arms. During the summer of 1348 he lost two of his largest arms. These were sound, and more than a foot in diameter at the points of breakage. . . .

It is doubtful if there is any portion of the earth upon which there are so many deadly struggles as upon the earth around the trunk of a tree. Upon this small arena there are battles fierce and wild; here nature is "red in tooth and claw." . . . Around the tree are daily almost merciless fights for existence. These death-struggles occur not only in the daytime, but in the night. Mice, rats, and rabbits destroy millions of young trees. . . . The owl, the faithful night-watchman of trees, often swoops down at night, and as a result some little tree is splashed with the blood of the very animal that came to feed upon it.

The lower section of Old Pine's trunk contained records which I found interesting. One of these in particular aroused my imagination. I was sawing off a section of this lower portion when the saw, with a *buzz-z-z-z*, suddenly jumped. The object struck was harder than the saw. I wondered what it could be, and, cutting the wood carefully away, laid bare a flint arrowhead. . . . The outer ring which these arrowheads had pierced was the six hundred and thirtieth, so that the year of this occurrence was 1486.

Had an Indian bent his bow and shot at a bear that had stood at bay backed up against this tree? Or was there around this tree a battle among Indian tribes? Is it possible that at this place some Cliff-Dweller scouts encountered their advancing foe from the north and opened hostilities? It may be that around Old Pine was fought the battle that is said to have decided the fate of that mysterious race, the Cliff-Dwellers. . . .

III

After I had finished my work of splitting, studying, and deciphering the fragments of the old pine, I went to the sawmill and arranged for the men to come over that evening after I had departed, and burn every piece and vestige of the venerable old tree. I told them I should be gone by dark on a trip to the summit of Mesa Verde, where I was to visit a gnarled old cedar. Then I went back and piled into a pyramid every fragment of root and trunk and broken branch. Seating myself upon this pyramid, I spent some time that afternoon gazing through the autumn sun-glow at the hazy Mesa Verde, while my mind rebuilt and shifted the scenes of the long, long drama in which Old Pine had played his part and of which he had given us but a few fragmentary records. I lingered there dreaming until twilight. I thought of the cycles during which he had stood patient in his appointed place, and my imagination busied itself with the countless experiences that had been recorded, and the scenes and pageants he had witnessed but of which he had made no record. . . . More than a thousand times he had beheld the earth burst into bloom amid happy songs of mating birds; hundreds of times in summer he had worn countless crystal rain-jewels in the sunlight of the breaking storm, while the brilliant rainbow came and vanished on the near-by mountain-side. Ten thousand times he had stood silent in the lonely light of the white and mystic moon.

Twilight was fading into darkness when I arose and started on my night journey for the summit of Mesa Verde. When I arrived at the top of the Mesa, I looked back and saw a pyramid of golden flame standing out in the darkness.

Public Debate over the Hetch Hetchy Dam, 1913

Mr. Pinchot. . . . We come now face to face with the perfectly clean question of what is the best use to which this water that flows out of the Sierras can be put. As we all know, there is no use of water that is higher than the domestic use. Then, if there is, as the engineers tell us, no other source of supply that is anything like so reasonably available as this one; if this is the best, and within reasonable limits of cost, the only means of supplying San Francisco with water, we come straight to the question of whether the advantage of leaving this valley in a state of nature is greater than the advantage of using it for the benefit of the city of San Francisco.

Now, the fundamental principle of the whole conservation policy is that of use, to take every part of the land and its resources and put it to that use in which it will best serve the most people, and I think there can be no question at all but that in this case we have an instance in which all weighty considerations demand the passage of the bill. There are, of course, a very large number of incidental changes that will arise after the passage of the bill. The construction of roads, trails, and telephone systems which will follow the passage of this bill will be a very important help in the park and forest reserves. The national forest telephone system and the roads and trails to which this bill will lead will form an important additional help in fighting fire in the forest reserves. As has already been set forth by the two Secretaries, the presence of these additional means of communication will mean that the national forest and the national park will be visited by very large numbers of people who cannot visit them now. I think that the men who assert that it is better to leave a piece of natural scenery in its natural condition have rather the better of the argument, and I believe if we had nothing else to consider than the delight of the few men and women who would yearly go into the Hetch Hetchy Valley, then it should be left in its natural condition. But the considerations on the other side of the question to my mind are simply overwhelming, and so much so that I have never been able to see that there was any reasonable argument against the use of this water supply by the city of San Francisco. . . .

Mr. Raker [U.S. Congressman from California]. Taking the scenic beauty of the park as it now stands, and the fact that the valley is sometimes swamped along in June and July, is it not a fact that if a beautiful dam is put there, as is contemplated, and as the picture is given by the engineers, with the roads contemplated around the reservoir and with other trails, it will be more beautiful than it is now, and give more opportunity for the use of the park?

Mr. Pinchot. Whether it will be more beautiful, I doubt, but the use of the park will be enormously increased. I think there is no doubt about that.

Mr. Raker. In other words, to put it a different way, there will be more beauty accessible than there is now?

Mr. Pinchot. Much more beauty will be accessible than now.

Mr. Raker. And by putting in roads and trails the Government, as well as the citizens of the Government, will get more pleasure out of it than at the present time?

Mr. Pinchot. You might say from the standpoint of enjoyment of beauty and the greatest good to the greatest number, they will be conserved by the passage of this bill, and there will be a great deal more use of the beauty of the park than there is now.

Mr. Raker. Have you seen Mr. John Muir's criticism of the bill? You know him?

Mr. Pinchot. Yes, sir; I know him very well. He is an old and very good friend of mine. I have never been able to agree with him in his attitude toward the Sierras for the reason that my point of view has never appealed to him at all. When I became Forester and denied the right to exclude sheep and cows from the Sierras, Mr. Muir thought I had made a great mistake, because I allowed the use by an acquired right of a large number of people to interfere with what would have been the utmost beauty of the forest. In this case I think he has unduly given away to beauty as against use. . . .

Mr. Phelan [former mayor of San Francisco] . . . I will only emphasize the fact that the needs of San Francisco are pressing and urgent. San Francisco is expanding with tremendous rapidity due to the development of the interior of California and to the prospect of the early opening of the canal and the building of the exposition, and already, not withstanding the threat of a water famine, the outlying district, which never before was developed, is being cut up into suburban tracts.

A large number of our population has been lost to Oakland, Alameda, and Berkeley, by reason of the fact that we have never had adequate facilities either of transportation or of water supply to meet what would otherwise be a demand for residences on the peninsula. There are disadvantages in crossing the bay. So San Francisco, the chief Federal city on the Pacific coast, asks the Federal Government for assistance in this matter of grant and not by money. It has obligated itself to pay $70,000,000 for a water supply. We have endeavored to satisfy the needs of the irrigationists in good faith, as well as the local water monopoly, and we come this year to Washington, I think, with the good will of those heretofore opposed, possibly with the exception of the gentlemen who are devoted to the preservation of the beauties of nature.

As Californians, we rather resent gentlemen from different parts of the country outside of California telling us that we are invading the beautiful natural resources of the State or in any way marring or detracting from them. We have a greater pride than they in the beauties of California, in the valleys, in the big trees, in the rivers, and in the high mountains. We have the highest mountain in the United States in California, Mount Whitney, 15,000 feet above the sea, as we have the lowest land, in Death Valley, 300 feet below the sea. We have the highest tree known in the world, and the oldest tree. Its history goes back 2,000 years, I believe, judged by the internal evidences; as we have the youngest in the world, Luther Burbank's plumcot.

All of this is of tremendous pride, and even for a water supply we would not injure the great resources which have made our State the playground of the world. By constructing a dam at this very narrow gorge in the Hetch Hetchy Valley, about 700 feet across, we create, not a reservoir, but a lake, because Mr. Freeman, who has studied the situation in Manchester or Birmingham, where there is a similar case, has shown that by planting trees or vines over the dam, the idea of a dam, the appearance of a dam, is entirely lost; so, coming upon it will look like an emerald gem in the mountains; and one of the few things in which California is deficient, especially in the Sierras, is lakes, and in this way we will contribute, in large measure, to the scenic grandeur and beauty of California. I suppose nature lovers, suspecting a dam there not made by the Creator, will think it of no value, in their estimation, but I submit, man can imitate the Creator—a worthy exemplar. . . .

Mr. Graham [U.S. Congressman from Illinois]. In that they are mistaken by a dam site?

Mr. Phelan. They are mistaken by a dam site, and after it is constructed, as somebody said, not wishing to be outdone in profanity, "It will be the damdest finest sight you ever saw."

I remember the story of John Hay's Little Breeches, which describes the old fellow, who, believing in nothing that was religious or good, and having been told, after his child recovered, that he had wandered away in the woods and must have been restored by the angels, said:

> To restore the life of a little child and to bring him back to his own,
> Is a darn sight better business than loafing 'round the throne.

To provide for the little children, men, and women of the 800,000 population who swarm the shores of San Francisco Bay is a matter of much greater importance than encouraging the few who, in solitary loneliness, will sit on the peak of the Sierras loafing around the throne of the God of nature and singing His praise. A benign father loves his children above all things. There is no comparison between the highest use of the water—the domestic supply—and the mere scenic value of the mountains. When you decide that affirmatively, as you must, and then, on top of that, that we are not detracting from the scenic value of the mountains, but enhancing it, I think there is nothing left to be said. That is all. . . .

Mr. Whitman [U.S. Congressman from Washington]. You are asked to consider this park as it is at present, with almost nobody using it. Very little attention has been given to what may happen to this park by the year 2000. On the other hand, the city desires to focus your attention to the year 2000 for its water supply. They are getting along and can get along perfectly comfortably for a good many years for their local supply, but it is the year 2000 they want you to look to. If you look to the year 2000 in one way, I pray you to look to it in the other. What will that park be and what will the use of it be to the American public, winter and summer, in the year 2000?

Now, I have said nothing about nature. I have tried to put this thing on a practical ground, which will appeal to the American citizen, and I do not want to add anything as to nature. But I have a letter here addressed to the chairman of this committee from Robert Underwood Johnson, who was, with Mr. John Muir, the original cause of the establishment of this park, and he has put this matter so admirably in his letter that, as a few concluding words, I should like to read it. There is not very much of it. He says:

New York, June 25, 1913

Hon. Scott Ferris, M. C.,
Chairman House Committee on the Public Lands,
Washington, D.C.

What is at stake is not merely the destruction of a single valley, one of the most wonderful works of the Creator, but the fundamental principle of conservation. Let it be established that these great parks and forests are to be held at the whim or advantage of local interests and sooner or later they must all be given up. One has only to look about to see the rampant materialism of the day. It can only be overcome by a constant regard for ideas and for the good of the whole country now and hereafter. The very sneers with which this type of argument is received are a proof of the need of altruism and imagination in dealing with the subject. The time has not yet come to substitute for our national motto those baleful words, "let us eat, drink, and be merry, for to-morrow we die."

The opponents of the Hetch Hetchy scheme maintain that their position is not inimical to the true interests of San Francisco. They say if there were no other source of good and abundant water for the city they would willingly sacrifice the valley to the lives and the health of its citizens. The records of the hearing before the Senate Committee on Public Lands two or three years ago show that two official representatives of the city (one, ex-Mayor Phelan) confessed that the city could get water anywhere along the Sierra if she would pay for it. This is the crux of the whole matter. The assault upon the integrity of the park has this purpose— to get something for nothing. Mr. Freeman, the engineer employed by the city, has also stated that it is physically possible to get water anywhere along the Sierra. The elaborate published examination of the Hetch Hetchy resources bears the proportion, let us say, of 30 or 50 to 1 to all the information concerning other sources. It has not been demonstrated that Hetch Hetchy is the only available source, but only that it might be the cheapest. On this point we hold that while we are willing to die for the lives or the health of the citizens of San Francisco, we are not willing to die for their pockets.

We believe, moreover, that a larger measure of attention should be given to the question of filtration. I have already called your attention to the system in operation at Toledo, under which typhoid fever has almost disappeared, and to the abandonment by the city of London of its project of a supply from the Welsh Mountains in favor of the same system of filtration. I earnestly suggest that the advantages of this method be made the subject of an official examination during the present summer by United States Government experts, for if such a system be feasible, it would be folly to destroy the valley and dismember the park to have it discovered later that they must, after all, be abandoned for a method both better and cheaper.

The opponents of the bill invite your careful attention to the fact that whereas at first the scheme was put forward as one appealing to humane instincts—to provide a great city with potable water—it is now clearly seen to be aiming at quite another purpose—the production of power for use and for sale. This is commercialism pure and simple, and the far-reaching results of this disposition of the national parks when the destruction of their supreme features is involved, is something appalling to contemplate.

I have not yet spoken of the great recreative, curative, and hygienic uses of the park. It contains three considerable camping spots—the Yosemite Valley, now greatly crowded every summer; the Tuolumne Meadows, and the Hetch Hetchy. The second is much more difficult of access than the third, and both would be withdrawn from public use by the operation of the proposed bill, for it would be idle to take the valley for a reservoir without giving to the city full control of the watershed, since a single case of typhoid infection would endanger the health of the city. The population of the San Joaquin Valley, in the hot and dusty summer, increasingly frequent the park as campers. These would be deprived of the use of these wonderful scenes. As for the general public of travelers, that take so much money to California in quest of beauty—for it, there would be only a phantom valley, sunken, like the fabled city of Brittany, while the 20 miles of the most wonderful rapids in the world, the cascades of the Tuolumne, would be virtually eclipsed. I am aware that in certain quarters one who contends for the practical value of natural beauty is considered a "crank," and yet the love of beauty is the most dominant trait in mankind. The moment anyone of intelligence gets enough to satisfy the primal needs of the physical man, he begins to plan for something beautiful—house, grounds, or a view of nature. Could this be capitalized in dollars, could some alchemy reveal its value, we should not hear materialists deriding lovers of nature, with any effect upon legislators. Without this touch of idealism, this sense of beauty, life would only be a race for the trough.

I have only time for one other point. In 1890 when I appealed to Senator George Hearst to support the bill creating the Yosemite National Park, a project which, as is well known, was first proposed by me to Mr. Muir in 1889, and was jointly urged by us upon Congress, that practical Senator assented with alacrity, and in effect said: "The chief use of that region is for water for irrigation purposes and for its scenery. It has been prospected over many times and there are no precious metals worth speaking of. The forests are more valuable to hold water for irrigation than as timber. Indeed I should favor reserving the whole of the Sierra down to Mount Whitney." I reported this last remark to Gen. Noble, President Harrison's Secretary of the Interior, and toward the close of the administration the whole of that region was reserved. I believe California would not consent to give up the great reservations. Moreover, I believe that the people of the State are opposed to the destruction of the Hetch Hetchy, and that this can be demonstrated if the bill can be delayed until the December session.

I have the honor to remain, respectfully yours,

Robert Underwood Johnson

ℰ E S S A Y S

The essays reflect this chapter's dual focus on natural and urban environmentalism. In the first selection (which neatly extends the Maury Klein–Harvey A. Kantor argument of Chapter 5), Martin V. Melosi, a historian at the University of Houston, describes the belated public alarm and the first steps taken to ameliorate the environmental crisis caused by urban technology. In the second essay, historian Suellen M. Hoy, of St. Mary's College, South Bend, Indiana, places women in the forefront of the drive for urban sanitation. In the final selection, historian Roderick Nash of the University of California, Santa Barbara, considers the motives of the main actors in the Hetch Hetchy controversy and assesses the impact of their battle.

The Urban Environmental Crisis

MARTIN V. MELOSI

The industrial city was the most visible sign of the nineteenth-century economic revolution in the United States. Between 1870 and 1920, it became the dominant urban form in the country. As Sam Bass Warner, Jr., has suggested, "The ubiquity of power and machines in the late nineteenth and early twentieth centuries had profound effects on the American urban system." In earlier times, large American cities had chiefly been centers of commerce and finance. As early as 1820, urban development and industrial growth were becoming immutably linked. Relatively new cities, such as Pittsburgh, Cleveland, and Milwaukee, began to experience rapid growth and vast economic prosperity by producing such products as iron and steel, petroleum, and beer. Industrialization also transformed many older commercial cities, such as New York, Boston, and Philadelphia, which attracted major industries of their own.

As the undisputed centers of economic dynamism in the United States, industrial cities flourished. Yet their overcrowded tenements, congested traffic, critical health problems, smoky skies, mounds of putrefying wastes, polluted waterways, and unbearable noise levels attested to the price they had to pay for such success. Unlike the commercial cities, which had not suffered such massive physical defilement (because agriculture, decentralized manufacturing, and trade had dominated the preindustrial economy), the industrial cities were experiencing an environmental crisis on a scale not encountered before in America. . . .

Many of [the] factors, [that] did in fact encourage industrial expansion in the nineteenth century also contributed directly to the creation or aggravation of urban pollution. Chief among these were the use of coal as a major industrial energy source, the nature of the factory system, the process of industrial specialization and concentration, and the steadily increasing labor force.

The smoky skies of the industrial city were a constant reminder of the dominance of coal as an energy source in the late nineteenth and early twentieth centuries. The need for a plentiful, inexpensive, and effective source of energy to provide power to run factory machinery and locomotives led to the preeminence of coal. . . . By 1895, coal consumption began to surpass wood use, because of the high demand for bituminous (or soft) coal by the steel and railroad industries. Wood continued to supply a substantial portion of the energy for domestic heating, but coal became the primary fuel for manufacturing and transportation.

Using coal as a major energy source, industrial development increased markedly, which, in turn, contributed to the severity of air pollution in urban areas. The most serious problem with coal, especially bituminous coal, was its devastating smoke, which left its mark on buildings, on laundry, and in the lungs of urbanites. Since only a small portion of bituminous coal was consumed in the generation of heat or power, much of the residue went directly into the air. The problem was greatest for cities with high concentrations of primary industries, such as Pittsburgh or St. Louis. . . . The Edison Company, which generated electricity for New York City, was a constant source of smoke pollution in the 1910s and was repeatedly cited by sanitary inspectors. During times when hard coal was in short supply, New York Edison would use soft coal, thereby increasing its smoke output markedly. Often, to deter sanitary inspectors from photographing Edison's smokestacks for use as evidence in legal proceedings, the company placed scouts on the roof who warned the engineers to stop feeding the coal into the furnaces. Even so, the New York Health Department was able to institute twenty-eight actions against the company in the early 1900s. Not until alternative fuels, such as natural gas, replaced coal, did the smoke problem begin to dissipate.

Coal provided the basic source of energy for large-scale industrial development, but the factory system created the managerial and operational means for the mass production of goods. By the 1850s, factories had become the dominant form of industrial enterprise, and they continued to expand in size as well as number into the twentieth century. In 1899, 40 percent of the approximately 500,000 industrial establishments of the country were factories. The scale of production was no less spectacular. Between 1879 and 1899, production of shoes and boots, for example, increased from 64,053 to 136,313. Between 1876 and 1899, raw steel production increased from 597,000 to 11,227,000 short tons. . . . By its very nature, the factory system encouraged the centralization of production in or near urban centers. Modern factories produced goods on a large scale, and location was of primary importance. Factories had to be near, or have ready access to, sources of raw materials, a sufficient labor force, and sizeable markets. Efficient transportation could compensate for some deficiencies, especially access to raw materials, but for the most part proximity to large cities meant the difference between economic success and failure.

These requirements for location of factories and their operational practices, however, contributed greatly to urban pollution. Factories, especially those in the textile, chemical, and iron and steel industries, were often constructed near waterways, since large quantities of water were needed to supply steam boilers or for various production processes such as cooling hot surfaces of metals or making chemical solutions. Waterways also provided the easiest and least expensive means of disposing of soluble or suspendable wastes. Studies of the impact of factories upon the environment suggest that, in 1900, 40 percent of the pollution load on American rivers was industrial in origin. (By 1968 that figure had increased to 80 percent.) The "death" of New Jersey's Passaic River in the late nineteenth century was a classic illustration of how factories defiled their environment. Before it became badly polluted, the Passaic was a major recreational area and also the basis for a thriving commercial fishing industry. As urbanization and industrialization expanded after the Civil War, the volume of sewage and industrial waste that poured into the river forced the city of Newark to abandon the Passaic as a water supply. Pollution also ruined commercial fishing in the area, and soon homes along the waterway disappeared. During hot weather the river emitted such a stench that many factories were forced to close. . . .

The presence of a factory in a given location most often meant the deterioration of physical surroundings. yet factories also contributed an even more insidious, if not so obvious, form of pollution—noise. Many factories produced excessively high noise levels, attributable to machinery that was inadequately lubricated or not equipped with mufflers or noise arresters. These high noise levels not only impaired the hearing of employees but also annoyed adjacent residential communities. . . . Businessmen . . . [mostly] tolerated the din since production, not conservation, was the raison d'être for their factories. . . .

Industrial specialization in certain urban communities compounded the problems created by factory operations and concentration. Industrial special-ization implies specialization of function and location—that is, special types of industry clustered in a single geographic location. Especially after 1870, there was a growing tendency for certain industries to congregate in or near specific urban centers for the sake of efficiency. Although this arrangement was economically sound, it often had disastrous environmental effects, especially if the industry was a blatant polluter. The Pennsylvania cities of McKeesport, Johnstown, and Pittsburgh, which produced large quantities of iron and steel, were inundated with environmental pollution. For instance, Pittsburgh in 1904 produced 63.8 percent of the national total of pig iron and 53.5 percent of the nation's steel. Little wonder that Pittsburgh had the reputation of being "the smoky city." As the chamber of commerce explained during debate over a 1906 anti-smoke ordinance, "With the palls of smoke which darken our sky continually and the almost continuous deposits of soot, our dirty streets and grimy buildings are simply evidences of the difficulty under which we labor in any endeavor to present Pittsburgh as an ideal home city." Slaughtering and meat packing, another industry notorious for pollution, was also highly con-centrated in such cities as Chicago, St. Louis, and Kansas City. Chicago alone was responsible for 35.6 percent of the national market. . . .

Human concentration in the cities matched industrial concentration as a major cause of pollution. The phenomenal increase in the American popula-tion in general and the urban population in particular during the nineteenth century is well known. . . . In 1850, the total population of the United States was approximately 23 million; by 1920 it was 106 million. As the population continued to enlarge, it concentrated increasingly in the cities. . . . Also by 1920, the number of urban areas rose from 392 to 2,722, and the number of cities with a population of 50,000 or more increased from 16 to 144.

The amazing growth of the population was due primarily to spectacular increases in immigration and rural-to-urban migration. During these years almost 32 million people came to the United States, largely from southern and eastern Europe. By 1910, 41 percent of all urbanites in the nation were foreign-born, and approximately 80 percent of the new immigrants settled in the Northeast. Migration from countryside to city was also impressive; a conservative estimate is 15 million between 1880 and 1920. During those years, the proportion of the population living in rural America fell from 71.4 percent to 48.6 percent. . . .

With the urban population steadily on the rise and the bulk of the working force being attracted to industrial jobs, the cities underwent an incredible physical strain. None suffered the repercussions of the environmental crisis more than the working class. Overcrowding was the worst of the problems. Forced to live close to their places of employment, many workers found themselves crammed into the burgeoning slums in the central city. Housing was at a premium; few could afford to buy single-unit dwellings, so they rented what they could. . . . In a seller's market, landlords did little to upgrade the deteriorating tenements and converted buildings that many workers were forced to use as residences. Often families would share quarters with other individuals or groups. David Brody describes living conditions of Slavic steelworkers in Pennsylvania:

> The inadequate dwellings were greatly overcrowded. The boarding boss and his family slept in one downstairs room in the standard four-room farm house. The kitchen was set aside for eating and living purposes, although it, too, often served as a bedroom. Upstairs the boss crammed double beds which were in use night and day when the mill was running full. Investigators came upon many cases of extreme crowding. Thirty-three Serbians and their boarding boss lived in a five-room house in Steelton. In Sharpsburg, Pennsylvania, an Italian family and nine boarders existed without running water or toilet in four rooms on the third floor of a ramshackle tenement.

Brody went on to state, according to an Immigration Commission report, that the number per sleeping room in immigrant households averaged about three, with quite a few having four or as many as six or more per sleeping room.

Not only were individual dwellings overcrowded, but neighborhood densities were staggering. The average block density in lower Manhattan increased from 157.5 persons in 1820 to 272.5 persons in 1850. New York City's Sanitary District "A" averaged 986.4 people to the acre. . . . In comparison, Bombay, India—the next most crowded area in the world—had 759.7 people per acre, and Prague, the European city with the worst slum conditions, had only 485.4 people per acre.

Such crowded conditions and such limited city services provided fertile ground for health and sanitation problems. Many workers had little choice but to live in the least desirable sections of the city, usually close to the smoke-belching factories where they worked or near marshy bogs and stagnant pools, which speculators could not develop into prime residential communities. City services, especially sewage and refuse collection, failed to keep up with the demand. Smoke from wood-burning and coal-burning stoves and fireplaces fouled the air of the inner city, and the noise level in some areas reached a roar. . . . Jane Addams, in *Twenty Years at Hull House,* recalled the shock of English visitors over living conditions in Chicago:

> . . . That a group of Greeks should be permitted to slaughter sheep in a basement, that Italian women should be allowed to sort over rags collected from the city dumps, not only within the city limits but in a court swarming with little children, that immigrant bakers should continue unmolested to bake bread for their neighbors in unspeakably filthy spaces under the pavement, appeared incredible to visitors accustomed to careful city regulations.
> . . .

These impressions of living conditions were only the most dramatic recountings of life in the slums. The statistics on health problems, disease, and high mortality rates were even more sobering. In one of the most widely publicized epidemics of its day, Memphis lost almost 10 percent of its population in 1873 to yellow fever, which ostensibly originated in its slums. In New Orleans, typhoid was spread through the city by sewage that oozed from the unpaved streets. In "Murder Bay," not far from the White House in Washington, D.C., black families picked their dinners out of garbage cans and dumps. Mortality figures for the area were consistently twice as high as in white neighborhoods; infant mortality in 1900 ranged as high as 317 per thousand. By 1870, the infant mortality rate in New York was 65 percent higher than in 1810. . . .

Industrial expansion alone does not explain the severity and complexity of the environmental crisis of the cities. . . . Certainly the compulsion for limitless economic growth and prosperity, which underlay industrial expansion, blinded the so-called robber barons and their supporters to the deterioration of the environment which that development produced. . . . Numerous factors, other than the impact of industrial development, threatened the preservation of a palatable urban quality of life, none more significantly than the physical form that the industrial cities took and their distinctive patterns of growth.

The industrial city, characterized by urban sprawl, rapidly multiplying suburbs, an ever-rising skyline, and a congested downtown area, contrasted sharply with the "walking city" of the previous era. After the 1870s, the intimacy and homogeneity of the walking city virtually disappeared. Preindustrial urban areas were small enough that citizens could walk or ride in carriages or omnibuses to most places, but in the industrial city vast growth made mass transit the only viable means of travel. The relatively spacious neighborhoods in the walking city had allowed for at least some casual contact among social classes. Rigid segregation of residences was avoided, and people, both rich and poor, tended to live close to where they worked. In the industrial city, rapid growth constantly shifted residential neighborhoods and economic districts, eventually producing more rigid class delineations. With the extension of efficient transit lines into surrounding districts, relatively affluent urbanites moved out of the walking city into the more spacious suburbs. This tendency quickly produced well-defined residential subdivisions, divided primarily along income lines. Those who lacked the economic means to move to suburbia were relegated to the central city residential areas, which often degenerated into slums. . . . As a result, the downtown area of the walking city, which had once been distinguished by warehouses, small financial establishments, and shops, was transformed into a congested business district, where retailing became the major function. . . . Many of the larger manufacturers relocated away from the downtown area along intercity transportation routes. . . . In his pioneering study of the process of urban growth, *Streetcar Suburbs,* Sam Bass Warner, Jr., concludes, "With the new metropolis and all its changes the ancient problems of the large cities once more came to life: the individual members of urban society became isolated within a physical and social network which had passed their comprehension and control.". . .

The pollution problems of the central city were much more obvious, and initially more serious, than those of the suburbs. The growth of the local consumer market and technological innovations in transportation, communication, and construction made possible the high concentration of retail stores and service-oriented firms in the central business district. The industrial city reversed the previous wide dispersal of retail establishments that had characterized the walking city. . . . Not until the 1920s, when the automobile began to dominate urban transportation, did specialty stores and sprawling shopping centers and malls situated in the suburbs begin to wrest shoppers away from the central business districts.

City governments were ill-prepared to provide adequate sanitation services in the central city. Garbage and rubbish accumulated in the streets faster than it could be collected. Street cleaning crews in Manhattan collected as much as 1,100 tons of garbage a day during the summer months. . . . [They] carelessly collected the garbage, loaded it on barges, and dumped it at sea. . . . In Cleveland, no public provision was made for gathering household garbage until the late 1880s. . . .

The technological advances that made possible the physical development of the central business districts also contributed to pollution problems. The balloon frame, the steel girder, and the elevator facilitated the construction of multistory buildings, thus making land use more economical. Yet these innovations encouraged high-density building, which further strained meager city services and added to congestion problems. Advances in transportation—the horsecar, trolley, and electric streetcar—exacerbated congestion and sometimes contributed directly to pollution. Horsecars had several drawbacks, the most serious being disposal of manure. A single horse discharged gallons of urine and nearly twenty pounds of fecal matter into the streets daily, which not only posed a health hazard but also deteriorated streetcar rails. . . .

Phasing out the horsecar did not end pollution problems stemming from inner-city transportation. Steam-driven commuter trains produced dense smoke and encountered substantial public opposition. . . . Even though the electric streetcar alleviated some of the air pollution problems in the streets (coal-generated power produced other sources), it was not free of difficulties.

For a time, the public was quite fearful of electricity, and this fear was aggravated by several fatal electrical accidents. . . . Increased transportation in the inner city substantially raised the general noise level, adding screeching brakes, grinding gears, whining motors, and clanging bells to the din. As traffic congestion became more serious, cities had to construct new and wider streets and alleys. And, while improved surfaces reduced mud and dust, they also contributed to greater noise and added more surface area for street crews to keep clean.

Needless to say, contemporaries had little inkling of the long-term effects of high-density building on the urban ecology. The wholesale uprooting and destruction of plants and trees to make way for stores, terminals, houses, and streets reduced oxygen generation in the city's core. Also, wildlife in the area lost its natural protection and habitat. The park movement, which began in New York City in the 1850s with the authorization for Central Park, helped somewhat in reducing the wanton destruction of natural life in urban areas. The great landscape architect, Frederick Law Olmsted, was one of a few Americans who emphasized that parks were a "palliative" for urban ills. Believing that the movement of people "townward" was a permanent phenomenon, Olmsted became concerned with the debilitating effects of the city upon the health and well-being of its citizenry. . . . Parks and parkways were a major way to relcaim the urban atmosphere from the effects of the noxious elements poured into it, but even Olmsted's exhortations and the success of the park movement throughout the United States could not repair the damage already done or to be done in the future.

Outward expansion of the industrial cities, in the form of suburbs, produced a variant to the environmental problems of the inner cities. The greatest cliché about suburban development in the nineteenth century is that middle- and upper-income people, who wished to escape the inner cities, fled to pristine suburbs where the urban blight could not engulf them. . . .

The initial detachment from the central city, which suburbanites prized, sometimes worked as a disadvantage. The need to extend services to the suburbs was crucial. Sometimes the building of sewer lines, like good transportation lines, was a precondition of suburban expansion, but sometimes it was not. . . . Finding adequate water supplies was a related problem, which was intensified by the competition between suburbs and industrial cities. Many waterways became overtaxed from being required to absorb wastes from the inner city as well as from nearby suburbs; they were often lost as water supplies to both. . . . One solution, which became an inevitability for some suburbs, was *annexation* to the city in order to get adequate services. For example, the suburbs of Morrisania and West Farms, finding it difficult to locate a source of high-quality water on their own, voted to join New York City in 1873. . . .

. . . The continual growth in number and size of suburbs insured that many [suburbs] would ultimately suffer the same congestion and density problems of the inner cities. It should be remembered that the transit lines, which had helped produce the nineteenth-century suburbs, tended to cluster people rather than to scatter them along the commuter routes. Often the result was a series of densely populated smaller communities strewn along the periphery of the urban core. For instance, the Boston suburbs of Roxbury, West Roxbury, and Dorchester grew dramatically. In 1870, after about fifteen years of the horsecar lines, the population of the three towns was 60,000; by 1900, it was 227,000. If these suburbs had been combined into a single city, it would have rivaled Minneapolis, Louisville, and Jersey City in size. . . .

By the late nineteenth century, the saturation of cities and suburbs with air, water, refuse, and noise pollution finally produced an environmental consciousness among the complacent citizenry. Until this time, almost everyone had ignored questions of environmental quality. . . . However, it soon became evident that industrial expansion, which made urban centers advantageous places to work, also made them unbearable places to live. Predictably, frustration over the quality of life in the cities was greatest for those who did not have the means of separating their working environment from their residential environment. However, even those who fled the inner city for the suburbs could not be assured of escaping pollution. . . . Early protests against pollution, therefore, tended to be responses to the obvious irritations, such as bad-tasting water, eye-smarting smoke, stench-ridden garbage, or noisy machinery. The concept of pollution as "nuisance" dominated these early complaints. Indeed, "nuisance" was a popular contemporary term, which urbanites applied indiscriminately to any more serious environmental problems. Contemporary observers often referred to all manner of ills in this way: "the noise nuisance," "hooting nuisance," "the garbage nuisance," "the smoke nuisance." As the noted sanitarian, John S. Billings, stated,

> The great majority of the dwellers in our cities have not, heretofore, taken any active personal interest in the sanitary condition of their respective towns. They may grumble occasionally when some nuisance is forced on their notice, but, as a rule, they look on the city as a sort of hotel, with the details of the management of which they have no desire to become acquainted.

Their ignorance, as well as their acceptance of unrestrained industrial growth as a positive good, produced the urbanites' initial mild response to pollution. Few city dwellers possessed a broad ecological perspective about pollution problems because such an outlook did not exist at the time, even within the scientific community. . . . Not until the twentieth century did the scientific community begin to acquire sophisticated notions about the relationship between pollutants and health problems. . . . Social scientists had yet to analyze the complex interrelationships between urban/industrial growth and environmental degradation. No wonder most Americans were unprepared to confront urban pollution—no one had a total grasp of the problem.

By the turn of the century, however, sporadic protests against the irritations of a dirty city led to individual and group efforts to deal with smoke, sewage, garbage, and noise. Demands for cleansing the environment grew out of citizens' complaints for the most part, but reformers occasionally pursued substantive changes in nuisance laws, industrial operations, municipal services, and even public behavior and conduct. Sometimes reform came from within municipal health and public works departments. Environmental reform never took the shape of a permanent or comprehensive movement during the period. Instead, it was an outgrowth of protests against specific problems, usually on the local level, but occasionally state-, region-, or nationwide. . . .

By the 1890s, . . . reformers were beginning to see pollution not simply as an irritant but as an unwanted by-product of industrialization. However, pollution was linked with wastefulness and inefficiency in such a way as to avoid the conclusion that industrial activity was intrinsically responsible for despoiling the environment. Smoke abatement advocates, for example, often charged that air pollution not only produced a health hazard but graphically demonstrated the squandering of natural resources. One observer, extolling the virtues of technical improvements made to a furnace of the Power Building in Cincinnati, stated: "The large Power Building at Eighth and Sycamore for the past year has been a standing monument of what a good appliance and careful firing will do. The stack has been and is absolutely smokeless, and the saving in coal bills has been over twenty-five percent." Anti-noise advocates also drew ammunition from the link between pollution and inefficiency. They often argued that excessive noise in factories worked against high productivity by employees. As Raymond Smilor suggests, "Noise was a liability in business; it cost money. Although it failed to appear on the balance sheet, noise showed in the profit-and-loss statement as an unrealized economy. . . .

. . . To many reformers, the curtailing of pollution was one measure of civilization. The "White City" of the 1893 Chicago World's Fair and "Hygeia," the mythical Victorian city of health, were standards toward which to strive. After all, the city was supposed to put in order what was chaotic in nature. Citizens who littered the streets or defiled their physical surroundings were classified with cavemen or even animals. The interest in the City Aesthetic, best expressed in the City Beautiful movement of the 1890s, was a very subjective indictment of pollution. Many people continued to equate pollutants, such as factory smoke, with material progress. But advocacy of the aesthetic elevated concern about the environment from the purely utilitarian realm.

What gave environmental reform a broader appeal and national attention was its almost inevitable association with progressivism in the 1890s and beyond. Since progressive reform was rooted in the industrial city, environmental protesters had little trouble associating themselves with the larger movement. Despite the diversity of the Progressives, they shared several common beliefs and values that environmental reformers could readily accept. Progressives were trying to bring order out of the chaos caused by the transition of the United States from a rural/agrarian to an urban/industrial society. They had faith in the inherent good of humankind and believed progress was possible by eliminating evils produced by the physical and social environment. They placed great confidence in the ability to measure problems scientifically and to resolve them through the efforts of an expert elite. Of course, the Progressives' limitations were as unbounded as their optimism. . . . Their faith in simplistic solutions to complex problems was naive at best, and, although they decried poverty, injustice, and corruption, they were paternalistic and even hostile to those who fell outside their societal norms.

Yet the conviction of Progressives that the environment in which humans lived could be improved and their adherence to scientific solutions gave substantial support to the protest against urban degradation. Several leading Progressives, especially those with strong interests in urban affairs, were important advocates of environmental reform. Among these were Theodore Roosevelt; Albert Shaw, editor of *Review of Reviews;* Hazen Pingree, mayor of Detroit and governor of Michigan; "Golden Rule" Jones, mayor of Toledo; and Tom Johnson, mayor of Cleveland. Likewise, environmental reformers often became strong adherents to various progressive reforms. The link to progressivism is clear in the following statement by municipal engineer William Mayo Venable:

> . . . The same spirit that leads men to realize the corruption of politics and business, and to attempt to remedy those conditions by adopting new methods of administration and new laws, also leads to a realization of the primitiveness of the methods of waste disposal still employed by many communities, and to a consequent desire for improvement.

By the early twentieth century, environmental protest had undergone some important changes. . . . Major cities began to grapple with the problems of sewage and garbage collection and disposal. Civic and professional organizations, including smoke and noise abatement committees, were putting pressure on city government for change. And the association of environmental reform with progressivism had brought some national attention to several urban problems. Yet environmental reform had serious limitations during this period. . . . The most severe restriction was the lack of what might be called "environmental perspective." Pollution problems were most often approached as isolated cases. The smoke problem was considered independent of the noise problem and the noise problem independent of the sewage problem. Rarely did environmental protest groups confront pollution comprehensively, as part of an overall urban crisis. In fact, other than civic reform groups, which developed interests in many phases of uban life, there were no organizations that were broadly concerned with environmental quality. Urban reformers had yet to consider pollution in terms of its root causes—the processes of urbanization and industrialization; instead, they concentrated on the results and consequences of pollution. As commendable as their efforts were, the reformers, as the well-worn cliché states, "could not see the forest for the trees.". . .

Rallying to combat the most flagrant pollution problems, protesters and reformers rarely found it easy to agree on solutions. As stated above, environmental reformers shared many of the characteristics of the middle-class reformers of the period. Various factors, especially occupation, influenced the environmental goals of the reformers and often limited collective action. Sanitarians and public health officials, who played a central role in many reform efforts, tended to give priority to high standards of health as a goal of pollution control. . . . Civic reform groups, especially those dominated by women, represented the nonspecialist's interest in the health question; they generally accepted the efficacy of a technical solution to pollution and placed substantial emphasis upon aesthetic benefits of improving the urban environment. . . . Similarly, the occupational interests of other groups dictated their behavior. For instance, political leaders had to consider environmental issues that would appease their constituencies, and businessmen sought to protect their special interests. Efforts at compromise were always difficult. Overlapping interests made clear environmental goals almost impossible to achieve.

Of all those involved with environmental problems, *city planners* seemed the most likely group to combine the myriad interests of reformers and devise a plan of action. But even this group contributed little to a comprehensive solution to environmental problems between 1870 and 1920. . . . Planners, of course, were deeply involved in housing reform, land-use controls, and social manipulation in the form of zoning regulations, but not as chief architects of a comprehensive anti-pollution plan. After 1920, the profession was gradually transforming the planners' role from that of reformer to that of technician. As Roy Lubove argues:

> Increasingly . . . the professional planner evolved into a technician who minimized normative goals—structural or institutional innovation—and became the prophet of the "City Scientific" or "City Efficient." Technical matters relating to zoning, law, finance, capital expenditure, and transportation became his province. He did not seek fundamental changes in urban form and stucture, but projected existing demographic and institutional trends into the future as a basis for planning.

. . . Reform was worthless without implementation, and implementation was difficult at a time when the line between individual and municipal responsibility was still unclear. Few government officials could make a distinction between environmental degradation as a citywide problem requiring community action and as a problem of personal discomfort requiring private action. Between 1870 and 1920, many cities were just attempting to establish home rule in basic areas of governance. In the 1850s, rural-dominated state legislatures began to exercise extensive control over the major cities in their states, especially by creating independent departments and boards as a means of decentralizing authority. The industrial cities were not very successful in restoring home rule and often were vulnerable to control by political machines that simply overlooked the directives of the legislatures. Machine—or boss—rule was based upon personal loyalties. Bosses actually sustained themselves through the disorder of the industrial cities and used political power as a marketable commodity, with patronage going to the highest bidder. In this kind of system, large-scale environmental reform, based on notions of community responsibility, was virtually impossible. Even with the establishment of so-called reform governments, a solution to environmental problems was no easy task. Commission and city manager systems of government, for instance, which were intended to allow efficient execution of municipal responsibilities, often swapped the working-class constituency of the boss for a middle- or upper-class constituency. . . . The special interests that influenced most municipal governments of the period played a large part in determining municipal priorities and could work against communitywide solutions. . . .

. . . Most cities responded fairly rapidly and effectively in those areas where solutions had to be found in order to avoid rampant health hazards. This was especially true with respect to the search for pure water supplies and improved sewerage systems. However, water pollution per se was not eliminated; industrial wastes and raw household sewage continued to pour into waterways without proper treatment or filtration. Numerous cities adopted new methods of collection and disposal of refuse, but these methods did nothing to reduce ever-growing quantities of solid waste and often created alternate forms of pollution, such as smoke from incineration of rubbish. . . . The successes of environmental reform efforts, therefore, were often ephemeral or incomplete. A comprehensive solution to environmental blight in the cities was still a dream. Yet it would be unfair to overlook the major accomplishment of environmental protests of the era—a heightened environmental awareness or consciousness that made urbanites take notice of many of the threats posed by this first environmental crisis in the cities. . . .

Women as Municipal Housekeepers

SUELLEN M. HOY

As society grows more complicated it is necessary that woman shall extend her sense of responsibility to many things outside of her home, if only in order to preserve the home in its entirety.

Jane Addams, "Woman's Conscience and Social Amelioration" (1908)

During the late nineteenth and early twentieth centuries, Americans witnessed the transformation of the United States from a predominantly rural-agricultural society to a primarily urban-industrial one. Many Americans,

Suellen Hoy, *Pollution and Reform in American Cities, 1870–1930*, pp. 173–176, edited by Martin V. Melosi, Copyright © 1980. Reprinted by permission of University of Texas Press.

especially those living in cities, were disturbed by the rapidity and complexity of the change and were anxious about the future of traditional American values and institutions. Women, as individuals and in groups, found themselves particularly concerned about their homes and families. It is not surprising that many of them took on the important task of improving the urban environment.

Men and women alike believed that it was only natural for women to serve as "municipal housekeepers" in their communities. George E. Waring, the well-known sanitary engineer, was convinced that "city cleansing" was above all "woman's work." It required the "sort of systematized attention to detail, especially in the constantly recurring duty of 'cleaning-up,' that grows more naturally out of the habit of good housekeeping than out of any occupation to which man is accustomed." Dr. Katherine Bement Davis, New York City's commissioner of correction, agreed. She observed that it had always been woman's responsibility "to do the spanking and the house-cleaning."

Countless women in the United States joined a multiplicity of civic leagues, women's clubs, and village improvement societies. Discussions at meetings and club publications reinforced the conviction that "city housekeeping was quite as much their vocation as taking care of the home" and that their own health and happiness as well as that of their families depended in large part on the sanitary conditions of their communities. Club officers also reminded members that women "are no less good mothers and devoted wives because they realize that many outside influences touch their domestic life." Thus, women in large numbers came to believe that "the one calling in which they were, as a body, proficient, that of housekeeping and homemaking, had its outdoor as well as its indoor application." This knowledge led them into the movement for sanitary reform.

In nearly every region of the country, groups of women became involved in activities that, among other things, included cleaning streets, inspecting markets, abating smoke, purifying water, and collecting and disposing of refuse. Several women were appointed to positions in local government and made responsible for improving the cleanliness of their cities. One woman, Caroline Bartlett Crane of Kalamazoo, Michigan, was hired as a consultant by over sixty municipalities to prepare sanitary surveys. And Mary E. McDowell, commonly referred to as the "Garbage Lady," was instrumental in effecting substantial changes in the solid waste disposal practices of Chicago, Illinois.

The early women's groups were rather exclusive, with membership ordinarily restricted to women of the upper- and upper-middle classes who had extended periods of leisure, common interests, and congenial tastes. Women in these clubs typically met at each others' homes and at other social gatherings and discussed art, literature, and related subjects. Not until the late nineteenth century did they begin to concern themselves with philanthropic and civic affairs.

Middle-class housewives made up the majority of club women interested in improving urban sanitary conditions. Many were middle-aged, had children in school, and often hired servants to clean their homes. There remained, however, a strong contingent of upper- and upper-middle-class women who kept active in civic affairs and who frequently retained leadership positions in women's organizations. For example, many of the women who followed Jane Addams's example and ran settlement houses in the nation's largest cities (Mary McDowell, Mary Simkhovitch, Lillian Wald, and others) belonged to the upper class.

As early as 1894, the Civic Club of Philadelphia made its initial attack on littered and garbage-strewn gardens and streets. Established "to promote by education and active co-operation a higher public spirit and a better social order," the club obtained permission from city officials to place baskets for wastepaper and refuse in the zoological gardens, which visitors badly littered. The experiment proved so successful that the women devised a plan to place receptacles in other areas of the city. In 1896, after obtaining permission from the Philadelphia Department of Public Works, they purchased forty-five receptacles and positioned them on carefully selected street corners in the city's Seventh Ward. At the year's end, there had been a marked improvement in the appearance of the area. In June 1897, the club offered the receptacles to the city council, which accepted them with gratitude. The council also made a $400 appropriation for purchasing similar receptacles to be placed in other parts of the same district.

The work of the Civic Club did not end with the council's action. Members were encouraged to become acquainted with municipal regulations on the collection of ashes and garbage and to report infringements to the Department of Public Works. Although their complaints "received prompt and courteous attention," the women of Philadelphia did not slacken their voluntary efforts on behalf of a clean community. They were rewarded for their service in 1913 when Edith W. Pierce became the first female city inspector of street cleaning. In appointing Pierce to this position, Morris L. Cooke, the director of public works, noted that her responsibilities would be "somewhat different from that of the men inspectors." She was to inspect the entire city rather than a single district. Motivated by what she called the "three C's"— "Care, Common-sense, and Co-operation"—Pierce efficiently carried out her official assignments. She also organized sectional associations for keeping streets, sidewalks, homes, and schools clean and founded a Junior Sanitation League, modeled after George E. Waring's New York City organization.

The Civic Club of Philadelphia was not the only women's club on the eastern seaboard to educate cities to "a sense of . . . their own needs" during the late nineteenth century. In 1884 a Ladies' Health Protective Association (LHPA) was formed in New York City to confront the problem of the ever-increasing amount of garbage, manure, and rubbish left in the streets. In the introduction of an appeal to Mayor Abram S. Hewitt, the women explained why they had become involved:

> It is the climax of aggravation to the painstaking housekeeper to look out of her windows and see ash barrels standing forgotten on the sidewalk from hour to hour and often from day to day; to have those barrels toppled over by sportive boys or raked over by grimy ragpickers, and the contents left in hillocks in the street from

one month's end to another; and supposing even that she personally . . . carefully sweeps and washes her own area flags and space of sidewalk, to have these covered within two hours by the sticks, loose papers and powdered manure that blow upon them from all quarters alike.

The women recommended to the mayor ways of improving the sanitary conditions of New York City's streets. They asked that the annual appropriation for street cleaning be adequate for the work; that street sweeping machines be used late in the night; that neither ashes nor garbage be allowed on pavements in front of residences; that householders be required to own galvanized iron receptacles; that crematories be built to dispose of house ashes, garbage, and street sweepings; and that the city be divided into convenient sections managed by foremen, responsible to a street commissioner-in-chief, and cleaned by laborers, paid by the piece and not by the day. The Ladies' Health Protective Association also suggested that women be appointed as inspectors, since "keeping things clean, like the training of children and the care of the sick, has ever been one of the instinctive and recognized functions of women.". . .

The Hetch Hetchy Controversy

RODERICK NASH

As to my attitude regarding the proposed use of Hetch Hetchy by the city of San Francisco . . . I am fully persuaded that . . . the injury . . . by substituting a lake for the present swampy floor of the valley . . . is altogether unimportant compared with the benefits to be derived from its use as a reservoir.

Gifford Pinchot, 1913

These temple destroyers, devotees of ravaging commercialism, seem to have a perfect contempt for Nature, and instead of lifting their eyes to the God of the Mountains, lift them to the Almighty Dollar.

John Muir, 1912

Situated on a dry, sandy peninsula, the city of San Francisco faced a chronic fresh-water shortage. In the Sierra, about one hundred and fifty miles distant, the erosive action of glaciers and the Tuolumne River scooped the spectacular, high-walled Hetch Hetchy Valley. As early as 1882, city engineers pointed out the possibility of damming its narrow, lower end to make a reservoir. They also recognized the opportunity of using the fall of the impounded water for the generation of hydroelectric power. In 1890, however, the act creating Yosemite National Park designated Hetch Hetchy

From *Wilderness and the American Mind* by Roderick Nash, pp. 161–81. Copyright © 1973, reprinted by permission of Yale University Press.

and its environs a wilderness preserve. Undaunted, San Francisco's mayor James D. Phelan applied for the valley as a reservoir site shortly after the turn of the century. Secretary of the Interior Ethan A. Hitchcock's refusal to violate the sanctity of a national park was only a temporary setback, because on April 18, 1906, an earthquake and fire devastated San Francisco and added urgency and public sympathy to the search for an adequate water supply. The city immediately reapplied for Hetch Hetchy, and on May 11, 1908, Secretary James R. Garfield approved the new application. "Domestic use," he wrote, "is the highest use to which water and available storage basins . . . can be put."

John Muir, Robert Underwood Johnson, and those whom they had won to the cause of wilderness preservation disagreed. Secretary Garfield's approval stimulated them to launch a national protest campaign. Given the flourishing cult of wilderness on the one hand and the strength of traditional assumptions about the desirability of putting undeveloped natural resources to use on the other, the battle over Hetch Hetchy was bound to be bitter. Before Congress and President Woodrow Wilson made a final decision in 1913, the valley became a *cause célèbre*. The principle of preserving wilderness was put to the test. For the first time in the American experience the competing claims of wilderness and civilization to a specific area received a thorough hearing before a national audience.

When the preservationists first learned of San Francisco's plans for Hetch Hetchy, Theodore Roosevelt occupied the White House, and the choice of reservoir or wilderness placed him in an awkward position. There were few Americans so committed to a belief in the value of wild country. Yet Roosevelt appreciated the importance of water, lumber, and similar commodities to national welfare and as President felt responsible for providing them. The result of this ambivalence was inconsistency in Roosevelt's early policy statement. In 1901 he declared in his first annual message that "the fundamental idea of forestry is the perpetuation of forests by use. Forest protection is not an end in itself; it is a means to increase and sustain the resources of our country and the industries which depend on them." But later in the message, he revealed his hope that some of the forest reserves could be made "preserves for the wild forest creatures." . . .

In this seesaw manner Roosevelt hoped to hold the two wings of the conservation movement together on a united front. The task was formidable: Muir already had found his position incompatible with Gifford Pinchot's. But after 1905 Pinchot was Chief Forester and the principal spokesman of the utilitarian conception of conservation. Moreover, he enjoyed a close friendship with Roosevelt. According to Johnson, the President went so far as to declare that " 'in all forestry matters I have put my conscience in the keeping of Gifford Pinchot.' " And Pinchot favored converting Hetch Hetchy into a reservoir. Yet Roosevelt had camped in Yosemite with Muir and appreciated the growing political strength of the preservationist position. Early in September 1907, he received a letter from Muir that brought the issue to a head. Reminding the President of their 1903 trip into the Sierra wilderness, Muir expressed his desire that the region "be saved from all sorts of commercialism and marks of man's works." While acknowledging the need for an adequate municipal water supply, he maintained that it could be secured outside "our wild mountain parks." Concluding the letter, Muir expressed his belief that over ninety per cent of the American people would oppose San Francisco's plans if they were apprised of their consequences.

Roosevelt's initial reaction, made even before Muir's communication, was to seek advice from engineers about alternative reservoir sites. The report, however, was that Hetch Hetchy offered the only practical solution to San Francisco's problem. Reluctantly Roosevelt made up his mind. While assuring Muir that he would do everything possible to protect the national parks, the President reminded him that if these reservations "interfere with the permanent material development of the State instead of helping . . . the result will be bad." Roosevelt ended with an expression of doubt that the great majority would take the side of wilderness in a showdown with the material needs of an expanding civilization. . . . Still Roosevelt was not comfortable in his decision against wilderness, and confessed to Johnson that Hetch Hetchy was "one of those cases where I was extremely doubtful."

In spite of his doubts Roosevelt had made a choice, and in the spring of 1908 the Garfield permit opened the way for the development of the valley. Muir was discouraged but not defeated. He believed it still was possible to arouse a national protest and demonstrate to federal authorities that Roosevelt was mistaken in his judgment about the lack of public sentiment for keeping Hetch Hetchy wild. But Muir fully realized that "public opinion is not yet awakened." The first task of the preservationists was to capitalize on the wilderness cult and replace ignorance with anger. Telling arguments against the reservoir were needed. As the basis for their protest, the friends of wilderness turned to the old Romantic case against "Mammon." They made Hetch Hetchy into a symbol of ethical and aesthetic qualities, while disparaging San Francisco's proposal as tragically typical of American indifference toward them. This line of defense took advantage of national sensitivity to charges of being a culture devoted entirely to the frantic pursuit of the main chance. It criticized the commercialism and sordidness of American civilization, while defending wilderness.

John Muir opened the argument for the Valley on aesthetic grounds with an article in [the radical magazine] *Outlook*. After describing its beauties, he declared that its maintainence as a wilderness was essential, "for everybody needs beauty as well as bread, places to play in and pray in where Nature may heal and cheer and give strength to body and soul alike." . . .

[The] president of the American Civic Association, J. Horace McFarland, . . . believed the aesthetic should have a place in the conservation movement, and in 1909 expressed his displeasure at its concentration on utilitarian aims. In the same year he told Pinchot that "the conservation movement is now weak, because it has failed to join hands with the preservation of scenery." For McFarland, Hetch Hetchy was a test case, and he spoke and wrote widely in its defense. If even national parks were to be given over to utilitarian purposes, there was no guarantee that ultimately all the beauty of unspoiled nature would be destroyed. Speaking before the Secretary of the Interior on the Hetch Hetchy question, McFarland contended that such undeveloped places would become increasingly valuable for recreation as more and more Americans lived in cities. Yet when the preservation of wilderness conflicted with "material interests," those financially affected cried: " 'that is sentimentalism; that is aestheticism; that is pleasure-loving; that is unnecessary; that is not practical.' " Usually such resistance carried the day and wildness was sacrificed. McFarland objected because "it is not sentimentalism, Mr. Secretary; it is living." . . .

Lyman Abbott, the editor of *Outlook,* also felt it was a mistake "to turn every tree and waterfall into dollars and cents." His magazine found most of its readers among a class of people concerned over what they thought was the eclipse of morality, refinement, and idealism by urbanization, industrialization, and an emphasis on business values. The defense of wilderness attracted them because it permitted making a positive case—they could be for something (wilderness) rather than merely against amorphous forces. Protecting the wild from an exploitative civilization, in short, represented the broader struggle to maintain intangibles against the pressure of utilitarian demands. . . .

Another tactic of the preservationists emphasized the spiritual significance of wild places and the tendency of money-minded America to ignore religion. Hetch Hetchy became a sanctuary or temple in the eyes of the defenders. John Muir, for one, believed so strongly in the divinity of wild nature that he was convinced he was doing the Lord's battle in resisting the reservoir. The preservationists' innumerable puns about "damning" Hetch Hetchy were only partly in jest. John Muir and his colleagues believed they were preaching "the Tuolumne gospel." San Francisco became "the Prince of the powers of Darkness" and "Satan and Co." Muir wrote: "we may lose this particular fight but truth and right must prevail at last. Anyhow we must be true to ourselves and the Lord." . . .

Using these arguments, and the especially effective one (unrelated to wilderness) that the valley as part of Yosemite National Park was a "public playground" which should not be turned over to any special interest, the preservationists were able to arouse considerable opposition to San Francisco's plans. Members of the Sierra and Appalachian Mountain Clubs took the lead in preparing pamphlet literature for mass distribution. *Let All the People Speak and Prevent the Destruction of the Yosemite Park* of 1909, for example, contained a history of the issue, reprints of articles and statements opposing the dam, a discussion of alternative sources of water, and photographs of the valley. Preservationists also obtained the sympathies of numerous newspaper and magazine editors in all parts of the nation. Even Theodore Roosevelt retreated from his earlier endorsement of the reservoir and declared in his eighth annual message of December 8, 1908, that Yellowstone and Yosemite "should be kept as a great national playground. In both, all wild things should be protected and the scenery kept wholly unmarred."

Evidence of the effectiveness of the protest appeared in the action of the House after its 1909 hearings. Although the Committee on the Public Lands had approved the grant in a close vote, a strong minority report dissented on the grounds that such action would deny the public's right to the valley for recreational purposes. Testifying to the amount of popular opposition, the report observed that "there has been an exceedingly widespread, earnest, and vigorous protest voiced by scientists, naturalists, mountain climbers, travelers, and others in person, by letters, and telegrams, and in newspaper and magazine articles." In the face of this expression of public opinion, the House pigeonholed and killed San Francisco's application in the Sixtieth Congress.

San Francisco was bewildered and incensed at the public unwillingness that it should have Hetch Hetchy as a reservoir. Was not supplying water to a large city a worthy cause, one that certainly took priority over preserving wilderness? The San Francisco *Chronicle* referred to the preservationists as "hoggish and mushy esthetes," while the city's engineer, Marsden Manson, wrote in 1910 that the opposition was largely composed of "short-haired women and long-haired men." San Francisco argued that the beauties of wilderness were admirable, but in this case human health, comfort, and even human life were the alternatives. Phrased in these terms, even some of the members of the Appalachian Mountain Club and the Sierra Club felt compelled to place the needs of civilization ahead of protecting wild country. In the Sierra Club, Warren Olney, one of the founders, led a faction which supported the city. In 1910 the Club held a referendum in which preservation won 589 to 161, but in order to prosecute the defense of Hetch Hetchy, the preservationists were obliged to act in a separate organization: the California Branch of the Society for the Preservation of National Parks. The wilderness enthusiasts in the Appalachian group formed an Eastern Branch of the Society.

At every opportunity the proponents of the dam expressed their belief that a lake in Hetch Hetchy would not spoil its beauty but, rather, enhance it. A prominent engineer reported on the City's behalf that roads and walks could be built which would open the region for public recreation in the manner of European mountain-lake resorts. Since the preservationists frequently based their opposition on the need to maintain a "scenic wonder" or "beauty spot," and on the desirability of maintaining a public playground, the claims of San Francisco were difficult to dismiss. If, instead, more attention had been paid specifically to the wilderness qualities of Hetch Hetchy— which *any* man-made construction would have eliminated—San Francisco's point about the scenic attraction of an artificial lake could have been more easily answered. As it was, this tactical error cost the preservationists considerable support.

The Hetch Hetchy controversy entered its climactic stage on March 4, 1913, when the Woodrow Wilson administration took office. San Francisco's hopes soared, because the new Secretary of the Interior, Franklin K. Lane, was a native, a former attorney for the city, and a proponent of the reservoir. But Lane upheld the policy of previous Secretaries that in cases involving national parks Congress must make the final decision. On behalf of

San Francisco, Representative John E. Raker immediately introduced a bill to the Sixty-third Congress approving the grant. The preservationists prepared to send protest literature to 1418 newspapers and to make known their views before Congress. Robert Underwood Johnson distributed an *Open Letter to the American People* in which he declared Hetch Hetchy to be "a veritable temple of the living God" and warned that "again the money-changers are in the temple." The stage was set for a showdown.

On June 25 the House Committee on the Public Lands opened hearings on the Hetch Hetchy issue, with Gifford Pinchot as the star witness. Pinchot simplified the question into "whether the advantage of leaving this valley in a state of nature is greater than . . . using it for the benefit of the city of San Francisco." He admitted that the idea of preserving wilderness appealed to him "if nothing else were at stake," but in this case the need of the city seemed "overwhelming." . . . Former San Francisco mayor James D. Phelan told the Committee that the criteria for a decision should be the needs of the "little children, men and women . . . who swarm the shore of San Francisco Bay" rather than the few who liked "solitary loneliness" and "the mere scenic value of the mountains."

Since the House hearings were called on short notice, Edmund D. Whitman of the Appalachian Mountain Club was the only preservationist to testify. He attempted to show that the reservoir would substantially reduce the value of Yosemite National Park as a public recreation ground and beauty spot. But Whitman did not bring out the fact that wilderness was at stake in Hetch Hetchy. As a result Phelan's rejoinder that San Francisco would cover the dam with moss, vines, and trees and would build picnic spots and trails around the reservoir seemed to answer his objections. . . .

On the basis of the June hearings, the Committee submitted a report unanimously endorsing the reservoir plans. When the bill reached the floor of the House on August 29, 1913, strong support immediately developed for its passage. Applying the time-honored utilitarian yardstick to the problem, Representative Raker of California asserted that the "old barren rocks" of the valley have a "cash value" of less than $300,000 whereas a reservoir would be worth millions. But most proponents of the dam were not so positive. They prefaced their support of the dam with a declaration of their love of wilderness and reluctance to have it destroyed. Finly H. Gray of Indiana, for example, explained: "Mr. Chairman, much as I admire the beauties of nature and deplore the desecration of God's Creation, yet when these two considerations come in conflict the conservation of nature should yield to the conservation of human welfare, health, and life."

The choice Representative Gray made between wilderness and the needs of civilization was especially difficult for William Kent, a Representative from California. Independently wealthy, he had chosen a career as a reformer in politics, first in Chicago and after 1906 in Marin County, north of San Francisco, where he had lived as a boy. Kent's devotion to wild country had the same characteristics as Theodore Roosevelt's. "My life," he declared in an autobiographical fragment, "has been largely spent outdoors . . . I have ridden the prairies, the mountains and the desert." A skilled hunter who deprecated the softness of his contemporaries, Kent called for a revitalization of the savage virtues. Understandably, he believed in the wisdom of preserving wilderness, and in 1903 bought several hundred acres of virgin redwood forest on the shoulder of Marin County's Mt. Tamalpais. In December 1907 Kent informed the Secretary of the Interior of his desire to give this land to the federal government as a national monument under the provisions of the Antiquities Act. His purpose was to keep in a primitive condition "the most attractive bit of wilderness I have ever seen." Kent requested the area be named in honor of John Muir, and on January 9, 1908, President Roosevelt issued a proclamation designating the Muir Woods National Monument.

In view of this record, preservationists believed they had found a champion in William Kent. The Sierra Club made him an honorary member while letters poured in from all parts of the country applauding him for upholding aesthetic and spiritual values in a materialistic age. . . . Protecting the redwoods, Muir thought, was "a much needed lesson to saint and sinner alike, and a credit and encouragement to God." It astonished Muir that "so fine divine a thing should have come out of money-mad Chicago. . . .

A few weeks after arriving in Washington in 1911 to begin his first term as a California Congressman, William Kent received a letter from his friend John Muir about Hetch Hetchy. Assuming that Kent, the donor of Muir Woods, would champion the cause of wilderness preservation, Muir simply encouraged him to follow the Hetch Hetchy issue and "do lots of good work." But for Kent the matter was not so simple. While he realized that Hetch Hetchy was valuable as wilderness and part of a national park, he also knew that the powerful Pacific Gas and Electric Company wanted the valley as a step toward consolidating its control over California hydroelectric resources. Municipal control of Hetch Hetchy's water by San Francisco would block this plan, be a significant victory for the ideal of public ownership, and, beyond that, assert the democratic principle. Moreover, Kent had decided with his political friend Gifford Pinchot that "real conservation meant proper use and not locking up of natural resources." The sacrifice of Hetch Hetchy's wilderness qualities, Kent concluded, was regrettable but in this case necessary for a greater good. Answering Muir indirectly in a letter to Robert Underwood Johnson, Kent stated his conviction that conservation could best be served by granting the valley to San Francisco.

In 1913, as a key member of the House Committee on the Public Lands, William Kent was in a position to exert considerable influence. He began by helping draft a bill permitting San Francisco to build its reservoir; then opened his home to the city's supporters as a campaign headquarters. The fact that Kent was widely known as the donor of Muir Woods lent extra weight to his opinions. Certainly *he* would not dismiss the claims of wilderness preservation lightly. Kent exploited this advantage fully. When the Hetch Hetchy bill came to the floor of the House, he stated simply: "I can lay claim to being a nature lover myself. I think that is a matter of record." . . .

It remained for Kent, as an acknowledged admirer of Muir, to provide public explanation for their divergence over Hetch Hetchy. He did so in the summer of 1913 in a series of letters to his Congressional colleagues. To

Representative Sydney Anderson of Minnesota he wrote: "I hope you will not take my friend, Muir, seriously, for he is a man entirely without social sense. With him, it is me and God and the rock where God put it, and that is the end of the story. I know him well and as far as this proposition is concerned, he is mistaken." Similarly, Kent wired Pinchot that the Hetch Hetchy protest was the work of private waterpower interests using "misinformed nature lovers" as their spokesmen. In October Kent told a meeting in California that because Muir had spent so much time in the wilderness he had not acquired the social instincts of the average man.

It was not the case that Kent changed his mind about the value of wilderness between 1908 and 1913. In fact, at the very time he was advocating development of Hetch Hetchy, he asked Gifford Pinchot for a statement in support of a state park on Mt. Tamalpais. . . . Kent's problem was that the necessity of deciding about Hetch Hetchy left no room for an expression of his ambivalence. The valley could not be a wilderness and a publicly owned reservoir simultaneously. And, ultimately, Kent and Muir gave wilderness preservation a different priority at the price of their earlier friendship.

As the consideration of the Hetch Hetchy question in the House continued into September, 1913, the sentiments of William Kent and other supporters of San Francisco encountered stiffer opposition. Halvor Steenerson of Minnesota declared it was nonsense to claim that an artificial lake would add to the beauty of the valley. "You may as well improve upon the lily of the field by handpainting it," he pointed out, and added that all the city offered was a power plant making a "devilish hissing noise" and a "dirty muddy pond." Concluding his remarks, Steenerson spoke in the agrarian tradition, deploring the tendency of Americans to live in cities, and in the Romantic manner, hoping that some day a poet would use the "pristine glory" of Hetch Hetchy "to produce something more valuable than money." . . .

On September 3 the House passed the Hetch Hetchy bill 183 to 43, with 203 Representatives not voting. No Congressman from a Western state voted against it. Most of its support came from Southern and Middle Western Democrats. In fact, the bill was rumored to be an administration measure, connected, in some minds, with the votes California had given to Wilson in the recent election. . . .

Between the time of the House passage and early December when the Senate began its debate, the destruction of the wilderness qualities of Hetch Hetchy Valley became a major national issue. Hundreds of newspapers throughout the country, including such opinion leaders as the New York *Times,* published editorials on the question, most of which took the side of preservation. Leading magazines, such as *Outlook, Nation, Independent,* and *Collier's,* carried articles protesting the reservoir. A mass meeting on behalf of the valley took place at the Museum of Natural History in New York City. Mail poured into the offices of key Senators: Reed Smoot of Utah estimated late in November that he had received five thousand letters in opposition to the bill, and other Senators were likewise besieged. The protests came from women's groups, outing and sportsmen's clubs, scientific societies, and the faculties of colleges and universities as well as from individuals. The American wilderness had never been so popular before.

The arguments the preservationists used against the dam followed the lines laid down in the earlier stages of the controversy. The issue was represented to be between the intangible values of wilderness and the insensitivity of utilitarianism. . . . Frederick Law Olmsted, Jr., who had succeeded to his father's place as a leader in the field of landscape architecture, also published a defense of the valley. After distinguishing between the "beauty-value" and the "use-value" of nature, he observed that the previous century "has shown . . . an enormous increase in the appreciation of and resort to the wilder and less man-handled scenery as a means of recreation from the intensifying strain of civilization." As a consequence, Olmsted contended, wildernesses like Hetch Hetchy had great importance to modern society. . . .

The wilderness advocates looked forward hopefully to the Senate debate and vote. They had succeeded in demonstrating that a large number of Americans resented the proposed alteration of Yosemite National Park. In mid-November 1913, Muir cheered the hard-working Johnson: "we're bound to win, enemy badly frightened, Up and smite em!" But when the Senate began its consideration of the bill on December 1, it was apparent that San Francisco's representatives, who had not campaigned nationally but rather lobbied quietly in Washington, had done effective work. As was the case with many Representatives, most Senators first made clear that they too appreciated the values of unspoiled nature but went on to support the dam. "I appreciate the importance of preserving beautiful natural features of a landscape as much as anybody else," Frank B. Brandegee of Connecticut declared. Yet ultimately civilization won out because the "mere preservation of a beautiful, romantic, and picturesque spot . . . for esthetic purposes" could not conceivably take precedence over "the urgent needs of great masses of human beings for the necessities of life." . . .

A decision had been made to vote on December 6, and when the Senators entered their chamber that morning they found copies of a "Special Washington Edition" of the San Francisco *Examiner* on their desks. Skillful drawings showed how the valley might appear as a man-made lake with scenic drives for automobiles and boating facilities for happy family groups. The *Examiner* also published experts' testimony justifying the grant in a variety of ways. In comparison, the preservationists' campaign literature was considerably less impressive.

At three minutes before midnight on December 6, the Senate voted. Forty-three favored the grant, twenty-five opposed it, and twenty-nine did not vote or were absent. Eighteen votes from Southern Democrats were the decisive factor, and suggested, as in the case of the House, that the Wilson administration was behind San Francisco. Only nine of the "yeas" came from Republicans.

A Presidential veto was the last hope of the preservationists. After the Senate passage, Wilson received numerous letters calling upon him to defend Yosemite National Park. Robert Underwood Johnson wrote, characteristically, that "God invented courage for just such emergencies. The moral effect of a veto would be immense." He even called in person on the President, but when he left the office, William Kent was waiting to enter! On December 19, 1913, Wilson approved the Hetch Hetchy grant. In signing he declared that "the bill was opposed by so many public-spirited men . . . that I have naturally sought to scrutinize it very closely. I take the liberty of thinking that their fears and objections were not well founded."

The preservationists had lost the fight for the valley, but they had gained much ground in the larger war for the existence of wilderness. A deeply disappointed John Muir took some consolation from the fact that "the conscience of the whole country has been aroused from sleep." Scattered sentiment for wilderness preservation had, in truth, become a national movement in the course of the Hetch Hetchy controversy. Moreover, the defenders of wilderness discovered their political muscles and how to flex them by arousing an expression of public opinion, and in Hetch Hetchy they had a symbol which, like the *Maine,* would not easily be forgotten. In fact, immediately after the Hetch Hetchy defeat the fortunes of wilderness preservation took an abrupt turn for the better. Early in 1915 Stephen T. Mather, a highly successful businessman and wilderness enthusiast, became director of the national parks. Along with Horace M. Albright, Robert Sterling Yard, J. Horace McFarland, and the Sierra Club, Mather generated a campaign on the park's behalf that resulted in the enactment in 1916 of the National Park Service Act. The publicity that accompanied its passage did much to increase the national interest in preserving wilderness that the Hetch Hetchy fight had aroused.

Near the close of the Senate debate on Hetch Hetchy, James A. Reed of Missouri arose to confess his incredulity at the entire controversy. How could it be, he wondered, that over the future of a piece of wilderness "the Senate goes into profound debate, the country is thrown into a condition of hysteria." Observing, accurately, that the intensity of resistance to the dam increased with the distance from Yosemite, he remarked that "when we get as far east as New England the opposition has become a frenzy.". . .

Indeed the most significant thing about the controversy over the valley was that it occurred at all. One hundred or even fifty years earlier a similar proposal to dam a wilderness river would not have occasioned the slightest ripple of public protest. Traditional American assumptions about the use of undeveloped country did not include reserving it in national parks for its recreational, aesthetic, and inspirational values. The emphasis was all the other way—on civilizing it in the name of progress and prosperity. Older generations conceived of the thrust of civilization into the wilderness as the beneficent working out of divine intentions, but in the twentieth century a handful of preservationists generated widespread resistance against this very process. What had formerly been the subject of national celebration was made to appear a national tragedy. . . .

✣ *F U R T H E R   R E A D I N G*

Kendall E. Bailes, ed., *Environmental History* (1985)
Michael P. Cohen, *The Pathless Way: John Muir and the American Wilderness* (1984)
Edward Greer, "Air Pollution and Corporate Power: Municipal Reform Limits in a Black City," *Politics and Society* 4(1974), 483–510

Dolores Hayden, *The Grand Domestic Revolution: A History of Feminist Designs for American Homes, Neighborhoods and Cities* (1981)
Samuel P. Hays, *Conservation and the Gospel of Efficiency* (1975)
Melvin Kalfus, *Frederick Law Olmsted* (1990)
Martin V. Melosi, ed., *Pollution and Reform in American Cities, 1870–1930* (1980)
Roderick Nash, *The American Environment* (1976)
———, *The Call of the Wild* (1970)
———, *Wilderness and the American Mind* (1973)
David Schuyler, *The New Urban Landscape* (1986)
Robert C. Twombly, *Louis Sullivan* (1986)
Peter Wild, *Enos Mills* (1979)
Donald Worster, *Nature's Economy* (1985)

CHAPTER

13

Commercialized Leisure

and Spectator Sports

⚭

In its train the industrial revolution in the United States brought not merely new work habits but also new play habits—indeed, an entire reorganization of Americans' leisure time. Whereas work and communal socializing once had been intertwined in agrarian activities like barn raisings and quilting bees, the pace and noise of the factory set a new barrier between the two. Now more than ever, people worked in order to "live," not vice versa, even as workers demanded—and gradually received—a shortened working day.

But what Americans, especially city dwellers, did with their "time off" changed drastically. The very marketplace that replaced the artisan with the factory worker also created the professional athlete and the athletic spectator, the shopper, and a national moviegoing audience. Instead of localized, neighborhood-based, and informally organized recreational pursuits, Americans by 1920 were fully enmeshed in a commercialized leisure and entertainment network. Collapsing older social divisions based on region, ethnicity, class, and sex, the new mass leisure and communication empire exercised a powerful nationalizing force within the culture. Among sports that captured the national imagination, two—baseball and boxing—may be said to have fully matured as professional mass spectacles by the time of World War I. Baseball, in particular, suggested the opposite tuggings on the popular psyche toward a pastoral idealism on the one hand and a modern, competitive, rulebound world on the other.

⚭ D O C U M E N T S

The five documents that follow testify to the encompassing diversity as well as the inner texture of commercialized leisure pursuits. The first two selections are drawn from the contemporary saga of professional baseball. A reporter's dispatch from a famous Giants-Cubs game in 1908, the first document reveals an already popular fascination with the adjudication of sports rules and a highly developed and colorful sports lingo. In 1914 humorist Ring Lardner spoofed the growing cult of the professional baseball player. In an engaging serial in the the *Saturday Evening*

Post, Lardner's Jack Keefe, "the busher," presented himself and his fellow players as a "childish and stupid and not a little mean-spirited"—but still lovable —collection of ordinary human beings.

In the third document, taken from his novel *Sister Carrie,* the American exemplar of hard social realism, or "naturalism," Theodore Dreiser, provides an immortal portrait of a poor country girl's confrontation with the lure of the department store. The fourth document, a 1910 article from New York's lively *Independent* magazine, speculates on the advantages of the motion picture over the traditional stage production. And finally, in an excerpt from *Everybody's Magazine,* Coney Island's master amusement park promoter Frederic Thompson explains the secret of his success.

The New York Giants Lose a Pennant, 1908

New York, Sept. 23, 1908—Minor league brains lost the Giants' game today after they had it cleanly and fairly won by a score of 2 to 1. In the ninth round, Fred Merkle did a bonehead base-running stunt identical with the recent exhibition which Mr. Gill, also a minor leaguer, gave at Pittsburgh three weeks ago. But this time Hank O'Day had his eagle eye peeled, and the winning run which the Giants compiled in the ninth inning was tossed into the discard.

O'Day ruled "no contest" and, as the field could not be cleared, the game may be forfeited to the Cubs.

It must chagrin the Giants aplenty to think how they kiboshed themselves. In a swell combat, worth going miles to see, Mathewson had the better of Pfiester, and the game looked as safe as the Bank of England when Bridwell tore off what should have been a hit in the ninth.

Tinker's home run in the fifth was all the Cubs had in the way of visible assets. Steinfeldt's bum heave and a couple of singles knotted the count in the sixth after a most gallant defense. Then came the bonehead finish, which left the bugs puzzled and wondering. And they won't know what happened until they see the public prints—i.e., newspapers—in the morning.

President Pulliam would not make a statement tonight, but he intimated the game would not be played over. That means either that the contest goes to the Cubs by forfeit because of the crowd on the field, or that Pulliam will overrule O'Day's decision that the run in the ninth did not count. This would give the game to New York.

Round nine for the Giants opened with the out of Seymour. Then Devlin singled and McCormick forced him. Merkle's safety to right put McCormick on third. On the first ball pitched, Bridwell pasted a neat but not gaudy single to center. McCormick crossed the plate, but Merkle, who was on first base, ran half way down to second, then turned, and hotfooted it for the clubhouse.

Unless the said Merkle planted a hoof on second base, Bridwell could not be credited with a hit, and McCormick could not score. The Cubs and Hank O'Day were primed for the situation, having been through it once before in Pittsburgh. With one voice the Cubs set up a yelp like a cage of hungry hyenas, and O'Day, working behind the plate, ran to the pitching slab to see what had come off at second base. Capt. Donlin realized the danger about to overtake the Giants, so he set off after the fat-headed Merkle, while McGinnity, who was coaching at third base, butted into the fracas coming off at the middle cushion.

The facts in the case gleaned from active participants and survivors are these: Hoffman fielded Bridwell's knock and threw to Evers for a force play on the absent Merkle. But McGinnity, who was not in the game, cut in ahead and grabbed the ball before it reached the eager Trojan. Three Cubs from as many directions landed on the iron man at the same time and jolted the ball from his cruel grasp. It rolled among the spectators who had swarmed upon the diamond like an army of starving potato bugs.

At this thrilling juncture "Kid" Kroh, the demon southpaw, swarmed upon the human potato bugs and knocked six of them galley-west. The triumphant Kroh passed the ball to Steinfeldt after cleaning up the gang that had it. Tinker wedged in and the ball was conveyed to Evers for the force out of Merkle, while Capt. Donlin was still some distance off towing that brilliant young gent by the neck.

Some say Merkle eventually touched second base, but not until he had been forced out by Hoffman to McGinnity, to six potato bugs, to Kroh, to some more Cubs, and the shrieking, triumphant Mr. Evers, the well-known Troy shoe dealer. There have been some complicated plays in baseball, but we do not recall one just like this in a career of years of monkeying with the national pastime.

Meanwhile a more turbulent scene was being enacted elsewhere. Peerless Leader Chance ran at O'Day to find out what Hank had to say, but the sparrow cops, specials, two hundred cops and Pinks—slang for Pinkertons—thought Chance was going to bite Hank on the ankle. Half a hundred men in uniform surrounded the P.L., and thousands of bugs surrounded them. Bill Marshall, an expert on bacteria, and Del Howard rushed in to help the Peerless Leader. Another squad of cops had O'Day in tow several yards away.

Hank didn't know Chance wanted to converse with him, and they couldn't get together anyhow. Finally the cops got O'Day into a coop under the stand and tried to slam the door in the face of the Peerless Leader. He jammed his robust frame in the opening and defied the sparrow chasers. Chance later got to O'Day who, said Emslie, working on the bases, did not see the second-base play because of the crowd, but Hank informed Chance that McCormick's run didn't count.

Still later, Hank submitted gracefully to an interview by the war scribes. He said Merkle was forced at second base and the game ended in a tie, 1 to 1. None of the Giants remained to make public statements. Part of the crowd lifted a player in white to their shoulders and bore him to the clubhouse. The Giant thus honored was not Mr. Merkle. He left long before the trouble started, and his departure caused it. Some base runners should have a groove cut for them so they couldn't go wrong.

O'Day made the correct ruling. He had been through one harrowing experience along the same lines at Pittsburgh, where a situation similar in every respect came up, including the minor leaguer on first base, and Hank stood by to see what came off. President Pulliam was present and saw what transpired. Under the rules of baseball, a run cannot score when the third out is forced out, even if private citizens, née bugs, and players not in the game assist in the final play.

New York, Sept. 24—Following a sleepless night of agony throughout the length and breadth of Manhattan, haggard bugs waited all morning for the decision from President Pulliam on the riotous wind-up of Wednesday's tie game. Scribes from far and near assembled in Pulliam's outer office, where he conversed on general topics in his usual affable manner. Then he retired to the inner sanctum and sent out a neatly typewritten ruling. In effect, H. Pulliam said he had received a written report from Umpires O'Day and Emslie stating the game resulted in a tie score, 1 to 1, and that it was impossible to continue after the ninth inning.

"Without entering, at this time, into the merits of the controversy or passing upon the legality of any decision," the ruling continued, "the game will be recorded as reported, namely, a tie score."

Barring himself within the inner precincts, Mr. Pulliam declined to see anybody, nor would he come forth to reveal the future. Questions sent in by scribes came back in original state—i.e., unanswered. Nothing was said about playing off the tie game, as provided by the league constitution, which states such games shall be played. As this is the last day that the game can be played, the Giants are subject to a fine. It rests with the home club to arrange such matters, but McGraw announced last night the contest would not be played over.

Editor's note: When the season's play ended with the Giants and the Cubs tied, the National League's board of directors ordered the tie game replayed in New York. The Cubs won, 4 to 2, on October 8.

A Busher's Letters Home, 1914

TERRE HAUTE, INDIANA, September 6

FRIEND AL: Well, Al old pal I suppose you seen in the paper where I been sold to the White Sox. Believe me Al it comes as a surprise to me and I bet it did to all you good old pals down home. You could of knocked me over with a feather when the old man come up to me and says Jack I've sold you to the Chicago Americans.

I didn't have no idea that anything like that was coming off. For five minutes I was just dum and couldn't say a word.

He says We aren't getting what you are worth but I want you to go up to that big league and show those birds that there is a Central League on the map. He says Go and pitch the ball you been pitching down here and there won't be nothing to it. He says All you need is the nerve and Walsh or no one else won't have nothing on you.

So I says I would do the best I could and I thanked him for the treatment I got in Terre Haute. They always was good to me here and though I did more than my share I always felt that my work was appresiated. We are finishing second and I done most of it. I can't help but be proud of my first year's record in professional baseball and you know I am not boasting when I say that Al.

Well Al it will seem funny to be up there in the big show when I never was really in a big city before. But I guess I seen enough of life not to be scared of the high buildings eh Al?

I will just give them what I got and if they don't like it they can send me back to the old Central and I will be perfectly satisfied.

I didn't know anybody was looking me over, but one of the boys told me that Jack Doyle the White Sox scout was down here looking at me when Grand Rapids was here. I beat them twice in that serious. You know Grand Rapids never had a chance with me when I was right. I shut them out in the first game and they got one run in the second on account of Flynn misjuging that fly ball. Anyway Doyle liked my work and he wired Comiskey to buy me. Comiskey come back with an offer and they excepted it. I don't know how much they got but anyway I am sold to the big league and believe me Al I will make good.

Well Al I will be home in a few days and we will have some of the good old times. Regards to all the boys and tell them I am still their pal and not all swelled up over this big league business.

Your pal,

Jack

PASO ROBLES, CALIFORNIA, March 2

OLD PAL AL: Well Al we been in this little berg now a couple of days and its bright and warm all the time just like June. Seems funny to have it so warm this early in March but I guess this California climate is all they said about it and then some.

It would take me a week to tell you about our trip out here. We came on a Special Train De Lukes and it was some train. Every place we stopped there was crowds down to the station to see us go through and all the people looked me over like I was a actor or something. I guess my hight and shoulders attracted their attention. Well Al we finally got to Oakland which is across part of the ocean from Frisco. We will be back there later on for practice games.

We stayed in Oakland a few hours and then took a train for here. It was another night in a sleeper and believe me I was tired of sleepers before we got here. I have road one night at a time but this was four straight nights. You know Al I am not built right for a sleeping car birth.

The hotel here is a great big place and got good eats. We got in at breakfast time and I made a B line for the dining room. Kid Gleason who is a kind of asst. manager to Callahan come in and sat down with me. He says

Leave something for the rest of the boys because they will be just as hungry as you. He says Ain't you afraid you will cut your throat with that knife. He says There ain't no extra charge for using the forks. He says You shouldn't ought to eat so much because you're overweight now. I says You may think I am fat, but it's all solid bone and muscle. He says Yes I suppose it's all solid bone from the neck up. I guess he thought I would get sore but I will let them kid me now because they will take off their hats to me when they see me work.

Manager Callahan called us all to his room after breakfast and give us a lecture. He says there would be no work for us the first day but that we must all take a long walk over the hills. He also says we must not take the training trip as a joke. Then the colored trainer give us our suits and I went to my room and tried mine on. I ain't a bad looking guy in the White Sox uniform Al. I will have my picture taken and send you boys some.

My roommate is Allen a lefthander from the Coast League. He don't look nothing like a pitcher but you can't never tell about them dam left handers. Well I didn't go on the long walk because I was tired out. Walsh stayed at the hotel too and when he seen me he says Why didn't you go with the bunch? I says I was too tired. He says Well when Callahan comes back you better keep out of sight or tell him you are sick. I says I don't care nothing for Callahan. He says No but Callahan is crazy about you. He says You better obey orders and you will git along better. I guess Walsh thinks I am some rube.

When the bunch come back Callahan never said a word to me but Gleason come up and says Where was you? I told him I was too tired to go walking. He says Well I will borrow a wheel-barrow some place and push you round. He says Do you sit down when you pitch? I let him kid me because he has not saw my stuff yet.

Next morning half the bunch mostly vetrans went to the ball park which isn't no better than the one we got at home. Most of them was vetrans as I say but I was in the bunch. That makes things look pretty good for me don't it Al? We tossed the ball round and hit fungos and run round and then Callahan asks Scott and Russell and I to warm up easy and pitch a few to the batters. It was warm and I felt pretty good so I warmed up pretty good. Scott pitched to them first and kept laying them right over with nothing on them. I don't believe a man gets any batting practice that way. So I went in and after I lobbed a few over I cut loose my fast one. Lord was to bat and he ducked out of the way and then throwed his bat to the bench. Callahan says What's the matter Harry? Lord says I forgot to pay up my life insurance. He says I ain't ready for Walter Johnson's July stuff.

Well Al I will make them think I am Walter Johnson before I get through with them. But Callahan come out to me and says What are you trying to do kill somebody? He says Save your smoke because you're going to need it later on. He says Go easy with the boys at first or I won't have no batters. But he was laughing and I guess he was pleased to see the stuff I had.

There is a dance in the hotel to-night and I am up in my room writing this in my underwear while I get my suit pressed. I got it all mussed up coming out here. I don't know what shoes to wear. I asked Gleason and he says Wear your baseball shoes and if any of the girls gets fresh with you spike them. I guess he was kidding me.

Write and tell me all the news about home.

Yours truly,

JACK

Theodore Dreiser's Carrie Discovers the Department Store, 1900

At that time the department store was in its earliest form of successful operation, and there were not many. The first three in the United States, established about 1884, were in Chicago. Carrie was familiar with the names of several through the advertisements in the "Daily News," and now proceeded to seek them. The words of Mr. McManus had somehow managed to restore her courage, which had fallen low, and she dared to hope that this new line [of department store work] would offer her something. Some time she spent in wandering up and down, thinking to encounter the buildings by chance, so readily is the mind, bent upon prosecuting a hard but needful errand, eased by that self-deception which the semblance of search, without the reality, gives. At last she inquired of a police officer, and was directed to proceed "Two blocks up," where she would find "The Fair."

The nature of these vast retail combinations, should they ever permanently disappear, will form an interesting chapter in the commercial history of our nation. Such a flowering out of a modest trade principle the world had never witnessed up to that time. They were along the line of the most effective retail organisation, with hundreds of stores coordinated into one and laid out upon the most imposing and economic basis. They were handsome, bustling, successful affairs, with a host of clerks and a swarm of patrons. Carrie passed along the busy aisles, much affected by the remarkable displays of trinkets, dress goods, stationery, and jewelry. Each separate counter was a show place of dazzling interest and attraction. She could not help feeling the claim of each trinket and valuable upon her personally, and yet she did not stop. There was nothing there which she could not have used—nothing which she did not long to own. The dainty slippers and stockings, the delicately frilled skirts and petticoats, the laces, ribbons, hair-combs, purses, all touched her with individual desire, and she felt keenly the fact that not any of these things were in the range of her purchase. She was a work-seeker, an outcast without employment, one whom the average employee could tell at a glance was poor and in need of a situation.

It must not be thought that any one could have mistaken her for a nervous, sensitive, high-strung nature, cast unduly upon a cold, calculating, and unpoetic world. Such certainly she was not. But women are peculiarly sensitive to their adornment.

Not only did Carrie feel the drag of desire for all which was new and pleasing in apparel for women, but she noticed too, with a touch at the heart, the fine ladies who elbowed and ignored her, brushing past in utter disregard of her presence, themselves eagerly enlisted in the materials which the store contained. Carrie was not familiar with the appearance of her more fortunate sisters of the city. Neither had she before known the nature and appearance of the shop girls with whom she now compared poorly. They were pretty in the main, some even handsome, with an air of independence and indifference which added, in the case of the more favoured, a certain piquancy. Their clothes were neat, in many instances fine, and wherever she encountered the eye of one it was only to recognize in it a keen analysis of her own position— her individual shortcomings of dress and that shadow of *manner* which she thought must hang about her and make clear to all who and what she was. A flame of envy lighted in her heart. She realized in a dim way how much the city held—wealth, fashion, ease—every adornment for women, and she longed for dress and beauty with a whole heart. . . .

Democracy at the Movies, 1910

The cinematograph is doing for the drama what the printing press did for literature, bringing another form of art into the daily life of the people. Plays are now within the reach, literally, of the poorest, as are good books and good pictures. The secret of cheapness in art as in other things is mechanical multiplication. So long as a play required for each presentation the active co-operation of a considerable number of more or less talented persons it could never be cheap, and in its better forms it was necessarily accessible to a comparatively small part of the population. But once on a celluloid film a spectacle can be reproduced indefinitely, the good as cheaply as the poor, and superiority is no longer handicapped. The same effect is shown in the field of literature. Among the dollar and a half books published every year there is a large proportion of trash or worse, but the volumes sold for fifty cents or less comprise the world's best literature.

The moving picture shows are in general superior, both artistically and morally, to the vaudeville and melodrama that they have driven out of business. It is a mistake to suppose that their amazing popularity is due altogether to their low price of admission. On the contrary the cinematograph has some advantages, not only over the cheap shows which it at first rivaled, but over any previous form of dramatic art. The most conspicuous of these advantages is spaciousness, distance. The stage is at the best but a narrow platform. The characters must dodge out of the wings or pop out of a door at the back. They have their exits and their entrances, but all both necessarily sudden, more "dramatic" than lifelike.

But the moving picture show has a third dimension. The characters have a gradual approach and recession. The railroad train rushes out toward the spectator; the horseman rides off thru the woods or across the plain until he disappears in the distance. . . .

The abolition of the painted scenery of the backdrop gives to the drama a sense of reality, a solidity, that it never had before. The mountains and clouds do not now show spots of threadbare canvas. The tumbling waves do not throw up a dust. The rocks and trees do not shiver at the touch of the actors.

The sunshine is such as never came from calcium or carbon, and the wind that blows about loose hair and garments is not that of the electric fan. . . .

On the ordinary stage there is no good way of showing what is being written or read, however essential this may be to the plot. The actor has to read aloud his letter as he writes it as tho he was not sure of its grammar. This device is no longer necessary. The incriminating note, the long lost will, the visiting card, the portrait, and the newspaper paragraph are shown to us directly and we do not have to hear of them at second hand. We see instantly what the hero sees when he puts the spyglass to his eye, and what the housemaid is looking at thru the keyhole. Ghosts, visions, and transformation scenes are accomplished in a manner truly magical, without the aid of the old stage contrivances, the steam curtain, the trap and the *deus ex machina*. Flying is as easy as walking. Acrobatic feats are unlimited. All miracles are possible, even that most marvelous of miracles, the reversal of the course of life. . . .

The disadvantages of the cinematograph in comparison with the ordinary drama cannot well be discussed at present because we do not know which of them are inherent and which remediable. The flickering and jerky action, now often so disagreeable, can be obviated by more rapid exposures and better adjustment of apparatus. The cinematograph drama is still pantomime as was all drama everywhere in its primitive form. But the phonograph is losing its metallic twang and may soon be satisfactorily synchronized with the running film. The problem of photography in natural colors may be regarded as solved altho it cannot in its present stage stand the quick exposure and great enlargement necessary for moving pictures. If once the cinematograph drama can be made vocal and given lifelike color, the only thing further required for a perfect illusion of reality is a real perspective. It can be done by giving our two eyes different pictures and this is not impossible. It has been accomplished for small stationary pictures by means of red and blue spectacles and other contrivances. How it can be managed we do not know. If we did we would not be engaged in writing editorials for a living. But we expect to see some time a stereoscopic colored speaking moving picture drama and it will be well worth seeing. It will be a new form of fine art not unworthy to rank with the elder arts.

Frederic Thompson Creates the Carnival Spirit, 1908

The difference between the theatre and the big amusement park is the difference between the Sunday-school and the Sunday-school picnic. The people are the same; the spirit and the environment are wholly different. It is harder to make the picnic successful than successfully to conduct a session of the school; and it is harder to make a success of a big amusement park than of a theatre. There isn't any irreverence in this comparison with the Sunday-school, for if the amusement park doesn't attract people who are interested in the Sunday-school, it isn't going to succeed.

For I want to say at the beginning that ninety-five percent of the American public is pure and good, and it is this public that it pays to serve. This isn't just a general statement. I always believed it. I have proved it by studying the twenty-five million people that have visited Luna Park in the past five years. I haven't any use for the bad five percent. As a showman I don't want them to come near my enterprises.

In the theatre and in the Sunday-school conventional standards of behavior are accepted as a matter of course. The picnic and the open-air park are designed to give the natural, bubbling animal spirits of the human being full play, to give people something fresh and new and unusual, to afford them respite from the dull routine of their daily lives.

The one thing that makes a picnic or an amusement park a success—it doesn't make any difference whether the picnic is made up of ten people or ten thousand, whether the park is a little one or a great international exposition—the one thing absolutely necessary is the carnival spirit. Without that no show in the open, nothing that has to do with people in the mass, can hope to succeed. Whenever any enterprise that is intended to appeal to the million fails, the failure can always be traced to the lack of carnival enthusiasm.

This spirit of gaiety, the carnival spirit, is not spontaneous, except on extraordinary occasions, and usually its cause can be easily traced. Almost always it is manufactured. Take a big political meeting, for instance. Ninety-nine times out of a hundred the steps that culminate in a great outburst are carefully planned. There are men who make it a business to insure the success of great mass meetings. When you get right down to it, the fundamentals are the same, whether the application is to a church picnic, a political meeting, a circus, or a big exposition. . . .

In the year 1901 I had a show called "A Trip to the Moon" on the Midway at the Pan-American Exposition in Buffalo. Architecturally and from an educational standpoint this exposition was one of the most remarkable in all the history of world's fairs. It was beautiful; it was tremendous; but it wasn't paying. After several months I went to the executive committee and to the president and told them why their outlay of millions of dollars was attracting only thirty thousand people a day. I told them they were failing miserably because there wasn't a regular showman in the lot. I told them about the carnival spirit, and they came back by telling me about the educational value of the exposition.

"But what's the use of a college if there are not students?" I asked. "Before we talk of educational benefits let's get in the crowd to educate."

They didn't take kindly to my notions at first. Then I suggested that they turn over the show to me for one day, which would be sufficient to test what the executive gentlemen were pleased to call my theories. President Milburn was with me, and I finally won the point. The exposition was to be mine for August 3, and I told them that it would be known as "Midway Day."

Within six hours after the final interview I had four printing-houses at work getting out the paper with which I was going to plaster the country. I and my side-show associates sent ten advance men on the road to herald the coming of the big day, and within a week a large part of the eastern half of the United States was screaming: "August third! Midway Day at the Pan-American! Don't miss it!"

They didn't. On the night of August 2 a crowd of would-be excursionists was left on every railway station within twenty-four hours' ride of Buffalo, and when the gates of the exposition were thrown open, the police reserves had to be summoned to stop a panic. They arrived too late to prevent ten thousand people from forcing their way in without paying. There were more than enough left to make the gate receipts satisfactory. . . .

How was it done? By paying no attention to Machinery Hall, the architectural beauty of the State Building, or the interesting exhibits of Trade and Industry; and by smearing the sign-boards of forty-five states with the carnival spirit. Instead of advertising an organ concert in Music Hall we yelled ourselves hoarse about high diving, greased poles, parades, and every other crazy thing we could think of. I instructed all bands to play marching and to go to the band-stands only when they wished to rest. To the Stadium, which had never held a quarter of its capacity, I drew 23,000 people to see a race contested by an ostrich, a camel, an elephant, a man on a bicycle, another on a horse, an automobile, and a zebra. I had a man sliding by his teeth from the top of the sky-scraping electric tower to the esplanade below. True, he had never before traveled more than thirty feet in that fashion, but we tied him on, so there was no danger. The illusion was great, and the stunt made a sensation.

In every part of the grounds something extraordinary was going on all the time. There were speed, light, gaiety, color, excitement. The crowd entered into it. They didn't sit on the benches and admire the sculptural work with the aid of official guides—not a bit of it. They joined in the spirit of the occasion—they caught the carnival spirit—and the Pan-American was "made," as far as any exposition could be made at such a late day.

To create a carnival spirit a showman may use other means than ballyhoos—which means the sample shows on the outside, with the patter of the barkers—bands, freak shows, and free circuses. I use architecture. It's all right to copy the capitol at Washington in making a state building at an exposition, and there is no objection to constructing Machinery Hall and the House of Manufactures with an outward indication of the staid and serious exhibits within—if the heads of the exposition are philanthropists. But if they are trying to have their enterprise make both ends meet it is suicidal. The scenery of a comic opera suggests the spirit and the environment of the piece, and the scenery of an exposition or an amusement park must do the same if the place is to score what in theatrical parlance is known as a "hit." Straight lines are necessarily severe and dead. They have no right in the place of honor of a great outdoor show. The very architecture must be in keeping with the spirit of carnival. It must be active, mobile, free, graceful, and attractive. It must be arranged so that visitors will say, "What is this?" and "Why is that?"

When I was studying architecture I paid a great deal of attention to the vignola and to the other classically conventional standards of construction. I was like every other architect. But when I started to build I realized that I, like every one else, was obtaining absolutely conventional results. So one day I threw all my books and plans on to the ash-heap and decided to start after something new. I began designing, not after classical models, but with a sense of their proportions. I stuck to no style. I adopted what I thought was best in Free Renaissance, but reserved the right to use all the license in the world and to inject into everything I did the graceful, romantic curves of the Oriental.

One result is Luna Park, the sky-line of which is utterly unlike anything else of its kind in the two Americas. The architecture of Luna Park helps rather than hinders the spirit of carnival. Luna Park has been, and is, tremendously successful. There are other amusement parks in its vicinity that are chastely beautiful from an artistic standpoint, but that so far as dollars and cents are concerned are utter failures. Visitors admire the buildings—and don't go near the shows. I have built their sort of buildings, too, but not for a Luna Park. They don't pay. An exposition is a form of festivity, and serious architecture should not enter into it if it will interfere with the carnival spirit.

In amusing the million there are other essential elements besides gaiety. One is decency—the absolutely necessary quality in every line of the world's business. There is nothing that pays so well. . . .

The first rowdy I caught in Luna Park was soundly thrashed, and before he was thrown out of the grounds I told him the place was not run for him, but for his mother and sister. I think that did him more good than the punishment. For several seasons I advertised the park as "the place for your mother, your sister, and your sweetheart." If I hadn't believed it was that I wouldn't have spent upward of a hundred thousand dollars in impressing the fact upon the public.

Courtesy on the part of the employee is as necessary as decency on the part of the visitor. If I hear of one of my employees resenting an insult offered by a visitor, I dismiss him. I tell him that so long as he wears my uniform he is representing me, and that I am the only person who can be insulted inside the gates.

An amusement park is a condensed Broadway, if that is understood to represent metropolitan theatreland. In a park the best things of a theatrical nature must be presented in capsule form. The shows must be diversified because the appeal must be universal. The whole gamut of the theatre must be run, and no show can last more than twenty minutes. If you have a two-hour show, it should be boiled down to a quarter of an hour. It is foolish to make people serious or to point a moral, for you are dealing with a moral people. Nor is it worth while to try to educate the amusement-seeking public. It is better to take it for granted that they are educated, and if you start out to amuse them, to stick to that.

People are just boys and girls grown tall. Elaborated child's play is what they want on a holiday. Sliding down cellar doors and the make-believes of youngsters are the most effective amusements for grown-ups. An appreciation of that fact made "The Trip to the Moon" possible, and "The Trip to the Moon" made for me and my partner, Dundy, half a million dollars. "The Tickler," "Bump the Bumps," and "The Virginia Reel" are nothing more than improved cellar doors. "The Trip to the Moon," "Night and Morning," "The Witching Waves," and "The Lost Girl" are only elaborations of the doll-house stunts of childhood, and they are successful largely for that reason. But they must be short and decisive. I would rather have a good show that lasts three minutes than a better one that runs an hour. And I prefer one that is over in a minute but enables the spectator to become a part of it to one that runs three minutes and never permits him to become more than an onlooker.

Speed is almost as important a factor in amusing the millions as is the carnival spirit, decency, or a correct recollection of school days. Speed has become an inborn American trait. We as a nation are always moving, we are always in a hurry, we are never without momentum. "Helter Skelters," "Scenic Railways," "Shoot the Chutes," "The Dragon's Gorge," the thousand and one varieties of roller-coasters are popular for the same reason that we like best the fastest trains, the speediest horses, the highest powered motor-cars, and the swiftest sprinters.

Not only must some rides be speedy and all shows be short, but the employees must work fast visibly, thereby promoting by suggestion speed in the mind, heart, and steps of the most laggard visitors. Throughout Luna Park and all exposition grounds there are benches for the weary. I want the benches there, but I don't want people to sit on them. Whenever, on my frequent tours of the grounds, I find men and women seated watching the lights or the crowds or the free shows, I order out a band, make the musicians march about playing the liveliest tunes, and inject into the very atmosphere such excitement, gaiety, and speed that the resters get up and again take an interest in things. I have never seen this ruse fail.

To keep up the carnival spirit everybody and everything must be on the "go." There can be no carnival without speed. The moment a crowd of folk who are slowly meandering around catch this spirit they walk faster, they laugh, they spend money, they have a good time. I instruct my "talkers" to be always on the alert and to interest people while they are approaching. "Mills won't grind with water that's past" is an old motto, but a good one. It applies to the business of amusing the millions perhaps more than to any other kind of human activity.

Bad weather kills the carnival spirit, and on rainy days the showman must fight hardest to maintain a pretense of gaiety. I have made it a rule to keep my attractions running just the same in a rain-storm as in the sunshine, and as an evidence of the curious and timely reward the allegiance to this principle has frequently brought me I need tell only one story.

I reached the gates of Luna at half past nine one night two years ago when rain was falling in torrents. Just as I entered the park all the lights went out and I met a crowd of employees on their way home. I told them to stop, ordered them back to their posts, sent for the manager, told him to turn on the lights, and sent word to the five bands to get back into their uniforms and start playing. I had made it a rule to keep faith with my public, and, although it costs eight hundred dollars a night to light Luna, I thought the chance that the next train might bring to Coney Island half a dozen people who would expect to find my place open and ablaze with electricity was worth taking. Within five minutes, as if by miracle, the weather changed, the rain ceased, the stars came out, and people began to stream in. Within the next hour nearly eleven thousand people paid admissions to Luna. If I had not insisted on a pretense at gaiety they would have gone somewhere else.

There was another time when it didn't work so well. It rained hard, with no prospect of letting up. I insisted upon the bands' playing—the big band of sixty pieces and the smaller ones as well—we have six in all. After a while the big band started to play:

> Ain't it a shame, a measly shame
> To keep me standing out in the rain.

The other bands took it up and for an hour they played nothing else. I gave in.

Here is another incident that illustrates my practice of never disappointing people: While "The Trip to the Moon" was running I insisted that a performance be given every fifteen minutes, despite the frequently expressed opinion that some day there would be an audience of only one person. And it finally happened. The fifteen minutes were up, and the lecturer, upon making his entrance, found a little wizened old man the sole occupant of the auditorium. He was a bit of a joker—this lecturer—and taking a seat alongside the audience, he started to deliver his talk in a conversational tone.

"The principles of aerial navigation have never been properly understood," said he.

"You don't say," replied the audience. "Why haven't they?"

The rest of the lecture was made in the same question and answer style, and both gentlemen enjoyed the affair immensely.

It costs a lot of money to build and operate an amusement park on a large scale.

I suppose that more than twenty-five million dollars are invested in these parks in this country. Dreamland on Coney Island cost about $2,500,000; Riverview Park and the White City in Chicago cost about a million each.

Luna Park cost $2,400,000. The total annual expenses, including the cost of rebuilding, of putting in new shows, and the operating expenses, average about a million dollars, and the season lasts four months. I spent $240,000 on one show alone, of which $68,000 was for animals, mostly elephants and camels—it was the representation of the Indian Durbar—and I lost $100,000 on it. I charged the loss up to education, and it was worth it. It costs $5,600 a week to light Luna Park, and $4,500 for the music. The salaries of the free performers this season are $2,300 a week. And all of these expenditures, as well as a good many others, go simply to manufacture the carnival spirit.

❧ *E S S A Y S*

The interaction between sport and a changing society is the focus of the essays following. Historian Gunther Barth of the University of California, Berkeley, speculates that baseball's soothing answers to a worried public in an industrial age had much to do with its emergence as the national pastime. Then Kathy Peiss, a historian at the University of Massachusetts, Amherst, examines the effect of commercial amusement parks on working-class leisure and sexual culture.

Baseball and the Values of Industrial America

GUNTHER BARTH

Old men, young men, and small boys, usually "confined in offices, shops, and factories," packed the Polo Grounds on May 30, 1888, for a baseball game between New York and Pittsburgh, "and saw the popular sport to their hearts' content." . . . The spectators yelled, "jumped like colts, clapped their hands, threw their hats into the air, slapped their companions on the back, winked knowingly at each other, and . . . enjoyed themselves hugely." On that afternoon, according to the account of a New York *Times* reporter, 13,333 "anxious sightseers" experienced in the ball park the quintessence of urban leisure: watching others do things.

The scene, barely a few years old, seemed timeless to the spectators. Engulfed by the surging city, . . . the baseball field exposed within its boundaries the remnants of a ravaged countryside in the form of scarred ravines protected by their ugliness from building construction. Here, with weathered wooden grandstands and solid clapboard fences as dikes, a lake of grass contrasted with the surrounding shades of brown. Its green faded away around the bases, where the intense play had turned the grass to dirt, a baseball diamond without a diamond's glitter. Oblivious of this, however, thousands of spectators looked only for the sparkle of perfection in the play on the field. To them going to the ball park meant surrender to the spell of baseball and to the motions of the players. . . .

In addition to the excitement, a visit to the ball park provided men with a new perspective on life in the modern city. . . .

Thousands and thousands of men, frequently mystified by the operation of the economic sphere or the actions of their fellowmen in public office, saw in the ball park how rules affected one sector of modern city life, the athletic contest. In ways they could perceive, the spectacle demonstrated the regulation of one of their elementary drives—competition. When their knowledge of the rules of baseball put them in a position to detect how at times some players tried to win by getting away with infractions, city people came to an understanding of how regulations operated in the free-for-all of the modern world. A quick assessment of the swift action on the diamond revealed that restraints curbed the struggle for success, ordinarily pursued obtrusively by reckless men or obscured by the hustle of daily life. This insight reassured the spectators that elements of order permeated the turmoil of the modern city. . . .

The practice of conducting an entire game according to established rules signaled the arrival of spectator sports as big business in the nineteenth century. Apart from their basic function of distinguishing one sport from another, rules made a game a socially acceptable outlet for emotions. By regularizing procedures, they fostered interest, shaped the sport to the liking of spectators, and provided the framework for a sequence of related events leading to a championship. The use of rules set the big-city spectacle apart from impromptu play, which is attractive because it is freely improvised, utilizes make-believe instead of rules, and provides the pleasure of assuming roles. Rules also heightened enormously the popularity of a contest because they facilitated betting on the results. . . .

Although the fans paid admissions to sports spectacles and thus influenced their development, general social and cultural trends also affected the diversions of nineteenth-century urbanites. The disintegration of traditional society that accompanied the rise of the modern city undermined forms of popular recreation that were rooted in a predominantly agrarian social system. The newly emerging leisure culture was molded according to the requirements of capitalist society and industrial production. Unlike their ancestors in pre-industrial societies, relieved from incessant labor by climatic vicissitudes and rewarded for prolonged toil by seasonal feast days, in general the residents of the modern city learned to be satisfied with brief but more frequent opportunities to enjoy themselves.

This formula suited their working hours, which could stretch through day and night, with some workers idle while others toiled if factory shifts required several sets of men. In consequence, the sporting events which attracted the most attention came to be reduced in length. However, the number of contests and of competitors increased and provided a steady stream of excitement that fitted most people's schedules and directed the use of leisure time toward relaxation rather than rest. . . .

Popular sports, connecting the urban population with a rising sports industry, shared a potential for educating as well as entertaining crowds of spectators. Among these spectacles, baseball occupied a special position as the most popular and most organized of all spectator sports in the last decades of the nineteenth century. It was the most convenient way for city people to enjoy themselves and also to demonstrate a commitment to standards of excellence in a leisure-time activity. Within a generation the game had made the transition from a pastime for gentlemen to a social institution illuminating the inner workings of new patterns of urban life.

Baseball conquered the United States in the decades between 1840 and 1870, which saw the standardization of the diamonds, the organization of teams, the refinement of rules, the establishment of game schedules, and the first grand tour by a professional baseball team. . . .

Historical evidence links baseball, as we know it, with the modern city. In the early 1840's a group of New York gentlemen who on sunny days enjoyed playing ball games in a lot at the corner of Madison Avenue and Twenty-Seventh Street formed the first association and in 1845 adopted the first set of modern rules. These merchants, brokers, and physicians enjoyed dining and playing together. In 1846 their Knickerbocker Baseball Club played its first match against another team of gentlemen, the New York Nine, in a popular summer resort across the Hudson River. The New York *Clipper* considered that contest the beginning of baseball "as now played" in its preview of the Centennial Year season of 1876. Social as well as athletic exclusiveness distinguished these early gatherings. More often than not, formal challenges initiated the contests and social events concluded them. Soon uniforms—white shirts, blue trousers, and straw hats in the case of the Knickerbockers—added another stylish note.

Despite several efforts to create a uniform game, there were no generally accepted rules regulating strikes and balls until the Civil War. The time the play consumed was still of little consequence, and games often dragged on, endlessly it appeared, because the man at bat, the "striker," waited for the pitch that suited him or hoped to tire out the pitcher. Often, local circumstances dictated the number of passes as well as the layout of the field, the distance between bases, the size of the diamond, and the position of the umpire.

The aristocratic setting of the game vanished during the 1850's when new clubs sprang up in New York, Brooklyn, Philadelphia, Baltimore, and Boston. Fascinated with baseball, laborers, mechanics, and clerks put onto diamonds teams that rejected the assumption that the Knickerbockers arbitrated the game simply because they had organized it first. . . . In 1858, the search for more order brought together delegates from twenty-two clubs who established the National Association of Base Ball Players. Although a far cry from a national unit, the Association placed all clubs on an equal basis by forming a rules committee, establishing procedures for new clubs to join the group, and regulating players, umpires, and scorers. Following the time-honored American practice demonstrated by churches, political parties, labor unions, and charity groups, it grew from the local level to a state, regional, and ultimately a national organization. . . .

The Civil War . . . hasten[ed] the emergence of baseball as a game that was played everywhere in the same way. The young men liked to throw, hit, and catch, and when they met on a field as strangers they needed a standard game so that they could enjoy a contest without prolonged arguments. Whether bored by army life, ordered by officers to attend games, or fascinated by baseball, soldier specators contributed to the emergence of a standard game because they needed to know not only what went on but also what to anticipate in order to enjoy themselves. Far from home, they watched strangers, and their interest centered more on the play as a whole than on an individual player in the field. When these captive audiences vanished with the end of the war, the systematic baseball reports in the sports press and the metropolitan newspapers sealed the uniform character of the game and contributed to the emergence of professional baseball as the great urban spectator sport.

The reports, tables, and statistics that the leading American sports journalists compiled in the 1860's and 1870's enabled thousands of spectators who flocked into the ball parks of the big cities after the Civil War to follow both teams and games methodically. An English immigrant, Henry Chadwick, saw himself in his old age as the "head gardener" who had raised the "now giant oak of the American game of baseball." . . . He considered it "important and necessary" to give "the full record of each season," and his readers' responses reinforced his view. The accuracy of his scientifically oriented approach underpinned the emotional support given the game during the 1850's by William Trotter Porter in the New York *Spirit of the Times*. This editor, also credited with publishing the first box scores, had put emphasis on "inside" human interest stories and called baseball "our National Game." . . .

The writings of Henry Chadwick and his colleagues gave baseball an identity and helped popularize game and players. They upheld faith in baseball as a noble and clean game when the fans' enthusiasm lagged in the face of reports about fixed games, gambling scandals, warring leagues, and protracted infighting between owners and players for shares in the new sports bonanza. . . .

In the 1880's, Chicago reporters expressing the raw energies of the wildly growing city added slang and frivolity, metaphor and simile to baseball reports and turned them into news that at times qualified as lead stories. In 1913, the Charleston *News and Courier* called the resulting style "a distinctive and peculiar tongue, . . . not English, . . . not precisely slang, . . . full of idiomatic eccentricities, rich in catch-phrases and technical terms, wonderfully expressive and in the highest degree flexible." This novel approach gave such a remarkable importance to baseball that in the same year the *Nation* slyly wondered why the baseball language "should so far outdo the feats of the players whom it glorifies." It also affected general reporting.

In 1896 a Chicago newspaper editor sent one of his baseball reporters to help cover the Democratic National Convention and to write a follow-up on the reception of William Jennings Bryan's "Cross of Gold" speech. The language of the sportswriter's story on the front page of the Chicago *Daily News* on July 9, 1896, documents one aspect of the impact of baseball on modern city culture. It enlivened what had been the rather staid and dull form of political reporting in an attempt to describe the "almost indescribable":

HOW BRYAN SWAYED THE CROWD
SCENE AFTER HIS REMARKABLE ORATION WAS ALMOST INDESCRIBABLE

When Bryan's words: "You shall not crucify mankind upon the cross of gold" rang out over the throng there was a pause, a break of the smallest fraction of a second. The orator turned and made ready to leave the stand.

Then from the rearmost wall to the speaker's stand, from end to end of the gigantic hall, came like one great burst of artillery the answer of the convention: "You shall not crucify mankind upon the cross of gold." Roar upon roar, crash upon crash of fierce, delirious applause.

The people, men and women, were upon their chairs, their hats were in the air, their handkerchiefs tossing like whitecaps on the winter sea. Flags were flying, waving, streaming; the broad stripes of old glory were intermixed with the banners of states and territories and the pennons of the candidates.

Far down in the rear of the hall a woman was on her chair waving her cloak, blue with red lining, and the alternate flashes of red and blue blazed more conspicuous than any other banner in the hall.

People sprung upon Bryan as he struggled toward his chair. They leaped at him like hungry wolves and hugged him and crushed him in their strong arms. Old men, white with age and with the frenzy of the hour, tottered to him to grasp his hand.

Young men stood on the seats and strove to strike approving hands upon his shoulders as he passed by. His progress to his seat was such as never any Roman coming home to triumph had—the orator was literally whirled off his feet and borne on by the struggling masses of frantic friends.

Then some one in a western delegation uprooted the blue guidon that marked the place of his colleagues. In a second twenty other guidons were twisted from their sockets, and the men who tore them free were crowding toward the spot, where Bryan, bewildered, half frightened, panting, yet proud and satisfied, was fighting off the caresses, the adoration of his myriad friends. Over the head of the Nebraska man the blue guidons were clustered. More and more the group grew in numbers every second.

As each blue guide post was added to the throng the crowd simply joined delirium to its previous frenzy. Round the hall, waving the guidons on high, marched the men of Florida, of Illinois, of Idaho.

Twenty other states followed and there would have been but one man before the public eye could a vote have been taken then. Presently, exhausted, the banner-bearers sought their places—Bryan sunk utterly wearied into his seat—the mightiest demonstration of many a convention year was over.

. . . Joseph Pulitzer's *World* had produced the first sports page in the 1880's, and William Randolph Hearst's interest "in stories of the great American game" led to the development of the modern sports section in his New York *Journal* in the 1890's. . . .

Commercialization and professionalization went hand in hand. Young men quickly spotted baseball as a new road to fortune and fame. The growing demand for good baseball put a premium on good players and induced more and more clubs to offer gifts or money to attract them. The practice violated the Association rule against paying players, so that at times clubs used unrelated salaried jobs to attract athletes who were in effect being paid for playing baseball, thus evading the regulation. Rumors about a player getting money under the table circulated as early as 1860. . . .

In 1868, the National Association of Base Ball Players terminated its futile struggle against the monetary practices that produced professional players. The group accepted a recommendation of its rules committee to recognize two distinct classes of players, amateurs and professionals, in an attempt to straighten out the confusing variety of players.

Similar considerations motivated Henry Chadwick to champion an all-professional team. The New York *Clipper* writer realized that the game could survive as a big spectator sport only if played by professionals. In his preview of the 1868 season he stressed the professional status that distinguished the Cincinnati Red Stockings from the other good teams he discussed: the New

York Mutuals, the Brooklyn Athletics, the Troy Haymakers, the Chicago White Stockings, the Philadelphia Athletics, and the Baltimore Marylands. He strongly supported the Cincinnati arrangement, which had each player under contract for the entire season at a negotiated rate of pay ranging from $800 to $1,400.

The new industry experienced dismal years, but open and definite professionalism also made the conduct of the game into something approaching a system. The momentum of money squelched the hopes of small-scale speculators who had dreamed of exploiting the new bonanza by luring players and spectators to their own teams. The big clubs built or took over ball parks and clubhouses and organized a game schedule that glorified inter-urban competition on a national basis. . . .

Although breach of contract and bribery, drinking and gambling tarnished the image of baseball, in Boston Harry Wright and other members of the disbanded Cincinnati super-team maintained discipline and won the Association championship for four consecutive years. In 1875, when the original clubs had shrunk to seven, the first major professional baseball league folded, but the presence of the professional players it had developed and the economic potential of professional baseball brought the National League into existence in the following year.

The modern business structure of big-time American baseball grew around the organizational framework conceived in the 1870's. Attempts to break the monopoly of the National League gave rise to the American Association in 1882. Within two years the rivals were able to agree to end competition over cities and for players. The Association failed in 1890; however, ten years later, another major league formed—the American League. From 1900 on, big-time baseball operated within the context of two league championships, figuratively called the Pennants, and soon added a play-off series between the champions called the World Series.

From its start in 1876, the National League of Professional Baseball Clubs, to give it its full title, meant business. Its owners established themselves as masters of the game. William A. Hulbert, the first League president, engineered the developments. In contrast to some of the gentlemen players, political bosses, or gambling operators who had previously dabbled in managing baseball, he was a member of the Chicago Board of Trade who used his managerial experience to lay the foundation for another flourishing business. Hulbert was "a typical Chicago man" in the eyes of Albert G. Spalding, who pitched for him before becoming a successful manufacturer of sporting goods. As booster of his city, Hulbert "never spoke of what *he* would do, or what *his* club would do, but it was always what *Chicago* would do." He set up an oligarchy of club owners who ran the game efficiently. With draconic measures he restored the surface honesty of the sport and the public confidence in its operation that seemed so essential for good business.

The governmental and economic structure of baseball became autocratic, but the atmosphere of the ball park preserved the appearance of freedom. The public, fed up with corrupt practices, largely ignored the undemocratic features of the new regime, which, in turn, struggled to square the owners' business monopoly with democracy and even make baseball its symbol. . . .

Any notion that gentlemen may once have had about the proper conduct of a ball player or the correct form of making a play vanished with the emergence of professionalism. The idea governing the related game of cricket—that some behavior on the field was "not cricket"—never took hold in professional baseball. Its players, Bruce Catton concluded in his reflections on the game, "have borrowed nothing from the 'sportsmanship' of more sedate countries; they believe that when you get into a fight you had better win, and the method by which you win does not matter very much." As soon as the skills of the professionals turned the drama of sport into an exhibition, Lewis Mumford stressed in his assessment of mass sport, the rule became "Success at Any Price" instead of "Fair Play." The disappearance of a tacit understanding about the conduct of the game, as well as the necessity of basing a judgment call on an observation made in a fraction of a second, increased the interaction between player and umpire on the field.

The intense rivalry encouraged the player constantly to seek advantages by bending a rule or trying to get away with an infraction. "Boys, you've heard the new rules read," the captain of the New York Giants would say in beginning his annual talk at the opening of the season during the 1880's; "now the question is: what can we do to beat them?" A generation seasoned by the Civil War began to assume that any behavior, however outrageous, was acceptable in baseball, too, and this feeling may have generated the metaphor that spoke of baseball as war. "Infractions are expected by the crowd, and hence by players, umpires and managers," explained Walter Camp, who almost singlehandedly shaped the rules of American football, in 1910. "In the long run, the people make the law," he added, unwittingly identifying the spectators' influence over the enforcement of the rules with the workings of rules committees eager to attract the largest crowds.

For the people in the ball park, the umpire represented the voice of authority. To the spectators he was a convenient target for their frequent irritations and deep-seated frustrations both within and outside the ball park. The umpire became a personification of the rulers of their lives, who in the workaday world remained hidden behind the whirl of urban life, the faceless corporate structures, the anonymity of technocracy, and the mystery of public affairs. During the strife-ridden 1880's and 1890's, in their urge to identify and challenge a villain in the drama they lived, the crowds ignored any distinction between the rules committee of the league that had made the regulations and the umpire on the field calling a play.

Thus the grandstand crowds had a field day in exploiting to their hearts' content the pressure put on the umpire. Over decades of changing styles of play he was called on to decide the legality of the tricky delivery (a new overhand pitching style), unusual batting tactics, fielding aberrations, and base-running maneuvers. What mattered was that all decisions allowed the spectators to challenge vehemently and vociferously the ruler, clearly identified from the 1880's on by his dark blue coat and cap.

On the surface the umpire appeared to exercise an authority like that of some other powers that regulated life. Like constables and clerks, he also lost his standing as a gentleman. Though he had once been specifically honored because refereeing evidenced his intimate knowledge of the game, the rise of baseball as a specator sport had made him just another member of the cast of characters in the show—at times a villainous buffoon. Before the introduction of the double umpire system at the beginning of the twentieth century, the single man working behind either the pitcher or the catcher frequently cut a pathetic figure.

Definitely not omnipotent and hardly ominipresent, the umpire was abused or even mobbed on the field by spectators and players, and ridiculed or slandered in the sports papers as "the mortal enemy" of everyone, if "he does not especially favor the local club." Among the many fatuous comments on umpire-baiting, few rivaled the explanation that rowdy fans were merely exercising their democratic right to protest tyranny. Any protection the league might have extended to the umpire, and he received none, would have interfered with his actual role. Shaping the game to maximize attendance was of utmost significance to the club owners, so that they tolerated the rowdy behavior of players, managers, and spectators as long as it enhanced the excitement of the game.

This desire for an exciting spectacle eventually led to new rules speeding up the moments of spectacular action in the game and also to the introduction of protective equipment, because gloves and face masks allowed men to make without injury the rough, fast, and exciting plays of the game, in bursts of speed, that most people waited for. Speed occupied the spectators, who were constantly under pressure to match the hectic tempo of the modern city. The action in the ball park demonstrated to them that it was possible, after all, to keep up with the fleeting moment. . . .

Although the players' concern for protection introduced gloves and catcher's masks into baseball, these innovations escaped being ridiculed as unmanly because the age worshipped the result they produced—memorable moments packed with action. Baseball had been played with bare hands until the glove began appearing in the early 1880's, supposedly after a shortstop had used a crude version to protect his hand. Other players followed his example when they noticed that he did not have to ease off catching the ball, could meet it solidly, and got his throw away faster than the other infielders. The spectators, who liked what they saw, supported the change, and sporting goods firms soon began furnishing gloves to professionals. A few years earlier, the first body shields had permitted the umpire to stand behind the catcher and enforce the strike and ball rules in a way that heightened the game's drama. The introduction of the mask and the fingerless glove with light padding on the palm in 1877 allowed the catcher to become the director of team action on the field, an effective way to coordinate the play.

In addition to the protective devices, the change from the large six-ounce elastic ball to the hard regulation ball hastened the transformation of a pastime into a spectacle. An ironic twist of circumstances accompanied these developments. While the new equipment opened up baseball to everyone it also made the professional game the exclusive domain of specialists. Hundreds of agile, hard-throwing men who had not qualified for old-time baseball because they were not born with hands and arms for barehanded fielding replaced the so-called natural players. They did not have to worry about protecting their hands while catching the ball, and their swift plays quickened the pace of the game. New waves of players, each raising the standards of performance, quickly drove each other out of big-league baseball. They constantly advanced the quality of the game, heightened the level of competition, and increased the expectations of spectators until only a handful of big-league-caliber experts could participate.

Less became more early in professional baseball, but the enthusiastic spectators caught on quickly and watched more carefully. Gloves and masks contributed to the decline of the high scores that characterized mid-nineteenth century baseball by allowing steady improvement in pitching and fielding. This intensified a trend marked by revoking the old straight-arm delivery restriction which had forced pitchers to obtain speed only by an underhand throw or a wristy jerk of the ball. In 1900, Adrian C. ("Cap") Anson, after his retirement as manager and captain of the Chicago club, called the high scores of old-time baseball "performances impossible in these days of great speed and curve pitching." In 1859, in the first inter-collegiate baseball game on record, Amherst beat Williams 73 to 32. When the celebrated Cincinnati Red Stockings ruled in 1869, they trounced an opponent 103 to 8, and that was only about half the largest number of runs ever scored in an old-style game. However, at the turn of the twentieth century big-league teams rarely scored more than 10 runs per game.

By that time only sandlot baseball, with the help of the mitt and, from 1896 on, such literary embellishment of baseball virtues as the feats recorded in *Frank Merriwell* by Gilbert Patten, had acquired some of the free and open features that many people identified with the sport. Boys and men tried to emulate the professionals on empty streets and vacant lots, in parks and on playgrounds. In big cities amateur clubs sometimes attracted more fans than the professionals. Eighty thousand people saw the game between the Telling Strollers and the Hanna Street Cleaners for the Cleveland championship of 1914. One year later, in the same natural amphitheater, more than 100,000 cheered the victory of the Cleveland Indians over the Omaha Luxus for the world amateur championship. In 1917 Frederic L. Paxson saw the rise of sports in the United States as another "safety valve" replacing Frederick Jackson Turner's frontier. Baseball "succeeded as an organized spectator sport," he observed, but it contributed something neither racing nor boxing could "in turning the city lot into a playground and the small boy into an enthusiastic player." . . .

While street baseball reaffirmed the social importance of play in the city, professional baseball followed "the individualistic tendencies of America" that left leisure to commerce, giving everyone who could buy a ticket the choice of watching the kind of sport he or she liked best, without making an effort to persuade a group of people to agree on playing one specific game, as an urban reformer of the age commented. It ignored any urge to participate in the play and, like urban politics, followed representational lines. Professional experts took places on the field which from time to time many men in the grandstands dreamed of occupying themselves. . . .

The hazards of the game opened up baseball to gifted players from major immigrant groups. In addition to the many athletes of English and Irish ancestry who had always been present in major-league baseball, American Indians, Frenchmen, Germans, Jews, Poles, Italians, and Latin Americans entered the game. At the turn of the century some of these players had risen beyond any narrow immigrant identity to become some of the great heroes of the sport. Big Ed Delahanty, Louis Francis "Chief" Sockalexis, Napoleon "Larry" Lajoie, and John Peter "Honus" Wagner represented these giants of the game. However, black players remained barred from major-league teams, perpetuating the discrimination officially introduced in 1867 when the rules of the National Association of Base Ball Players barred black players and black clubs from membership. In this respect, too, baseball mirrored life in the modern city. . . .

City people, at the turn of the century, considered the ball park not as a testing ground for the egalitarian promises of their society but as a source of diversion. As with their limited role in urban politics, they were satisfied with being represented on the field by their sports idols.

In the ball park they watched a spectacle that responded to their concerns. The game enriched their dreary urban existence by providing a few leisure hours in the outdoors. In the warmth of the afternoon sun, the spectators transcended temporarily the physical limitations urban life imposed upon them and experienced relief from the tension of their complex surroundings. They saw plays that reduced their bewildering struggle for success to a game of one-thing-at-a-time and to the measurable progress of a successful athlete mastering one obstacle after another. They detected few gray areas in the ball park. The game presented immediate and clear-cut wins and losses and pitted good guys against bad guys.

During a few hours in the ball park, city people saw plays that they could remember afterwards because of the way specific events built up to a memorable moment—the sudden skillful triumph over an adversary. By making intense competition against an opponent its essential feature, baseball seemed to legitimize and extoll each spectator's daily struggle for success. Watching the rivalry on the diamond introduced standards of competition into the spectators' lives. The game also reduced their daily tensions because its ups and downs seemed more momentous than their own lives.

The spectators learned to appreciate baseball's demonstrations of efficiency and excellence—qualities many of them took as keys to success in industrial America. They followed the dynamic between individual competition and cooperative triumph. Their involvement in the lessons of the diamond thrived on an appreciation of a faster throw, a better catch, or a longer hit. . . .

Mark Twain, in a "Welcome Home" speech to a team returning from a world tour in 1889, hailed baseball as "the very symbol, the outward and visible expression, of the drive and push and rush and struggle of the raging, tearing, booming nineteenth century.'' He went on to use baseball as a sign to delineate the "modern world," describing the game as a new, visible equator separating the part that mattered from the remainder of the globe where men did not steal "bases on their bellies." The title "world champion," given to the most successful big-league team, confirmed this new geography. It came to designate the winner of the first seven World Series, played between the champions of the National League and the Association in the 1880's. Later, the title was awarded the victor in the annual World Series between the champions of the National League and the American League—established in the first decade of the twentieth century. . . .

With the great expanse of greenery that it required, baseball also appeared to bring the countryside into the metropolis. It radiated the wholesome air of a timeless country sport which, each spring, cleansed anew the foul atmosphere of the modern city. From the 1880's on, a new feature of the baseball year strengthened the effect of conjuring up a bit of countryside. Big-league teams began to go into rural isolation, preferably a fashionable resort in the South, to get over the effects of a winter of loafing with "the hardest five weeks' grind in the world," thus seeming to extend baseball's links with country life and sunshine. Big-time baseball now returned every year to the country, whence many enthusiasts assumed it had come, to recharge its energy.

Baseball's manipulation of reality extended to man-made time, too. Although its spectacular plays were the epitome of swift motion and speedy action, baseball rose above any ordinary concern for an economy of time. If the score was tied after nine innings, the game continued as long as it took to achieve victory. While mechanical time prevailed almost everywhere in the modern city, with the factory whistle and the time clock regulating laborers in factories and clerks in stores, natural time regulated baseball. Only nature itself, requiring postponement on account of rain or termination of play after sundown, could interfere with the course of play.

The game's close ties with nature were used to underscore its virtue. In order to make sure that the tangible blessings of baseball were recognized, apologists extolled those of its features that filled the needs of city people. Untouched by logic or evidence, they stressed that getting out into the fresh air of the ball park promised to open men's eyes to their "business interests" and to protect boys from "immoral association." Despite news stories about dishonest games, umpire baiting, rowdy behavior on and off the field, and shady business deals, the importance of baseball as an inspiration for moral and upright behavior was rarely contested. Nothing was allowed to shatter the mystique of the popular game: upright young men fighting to excel on a green field under a clear sky in the big city. Clergymen of all denominations seemed to agree on the value of the game, and testified to their faith in baseball or used baseball as a testimony of their faith. . . .

Baseball offered a lesson in modern living in an imitation of a pastoral setting. Its features of intense rivalry as well as a limited amount of sportsmanship, general enthusiasm as well as rabid partisanship oriented crowds of people toward an acceptance of competition as a part of daily life, an awareness of a distinct urban vitality, and an appreciation for recreation. Spectators packing grandstands and bleachers intensified the pressure on factories and stores for a half-holiday once a week, lightening the routine of living and working. Seeing others play ball for a living encouraged them to play sandlot baseball or to take up other sports. In the 1890's, the *Nation* called the growing interest in sports "the athletic craze" and likened its intensity to preceding crazes involving greenbacks, silver, and grangers. . . .

The feeling of community that the ball park could evoke among crowds of city people struck a young Harvard graduate writing a newspaper column for a college pal in the late 1880's as incongruous with the diversity of the modern city. Ernest Lawrence Thayer set his baseball ballad, "Casey at the Bat," in Mudville, a rural heaven of shared sentiments. His lines about the luckless batter appeared in the Sunday edition of the San Francisco *Examiner,* next to the column of the avowed cynic Ambrose Bierce. Together with "Casey's Revenge," which followed several weeks later, it might have been lost with the weekend, had it not found a stage larger than the ball park.

A few weeks later, a young vaudeville performer recited the poem, fortuitously clipped by a friend, as entr'acte in a comic opera at the baseball night of a New York theater, when he had to acknowledge the presence among the spectators of members of the New York Giants and the Chicago White Stockings. The audience "shouted its glee," De Wolf Hopper recalled, because it "had expected, as any one does on hearing 'Casey' for the first time, that the mighty batsman would slam the ball out of the lot." With "Casey," baseball reached the stage of the popular theater that provided a setting where people could not only laugh about their own frustrated hopes and the shattered illusions of others but also learn to bridge some of the conflicts inherent in the modern city.

Coney Island Culture

KATHY PEISS

If dancing was working women's winter passion, then excursions were the height of the summer season. A network of picnic grounds, beach resorts, and amusement parks ringed Manhattan, attracting thousands of young women like Agnes M., a twenty-year-old German immigrant who had worked as a milliner, dressmaker, and domestic servant. "I have a great many friends in New York and I enjoy my outings with them," she observed in 1903. "We go to South Beach or North Beach or Glen Island or Rockaway or Coney Island. If we go on a boat we dance all the way there and all the way back, and we dance nearly all the time we are there." Her favorite resort, though, was Coney Island, "a wonderful and beautiful place." The special appeal of

From *Cheap Amusements: Working Women and Leisure in Turn-of-the Century New York* by Kathy Peiss, pp. 115–38. Copyright © 1986, reprinted by permission of Temple University Press.

Coney's amusement resorts to working women is suggested in Agnes' description of an outing with a German friend, newly arrived in New York. "When we had been on the razzle-dazzle, the chute and the loop-the-loop, and down in the coal mine and all over the Bowery, and up in the tower and everywhere else, I asked her how she liked it. She said: 'Ach, it is just like what I see when I dream of heaven.' " Coney took young women out of the daily round of tenement life and work, but at the same time, it allowed them to extend their culture to the resort, whose beaches, boardwalk, and dancing pavilions were arenas for diversion, flirtations, and displays of style.

Agnes did note that her passion for Coney Island was not shared by those of higher social standing, who questioned the resort's respectability and gentility. "I have heard some of the high people with whom I have been living say that Coney Island is not tony." Symbolically understanding this cultural issue in terms of dance, she implied that her betters repressed desire and were unable to express or enjoy themselves. "The trouble is that these high people don't know how to dance," she exclaimed. "I have to laugh when I see them at their balls and parties. If only I could get out on the floor and show them how—they would be astonished."

In the early twentieth century, many middle-class people, if not Agnes' employers, began to go to Coney Island and enjoy it. In his study of Coney Island, John Kasson brilliantly traces its evolution from a Victorian resort to the home of the modern amusement park. This transformation, Kasson argues, both exemplified and fostered the decline of genteel cultural hegemony and the rise of a new, expressive urban culture. Coney's thrilling mechanical devices and spectacular exhibits constituted a liberating experience for the middle class, a contrast to the normative demands of conventional bourgeois society. In this way, amusement parks "emerged as laboratories of the new mass culture," where middle-class attitudes toward leisure, sexuality, and the social relations of women and men were forged.

As Agnes' narrative suggests, however, Coney Island's amusement parks also resonated with pleasure for working-class people, particularly its youth subculture. Working-class participation at Coney followed a different trajectory from that of the middle-class patrons who rejected Victorian gentility and adopted a new expressive culture. Rather, Coney Island was initially incorporated into tradition of working-class excursions and outings, which like other forms of leisure were closely integrated into the life of the community. However, the way laboring people experienced the beach resort changed with the intensified commercialization of leisure. Less obvious, perhaps, is the impact of working-class culture on the design of the new "mass culture" realized in the amusement parks. Not only did Coney symbolize the conflict between Victorian and "modern" culture, it embodied a subtle debate over what forms that new culture should take. Amusement entrepreneurs and showmen developed different strategies for attracting the crowds, drawing upon alternative traditions of popular amusements that were linked to class-based cultures. In this debate, the desires of such working women as Agnes M., who loved to dance, see the men, and have a good time, shaped the emergent mass culture.

The Working-Class Excursion

Saloons, clubs, dance halls, and the streets figured prominently in the everyday recreation of working-class New Yorkers; the excursion was a special occasion. The outing to a picnic park or beach resort was a brief outdoor respite from tenement apartments, crowded neighborhoods, and busy workshops. On their days of rest—Sundays and summer holidays and, for increasing numbers, the Saturday half-holiday—working people relished a day of fresh air, eating, games, and socializing. Unlike a visit to a local park or square, the excursion usually involved some expense, at least the cost of carfare. Robert Coit Chapin found that three-quarters of the working-class families he questioned went on excursions. While many reported excursions simply to parks or friends' homes, typically families took a major outing—to Coney Island or Fort George—once or twice during the summer months. Such trips were even more common among the more prosperous households, as well as the American, German, and Italian populations of Manhattan. Nevertheless, poorer households could manage to afford excursions by some cost-saving strategies. As one West Side boy observed, "When our whole family goes to Jersey, . . . all of us kids sneak in that way. My father buys tickets and then we walk through the gates and he refuses to pay for us because he don't know us."

Family outings often took the form of day excursions, particularly to the public parks. The huge expanse of Central Park was a preeminent location for picnics and outdoor fun, accessible to working-class visitors by foot or streetcar. "The working classes fill the street-cars, and throng the Central Park," observed one writer in the 1870's. "In the summer whole families of laboring people go to the park early in the morning, taking a lunch with them, and there spend the entire day." Several decades later, Rachel Levin, a Russian immigrant, recalled the special quality of such outings: "Sunday usually you know we'd get the family together and go to Central Park—that was a holiday."

Besides the family get-together, there were massive outdoor gatherings sponsored by fraternal and social organizations for their members' families and friends. Like the lodge affair and benefit society ball, these excursions and picnics were incorporated into the working-class social system that provided insurance and mutual aid, integrating recreation with social services and community welfare. In the summertime, banners and posters advertising picnics were hung in the tenement districts, parades would form, and thousands boarded boats to enjoy inexpensive recreation, sociability, and a brief escape from the hot city. These excursions cost their participants relatively little. "The voluntary societies," Robert Coit Chapin observed, "often furnish means of recreation, such as social gatherings, picnics and excursions, and expenditure for recreation is sometimes not differentiated from dues and payments to the society."

Political organizations, unions, and social clubs also organized outings. To encourage tenement dwellers to support their ticket, Tammany Hall ran free excursions every two weeks in the summer. "So many people, especially children and their mothers, desired to go on an excursion,'' recalled Samuel Chotzinoff, ''that by five in the morning a queue many blocks long had already formed at the wharf.'' Unions sponsored annual picnics for their members, and these events often attracted masses of people. ''The picnic on Sunday was the most successful affair our local ever held,'' Timothy Healy, the president of the Brotherhood of Stationary Firemen, reported. ''We sold nearly six thousand tickets at the gate, and had in the neighborhood of ten thousand out before the affair came off.'' . . .

The Commercialization of Excursions

By the 1890's, the development of commercial excursions and the extension of transportation lines had begun to alter the working-class outing. New transportation networks made day trips cheaper and easier for families and individuals. Steamship companies continued to rent their facilities to organizations, but they also started to run regular excursion boats for anyone paying the price of admission. These charged fifteen to twenty-five cents for a round trip to Coney Island in 1901, and other commercial boats took passengers up the Hudson or to New Haven for outings. Streetcar lines were extended to the outer regions of the city, and by 1895, one could reach Coney Island for only five or ten cents by trolley.

Young women's opportunities for the pursuit of pleasure were heightened as excursions became commercialized. Irma Stein, who took outings with her family, recalled that ''at that time everything was so cheap. . . . We took subway rides, double-decker trolley, boat riding.'' Some trolley lines connected directly with picnic groves and amusement parks like Fort George, where a woman could enjoy an unsupervised afternoon or evening. Women could afford to use trolleys much as they had the streets, as spaces to court and socialize with men. Like Zetta, a woman with little spending money was ''obliged to turn to trolley rides and walks and various kinds of excursions,— literally to the streets,—for hospitality, when she received a man's visit.''

With the development of inexpensive and regular commercial excursions, young women travelled on their own to beach resorts. At North Beach, one of the more notorious amusement resorts, [Belle] Israels interviewed a young girl who observed, ''My mother doesn't know I go out here; but I want some fun, and it only costs ten cents.'' The excursion boats themselves also provided an opportunity for flirtations and amusement, without the chaperonage of parents. Israels' committee condemned the moral atmosphere of the all-day excursion boats as far worse than that of the late weekend boats from Coney Island or Rockaway Beach, charging that some boats rented staterooms to couples for short periods and ''their purpose is not one of rest or comfort.'' Like other forms of working women's amusements that took place outside of a familial or community context, the excursion boats combined sexual perils with the pleasures women craved.

Commercialization not only altered the mode of transportation; it also affected the social spaces in which young women and men enjoyed their outings. The number of old-fashioned picnic grounds began to decline in the early twentieth century; in 1910, there were only ten remaining in Manhattan and the Bronx, as residential and commercial development transformed the metropolis. Trying to meet a growing demand for new sensations and entertainment, many picnic parks began to offer a wide range of popular amusements, including concert halls, penny arcades, and mechanical rides. By the 1890's, the organized working-class excursion to a picnic grove increasingly gave way to a new cultural and commercial phenomenon, a trip to a modern amusement park.

The Working-Class Presence at Coney Island

The changes wrought by the commercialized outing are most evident at Coney Island, whose checkered history involved an important working-class presence even before the advent of its famous amusement parks. In the mid-nineteenth century, Coney Island was a desolate beach, attracting only a few wealthy patrons who sought quietude and the sea air. By 1870, small inns and bathhouses dotted the shore, but tales of swindlers and roughnecks roaming the island deterred many travellers. Not until the late 1870's did Coney emerge as New York's leading amusement resort. Railroads linked the beaches with Manhattan, while regular steamship service began by 1880. On the east end of the island, exclusive hotels and restaurants sprang up along Manhattan Beach, where society's upper crust, "chiefly New York and Boston nabobs," frequented the elegant Oriental Hotel. Just to the west, Brighton Beach beckoned middle-class vacationers to its family hotels, shore dinners, and open-air bands.

Discernible patterns of participation by class and sex marked Coney Island's early days. Middle- and upper-class women and children summered at the exclusive hotels and beaches, while businessmen remained in the city, paying occasional weekend visits to their families. While the east end of Coney Island catered solely to the respectable, its far west end was notorious as a hangout for underworld figures and gangs. Norton's Point became a center for horse racing, prize-fighting, and prostitution, offering leisure activities oriented to a "sporting" male subculture that crossed class lines. In the late nineteenth century, Coney Island's geography not only offered a "linear, visual study in American class structure," as Robert Snow and David Wright have written; it also reflected the Victorian organization of social life by gender.

Between these two poles, West Brighton, at the midpoint of the island, emerged as the playground of the masses. More than 80 percent of Coney's sixty thousand visitors clustered there on hot Sunday afternoons. Ignored by big real estate developers in the 1870's and 1880's, West Brighton was an amalgam of different amusements, including restaurants, saloons, bathhouses, and circus sideshows, dominated by Lucy the Elephant, at once a hotel and a major landmark of the area. Some of these resorts, like Feltman's Pavilion, catered primarily to middle-class lodges and voluntary organizations. Other attractions, however, appealed to the sensibilities and pocketbooks of the laboring classes. "Seeing the elephant" involved incorporating Coney's resorts into working-class culture.

Even in the days before the modern amusement parks dominated Coney Island, working women and men sought out its rollicking resorts and cool beaches. Their presence is impossible to document statistically, but a number of witnesses confirm the popularity of working-class outings to Coney Island. As early as the 1870's and 1880's, three hundred different societies were said to "indulge in at least one pic-nic during the summer" there. The cool sea air attracted crowds of women and children, who would wait until the last train or steamship to take them back to Manhattan. On one particularly steamy day, one thousand "apparently respectable" workingmen were permitted to sleep overnight on the beach. "The crowd was so great," observed the New York *Tribune*, "that extra cars were put on to accommodate those who wanted to start for the city to their work." By 1900, Coney Island was thronged with as many as 300,000 to 500,000 on Saturday afternoons, Sundays, and holidays.

Not only did working-class people flock to West Brighton, but by the 1890's, many of the resorts had taken their character from working-class cultural activities and commercial amusements popular in the tenement districts. Variety shows, inexpensive beer saloons, and penny arcades beckoned to the working-class crowds, while boardwalk pushcarts hawked such popular Coney Island cuisine as clams, hot corn, and chowder to the passing throngs. Like men of other classes, workingmen went to the prize fights, concert saloons, and other arenas of male culture, causing one union leader to complain, "If the working man would only show half the interest in the bread and butter question that he showed in the recent slugging battle at Coney Island, he would be doing something to benefit himself and those dependent upon him." People from the tenement districts, a journalist observed, particularly liked the free dancing pavilions and bathing beaches, where they revelled in such indecorous behavior as screaming and chasing through crowds. The free-and-easy culture of working-class Manhattan's streets, clubs, saloons, and public halls found expression at this summer resort.

The nature of West Brighton before the rise of the great amusement parks is best characterized by the Bowery, a lane of amusement concessions laid out by the area's leading entrepreneur, George Tilyou. Like its Manhattan namesake, it teemed with arcades, penny slot machines, shooting galleries, kinetoscope shows, freak shows, and dime museums, as well as numerous dance halls and variety houses. And while its visitors were of many classes, its hurly-burly ambience was much like the Bowery in the city, a street mingling working-class saloons, commercial amusements, and a rowdy and gregarious atmosphere. "Life is strenuous on the Bowery," one guidebook warned. "It is no place for the weak-hearted or the languid." The cultural style of West Brighton mimicked that of its working-class visitors rather than the more high-flown tastes of the middle-class end of the island. A journalist observed that West Brighton's patrons "have set aside money sufficient for a day within sound of Seidl's orchestra, yet they prefer the oom-pah bands of rusted brass. They would rather have a luncheon of Frankfurters and lager and a dinner of roasted clams and melted butter.'' This area was the center of attraction to Coney's visitors before the creation of the large amusement parks and, even after, drew crowds loving uninhibited excitement.

At the same time that a working-class presence developed at West Brighton, its patronage subtly changed in terms of gender. Many resorts at Coney Island had been havens for a male subculture of gambling houses, saloons, brothels, and taxi-dance houses. By the 1890's, the concert halls, dance pavilions, and variety shows sought members of both sexes. Open-air stages and beach pavilions were particularly popular, offering melodrama, sentimental plays, and slapstick comedy. Originally entertainment for men only, concert halls like Koster's emphasized risque titillation, having its soubrettes wear short skirts and sing suggestive lyrics. By the 1890's, such shows were drawing a mixed-sex audience. Men continued to attend, but were joined by ''mothers with babies and whole hordes of youngsters [who] would suddenly pounce upon and occupy a table in these halls.'' The entertainment had become tamer, but still challenged proper middle-class sensibilities. ''The singers in the concert halls and the variety shows have lengthened their dresses and abbreviated their misbehavior,'' noted one journalist, ''but it is still the seat of a delirium of raw pleasure.''

Working Women's Culture at Coney Island

For young working women, an excursion to Coney Island was the apotheosis of summer entertainment. The diversions ranged from sideshow attractions and vaudeville shows to restaurants and the boardwalk. Not unexpectedly, the most popular gathering places were dancing pavilions, open-air structures built on piers or on the beach, which rollicked with music and spieling from 7:00 P.M. until the last boat back to the city each night. The pavilions attracted ''pivoters,'' those ''thousands of girls who are seized with such madness for dancing that they spend every night in the dance halls and the picnic parks.'' Working women could find eight large dance halls at Coney Island, ranging from regulated places to more disreputable saloons with a dance floor, each having a discernible cultural style. Beatrice Stevenson, examining the working girls' amusements at Coney Island, catalogued these halls:

> At the largest and most exclusive, Saturday night sees an enormous crowd of elaborately dressed girls and men of good appearance and grooming. At other places girls are more plainly dressed, wear shirt waists and street hats, and at still others the girls are of coarse appearance and are flashily dressed. The forms of dancing and behavior vary at the three grades of halls; in the most fashionable there is a good deal of promiscuous intercourse, flirting and picking up of acquaintances, but the dancing itself is usually proper and conventional; in the most Bohemian, behavior is free and pronouncedly bad forms of dancing are seen.

Even after the new amusement parks were built, numerous dance houses and concert halls could be found in the seedy places of the Bowery that continued to attract young working women on Saturday and Sunday nights. "They know the bad reputation of some of them," Belle Israels observed in 1909, "but the dancing floor is good, there are always plenty of men and there are laughter and liberty galore."

Many of the social forms so familiar to young women in the city's dance halls and streets simply carried over to Coney Island. By relying on the system of treating, women could enjoy a day at Coney's resorts with their only expense being transporation: "It only costs fare down and back, and for the rest of it the boys you 'pick up,' 'treat.'" Some working women's manipulation of this relationship was suggested by a journalist, who overheard two young women at an unguarded moment discussing their male escorts:

"What sort of time did you have?"
"Great. He blew in $5.00 on the blow-out."
"You beat me again. My chump only spent $2.55."

Such customary practices as picking up a date and breaking dancers could be seen in the dancing pavilions of West Brighton. "Any well-seeming youngster may invite any girl to dance" at Coney Island, observed one journalist, "an arrangement long since sanctioned by the maelstrom of proletarian jollity, the 'social,' where tickets . . . connote partners and more partners, till everybody knows everybody else." Lillian Betts concurred, noting that at dancing pavilions "the buying of a drink gives the right of the floor to any man."

West Brighton's Bowery, the dancing pavilions, and the boardwalk were social spaces women used for flirtations and adventure, but like their urban counterparts, they held sexual risks. The typical shopgirl at Coney, one journalist asserted, was "keen and knowing, ever on the defensive, she discourages such advances as perplex her. . . . Especially she distrusts cavaliers not of her own station." At other amusement parks, too, unescorted women could expect verbal harassment and advances. At Fort George, claimed Israels, "no girl or group of girls can walk along the street there or through the park without being repeatedly accosted by men." Young women sought Coney's diversions with a friend of the same sex, the protective arrangement that better allowed them to strike up innocuous acquaintances with young men.

The Modern Amusement Park

By 1900, commercialization had altered the customary patterns of working-class leisure at the beach resort with the development of the amusement park. In 1896, Captain Paul Boyton's Seal Lion Park became the first amusement park at Coney Island, drawing in the crowds with marine animals and shoot-the-chutes. For the first time, a developer had enclosed a large area of land at West Brighton and established a variety of mechanical and other amusements based on a specific theme. Witnessing the commercial potential of this venture, George Tilyou purchased Coney Island property and created Steeple-chase Park in 1897, cramming it with mechanical rides and fun-house laughs. Steeplechase was followed by two spectacular parks, Luna Park and Dreamland.

The amusement parks brought a new measure of permanence to Coney's amusements. Owners invested heavily in land, buildings, and machinery. They consolidated control over entertainment in the parks by leasing the amusement concessions within their boundaries, which allowed them to determine the content and style of the exhibitions. Charging only ten to fifteen cents for admission, they sought the common denominator of the crowds, knowing that large profits would come from people who would return again and again to the parks. These entrepreneurs consciously created entertainment to fit their conception of a mass audience and what it wanted to experience.

In the eyes of the middle-class commentators who travelled yearly to West Brighton, the creation of the amusement park produced unexpected—and welcome—results. Not only did the parks offer mechanical thrills, hilarity, and new sensations, but they apparently engineered the social and moral transformation of Coney Island. Journalists tested the moral tenor of the amusement park and judged it wholesome. To court a new public, showmen now eschewed the old con games, the fake sideshows, and the criminal element. "Its laundered diversions attract a laundered constituency," one writer observed. "A permanent amusement park can't afford out-and-out swindles." The new moral atmosphere even extended to West Brighton's rollicking saloons and concessions, where another journalist found that "a careful scrutiny of the Bowery and adjacent lanes fails to discover evidences of the vicious resorts found there in recent years."

The result of the improvements, observed these commentators, was a new clientele for Coney Island, a shift in its composition by class and gender. "Time was when the place was shunned by ultra-respectable New Yorkers, who went instead to Manhattan Beach," one wrote, "but nowadays Coney is visited by all classes." Journalists were impressed with the refinement and courtesy of this new crowd, "as handsome and charming to gaze upon as any to be found at Newport or Long Branch or along the board walk of Atlantic City" and a far cry from the rowdy pleasure-seekers of previous decades. The new amusement parks were seen as family entertainment, and the male culture that permeated the resorts and sideshows abated. One writer observed, "The man who formerly came with a gang of fellows from his office or shop to enjoy a relapse into rowdyism now brought his womenfolk and was decent."

There is no doubt that the owners of Steeplechase, Luna, and Dreamland energetically sought to attract a respectable audience, wooing the middle-class patrons who had formerly attended Manhattan and Brighton Beaches. In a departure from the old Coney Island, several parks sold only soft drinks within their boundaries and entertainment was toned down for a family audience. Determined to offend no one, George Tilyou posted the following warning to vaudeville performers appearing at Steeplechase Park:

Performers playing in this house are requested not to use any *Vulgarity* or *Slang* in their act and to kindly omit the words *Damn* or *Liar* or any saying not fit for *Ladies* and children to hear. . . . Our audiences are mostly ladies and children, and what we want is only *Polite Vaudeville*.

Within the category of "respectability," however, the showmen and park owners sought the widest possible range, including working-class women and men in their idea of a mass audience. One guidebook stressed that "it is now possible for every sort and condition of people to find opportunities for rest and healthful recreation and all without the expenditure of too much money."

Amusement park owners used different strategies to attract the new mass audience, with differing degrees of success. The three large amusement parks, Steeplechase, Luna Park, and Dreamland, did not wage a unified assault on vulgarity and immorality, but rather fought a subtle battle over the nature of popular amusements and early mass entertainment. These parks drew upon different cultures in designing and presenting their amusements, with Luna and especially Dreamland oriented toward a middle-class model and Steeplechase using and transforming cultural forms prevalent in working-class life, especially in its youth subculture. These choices particularly affected the ways in which park owners handled sexual expression and social relationships in their mixed-sex amusements. . . .

Sexual Culture at Coney

Luna and Dreamland based much of their appeal on spectacle and sensation, inspiring surprise, awe, laughter, and delight in the experiences they orchestrated for the public. They intentionally rejected the "old" Coney Island's sexual culture. Still, many of Coney's visitors, including working women, continued to gravitate to the rowdy streets, alluring concession stands, and bawdy sideshows that flourished under the shadow of the big amusement parks. Hundreds of questionable dance resorts and music halls remained in the Bowery, Belle Israels charged in 1909: "Not even belittling the fact that 'nice' people dance in the Dreamland ball room, the fact remains that the average girl has small powers of discrimination."

While journalists touted the wholesome respectability of the "new" Coney Island, middle-class reform groups found much to criticize. In 1901, the Women's Branch of the Brooklyn City Mission crusaded against immorality and prostitution at Coney. When police denied that such activities occurred, a New York *Tribune* reporter investigated the moral condition of the resort. He condemned the "disgusting photographs" displayed in kinetoscope shows, noting that "the most pathetic sight was the number of women with daughters and sons that patronized the places where these machines were." Another study of vice at the island's resorts was conducted in 1910, while in 1912, a reform group called the West End Improvement League of Coney Island crusaded for more beach front, a boardwalk, and an improved moral tone. One Reverend Mortenson, of the Society of Inner Mission and

Rescue Work, was outraged by the rowdyism at night, the sideshows and bawdy concert halls, the suggestive moving picture machines, and, not least, the immorality of the beach on Sunday afternoons: "The nudity and unproper behavior of many of the people there are, mildly speaking, shocking." Indeed, some New York City guidebooks continued to advise middle-class tourists to stick to the safe and refined Manhattan and Brighton Beaches, warning that the individual who went to West Brighton "should look out for his pocket-book and not be too curious to visit all the 'midway attractions,' some of which are to be avoided."

The freer sexual expression of the dance halls, beaches, and boardwalk, which had long appealed to working women, increasingly became commodified in the amusement concessions of West Brighton. Many sideshows promoted familiarity between the sexes, romance, and titillation to attract crowds of young women and men. Penny arcades, for example, had machines to measure the ardor of a couple's kiss. The Cannon Coaster, which shot people out of a cannon onto a slide, advertised itself with the come-on, "Will she throw her arms around your neck and yell? Well, I guess, yes." Rides that sent their patrons into dark, winding passages—the Canals of Venice and the Tunnel of Love, for example—proliferated. Said the manager of one of these mazes, "The men like it because it gives them a chance to hug the girls, the girls like it because it gives them a chance to get hugged." One Coney Island dance master summed up the prevailing commercial attitude: "If you haven't got the girls, you can't do business! Keep attracting 'em. The fellows will come if the girls are there."

Steeplechase

George Tilyou's Steeplechase Park, the third of the large amusement parks of Coney Island, exemplifies the commercial potential of making sexuality and romance the focal point of amusement. Tilyou's inspiration came as much from the world of cheap amusements as it did from the middle-class exposition. He built Steeplechase in 1897 on different principles from those underlying Luna and Dreamland, being much less concerned with grandeur, artistic design, and awe-inspiring sensation. Advertised as "The Funny Place," Steeplechase featured hilarity, symbolized by a vulgar, grinning, slightly sinister clown face above its entrance gates, which by 1905 "was causing sensitive folk to wince as they passed by." With none of the attractions of Luna Park or Dreamland—no exotic villages, scenes of natural disasters, or re-enactments of current events, Steeplechase relied on fun houses, mechanical sensations, and circus-type sideshow attractions. Tilyou rarely allowed his patrons to be passive viewers. Instead, the patrons were whirled through space and knocked off balance, their hats blown off, skirts lifted, sense of humor tried. The patrons themselves became the show, providing interest and hilarity to each other.

At Steeplechase, visitors often experienced the unexpected in a sexual context. Some attractions simply encouraged closeness and romance. Men and women customarily sat together on the mechanical horses for the

Steeplechase Ride. More inventive were such novelties as the Razzle-Dazzle, also known as the Wedding Ring. This attraction was simply a large circle of laminated wood suspended from a pole, which would be rocked back and forth, causing the patrons to lose their balance. The Wedding Ring made instant acquaintances of strangers and gave women and men a perfect excuse to clutch each other. Similarly, the Barrel of Love was a slowly revolving drum that forced those in it to tumble into each other. Tilyou's intentions were made clear in the advertisement, "Talk about love in a cottage! This has it beat a mile." Meanwhile, the Dew Drop, a parachute ride, never failed to lift women's skirts to the delight of onlookers. Audience participation, the interaction of strangers, and voyeurism were incorporated into Tilyou's conception of mass entertainment.

Significantly, Tilyou never changed this formula, even with the moral cleansing of Coney Island and competition from the other amusement parks after 1900. Fire destroyed much of Steeplechase in 1907, and Tilyou energetically rebuilt it, playfully constructing a temple to exhibitionism, humor, and heterosocial relations called the Pavilion of Fun. The Pavilion featured novel and ingenious methods of placing people in compromising positions, never giving its victims any relief. The human pool table, for example, was placed at the foot of the Dew Drop. Instead of landing safely on solid ground after the parachute ride, the patrons found themselves on a spinning disk that threw them wildly into one another, with the expected results of flying clothes and revealed limbs.

Tilyou's most inspired and popular work, built after the 1907 fire, was known as the Blow-Hole Theater. The stage was placed at the end of the Steeplechase Ride, and the only exit from the ride was through a tunnel leading into the theater. The suspicious patrons would move onto a stage, dimly perceiving an expectant audience in the darkness. They were soon confronted by a dwarf and clown, who urged them forward toward the exit sign. As they walked across, the embarrassed victims encountered innumerable obstacles and tricks, the most popular being a system of compressed air jets that raised women's skirts and blew off men's hats. Eventually the confused participants were allowed to stumble their way off stage, where they found that they could enter the theater as members of the audience and watch the next group of unsuspecting victims. . . .

Coney and Cultural Change

At Coney Island, the commercialization of leisure entailed a complex cultural process. Steeplechase, the Bowery, and, to a lesser extent, the other amusement parks articulated new attitudes toward sexuality, gender, personal expressiveness, and pleasure. Entrepreneurs like Tilyou encouraged working-class women's participation by appealing to this cultural constellation, at the same time that they sought to tame and contain it for a middle-class clientele. The sexual culture of these commercial amusements affirmed many aspects of working-class youth culture in its encouragement of flirtation, permissiveness, and sexual humor. But in managing female-male relations, Steeplechase's formula allowed for a nonthreatening sexuality that excited but never crossed "forbidden" limits, a sexual ideology that would be increasingly accepted by the middle class. Tied to this was the notion of packaging sexuality and romance for the paying public, a concept that would become a primary tool of consumer industries. The commercialization of leisure, at least in the amusement parks, made playing with heterosexual expressiveness not only respectable but a privilege for which women and men gladly paid.

Thus Coney Island exemplifies not only the decline of a genteel middle-class cultural hegemony, as John Kasson has persuasively argued, but the rise of a heterosocial culture that owed its form in part to the structure of working-class social life. The cultural transformation of these decades must be seen not only in terms of changes within middle-class culture but in terms of changing relationships among class- and gender-based cultures. The Coney Island of the nineteenth century offered amusements that were geographically delineated by social group. For middle-class families, especially women and children, its east end provided a comfortable retreat from the city. For excursionists, West Brighton was an extension—albeit a spectacular one—of the social organizations, picnics, and outings that formed an integral part of working-class life. For men across class lines, the west end preserved the male subculture of gambling, athletics, and prostitution.

With the creation and expansion of the amusement park, a new phase began. Class distinctions did not entirely disappear, for the three amusement parks, as well as the Bowery sideshows, catered to somewhat different social groups. But the incorporation of the amusements into specific class and gender cultures lessened. The fashionable resorts on Manhattan and Brighton Beaches began to decline, with the two landmark hotel-palaces, the Manhattan Beach and the Oriental, closing in the 1910's. The male subculture also diminished as a separate entity on Coney Island and seems rather to have been toned down and mingled with the other amusements. Finally, Coney's place in the organization of working-class amusements changed. Increased numbers of working-class patrons visited the resort in the early twentieth century, and with the extension of the subway from Manhattan to Coney Island in 1920, it became an easily reached haven for the masses. With this new access, however, the group experience of the excursion and outing declined, and working-class people increasingly went to Coney as individuals or as family groups.

These changes grew out of the commercial transformation of popular amusements, including those of a new middle class that gloried in the midway and rejected genteel culture. Just as significant to this development, however, were the popular amusements of working-class youth. In Coney Island's Bowery they recognized their street life, in the dance halls and variety shows familiar customs and behavior, and in the new amusement parks the celebration of sexuality and romance that was so much a part of youthful social life. Amusement park owners adopted these cultural forms and tamed them for a new mass audience that was more repsonsive to an expressive, heterosocial culture.

❧ *F U R T H E R   R E A D I N G*

Gunther Barth, *City People* (1980)

Susan Porter Benson, *Counter Cultures* (1986)

Francis G. Couvares, *The Remaking of Pittsburgh* (1984)

John T. Cumbler, *Working-Class Community in Industrial America* (1979)

Elliot J. Gorn, *The Manly Art: Bare Knuckle Prize Fighting in America* (1986)

Stephen Hardy, *How Boston Played* (1982)

Daniel Horowitz, *The Morality of Spending* (1985)

John F. Kasson, *Amusing the Millions: Coney Island at the Turn of the Century* (1978)

William Leach, ''Transformations in the Culture of Consumption,'' *Journal of American History* 71 (September 1984), 319–342

Lawrence Levine, *Black Culture, Black Consciousness* (1977)

Donald J. Mrozek, *Sport and American Mentality, 1880–1910* (1983)

Kathy Peiss, *Cheap Amusements* (1986)

Robert Peterson, *Only the Ball Was White* (1970)

Roy Rosensweig, *Eight Hours for What We Will* (1983)

David Q. Voigt, *American Baseball* (1966)

CHAPTER 14

The Language of Empire

ॐ

*In the final decade of the nineteenth century, American policy and public opinion
foresook their traditional isolationism and adopted an increasingly assertive stance
toward the rest of the world. Together, depression-related fears of economic
overproduction, anxieties over the closing of the frontier (see Frederick Jackson
Turner, Chapter 3), Social Darwinian concern with survival of the white (Anglo-
American) race, and a desire to match the nation's industrial might with
commensurate strength in the world's trading lanes fueled an expansionist fever.
Reflecting diverse origins, the language of empire was marked by different accents.
In practice, America's early international muscle flexing, focusing on Cuba,
Central America, the Philippines, and island steppingstones to China, was a
comparatively constricted affair. Indeed, the inflated rhetoric and great
expectations attached to international adventures indirectly addressed domestic
tensions—over race, immigration, and even the renewal of manhood—as well as
substantive foreign engagement.*

ॐ *D O C U M E N T S*

The following selections feature some of the most influential voices in the debate
over American expansionism. Captain Alfred T. Mahan of the Naval War College,
in *The Influence of Sea Power upon History* (1890), from which the opening
document is taken, was one of the first to link the need for a bigger navy with an
analysis of the growth of overseas trade. In the second document, Rough Rider
Theodore Roosevelt, in an address to a Chicago men's club in 1899, connects the
application of American firmness abroad to the quality of moral fiber at home. In
the third and fourth documents, Democratic standard-bearer and anti-imperialist
William Jennings Bryan matches arguments in 1890 with proimperialist Republican
senator Albert J. Beveridge of Indiana over U.S. policy in the Philippines. Finally,
in the famous Roosevelt Corollary to the Monroe Doctrine, issued by way of a
presidential message in 1904, President Roosevelt establishes the official
justification for U.S. intervention in Latin America.

Alfred T. Mahan on the Importance of Sea Power, 1890

To turn now from the particular lessons drawn from the history of the past to the general question of the influence of government upon the sea career of its people, it is seen that that influence can work in two distinct but closely related ways.

First, in peace: The government by its policy can favor the natural growth of a people's industries and its tendencies to seek adventure and gain by way of the sea; or it can try to develop such industries and such sea-going bent, when they do not naturally exist; or, on the other hand, the government may, by mistaken action check and fetter the progress which the people left to themselves would make. In any one of these ways the influence of the government will be felt, making or marring the sea power of the country in the matter of peaceful commerce; upon which alone, it cannot be too often insisted, a thoroughly strong navy can be based.

Secondly, for war: The influence of the government will be felt in its most legitimate manner in maintaining an armed navy, of a size commensurate with the growth of its shipping and the importance of the interests connected with it. More important even than the size of the navy is the question of its institutions, favoring a healthful spirit and activity, and providing for rapid development in time of war by an adequate reserve of men and of ships and by measures for drawing out that general reserve power which has before been pointed to, when considering the character and pursuits of the people. Undoubtedly under this second head of warlike preparation must come the maintenance of suitable naval stations, in those distant parts of the world to which the armed shipping must follow the peaceful vessels of commerce. The protection of such stations must depend either upon direct military force, as do Gibraltar and Malta, or upon a surrounding friendly population, such as the American colonists once were to England, and, it may be presumed, the Australian colonists now are. Such friendly surroundings and backing, joined to a reasonable military provision, are the best of defences, and when combined with decided preponderance at sea, make a scattered and extensive empire, like that of England, secure; for while it is true that an unexpected attack may cause disaster in some one quarter, the actual superiority of naval power prevents such disaster from being general or irremediable. History has sufficiently proved this. England's naval bases have been in all parts of the world; and her fleets have at once protected them, kept open the communications between them, and relied upon them for shelter.

Colonies attached to the mother-country afford, therefore, the surest means of supporting abroad the sea power of a country. In peace, the influence of the government should be felt in promoting by all means a warmth of attachment and a unity of interest which will make the welfare of one the welfare of all, and the quarrel of one the quarrel of all; and in war, or rather for war, by inducing such measures of organization and defence as shall be felt by all to be a fair distribution of a burden of which each reaps the benefit.

Such colonies the United States has not and is not likely to have. As regards purely military naval stations, the feeling of her people was probably accurately expressed by an historian of the English navy a hundred years ago, speaking then of Gibraltar and Port Mahon. "Military governments," said he, "agree so little with the industry of a trading people, and are in themselves so repugnant to the genius of the British people, that I do not wonder that men of good sense and of all parties have inclined to give up these, as Tangiers was given up." Having therefore no foreign establishments, either colonial or military, the ships of war of the United States, in war, will be like land birds, unable to fly far from their own shores. To provide resting-places for them, where they can coal and repair, would be one of the first duties of a government proposing to itself the development of the power of the nation at sea. . . .

The question is eminently one in which the influence of the government should make itself felt, to build up for the nation a navy which, if not capable of reaching distant countries, shall at least be able to keep clear the chief approaches to its own. The eyes of the country have for a quarter of a century been turned from the sea; the results of such a policy and of its opposite will be shown in the instance of France and of England. Without asserting a narrow parallelism between the case of the United States and either of these, it may safely be said that it is essential to the welfare of the whole country that the conditions of trade and commerce should remain, as far as possible, unaffected by an external war. In order to do this, the enemy must be kept not only out of our ports, but far away from our coasts.

Theodore Roosevelt Links War in the Philippines to the Ideal of the Strenuous Life, 1899

In speaking to you, men of the greatest city of the West, men of the State which gave to the country Lincoln and Grant, men who preëminently and distinctly embody all that is most American in the American character, I wish to preach, not the doctrine of ignoble ease, but the doctrine of the strenuous life, the life of toil and effort, of labor and strife; to preach that highest form of success which comes, not to the man who desires mere easy peace, but to the man who does not shrink from danger, from hardship, or from bitter toil, and who out of these wins the splendid ultimate triumph.

A life of slothful ease, a life of that peace which springs merely from lack either of desire or of power to strive after great things, is as little worthy of a nation as of an individual. I ask only that what every self-respecting American demands from himself and from his sons shall be demanded of the American nation as a whole. Who among you would teach your boys that ease, that peace, is to be the first consideration in their eyes—to be the ultimate goal after which they strive? You men of Chicago have made this city great, you men of Illinois have done your share, and more than your share, in making America great, because you neither preach nor practise such a doctrine. You work yourselves, and you bring up your sons to work. If you are rich and are worth your salt, you will teach your sons that though they may have leisure, it is not to be spent in idleness; for wisely used leisure merely means that those who possess it, being free from the necessity of working for their livelihood, are all the more bound to carry on some kind of non-remunerative work in science, in letters, in art, in exploration, in historical research—work of the type we most need in this country, the successful carrying out of which reflects most honor upon the nation. We do not admire the man of timid peace. We admire the man who embodies victorious effort; the man who never wrongs his neighbor, who is prompt to help a friend, but who has those virile qualities necessary to win in the stern strife of actual life. It is hard to fail, but it is worse never to have tried to succeed. In this life we get nothing save by effort. Freedom from effort in the present merely means that there has been stored up effort in the past. A man can be freed from the necessity of work only by the fact that he or his fathers before him have worked to good purpose. If the freedom thus purchased is used aright, and the man still does actual work, though of a different kind, whether as a writer or a general, whether in the field of politics or in the field of exploration and adventure, he shows he deserves his good fortune. But if he treats this period of freedom from the need of actual labor as a period, not of preparation, but of mere enjoyment, even though perhaps not of vicious enjoyment, he shows that he is simply a cumberer of the earth's surface, and he surely unfits himself to hold his own with his fellows if the need to do so should again arise. A mere life of ease is not in the end a very satisfactory life, and, above all, it is a life which ultimately unfits those who follow it for serious work in the world.

In the last analysis a healthy state can exist only when the men and women who make it up lead clean, vigorous, healthy lives; when the children are so trained that they shall endeavor, not to shirk difficulties, but to overcome them; not to seek ease, but to know how to wrest triumph from toil and risk. The man must be glad to do a man's work, to dare and endure and to labor; to keep himself, and to keep those dependent upon him. The woman must be the housewife, the helpmeet of the homemaker, the wise and fearless mother of many healthy children. In one of Daudet's powerful and melancholy books he speaks of "the fear of maternity, the haunting terror of the young wife of the present day." When such words can be truthfully written of a nation, that nation is rotten to the heart's core. When men fear work or fear righteous war, when women fear motherhood, they tremble on the brink of doom; and well it is that they should vanish from the earth, where they are fit subjects for the scorn of all men and women who are themselves strong and brave and high-minded.

As it is with the individual, so it is with the nation. . . .

If we are to be a really great people, we must strive in good faith to play a great part in the world. We cannot avoid meeting great issues. All that we can determine for ourselves is whether we shall meet them well or ill. In 1898 we could not help being brought face to face with the problem of war with Spain. All we could decide was whether we should shrink like cowards from the contest, or enter into it as beseemed a brave and high-spirited people; and, once in, whether failure or success should crown our banners. So it is now. We cannot avoid the responsibilities that confront us in Hawaii, Cuba, Porto Rico, and the Philippines. . . . The timid man, the lazy man, the man who distrusts his country, the over-civilized man, who has lost the great fighting, masterful virtues, the ignorant man, and the man of dull mind, whose soul is incapable of feeling the mighty lift that thrills "stern men with empires in their brains"—all these, of course, shrink from seeing the nation undertake its new duties; shrink from seeing us build a navy and an army adequate to our needs; shrink from seeing us do our share of the world's work, by bringing order out of chaos in the great, fair tropic islands from which the valor of our soldiers and sailors has driven the Spanish flag. These are the men who fear the strenuous life, who fear the only national life which is really worth leading. . . .

I preach to you, then, my countrymen, that our country calls not for the life of ease but for the life of strenuous endeavor. The twentieth century looms before us big with the fate of many nations. If we stand idly by, if we seek merely swollen, slothful ease and ignoble peace, if we shrink from the hard contests where men must win at hazard of their lives and at the risk of all they hold dear, then the bolder and stronger peoples will pass us by, and will win for themselves the domination of the world. Let us therefore boldly face the life of strife, resolute to do our duty well and manfully; resolute to uphold righteousness by deed and by word; resolute to be both honest and brave, to serve high ideals, yet to use practical methods. Above all, let us shrink from no strife, moral or physical, within or without the nation, provided we are certain that the strife is justified, for it is only through strife, through hard and dangerous endeavor, that we shall ultimately win the goal of true national greatness.

William Jennings Bryan Opposes U.S. Occupation of the Philippines, 1900

The young man upon reaching his majority can do what he pleases. He can disregard the teaching of his parents; he can trample upon all that he has been taught to consider sacred; he can disobey the laws of the State, the laws of society and the laws of God. He can stamp failure upon his life and make his very existence a curse to his fellow men, and he can bring his father and mother in sorrow to the grave; but he cannot annul the sentence, "The wages of sin is death."

And so with the nation. It is of age and it can do what it pleases; it can spurn the traditions of the past; it can repudiate the principles upon which the nation rests; it can employ force instead of reason; it can substitute might for right; it can conquer weaker people; it can exploit their lands, appropriate their property and kill their people; but it cannot repeal the moral law or escape the punishment decreed for the violation of human rights. . . .

Some argue that American rule in the Philippine Islands will result in the better education of the Filipinos. Be not deceived. If we expect to maintain a colonial policy, we shall not find it to our advantage to educate the people. The educated Filipinos are now in revolt against us, and the most ignorant ones have made the least resistance to our domination. If we are to govern them without their consent and give them no voice in determining the taxes which they must pay, we dare not educate them, lest they learn to read the Declaration of Independence and Constitution of the United States and mock us for our inconsistency.

The principal arguments, . . . advanced by those who enter upon a defense of imperialism are:

First—That we must improve the present opportunity to become a world power and enter into international politics.

Second—That our commercial interests in the Philippine Islands and in the Orient make it necessary for us to hold the islands permanently.

Third—That the spread of the Christian religion will be facilitated by a colonial policy.

Fourth—That there is no honorable retreat from the position which the nation has taken.

The first argument is addrest to the nation's pride and the second to the nation's pocket-book. The third is intended for the church member and the fourth for the partisan.

It is sufficient answer to the first argument to say that for more than a century this nation has been a world power. For ten decades it has been the most potent influence in the world. Not only has it been a world power, but it has done more to shape the politics of the human race than all the other nations of the world combined. Because our Declaration of Independence was promulgated others have been promulgated. Because the patriots of 1776 fought for liberty others have fought for it. Because our Constitution was adopted other constitutions have been adopted.

The growth of the principle of self-government, planted on American soil, has been the overshadowing political fact of the nineteenth century. It has made this nation conspicuous among the nations and given it a place in history such as no other nation has ever enjoyed. Nothing has been able to check the onward march of this idea. I am not willing that this nation shall cast aside the omnipotent weapon of truth to seize again the weapons of physical warfare. I would not exchange the glory of this Republic for the glory of all the empires that have risen and fallen since time began. . . .

A war of conquest is as unwise as it is unrighteous. A harbor and coaling station in the Philippines would answer every trade and military necessity and such a concession could have been secured at any time without difficulty.

It is not necessary to own people in order to trade with them. We carry on trade today with every part of the world, and our commerce has expanded more rapidly than the commerce of any European empire. We do not own Japan or China, but we trade with their people. We have not absorbed the republics of Central and South America, but we trade with them. It has not been necessary to have any political connection with Canada or the nations of Europe in order to trade with them. Trade cannot be permanently profitable unless it is voluntary.

When trade is secured by force, the cost of securing it and retaining it must be taken out of the profits, and the profits are never large enough to cover the expense. Such a system would never be defended but for the fact that the expense is borne by all the people, while the profits are enjoyed by a few.

Imperialism would be profitable to the army contractors; it would be profitable to the ship owners, who would carry live soldiers to the Philippines and bring dead soldiers back; it would be profitable to those who would seize upon the franchises, and it would be profitable to the officials whose salaries would be fixt here and paid over there; but to the farmer, to the laboring man and to the vast majority of those engaged in other occupations it would bring expenditure without return and risk without reward.

Farmers and laboring men have, as a rule, small incomes and under systems which place the tax upon consumption pay much more than their fair share of the expenses of government. Thus the very people who receive least benefit from imperialism will be injured most by the military burdens which accompany it.

In addition the evils which he and the farmer share in common, the laboring man will be the first to suffer if oriental subjects seek work in the United States; the first to suffer if American capital leaves our shores to employ oriental labor in the Philippines to supply the trade of China and Japan; the first to suffer from the violence which the military spirit arouses and the first to suffer when the methods of imperialism are applied to our own Government. . . .

The religious argument varies in positiveness from a passive belief that Providence delivered the Filipinos into our hands, for their good and our glory, to the exultation of the minister who said that we ought to "thrash the natives (Filipinos) until they understand who we are," and that "every bullet sent, every cannon shot and every flag waved means righteousness."

We cannot approve of this doctrine in one place unless we are willing to apply it everywhere. If there is poison in the blood of the hand it will ultimately reach the heart. It is equally true that forcible Christianity, if planted under the American flag in the far-away Orient, will sooner or later be transplanted upon American soil.

If true Christianity consists of carrying out in our daily lives the teachings of Christ, who will say that we are commanded to civilize with dynamite and proselyte with the sword? . . .

There is an easy, honest, honorable solution of the Philippine question. It is set forth in the Democratic platform and it is submitted with confidence to the American people. This plan I unreservedly indorse. If elected, I will convene Congress in extraordinary session as soon as inaugurated and recommend an immediate declaration of the nation's purpose, first, to establish a stable form of government in the Philippine Islands, just as we are now establishing a stable form of government in Cuba; second, to give independence to the Filipinos as we have promised to give independence to the Cubans; third, to protect the Filipinos from outside interference while they work out their destiny, just as we have protected the republics of Central and South America, and are, by the Monroe doctrine, pledged to protect Cuba.

A European protectorate often results in the plundering of the ward by the guardian. An American protectorate gives to the nation protected the advantage of our strength, without making it the victim of our greed. For three-quarters of a century the Monroe doctrine has been a shield to neighboring republics and yet it has imposed no pecuniary burden upon us. After the Filipinos had aided us in the war against Spain, we could not honorably turn them over to their former masters; we could not leave them to be the victims of the ambitious designs of European nations, and since we do not desire to make them a part of us or to hold them as subjects, we propose the only alternative, namely, to give them independence and guard them against molestation from without.

When our opponents are unable to defend their position by argument they fall back upon the assertion that it is destiny, and insist that we must submit to it, no matter how much it violates our moral precepts and our principles of government. This is a complacent philosophy. It obliterates the distinction between right and wrong and makes individuals and nations the helpless victims of circumstance.

Destiny is the subterfuge of the invertebrate, who, lacking the courage to oppose error, seeks some plausible excuse for supporting it. Washington said that the destiny of the republican form of government was deeply, if not finally, staked on the experiment entrusted to the American people. How different Washington's definition of destiny from the Republican definition! . . .

Albert Beveridge Defends U.S. Imperialism, 1900

Mr. President, the times call for candor. The Philippines are ours forever, "territory belonging to the United States," as the Constitution calls them. And just beyond the Philippines are China's illimitable markets. We will not retreat from either. We will not repudiate our duty in the archipelago. We will not abandon our opportunity in the Orient. We will not renounce our part in the mission of our race, trustee, under God, of the civilization of the world. And we will move forward to our work, not howling out regrets like slaves whipped to their burdens, but with gratitude for a task worthy of our strength, and thanksgiving to Almighty God that He has marked us as His chosen people, henceforth to lead in the regeneration of the world.

This island empire is the last land left in all the oceans. If it should prove a mistake to abandon it, the blunder once made would be irretrievable. If it proves a mistake to hold it, the error can be corrected when we will. Every other progressive nation stands ready to relieve us.

But to hold it will be no mistake. Our largest trade henceforth must be with Asia. The Pacific is our ocean. More and more Europe will manufacture the most it needs, secure from its colonies the most it consumes. Where shall we turn for consumers of our surplus? Geography answers the question. China is our natural customer. She is nearer to us than to England, Germany, or Russia, the commercial powers of the present and the future. They have moved nearer to China by securing permanent bases on her borders. The Philippines give us a base at the door of all the East.

Lines of navigation from our ports to the Orient and Australia; from the Isthmian Canal to Asia; from all Oriental ports to Australia, converge at and separate from the Philippines. They are a self-supporting, dividend-paying fleet, permanently anchored at a spot selected by the strategy of Providence, commanding the Pacific. And the Pacific is the ocean of the commerce of the future. Most future wars will be conflicts for commerce. The power that rules the Pacific, therefore, is the power that rules the world. And, with the Philippines, that power is and will forever be the American Republic. . . .

Nothing is so natural as trade with one's neighbors. The Philippines make us the nearest neighbors of all the East. Nothing is more natural than to trade with those you know. This is the philosophy of all advertising. The Philippines bring us permanently face to face with the most sought-for customers of the world. National prestige, national propinquity, these and commercial activity are the elements of commercial success. The Philippines give the first; the character of the American people supply the last. It is a providential conjunction of all the elements of trade, of duty, and of power. If we are willing to go to war rather than let England have a few feet of frozen Alaska, which affords no market and commands none, what should we not do rather than let England, Germany, Russia, or Japan have all the Philippines? And no man on the spot can fail to see that this would be their fate if we retired. . . .

Here, then, Senators, is the situation. Two years ago there was no land in all the world which we could occupy for any purpose. Our commerce was daily turning toward the Orient, and geography and trade developments made necessary our commercial empire over the Pacific. And in that ocean we had no commercial, naval, or military base. To-day we have one of the three great ocean possessions of the globe, located at the most commanding commercial, naval, and military points in the eastern seas, within hail of India, shoulder to shoulder with China, richer in its own resources than any equal body of land on the entire globe, and peopled by a race which civilization demands shall be improved. Shall we abandon it? That man little knows the common people of the Republic, little understands the instincts of our race, who thinks we will not hold it fast and hold it forever, administering just government by simplest methods. . . .

But, Senators, it would be better to abandon this combined garden and Gibraltar of the Pacific, and count our blood and treasure already spent a profitable loss, than to apply any academic arrangement of self-government to these children. They are not capable of self-government. How could they be? They are not of a self-governing race. They are Orientals, Malays, instructed by Spaniards in the latter's worst estate.

They know nothing of practical government except as they have witnessed the weak, corrupt, cruel, and capricious rule of Spain. What magic will anyone employ to dissolve in their minds and characters those impressions of governors and governed which three centuries of misrule has created? What alchemy will change the oriental quality of their blood and set the self-governing currents of the American pouring through their Malay veins? How shall they, in the twinkling of an eye, be exalted to the heights of self-governing peoples which required a thousand years for us to reach, Anglo-Saxon though we are? . . .

The three best educators on the island at different times made to me the same comparison, that the common people in their stupidity are like their caribou bulls. They are not even good agriculturists. Their waste of cane is inexcusable. Their destruction of hemp fiber is childish. They are incurably indolent. They have no continuity or thoroughness of industry. They will quit work without notice and amuse themselves until the money they have earned is spent. They are like children playing at men's work.

No one need fear their competition with our labor. No reward could beguile, no force compel, these children of indolence to leave their trifling lives for the fierce and fervid industry of high-wrought America. The very reverse is the fact. One great problem is the necessary labor to develop these islands—to build the roads, open the mines, clear the wilderness, drain the swamps, dredge the harbors. The natives will not supply it. A lingering prejudice against the Chinese may prevent us from letting them supply it. Ultimately, when the real truth of the climate and human conditions is known, it is barely possible that our labor will go there. Even now young men with the right moral fiber and a little capital can make fortunes there as planters. . . .

The Declaration of Independence does not forbid us to do our part in the regeneration of the world. If it did, the Declaration would be wrong, just as the Articles of Confederation, drafted by the very same men who signed the Declaration, was found to be wrong. The Declaration has no application to the present situation. It was written by self-governing men for self-governing men. . . .

Senators in opposition are estopped from denying our constitutional power to govern the Philippines as circumstances may demand, for such power is admitted in the case of Florida, Louisiana, Alaska. How, then, is it denied in the Philippines? Is there a geographical interpretation to the Constitution? Do degrees of longitude fix constitutional limitations? Does a thousand miles of ocean diminish constitutional power more than a thousand miles of land? . . .

Mr. President, this question is deeper than any question of party politics; deeper than any question of the isolated policy of our country even; deeper even than any question of constitutional power. It is elemental. It is racial. God has not been preparing the English-speaking and Teutonic peoples for a thousand years for nothing but vain and idle self-contemplation and self-admiration. No! He has made us the master organizers of the world to establish system where chaos reigns. He has given us the spirit of progress to overwhelm the forces of reaction throughout the earth. He has made us adepts in government that we may administer government among savage and senile peoples. Were it not for such a force as this the world would relapse into barbarism and night. And of all our race He has marked the American people as His chosen nation to finally lead in the regeneration of the world. This is the divine mission of America, and it holds for us all the profit, all the glory, all the happiness possible to man. We are trustees of the world's progress, guardians of its righteous peace. The judgment of the Master is upon us: "Ye have been faithful over a few things; I will make you ruler over many things.". . .

The Roosevelt Corollary to the Monroe Doctrine, 1904

It is not true that the United States feels any land hunger or entertains any projects as regards the other nations of the Western Hemisphere save such as are for their welfare. All that this country desires is to see the neighboring countries stable, orderly, and prosperous. Any country whose people conduct themselves well can count upon our hearty friendship. If a nation shows that it knows how to act with reasonable efficiency and decency in social and political matters, if it keeps order and pays its obligations, it need fear no interference from the United States. Chronic wrongdoing, or an impotence which results in a general loosening of the ties of civilized society, may in America, as elsewhere, ultimately require intervention by some civilized nation, and in the Western Hemisphere the adherence of the United States to the Monroe Doctrine may force the United States, however reluctantly, in flagrant cases of such wrongdoing or impotence, to the exercise of an international police power. If every country washed by the Caribbean Sea would show the progress in stable and just civilization which with the aid of the Platt amendment Cuba has shown since our troops left the island, and which so many of the republics in both Americas are constantly and brilliantly showing, all question of interference by this Nation with their affairs would be at an end. Our interests and those of our southern neighbors are in reality identical. They have great natural riches, and if within their borders the reign of law and justice obtains, prosperity is sure to come to them. While they thus obey the primary laws of civilized society they may rest assured that they will be treated by us in a spirit of cordial and helpful sympathy. We would interfere with them only in the last resort, and then only if it became evident that their inability or unwillingness to do justice at home and abroad had violated the rights of the United States or had invited foreign aggression to the detriment of the entire body of American nations. It is a mere truism to say that every nation, whether in America or anywhere else, which desires to maintain its freedom, its independence, must ultimately realize that the right of such independence can not be separated from the responsibility of making good use of it. . . .

⚘ *E S S A Y S*

The following essays probe the realities of U.S. foreign policy and the political assumptions and projections of American leaders as they set out to reorder the wider world. In the opening selection, historian Paul Kennedy of Yale University succinctly analyzes the connections between national economy and foreign affairs in the emergence of the United States as a world power, 1890–1940. Next, historian Peter W. Stanley of Carleton College, Northfield, Minnesota, monitors the contradictory and ultimately self-disillusioning course of U.S. policy in the Philippines, a set of actions that first stirred the pot for progressive change and then clamped a brutal lid on indigenous revolutionaries. In the final selection, Walter LaFeber, a professor of history at Cornell University, diagnoses Theodore Roosevelt's fateful commitment to a U.S. protectorate over the Panama Canal Zone as well as the larger consequences of the Roosevelt Corollary.

The United States as New Kid on the Block, 1890–1940

PAUL KENNEDY

Of all the changes which were taking place in the global power balances during the late nineteenth and early twentieth centuries, there can be no doubt that the most decisive one for the future was the growth of the United States. With the Civil War over, the United States was able to exploit . . . many advantages . . . rich agricultural land, vast raw materials, and the marvelously convenient evolution of modern technology (railways, the steam engine, mining equipment) to develop such resources; the lack of social and geographical constraints; the absence of significant foreign dangers; the flow of foreign and, increasingly, domestic investment capital—to transform itself at a stunning pace. Between the ending of the Civil War in 1865 and the outbreak of the Spanish-American War in 1898, for example, American wheat production increased by 256 percent, corn by 222 percent, refined sugar by 460 percent, coal by 800 percent, steel rails by 523 percent, and the miles of railway track in operation by over 567 percent. "In newer industries the growth, starting from near zero, was so great as to make percentages meaningless. Thus the production of crude petroleum rose from about 3,000,000 barrels in 1865 to over 55,000,000 barrels in 1898 and that of steel ingots and castings from less than 20,000 long tons to nearly 9,000,000 long tons." This was not a growth which stopped with the war against Spain; on the contrary, it rose upward at the same meteoric pace throughout the early twentieth century. Indeed, given the advantages listed above, there was a virtual inevitability to the whole process. That is to say, only persistent human ineptitude, or near-constant civil war, or a climatic disaster could have checked this expansion—or deterred the millions of immigrants who flowed across the Atlantic to get their share of the pot of gold and to swell the productive labor force.

The United States seemed to have *all* the economic advantages which *some* of the other powers possessed *in part,* but *none* of their disadvantages. It was immense, but the vast distances were shortened by some 250,000 miles of railway in 1914 (compared with Russia's 46,000 miles, spread over an area two and a half times as large). Its agricultural yields per acre were always superior to Russia's; and if they were never as large as those of the intensively farmed regions of western Europe, the sheer size of the area under cultivation, the efficiency of its farm machinery, and the decreasing costs of transport (because of railways and steamships) made American wheat, corn, pork, beef, and other products cheaper than any in Europe. Technologically, leading American firms like International Harvester, Singer, Du Pont, Bell, Colt, and Standard Oil were equal to, or often better than, any in the world; and they enjoyed an enormous domestic market and economies of scale, which their German, British, and Swiss rivals did not. "Gigantism" in Russia was not a good indicator of industrial efficiency; in the United States, it usually was. For example, "Andrew Carnegie was producing more steel than the whole of England put together when he sold out in 1901 to J. P. Morgan's colossal organization, the United States Steel Corporation." When the famous British warship designer Sir William White made a tour of the United States in 1904, he was shaken to discover fourteen battleships and thirteen armored cruisers being built simultaneously in American yards (although, curiously, the U.S. merchant marine remained small). In industry *and* agriculture *and* communications, there was both efficiency and size. It was therefore not surprising that U.S. national income, in absolute figures and per capita, was so far above everybody else's by 1914.

The consequences of this rapid expansion are reflected in Table 1, and in the pertinent comparative statistics. In 1914, the United States was producing 455 million tons of coal, well ahead of Britain's 292 million and Germany's 277 million. It was the largest oil producer in the world, and the greatest consumer of copper. Its pig-iron production was larger than those of the next three countries (Germany, Britain, France) combined, and its steel production almost equal to the next four countries (Germany, Britain, Russia, and France). Its energy consumption from modern fuels in 1913 was equal to that of Britain, Germany, France, Russia, and Austria-Hungary together. It produced, and possessed, more motor vehicles than the rest of the world together. It was, in fact an entire rival continent and growing so fast that it was coming close to the point of overtaking all of Europe. According to one calculation, indeed, had these growth rates continued and a world war been avoided, the United States would have overtaken Europe as the region possessing the greatest economic output in the world by 1925. What the First

Table 1   National Income, Population, and per Capita Income of the Powers in 1914

	NATIONAL INCOME	POPULATION	PER CAPITA INCOME
United States	$37 billion	98 million	$377
Britain	11	45	244
France	6	39	153
Japan	2	55	36
Germany	12	65	184
Italy	4	37	108
Russia	7	171	41
Austria-Hungary	3	52	57

World War did, through the economic losses and dislocations suffered by the older Great Powers, was to bring that time forward, by six years, to 1919. The "Vasco da Gama era"—the four centuries of European dominance in the world—was coming to an end even before the cataclysm of 1914.

The role of foreign trade in the United States' economic growth was small indeed (around 8 percent of its GNP derived from foreign trade in 1913, compared with Britain's 26 percent), but its economic impact upon other countries was considerable. Traditionally, the United States had exported raw materials (especially cotton), imported finished manufactures, and made up the usual deficit in "visible" trade by the export of gold. But the post–Civil War boom in industrialization quite transformed that pattern. Swiftly becoming the world's largest producer of manufactures, the United States began to pour its farm machinery, iron and steel wares, machine tools, electrical equipment, and other products onto the world market. At the same time, the Northern industrialists' lobby was so powerful that it ensured that foreign products would be kept out of the home market by higher and higher tariffs; raw materials, by contrast, or specialized goods (like German dyestuffs) were imported in ever-larger quantities to supply American industry. But while the surge in the country's industrial exports was the most significant change, the "transportation revolution" also boosted American farm exports. With the cost of carrying a bushel of wheat from Chicago to London plummeting from 40 cents to 10 cents in the half-century before 1900, American agricultural produce streamed across the Atlantic. Corn exports peaked in 1897 at 212 million bushels, wheat exports in 1901 at 239 million bushels; this tidal wave also included grain and flour, meat and meat products.

The consequences of this commercial transformation were, of course, chiefly economic, but they also began to affect international relations. The hyperproductivity of American factories and farms caused a widespread fear that even its enormous domestic market might soon be unable to absorb these goods, and led powerful interest groups (midwestern farmers as well as Pittsburgh steel producers) to press the government to give all sorts of aid to opening up, or at least keeping open, markets overseas. The agitation to preserve an "open door" in China and the massive interest shown in making the United States the dominant economic force in Latin America were only two of the manifestations of this concern to expand the country's share of world trade. Between 1860 and 1914 the United States increased its exports more than sevenfold (from $334 million to $2.365 billion), yet because it was so protective of its own market, imports increased only fivefold (from $356 million to $1.896 billion). Faced with this avalanche of cheap American food, continental European farmers agitated for higher tariffs—which they usually got; in Britain, which had already sacrificed its grain farmers for the cause of free trade, it was the flood of American machines, and iron and steel, which produced alarm. While the journalist W. T. Stead wrote luridly of "the Americanization of the world"—the phrase was the title of his book of 1902—Kaiser Wilhelm and other European leaders hinted at the need to combine against the "unfair" American trading colossus.

Perhaps even more destabilizing, although less well understood, was the impact of the United States upon the world's financial system and monetary flows. Because it had such a vast surplus in its trade with Europe, the latter's deficit had to be met by capital transfers—joining the enormous stream of direct European investments into U.S. industry, utilities, and services (which totaled around $7 billion by 1914). Although some of this westward flow of bullion was reversed by the returns on European investments and by American payments for services such as shipping and insurance, the drain was a large one, and constantly growing larger; and it was exacerbated by the U.S. Treasury's policy of accumulating (and then just sitting on) nearly one-third of the world's gold stock. Moreover, although the United States had by now become an integral part of a complete global trading system—running a deficit with raw-materials-supplying countries, and a vast surplus with Europe—its own financial structure was underdeveloped. Most of its foreign trade was done in sterling, for example, and London acted as the lender of last resort for gold. With no central bank able to control the financial markets, with a stupendous seasonal outflow and inflow of funds between New York and the prairie states conditioned solely by the grain harvest and that by a volatile climate, and with speculators able to derange not merely the domestic monetary system but also the frequent calls upon gold in London, the United States in the years before 1914 was already becoming a vast but unpredictable bellows, fanning but also on occasions dramatically cooling the world's trading system. The American banking crisis of 1907 (originally provoked by an attempt by speculators to corner the market in copper), with consequent impacts on London, Amsterdam, and Hamburg, was merely one example of the way the United States was impinging upon the economic life of the other Great Powers, even before the First World War.

This growth of American industrial power and overseas trade was accompanied, perhaps inevitably, by a more assertive diplomacy and by an American-style rhetoric of *Weltpolitik*. Claims to a special moral endowment among the peoples of the earth which made American foreign policy superior to those of the Old World were intermingled with Social Darwinistic and racial arguments, and with the urging of industrial and agricultural pressure groups for secure overseas markets. The traditional, if always exaggerated, alarm about threats to the Monroe Doctrine was accompanied by calls for the United States to fulfill its "Manifest Destiny" across the Pacific. While entangling alliances still had to be avoided, the United States was now being urged by many groups at home into a much more activist diplomacy—which, under the administrations of McKinley and (especially) Theodore Roosevelt, was exactly what took place. The 1895 quarrel with Britain over the Venezuelan border dispute—justified in terms of the Monroe Doctrine—was followed three years later by the much more dramatic war with Spain over the Cuban issue. Washington's demand to have sole control of an isthmian canal (instead of the older fifty-fifty arrangement with Britain), the redefinition of the Alaskan border despite Canadian protests, and the 1902–1903 battle-fleet preparations in the Caribbean following the German actions against

Venezuela were all indications of U.S. determination to be unchallenged by any other Great Power in the western hemisphere. As a "corollary" of this, however, American administrations showed themselves willing to intervene by diplomatic pressure *and* military means in Latin American countries such as Nicaragua, Haiti, Mexico, and the Dominican Republic when their behavior did not accord with United States norms.

But the really novel feature of American external policy in this period were its interventions and participation in events *outside* the western hemisphere. Its attendance at the Berlin West Africa Conference in 1884–1885 had been anomalous and confused: after grandiose speeches by the U.S. delegation in favor of free trade and open doors, the subsequent treaty was never ratified. Even as late as 1892 the *New York Herald* was proposing the abolition of the State Department, since it had so little business to conduct overseas. The war with Spain in 1898 changed all that, not only by giving the United States a position in the western Pacific (the Philippines) which made it, too, a sort of Asiatic colonial power, but also by boosting the political fortunes of those who had favored an assertive policy. Secretary of State Hay's "Open Door" note in the following year was an early indication that the United States wished to have a say in China, as was the commitment of 2,500 American troops to the international army sent to restore order in China in 1900. Roosevelt showed an even greater willingness to engage in *grosse Politik,* acting as mediator in the talks which brought an end to the Russo-Japanese War, insisting upon American participation in the 1906 conference over Morocco, and negotiating with Japan and the other Powers in an attempt to maintain the "Open Door" in China. Much of this has been seen by later scholars less as being based upon a sober calculation of the country's real interests in the world than as reflecting an immaturity of foreign-policy style, an ethnocentric naiveté, and a wish to impress audiences both at home and abroad—traits which would complicate a "realistic" American foreign policy in the future; but even if that is true, the United States was hardly alone in this age of imperialist bombast and nationalist pride. In any case, except in Chinese affairs, such diplomatic activism was not maintained by Roosevelt's successors, who preferred to keep the United States free from international events occurring outside the western hemisphere.

Along with these diplomatic actions went increases in arms expenditures. Of the two services, the navy got the most, since it was the front line of the nation's defenses in the event of a foreign attack (or a challenge to the Monroe Doctrine) and also the most useful instrument to support American diplomacy and commerce in Latin America, the Pacific, and elsewhere. Already in the late 1880s, the rebuilding of the fleet had commenced, but the greatest boost came at the time of the Spanish-American War. Since the easy naval victories in that conflict seemed to justify the arguments of Admiral Mahan and the "big navy" lobby, and since the strategists worried about the possibility of a war with Britain and then, from 1898 onward, with Germany, the battle fleet was steadily built up. The acquisition of bases in Hawaii, Samoa, the Philippines, and the Caribbean, the use of naval vessels to act as "policemen" in Latin America, and Roosevelt's dramatic gesture of sending his "great white fleet" around the world in 1907 all seemed to emphasize the importance of sea power.

Consequently, while the naval expenditures of $22 million in 1890 represented only 6.9 percent of total federal spending, the $139 million allocated to the navy by 1914 represented 19 percent. Not all of this was well spent—there were too many home fleet bases (the result of local political pressures) and too few escort vessels—but the result was still impressive. Although considerably smaller than the Royal Navy, and with fewer *Dreadnought*-type battleships than Germany, the U.S. Navy was the third largest in the world in 1914. Even the construction of a U.S.-controlled Panama Canal did not stop American planners from agonizing over the strategical dilemma of dividing the fleet, or leaving one of the country's coastlines exposed; and the records of some officers in these years reveal a somewhat paranoid suspicion of foreign powers. In fact, given its turn-of-the-century *rapprochement* with Great Britain, the United States was immensely secure, and even if it feared the rise of German sea power, it really had far less to worry about than any of the other major powers.

The small size of the U.S. military was in many ways a reflection of that state of security. The army, too, had been boosted by the war with Spain, at least to the extent that the public realized how minuscule it actually was, how disorganized the National Guard was, and how close to disaster the early campaigning in Cuba had come. But the tripling of the size of the regular army after 1900 and the additional garrisoning tasks it acquired in the Philippines and elsewhere still left the service looking insignificant compared with that of even a middle-sized European country like Serbia or Bulgaria. Even more than Britain, the United States clung to a laissez-faire dislike of mass standing armies and avoided fixed military obligations to allies. Less than 1 percent of its GNP went to defense. Despite its imperialist activities in the period 1898–1914, therefore, it remained what the sociologist Herbert Spencer termed an "industrial" society rather than a "military" society like Russia. Since many historians have suggested that "the rise of the superpowers" began in this period, it is worth noting the staggering *differences* between Russia and the United States by the eve of the First World War. The former possessed a front-line army about ten times as large as the latter's; but the United States produced six times as much steel, consumed ten times as much energy, and was four times larger in total industrial output (in per capita terms, it was six times more productive). No doubt Russia seemed the more powerful to all those European general staffs thinking of swiftly fought wars involving masses of available troops; but by all other criteria, the United States was strong and Russia weak.

The United States had definitely become a Great Power. But it was not part of the Great Power system. Not only did the division of powers between the presidency and the Congress make an active alliance policy virtually impossible, but it was also clear that no one was in favor of abandoning the existing state of very comfortable isolation. Separated from other strong nations by thousands of miles of ocean, possessing a negligible army, content to have achieved hemispheric dominance and, at least after Roosevelt's departure, less eager to engage in worldwide diplomacy, the United States in 1913 still stood on the edges of the Great Power system. And since most of the other countries after 1906 were turning their attention from Asia and Africa to developments in the Balkans and North Sea, it was perhaps not surprising that they tended to see the United States as less a factor in the international power balances than had been the case around the turn of the century. That was yet another of the common pre-1914 assumptions which the Great War itself would prove wrong.

U.S. Misunderstanding of the Philippines

PETER W. STANLEY

One's first inclination is to consider the Philippine Islands only a marginal participant in American–East Asian history. There are persuasive reasons for feeling this way. Geographically, the archipelago is literally marginal, or peripheral, to East Asia; ethnically and culturally, it belongs to Southeast Asia. Moreover, it came to prominence relatively late in the course of America's dealings with that part of the world and was always seen by most Americans as merely an adjunct to more critical involvements elsewhere. Seldom have the Philippines attracted much interest in their own right.

This is true as far as it goes, but fundamentally misleading. The real importance of the Philippines to the United States has been moral and exemplary, rather than strategic or economic. The American empire in those islands gives an insight into America.

The Philippines were the only place in Asia—indeed, the only place outside the Western Hemisphere—that the United States ever ruled as an imperial possession. Although a few elite Filipinos hoped otherwise, it was always clear to Americans that the inhabitants of the islands would never become citizens of the United States, nor the archipelago itself be brought fully into the union. The Filipinos and their islands thus became that rarest of phenomena under the republican form of government, subjects.

Sovereignty opened up the possibility for Americans directly to affect every aspect of Philippine public life. And this immense potential power was actually used in a variety of ways, from shooting revolutionaries and deporting political dissenters, to improving public health, building roads, establishing school curricula, defining political institutions and economic structures, and sanctioning power relationships within the society at large. With the possible exceptions of the occupation of Cuba early in the twentieth century and the occupation of Japan after World War II, there is no other instance of America's exercising such power over people recognized to be permanently ineligible for American citizenship and outside the protection of the Bill of Rights. There is literally no other case in which the United States exercised such power for so long a period of time.

The Philippines, then, were the place where the United States came closest to enjoying free rein to do whatever it wished with the lives of another people. This in itself made the Philippine-American encounter different in kind from the relationship between Americans and Chinese or Japanese. The insular empire in the Philippines revealed at its most unfettered the early-twentieth-century American style in dealing with less developed Asian societies.

The first Americans to visit these islands went as merchants in the 1790s, more than a century before the Spanish-American War. Spain, which had governed them since the sixteenth century, made it a policy to discourage foreign trade or settlement; and as a result, the earliest Philippine-American contacts were usually brief and clandestine. Vessels trading principally with some other part of Asia would simply call at Manila to try to fill out incomplete cargoes. The products of the islands were attractive in their own right, however; and in 1796 a vessel named *Astrea* opened a direct trade between Salem and Manila, exchanging hats, wooden compasses, and Madeira for sugar, indigo, pepper, and hides that had been produced in the archipelago.

This trade caught on. It spread from Salem to Boston and New York. By the turn of the century, although it was still technically illegal for foreigners to live or own property in the Philippines, there was enough business involved to make it worthwhile for several American commission merchants to establish themselves informally in Manila as agents for the trade. Eventually, in 1814, Spain reconciled itself to the new order of things and opened the port of Manila officially to foreign trade and residence.

These early American traders arrived at one of the great turning points of Philippine history; and by their presence and economic activity, they and their successors during the nineteenth century played a major role in creating social and cultural forces that ultimately undermined Spanish sovereignty. To understand this, one must first appreciate the philosophy and character of the Spanish empire in the Philippines.

The Philippines were unique in East Asia, because they did not have a highly developed civilization at the time of their original contacts with the West. When the Spaniards came to stay, in 1565, they found a society, economy, and culture that were locally oriented toward extended kinship groups called *barangays*. The people who lived in these communities were relatively peaceful in their relations with each other, literate in a variety of dialects, and talented at various crafts and skills ranging from metalworking to boatbuilding. . . . But there was no superstructure of law or administration, no artistic or literary tradition of high culture, and no power of political or military organization adequate to resist a European army.

Even though the Spaniards were few in number, Filipinos (whom the Spaniards called *indios*) could not mount an effective resistance. By the end of the sixteenth century, Spaniards had overrun most populated parts of the archipelago. . . . In the process, the Spaniards chronically disrupted the indigenous society and economy—by violence, evangelization, the introduction of a system of forced labor, the creation of quasi-feudal fiefdoms called *encomiendas*, and by depleting the food supply.

The effect was devastating. Witnesses reported that as a result of the Spanish presence, traditional patterns of authority were eroding, crime and disorder increasing, villages being abandoned in favor of a return to the safety of the hills. In some places, agriculture was deliberately neglected in hopes of starving out the Spanish invaders and the Chinese merchants who quickly followed in their wake.

Under the prodding of the clergy, Spain imposed a regime designed to protect the Philippines and the Filipinos against further destructive exploitation. It closed the islands, as a whole, to foreigners; and, within the archipelago, closed the countryside and the villages to all Europeans, including Spaniards, except for the clergy and a small number of governmental officials. There were complicated reasons for this. (It was, among other things, part of a power struggle between Spanish clergy and laity in the islands.) What matters for our purposes, however, is the effect: the Spanish policy of isolation . . . froze Filipino life midway through a period of acute disruption, throwing the society back upon its own badly battered cultural resources.

For the next 250 years, until the second half of the nineteenth century, Spain governed the Philippines through Spanish priests and the descendants of the traditional *indio* elite. As late as 1848, apart from a small military and naval contingent, only a few hundred Spanish laymen lived anywhere in the islands, outside Manila and its immediate periphery.

Early in the second half of the eighteenth century, however, the artificial isolation of the Philippines was pierced. Here, as in China, the British led the way. British forces occupied Manila between 1762 and 1764, and during their stay Philippine commerce was opened for the first time to Europeans from outside Spain. Confined to Manila and a few other cities by their own law, Spaniards had devoted their economic energies to the celebrated galleon that made an annual voyage to Acapulco and back. The galleon trade was essentially an exchange of Mexican silver for various Chinese and other Asian products amassed at Manila during the year. The Philippines were simply an entrepot, not the source of the wealth. The British, unlike the Spaniards, were interested in native Philippine products such as sugar and hemp. They continued to seek them out—bribing and smuggling where necessary—even after the occupation was over.

This started the commercial development of the Philippine countryside. In particular, it pushed up land values by making it profitable for landowners to specialize and produce for an export market. As a result, new wealth began to appear in the provinces, much of it in the hands of new men who were not part of the traditional elite. With this wealth came aspirations to lead a less parochial and specifically a more Westernized style of life.

This was the situation into which Americans projected themselves in the 1790s. They went to the Philippines seeking profits; but in the process they became, like the British, catalysts of social and economic change. The commission merchants who had established themselves illegally in Manila around the turn of the century put out connections to the American firms doing business at Canton and eventually coalesced into two major trading houses— Russell & Sturgis; and Peele, Hubbell & Company.

As Spain's own efforts at economic development lagged, these two American firms and their British counterparts became the principal dynamic element in the Philippine economy, the locus of initiative. In the absence of modern banking and credit facilities, they not only acted as commission merchants but as bankers, investors, shipping and insurance agents, and landowners. By the middle of the nineteenth century, Russell & Sturgis had come to play so pivotal a role in these respects that it was commonly referred to in the islands simply as "the great company." . . .

Had the Spanish government accommodated itself to change—for example, by liberalizing and secularizing its administration, improving public services, and recognizing that a new group of economic and cultural leaders had replaced many members of the traditional elite—it is conceivable that the Spanish empire might have survived in the archipelago for decades more.

Instead, however, the Spanish community and the church-state through which Spain ruled remained to the end the chief support of the status quo and the foremost obstacle to change. As a result, reforms that could have been dealt with under Spanish sovereignty—reforms such as liberalizing the government—became fused with highly emotional issues of racial dignity and national pride that deepened Filipinos' alienation from Spain.

So in the end, across the whole spectrum of reform and discontent, advocates of economic development, improved government services, racial dignity, class interest, and political or educational liberalization all found in the Spanish regime a common target. . . .

Accordingly, in 1896, after years of unsuccessful reformist agitation by the economic and social elite of the islands, a group of urban lower- and lower-middle-class conspirators launched an armed rebellion under the leadership of a romantic figure named Andres Bonifacio. The organization he formed was named *Katipunan,* a Tagalog acronym. Bonifacio was a talented conspirator, versed in the writings of European social revolutionaries, but an incompetent general. He was replaced and eventually executed, after a shabby trial for treason, by Emilio Aguinaldo, a minor official from Cavite province who had enjoyed some success against Spanish military forces. After months of sharp fighting, Aguinaldo accepted a large payment from the Spanish government and retired to Hong Kong in 1897. But the social forces behind the revolution remained. When the United States declared war on Spain in 1898 and transported Aguinaldo back to the islands to help Americans destroy Spanish power there, the Filipino people rose anew and seized control of virtually the entire archipelago outside Manila on their own, before American ground forces could be deployed.

This posed a serious problem for American policymakers. At the outset of the war, the McKinley administration still had limited and uncertain goals in the Philippines. Its immediate aims were to attack and defeat Spanish military and naval forces and seize the city of Manila. As the seat of Spanish government in the islands, Manila would be a valuable bargaining chip in the eventual peace negotiations. Beyond this, many people felt that Manila would make an admirable base of operations for American naval and commercial activities in the western Pacific, an American equivalent of Hong Kong.

Certain individual exceptions notwithstanding, neither the administration nor Congress had originally intended to take the whole archipelago from Spain. Apart from Manila and whatever surrounding territory might be required to make the city defensible, the islands did not seem intrinsically attractive.

Even after Dewey's victory, on May 1, 1898, the initial response of the leading American expansionists remained guarded and ambivalent. Theodore Roosevelt came out briefly against annexation, arguing that the islands were too far away. Captain Mahan recommended taking Manila and possibly the island of Luzon, upon which it was located, but nothing else. Henry Cabot Lodge thought it might be well to acquire the whole archipelago, and then trade everything except Luzon to Britain for various Caribbean islands. The leaders of both wings of the Democratic party—William Jennings Bryan and former President Grover Cleveland—opposed taking anything at all.

Most of these people assumed that residual sovereignty and power in the Philippines would continue to be exercised by Spain, except in those places the United States either seized or acquired in the treaty. McKinley's original peace proposal, presented to Spain a month after Dewey's victory, was simply that Spain convey to the United States "a port and necessary appurtenances." Everything else, implicitly, was to be at Spain's disposal.

The astounding success of the Philippine revolution invalidated this assumption. Actual control of the islands outside of Manila and a few other spots was now in the hands of Filipinos. This raised vexatious questions as to what the United States should do. Nobody seriously thought that the Spaniards could reconquer the Philippines, but it was clear that if the United States recognized Spanish sovereignty there in the peace treaty, they would try. This would lead to a great deal of death, destruction, and political instability in the region, for which Americans would have to bear much of the responsibility.

On the other hand, nobody seriously supposed that an independent Philippine government could survive by itself in that age of high imperialism. In both Washington and London, it was widely held that if the United States should leave, Japan or Germany would move in; and the British, who would have found German control of the islands a serious threat to their own position in East Asia, informally urged the United States to keep the Philippines for itself.

There was a third option besides independence and outright acquisition. The United States could have recognized Philippine independence and then established a protectorate over the archipelago to warn off other foreign powers. This would have been acceptable to at least some elements in the Philippine revolutionary government; and it was actually recommended by a number of anti-imperialists in the United States Senate. But it was not a credible alternative in the eyes of the McKinley administration, because a protectorate of this sort would have left the United States responsible to other nations for the Filipinos' behavior toward foreign citizens and interests. Since the administration, like most Americans of the time, considered the Filipinos a backward people likely to behave erratically or even violently to foreigners living among them, it did not want to accept such a responsibility. In the phrase of the time, it maintained that it would accept "no responsibility without control."

This lack of credible alternatives increased the administration's receptivity to frankly imperialistic, annexationist arguments. Acquiring the whole archipelago, it was said, would improve American trade and the American strategic position in the Orient; it would fulfill American obligations to international society and at the same time signal American arrival in the ranks of the great powers. By autumn of 1898, the administration had reversed its former policy and instructed its negotiators in Paris to get a treaty giving the United States sovereignty over the whole of the Philippine Islands.

In the meantime, an extremely ugly situation had developed at Manila. An American army had been dispatched to the Philippines even before news of Dewey's victory had been received. (The reasoning behind this was that the slow-sailing transports could be called back if Dewey had been defeated, but that the army would be needed promptly if he had won, in order to establish support facilities on shore and maintain an American presence.) This army, swelled by reinforcements, took possession of Manila from its Spanish garrison in August after a mock battle meant to save Spanish honor. Farcical in its theatrics, this arrangement nevertheless reflected certain realities: the Americans wanted Manila; and the Spaniards, realizing that they could hold out no longer, preferred to surrender to a white Western power rather than their own former subjects.

Predictably, this deal between Americans and Spaniards infuriated the Filipinos, who were at the time besieging Manila, which they considered the natural capital of their independent government. The result of the maneuver, therefore, was to place the Americans inside Manila looking out, and the Filipinos outside Manila looking in—the two armies facing each other with increasing hostility and suspicion across the cordon surrounding the city. As it became clear that the United States intended to take over the entire archipelago, tensions along this line rose to great intensity. Troops jeered at and baited each other; commanders on each side became convinced that the other was about to attack. The situation made an outbreak of actual fighting almost inevitable. On the night of February 4, 1899, two days before the peace treaty with Spain was ratified by the American Senate, a minor incident set off general firing between the two armies and quickly escalated into a full-scale war.

This war—which Americans then and now have called an insurrection, thereby evading the Filipinos' claim to be resisting a foreign invasion—was bound to be won militarily by the United States sooner or later. This was so partly because of the overwhelming strategic power of the United States, but more because of the weaknesses and inadequacies of the Philippine government. The latter was, after all, a new creation with only the most rudimentary administrative and financial machinery, headed by the increasingly dictatorial General Aguinaldo. It was being torn apart internally by regional, linguistic, religious, and class tensions.

Nevertheless, the disadvantages under which the Filipinos labored had their compensations; and these have given this vicious war—which was filled with the most dreadful atrocities on both sides—a special fascination ever since the Vietnam War. For one thing, the enormous imbalance in regular forces compelled the Filipinos, who would have preferred to wage conventional warfare, to adopt instead guerrilla tactics that proved far more vexing and punishing to the American invaders.

Concomitantly, the expendability of the central government and the diffuse character of social and political organization in the islands deprived Americans of convenient targets against which to use their admittedly overwhelming power. This sustained the spread of a guerrilla, or what in the future would be called a people's, war. In the circumstances, a conventional military victory could not by itself establish American control. It would still leave at the local level a combustible polity governable only by the recurrent, overt use of force. This was a higher price for empire than it seemed likely the American public would be willing to pay.

This was all the more true because the American empire in the islands had been politically vulnerable at home all along. Right from the beginning, there had been a strong anti-imperialist movement in the United States. It was a strange alliance of people who had little else in common. Some were idealists who thought that ruling another people against their will was incompatible with the tenets of America's own Declaration of Independence and that enslaving a colored people, in particular, was tantamount to repudiating the outcome of the Civil War. Others were isolationists who wanted to avoid involvement in the strategic rivalries of the western Pacific, or nativists and racists who didn't want Filipinos in the American electorate or labor force. Many of the anti-imperialists were simply Democrats who wanted to embarrass a Republican administration.

Whatever their motives may have been, they were a powerful political force. They came within two votes of defeating the peace treaty with Spain. A week after that, on February 14, 1899, they produced a tie vote in the Senate on the Bacon Resolution, which would have promised Filipinos full independence as soon as they could establish a stable government of their own. The Bacon Resolution was defeated only by the tie-breaking vote of the Vice President. . . .

By the summer of 1900, two-thirds of the United States Army was engaged in the Philippines. The war there was proving costly both in lives and money, disgraceful in the atrocities committed by Americans, shocking as evidence of the intensity of Filipino opposition. It was impossible to ignore the reality that tens of thousands of Filipinos were prepared to die rather than be annexed to the United States. This took the bloom off the idea of territorial imperialism for many Americans whose original approach to the question had been romantic, idealized, or even simply casual.

Then, too, there was the international context. While the United States was bogged down in the Philippines, the British were similarly mired fighting the Boers in South Africa. Africa had just been divided among rival European empires; China seemed on the brink of a similar fate. War scares and alliance-mongering were in the air. This led many people on both sides of the Atlantic to re-examine imperialism. The result was a new form of anti-imperialism more sophisticated than that of the moralists and idealists, more comprehensive than that of the nativists and isolationists.

The classic intellectual formulation of this new anti-imperialism was John A. Hobson's *Imperialism: A Study,* published in 1902. An English "radical" economist, profoundly humanistic in his values, Hobson argued that the many groups that either benefited or thought they would benefit from imperialism were really only pawns of the world's finance capitalists. Having spoiled their own domestic markets by taking too large a share of corporate earnings for profits and reinvestment at the expense of wages, these investors were driven to use the power of the state to open safe, attractive new investment opportunities abroad.

Hobson's ideas—though not his great book, which caught on slowly in the United States—were well known in early twentieth-century America, even by arch-imperialists such as Henry Cabot Lodge. For most people who knew them, they too compromised the imperial pretension unfolding in the Pacific. They complemented and helped to shape a new moral critique of imperialism arising from the progressive reform movement in America.

Yet there were still many Americans who wanted not only to defeat the Philippine "insurrection" but also to establish a permanent and formal empire in the islands for the economic and strategic advantage of the United States and, conceivably, the benefit of the Filipino people. The cleverest tacticians among these remaining imperialists realized that they could retain the Philippines only if they defused the political opposition of Filipinos to American rule. In order to neutralize the political threat to imperialism at home in America, Filipinos had not only to be conquered but converted. This was the origin of what William Howard Taft called the policy of "attraction."

Attraction began as a tactic for pacification. Originally the carrot to offset the stick of military repression, it eventually superseded the military approach altogether as the principal American strategy for dealing with the Filipino people.

The policy grew out of the experience of the Schurman Commission, a body composed of three civilians (including Dean C. Worcester) and the ranking military and naval officers in the islands. Ordered by President McKinley in 1899 to gather information about the islands and to recommend policy, the commissioners held public hearings in Manila to solicit informed opinions. Because fighting was already in progress, however, the sampling of opinion that could be obtained in this way was highly unrepresentative: only persons inside American lines could appear to testify. What the commissioners heard, therefore, was primarily the opinion of conservative

Westernized Filipinos, many of whom resented Aguinaldo's new prominence and feared that the revolutions against Spain and America might lead to social and economic agitation against their own interests.

Taken at face value, their testimony suggested the existence of a widespread desire in the Philippines for order, reform, and modernization—a secularized government, for example, more infrastructure, improved public education, guaranteed personal liberties, steps to encourage economic growth. This was a gratifying discovery for the Americans, because it implied that the interests shared by Americans and Filipinos might be more important than those which divided them. "The very thing they yearn for is what of all others our Government will naturally desire to give them," the commissioners concluded in their report.

As the Philippine-American war continued, the views of the Manila elite gained adherents in the countryside, as well. . . . Provincial elites, who had once dreamed of dominating the revolution, found themselves instead caught in a cross fire between the United States Army and local guerrilla groups. So did many peasants. Reluctantly, growing numbers of people concluded that since the Americans could not be driven away, collaboration with them for agreed ends was preferable to a continuation of the fighting.

In this way, a structure of accommodation, or collaboration, emerged, linking the American government and the Filipino elite. The Americans needed the elite to mediate with the mass of the people; the elite needed the Americans to impose order and restore their leadership of society. By cooperating, each could achieve what neither could bring about alone.

The architects of the collaborative empire were William Howard Taft, on the American side, and a group of the Filipino elite who founded the Partido Federal late in 1900. Taft, the first civil governor of the islands, led a new commission to the Philippines earlier that year. Originally functioning as both the legislature and the executive, the commission took over the government of the archipelago province by province, as the Army progressed with pacification. It needed safe, talented, cooperative Filipinos through whom to work.

Active participation by Filipinos in their own government was a cornerstone of the policy of attraction. Over the years, the personnel changed, but the progress of political devolution continued. In 1907, only five years after the formal end of the Philippine-American war, an elected assembly was inaugurated. Nine years later, the Jones Act promised eventual independence at some unspecified date in the future. Although these developments moved faster and sacrificed more control than Taft and his colleagues had originally intended, they did disarm opposition to short-term American sovereignty. During the administration of Woodrow Wilson and his governor-general, Francis Burton Harrison, prominent Filipino politicians actually intrigued behind the scenes to slow the juggernaut of independence, lest the American military and economic presence be withdrawn too quickly.

Beyond this, the cement of collaboration was a number of shared interests in development and reform. Building upon the testimony before the Schurman Commission, the Americans inaugurated popular programs to modernize and extend public education, secularize the state, build roads and other infrastructure, and secure preferential access to the American market as a stimulus to Philippine agriculture. Many of these programs have since come under serious criticism: education for being irrelevant and denaturalizing, free trade for distorting the Philippine economy and making it dependent upon the United States. At the time, however, they won gratitude and support from most of the Filipino people, as evidence of American good faith.

The result was, in many respects, a success. Americans gained a governable colony that was never again an issue, let alone an embarrassment, in domestic politics; Filipinos achieved substantial control of their own development; numerous useful projects were undertaken cooperatively; and, not the least of accomplishments in a colonial relationship, both sides were spared the agonies of large-scale political violence. Between roughly 1906 and 1941, there was only one large-scale revolutionary outbreak, and that was directed against Filipino political and economic leaders more than Americans. As the original generation of American imperialists passed from power, even formal independence ceased to be an issue between the two peoples.

An internally autonomous commonwealth was established in 1935 (it could have come several years earlier but for bickering among Filipino politicians as to who should get the credit); and complete independence followed in 1946, making the Philippines the first major Western colony to reclaim its sovereignty. A tactical gamble initiated to pacify and retain the islands had, in practice, paved the way to national freedom.

But there was a hidden price for all of this. America's reliance upon collaboration and suasion to maintain its insular empire made the collaborators a privileged group. Positioning themselves between the two real loci of power and authority in the islands, the American government and the mass of the Filipino people, they became indispensable mediators. Since the only credible collaborators—the only people with the authority, outlook, and education necessary both to deal with the Americans and to deliver the allegiance of the people—were the members of the established elite, the imperialism of suasion thus became a bulwark of class interest.

Within the government, elite collaborators used their offices to frustrate Americans' occasional attempts to move beyond nation-building programs to a kind of reform that would have redistributed wealth and power. Outside, in the political life of the people, they used their role as spokesmen of the nation to identify themselves with popular issues such as nationalism and independence. . . . Campaigning for independence and running against imperialism were easy ways for the elite of the islands to rally public support without having to address issues of social or economic equity that might have compromised their own interests.

Moreover, the elite said, the "discipline of the independence movement" required solidarity behind the nation's leaders. In this way, issues that were legitimate but remote from the daily lives of most Filipinos were manipulated as symbols to purge politics of its social and economic content.

Behind the facade of liberal devolution and developmental benevolence, America thus became a dual sanction for elite rule in its Philippine colony— buttress and target simultaneously. While protecting and institutionalizing the power of the Filipino elite, Americans also allowed themselves to be used as an external device for deflecting criticism of their regime. This led to a surrender of initiative and an evasion of responsibility by the United States without actually ending American intervention in Philippine life. The result compromised everyone involved, corrupting and vitiating Philippine public life, setting back many of the causes to which one side or the other was ostensibly committed, making a mockery of nationalism, and defining Philippine-American relations as an exercise in illusion. "Damn the Americans," said Manuel Quezon, Sergio Osmeña's successor as leader of the Nacionalista party and chief tactician of independence, "why don't they tyrannize us more?"

Teaching Panama to Behave

WALTER LaFEBER

The 1898 war introduced the United States as a great world power. Specifically, the conflict made the nation supreme in the Caribbean region. The country emerged from "the splendid little war," as Secretary of State John Hay aptly called it, with Cuba, Puerto Rico, a great (if little tested) fleet, and British recognition that the days of the Clayton-Bulwer treaty* were numbered. The cry for a canal intensified. Brooks Adams, John Quincy Adams's brilliant if eccentric grandson, and close friend of arch-expansionists Theodore Roosevelt and Senator Henry Cabot Lodge, had prophesied North American "economic supremacy" in world markets. The apparent fulfillment of that prophecy after 1898, Adams bragged, "knocked the stuffing out of me." "America has been irresistibly impelled to produce a large industrial surplus," he argued. "The expansion of any country must depend on the markets for its surplus product." Since "China is the only region which now provides almost boundless possibilities of absorption," an isthmian canal "to the Pacific must be built."

President William McKinley was equally direct in his Annual Message of December 1898. A canal, McKinley observed, was "demanded by the annexation of the Hawaiian Islands and the prospective expansion of our influence and commerce in the Pacific." He emphasized the waterway must be controlled by the United States. Brooks Adams and other acute observers believed Great Britain actually had little choice but to become the junior partner in an Anglo-Saxon empire. Not only did United States power appear awesome, but the London government was increasingly preoccupied with a rising Germany and a rebellion in South Africa where the Boer farmers were unexpectedly humiliating British troops.

With Great Britain busy elsewhere, in 1900 the United States Senate considered a bill that would build a Nicaraguan canal without regard for the

Excerpted from *The Panama Canal: The Crisis in Historical Perspective* by Walter LaFeber. Copyright © 1978 by Scott LaFeber. Used by permission of Oxford University Press, Inc.

* This 1850 treaty between the United States and Great Britain stipulated neither country would ever exercise exclusive control over a projected Isthmian passageway.

Clayton-Bulwer treaty. That threat prodded British officials to negotiate with Secretary of State Hay (a noted Anglophile), to work out an alternative. Hay finally agreed with British Ambassador Lord Pauncefote that under a new treaty the United States could build and control a canal, but would not fortify it. The Senate rebelled against the non-fortification pledge, as did a hero of the 1898 war, a self-proclaimed expansionist, and Republican candidate for Vice-President of the United States in 1900, Theodore Roosevelt. Though a close friend of Hay, Roosevelt warned that a fresh treaty was necessary. . . . The agreement directly abrogated the 1850 pact and implicitly gave the United States the sole right to fortify a canal. The treaty was negotiated during the weeks that President William McKinley, who had been shot, lingered near death, and then passed away. The White House was now in the hands of that "wild man," as one of McKinley's advisers called Theodore Roosevelt.

The only remaining question concerned the location of the passageway. Since the 1870s most knowledgeable observers had assumed the site would be Nicaragua. In 1901 the Walker Commission, a group of engineers named by McKinley to examine the prospects for a canal, also reported favorably on the Nicaraguan route. . . . But the Walker Commission, . . . believing the Nicaragua river system too shallow for a large canal, agreed with most engineers (and Theodore Roosevelt) that the Panama route was preferable, especially since de Lesseps had completed part of the work on the Isthmus. The Commission nevertheless concluded that building the canal in Panama would be considerably more expensive than the Nicaraguan route, for the New Panama Canal Company—a group of Frenchmen [led by Phillipe Bunau-Varilla] who had bought out the ruined de Lesseps company— was asking $109 million for its assets and concessionary rights to build in Panama. . . .

[The threat of losing its contract] convinced the anxious New Panama Canal Company in Paris to drop its price from $109 million to $40 million, thereby making the Panama route less expensive than the Nicaraguan. The Walker Commission now recommended Panama to the Senate as the better buy. . . .

[The U.S. Senate] instructed President Roosevelt to buy the Canal Company's claims for $40 million and build the passageway in Panama if he could obtain a treaty from Colombia. If he failed, Roosevelt was to deal with Nicaragua. . . .

Happily following instructions, Roosevelt and Hay opened negotiations with Colombia. In January 1903, after a good deal of arm-twisting, Hay convinced the Colombian ambassador in Washington to sign a treaty that gave the United States a 99-year lease on a six-mile-wide canal zone. In return, the United States would pay Colombia $10 million plus an annual payment of $250,000. The United States Senate ratified the pact, but in August 1903 the Colombian Senate not only rejected it, but did so unanimously. The Bogotá government . . . feared the loss of sovereignty in Panama to the powerful North Americans, and believed itself entitled to a larger sum, particularly since the United States–owned isthmian railroad had earned millions in profits of which Colombia received nothing. Left unsaid was that the Colombians hoped to stall until October 1904 when the Canal Company's rights would expire. Colombia could then collect all of the $40 million ticketed for Bunau-Varilla's . . . organization.

Roosevelt was livid. During the next several months he exhausted his rich vocabulary, calling the Colombians everything from "inefficient bandits" to "a corrupt pithecoid community." . . . In August 1903 the Secretary of State wondered whether he should turn to deal with Nicaragua or instead begin "the far more difficult and multifurcate scheme of building the Panama Canal *malgré* Bogotá."

Roosevelt's mind began to move in the same direction. He would be "delighted" if Panama became independent, TR wrote a friend in October. . . . "Whatever other governments can do, the United States cannot go into securing by such underhand means, the secession." As usual, he worked more directly. Roosevelt began drafting a message to Congress suggesting that the simpler method would be to send the navy to seize the Isthmus.

Roosevelt never sent that particular message, for Panamanian nationalists had long been awaiting such an opportunity. These nationalists, contrary to North American myths too long propagated in textbooks, did not suddenly spring up full-grown at Roosevelt's command. The belief that Panama should exist as a separate, independent country was neither artificially created suddenly in 1903 nor propagated in Washington before it took hold in Panama City. The Panamanian nationalism of 1902–03 formed only one part of an ancient story, although, as it turned out, the most important chapter. . . .

After Colombia declared its independence from Spain in 1821, it was never able to control Panama completely. In part this failure was due to the type of person the Isthmus attracted—the rootless, lawless, transient who obeyed no authority. This element remained in Panama, as a later observer noted, becoming "a community of gamblers, jockeys, boxers, and cockfighters." At the other end of the social spectrum a small propertied elite—an "oligarchy"—developed that resembled the North American elite of 1776; both developed valuable economic and political interests apart from the mother country, and neither saw any reason to share their wealth with colonizers. Colombia, moreover, was separated from the Isthmus as the United States was from England. The mountains and jungles in eastern Panama that bordered Colombia were so dense that in 1903 North Americans could reach Panama more easily and quickly by steamer than Colombians could by horse. . . .

Separated from the supposed mother country, holding a mobile, rebellious, independent population, Panama never developed the quasi-feudal, mercantilist characteristics of neighboring Latin American nations. Movement and trade were freer, liberalism seemed more natural. The land-owning oligarchs notably profited from such laissez-faire sentiment, but it also shaped the thought of most politically active Panamanians. They were individualistic, nationalistic, and ripe for revolt. . . .

Colombia's claim [to control over Panama] had been proven wrong throughout the nineteenth century. Indeed the Bogotá government itself had admitted failure. At least four times . . . between 1846 and 1903 Colombia asked the United States to restore order on the Isthmus. The settlement of the Thousand Days' War aboard a United States warship in November 1902 was only the last in a long line of North American interventions into affairs between Colombia and its raucous, hell-bent-for-independence province. A distinguished Panamanian diplomat later remarked that his country emerged as an independent nation because of its geography, economy, history, and "the interest and the sentiments of the people of Panama"—not "the arbitrariness of Theodore Roosevelt." . . .

That was one important lesson to be drawn from four hundred years of Panamanian experience. There were others. Panama's prosperity historically depended on traffic through the Isthmus. . . . Without vast arable lands or mineral wealth, the people's fortunes rose and fell with the use outsiders made of the major resource—geographical location. The Panamanians have been historically conditioned to think of this as the key to their welfare. That perception has been sharpened by the nationalist, anti-imperialist ideology that began to take hold in the mid-nineteenth century. In the end, Colombia could not control a nationalism that was rooted in the historical memory of four centuries and expressed in the demands of a revolutionary elite. . . .

With an isthmian canal virtually within his grasp, Roosevelt refused to allow those "contemptible little creatures" in Colombia to frustrate his grand plan. But TR could not decide how to deal with the Colombians. He apparently held little hope the deadlock would be broken by a successful Panamanian revolt. As the President searched desperately for alternatives, Bunau-Varilla and the Panamanian nationalists were devising a solution. That solution, together with a 1904 agreement negotiated between Washington and Panama City by Secretary of War William Howard Taft, created the framework for sixty years of relations between the two countries and shaped the crisis of the 1970s.

[Frenchman] Bunau-Varilla, with considerable help from top State Department officials, took the lead in solving Roosevelt's dilemma. During September and October 1903, [he] held a series of talks with Hay, Assistant Secretary of State Francis B. Loomis (whom Bunau-Varilla had known since a meeting in Paris two years before), and John Bassett Moore, a former Assistant Secretary of State. . . . Out of the conversations grew Bunau-Varilla's conviction that if the Panamanians tried to declare their independence the United States would use force, ostensibly to uphold its 1846 commitment to maintain transit rights across the Isthmus, but in reality to prevent Colombia from quashing the revolution. . . .

Plans again moved forward on the Isthmus. The revolutionaries comprised an odd but not illogical assortment, for a number of them had one association in common. Other than Amador (the Panama Railroad's physician), the group included José Agustín Arango (the railway's attorney), James R. Shaler (superintendent of the railway), and James R. Beers (the railway's freight agent). It might have been Beers who first assured Arango that a Panamanian revolt would be supported by the United States. Amador and Arango were joined by the oligarchy's leaders: C. C. Arosemena,

Ricardo Arias, Federico Boyd, and Tomás Arias. Once free of Colombian control—once they could develop their already extensive economic and political power according to their own interests and without concern for Bogotá—these oligarchs, their sons, and grandsons dominated Panama for sixty years. The motives varied, but for good reasons the railway officials and the Panamanian nationalists remained closely allied. As Roosevelt understood, "You don't have to foment a revolution. All you have to do is take your foot off and one will occur." . . .

The junta was preparing to provide the leadership, but the timing would be crucial. Closely following ship movements in the newspapers, Bunau-Varilla learned on October 30 that the *Nashville* was leaving Jamaica for an unspecified port. He correctly guessed it was heading for Colon and would arrive in two or three days. . . .

Bunau-Varilla wired this news to Amador, who had returned to the Isthmus to lead the revolt. Both men now believed the United States was moving into a position to support their revolution. . . .

Late that day the Panamanians struck, quickly seizing control of the Isthmus. The governor appointed by Colombia to rule the province, José Domingo de Obaldía, had long been sympathetic to Panamanian autonomy and gladly joined the revolutionaries. For his understanding he became one of Panama's first Vice-Presidents. Colombian army detachments were apparently bought off by Cromwell and the New Panama Canal Company; the commander received $30,000, other officers $10,000, and rank-and-file $50 each in gold.

Commander Hubbard aboard the *Nashville* received no orders regarding the uprising until late on November 2. Roosevelt and Loomis apparently did not trust the navy with their plans. Thus when 2500 Colombian soldiers appeared off Colon on November 2 to prevent the rumored revolution, a confused Hubbard allowed them to land. . . . The next day U.S. sailors finally landed to ensure that the Colombian troops behaved. An independent Panama had already been proclaimed by Amador. A new nation the size of South Carolina was born, and the labor pains had been easy. None of the belligerents was killed. The only deaths were a Chinese citizen who had gotten trapped in some desultory shelling, a dog, and, according to some reports, a donkey.

Roosevelt justified his aid to the revolutionaries by citing the 1846 commitment, a justification that had no legal or historical basis. The treaty certainly did not give the United States the right to use force against Colombia, with whom the pact had been made, in order to build a canal. Nor did it require Colombia to allow a canal to be constructed. The treaty indeed justified United States intervention in order to preserve Colombia's sovereignty on the Isthmus. TR intervened, however, to destroy that sovereignty. . . .

The President later argued that the seizure had been for the sake of "civilization," thereby adopting the proposition that since North American actions were justified morally they were justified legally. . . . Soon Roosevelt began a campaign, backed by force, to compel Latin American governments to uphold their own legal obligations as he defined those obligations.

In one sense, TR acted quite uncharacteristically: he aided a revolution. For a man whose central political tenet was stability, and for a nation that had fought revolutionaries and secessionists at least since 1861, unleashing revolution marked an abrupt change. It was also a short-lived change. Roosevelt possessed his canal territory and recognized the new Panamanian government led by Amador, Pablo Arosemena, and Obaldía on November 6. But when the Panamanian army attempted to land at Colon to claim the city, TR stopped it. A little revolution was sufficient. Washington needed time to sort things out. The Panamanian government would have to wait a while before its army could enter the country's second largest city. In the first moments after recognition, Panama and the United States were at loggerheads.

Nor did Roosevelt try to reconcile the Colombians. On November 6 he told them he had intervened because "treaty obligations" and the "interest of civilization" required that the Isthmus not endure "a constant succession of . . . wasteful civil wars." TR urged Bogotá to recognize the new government. . . . As Roosevelt later noted, he viewed Colombians as similar to "a group of Sicilian or Calabrian bandits. . . . You could no more make an agreement with the Colombian rulers than you could nail currant jelly to a wall." . . .

The new government . . . instructed the Frenchman that the negotiations were to be guided by three principles. First, no deals could be made that affected "the sovereignty of Panama, which [was] free, independent, and sovereign." Second, the United States should pledge to uphold the new nation's "sovereignty, territorial integrity, and public order." That clause would place North American troops, if necessary, between Panama and a vengeful Colombia. Third, a canal treaty would be drafted, but only after consultation with Amador and Boyd. "You will proceed in everything strictly in agreement with them," the Frenchman was told.

The instructions did not reach Bunau-Varilla in time, nor did Amador and Boyd. The minister made certain of that. On Friday the 13th of November he began talks with Roosevelt and Hay. Bunau-Varilla emphasized that time was all-important. If the treaty was not rushed to completion, he argued, a number of events would occur, all of them bad: a restless United States Senate . . . might turn back to Nicaragua; Colombia might seduce Panama back into the fold (the suave Reyes was on his way to Panama City); and isthmian politics might turn chaotic, forcing delays in the talks. . . .

Heartily sharing the Frenchman's mistrust of the Senate, Hay quickly prepared a treaty draft. It was largely the Hay-Herrán agreement that Colombia had rejected. The draft explicitly recognized Panamanian sovereignty in a canal zone, and even went further than the Hay-Herrán agreement by increasing Panama's judicial authority in a zone. Panamanian troops would protect the canal, and United States forces would be used in the area only with Panama's consent. The proposed treaty would run 99 years, or until about 2002.

Then, in what proved to be one of the most momentous twenty-four-hour periods in American diplomatic history, Bunau-Varilla worked all night and all day on November 16 to rewrite Hay's paper. The minister was afraid that the draft would not sufficiently appease the Senate, at least not enough to have the body act quickly on the treaty. Bunau-Varilla also wanted to complete the treaty before Amador and Boyd arrived. . . . On November 17, Bunau-Varilla told the two Panamanians to remain in New York for another day, then rushed to the State Department to consummate the deal.

Hay could hardly believe his eyes. Bunau-Varilla's treaty ensured the canal's neutrality, proposed payment to Panama of an amount equal to that which the United States would have paid Colombia, and guaranteed Washington's protection of Panama's independence. The United States was to assume a virtual protectorate over the new country. But in return, the treaty gave the United States extensive powers in the Canal Zone, for Washington would have "all the rights, power, and authority within the zone . . . which the United States would possess and exercise if it were the sovereign of the territory within which said lands and waters are located to the entire exclusion of the exercise by the Republic of Panama of any such sovereign rights, power, and authority."

That was the most radical change, a change that has caused continual crises in U.S.-Panamanian relations for the next three-quarters of a century. But there was more. Bunau-Varilla surrendered Panamanian judicial power in the Zone, widened the zone area from ten kilometers (or six miles) to ten miles, and lengthened Hay's 99-year lease to "perpetuity." . . .

The Panamanian government angrily protested "the manifest renunciation of sovereignty" in the treaty. That protest echoed down through the years, becoming ever more magnified. If the new government rejected the pact, however, it faced bitter alternatives: the United States might seize the canal area without either paying for it or undertaking to protect the new republic, or Roosevelt might build in Nicaragua and leave the Panama City revolutionaries to the tender mercies of the Colombian army. In truth, the Panamanians had no choice. . . .

. . . Having a French citizen disobey the Panamanian government's instructions, and then having no choice but to accept the Frenchmen's treaty, compounded the humiliation. In the 1970s a documentary film made in Panama about the 1903 affair was entitled, "The Treaty that No Panamanian Signed." . . .

. . . A surprising number of Senators and important newspapers condemned TR's action. The division was partially along party lines. William Randolph Hearst's Democratic papers attacked the President's action as "nefarious." Hearst's Chicago *American* called it "a rough-riding assault upon another republic over the shattered wreckage of international law and diplomatic usage." Such widely circulated urban dailies as the *New York Times*, New York *Evening Post*, Philadelphia *Record*, Memphis *Commercial Appeal*, and *Springfield Republican* agreed with Hearst's assessment. . . .

Even the newspapers and public spokesmen who supported TR refused to justify his action on moral grounds. Instead, as *Public Opinion* noted, since the majority of the country wanted "an isthmian canal above all things," it was willing to overlook moral issues in order to justify taking the canal as strictly "a business question."

Roosevelt refused to take that approach. As have most rulers who aggressively used naked force, he wanted it masked with morality. In an outspoken special message to the Senate on January 4, 1904, the President submitted the treaty and justified his actions in November on the grounds of the 1846 pact, "our national interests and safety," and the usual Rooseveltian claim of "the interests of collective civilization." He suffered no doubts that the United States had "received a mandate from civilization" to build a canal, although he could not tell exactly how that mandate had been expressed. One problem, of course, was that "the interests of collective civilization" had never been seen or defined (was Colombia, for example, a part of "collective civilization"?). . . .

After early 1904, politicians who opposed United States control of the canal were committing political suicide. Bunau-Varilla had triumphed. Although, as the *Pittsburgh Post* remarked, TR's methods in Panama "were subversive of the best principles of the republic," the Frenchman had made the treaty so attractive that the United States, as he hoped, quickly chose power over principle. . . .

. . . The Panamanians immediately began protesting the mushrooming North American control over their country. A first clash occurred in early 1904 when the State Department insisted that Panama must acknowledge in its new constitution (and not merely in the treaty), the United States right of intervention. William Buchanan, the U.S. Minister, wanted the widest possible power to control "pests" through Panama, and brought great presssure to bear on the Panamanian constitutional convention. Finally, Article 136 gave the United States the right to "intervene, in any part of Panama, to reestablish public peace and constitutional order." The North Americans could apparently unilaterally determine when public peace and order were jeopardized. . . .

Article III of the treaty, however, has most disrupted relations. It gave the United States the rights, powers, and authority in the zone "as if it were the sovereign of the territory." From the outset Panama argued that it remained the actual sovereign in the area. Bunau-Varilla agreed, perhaps out of conscience. "The United States, without becoming the sovereign, received the exclusive use of the rights of sovereignty," the Frenchman wrote, "while respecting the sovereignty itself of the Panama Republic." . . .

The United States wanted to compromise none of the vast powers Bunau-Varilla wrote into Article III. Attempting to placate the Panamanians while retaining all the power, in 1904 John Hay coined the phrase "titular sovereignty" to describe Panama's rights in a canal zone, . . . but on October 18, 1904, Roosevelt recognized the limitations of United States rights in the canal area when he instructed Secretary of War William Howard Taft:

We have not the slightest intention of establishing an independent colony in the middle of the State of Panama, or exercising any greater governmental functions than are necessary to enable us conveniently and safely to construct, maintain and operate the canal, under the rights given us by the treaty. Least of all do we desire to interfere wih the business and prosperity of the people of Panama. . . .

Roosevelt's term, "the equivalent of sovereignty," and the limitations placed upon United States power before and after the phrase, indicated that the President interpreted his nation's right in the Canal Zone to be short of sovereignty itself. . . .

The provisions [of the canal treaty] made Panama a potential colony of the United States. Article II—giving Washington officials the right "in perpetuity" to occupy and control any lands outside the Zone which, in their own opinion, they needed—was a virtual blank check. The cost of the lands would be determined by a joint U.S.-Panamanian commission, but under no circumstances could it delay canal construction while deliberating. The North Americans seized large chunks of Panamanian territory. Numerous requests for additional land were made between 1908 and 1930. Fourteen military bases were ultimately established, ostensibly to protect the Canal although some were for purposes outside Panama; several of the bases occupied land outside the Zone. Panamanian protests grew with the development of the military complex, particularly when United States–owned land later prevented orderly growth of Panama City and Colon. . . .

In a country possessing little experience in democratic politics, but of which democratic procedures were somehow expected, the United States placed an elite white oligarchy firmly in control. Washington officials helped create the conditions for an economically bipolarized, undemocratic, and potentially unstable country. When Panama later appeared as bipolarized, undemocratic, and unstable, North Americans could not understand why. . . .

TR's policy was the logical continuation of a century-long North American involvement that was turning Washington into a self-appointed policeman in the Caribbean. Since the eighteenth century the United States had been driving southward, first to conquer a continent, then, after the Civil War, to seize economic and strategic prizes. Its financial power increasingly penetrated the Caribbean area after the 1870s. Victory in the War of 1898 brought Puerto Rico and the Cuban naval base of Guantanamo. The Caribbean was becoming a North American lake, and obtaining the Canal Zone marked one more step in that direction.

Within a year after construction of the Canal began, however, Roosevelt announced a new policy, the so-called Roosevelt Corollary to the Monroe Doctrine. In his Annual Messages to Congress in 1904 and 1905, the President hoped that Latin American nations would be happy and prosperous, but he believed they could not share such joys "unless they maintain order within their boundaries and behave with a just regard for their obligations towards outsiders." To help them, the United States would become the policeman throughout the area. . . . The policeman, TR proclaimed, would ensure that the countries met their "obligations," so the "outsiders" would have no excuse to intervene. The "outsider" most feared in Washington was

Germany, whose businessmen, diplomats, and naval officers seemed overly ambitious in the Western Hemisphere. . . .

The Roosevelt Corollary triggered the most ignoble chapter in United States–Latin American relations. Believing, as TR said, that "a civilized nation" such as the United States possessed the right to stop "chronic wrongdoing," North Americans sent troops into a half-dozen Caribbean nations during the next twelve years, and within two decades dominated at least fourteen of the twenty Latin American countries through either financial controls or military power—and, in some instances, through both.

Officials at the time argued that the Roosevelt Corollary was necessary to protect the new canal. As John Hay's successor in the State Department, Elihu Root, wrote a friend in 1905, "The inevitable effect of our building the Canal must be to require us to police the surrounding premises." It became an early version of the domino theory: if unfriendly, powerful Europeans settled in one part of the Caribbean, their influence could spread until the Canal would be endangered.

Root's explanation of the Roosevelt Corollary cannot withstand historical analysis. That the Canal increased United States interest in the Caribbean cannot be disputed. But the Corollary's principles were formed long before the Isthmus was seized—as early as the 1870s, 1880s, and 1890s, when such Washington officials as Ulysses S. Grant, "Jingo Jim" Blaine, and Richard Olney bluntly told Europeans that the Caribbean should be considered a North American lake. . . .

TR's inspiration to act as a "civilized" policeman occurred before the Canal Zone was seized, and quite independently of events on the Isthmus. In 1900–1901, for example, the United States imposed on Cuba the Platt Amendment, giving Washington the right to intervene any time at its discretion to maintain order in the newly independent island. The provision established a precedent and a rationale for the later Corollary. In 1902–03 Germany and Great Britain intervened in Venezuela to collect overdue debts. An uproar resulted in the United States, and the British shrewdly suggested to Roosevelt that if he did not want the Europeans to protect their legal rights in the Western Hemisphere, he should do it for them. Grumbling that "These wretched republics cause me a great deal of trouble," TR believed a second foreign intervention "would simply not be tolerated here. I often think that a sort of protectorate over South and Central America is the only way out."

His opportunity finally arose in Santo Domingo. For over five years New York City bankers had fought French and German financiers for control of the country's resources. By early 1904 Santo Domingo seemed to be moving toward a state of permanent revolutionary instability. Roosevelt ordered the navy to seize the country's customs houses, pay off the foreign debt, and under no circumstances allow any revolutionary activity to interrupt the country's development. He publicly rationalized the seizure by announcing the Roosevelt Corollary.

These affairs in Cuba, Venezuela, and Santo Domingo had little or nothing to do with the Isthmus. Taking the Canal Zone by no means led to the Roosevelt Corollary. Instead, Roosevelt's Panama policy can be interpreted as fitting into a larger Latin American policy that was evolving long before the Panamanian revolution. To confuse the Canal as the cause of the Corollary, therefore, is to confuse fundamental motivations of American foreign policy.

Two motives shaped Roosevelt's Corollary. First, he hated disorder, especially disorder that might lead to political bipolarization or an opportunity for European economic and/or political intervention. . . . A second motivation was Roosevelt's belief that the United States had been entrusted with a "civilizing" mission which it should bear proudly. This belief seemed particularly applicable to the Caribbean, including Panama, where the people were largely a mixture of Indian, Spanish, and black. This motivation, of course, had its ironies. As sociologist William Graham Sumner observed at the time, "We talk of civilizing lower races, but we have never done it yet. We have exterminated them." . . .

. . . Historical circumstances made [TR] President precisely at the point when the European-dominated world system, which he so admired, was disintegrating. In 1904–05 Japan's dramatic victory over Russia surprised the white races and encouraged non-whites, especially those who lived in Asian and African colonial areas. The Chinese, Turkish, and Russian revolutions formed roots in those years. Roosevelt prided himself on his understanding of historical change and his sensitivity to the nuances of a global balance of power, but he never comprehended the significance of these shattering events. TR was unable to see that the world was comprised of more than simply the "civilized" versus the "wicked and inefficient types."

After he intervened in Panama in 1903, Roosevelt painstakingly explained his actions to the Cabinet, then demanded to know whether the explanation would silence his opponents. "Have I defended myself?" he asked. "You certainly have," replied a brave Elihu Root. "You have shown that you were accused of seduction and you have conclusively proved that you were guilty of rape." Roosevelt never understood how his policies and explanations worsened the problems in the Caribbean area that he tried to stabilize. He, Taft, and Bunau-Varilla were making Panama as well as the Canal Zone a virtual colony of the United States, but the North American leaders refused to assume even the responsibilities of enlightened colonialism, save that of using force or the threat of force to maintain order. That solution worsened, not ameliorated, Panama's problem and, consequently, Panamanian relations with the United States.

ॐ *F U R T H E R   R E A D I N G*

Howard K. Beale, *Theodore Roosevelt and the Rise of America to World Power* (1956)
Robert L. Beisner, *Twelve Against Empire* (1968)
W. B. Gatewood, Jr., *Black Americans and the White Man's Burden* (1975)
David Healy, *Gunboat Diplomacy in the Wilson Era* (1976)
Michael Hunt, *Ideology and U.S. Foreign Policy* (1987)

Walter LaFeber, *Inevitable Revolutions: The United States in Central America* (1983)

———, *The New Empire* (1963)

———, *The Panama Canal* (1979)

———, *The Making of a Special Relationship: The United States and China to 1914* (1983)

Lester D. Langley, *The United States and the Caribbean in the Twentieth Century* (1982)

Ernest R. May, *American Imperialism* (1968)

James C. Thomson, Jr., Peter W. Stanley, and John C. Perry, *Sentimental Imperialists* (1981)

William A. Williams, *The Roots of the American Empire* (1969)

Marilyn Blatt Young, *The Rhetoric of Empire* (1968)

America and the Great War

The First World War captured in sharp relief both the material benefits and the social cost of America's Great Leap Forward since 1880. When the United States finally entered the war in 1917, the unsurpassed productive capacity and technical efficiency of the world's largest democracy was vividly on display. So was the lagging, but rapidly improving administrative capacity of its government. Yet it was the peculiarity of the United States' political culture—mixing devout moralism with narrow self-interest, social pluralism with coercive conformity—that faced the biggest challenge as U.S. leaders tried both to manage a nation at war and later, in victory, to contend with a larger world beyond their control.

❧ D O C U M E N T S

The two main arguments that brought the United States into the war and the key domestic issues triggered by a wartime mobilization are treated in the selections following. In the first and second documents, respectively, President Woodrow Wilson reluctantly declares war against Germany, and Senator Robert M. La Follette of Wisconsin unhesitatingly dissents. In the third document, George Creel, head of the Committee on Public Information, recalls the government's unprecedented effort to rally prowar opinion. The fourth selection bares the teeth behind the domestic mobilization for war, with tightened control of protest in the Espionage Act of 1918. The penalties—both legal and extralegal—for resistance were imposed on groups like the radical Industrial Workers of the World, or "Wobblies," whose report of a vigilante beating is the subject of the fifth document. The sixth document captures a dramatic, no less domestic effect of the war in a humorous exchange of verse. In the penultimate selection, skilled male machinists at a Vermont machine-tool company ridicule their newly recruited female workmates, and the women respond in kind. The final document presents President Wilson's Fourteen Points for world peace, the program that would become the controversial basis for a postwar world order.

President Woodrow Wilson's War Message, 1917

Gentlemen of the Congress: I have called the Congress into extraordinary session because there are serious, very serious choices of policy to be made, and made immediately, which it was neither right nor constitutionally permissible that I should assume the responsibility of making.

On the third of February last I officially laid before you the extraordinary announcement of the Imperial German Government that on and after the first day of February it was its purpose to put aside all restraints of law or of humanity and use its submarines to sink every vessel that sought to approach either the ports of Great Britain and Ireland or the western coasts of Europe or any of the ports controlled by the enemies of Germany within the Mediterranean. That had seemed to be the object of the German submarine warfare earlier in the war, but since April of last year the Imperial Government had somewhat restrained the commanders of its undersea craft in conformity with its promise then given to us that passenger boats should not be sunk and that due warning would be given to all other vessels which its submarines might seek to destroy, when no resistance was offered or escape attempted, and care taken that their crews were given at least a fair chance to save their lives in their open boats. The precautions taken were meager and haphazard enough, as was proved in distressing instance after instance in the progress of the cruel and unmanly business, but a certain degree of restraint was observed. The new policy has swept every restriction aside. Vessels of every kind, whatever their flag, their character, their cargo, their destination, their errand, have been ruthlessly sent to the bottom without warning and without thought of help or mercy for those on board, the vessels of friendly neutrals along with those of belligerents. Even hospital ships and ships carrying relief to the sorely bereaved and stricken people of Belgium, though the latter were provided with safe conduct through the proscribed areas by the German Government itself and were distinguished by unmistakable marks of identity, have been sunk with the same reckless lack of compassion or of principle.

I was for a little while unable to believe that such things would in fact be done by any government that had hitherto subscribed to humane practices of civilized nations. International law had its origin in the attempt to set up some law which would be respected and observed upon the seas, where no nation had right of dominion and where lay the free highways of the world. By painful stage after stage has that law been built up, with meager enough results, indeed, after all was accomplished that could be accomplished, but always with a clear view, at least, of what the heart and conscience of mankind demanded. This minimum of right the German Government has swept aside, under the plea of retaliation and necessity and because it had no weapons which it could use at sea except these which it is impossible to employ as it is employing them without throwing to the wind all scruples of humanity or of respect for the understandings that were supposed to underlie the intercourse of the world. I am not now thinking of the loss of property involved, immense and serious as that is, but only of the wanton and wholesale destruction of the lives of non-combatants, men, women, and children, engaged in pursuits which have always, even in the darkest periods of modern history, been deemed innocent and legitimate. Property can be paid for; the lives of peaceful and innocent people cannot be. The present German submarine warfare against commerce is a warfare against mankind.

It is a war against all nations. American ships have been sunk, American lives taken, in ways which it has stirred us very deeply to learn of, but the ships and people of other neutral and friendly nations have been sunk and overwhelmed in the waters in the same way. There has been no discrimination. The challenge is to all mankind. Each nation must decide for itself how it will meet it. The choice we make for ourselves must be made with a moderation of counsel and a temperateness of judgment befitting our character and our motives as a nation. We must put excited feeling away. Our motive will not be revenge or the victorious assertion of the physical might of the nation, but only the vindication of right, of human right, of which we are only a single champion.

When I addressed the Congress on the twenty-sixth of February last I thought that it would suffice to assert our neutral rights with arms, our right to use the seas against unlawful interference, our right to keep our people safe against unlawful violence. But armed neutrality, it now appears, is impracticable. Because submarines are in effect outlaws when used as the German submarines have been used against merchant shipping, it is impossible to defend ships against their attacks as the law of nations has assumed that merchantmen would defend themselves against privateers or cruisers, visible craft giving chase upon the open sea. It is common prudence in such circumstances, grim necessity indeed, to endeavor to destroy them before they have shown their own intention. They must be dealt with upon sight, if dealt with at all. The German Government denies the right of neutrals to use arms at all within the areas of the sea which it has proscribed, even in the defense of rights which no modern publicist has ever before questioned their right to defend. The intimation is conveyed that the armed guards which we have placed on our merchant ships will be treated as beyond the pale of law and subject to be dealt with as pirates would be. Armed neutrality is ineffectual enough at best; in such circumstances and in the face of such pretensions it is worse than ineffectual; it is likely only to produce what it was meant to prevent; it is practically certain to draw us into the war without either the rights or the effectiveness of belligerents. There is one choice we cannot make, we are incapable of making; we will not choose the path of submission and suffer the most sacred rights of our nation and our people to be ignored or violated. The wrongs against which we now array ourselves are no common wrongs; they cut to the very roots of human life.

With a profound sense of the solemn and even tragical character of the step I am taking and of the grave responsibilities which it involves, but in unhesitating obedience to what I deem my constitutional duty, I advise that the Congress declare the recent course of the Imperial German Government to be in fact nothing less than war against the Government and people of the United States; that it formally accept the status of belligerent which has thus been thrust upon it; and that it take immediate steps not only to put the country in a more thorough state of defense, but also to exert all its power and employ all its resources to bring the Government of the German Empire to terms and end the war. . . .

While we do these things, these deeply momentous things, let us be very clear, and make very clear to all the world, what our motives and our objects are. My own thought has not been driven from its habitual and normal course by the unhappy events of the last two months, and I do not believe that the thought of the nation has been altered or clouded by them. I have exactly the same things in mind now that I had in mind when I addressed the Senate on the twenty-second of January last; the same that I had in mind when I addressed the Congress on the third of February and on the twenty-sixth of February. Our object now, as then, is to vindicate the principles of peace and justice in the life of the world as against selfish and autocratic power, and to set up among the really free and self-governed peoples of the world such a concert of purpose and of action as will henceforth ensure the observance of those principles. Neutrality is no longer feasible or desirable where the peace of the world is involved and the freedom of its peoples, and the menace to that peace and freedom lies in the existence of autocratic governments, backed by organized force which is controlled wholly by their will, not by the will of their people. We have seen the last of neutrality in such circumstances. We are at the beginning of an age in which it will be insisted that the same standards of conduct and of responsibility for wrong done shall be observed among nations and their governments that are observed among the individual citizens of civilized States.

We have no quarrel with the German people. We have no feeling towards them but one of sympathy and friendship. It was not upon their impulse that their government acted in entering this war. It was not with their previous knowledge or approval. It was a war determined upon as wars used to be determined upon in the old, unhappy days when peoples were nowhere consulted by their rulers and wars were provoked and waged in the interest of dynasties or of little groups of ambitious men who were accustomed to use their fellow-men as pawns and tools. . . .

We are accepting this challenge of hostile purpose because we know that in such a government, following such methods, we can never have a friend; and that in the presence of its organized power, always lying in wait to accomplish we know not what purpose, there can be no assured security for the democratic governments of the world. We are now about to accept the gauge of battle with this natural foe to liberty and shall, if necessary, spend the whole force of the nation to check and nullify its pretensions and its power. We are glad, now that we see the facts with no veil of false pretense about them, to fight thus for the ultimate peace of the world and for the liberation of its peoples, the German peoples included; for the rights of nations, great and small, and the privilege of men everywhere to choose their way of life and of obedience. The world must be made safe for democracy. Its peace must be planted upon the tested foundations of political liberty. We have no selfish ends to serve. We desire no conquest, no dominion. We seek no indemnities for ourselves, no material compensation for the sacrifices we shall freely make. We are but one of the champions of the rights of mankind. We shall be satisfied when those rights have been made as secure as the faith and the freedom of nations can make them. . . .

It is a distressing and oppressive duty, Gentlemen of the Congress, which I have performed in thus addressing you. There are, it may be, many months of fiery trial and sacrifice ahead of us. It is a fearful thing to lead this great peaceful people into war, into the most terrible and disastrous of all wars, civilization itself seeming to be in the balance. But the right is more precious than peace, and we shall fight for the things which we have always carried nearest our hearts—for democracy, for the right of those who submit to authority to have a voice in their own governments, for the rights and liberties of small nations, for a universal dominion of right by such a concert of free peoples as shall bring peace and safety to all nations and make the world itself at last free. To such a task we can dedicate our lives and our fortunes, everything that we are and everything that we have, with the pride of those who know that the day has come when America is privileged to spend her blood and her might for the principles that gave her birth and happiness and the peace which she has treasured. God helping her, she can do no other.

Senator Robert M. La Follette's Antiwar Dissent, 1917

The poor, sir, who are the ones called upon to rot in the trenches, have no organized power, have no press to voice their will upon this question of peace or war; but, oh, Mr. President, at some time they will be heard. I hope and I believe they will be heard in an orderly and a peaceful way. I think they may be heard from before long. I think, sir, if we take this step, when the people to-day who are staggering under the burden of supporting families at the present prices of the necessaries of the life find those prices multiplied, when they are raised a hundred percent, or 200 percent, as they will be quickly, aye, sir, when beyond that those who pay taxes come to have their taxes doubled and again doubled to pay the interest on the nontaxable bonds held by Morgan and his combinations, which have been issued to meet this war, there will come an awakening; they will have their day and they will be heard. It will be as certain and as inevitable as the return of the tides, and as resistless, too. . . .

Just a word of comment more upon one of the points in the President's address. He says that this is a war "for the things which we have always carried nearest to our hearts—for democracy, for the right of those who submit to authority to have a voice in their own government." In many places throughout the address is this exalted sentiment given expression.

It is a sentiment peculiarly calculated to appeal to American hearts and, when accompanied by acts consistent with it, is certain to receive our support; but in this same connection, and strangely enough, the President says that we have become convinced that the German Government as it now exists—"Prussian autocracy" he calls it—can never again maintain friendly relations with us. His expression is that "Prussian autocracy was not and could never be our friend," and repeatedly throughout the address the suggestion is made that if the German people would overturn their Government it would probably be the way to peace. So true is this that the dispatches from London all hailed the message of the President as sounding the death knell of Germany's Government.

But the President proposes alliance with Great Britain, which, however liberty-loving its people, is a hereditary monarchy, with a hereditary ruler, with a hereditary House of Lords, with a hereditary landed system, with a limited and restricted suffrage for one class and a multiplied suffrage power for another, and with grinding industrial conditions for all the wageworkers. The President has not suggested that we make our support of Great Britain conditional to her granting home rule to Ireland, or Egypt, or India. We rejoice in the establishment of a democracy in Russia, but it will hardly be contended that if Russia was still an autocratic Government, we would not be asked to enter this alliance with her just the same. Italy and the lesser powers of Europe, Japan in the Orient; in fact all of the countries with whom we are to enter into alliance, except France and newly revolutionized Russia, are still of the old order—and it will be generally conceded that no one of them has done as much for its people in the solution of municipal problems and in securing social and industrial reforms as Germany.

Is it not a remarkable democracy which leagues itself with allies already far overmatching in strength the German nation and holds out to such beleaguered nation the hope of peace only at the price of giving up their Government? I am not talking now of the merits or demerits of any government, but I am speaking of a profession of democracy that is linked in action with the most brutal and domineering use of autocratic power. Are the people of this country being so well represented in this war movement that we need to go abroad to give other people control of their governments? Will the President and the supporters of this war bill submit it to a vote of the people before the declaration of war goes into effect? Until we are willing to do that, it ill becomes us to offer as an excuse for our entry into the war the unsupported claim that this war was forced upon the German people by their Government "without their previous knowledge or approval."

Who has registered the knowledge or approval of the American people of the course this Congress is called upon in declaring war upon Germany? Submit the question to the people, you who support it. You who support it dare not do it, for you know that by a vote of more than ten to one the American people as a body would register their declaration against it.

In the sense that this war is being forced upon our people without their knowing why and without their approval, and that wars are usually forced upon all peoples in the same way, there is some truth in the statement; but I venture to say that the response which the German people have made to the demands of this war shows that it has a degree of popular support which the war upon which we are entering has not and never will have among our people. The espionage bills, the conscription bills, and other forcible military measures which we understand are being ground out of the war machine in this country is the complete proof that those responsible for this war fear that it has no popular support and that armies sufficient to satisfy the demand of the entente allies can not be recruited by voluntary enlistments.

George Creel on the Selling of the War, 1920

Back of the firing-line, back of armies and navies, back of the great supply-depots, another struggle waged with the same intensity and with almost equal significance attaching to its victories and defeats. It was the fight for the *minds* of men, for the "conquest of their convictions," and the battle-line ran through every home in every country. . . .

We strove for the maintenance of our own morale and the Allied morale by every process of stimulation; every possible expedient was employed to break through the barrage of lies that kept the people of the Central Powers in darkness and delusion; we sought the friendship and support of the neutral nations by continuous presentation of facts. We did not call it propaganda, for that word, in German hands, had come to be associated with deceit and corruption. Our effort was educational and informative throughout, for we had such confidence in our case as to feel that no other argument was needed than the simple, straightforward presentation of facts.

There was no part of the great war machinery that we did not touch, no medium of appeal that we did not employ. The printed word, the spoken word, the motion picture, the telegraph, the cable, the wireless, the poster, the sign-board—all these were used in our campaign to make our own people and all other peoples understand the causes that compelled America to take arms. All that was fine and ardent in the civilian population came at our call until more than one hundred and fifty thousand men and women were devoting highly specialized abilities to the work of the Committee, as faithful and devoted in their service as though they wore the khaki.

While America's summons was answered without question by the citizenship as a whole, it is to be remembered that during the three and a half years of our neutrality the land had been torn by a thousand divisive prejudices, stunned by the voices of anger and confusion, and muddled by the pull and haul of opposed interests. These were conditions that could not be permitted to endure. What we had to have was no mere surface unity, but a passionate belief in the justice of America's cause that should weld the people of the United States into one white-hot mass instinct with fraternity, devotion, courage, and deathless determination. The *war-will*, the will-to-win, of a democracy depends upon the degree to which each one of all the people of that democracy can concentrate and consecrate body and soul and spirit in the supreme effort of service and sacrifice. What had to be driven home was that all business was the nation's business, and every task a common task for a single purpose. . . .

. . . A speaking division toured great groups like the Blue Devils, Pershing's Veterans, and the Belgians, arranged mass-meetings in the communities, conducted forty-five war conferences from coast to coast, co-ordinated the entire speaking activities of the nation, and assured consideration to the crossroads hamlet as well as to the city.

The Four Minute Men, an organization that will live in history by reason of its originality and effectiveness, commanded the volunteer services of 75,000 speakers, operating in 5,200 communities, and making a total of 755,190 speeches, every one having the carry of shrapnel.

With the aid of a volunteer staff of several hundred translators, the Committee kept in direct touch with the foreign-language press, supplying selected articles designed to combat ignorance and disaffection. It organized and directed twenty-three societies and leagues designed to appeal to certain classes and particular foreign-language groups, each body carrying a specific message of unity and enthusiasm to its section of America's adopted peoples.

It planned war exhibits for the state fairs of the United States, also a great series of interallied war expositions that brought home to our millions the exact nature of the struggle that was being waged in France. In Chicago alone two million people attended in two weeks, and in nineteen cities the receipts aggregated $1,432,261.36.

The Committee mobilized the advertising forces of the country—press, periodical, car, and outdoor—for the patriotic campaign that gave millions of dollars' worth of free space to the national service.

It assembled the artists of America on a volunteer basis for the production of posters, window-cards, and similar material of pictorial publicity for the use of various government departments and patriotic societies. A total of 1,438 drawings was used.

It issued an official daily newspaper, serving every department of government, with a circulation of one hundred thousand copies a day. For official use only, its value was such that private citizens ignored the supposedly prohibitive subscription price, subscribing to the amount of $77,622.58.

It organized a bureau of information for all persons who sought direction in volunteer war-work, in acquiring knowledge of any administrative activities, or in approaching business dealings with the government. In the ten months of its existence it gave answers to eighty-six thousand requests for specific information.

It gathered together the leading novelists, essayists, and publicists of the land, and these men and women, without payment, worked faithfully in the production of brilliant, comprehensive articles that went to the press as syndicate features.

One division paid particular attention to the rural press and the plate-matter service. Others looked after the specialized needs of the labor press, the religious press, and the periodical press. The Division of Women's War Work prepared and issued the information of peculiar interest to the women of the United States, also aiding in the task of organizing and directing.

Through the medium of the motion picture, America's war progress, as well as the meanings and purposes of democracy, were carried to every community in the United States and to every corner of the world. "Pershing's Crusaders," "America's Answer," and "Under Four Flags" were types of feature films by which we drove home America's resources and determinations, while other pictures, showing our social and industrial life, made our free institutions vivid to foreign peoples. . . .

The U.S. Government Punishes War Protestors: The Espionage Act, 1918

Be it enacted by the Senate and House of Representatives of the United States of America in Congress assembled, That section three of title one of the Act entitled, "An Act to punish acts of interference with the foreign relations, the neutrality, and the foreign commerce of the United States, to punish espionage, and better to enforce the criminal laws of the United States, and for other purposes," approved June fifteenth, nineteen hundred and seventeen, be, and the same is hereby, amended so as to read as follows:

"SEC. 3. Whoever, when the United States is at war, shall willfully make or convey false reports or false statements with intent to interfere with the operation or success of the military or naval forces of the United States, or to promote the success of its enemies, or shall willfully make or convey false reports or false statements, or say or do anything except by way of bona fide and not disloyal advice to an investor or investors, with intent to obstruct the sale by the United States of bonds or other securities of the United States or the making of loans by or to the United States, and whoever, when the United States is at war, shall willfully cause or attempt to cause, or incite or attempt to incite, insubordination, disloyalty, mutiny, or refusal of duty, in the military or naval forces of the United States, or shall willfully obstruct or attempt to obstruct the recruiting or enlistment service of the United States, and whoever, when the United States is at war, shall willfully utter, print, write, or publish any disloyal, profane, scurrilous, or abusive language about the form of government of the United States, or the Constitution of the United States, or the military or naval forces of the United States, or the flag of the United States, or the uniform of the Army or Navy of the United States, or any language intended to bring the form of government of the United States, or the Constitution of the United States, or the military or naval forces of the United States, or the flag of the United States, or the uniform of the Army or Navy of the United States into contempt, scorn, contumely, or disrepute, or shall willfully utter, print, write, or publish any language intended to incite, provoke, or encourage resistance to the United States, or to promote the cause of its enemies, or shall willfully display the flag of any foreign enemy, or shall willfully by utterance, writing, printing, publication, or language spoken, urge, incite, or advocate any curtailment of production in this country of any thing or things, product or products, necessary or essential to the prosecution of the war in which the United States may be engaged, with intent by such curtailment to cripple or hinder the United States in the prosecution of the war, and whoever shall willfully advocate, teach, defend, or suggest the doing of any of the acts or things in this section enumerated, and whoever shall by word or act support or favor the cause of any country with which the United States is at war or by word or act oppose the cause of the United States therein, shall be punished by a fine of not more than $10,000 or imprisonment for not more than twenty years, or both. . . .

Title XII of the said Act of June fifteenth, nineteen hundred and seventeen, be, and the same is hereby, amended by adding thereto the following section:

"SEC. 4. When the United States is at war, the Postmaster General may, upon evidence satisfactory to him that any person or concern is using the mails in violation of any of the provisions of this Act, instruct the postmaster at any post office at which mail is received addressed to such person or concern to return to the postmaster at the office at which they were originally mailed all letters or other matter so addressed, with the words 'Mail to this address undeliverable under Espionage Act' plainly written or stamped upon the outside thereof, and all such letters or other matter so returned to such postmasters shall be by them returned to the senders thereof under such regulations as the Postmaster General may prescribe."

Approved, May 16, 1918.

A Wobbly Testifies to Vigilante Attack, 1917

"On the night of November 5, 1917, while sitting in the hall at No. 6 W. Brady Street, Tulsa, Okla. (the room leased and occupied by the Industrial Workers of the World, and used as a union meeting room), at about 8:45 P.M., five men entered the hall, to whom I at first paid no attention, as I was busy putting a monthly stamp in a member's union card book. After I had finished with the member, I walked back to where these five men had congregated at the baggage-room at the back of the hall, and spoke to them, asking if there was anything I could do for them.

"One who appeared to be the leader, answered 'No, we're just looking the place over.' Two of them went into the baggage-room flashing an electric flashlight around the room. The other three walked toward the front end of the hall. I stayed at the baggage-room door, and one of the men came out and followed the other three up to the front end of the hall. The one who stayed in the baggage-room asked me if I was 'afraid he would steal something.' I told him we were paying rent for the hall, and I did not think anyone had a right to search this place without a warrant. He replied that he did not give a damn if we were paying rent for four places, they would search them whenever they felt like it. Presently he came out and walked toward the front end of the hall, and I followed a few steps behind him.

"In the meantime the other men, who proved to be officers, appeared to be asking some of our members questions. Shortly after, the patrol-wagon came and all the members in the hall—10 men were ordered into the wagon. I turned out the light in the back end of the hall, closed the desk, put the key in the door and told the 'officer' to turn out the one light. We stepped out, and I locked the door, and at the request of the 'leader of the officers,' handed him the keys. He told me to get in the wagon, I being the 11th man taken from the hall, and we were taken to the police station. . . .

After some argument by both sides the cases were continued until the next night, November 8th, and the case against Gunnard Johnson, one of our men, was called. After four and a half hours' session the case was again adjourned until November 9th at 5 P.M., when we agreed to let the decision in Johnson's case stand for all of us. . . .

"Johnson said he had come into town Saturday, November 3d, to get his money from the Sinclair Oil & Gas Co. and could not get it until Monday, the 5th, and was shipping out Tuesday, the 6th, and that he had $7.08 when arrested. He was reprimanded by the judge for not having a Liberty Bond, and as near as anyone could judge from the closing remarks of Judge Evans, he was found guilty and fined $100 for not having a Liberty Bond.

"Our lawyer made a motion to appeal the case and the bonds were then fixed at $200 each. I was immediately arrested, *as were also five spectators in the open court-room,* for being I.W.W.'s. One arrested was not a member of ours, but a property-owner and citizen. I was searched and $30.87 taken from me, as also was the receipt for the $100 bond, and we then were all placed back in the cells.

"In about forty minutes, as near as we could judge about 11 P.M., the turnkey came and called 'Get ready to go out you I.W.W. men.' We dressed as rapidly as possible, were taken out of the cells, and the officer gave us back our possessions, Ingersoll watches, pocketknives and money, with the exception of $3 in silver of mine which they kept, giving me back $27.87. I handed the receipt for the $100 bond I had put up to the desk sergeant and he told me he did not know anything about it, and handed the receipt back to me, which I put in my trousers' pocket with the 87 cents. Twenty-seven dollars in bills was in my coat pocket. We were immediately ordered into automobiles waiting in the alley. Then we proceeded one block north to 1st Street, west one-half block to Boulder Street, north across the Frisco tracks and stopped.

"Then the masked mob came up and ordered everybody to throw up their hands. Just here I wish to state I never thought any man could reach so high as those policemen did. We were then bound, some with hands in front, some with hands behind, and others bound with arms hanging down their sides, the rope being wrapped around the body. Then the police were ordered to 'beat it,' which they did, running, and we started for the place of execution.

"When we arrived there, a company of gowned and masked gunmen were there to meet us standing at 'present arms.' We were ordered out of the autos, told to get in line in front of these gunmen and another bunch of men with automatics and pistols, lined up between us. Our hands were still held up, and those who were bound, in front. Then a masked man walked down the line and slashed the ropes that bound us, and we were ordered to strip to the waist, which we did, threw our clothes in front of us, in individual piles— coats, vests, hats, shirts and undershirts. The boys not having had time to distribute their possessions that were given back to them at the police stations, everything was in the coats, everything we owned in the world.

"Then the whipping began, a double piece of new rope, $\frac{5}{8}$ or $\frac{3}{4}$ hemp, being used. A man, 'the chief' of detectives, stopped the whipping of each man when he thought the victim had had enough. After each one was whipped another man applied the tar with a large brush, from the head to the seat. Then a brute smeared feathers over and rubbed them in.

"After they had satisfied themselves that our bodies were well abused, our clothing was thrown into a pile, gasoline poured on it and a match applied. By the light of our earthly possessions, we were ordered to leave Tulsa, and leave running and never come back. The night was dark, the road very rough, and as I was one of the last two that was whipped, tarred and feathered, and in the rear when ordered to run, I decided to be shot rather than stumble over the rough road. After going forty or fifty feet I stopped and went into the weeds. I told the man with me to get in the weeds also, as the shots were coming very close over us and ordered him to lie down flat. We expected to be killed, but after 150 or 200 shots were fired they got in their autos.

"After the last one had left, we went through a barbed-wire fence, across a field, called to the boys, collected them, counted up, and had all the 16 safe, though sore and nasty with tar. After wandering around the hills for some time—ages it seemed to me—we struck the railroad track. One man, Jack Sneed, remembered then that he knew a farmer in that vicinity, and he and J. F. Ryan volunteered to find the house. I built a fire to keep us from freezing.

"We stood around the fire expecting to be shot, as we did not know but what some tool of the commercial club had followed us. After a long time Sneed returned and called to us, and we went with him to a cabin and found an I.W.W. friend in the shack and 5 gallons of coal oil or kerosene, with which we cleaned the filthy stuff off of each other, and our troubles were over, as friends sent clothing and money to us that day, it being about 3 or 3:30 A.M. when we reached the cabin.

"The men abused, whipped and tarred were Tom McCaffery, John Myers, John Boyle, Charles Walsh, W. H. Walton, L. R. Mitchell, Jos. French, J. R. Hill, Gunnard Johnson, Robt. McDonald, John Fitzsimmons, Jos. Fischer, Gordon Dimikson, J. F. Ryan, E. M. Boyd, Jack Sneed (not an I.W.W.).

"This is a copy of my sworn statement and every word is truth."

"It was very evident that the police force knew what was going to happen when they took us from jail, as there were extra gowns and masks provided *which were put on by the Chief of Police and one detective named Blaine, and the number of blows we received were regulated by the Chief of Police himself, who was easily recognizable by six of us at least.*"

Factory Workers' Poetical Debate on Women's Wartime Employment, 1918

The Reason Why

> The shop girls had a meeting
> They came from far and near
> Some came from Bryant's J and L
> And some from Fellows Gear.

But before inside the hall
They were allowed to look
They had to take their bloomers off,
And hang 'em on a hook.

Then into the hall they went at once
With courage ever higher
But hardly were they seated
When someone shouted "Fire."

Then out they ran all in a bunch,
They had no time to look,
And each one grabbed a bloomer
At random from the hook.

They got their bloomers all mixed up,
And they were mighty sore,
To think they couldn't have the one
They had always had before.

And that's the reason that you see
As you go 'round the streets,
Each one will stop and take a look
At every girl she meets.

And hence the reason that the girls
Who are not so very stout,
Have to take 'em in a bit,
And the fat ones, let 'em out.

The women replied in kind:

She Hands Him a Lemon

My man, you're really out of date
And now before it is too late,
I'll try to set you right;
We never mixed our bloomers, clown,
They fit just like a Paris gown,
They're neither loose nor tight.
The simple, tender, clinging vine,
That once around the oak did twine,
Is something of the past;
We stand erect now by your side,
And surmount obstacles with pride,
We're equal, free, at last.

We're independent now you see,
Your bald head don't appeal to me,
I love my overalls;
And I would rather polish steel,

Than get you up a tasty meal,
Or go with you to balls.
Now, only premiums good and big,
Will tempt us maids to change our rig,
And put our aprons on;
And cook up all the dainty things,
That so delighted men and kings
In days now past and gone.

Now in your talk of shouting "fire,"
You really did arouse my ire,
I tell you, sir, with pride,
That you would be the one to run
While we would stay and see the fun,
And lend a hand beside.
To sit by your machine and chew
And dream of lovely Irish stew,
Won't work today you'll find.
Now, we're the ones who set the pace,
You'll have to bustle in the race
Or you'll get left behind.

We're truly glad we got the chance
To work like men and wear men's pants,
And proved that we made good.
My suit a badge of honor is.
Now, will you kindly mind your "biz"
Just as you know you should.

Wilson's Fourteen Points for World Peace, 1918

Gentlemen of the Congress:

. . . It will be our wish and purpose that the processes of peace, when they are begun, shall be absolutely open and that they shall involve and permit henceforth no secret understandings of any kind. The day of conquest and aggrandizement is gone by; so is also the day of secret covenants entered into in the interest of particular governments and likely at some unlooked-for moment to upset the peace of the world. It is this happy fact, now clear to the view of every public man whose thoughts do not still linger in an age that is dead and gone, which makes it possible for every nation whose purposes are consistent with justice and the peace of the world to avow now or at any other time the objects it has in view.

We entered this war because violations of right had occurred which touched us to the quick and made the life of our own people impossible unless they were corrected and the world secured once for all against their recurrence. What we demand in this war, therefore, is nothing peculiar to ourselves. It is that the world be made fit and safe to live in; and particularly that it be made safe for every peace-loving nation which, like our own, wishes to live its own life, determine its own institutions, be assured of justice and fair dealing by the other peoples of the world as against force and selfish aggression. All the peoples of the world are in effect partners in this interest, and for our own part we see very clearly that unless justice be done to others it will not be done to us. The program of the world's peace, therefore, is our program; and that program, the only possible program, as we see it, is this:

I. Open covenants of peace, openly arrived at, after which there shall be no private international understandings of any kind but diplomacy shall proceed always frankly and in the public view.

II. Absolute freedom of navigation upon the seas, outside territorial waters, alike in peace and in war, except as the seas may be closed in whole or in part by international action for the enforcement of international covenants.

III. The removal, so far as possible, of all economic barriers and the establishment of an equality of trade conditions among all the nations consenting to the peace and associating themselves for its maintenance.

IV. Adequate guarantees given and taken that national armaments will be reduced to the lowest point consistent with domestic safety.

V. A free, open-minded, and absolutely impartial adjustment of all colonial claims, based upon a strict observance of the principle that in determining all such questions of sovereignty the interests of the populations concerned must have equal weight with the equitable claims of the government whose title is to be determined.

VI. The evacuation of all Russian territory and such a settlement of all questions affecting Russia as will secure the best and freest cooperation of the other nations of the world in obtaining for her an unhampered and unembarrassed opportunity for the independent determination of her own political development and national policy and assure her of a sincere welcome into the society of free nations under institutions of her own choosing; and, more than a welcome, assistance also of every kind that she may need and may herself desire. The treatment accorded Russia by her sister nations in the months to come will be the acid test of their good will, of their comprehension of her needs as distinguished from their own interests, and of their intelligent and unselfish sympathy.

VII. Belgium, the whole world will agree, must be evacuated and restored, without any attempt to limit the sovereignty which she enjoys in common with all other free nations. No other single act will serve as this will serve to restore confidence among the nations in the laws which they have themselves set and determined for the government of their relations with one another. Without this healing act the whole structure and validity of international law is forever impaired.

VIII. All French territory should be freed and the invaded portions restored, and the wrong done to France by Prussia in 1871 in the matter of Alsace-Lorraine, which has unsettled the peace of the world for nearly fifty years, should be righted, in order that peace may once more be made secure in the interest of all.

IX. A readjustment of the frontiers of Italy should be effected along clearly recognizable lines of nationality.

X. The peoples of Austria-Hungary, whose place among the nations we wish to see safe-guarded and assured, should be accorded the freest opportunity of autonomous development.

XI. Rumania, Serbia, and Montenegro should be evacuated; occupied territories restored; Serbia accorded free and secure access to the sea; and the relations of the several Balkan states to one another determined by friendly counsel along historically established lines of allegiance and nationality; and international guarantees of the political and economic independence and territorial integrity of the several Balkan states should be entered into.

XII. The Turkish portions of the present Ottoman Empire should be assured a secure sovereignty, but the other nationalities which are now under Turkish rule should be assured an undoubted security of life and an absolutely unmolested opportunity of autonomous development, and the Dardanelles should be permanently opened as a free passage to the ships and commerce of all nations under international guarantees.

XIII. An independent Polish state should be erected which should include the territories inhabited by indisputably Polish populations, which should be assured a free and secure access to the sea, and whose political and economic independence and territorial integrity should be guaranteed by international covenant.

XIV. A general association of nations must be formed under specific covenants for the purpose of affording mutual guarantees of political independence and territorial integrity to great and small states alike.

In regard to these essential rectifications of wrong and assertions of right we feel ourselves to be intimate partners of all the governments and peoples associated together against the Imperialists. We cannot be separated in interest or divided in purpose. We stand together until the end.

For such arrangements and covenants we are willing to fight and to continue to fight until they are achieved; but only because we wish the right to prevail and desire a just and stable peace such as can be secured only by removing the chief provocations to war, which this program does not remove. We have no jealousy of German greatness, and there is nothing in this program that impairs it. We grudge her no achievement or distinction of learning or of pacific enterprise such as have made her record very bright and very enviable. We do not wish to injure her or to block in any way her legitimate influence or power. We do not wish to fight her either with arms or with hostile arrangements of trade if she is willing to associate herself with us and the other peace-loving nations of the world in covenants of justice and law and fair dealing. We wish her only to accept a place of equality among the peoples of the world,—the new world in which we now live,—instead of a place of mastery.

Neither do we presume to suggest to her any alteration or modification of her institutions. But it is necessary, we must frankly say, and necessary as a preliminary to any intelligent dealings with her on our part, that we should know whom her spokesmen speak for when they speak to us, whether for the Reichstag majority or for the military party and the men whose creed is imperial domination.

We have spoken now, surely, in terms too concrete to admit of any further doubt or question. An evident principle runs through the whole program I have outlined. It is the principle of justice to all peoples and nationalities, and their right to live on equal terms of liberty and safety with one another, whether they be strong or weak. Unless this principle be made its foundation no part of the structure of international justice can stand. The people of the United States could act upon no other principle; and to the vindication of this principle they are ready to devote their lives, their honor, and everything that they possess. The moral climax of this the culminating and final war for human liberty has come, and they are ready to put their own strength, their own highest purpose, their own integrity and devotion to the test.

🕭 E S S A Y S

The two essays continue Chapter 15's focus on the precarious balance between American ideals and actions, both at home and abroad. In the first, historian Barry D. Karl of the University of Chicago suggests that wartime management provided a superficially successful but ultimately failed experiment in governmental centralism. In the second essay, historian Arthur S. Link of Princeton University argues that Wilson's moral diplomacy was more realistic and effective than posterity has acknowledged.

Managing War

BARRY D. KARL

The outbreak of war in Europe in August 1914 was not looked on by most Americans as an event that urgently affected the interests of the United States. Businessmen involved in international trade of course wondered what the consequences of so widespread a conflict might be, and when they saw foreign trade come to a virtual halt in the first few months of the war, they became intensely concerned. The general public followed the war in the newspapers, but it was probably more troubled by disturbances immediately to our southwest, where Mexican revolutions seemed threatening. Few serious observers would have predicted that in less than two and a half years American soldiers, drafted by an aroused and angry citizenry, would be crossing the Atlantic to fight on European soil. The transformation of popular attitudes in so brief a period of time was as remarkable as the experience of the war itself. American interest in international affairs entered a new phase as public opinion shifted from its familiar focus on protection of "our" hemisphere to salvation of the world. . . .

On 7 May 1915 a German submarine sank the British ship *Lusitania*. Among the 1,198 passengers and crew who died were 128 Americans. The fact that the vessel was British and hence, by German definition, an "enemy" did not mollify American feelings, which ran high. It was, moreover, a pas-

Barry D. Karl, *The Uneasy State: The United States from 1915 to 1945*, pp. 34–49. Copyright © 1983, reprinted by permission of the University of Chicago Press and the author.

senger vessel, not a purely merchant ship, a fact that occasioned much argument, not only in the United States but within the German General Staff, where it was clear that the novelty of the submarine as a weapon had reduced many of the formal definitions to rubble. The ship had been sunk without warning, despite the fact that it was unarmed. No effort had been made to find out what, in fact, it might have been carrying.

For Americans the event could be distinguished even from the sinking of vessels known to be carrying goods and supplies. The *Lusitania,* whatever its cargo, was loaded with passengers; and the freedom of Americans to travel the seas, even on the ships of nations at war, became the issue that galvanized popular response and began the crucial shift in the official position, which was no longer to be based on the freedom of neutral states to engage in trade in wartime but on the freedom of American citizens to travel as they chose. . . .

The debate that raged from May 1915 to the American declaration of war on 6 April 1917 reveals the gradual escalation of emotions on all sides. Great Britain was growing increasingly dependent on American supplies. Germany could not continue to allow its enemies to be supported by a supposed neutral. German strategy, dependent as it was on speed and surprise, could not be maintained indefinitely. The stalemated war in the trenches of Europe had developed into a ghastly inferno, where soldiers crawled in mud and darkness, lit only by the rocket flares, to achieve little but mutual destruction. The German decision to engage in unrestricted submarine warfare was based on an acceptance of the fact that the United States would probably intervene; but the Germans also calculated that internal divisions in the United States and the disorganized state of American industry, already revealed by Wilson's efforts at "preparedness," would render America's entry irrelevant. The benefits of halting Atlantic shipping, they reasoned, would outweigh any direct American involvement.

The Germans should have been right. The fact that they were not—and the resons why they were not—reveals important aspects both of America's experience in the war and of the ways that experience affected postwar American thought. The sinking of the *Lusitania* had shown the inherent weaknesses of "neutrality," but Wilson's attempts to persuade Americans to prepare themselves by adopting even a limited form of military conscription, like his attempts to get American industry to organize itself voluntarily for war production, had demonstrated the profound limits of presidential power over the nation's industrial system. What is more, it revealed that there was no national system capable of centralized management.

Readers of American newspapers and journals of various political persuasions and ethnic identifications would also have noted deep divisions in public opinion. It was, initially at least, not easy to hate the Germans. After all, they were Anglo-Saxons, like the English. Their contributions to American intellectual development were clear, not only to Americans of German origin but to the generation of American scientists and social scientists who had gone to Germany to work for higher degrees. Moreover, the American Irish sympathized with the Irish revolutionaries, who were seeking to win independence from Great Britain; they were contributing money as well as young fighters to what had become a bloody battle for the kind of freedom Americans of older English stock felt they had won from the mother country. Their concern for British interests on the continent of Europe were obviously very limited. . . . All in all, observers of the American scene from abroad would have had difficulty in detecting a national consensus on the war.

The American war machine gradually took shape, but it did so like a lumbering leviathan, willing to respond to the demands the new age was making upon it but slow and clumsy in its efforts to do so. The assumption that so vast a national program could be built on a voluntary basis, that Americans, from the top industrial managers down to the lowliest factory laborers, would organize themselves to serve the national war purpose, required the creation of a national will far more purposeful and far more self-sacrificing than Americans had ever before been asked to sustain. The insistence, too, that a significant portion of the cost of the war should be borne by public subscription through the sale of bonds also required a national consciousness different from that demanded by any previous crisis. The belief that all such things could be done with the minimum of legal coercion rested on a willingness to use the maximum of rhetorical persuasion and popular pressure to bring them about. Yet, long before the American decision to intervene, the tone had been irrevocably set. The war that no one could justify in 1914 had become a national crusade for aims no one could define in 1917; but everyone knew they were right. . . . The Great War had been transformed. A puzzle in international power relationships had become a new democratic revolution; for the world, as Wilson put it, was going to be made "safe for democracy."

The American declaration of war against Germany on 7 April 1917 could be viewed as the culmination of one process of development and its transformation into something else. . . . By asserting its rights not only to protect its own interests but to change the basic international structures that had presumably placed those interests under threat in the first place, the United States was seeking a new role for itself in international affairs, a role much closer to that of the sympathetic revolutionary state it had so often tried to be in nineteenth-century international politics. Whether Wilson and the military-industrial state he assembled reflected a national consensus was, as we have seen, highly questionable, but it was absolutely necessary that such a state be created, consensus or not. In fact, it became necessary that the consensus itself be created. Wilson's speeches were all calculated to produce a fervent national agreement, to call upon all Americans to help him fight not only the war but internal opposition to it. The Allied victory was produced by the power of an American industrial system created specifically for that purpose and placed under the command of a national administration with powers the United States had never before granted to its federal government. While the process of getting the system in place was slow and awkward, at the peak of its power, from December 1917 to November 1918, it exercised extraordinary control over American industrial life.

Wilson's decision to staff the war administration with volunteers recruited from the nation's industries was crucial not only to the way the war effort was ultimately organized but to the American approach to the war itself. Selecting leaders from the nation's railroad industry and its clothing and manufacturing concerns, as well as key figures in banking and finance, meant that Wilson would have an experienced cadre of industrial managers to work with. Given the fact that there was no alternative group in the federal government itself, the decision was less a matter of choice than a quickness to take advantage of the options open to him. These leaders in turn brought a younger group of executives with them. The top echelon consisted of men who, wealthy in their own right, could work for the government for "a dollar a year," the phrase used to characterize their patriotism.

Equally important, the private managerial system was inspired by a nationalism just as intense in its control of the life of the nation as the patriotism that justified wartime service. The need to "win the war" produced a sense of urgency that veiled a fear, not simply that the war might be lost or that the consequences of losing it would be dire, but that the cause of failure would be the internal divisions that the years from 1914 to 1917 had revealed so clearly. The war abroad had to be won; but that victory seemed to many to depend on winning the other war—the war at home.

On 14 April 1917, a week after his address requesting a declaration of war, President Wilson issued an executive order creating the Committee on Public Information. Headed by a newspaperman and magazine writer, George Creel, the committee was intended to organize the distribution of information required to keep the public properly informed on the course of the war. . . . The committee . . . became a propaganda agency; . . . it assumed responsibility not only for informing public opinion but for controlling it. Members of the new advertising industry joined with journalists and academicians to promote the war effort. The public schools were provided with pamphlets to distribute to schoolchildren, explaining America's role in the war and the need for loyalty to the American cause. Local committees tapped citizen volunteers to speak on behalf of the war effort to schoolchildren, clubs, and other organized citizen groups and in movie theaters between the end of the film and the beginning of the vaudeville acts. Such "four-minute men," as they were called (partly because they promised to speak for only four minutes and partly to recall the volunteer fighters of Revolutionary days), exhorted audiences to all forms of engagement in the war, from military service to volunteer activity. . . .

The promotion of Americanism and a spirit of wartime loyalty inevitably focused on the dissenters, the un-American and the disloyal, who opposed the war for whatever reason. . . . Freedom of the seas, rights of neutrals, competition of national empires for world markets—all of the issues that had been central to the debates of the previous three years—were pushed aside in the turmoil of the war effort, replaced now by a rage against Germans and things German. The German language was removed from school curricula, German operas and symphonies were cut from repertoires, German street names were changed, often being replaced with some form of the term "Liberty," and "von" vanished from family names, where it had once signified some proudly remembered identification with nobility. The British royal family of Saxe-Coburg-Gothas became Windsors, the Battenbergs became Mountbattens, and Americans with German names followed suit.

The actual organization of the war effort itself brought many of the progressives' arguments to the fore. . . . The possibility that the war would become dependent on the American public for funding was not seriously considered in advance. The income tax was still a novelty, and the initial rates were still set by the compromises made by the progressives. Thus it did not weigh heavily on the wealthy, and it bypassed all Americans with incomes of less than $4,000—the vast majority. By 1916, increases in military expenditures had begun to produce a national deficit, but Congress was unwilling to increase taxes.

The War Revenue Act of 4 October 1917 was in some respects a progressive triumph. It authorized a graduated income tax beginning at 4 percent on pesonal incomes of more than $1,000, raised the corporation tax, and placed an excess-profits tax on corporate and personal income. Excise taxes on alcohol and tobacco were increased, and new excise taxes were levied on luxuries, amusements, and transportation. This triumph was short-lived, but the progressive principle was nonetheless established: almost three-quarters of the cost of the war was to be borne by corporations and those with large incomes, not by the consumption taxes conservatives had tried to promote. The costs skyrocketed far beyond what was envisaged at the beginning. Ultimately, a third of the money came from war-bond subscriptions; the rest was charged to future generations of Americans. War-financing was a mixed experience, and few on either the progressive or the conservative side of the debate were satisfied. The issue was destined to return in the aftermath of the war as critics reexamined the experience and tried to assess its meaning.

The effective management of the war was again a subject of dispute. It was clear by the winter of 1917 that volunteerism was not working. The collapse of the nation's railroad system was the most threatening sign. It was also the oldest and most familiar example of American industrial inefficiency. . . . Reluctant pioneers, [the railroads] had been forced to face the development of a national labor force, the pressures of regional customer demand, the puzzles of technological innovation in materials and equipment, and, above all, the impact of federal regulation well ahead of their companions in the American technological revolution. They had also served as the most logical target of those who called for government ownership of public utilities. Even William Jennings Bryan had returned from Europe convinced that public ownership of the railroads was a national need, and, by the eve of the war, that conviction was shared by a sizable segment of informed public opinion.

By 1917, the American railroads had experienced almost thirty years of federal regulation, but this had been administered, by and large, with their advice and consent. As critics had been pointing out for more than two decades, railroad ownership had become centralized to a degree that had disturbed trust-busters without eliciting clear judicial decisions on what the government's response ought to be. The American railroad system was not a "system" in any serious sense. The lack of standardization in such obvious mechanisms as the couplings that attached one car to another made it impossible to ship a loaded car across the country without several reloadings into cars of different lines. Shippers complained about rates, while local railyards maintained platoons of workers whose job it was to reload cars. . . . The United States had a national railroad system in one sense only: the rail lines spanned the nation.

The war effort compelled the adoption of a national system. Shipments of troops and materials had to be organized for one basic purpose: support of the war effort. The demands of war exposed the inner workings of the rail system as they had never been seen before, and the strain on the system was already very great when the weather—December 1917 was an unusually snowy month—produced the straw that broke the old camel's back. The federal government took over the running of the railroads the day after Christmas. Secretary of the Treasury William Gibbs McAdoo became director-general of the Railroad Administration, which controlled almost 400,000 miles of track operated by 3,000 companies. The progressives cheered. Innovative managers moved in. They introduced technical improvements, modernized the system, rationalized rates, and raised wages, not only to keep the system going but to keep it going well. But again the progressives, who had seen all this as a needed revolution, turned out to be wrong; for the government did not choose to go on managing the reformed system after the war. The Transportation Act of 1920, against President Wilson's advice, returned the system to its private owners, much improved, more efficient, and more profitable. The war, and the public, had bailed out the railroads. They had also created the necessary transportation system for making the war effort work, and that, when all was said and done, was all they had intended to do.

The War Industries Board, established in July 1917, is another example of a centralized administrative control replacing a failed volunteer effort. In March 1918, President Wilson authorized a sweeping reorganization that placed financier Bernard M. Baruch in charge of the group that controlled war industry, set priorities, and fixed prices. Congress had already authorized strict presidential control over food production and fuel, and it moved now to take over patents and other property of enemy aliens and to control all trade with enemy nations. The creation of a War Finance Corporation to lend money to financial institutions, who would in turn lend money to industries engaged in war work, was another dramatic step in the process of government intervention, while the National War Labor Board and the War Labor Policies Board were presidential efforts to resolve labor disputes in war industries.

Progressives pressed all of the industrial boards and committees to follow progressive principles and to use their power to institute the reforms that progressives had long been advocating. Economists on the War Industries Board had their first opportunity to acquire systematic information on the economics of national industrial production and to push for standardized reporting. The Labor Board, under the joint chairmanship of Frank P. Walsh and former president William Howard Taft, committed itself to the ideal of a living wage, carrying a significant step further the argument against the treatment of labor as a commodity in the production system whose compensation was determined only by the law of supply and demand. . . . Presidential threats to use war power to take over industries whose management refused to negotiate with labor were effective in forcing bargaining and in gaining support from the leaders of the labor movement. Yet, as the experience in the twenties was to demonstrate, the balance between wartime fervor and commitment to progressive ideals was considerably more uneven than even the most knowledgeable of the progressives were inclined to believe in the heat of what some preferred to see as a wartime revolution. At the same time, the experience was there. It was intense, and it was available for later use in the New Deal decades. Even so, it was the sense of emergency, one could argue, that could be appealed to, not any commitment to reform. . . .

All in all, the war was a disruptive experience that swept across the American landscape like a firestorm feeding on every source of energy it touched. Prohibition had been an issue for more generations than anyone could remember. Wartime morality, plus the belief that most American manufacturers of alcohol were German, gave the Eighteenth Amendment movement the edge it needed. The intensity of the need to create and sustain a national sentiment in favor of the war was based on a fear that failure to do so would make victory impossible; but it led to repressive legislation that severely limited any criticism of the war or of the nation's conduct of it. The Espionage Act of June 1917 was intended to control treasonable or disloyal activities, and the coupling of treason and loyalty is the key to the difficulties that were encountered in interpreting and administering the law. Treason could be defined by forms of behavior determinable by law as treasonous. The same standard could not be applied to loyalty, a concept that depended on beliefs and on statements in speech or writing. The act empowered the postmaster general to exclude from the mails anything he deemed treasonable or seditious. Its constitutionality was upheld by the Supreme Court, even though Oliver Wendell Holmes's ringing dissent became the standard, ultimately, by which the Court would defend free speech. Before the war was over, the act was amended to make it even more severe, particularly in its penalties against socialists and pacifists.

Faced with congressional pressures to create a national war cabinet to build a more effective war machine, Wilson himself wrote the legislation that became the Overman Act of 1918, which granted the president greater administrative authority than any previous president had ever had. Passed in May 1918, the Overman Act gave Wilson enormous powers of reorganization and concentration of government where war activities were concerned. The American war machine had reached its peak. It could now win the war, but it would do so at a price that many were beginning to consider much more costly than anyone had anticipated. Americans had nationalized themselves to face threats that had gradually become more internal than external, although it grew increasingly difficult to see the distinction. . . . The enemy at home became the most visible enemy to attack.

The transformation of Wilson's attitude toward the war from "peace without victory" to "the war to end war" and then to a "war to make the world safe for democracy" was a transformation from the instrumental realism of much of the nineteenth century to a dramatic idealism that became much more of a religious crusade. Nor was this simply an American aberration, traceable to a unique American idealism or to Wilson's personal naïveté. Russia's withdrawal from the war, following the November 1917 revolution, led to the enunciation of similar criticisms of the aims of the war. Couched in Marxist terms, they held little appeal for Americans, even though they spoke to some of the same issues of international politics and to the ultimate uselessness of war as a policy instrument. Instead of arousing American sympathies, the Bolshevik position exacerbated American fears; for Russia's withdrawal liberated German troops for service on the Western front and underscored the growing fear that the antiwar movement, led by socialist and pacifist groups in other countries, would lead other allies to withdraw. . . . In the United States the hostility to socialism and to immigrant groups who were identified, rightly or wrongly, with leftist ideological positions came to be tied directly to the commitment to winning the war. It appeared to be a simple step in logic to argue that socialism and communism alike were pro-German.

The entry of the United States determined the outcome of the war; but the United States did not win the war. The victory went to the Allies, who dictated the terms of the peace. Germany had agreed to an armistice on the understanding that the United States would dictate the terms of the peace and that Wilson's Fourteen Points would serve as the basis of the terms. But Wilson joined the Versailles Conference as only one of the four heads of state who drafted the terms, and his influence was limited, especially given his inexperience and given the fact that the election in November 1918 had turned control of Congress over to the Republicans. Those who considered the election results a repudiation of Wilson seemed to forget that none of Wilson's political victories had been clear-cut. The Democrats had not been a majority party in 1912 and they were not one in 1918. The factors that had given them their slender margins had quite possibly been balanced by the experience of the war. The return to normal politics was on the way, and normal politics meant Republican majorities at the polls.

For so brief an experience, even if one dates it from 1914 rather than 1917, the American involvement in World War I was as intense and as significant as any since the Civil War. The regular army in 1917 consisted of about two hundred thousand men. By 1919 that number had reached more than four million, over two million of whom had gone to France. . . .

That Americans were fighting on the battlefields of Europe was something new and shocking, both for those who went and for those who joined the labor force to serve the nation's industrial needs. American industry responded, too, to its first major taste of government intervention; but even that was an experience of gradual escalation of control. One could remember the voluntary beginnings or the coercive last months and be remembering something quite different. The new industrial efficiency, developed along lines recommended by Frederick Winslow Taylor, gave some an opportunity to see what might come of scientific management; but the tests were too sporadic and too incomplete for anyone to draw clear conclusions.

The introduction of psychological testing brought professionals from a new academic field into consulting positions where industrial managers could see the possible effects of their methods. An experimental field hospital funded by the Rockefeller Foundation advanced medical knowledge of burn and wound treatment. . . . Yet, in virtually every field, the lesson was always the same. From the economists who worked for the War Industries Board to the historians and political scientists who advised the president at Versailles, the issue boiled down to one basic problem: American specialization in such fields was essentially in its infancy. American energy was great. The creation of the industrial machine that won the war had supplied an undeniable demonstration of that energy. But efficient management of the machine had depended entirely on the emergency of the war, on the fear of losing it, and on the support of a popular fervor the government worked desperately to sustain. The speed with which Congress dismantled the machine at the war's end, to the point of leaving Washington office workers to find money for their passage home when federal funds were abruptly cut off, suggests that national management was basically viewed as something temporary, even dangerous.

Yet progressives had argued, long before the war emergency gave them what they took to be their opportunity, that American society was seriously threatened by its inability to organize its resources and rationalize its industrial system. From the conservationists to the scientific industrial managers, the depth of concern was profound. The war had revealed the precarious condition of the American industrial system. Concerned Americans who lamented the closing of the frontier, the disorganization of the industrial labor force, the weaknesses of the transportation system, the pointless duplications and inefficiencies in agricultural and industrial production methods, the pockets of illiteracy and substandard health among the young, and the lack of technical information on national finance and industry found that they had indeed been correct in their assessment of conditions. They looked to the war to make their point for them, to prove to public opinion and even the most backward congressmen that their prescriptions would have to be followed. Nothing could have been further off the mark. All down the line, from their conviction that the new wave of American internationalism could not now be turned back to their belief that the war had put industrial management on a new course, with government firmly in command, the progressives simply turned out to be wrong.

The war had become a reform movement of its own, sweeping up all of the reform interests in one way or another but turning them to the one central purpose, winning the war. Still, what really destroyed the reform movement was not just the excesses generated by that purpose by the exhaustion produced by the war effort itself. Trench warfare had been a nightmare. As if to be certain that civilian populations would share the nightmare, an influenza pandemic, which originated on the Western front, spread to the United States with extraordinarily devastating effect in the winter of 1918–19. The high mortality rate from the disease accounted for more than half of the 112,432 American war fatalities and for thousands more at home.

The failure to consolidate, let alone to extend, wartime gains was nowhere more apparent than in the American labor movement. Spurred by an immediate postwar inflation, which by 1919 had driven the cost of living 77 percent above its prewar level, labor unions began to organize strikes. The most dramatic were the strike in the steel industry, where workers had for years suffered conditions among the worst in American industry, and the strike of the Boston police. Public reaction to both was colored by the antiradical hysteria of the period. Violence in the steel strike and the threat of violence in the police strike touched old nerves in the American public's general suspicion of unionization and its association with radical ideas. Yet these two were among 2,665 strikes involving more than four million workers, while the cost of living rose to 105 percent above prewar levels by 1920. Faced with the opposition first of state officials and ultimately of the United States attorney general, labor backed down. That it was forced to do so during the immediate period of postwar prosperity suggests something markedly antilabor in the public response. The Boston police strike became the symbol. Public protectors had no right to strike; they must have been led to do so by insidious forces. . . .

Former wartime managers, when writing of their part in the war effort, continued to extol the voluntarism with which Americans had joined together to forget their differences and win the war; but even many of those who praised that victory still insisted that the national industrial system should not be required to undertake such a burden again. Businessmen and labor leaders had not found government intervention in their interest, and neither side thought that the government had been even-handed. . . . The progressives' use of the war as an occasion for achieving the reforms they had failed to achieve in peacetime was more than a failure; for by linking the war with a fearful centralization, they proved the point about reformers that their critics had so often made: they were seen as oppressive zealots seeking to impress a national unity on an inherently free people. In the years to come, Prohibition would be taken as another proof of this point. And when the crisis of the thirties began, the reluctance to go back to wartime measures of national control was based in part on recollection of what had happened before. The fear that leaders used emergencies to justify the imposition of state controls was part of a historical experience with war that had nothing to do with voluntarism. Like children whistling past a cemetery, postwar memoirists praised voluntarism, but there was always a gnawing fear that it had not really worked. The truth of the matter was that it hadn't. . . .

Wilson and the War for Democracy

ARTHUR S. LINK

Never before had the tasks of leadership in foreign affairs been so difficult for Woodrow Wilson than they became after the adoption by Congress of the war resolution on April 6, 1917. His task was to articulate the war aims of the United States and to give voice to the aspirations of peoples everywhere for a hopeful future, without driving a fatal wedge between his country and the Allies in a war against a common foe. His was also the even more arduous and difficult task, once the war had ended, of achieving a "peace without victory," in spite of the primal passions set loose by years of bloodshed and by ambitions multiplied by victory. . . .

Wilson had a highly creative mind and was undoubtedly the chief innovator of what we will call, for purposes of brevity, the liberal peace program. But he made his chief contribution to the development of that program by synthesizing widely held hopes, plans, and programs; by expressing them in words that moved the hearts of people all over the world; and by devising the practical means to achieve them.

No sooner had the war begun in the summer of 1914 than men and women in Europe and the United States began to talk about peace and ways to prevent future wars. These international liberals drew upon common Judeo-Christian values and humanitarian traditions and, regardless of their nationality, proposed virtually the same plans for a peace settlement and reconstruction of the world over. First, all liberals demanded an end to entangling alliances, secret diplomacy, and attempts to maintain balances of power. Liberals were convinced that this—the old diplomacy—had made war inevitable in 1914. Instead they wanted open diplomacy, democratically controlled, and a concert of power instead of rival balances of power. For example, the platform of the Union of Democratic control, the leading British pacifist organization, read:

> The foreign policy of Great Britain shall not be aimed at creating alliances for the purpose of maintaining the "balance of power," but shall be directed to the establishment of a concert of the powers and the setting up of an international council whose deliberations and decisions shall be public.

Second, all international liberals were convinced that the existence of large armies and navies was a prime cause of war. Consequently, they demanded such sweeping reductions in armaments as would leave each nation with only that military power necessary to maintain domestic order. Some peace organizations, like the Women's Peace Party of the United States, also demanded the nationalization of the manufacture of armaments. . . . In addition, most liberals favored the internationalization of great waterways like the Panama, Suez, and Kiel canals and of strategic points like Gibraltar and the Bosporus.

Third, most liberals envisaged the creation of a postwar international organization strong enough to preserve peace and prevent aggression. . . . The League to Enforce Peace, organized in the United States in 1915, proposed a league whose members would be bound to use their economic and military resources against an aggressor. The League of Nations Association, founded in Great Britain in 1915, also worked for the creation of such an organization.

As a first step toward achieving these grand objectives, most international liberals demanded an end to the war and a settlement based on the principles of no indemnities, self-determination or autonomy for subject peoples, no transfer of territory without the consent of the peoples involved, and plebiscites to determine the fate of Alsace-Lorraine and Ireland.

Liberals in the belligerent countries worked against fearful odds, but Wilson kept in close communication with them, particularly the British, through Colonel House from 1914 to 1917. The wheels of history (or perhaps we should say of peace) began to move significantly when Wilson began to take leadership in the movement for a liberal peace program. . . .

Before House went to Europe in 1916, Sir Edward Grey said that the British government might be willing to accept Wilson's mediation, provided that the United States would agree to join a postwar league committed to disarmament and to the territorial integrity of member nations. . . .

Grey could not have put his questions to any person more likely to respond positively than Wilson. In mid-August 1914, he had said to Stockton Axson, his brother-in-law: "1. There must never again be a foot of ground acquired by conquest. 2. It must be recognized in fact that the small nations are on an equality of rights with the great nations. 3. Ammunition must be manufactured by governments and not by private individuals. 4. There must be some sort of an association of nations wherein all shall guarantee the territorial integrity of each." . . .

Wilson . . . took the public initiative in a move to implement the House-Grey plan by announcing, in his address to the League to Enforce Peace on May 27, 1916, that the United States was ready to join any feasible peace-keeping organization—as he put it, "an universal association of the nations to . . . prevent any war begun either contrary to treaty covenants or without warning and full submission of the causes to the opinion of the world—a virtual guarantee of territorial integrity and political independence."

Wilson was so encouraged by what seemed to be a nearly unanimous bipartisan approval of the league idea that he next incorporated a league plank into the Democratic platform of 1916 and made the league idea one of the chief features of his campaign speeches.

Wilson's third and most important step was to conjoin the league plan with the liberal peace program in his "Peace without Victory" speech of January 22, 1917. "I am proposing, as it were," he concluded, "that the nations should with one accord adopt the doctrine of President Monroe as the doctrine of the world: that no nation should seek to extend its polity over any other nation or people . . . that all nations henceforth avoid entangling alliances which would draw them into competitions of power.''

On March 7, 1917, Wilson told the French Ambassador to the United States, Jean Jules Jusserand, that he was above all eager to see a ''scientific'' and just peace, one that would not create any new Alsace-Lorraines to endanger the future peace of the world. He said that he had no illusions about the league of nations to be formed. It would have to develop slowly. It would be necessary to begin with a universal entente, with the mutual obligation to submit international disputes to a conference of countries not directly involved. Perhaps that would, little by little, create precedents which would break the habit of the recourse to arms. . . .

At about the same time, he set down for the guidance of the State Department what he called ''Bases of Peace'':

1. Mutual guarantee of political independence,—absolute in all domestic matters, limited in external affairs only by the rights of other nations.

2. Mutual guarantee of territorial integrity. NOTE: The application of this guarantee to the territorial arrangements . . . would . . . necessarily depend upon . . . their reasonableness and natural prospect of permanency; and . . . upon whether they were in conformity with the general principles of right and comity set forth in the address of the President of the Senate on the twenty-second of January last.

3. Mutual guarantee against such economic warfare as would in effect constitute an effort to throttle the industrial life of a nation or shut it off from equal opportunities of trade with the rest of the world. . . .

4. Limitation of armaments, whether on land or sea, to the necessities of internal order and the probable demands of cooperation in making good the foregoing guarantees. (NOTE:) *Provided* the nations which take part in this covenant may be safely regarded as representing the major force of mankind. . . .

Wilson's role and responsibilities of course changed drastically after the adoption of the war resolution. As the leader of one of the great belligerent powers he was now responsible for a massive mobilization of the country's entire resources for war. . . . Significantly, however, Wilson's supreme objective did not change. He had gone to war in order to wage peace. His objective, as he said in his war message, was still the attainment of a peace of justice and reconciliation. . . . Moreover, Americans had no quarrel with the great German people, only feelings of sympathy and friendship. . . .

[Wilson] had no desire to spare American resources and manpower, was prepared to continue the struggle to the bitter end if necessary, and strongly supported all proposals for closer Allied and American military cooperation. Yet he took assiduous pains to make it clear that the United States was in the war for its own reasons; and that it was fighting as an *associate,* not an ally, of the Entente powers.

This distinction reveals Wilson's fundamental thinking about the nature of the war and the role that the United States should play in it. He has often been misquoted as saying that the war was one for democracy; actually, he said that it was a war to make the world *safe* for democracy. He never deluded himself into thinking that the United States and the Allies were fighting for the same objectives. Wilson jealously guarded his freedom of action, first, by refusing to discuss peace terms with any Allied leader during the early months of the war and, second, by making it unmistakably clear in his public addresses all through the war what his, or the American, terms would be. . . .

There was much truth in a British contemporary's quip that Wilson was talking more like a mediator than a belligerent. He certainly hoped all through 1917 that the moderate forces in the Reichstag (the German parliament) and the civilian leaders in the Imperial government would take control from the High Command and appeal for a peace conference. Wilson correctly regarded the Kaiser as a figurehead of the military. Had such a turnover of power occurred in Berlin, then Wilson almost certainly would have responded eagerly, even if Allied refusal to cooperate had resulted in a separate peace between the United States and Germany.

Wilson had no fears of any such rupture with the Allies. He had great faith in his own ability to marshal world opinion behind a generous settlement. As he warned in his address of December 4, 1917:

Statesmen must by this time have learned that the opinion of the world is everywhere wide awake and fully comprehends the issues involved. No representative of any self-governed nation will dare disregard it by attempting any . . . covenants of selfishness and compromise. . . . The congress that concludes this war will feel the full strength of the tide that runs now in the hearts of consciences of free men everywhere.

There was, besides, the reassuring fact that the Allies were absolutely dependent economically and were growing militarily dependent upon the United States. Indeed, no one could foresee victory on the western front without a large American army to break the stalemate in the trenches. This meant, as Wilson wrote to Colonel House in July 1917, "When the war is over we can force them to our way of thinking, because by that time they [the Allies] will, among other things, be financially in our hands."

Growing confidence in his own power and leadership, evidence of war weariness everywhere in Europe (mutinies broke out in sixteen corps of the French army in the spring of 1917), and signs of revolt in the Reichstag against the High Command (the Reichstag adopted a no-annexation, no-indemnities resolution on July 19, 1917) all stimulated in Wilson the desire to strike for peace in some dramatic way. . . .

The opportunity, indeed the necessity, for a peace move came almost as soon as House arrived in London. The Bolsheviks seized control of the Russian government on November 7 and appealed to the Allies to begin negotiations at once looking toward a peace based upon the principles of no annexations and no indemnities. In Paris, House pleaded with the British and French leaders to approve a preliminary reply in the form of a simple announcement of liberal war aims. That, House urged, might at least persuade the Bolshevik authorities to try to maintain the Russian war effort. . . . The British and French were adamant. They would not even approve an innocuous declaration of war aims. . . .

Events of the next two weeks convinced Wilson that he himself would have to make an authoritative statement. The Bolsheviks signed a separate armistice with the Central Powers on December 15 and appealed for the assembling of a *general* peace conference at once. The new Russian leaders also published the secret treaties between the czarist government and the Allies negotiated since the beginning of the war; they pointed to the refusal of the Entente powers to join a peace conference as proof of their perfidious ambitions. Czernin, the Austrian Foreign Minister, speaking on Christmas Day, echoed the Bolshevik appeal and declared that the Central Powers desired no forcible annexations, would deprive no country of its independence, and wanted minorities to enjoy the right of self-determination. Liberals, idealists, labor leaders, and Socialists in the United States and Great Britain were excited. They denounced Allied intransigence, declared that the time for peace had come, and demanded that a frank reply be sent to the Russian and Austrian overtures.

It was in these circumstances that Wilson set to work with Colonel House on January 4, 1918, on what was to become the Fourteen Points Address. . . . He hammered out on his own typewriter a statement intended to appeal to German and Austrian moderates, to reply to the Bolsheviks, and, above all, to make clear to all the world the aspirations and ideals for which the American people were fighting.

The address was completed on January 7, and Wilson read it to a joint session of Congress on the following day. . . . It was evident, Wilson said, that the German military masters were bent upon the conquest and subjugation of the helpless Russian people. Therefore, the time had come for the peace-loving nations to avow their ideals and objectives, and these he summarized in fourteen points.

On the one hand there were the general points promising open diplomacy; . . . limitation of armaments to the lowest level consistent with domestic safety; the removal, insofar as possible, of barriers to international trade; an absolutely impartial and open-minded settlement of colonial claims; . . . and the establishment of a league of nations to protect great and small states alike.

On the other hand there were the points relating to specific issues. Two of these—the evacuation and restoration of Belgium and the evacuation of Russia and the self-determination of the Russian people—were, like the general points, indispensable to a peace settlement. The remaining six points were not quite as important, for in defining them Wilson said that they "should" rather than "must" be achieved. They were, presumably, negotiable. They were the return of Alsace-Lorraine to France. Wilson had great difficulty in framing this point—the chief French war objective—and in deciding whether to include it. House wanted him to leave it out altogether! The other five were autonomy for the subject peoples of the Austro-

Hungarian Empire; a readjustment of Italy's boundary along clearly recognizable lines of nationality; the evacuation of the Balkans and free development for the states of that region; security for the Turkish portions of the Ottoman Empire, but autonomy for the subject peoples of that empire and internationalization of the Dardanelles; and the creation of an independent Polish state with access to the sea and international guarantees of its independence.

There was an implied fifteenth point, one as important as any of the fourteen—that the United States had no jealousy of Germany's greatness and no desire to do her any injury. . . .

. . . The United States would be willing to go at once to the peace table if the Germans would accept the fourteen points as the basis for a settlement. It was not even necessary, Wilson said, for the Germans to alter their political institutions. But it was necessary for the United States to know who spoke for Germany—the majority of the Reichstag, or the military party whose creed was domination. The moral climax of the war had now come, and the American people were ready for the test. Germany, Wilson was saying, could obtain a generous settlement if she wanted one. . . .

. . . The Fourteen Points Address . . . immediately became the moral standard to which liberals, labor leaders, and Socialists in the United States and Europe rallied. British Labourites hailed Wilson as their own spokesman. The entire French Left, as one authority has written, were "galvanized into the President's most ardent supporter in the Entente." Even V. I. Lenin, head of the Bolshevik government, warmly responded that the address was "a potential agency promoting peace"; the address was printed in *Izvestiya*, the official Bolshevik daily, and distributed widely throughout Russia.

For a time it seemed that Wilson had begun transatlantic conversations that might lead to an armistice and peace negotiations. Czernin responded in an address . . . on January 24 . . . that the Austro-Hungarian government agreed for the most part with Wilson, and that the fourteen points provided an acceptable basis for peace negotiations. The new German Chancellor, Count Georg F. von Hertling, . . . said [that Germany], could certainly agree with many of the President's general points, but it would brook no interference in its negotiations with Russia. Hertling was evasive about Belgium, and said that Germany would never return Alsace-Lorraine to France. . . .

This brief transatlantic dialogue came to an abrupt end on March 3, 1918, when the Germans imposed a Carthaginian peace upon the Russians at Brest-Litovsk. Wilson expressed his disillusionment and despair in a speech at Baltimore on April 6. He had tried, he said, to judge Germany's purposes without hatred or vindictiveness. . . . The Treaty of Brest-Litovsk had revealed that Germany's real masters sought the domination of Europe. . . . He cried out that there was only one response that the American people could give: "Force, Force to the utmost, Force without stint or limit, the righteous and triumphant Force which shall make Right the law of the world, and cast every selfish dominion down in the dust."

The poignancy of Wilson's consternation at the Treaty of Brest-Litovsk becomes clearer when one recalls what that treaty portended. It meant that peace could be won only by smashing the power of the German military machine. This, in turn, meant a settlement, not negotiated among equals, but imposed by the victors—in short a situation of grave difficulty for the man who knew that it would be as necessary to restrain the ambitions of his associates as to defeat those of his enemies. But peace without victory was no longer possible after March 1918. With Russia prostrate, the German High Command decided to go for all-out victory on the western front. It transferred some forty divisions from the eastern front and launched a gigantic offensive to knock France out of the war before the trickle of American reinforcements could become a mighty stream. . . .

The French defenses held before Paris in mid-July. Soon afterward, with the help of an ever-growing American Expeditionary Force, the supreme Allied commander, Marshal Ferdinand Foch, began a counteroffensive. By October 1, the combined Allied and American armies had broken the Hindenburg Line and were nearing the Belgian and German frontiers. Panic-stricken, General Erich von Ludendorff then demanded that the Imperial government obtain an immediate armistice. . . .

The German government responded by appealing to Wilson, *not* to the Allied governments, for an armistice on the basis of the Fourteen Points and Wilson's subsequent war addresses. Wilson was not taken in by the German leaders. He deftly maneuvered them into acknowledgement of defeat and agreement to accept an armistice that would render them powerless to resume *offensive* operations. However, he wanted to maintain enough German power to serve as a counterbalance to Allied might. "It is certain," he advised Colonel House on October 28, "that too much success or security on the part of the Allies will make a genuine peace settlement exceedingly difficult, if not impossible." . . .

Wilson's decision to go forward with armistice negotiations carried heavy risks at home and abroad. In the United States, Theodore Roosevelt led the chorus demanding a drive to Berlin and a dictated peace. Abroad, the Allies were naturally reluctant to promise Germany to make peace upon a basis of the fourteen points and Wilson's later pronouncements, when total victory was so near.

Determined to end the bloodshed, Wilson sent Colonel House to Paris in mid-October to force a final showdown before the collapse of German resistance had emboldened the Allied leaders into taking peace negotiations into their own hands. From October 29 through November 4, House confronted the Allied prime ministers in a series of stormy meetings. When they threatened to repudiate the fourteen points, House countered with the warning that Wilson was prepared to make a separate peace. The result was an agreement to promise Germany terms as stipulated in the Fourteen Points Address. . . .

House, in a telegram to Wilson on November 5, boasted of his "great diplomatic victory," and so it was in a sense. However, Foch, aided by General John J. Pershing, . . . imposed such military and naval terms, most importantly, French occupation of the Rhineland and the internment of the German navy, as to put Germany completely at the mercy of the British and

French. Thus the armistice signed on November 11 was a shadow victory for House and a substantive victory for the Allies, particularly France. Although Wilson had questioned the necessity of occupying Alsace-Lorraine and opposed the occupation of the Rhineland, now he had no alternative but to accept the package that was known as the Pre-Armistice Agreement.

The opportunity for which Wilson had waited since 1914 was now almost at hand. . . . He had decided to go to Paris as the head of the American delegation. . . . No leader in history ever embarked upon a fateful undertaking with higher hopes or nobler ambitions. However, his bargaining position had been additionally weakened by the time he sailed for France on December 4, 1918. On October 25, he had made a frankly partisan appeal for the election of a Democratic Congress and had said that a Republican victory "would . . . certainly be interpreted on the other side of the water as a repudiation of my leadership." Republicans had won both houses of Congress, and their leaders were now saying that Wilson did not represent the American people on his fateful mission to France. Second, all of western Europe was in a state of nearly psychotic shock after more than four years of bloodletting. Passions of hatred and revenge were surging through the British, French, and Italian peoples and inevitably infected their spokesmen. These primeval forces, beyond Wilson's control, boded ill for one who wanted only to do what was right and just. Among other things, his suggestion that Germany be represented at the peace conference was rejected peremptorily.

The first stage of the Paris Peace Conference began when it opened on January 18, 1919, and ended when Wilson left for a visit to the United States on February 14. . . . The second stage lasted from Wilson's departure to his return to Paris on March 14. . . . The third stage lasted from March 24 until about May 7, when agreement on a treaty with Germany was reached. During this period, Wilson had his hardest struggles and made his most important compromises. The final stage lasted from May 7, when the Treaty was presented to the German delegation, to June 28, when it was signed in the Hall of Mirrors at Versailles. . . .

The overshadowing issue of the Paris Peace Conference was security for France against future German aggression. Wilson offered security in a Reich that was reformed because now democratic, and in the League of Nations that would provide machinery to prevent future German aggression. Such assurances were not enough for the French. Their territory had been invaded twice by Germany in less than half a century; France was still, in 1919, inferior in manpower, resources, and industry to Germany. The French were determined to destroy the German colossus once and for all and to guarantee their safety in the future. Thus Clemenceau followed plans devised by Marshal Foch and approved even before the United States had entered the war. These included, in addition to the recovery of Alsace-Lorraine, tearing the west bank of the Rhine from Germany and the establishment of one or more autonomous Rhenish republics under French control.

Wilson opposed this plan with grim determination. He argued that the dismemberment of Germany in the West would outrageously violate the

Pre-Armistice Agreement and create a wound that would fester until it produced another war. The tension reached its climax during late March and early April. Clemenceau accused Wilson of being pro-German; Wilson ordered his ship to raise steam and be prepared to take him back to the United States.

Compromise was the only alternative to the disruption of the conference. In the showdown, it was Clemenceau who made the vital concession—by yielding his demand for the creation of the Rhenish republics and permanent French occupation of the Rhineland. In return, Wilson and David Lloyd George, the British Prime Minister (who gave Wilson indispensable support at this juncture), agreed to permit a fifteen-year occupation of the Rhineland and signed with Clemenceau treaties promising that, for a limited period, the United States and Great Britain would come to France's aid if she was attacked by Germany. . . .

The issue of reparations and indemnities provoked the most protracted debates at the conference and the greatest bitterness in Germany afterward. In cynical disregard of the Pre-Armistice Agreement, which strongly implied that Germany should be liable only for civilian damages, Clemenceau and Lloyd George, under heavy pressure from their own peoples, demanded that Germany be made to shoulder the entire costs of the war to the Allied peoples as well as its partial costs to their governments. Wilson made his most important concessions at Paris on this issue. First, he agreed that Germany should be forced to bear the costs of disability pensions to Allied veterans and their families, on the ground that these were really civilian damages. Second, he agreed that the French should have the right to occupy the Rhineland if the Germans failed to meet their reparations obligations. The French demanded ownership of the Saar Valley in compensation for the wanton destruction wrought in France by the retreating German armies. Wilson fought this demand bitterly and successfully on the ground that the Saar was German territory. However, he did agree to French ownership of the Saar coal mines and French administration of the territory for fifteen years under the supervision of the League of Nations. . . . In addition, Wilson consented to the immediate seizure of some $5 billion worth of German property. Finally, Wilson agreed to the inclusion of the much-controverted Article 231 in the treaty, by which Germany and her allies acknowledged legal responsibility for all losses incurred during the war by the Allied peoples and governments. . . .

Perhaps Wilson made this, his most important concession at the conference, in the conviction that it would not matter much in the long run. He knew that the Allies would never be able to collect the astronomical sums that they expected. He knew that the Allies could not collect huge sums without bankrupting the German economy, the well being of which was absolutely essential to the prosperity of western Europe. He also knew that passions would eventually cool. And he must have thought that the Reparations Commission, under American leadership, would gradually handle the reparations problem in a sensible and realistic way. This, in fact, is what did occur in the 1920s with the establishment of the Dawes and Young commissions of

1923–1924 and 1929. Finally, in 1932, the European powers meeting in Lausanne, Switzerland, ended the problem altogether. They reduced Germany's obligations to some $700 million and tacitly acknowledged that this sum would never have to be paid. . . .

[A] large problem was disarmament, the key, Wilson believed, to peace and security in the future. Wilson proposed that the victors accept virtually the same limitations on ground forces that they were imposing upon the Germans and agree in the peace treaty itself to abolish conscription, prohibit private manufacture of the implements of war, and maintain armies sufficient only to preserve domestic order and fulfill international obligations. He encountered insuperable opposition from the French and won only a vague promise to undertake general disarmament in the future. He did not propose to restrict navies because, for one reason, he was forced to use the threat of American naval expansion as a bargaining tool to win British support for the League of Nations. He was also deeply suspicious of Japanese imperialism and did not want to weaken the chief potential deterrent to Japanese ambitions.

The issue that took precedence over all the others in Wilson's plans and purposes—the question of the League of Nations—is mentioned last because it was so pervasively involved in all the discussions at Paris. There were two divergent concepts of what the League should be and do, and they cast a revealing light upon the motives and objectives of the opposing forces at Paris. One was the French concept of a league of victors, which would be used to guarantee French military domination of the Continent. The French plan was embodied in a draft presented at the first meeting of the League of Nations Commission on February 3, 1919. It envisaged the creation of an international army and a general staff with startling supranational powers, not unlike those later given to NATO. The other was Wilson's concept of a league of *all* nations, the vanquished as well as the victors—a universal alliance for the purpose of creating a concert of power, not really a supranational agency, but one depending upon the leadership of the great powers, the cooperation of sovereign states, and the organized opinion of mankind for its effectiveness.

As chairman and with strong British support, Wilson controlled the meetings of the commission that drafted the Covenant, or constitution, of the League. The crucial conflicts came when the French, Italians, Japanese, and even the British at times, ruthlessly threatened to refuse to support Wilson's league in order to exact concessions on other issues. Time and again Wilson did retreat, but by thus yielding he won the larger goal—a League of Nations constructed almost exactly as he wanted it.

The Covenant of the League was firmly embedded in all the treaties signed at Paris; it bound its signatory members in an alliance of nonaggression and friendship; and it created the machinery for international cooperation in many fields and for the prevention of war. . . .

The structure erected was the League itself: an international parliament with an Assembly, in which all members were represented, and an executive Council, in which the great powers shared a larger responsibility with a minority of smaller states. In addition, there was a separate and independent judicial branch—a Permanent Court of International Justice, and an administrative arm—a Secretariat and various commissions charged with the responsibility to execute the peace treaties and to promote international cooperation in economic and social fields. It was, Wilson said when he first presented the Covenant to a full session of the conference, "a living thing . . . a definite guarantee of peace . . . against the things which have just come near bringing the whole structure of civilization into ruin."

Did Wilson fail at Paris? This is a question that has been asked and answered a thousand times by statesmen and scholars since the Versailles Treaty was signed in 1919. It will be asked so long as men remember Woodrow Wilson and the world's first major effort to prevent future aggressions and wars. The answer that one gives depends, not only upon the circumstances and mood prevailing at the time it is given, but also upon the view that one takes of history and of the potentialities and limitations of human endeavor. That is to say, it makes a great deal of difference whether one judges Wilson's work by absolute so-called moral standards, or whether one views what he did while remembering the obstacles that he faced, the pressures under which he labored, what was possible and what impossible to achieve at the time, and what would have happened had he not been present at the conference.

The Versailles Treaty, measured by the standards that Wilson had enunciated from 1916 to 1919, obviously failed to fulfill entirely the liberal peace program. It was not, as Wilson had demanded in his "Peace without Victory" speech and implicitly promised in the Fourteen Points Address, a peace among equals. It was, rather, as the Germans contended then and later, a *diktat* imposed by victors upon a beaten foe. It shouldered Germany with a reparations liability that was both economically difficult for Germany to satisfy and potentially a source of future international conflict. It satisfied the victors' demands for a division of the enemy's colonies and territories. In several important instances, it violated the principle of self-determination. Finally, it was filled with pinpricks, like Article 231 and the provision for the trial of the former German Emperor, that served no purpose except to humiliate the German people. It does not, therefore, require much argument to prove that Wilson failed to win the settlement that he had demanded and that the Allies had promised in the Pre-Armistice Agreement.

To condemn Wilson because he failed in part is, however, to miss the entire moral of our story. That moral is a simple one: The Paris peace settlement reveals more clearly than any other episode of the twentieth century both the tension between the ideal and the real in history, and the truth of the proposition that failure inheres in all human striving. It does not make much sense merely to list Wilson's failures. We can see their meaning only when we understand *why* he failed to the extent that he did.

Wilson did not succeed wholly at Paris because he did not fight with all his mind and strength for the liberal peace program. Never before had he fought more tenaciously or pleaded more eloquently. Nor did he fail because he was incompetent, uninformed, and "bamboozled" by men of superior wit and learning, as John Maynard Keynes, in *The Economic Consequences of the Peace,* and Harold Nicolson, in *Peacemaking 1919* (1933), have portrayed him in their unkind caricatures. Indeed, the records of the deliberations at Paris demonstrate conclusively that Wilson was the best-informed and on the whole the wisest man among the statesmen assembled there.

Wilson failed as he did because his handicaps and the obstacles he fought against made failure inevitable. First and foremost, he had lost most of his strategic advantages by the time the peace conference opened. German military power, upon which he had relied as a balance against Allied ambitions, was now totally gone. Wilson had no lever to use against Britain and France, for they were no longer dependent upon American men and resources for survival. His only recourse—withdrawal from the conference—would have resulted in a Carthaginian peace imposed by the French, as the British alone could have prevented the French from carrying out their plans to destroy Germany. In these circumstances, compromise was not merely desirable; it was a compelling necessity to avert, from Wilson's point of view, a far worse alternative.

To compound Wilson's difficulties, his claim to the right to speak in the name of the American people, already seriously weakened by the election of a Republican Congress in November 1918, was denied during the peace conference itself by Republican leaders like Senator Henry Cabot Lodge. In addition, Colonel House, upon whom Wilson had relied as his strong right arm, had failed to support liberal peace ideals during that period of the conference when he was still the President's spokesman. Not only did House become a captive of Clemenceau, he was so eager for harmony that he seriously undercut and compromised Wilson on several crucial occasions.

The character of Wilson's antagonists at Paris also posed a formidable obstacle. Clemenceau, Lloyd George, Orlando, Baron Sonnino, and the Japanese delegates were all tough and resourceful negotiators, masters of the game of diplomacy, quick to seize every advantage that the less experienced American offered.

To overcome such opposition, Wilson had at his command the threat of withdrawal, the promise of American support for the right kind of settlement and of leadership in the League of Nations, and the fact that he did speak for liberal groups, not only in his own country, but throughout the world as well. These were sources of considerable strength, to be sure, but they were not enough to enable Wilson to *impose his own settlement. . . .*

In spite of it all, Wilson won a settlement that honored more of the fourteen points than it violated and which to a large degree vindicated his liberal ideals. Belgium was restored, Alsace-Lorraine was returned to France, and an independent Poland with access to the sea was created. The claims of the Central European and Balkan peoples to self-determination were satisfied. German military power was destroyed, at least for a time. Most important, the Paris settlement provided machinery for its own revision through the League of Nations and the hope that the passing of time and American leadership in the League would help to heal the world's wounds and build a future free from fear.

As it turned out, many of Wilson's expectations were fulfilled even though the American people refused to play the part assigned to them. As intimated earlier, the reparations problem was finally solved in the 1920s and early 1930s in a way not dissimilar from the method that Wilson had proposed. Germany was admitted to the League in 1926, and that organization then ceased to be a mere league of victors. Substantial naval disarmament and limitation were accomplished in 1921 and 1930. Even the great and hitherto elusive goal of land disarmament and the recognition of Germany's right to military equality were seriously sought by international action in the early 1930s. In brief, the Paris settlement, in spite of its imperfections, did create a new international order that functioned reasonably well, relatively speaking.

It is time to stop perpetuating the myth that the Paris settlement made inevitable the rise to power of Mussolini, the Japanese militarists, and Hitler, and hence the Second World War. That war was primarily the result of the Great Depression, which wrought great havoc particularly in Japan and Central Europe and devastated the international economy. In turn, the depression caused all nations to follow selfish policies and eschew international cooperation. The Second World War was also caused by the failure of the United States and Great Britain, in the midst of the depression, to stop Japanese aggression in Manchuria in 1931, and by the loss of British and French nerve in dealing with Hitler from 1935 to 1938. It was, additionally, caused by British fear of the Soviet Union and the delusion that Hitler might be used as a counterweight to the Soviets. . . .

The Paris settlement . . . was not inevitably a "lost peace." On the contrary, it established the foundation of what could have been a viable and secure world order, if only the victors had maintained the will to build upon it.

⯲ *F U R T H E R   R E A D I N G*

John M. Blum, *Woodrow Wilson and the Politics of Morality* (1956)
Alfred E. Cornebise, *War as Advertised: The Four Minute Men and America's Crusade, 1917–1918* (1984)
Robert H. Ferrell, *Woodrow Wilson and World War I* (1985)
Peter G. Filene, *Him/Herself: Sex Roles in Modern America* (1986)
Paul Fussell, *The Great War and Modern Memory* (1975)
Lloyd C. Gardner, *Safe for Democracy: The Anglo-American Response to Revolution, 1913–1923* (1984)
Maurine W. Greenwald, *Women, War and Work* (1980)
Ellis W. Hawley, *The Great War and the Search for a Modern Order* (1979)
Barry D. Karl, *The Uneasy State: The United States from 1915 to 1945* (1983)
David M. Kennedy, *Over Here: The First World War and American Society* (1966)
Arthur S. Link, *Wilson the Diplomatist* (1965)
——, *Woodrow Wilson: Revolution, War and Peace* (1979)
William Preston, Jr., *Aliens and Dissenters: Federal Suppression of Radicals, 1903–1933* (1966)